History of Psychology

The Making of a Science

Edward P. Kardas

Southern Arkansas University

Los Angeles | London | New Delhi
Singapore | Washington DC | Melbourne

FOR INFORMATION:

SAGE Publications, Inc.
2455 Teller Road
Thousand Oaks, California 91320
E-mail: order@sagepub.com

SAGE Publications Ltd.
1 Oliver's Yard
55 City Road
London, EC1Y 1SP
United Kingdom

SAGE Publications India Pvt. Ltd.
B 1/I 1 Mohan Cooperative Industrial Area
Mathura Road, New Delhi 110 044
India

SAGE Publications Asia-Pacific Pte. Ltd.
18 Cross Street #10-10/11/12
China Square Central
Singapore 048423

Printed in the United States of America

Library of Congress Cataloging-in-Publication Data

ISBN: 978-1-0718-0609-8

This book is printed on acid-free paper.

Acquisitions Editor: Matt Wright

Product Associate: Yumna Samie

Production Editor: Vijayakumar

Copy Editor: Christobel Colleen Hopman

Typesetter: diacriTech

Cover Designer: Scott Van Atta

Marketing Manager: Victoria Velasquez

22 23 24 25 26 10 9 8 7 6 5 4 3 2 1

BRIEF CONTENTS

DETAILED CONTENTS

PREFACE

The world has changed since the previous version of this book came out. That is not news. The tragedy of the Covid-19 virus continues and shows little signs of abating. Nearly nine years have passed since the previous version of this text was published by a different house. I am happy to be working with SAGE in bringing out this revised edition. When I first began to teach the history course over 30 years ago I used a first edition text with a modest page count. Over the years that text grew fatter until it nearly doubled the number of pages of its first edition. That kind of bloat is one of the pitfalls I have tried to avoid. This new edition is only a little longer than the previous one. However, there are structural changes from the previous edition. Most obvious is the number of chapters. Now there are 14 instead of 16 and there is a new chapter on the history of cognitive psychology. This editing was accomplished by serious pruning of topics related to the early historical antecedents of psychology: Greek philosophy and the faith-based thinking that followed it. However, the main issues from both those eras are still covered. The model I use for my teaching goes back to Vince Lombardi, the football coach. At his first team meeting with the Green Bay Packers he was reputed to have started his presentation by holding up a football and saying, "Gentlemen, this is a football." He meant, of course, that success on the field depended on mastering the basics. So too is success in the classroom dependent on covering the topic *ab initio* or from the beginning. So, Chapters 3 to 4 now cover what formerly took Chapters 3 to 6. To me, the history of psychology, too, should start at the beginning. Thus, Chapter 2 begins by looking at prehistory.

Colleague Tracy Henley, after reading the original Chapter 2, inspired Matt Rossano, himself, and I to put together a presentation on psychology's prehistory for the 2017 Southwestern Psychological Association's meeting in San Antonio. After at lunch, we decided to edit a volume on that period and the result was the *Handbook of cognitive archeology: Psychology in prehistory* (Henley et al., 2020). There are now several references to the chapters in that book in the current version of the prehistory chapter in this volume. Those represent the belief that the proper study of psychology's history requires scholars and students to understand human behavior before our species was able to write about it. Chapter 2 testifies to a wider definition of human behavior, one that includes psychology but that also brings in the kinds of topics that Wundt himself believed constituted a full psychology, his *völkerpsychologie*. He believed that human behavior requires study from both a scientific viewpoint and a cultural one. Chapter 2, uniquely among history of psychology texts, pays homage to Wundt's vision of psychology but one mostly lost to history. Psychology chose Wundt's pioneering use of the laboratory but left his more complex definition of psychology behind.

This edition, once again, emphasizes the emergence of psychology as its own discipline from four parent disciplines: philosophy, biology, computational science, and social science.

The porous borders between psychology and those parent disciplines still exist and move. Philosophy is psychology's oldest precursor and it asked, for the first time in recorded history, some of the probing questions still of interest to psychologists today. For instance, "Is living a virtuous life humankind's top goal?" Philosophy, too, has changed recently. Knobe (2010) has proposed experimental philosophy or x-phi. He seems to be asking philosophers to become more like experimental psychologists and to leave their cherished armchairs and to begin collecting data. Along the border with biology researchers on both sides now actively seek answers about the once taboo topic of animal cognition. Darwin wrote about animal behavior. Comparative psychology enjoyed success early in psychology's history before interest in that area waned. Later in Europe, ethologists (biologists who study animal behavior) used behavior to better classify species. Today, the study of animal cognition is not exclusive to psychology, biology, and even Artificial Intelligence (AI). The computational sciences gave us geometry, algebra, analytical geometry, calculus and much more. Isaac Newton's *Principia Mathematica* provided a model for theorizing in the natural sciences that social scientists sought to emulate later. Today, the computational sciences are nearly running amok with advances in AI. Hardly a week goes by without a news story describing new ways of mathematizing behavior through algorithms or worrying about smart machines taking over the world. In the social sciences social media has become the buzzword. The world has gone from e-mail, html, FaceBook, Twitter, Tik Tok, Instagram, SnapChat, YouTube, Pinterest, Airbnb, Uber and so on. Covid has forced people indoors and has made social media much more influential. Social media's long-term effects are not yet known. Thus, the borders between psychology and its parent disciplines still exist; they are porous two-way highways. The fight for disciplinary territory continues. Psychology's emergence as an independent discipline was not a one-time thing, it is an ongoing struggle for its intellectual territory.

Although the content of the volume has been abridged in places it still includes all of the important historical information as before. The new chapter, "Cognitive Psychology: Revolution of Evolution?" Emphasizes that psychology's move toward cognition was not sudden or revolutionary. In truth, there was no revolution. I should know having witnessed the Cuban Revolution first hand as a child while my father served as an American diplomat there before, during, and after Fidel Castro came to power. The new chapter covers the how computers came to provide a new model for cognition. It examines the research in memory, problem solving, language, human neurophysiology, and animal cognition. Hopefully, this chapter adds a necessary component missing from the previous volume. Much reading precedes writing. In this volume I added 221 new references, most of those published after the appearance of the previous volume. The history of psychology is not yet writ in stone, instead it continues to be a fertile field for scholars who visit and revisit its acres seeking the true story of psychology's past.

Culture changes too. Since the first volume appeared American culture has been shocked by the murders of African-Americans by police, the #metoo movement, and cancel culture. Americans are much more cognizant and aware of the fissures in the body politic. Those concerns spilled over to the writing of psychology's history too. Take Edward Lee Thorndike, for example. Recently, Columbia University took his name off of a building on its campus because his racist views had come to light. At the APS meeting Kardas and Henley (2021) presented a virtual poster addressing history's problems with situations such as Thorndike's. Both of us agreed, as history of psychology textbook authors, that it was difficult to reconcile the scientific contributions of scholars such as Thorndike with the darker sides of their lives. In Chapter 1 is a warning against presentism and an introduction the concept of *zeitgeist*. But the problem remains: How to teach this course without nullifying, erasing, or cancelling people now found repugnant? Certainly, something must change. The course cannot be taught while ignoring yesterday's repugnant ideas. Fortunately, there are precedents to guide us. Psychologists no longer speak of the people they study as "subjects" (Roediger, 2004a). Smoking in public is nearly banned everywhere. So, change is possible. Simmons (2016) endorsed searching for self-cures for teaching the history of psychology, cures that stabilized it, reassembled new revelations with old, promoted care, and provided reparations when necessary. Morawski (2020, p. 191) wrote:

> Chronicling psychology's historical trajectory affords a way to better see where the science is, where it is moving, and how it could have been or could be otherwise.

Thus, the historian's job is not to censor the past but instead to explain it and demonstrate how the past led to the present. History is capable of rewriting itself, it always has, but now the task is to rewrite in a new and more ethical way.

The Greco-Roman world and it heritage is not the only one worthy of being called a civilization. Certainly, Egypt, Persia, China, Korea, Mexico, and Peru and others were homes to advanced ancient civilizations. But, they are not the focus of this text; psychology's earliest steps were taken in the eastern Mediterranean basin. That is why Chapters 3 and 4 cover some of the antecedents to modern psychology. Throughout the text the effects of "big history" are acknowledged, for example: urbanization, Christianity, Islam, Humanism, Astronomy, Measurement, Evolution, and Artificial Intelligence. In addition, the *Zeitgeists* that begin chapters cover big history topics such as: the history of ancient Greece, world religions, the Enlightenment, Europe after 1648, the scientific laboratory, the history of biology, 19th Century American universities, Russia from 1860 to 1917, the United States from 1914 to 1941, the history of modern Germany, the 19th Century, and World War II. All are designed to show that the history of psychology falls within much larger historical contexts.

As Ebbinghaus observed in his 1908 textbook, "Psychology has a long past, but only a short history." Thus, it is not until Chapter 6 that "psychologists" (Spencer, Bain, Herbart, and Lotze) begin to appear. In Chapter 7 Wundt (Voluntarism) and Titchener (Structuralism) step onstage and give early psychology its introspective bent. After comes a slight detour into biology (Chapter 8) and the influence of Darwinian thinking on psychology and the rest of the world, a tour of Functional psychology (Chapter 9) is next telling its truncated history. Two chapters on Behaviorism (10) and Neobehaviorism (11) follow. The stories of Gestalt psychology (12) and the history of personality and psychopathology (13) come next. Finally as noted earlier chapter (14) looks at the emergence of cognitive psychology.

Each chapter, starting with Chapter 2, includes a *Zeitgeist*, a Preview, an Introduction, and a Summary. This common structure provides a scaffold for the reader and helps crystallize the topics covered. Borders with philosophy, computational science, biology, and social science are also noted throughout the textbook. They show specific times and places where those disciplines interacted or presaged psychology. For instance, one border with biology discusses how the study of optics contributed to early psychological research in vision. Another, a border with social science, discusses Jung's wide-ranging interests (e.g., from mythology to flying saucers) in his attempts to understand personality. The text also lists Then and Now sections. They connect past research interests and data from the history of psychology to contemporary research results. They discuss a wide variety of topics including: birth order effects, latent learning, and the physiology of emotion. These connect the past to the present and show how scientists approached specific topics in the past and how they are seen now. They help students realize that how long psychologists have been working on understanding fundamental issues in the field. Lastly, each chapter displays definitions of important terms within each chapter as well as in a separate Glossary. It has been a long and productive effort for me to produce this revised edition. Hopefully, readers will find it readable, informative, and fun.

ACKNOWLEDGMENTS

It's hard to believe that work began on this revised edition in late January 2018. That was when I first heard from SAGE's Acquisitions Editor Abbie Rickard. She had noticed that the earlier version of my text had not been revised and expressed an interest in releasing a new edition under SAGE's imprint. After some legal necessities, SAGE and I contracted for this revised edition in August 2019. The first revised chapters were written and sent in mid-October 2019 with anonymous reviews completed before Christmas 2019. So, here is the place to thank those colleagues who took the time to review projects such as mine. Soon after came what Abbie called the "new normal." Covid had hit and everyone's lives changed. Given my extra work on quickly converting classes to online format, Abbie and I came up with a new schedule for chapter completions. Then, in early May 2020 Abbie delivered her first child, a girl named Jane Marie. At that point, Elizabeth Cruz, Abbie's Editorial Assistant stepped in as my main contact with SAGE. By November 2020 Abbie had come to a crossroads. The combination of living with Covid, raising a newborn, and having a father-in-law who lived in Barbados proved too hard to resist. She reluctantly resigned from SAGE and moved to the Caribbean. At that point Lara Parra and her assistant Yumna Samie became my partners and together we wrapped up the work that Abbie and Elizabeth had started. Lara, Yumna, and I met remotely from three different states to plan and discuss this volume. For the first time in years I had no summer school duties so I was able to spend more of my time completing the necessary chapter revisions. Those were completed by August 2021. I drafted the new final chapter, "Cognitive Psychology: Evolution or Revolution?," from scratch, a much different process than revision of old chapters. I thank all of the staff at SAGE for their help in getting this project done. I'm happy to report that the process was amicable and collegial.

Of course, any project of this size is not only one person's work or even the work of the publisher and its employees. Here at Southern Arkansas University I would be nearly helpless were it not for the unflagging work of our Donna McCloy, our Assistant Librarian for Reference. Many times did she find and procure needed documents at all hours. Our library's Director and Electronic Resources Manager also came to my aid numerous times. This work would still be in progress were it not for those two. Our president, Trey Berry, and the dean of my college, Helmut Langerbein, historians both, tried to keep me on even keel regarding their discipline. My direct reports, Provost David Lanoue and chair Deborah Wilson encouraged me and took up some of my slack when necessary. I direct our Honors College and David Wingfield, the assistant director, covered for me more than once during the revision process. I thank them all. Close colleagues Chris Spatz, Dan Fasko, and John Oxford served as sounding boards and dispensed helpful advice throughout the project. So too did Jon-David Hague, an editor with long experience in academic publishing; he provided me with insights about the publishing business only an insider would possess. My family only consists of my wife Julie now that our three children, Christian, Clayton, and Caraway have left the nest and have their own productive lives and families. Yet, those three children still provided advice when asked, albeit remotely. Julie, my dear companion and helpmate read nearly all I wrote. Her keen eye never yielded as she caught, again and again, many of my errors in early drafts. Beyond that simple service, however, she provided me with the necessary motivation to persevere in putting this edition to bed. She always encouraged and never cajoled. I could not have finished without her help. Regardless, the final responsibility for the book is mine. Any errors or missteps are mine too.

REVIEWERS TO ACKNOWLEDGE

Bradford Daly, Alfred University

Chris Dinwiddie, Southwest Baptist University

Amy Dombach, Felician University

Charles Fox, Worcester State University

Joseph Houpt, University of Texas at San Antonio

Maureen Mathews, Virginia Commonwealth University

Donna Nesbit-Veltri, University of Texas – El Paso

John Nestojko, Washington University in St. Louis

Robert Newby, Tarleton State University

Lorenz S. Neuwirth, SUNY Old Westbury

April Phillips, Northeastern State University

Warren Reich, Rutgers University – Newark

Miranda Richmond, University of Texas San Antonio

Wiliam Ellery Samuels, The Graduate Center at the City University

Jon Sigurjonsson, Caldwell University

Starlette Sinclair, Florida Gulf Coast University

Amy Skinner, Troy University

Nicole Taylor, University of Indianapolis

Albert Toh, University of Arkansas at Pine Bluff

Jessica Waesche, University of Central Florida

Yvonne Wells, Suffolk University

Lori Werdenschlag, Northern Vermont University

Kevin Woller, Rogers State University

ABOUT THE AUTHOR

Edward P. Kardas is distinguished professor of psychology and director of the Honors College at Southern Arkansas University (SAU) where he has worked since 1980. He received his PhD in Comparative-Developmental psychology from Louisiana State University. Before arriving at SAU he taught at Louisiana State University at Eunice and the University of Wisconsin-Milwaukee. He is the author or co-author (with Tommy Milford, formerly of SAU) of two books on using the Internet and the World Wide Web in teaching and two textbooks one on psychological research methods (with Chris Spatz of Hendrix College) and the other on the history of psychology. Along with Tracey Henley and Matt Rossano, he edited the Handbook of cognitive archeology: Psychology in prehistory. That volume's 27 chapters covered prehistoric human behavior under four headings: developmental psychology, cognitive psychology, social psychology, and personality and clinical psychology. Kardas has taught nearly all of the courses on the scientific side of psychology including research methods, learning, physiological and comparative psychology, and the history of psychology. He was an early adopter of computer technology moving from Apple II+ computers to Macs to iPads to iPhones and to online education. His current scholarly activity revolves around research about honors education. Prior to COVID he led student travel experiences to Paris, Italy, and Cuba. In Cuba, Juping Wang of the SAU Modern Languages department and he developed a formal educational exchange program with the University of Artemisa. SAU and Artemisa students and faculty participated in several programs in both countries and eventually painted two matching murals, one on each campus, to commemorate their relationship.

Kardas is the past president of the Magnolia Columbia County Literacy Council and a member of the First United Methodist Church where he has taught Sunday School on occasion. Always an avid sportsman, he played lacrosse at the University of Baltimore and cofounded (with Tommy Bennett) the LSU Lacrosse Club, still an ongoing enterprise. He has quit playing golf and collecting old trucks. In their place has come target shooting and advising the SAU Shooting Club.

He is married to the former Julie Anne McCuller since 1988. They have celebrated yearly the anniversary of their first date on October 4, 1987. They are the parents of two men and a woman who somehow grew up too quickly and all, somehow, ended up as engineers. All are married and our eldest and his wife recently made us the proud grandparents of John Edward Kardas.

1 21ST CENTURY PSYCHOLOGY

How did modern psychology come to be? Providing the answer to that question will be the task of this textbook. It will take quite a few pages to reveal the full answer to that question because 21st century psychology is the product of a long history of intellectual effort in a variety of fields that predate psychology itself.

The oldest and most venerable of those fields is philosophy. How did psychology evolve out of questions that interested philosophers? Questions such as: How do people know anything? How should people live their lives?

Biology is another older field with which psychology shares many questions and interests. It is also the field that opened psychology to the study of other species in an effort to better understand the commonalities between humans and the rest of the natural world.

Still another set of fields that influenced psychology are the computational sciences. Psychologists quantify many things: IQs, values of dependent variables, correlations between measurements, and much more. Some psychologists create mathematical models to explain experimental observations. Researchers in cognitive psychology and artificial intelligence may write computer programs designed to explain or simulate behavior. Statistics and psychology have a long history together as well.

The social sciences are a newer set of fields that include economics, sociology, anthropology, linguistics, geography, and political science. They are like close family because psychology, too, is a social science. The social sciences are relative newcomers compared to philosophy, biology, and the computational sciences but they also contributed much to the rise of psychology.

The chapters that follow will show how psychology emerged from all of these fields to claim a disciplinary territory of its own in between all of them. The text will first go back deep into human prehistory to discover the oldest vestiges of human behavior. From there it will visit psychology's "borders" with philosophy, biology, the computational sciences, and the social sciences. The goal of those visits will be to see how psychology incorporated questions from those disciplines and integrated them into a new, comprehensive, and integrated science. At the same time, the text will focus on the big ideas, the eminent thinkers, and the large-scale external forces that led to 21st century psychology. The goal of all that effort will be to answer the question: How did modern psychology come to be?

This chapter will begin by examining historiography, the study of history itself. In many ways this psychology course may be different from any other psychology course. For one thing, this course is history as well as psychology. So, knowing a little about how the study of history is conducted is necessary for a proper understanding of the dual nature of this course.

Next will come a brief look at the state of psychology today in order to give a clear picture of the endpoint of psychology's history. Historians already know the end of the story, but they wish to know the details that led to it. By the end of this chapter a clear picture of psychology's present should emerge. The text will then venture out to explore the details of psychology's past.

HISTORY AND PREHISTORY

Before looking at the history of psychology, an investigation of **history** itself is in order. History is more than the simple recounting of past events, and the study of history is not as simple as it might first seem. The recent attempts to "cancel" historical figures and to disallow the teaching of critical race theory speaks to the complexity of studying history. Historians depend on records and documents as their primary source materials. From their analyses of those materials, they attempt to reconstruct and interpret the past. Naturally, when such materials are nonexistent or lost, historians cannot accurately recount the past. Thus, the study of history is impossible prior to the advent of human records, the earliest of which are less than 10,000 years old. The earliest human writing may be symbols scratched on tortoise shells in China that are about 8,800 years old (Li et al., 2003). Anything in the past that happened before humans began keeping records falls into the realm of **prehistory**. The study of prehistory is primarily the province of archeologists and anthropologists; they slowly and patiently sift through ancient human sites searching for cultural artifacts (e.g., pots and weapons) or biological remains (e.g., teeth and bones) that are often the only evidence of humankind's distant past. Chapter 2 will recount that longest period of human existence and summarize the evidence of over four million years of human prehistory. Psychologists, too, are discovering an interest in the distant past (Henley et al., 2020).

Zeitgeist

So, history itself goes back less than 10,000 years. But *hominins* (human-like species) have existed for as long as four million years (Hobolth et al., 2007). Thus, the study of history only covers a tiny sliver of time that humans and predecessor species have lived on this planet. The study of history is further complicated by the inescapable fact that historians live in a particular culture and time, their own, as they attempt to document the past. This phenomenon, often labeled with the German word, *zeitgeist*, is extremely important to understanding the past. People live in a constantly changing cultural, moral, and intellectual matrix. Sometimes, *zeitgeist* changes are so gradual and subtle that they nearly go unnoticed. The world changes, but those changes are often subtle. In the movie *Bullitt* (D'Antoni & Yates, 1968), for example, it is possible to see how much the world has changed. In that movie, Steve McQueen plays a San Francisco detective working a complex murder case. Throughout, he must stop at pay phones to call into his police station. Today, of course, a detective might communicate by radio or cell phone; pay phones are now practically nonexistent. To put it another way, our *zeitgeist* no longer includes pay phones; they have become nearly as uncommon as buggy whips, boot scrapers, and lap blankets (all of which were common items during the Victorian Age). So, historians not only have to be faithful reporters of the past, they also must decipher and report the *zeitgeist* surrounding historical events. In the *Bullitt* example, that might mean explaining that wireless communication was extremely rare in 1968, that public telephones were much more available then than they are today, and that the nearly universal presence of cell phones today is a recent phenomenon. *Zeitgeist* also plays a large role in cancel culture where many historical figures, including psychologists, are being judged morally not by the era they lived in but, rather, in terms of the present. *Zeitgeist* is a word many psychology students learn for the first time while taking this course. In the course of your studies you may need to understand the *zeitgeist* of other times and places while temporarily leaving that of the early 21st century behind.

Another striking example of *zeitgeist* change over the last 50 years revolves around the issue of civil rights in the United States. In 2008, an African American, Barack Obama, was elected president. In his election night address at Grant Park, Chicago, he said:

> If there is anyone out there who still doubts that America is a place where all things are possible; who still wonders if the dream of our founders is alive in our time; who still questions the power of our democracy, tonight is your answer.

What Obama said, in other words, was that the *zeitgeist* of the United States had changed and that his election was the proof that it had. In 1964 in Philadelphia, Mississippi, three civil rights workers, James Chaney, Andrew Goodman, and Michael Schwerner were murdered because of their attempts to add African Americans to the voting rolls in Mississippi. Since then, the United States and Mississippi have changed in many ways. Few, if any, historians back then would have predicted that an African American man would be elected president as early as 2008. That early a date would have seemed highly unlikely in the *zeitgeist* of the United States in 1964.

Knowledge of history is necessary to appreciate how the *zeitgeist* changes. Often, the historical changes that take place during people's lifetimes are too subtle for them to sense a change in the *zeitgeist*. For example, nearly all cars have had four tires, a steering wheel, and an ignition key. Thus, it is hard to appreciate how people traveled before cars came along, or to imagine what kinds of vehicles they will be driving in the future.

THEN AND NOW
FIRST CAR IN TOWN

In the town where I live and teach, the first automobile arrived in 1912. Before then, most people walked, rode a horse or a mule, or traveled in a wagon drawn by an animal. Consequently, what to me today would be a short shopping trip to the next town, a distance of six miles, would have been an all day affair for people in my town before cars and paved roads became commonplace. It is hard for me to imagine devoting a whole day to a six-mile shopping trip, or to not have an automobile handy at all times. So, a six-mile trip now is not equivalent to a similar length trip in 1912. The *zeitgeists* are very different.

The *zeitgeist* of psychology, too, has changed in many ways over the course of its history. Some obvious examples include the role of women in psychology, discrimination against minorities, and changes in technology. Today, women in the Western world currently enjoy a newfound degree of freedom and opportunity. In other parts of the world, however, their status remains at or near traditional levels. The role of women is changing in the areas of equal rights, #MeToo, legal reform, and fighting gender-based poverty.

Racial discrimination, too, has a long history. In the United States the enslavement of African Americans and its abolition led to many long-term historical consequences that are still evident today. For example, Lee et al. (2008) find that rates of homicide among white Americans are higher in rural counties in states that were members of the Confederacy (1861–1865) than in those rural counties that were not. They believed that the frontier tradition of settling disputes violently remains a legitimate method today in the rural American South, and they contended that the culture of violence created by slavery has lingered into the present. They further argued that those cultural factors, and not resource deprivation, better explained their data. Perhaps the conviction of Minneapolis police sergeant Derek Chauvin for the murder of George Floyd may mark a change toward less discrimination in the history of race relations in the United States.

Technological change is yet another agent in history, one whose effects seem to accelerate over time. The pace of technology is quicker now than it ever has been. Note how quickly bulky car bag phones became all-purpose, palm-sized, smart phones. The study of cell phone use is a new topic in psychology. A recent search of PsycINFO, for instance, found 2,957 hits for "cell phone" with the earliest one written in 1998.

Historians of psychology, too, must convey the facts of the past but they must also describe the sociocultural matrix in which those facts first appeared. All of the following are more than facts: women were unable to matriculate in most colleges in the 1890s, African Americans shed the shackles of slavery but still suffered severe discrimination from then to the present, and the internet has changed how people communicate. Facts alone do not a history make. Those facts must be understood in their original contexts and also in how they changed today's *zeitgeist*. Every chapter after this one will begin with a *zeitgeist* section designed to set the larger historical scene for each chapter.

LEARNING OBJECTIVE

1. Imagine what the *zeitgeist* of where you live was like 100 years ago.

PERSONS IN HISTORY

Historians cannot study every last person who ever lived, even if they wanted to. Instead, historians must select certain individuals for study. Typically, those individuals tend to be members of elites, well documented, and males. Think of Julius Caesar, Isaac Newton, Napoleon Bonaparte, or Albert Einstein. Women, of course, are not entirely excluded from historical analysis but appear less often in histories of all types. Recall Celtic warrior-queen Boadicea, the scientist Marie Curie, Revolutionary War hero Molly Pitcher, or psychologist Mary Whiton Calkins. That historians select certain persons and exclude others is another reason why history is not just the simple recounting of past events. That being said, it is clear that some people from the past deserve more scholarly attention than others. Those people are more eminent. **Eminence** is prevalent in nearly every human endeavor, including psychology. Historians and others may ascribe greater eminence to one person over another. Much of the study of history consists of examining the lives of eminent people. The same is true in the history of psychology. Below is a list of some eminent psychologists from the 20th century. However, it is unwise to study history only via the lives of eminent people, be they warriors, kings or queens, scientists, or psychologists. Listed below those selected as eminent are many worthy and hard-working individuals. Not paying attention to them as well makes for an incomplete history. Historians of science, too, must balance the relative contributions of eminent scientists against other important factors like "social milieu . . . and the institutional structure of scientific investigation" (Lewontin, 2009, p. 19).

The history of psychology also includes the study of men and women who first discovered scientific facts or applied those facts to particular populations, or integrated facts or applications into theories. Again, it is all too easy to overstate the role and importance of psychology's pioneers. On the other hand, it would be a serious mistake to ignore them altogether. So, the many psychologists in this text represent only the visible tip of psychology's iceberg. Many more and mostly unknown psychologists have worked long and hard to create what psychology is today.

One problem is that there are so many psychologists out there. It's not possible to look at them all. Who deserves further examination? As in any discipline, some psychologists are more eminent than others. Psychologists have long been interested in studying what makes one person more prominent or eminent than another. Cattell (1905), for instance, began a project designed to identify eminent American scientists. Given the *zeitgeist* of his times, he titled his list "A biographical directory of American *men* (italics added) of science." In 2002, Haggbloom et al. published a list of the 99 most eminent psychologists of the 20th century. That list makes a convenient starting point for discussing the role of individuals in psychology. Table 1.1 lists those 99 psychologists. Interestingly, the highest-ranked woman on the list is Elizabeth Loftus, at number 58. Her ranking, along with the inclusion of only four other women, shows that the *zeitgeist* of psychology today is still not evenly balanced in terms of gender. However, that may change in the future as many more women than men are enrolled as psychology majors and graduate students in American universities today. In the chapters to come, many of the psychologists listed in Table 1.1 will appear as well as eminent men and women from other disciplines.

A newer list (Green & Martin, 2017) extended Haagbloom et al.'s by means of an online game that allowed players to rate the eminence of a pair of psychologists from a list of 402 historical individuals. They recorded responses from 892 game sessions that yielded 66,852 ratings. Participants gave their gender and age; the researchers deduced geographic region from IP addresses. Their top 20 list included nine names that appeared on Haagbloom et al.'s list (see Table 1.2). Green and Martin performed additional analyses separating out the results by gender, age of the respondent, and geographic differences. Women rated Elizabeth Loftus higher than did men (11ᵗʰ vs. 36ᵗʰ) and ranked the 33 female psychologists on the list higher in their mean rankings (121ˢᵗ to 213ᵗʰ). Women ranked Darwin, Watson, and Hull outside of their top 20 while all three were in men's top 20 lists. In terms of age of the respondents, only Skinner and Freud appeared on the lists of all four age ranges while Wundt, James, Bandura, Piaget, Edward Thorndike, Pavlov, and Watson appeared on three of the age ranges. There were 657 respondents from North America (United States and Canada), 111 from Europe, and 104 from South America. Only 20 participated from Asia and Oceania and those were not included in the analyses. Robert Thorndike, Piaget, and Watson were the only names that appeared from all four regions. Pavlov, Freud, James, Edward Thorndike, Milgram, Spearman, Skinner, Wundt, Darwin, and Bandura were named by two regions. The data for both Thorndikes, the two Allports, and the two Cattells were a methodological problem needing solution.

TABLE 1.1 ■ The 99 Most Eminent Psychologists of the 20th Century

1. B.F. Skinner	24. Ivan P. Pavlov	47. Arthur R. Jensen	70. Eleanor E. Maccoby
2. Jean Piaget	25. Walter Mischel	48. Lee J. Cronbach	71. Robert Plomin
3. Sigmund Freud	26. Harry F. Harlow	49. John Bowlby	72. 5.* G. Stanley Hall
4. Albert Bandura	27. J.P. Guilford	50. Wolfgang Köhler	73. Lewis M. Terman
5. Leon Festinger	28. Jerome S. Bruner	51. David Wechsler	74. 5.* Eleanor J. Gibson
6. Carl R. Rogers	29. Ernest R. Hilgard	52. S.S. Stevens	75. 74.5. Paul E. Meehl
7. Stanley Schachter	30. Lawrence Kohlberg	53. Joseph Wolpe	76. Leonard Berkowitz
8. Neal E. Miller	31. Martin E.P. Seligman	54. D.E. Broadbent	77. William K. Estes
9. Edward Thorndike	32. Ulric Neisser	55. Roger N. Shepard	78. Eliot Aronson
10. A.H. Maslow	33. Donald T. Campbell	56. Michael I. Posner	79. Irving L. Janis
11. Gordon W. Allport	34. Roger Brown	57. Theodore M. Newcomb	80. Richard S. Lazarus
12. Erik H. Erikson	35. R.B. Zajonc	58. Elizabeth F. Loftus	81. W. Gary Cannon
13. Hans J. Eysenck	36. Endel Tulving	59. Paul Ekman	82. Allen L. Edwards
14. William James	37. Herbert A. Simon	60. Robert J. Sternberg	83. Lev Semenovich Vygotsky
15. David C. McClelland	38. Noam Chomsky	61. Karl S. Lashley	84. Robert Rosenthal
16. Raymond B. Cattell	39. Edward E. Jones	62. Kenneth Spence	85. Milton Rokeach
17. John B. Watson	40. Charles E. Osgood	63. Morton Deutsch	86. 5.* John Garcia
18. Kurt Lewin	41. Solomon E. Asch	64. Julian B. Rotter	87. 5. James J. Gibson
19. Donald O. Hebb	42. Gordon H. Bower	65. Konrad Lorenz	88. 5. David Rumelhart
20. George A. Miller	43. Harold H. Kelley	66. Benton Underwood	89. 5. L.L. Thurston
21. Clark L. Hull	44. Roger W. Sperry	67. Alfred Adler	90. 5. Margaret Washburn
22. Jerome Kagan	45. Edward C. Tolman	68. Michael Rutter	91. 5. Robert Woodworth
23. Carl G. Jung	46. Stanley Milgram	69. Alexander R. Luria	

| 92. 5.* Edwin G. Boring | 94. 5. Amos Tversky | 96. Herman A. Witkin | 98. Orval Hobart Mowrer |
| 93. 5. John Dewey | 95. 5. Wilhelm Wundt | 97. Mary D. Ainsworth | 99. Anna Freud |

*Numbers with .5 indicate a tie in the ranking. In these cases, the mean is listed.

Source: Haggbloom, S.J., Warnick, R., Warnick, J., Jones, V.K., Yarbough, G.L., Russell, T.M., Borecky, C.M., McGahhey, R., Powell, J.L., Beavers, J., & Monte, E. (2002). The 100 most eminent psychologists of the 20th century. *Review of General Psychology*, 6, 139–152.

TABLE 1.2 ■ Overall Top 20 Rankings
NAME

1. **William James**	11. Elizabeth Loftus
2. **B. F. Skinner**	12. Stanley Milgram
3. Wilhelm Wundt	13. Hermann Helmholtz
4. **Sigmund Freud**	14. Harry Harlow
5. **Jean Piaget**	15. Robert L. Thorndike
6. Charles Darwin	16. **Abraham Maslow**
7. Ivan Pavlov	17. **Hans Eysenck**
8. **John B. Watson**	18. Charles Spearman
9. **Albert Bandura**	19. Lev Vygotsky
10. **Edward L. Thorndike**	20. Solomon Asch

Bold names appeared in top 20 of Haggbloom et al. (2002).

Source: Green, C. D., & Martin, S. M. (2017). Historical impact in psychology differs between demographic groups, *New Ideas in Psychology*, 47, 24–32.

Green and Martin (2017, p. 31) concluded:

historical impact is not a singular thing that extends homogeneously across the entire discipline. There are distinct, sizeable communities within the psychology for whom different historical figures have legitimately had greater impact than for other communities. Our efforts to measure impact should, going forward, include these differences so that we may attain a more accurate, more nuanced, more sophisticated understanding of our discipline and its history.

In the chapters that follow, only some of the eminent psychologists can become part of this history of psychology. Understand that there are many others who have contributed to psychology's path to the 21st century. That space does not allow them to be included in this text does not diminish their contributions.

TABLE 1.3 ■ Top 20 Rankings by Gender	
Rankings by Women	**Rankings by Men**
1. **B F Skinner**	1. **William James**
2. Erik Erikson	2. **Wilhelm Wundt**
3. **Jean Piaget**	3. **B.F. Skinner**
4. **Sigmund Freud**	4. **Ivan Pavlov**
5. **Albert Bandura**	5. Charles Darwin
6. Abraham Maslow	6. John B. Watson
7. **William James**	7. **Sigmund Freud**
8. Carl Rogers	8. **Jean Piaget**
9. Charles Spearman	9. **Edward L. Thorndike**
10. Robert L. Thorndike	10. Clark Hull
11. Elizabeth F. Loftus	11. Hermann Helmholtz
12. **Stanley Milgram**	12. **Albert Bandura**
13. Alfred Adler	13. Ulric Neisser
14. Solomon Asch	14. Gustav T. Fechner
15. **Wilhelm Wundt**	15. G. Stanley Hall
16. **Edward L. Thorndike**	16. Gordon W. Allport
17. Harry F. Harlow	17. Kurt Lewin
18. Floyd H. Allport	18. **Stanley Milgram**
19. **Ivan Pavlov**	19. **Harry F. Harlow**
20. Hans Eysenck	20. Stanley Schachter

N.B. Figures on both lists appear in bold.

Source: Green, C. D., & Martin, S. M. (2017). Historical impact in psychology differs between demographic groups, *New Ideas in Psychology, 47*, 24–32.

IDEAS IN HISTORY

History also includes the study of ideas. People think up ideas, but afterwards those ideas may take on a life of their own. Few historians concentrate on the study of ideas, perhaps because the topic is so abstract (Watson, 2005). Certainly history itself can be viewed as a large collection of ideas: fire, clothing, agriculture, language, religion, time, government, education, mathematics, and science, to name a few. Naturally, this text will focus more closely on ideas in psychology. Among some of the ideas covered will be: mind, evolution, morality, rationality, emotion, personality, and the unconscious. Many psychological ideas are also closely associated with the person who first had the idea (or, at least associated with the person historians link with the idea). The truth, however, is that most ideas do not have a one-to-one correspondence with only one person. Typically, ideas tend to be in the *zeitgeist* a while before someone comes along and synthesizes one or more ideas coherently. That is usually the person who becomes associated with the idea. History is full of such examples, both in general and in psychology. Darwin was not the first person to have the idea of evolution nor was Freud the first to think of the unconscious. Recall Pavlov's admonition, "If you want new ideas, read old books." Thus, the relationship of ideas and who first thought of them is anything but clear or simple. Truly original ideas emerging from a single mind are very rare.

TRENDS IN HISTORY

Just as historians cannot study every person, they cannot study every single event or idea either. So, historians conceptualize people, events, and ideas into higher-level categories or trends. Some of those categories may be familiar and include eras of history such as the Paleolithic (Old Stone Age) or Neolithic (New Stone Age), collections of related philosophical ideas such as empiricism or rationalism, or processes such as industrialization or globalization. Historical trends simplify the study of history by collecting similar events and ideas under higher-level categories. But, at the same time, doing so obscures the finer-grain details of history. Similarly, psychologists have long characterized their history with terms such as structuralism, functionalism, behaviorism, Gestalt psychology, humanism, and cognitivism. This text risks becoming a long list of *isms* and *ologies*. In the pages that follow, such an approach will be avoided and the attempt will be to relate the history of psychology as the exciting account it truly is.

PRESENTISM

One of the difficulties in writing history is presentism. Like everyone else, historians are captives of the present. They cannot travel back in time to view directly the people and events they wish to describe. At the same time, historians realize that they are also captives of their own *zeitgeist*. So, they must avoid interpreting the past using only their own experiences and knowledge. The trick then is to describe the past through the eyes of those alive at the time. Very often, the culture and mores of the past are so different from those of our own time that moral conflicts arise. For instance, how could George Washington have owned slaves? The answer is that the first president lived in a different time and place. He was a Virginia planter during a time when nearly all planters owned slaves. Should Washington's behavior be judged on the basis of today's morals? Many people today believe he should and that is one of the sources of cancel culture. Or, should Washington's owning of slaves be judged in light of the morals of his time? In today's world these are open questions.

Another view of presentism is that the present is the inevitable outgrowth of the past, or put another way, that the present is the only possible culmination of past events. This view, sometimes called "Whig History," interprets the past as justification for the conditions of the present. This view of presentism, too, is wrong. The present is not the triumphant and inevitable outcome of past events; so called "historical accidents" happen all the time. The present could easily have been quite different had someone made another decision or if something that did happen had not happened.

OBJECTIVITY

Psychologists know that objectivity is a necessary feature of research. The same is true for historians. However, many of the earliest histories were anything but objective. Some were written to flatter rulers, while others were written to glorify their own religious or political systems. Worse still, some historians believed they were writing objective histories but were not because they failed to realize their own inherent biases. So, history is not psychology. History has its own methods and problems. This text will try to respect history's methods (historiography) while telling the story of psychology. This text is, most of all, an intellectual history of psychology. As such, it will look at the history of ideas and how they contributed to the rise of modern psychology. At the same time, however, it will have to look closely at the thinkers who first contributed those ideas. It will also have to look at those ideas and thinkers in their own contexts and avoid framing those in the light of modern personal experiences or biases.

Why Study History?

Why study history? Philosopher George Santayana wrote, "Those who do not learn from history are doomed to repeat it." There are many lessons to be learned from history. One such lesson is fighting the last war. Soldiers and world leaders who fail to learn from past conflicts may prepare for future conflicts not realizing that conditions have changed. History is full of such examples. Generals in World War I, for instance, did not anticipate the devastating effects of the machine gun developed before World War I but never used in combat (Gilbert, 2004). Consequently, many millions of soldiers died unnecessarily prior to changes in military strategy and tactics. In psychology, Janis (1972) found that leaders made bad decisions under certain conditions. He called that phenomenon groupthink. The conditions that led to groupthink were the existence of a powerful, isolated, decision-making group, biased leadership, and the presence of high levels of stress. Janis discovered groupthink after analyzing the decisions that led to the disastrous Bay of Pigs invasion of Cuba in 1961. President Kennedy and his advisors were victims of groupthink during that historical episode. So, one important reason to study history is to avoid the repetition of past mistakes.

The American Historical Association (Stearns, 2008) suggests additional reasons to study history; to understand

- people and societies
- how historical change led to the present

- our own lives by comparing them to the lives of people in the past

- our own moral sense

- our own historical identity

With only minor modifications, these same reasons apply to the history of psychology; to understand

- psychologists and their ideas

- how psychology's past led to its present

- our ideas about psychology by comparing them to the ideas of people in the past

- the nature of morality and other longstanding questions

- psychology's historical identity

What is the relationship of the history of psychology to history itself? The history of psychology is a subfield of history but it is not independent of it. There are many instances where large-scale historical events (often labelled "big history") profoundly influenced the history of psychology.

Here are two examples of such large-scale historical interactions with the history of psychology. The first was the 1763 Treaty of Paris that concluded the French and Indian War (1754–1763). As a result of that treaty, the French government ceded all of North America east of the Mississippi river, except for New Orleans, to Great Britain (Schwartz, 1999). Among the many differences in 18th century French and British cultures was their dominant philosophies. French philosophy was dominated by rationalism while British philosophy was dominated by empiricism. (For now, think of rationalism as a philosophy that assumes that certain properties of mind need not be learned, and think of empiricism as a philosophy that emphasizes the environment's role in developing the mind. These philosophies will be examined in more detail inChapter 3.) Psychology enjoyed its greatest development in the United States, a part of North America settled by the British. Thus, American psychology owes much to British empiricism. American psychology today might be very different had the British lost the French and Indian War.

A second and more recent example was the exodus of Jewish intellectuals from Nazi Germany prior to World War II. When Hitler came to power in Germany in 1933, it was soon evident that Jews living in Germany were in mortal danger. One of the first signs of that danger was seen in German universities after the "Law for the Restoration of the Professional Civil Service" was enacted soon after Hitler came to power (Friedlander, 1997). Quickly, British and American scientists put together a plan to help prominent German (and later Austrian) scientists emigrate to Great Britain, the United States, and other countries. Before the Nazis came to power, Germany was the world's leader in science and about 25% of its scientists were Jews (Medawar & Pyke, 2001). Among the German psychologists who left Germany were: Charlotte Bühler, Kurt Goldstein, Kurt Lewin, Wolfgang Köhler, and Max Wertheimer. In addition, of the 20 chairs of psychology in Germany, seven emigrated (Sexton & Hogan, 1992).

Obviously, the future of German psychology was profoundly altered by Hitler's rise and Nazi policies. What would German psychology be like today had Hitler not come to power? On the other side of that coin is the question of what American psychology would look now if Hitler had never existed? Most of those European psychologists would likely have stayed home along with their ideas and insights. Had that been the case, American psychology would be much different. A closer look at psychology and its history is now in order.

LEARNING OBJECTIVE

3. Describe one or two events in your life that would represent "big history" or large scale events capable of altering history for many people.

21ST CENTURY PSYCHOLOGY

The first task will be to examine the present state of psychology. That analysis will serve as the beginning and endpoint of the text's look at psychology's history. Before looking at psychology's past, its present state must be understood.

Science and Psychology

Situating psychology within the larger framework of scientific disciplines is the first step. Psychology is a science. More specifically, it is a social science. Other social sciences include anthropology, criminology, linguistics, economics, geography, political science, and sociology. More broadly, and in addition to the social sciences, science can be further divided into categories of physical sciences, biological sciences, and computational sciences (see Table 1.4). Although these scientific disciplines study a wide variety of topics, they all share a common methodology: the scientific method.

Goldstein and Goldstein (1978) define science as an activity with three features:

1. searching for understanding

2. creating general laws and principles derived from those searches

3. testing those laws and principles experimentally

All sciences share the aforementioned features and also adhere to several other underlying principles: empiricism, replication, a public nature, and theory construction (Spatz & Kardas, 2008). All science is empirical, meaning that scientists strive to make unbiased observations about the universe. All sciences, including psychology, have developed methods and instruments for making those unbiased observations. What would you do in this class if your instructor suddenly asked you to produce a rock hammer? If you were taking a geology class that would not seem strange. Geologists use rock hammers to obtain samples to study. Similarly, cell biologists use petri dishes to grow microorganisms under controlled conditions. So, in that class using petri dishes would not seem strange. The message here is that all scientists adhere to the general principles of science mentioned earlier but the tools they use vary tremendously.

TABLE 1.4 ■ Categories of Science			
Scientific Disciplines (Modified from American Association for the Advancement of Science Membership Categories)			
Physical Science	**Biological Sciences**	**Social Sciences**	**Computational**
Astronomy	Agriculture	Anthropology	Information, Computer, and Communication
Atmospheric	Biology	Linguistics/Language	Mathematics
Chemistry	Medical	Psychology	Statistics
Geology	Neuroscience	Economics	
Geography	Pharmacological	Geography	
Physics		Political Science	
		Sociology	
		Criminology	

Source: © Cengage Learning 2014

Science also checks and rechecks its observations to ensure that they are reliable. That is the principle of replication and it assures scientists that the observations made are real. Scientists reject observations that cannot be replicated. In addition, the vast majority of scientific results are made public by design. Publishing the results of experiments in journals, books, and other media has been a part of the scientific enterprise since the 1600s. Publication of results, combined with later attempts by other scientists to replicate those published results, makes science self-correcting. Not all scientific results are published, usually due to reasons of national security or business competition. Negative results (e.g., failures to find differences or relationships) also are rarely published. Lastly, scientists create **theories** to explain the observations they have made and to point the direction for future observations. Depending on the discipline, theories may be verbal explanations, mathematical formulas, or analogies. Theories are very important to science and vary depending on the discipline involved. Much of what this text covers will be the number of paths that led to scientific psychology. Like scientists in other disciplines, psychologists, too, have developed specific methods designed to help them understand nature's secrets.

Applied Psychology

Psychology is also an applied discipline, meaning that many psychologists take the scientific findings made by themselves or others and use them in specific real-world situations. Clinical and counseling psychologies are probably the most prominent examples of applied psychology, but they are by no means the only ones. Educational psychology and forensic psychology are other important examples. Scientific psychology and applied psychology go hand in hand, meaning that many of the results from scientific psychology can be easily and readily applied in therapy, schools, on the job, or on the athletic field. In 1949, the Boulder Conference formalized the relationship between research (e.g., science) and therapy (e.g., application) in clinical psychology. The resulting Boulder model also designated the PhD, which is based on research, as the appropriate terminal degree for clinicians as well as specified that university psychology departments were the proper sites for clinical training. In 1973, an alternative model for clinical training, the Vail model, arose to promote training that emulated professional schools (e.g., medicine, dentistry, and law) instead of the more research-based approach of the Boulder model. In addition, the Vail model programs conferred a new degree, the PsyD (doctor of psychology), and their programs were no longer restricted to university psychology departments. In fact, some PsyD programs were housed in independent institutions (Norcross & Castle, 2002).

Today, the two models coexist in clinical psychology. Nathan (2000) argued that the Boulder model no longer applied because few practicing clinicians actually conduct their own research. Nevertheless, the Boulder model's basic premise, that research serves practice (and vice versa), still seems to apply. If nothing else, the requirement that clinicians and other practitioners maintain their knowledge base through regular and additional training throughout their careers reinforces the premise of the Boulder model. As Baker and Benjamin (2000, p. 247) noted, the Boulder model still makes up the "overwhelming majority" of clinical training programs today. Recently, Dautenhahn (2018) examined admission criteria, faculty modeling, structural factors, epistemology, and student factors to see if any predicted a specific clinical training model. She examined three models: clinical scientist, scientist–practitioner, and practitioner–scholar and found "the similarities are much more striking than the differences" (p. 41).

All of psychology's applied areas share the idea that the scientific results from psychology can be used in a wide variety of everyday practical settings. Today, applied psychology constitutes the largest portion of 21st century psychology.

Psychology's Borders

Gray (2008) noted that psychology fits neatly in the middle of nearly every academic discipline. Figure 1.1 shows how Gray placed psychology in a central position with the natural sciences, social sciences, and humanities arrayed around it. He added, "It would be impossible for people from any other department to draw a diagram nearly as elegant as mine that put their discipline in the center" (p. 30). The centrality of psychology creates *borders* between it and many nearby disciplines. Four disciplines: philosophy, biology, the computational sciences, and the social sciences have especially close borders with psychology. Over historical time those borders have moved and shifted. Those border realignments are historically important to understanding 21st century psychology, and this text will use those borders and their changes to explore psychology's history in later chapters.

One way to define psychology is to define what it is not. Psychology is not philosophy. But, psychology's oldest border is with philosophy. When humans freed themselves from simply existing day-to-day and were able to devote time to thinking about the universe, they

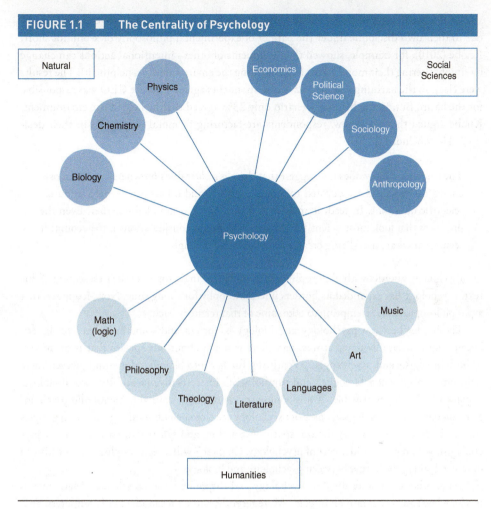

FIGURE 1.1 ■ The Centrality of Psychology

Natural

Social Sciences

Economics

Physics

Political Science

Chemistry

Sociology

Biology

Anthropology

Psychology

Music

Math (logic)

Art

Philosophy

Languages

Theology

Literature

Humanities

Redrawn from: *The value of Psychology 101 in liberal arts education: A psychocentric theory of the university.* Observer, 21(9), 29–32, 2008.

formulated questions that still remain unanswered. Some of those questions are well known: Who am I? What is true? What is the difference between right and wrong? What makes something beautiful? Those questions are of interest to nearly anyone and they are certainly of interest to psychologists. But, deep behind philosophy's border are topics that really only appeal to bona fide philosophers such as esthetics, logic, and metaphysics (the study of first principles such as the nature of being). The word around campus might be that philosophers think about problems while psychologists try to collect data in order to solve similar problems. In many ways, that oversimplification is true. However, along the border between psychology and philosophy, ideas still cross in both directions. Psychological research often causes philosophers to revisit old problems, and, more importantly, philosophical ideas continue to inspire psychologists to conduct research on problems that originate from the philosophical side of the border. Interestingly, some philosophers have begun to apply psychology's methods to their own discipline under the banner of experimental philosophy or x-phi, for short. Knobe (2010), for example, showed that judgments of other's intentional actions can change by simply altering their moral status (e.g., harming the environment vs. helping it). The results were clear, in the harming scenario 82% of respondents agreed that the CEO was responsible for the harm. But, in the helping scenario only 23% agreed that he helped the environment. Knobe argued that, somehow, respondents are factoring in moral judgments in their decisions. He concluded (p. 51):

> The evidence simply does not suggest that there is a clear division whereby certain psychological processes are devoted to moral questions and others are devoted to purely scientific questions. Instead, it appears that everything is jumbled together. Even the processes that look most 'scientific' actually take moral considerations into account. It seems that we are moralizing creatures through and through.

Psychology's border with philosophy will be one of the main topics of the first section of this text. Psychology has expanded its borders into philosophy for a long time. Now, it appears that x-phi philosophers are attempting to take some of that territory back.

The border between psychology and biology is ancient and sometimes hard to discern because humans are living creatures, and there is much about our species that is of interest to both biologists and psychologists. Venturing further into biology's domain, however, there will come a place where biologist's and psychologist's interests diverge and the two disciplines become clearly distinguishable. While zoologists interested in animal behavior and psychologists interested in the biological bases of psychology are close neighbors along this border, topics such as body temperature regulation, species extinction, and salt balance are ones most psychologists would not consider part of psychology. Chapter 7 will look more closely at the history of research along the border between psychology and biology.

Yet another old border divides psychology and the computational sciences. Mathematics has long been an area of human interest. More recently, and with the advent of computers, artificial intelligence has become a topic that straddles the border between computational science and psychology. As machines and technology became more complex, it was no longer possible to dismiss notions such as intelligent machines. Indeed, intelligent machines, long a popular topic in science fiction, now exist, albeit in primitive form. Already, a small number of cities have adopted driverless buses (Cottrell, 2005). In time, they may replace bus drivers everywhere. Expert systems, natural language processing, and robotics are other artificial intelligence topics further removed from psychology's border with the computational sciences. IBM's Deep Blue played chess well enough to defeat the best human grandmasters and "thought" about chess in ways vastly different than how people do (Newborn, 2003). Gary Kasparov (2010, p. 17), Deep Blue's first victim, noted, "Today, for $50 you can buy a home PC program that will crush most grandmasters." Futurists wonder if humans will eventually create machines smarter than ourselves and worry what might happen to us as a species then.

The border with the social sciences is the most recent. Sociologists study topics related to psychology but at a different level of analysis. They also use different methods. The old saw is that psychologists study people while sociologists study groups of people inside social structures (e.g., jails, hospitals, and subcultures). Deep beyond psychology's border with sociology are purely sociological topics such as culture, social class differences, and social problems.

Another set of social scientists, economists, study how human decision-making has small-scale and large-scale effects on the economy. It is no accident that psychologists Herbert Simon and Daniel Kahneman won Nobel Prizes in economics (see Chapter 13). Their research straddled the border between psychology and economics.

Anthropologists, linguists, geographers, and political scientists, social scientists all, also study human behavior and thinking. Research in anthropology, linguistics, and geography has much to say about prehistorical and historical aspects of human behavior and thinking. Modern elections are only one arena in which research in political science excels. Political science research also has created the very practical techniques of polling and electioneering. Any candidates for public office who do not avail themselves of the skills of a competent pollster will likely lose their elections.

All of these disciplinary borders are conceptual, not real; they are fuzzy and dynamic. Crossing them is not like crossing an international border. Those international borders, very often, clearly mark a change in country, customs, and values. The border between Quebec and Maine is dramatically clear. While Maine is thickly wooded, Quebec is nearly treeless. While the rocks in Maine still lie where the glaciers dropped them 12,000 years before, in Quebec generations of farmers have picked them up and piled them into long stone fences. In Maine, because of the omnipresent forest, driving into a town is nearly always a surprise. In Quebec, however, towns are evident far off because of the fewer trees and the tall spires of Catholic churches. Over hundreds of years the Quebecois transformed their province until it no longer resembled its primordial state.

Psychology's borders with philosophy, biology, the computational sciences, and the social sciences are less evident than are international borders, and psychology's borders are more readily changeable. It is not always obvious that a disciplinary border has been crossed or that it is still in the same place when last visited. Speaking of borders and landscapes, notice how one part of the United States is often indistinguishable from another part. Interstates, malls, street signs, and even houses all look alike. Some things are different, however. Car license plates can provide one clue. By the end of this course it should be easier to tell when a disciplinary border has been crossed and psychology left behind.

LEARNING OBJECTIVE

4. Compare the borders you have noticed in courses you have taken. What indicated to you that you were in a new or different territory?

DEFINITION OF 21ST CENTURY PSYCHOLOGY

What is the definition of psychology? That is not a question that is easily answered. The standard definition in general psychology texts goes something like: Psychology is the scientific study of behavior and mental processes. That definition is accurate but leaves out many details. Psychology is at once a science, a practice, a way of thinking, and an academic discipline with definable boundaries.

Psychology's Subdisciplines

One way to understand psychology is to look at all of the parts that constitute it. Psychology consists of a large number of subdisciplines; that is an important detail in its definition. All of those subdisciplines should fit the general definition of psychology. Fortunately, others have already spent considerable time and effort delineating psychology's subdisciplines. The two major organizations in American psychology, the American Psychological Association (APA) and the Association for Psychological Science (APS) have categorized the parts of psychology, albeit in differing ways (Figure 1.2). The APA uses a list of 74 top-level terms to help authors classify the work they submit to the annual convention. Like the APA, the APS also has a list of terms designed for authors submitting work to their annual convention. The APS list has 73 top-level terms, but only 39 of those are shared with the APA list. Table 1.5 shows 57 subdisciplines in four categories: listed by APA and APS (39), APA only (17), APS only (5), and PsycINFO (1). When these lists are carefully analyzed and compared a picture of the many parts of 21st century psychology emerges. The 39 topics in common on the APA and APS lists provide a starting point. When topics not held in common are added, the picture becomes clearer. Think of the topics in the first column (APA and APS) as the baseline of psychology. Of the 17 topics in the APA only column, six deal directly with problems: HIV/AIDS, child abuse, disasters/crisis, stress, suicide, and violence. Meanwhile, two of the five topics listed in the APS only column, behavioral genetics and epidemiology, are on psychology's border with biology. PsycINFO, includes all of the topics listed but adds a unique one: intelligent systems. APS divides psychology into nine larger

---

FIGURE 1.2 ■ Psychology's Subdisciplines

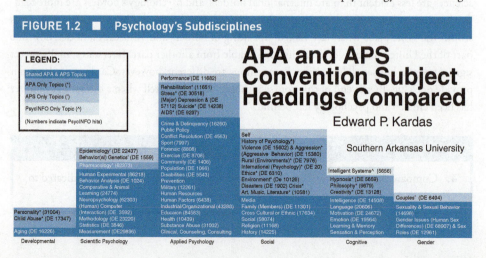

categories: biological/neuroscience, clinical, cognitive, developmental, gender, I/O (industrial/organizational), methodology, personality/emotion, and social.

TABLE 1.5 ■ Psychology's Subdisciplines			
APA & APS	**APA Only**	**APS Only**	**PsycINFO**
Aging	AIDS/HIV	Behavioral Genetics	Intelligent Systems
Behavior Analysis	Art/Music/Literature	Couples	
Clinical/Counseling/Consulting	Child Abuse	Epidemiology	
Community	Creativity	Performance	
Comparative & Animal Learning	Disasters/Crisis	Self	
Conflict Resolution	Environment		
Crime and Delinquency	Ethics		
Cross-cultural/Ethnic	Hypnosis		
Disabilities	International		
Education	Personality		
Emotion	Pharmacology		
Exercise	Philosophy		
Family	Rehabilitation		
Forensic	Rural		
Gender Issues and Sex Roles	Stress		
Health	Suicide		
History	Violence		
Human Experimental			
Human Factors			
Human Resources			
Intelligence			

(Continued)

TABLE 1.5 ■ Psychology's Subdisciplines *(Continued)*			
APA & APS	**APA Only**	**APS Only**	**PsycINFO**
Industrial/Organizational			
Language			
Learning and Memory			
Lifespan			
Measurement/Statistics/Methodology/Computer			
Media			
Military			
Motivation			
Neuropsychology			
Population			
Prevention			
Public Policy			
Religion			
Sensation and Perception			
Sexuality and Sexual Behavior			
Social			
Sport			
Substance Abuse			

LEARNING OBJECTIVE

5. Reorganize the subfields of psychology shown in Table 1.5 by coming up with different higher-order headings. You may re-use some of the existing ones, but try to find other ways of categorizing psychology's subfields.

Psychologists interested in topics on the border with biology include those studying the brain and its workings, genetics, and drug effects. Also included here are those working with animal behavior. Clinicians, counselors, therapists, schools, businesses, soldiers, police officers, community developers, and athletes all look to psychology for specific answers to problems in their respective areas. Think of the opioid epidemic or dealing with the daily stresses of living as examples. Cognitive psychologists follow psychology's original goal, understanding the mind. But, they pursue that goal very differently than did the earliest psychologists. Today's cognitive psychologists may be interested in studying intelligence and language, among other similar topics. They are also looking at AI, the creation of cognition in nonhuman systems such as robots. Developmental psychologists explore the dynamic nature of human and animal life spans. They also investigate processes such as aging, maturation, and death itself. Gender, the biological division of males and females, imposes differences between them because of their different but complementary reproductive systems. At the same time, because men and women are members of the same species, similarities also exist. Industrial/Organizational (I/O) psychologists apply psychological findings to the world of work. Nearly any business now has experts in human resources who help hire new workers or impose behavioral standards on the job (e.g., preventing gender discrimination or eliminating adverse working conditions). I/O psychologists have also long labored to make the world a safer place to live and work in. Human factors psychologists ensure that workers can perform their jobs within the limits of human abilities and do so without incurring short or long term injuries. Most psychology majors know well the methodological part of the discipline through their courses in statistics and research methods. The science of psychology would not exist without careful attention to measurement, research design, or proper use of scientific equipment. The "why" question is within the domain of psychologists who study personality or emotion. Why did nearly a thousand people drink Jim Jones' Kool-Aid in Guyana? Why are the personalities two children in the same family so different? These are the types of questions by these psychologists. Social psychologists look at a wide variety of topics related to sociality ranging from the antisocial (e.g., crime and delinquency) to the highly social (religion). Modern multicultural societies, for example, may be composed of people with different ethnic backgrounds or religions. Daily news reports from around the world tell of strife and conflict in places where ethnicity or religion differ. Samuel Huntington (1996) identified eight "civilizations" or large groups that were similar ethnically or religiously: Western (United States and Europe), Latin American, Islamic, African, Orthodox, Hindu, Japanese, and Sinic (China, Korea, and Vietnam). He argued that human conflicts and wars were more likely to occur along the "fault lines" where those civilizations met. A large swath of topics still remain and those may be lumped into the general category. General psychologists might look at special populations such as the disabled or pro athletes. They often examine wider topics: the effects of environmental change or international psychology. New or cutting edge topics such as media or public policy might be their focus. Historians of psychology fall into this last category too. All psychologists are interested in describing psychology's past and predicting its future. But, just knowing the subdisciplines is not enough. Another way to look at psychology is through the phenomena it attends to.

Psychology's Phenomena

There is much more involved in understanding 21st century psychology than simply listing and analyzing its many subdisciplines. Somehow, each of those subdisciplines must relate to the core subject matter of psychology itself in a clear and recognizable manner. Some phenomena must exist that are clearly and obviously psychological. Once again, someone else has already taken the time and effort to put together such a list. The National Library of Medicine's list of Psychological Phenomena and Processes identifies 12 high-level phenomena in psychology:

- Mental Competency
- Mental Health
- Mental Processes
- Parapsychology
- Personal Autonomy
- Psycholinguistics
- Psychological Theory
- Applied Psychology
- Psychomotor Performance
- Psychophysiology
- Religion and Psychology
- Resilience

The first two items relate to the phenomena of normal vs. psychopathological behavior and are clearly psychological. The next heading, mental processes, includes a large number of phenomena including awareness, learning, memory, and problem-solving. This heading includes a great number of psychological phenomena, some of which date back to the time when psychology began to intrude on philosophy at the end of the 19th century.

Parapsychology includes claims about near-death experiences, out-of-body experiences, precognition, and UFO sightings. Parapsychology is a set of hotly disputed psychological phenomena and, most likely, no amount of discouragement by scientists will reduce the frequency of parapsychological claims. Hynan (2007) provided methodological guidelines for evaluating such claims and suggested that no one method alone is likely to be suitable. Interestingly, psychologists as prominent as William James, C. J. Jung, and William McDougall spent much time investigating paranormal phenomena.

Personal autonomy relates to living independently of others. Most children eventually live autonomously while some adults lose autonomy through a variety of means (e.g., accidents or dementia). Psycholinguistics includes neurolinguistic programming (like parapsychology, neurolinguistic programming is controversial) and the semantic differential, a method for rating attitudes.

As already noted, theories are very important in science and psychology. There are a large number of theories in psychology. Some theories have seen their day, while others continue to thrive. The success of any theory is measured by the amount of research it generates. This text will examine many psychological theories in psychology. Sternberg and Grigorenko (2001, p. 1075) warned, "The student learns as well how...a host of –isms have come and gone, with each generation of researchers hoping that their –ism will somehow be the last." Theories really are provisional; becoming too attached to one can be counterproductive.

The next item, applied psychology, has already been explored in this chapter. It contains the largest part of the body of psychology. So, by popularity alone, it requires examination. Some phenomena within this topic include lie detection, underachievement, absenteeism, and job satisfaction. People look to psychologists to solve these and many other real world problems.

The next category, psychomotor performance includes motor skills and task performance. Humans exhibit a wide variability in their motor skills. Pro athletes represent one extreme and may be highly rewarded for their motor skills. It's amazing that professional golfers can hit drives well over 300 yards with such little apparent effort, or that Olympic gymnasts can perform their routines nearly flawlessly.

Psychophysiology contains a great many psychological phenomena. They range from consciousness to sensory capacities and sleep, through stress-related job burnout. Psychophysics arose at the border between biology and psychology in the 19th century and continues to be a prominent area for psychological research today.

Another of psychology's early interests was the psychology of religion. Nelson (2006) documented the history of the relationship of science (including psychology) and religion and recommended a return to a broader conception of science so that both psychology and religion can be examined from more similar points of view.

The last item, resilience, refers to how individuals differ in their responses to the same situation or stimulus. One example is mental toughness. Crust (2008) reviewed previous research on that phenomenon and concluded that more research is needed in order to better define it. Specifically, he recommended that mental toughness be examined by a variety of methodological approaches, and that populations other than elite athletes be included more often. Couzin-Frankel (2018, p. 971) following events such as hurricane Katrina wrote, "One psychologist coined the term ordinary magic to describe the mix of features that brews resilience. From our stories, we learned that no clear-cut recipe exists."

Hopefully, this brief examination of psychological phenomena has provided a clearer picture of 21st century psychology. The standard textbook definition of psychology still holds for all of these phenomena, but looking at the phenomena makes the definition clearer. Every one of these phenomena is somehow related to behavior or to mental processes.

Are There Laws of Psychology?

One of the factors that led Mjøset (2001, p.15) to differentiate social science from physical science was that the latter had succeeded in formulating laws of nature such as the Second Law of Thermodynamics. Such laws are undisputed, universal statements about how nature works. He noted that many early psychologists hoped to formulate similar laws of nature within psychology. Unfortunately, no such laws have yet been discovered nor may they ever be. In some ways, the physical sciences have far surpassed the social sciences because of the presence and reality of physical laws. The situation is somewhat similar between the biological sciences and the physical sciences. It is impossible to find biological laws either. In the face of these differences between the sciences, some social scientists, notably Merton (1949), simply decided to continue practicing science and forgo any hope of discovering universal laws. In psychology, a similar story exists. It is impossible to find results that apply in all situations. Instead, results must be carefully couched within disciplinary, subdisciplinary, or finer-grained contexts. There are no universal laws of psychology.

All is not lost, however. Some psychological results have stood the test of time and have been replicated again and again. While the examples to follow fail to reach the criterion of a scientific law, they serve to illustrate real and reliable psychological data. The first example is Ebbinghaus's research on human memory. His 1885 book, *Über das Gedächnis* (*Concerning Memory*), caused a sensation when first published. He was the first to show the relationship between memory and the passage of time. Simply put, people forget much more quickly soon after learning and forget much more slowly thereafter. Figure 1.3 shows the relationship between memory and time. Ebbinghaus's discovery does not rise to the level of a scientific law because other conditions (e.g., practice) can alter the relationship between memory and time. So, the relationship is real and reproducible but it does not apply to all types of memory.

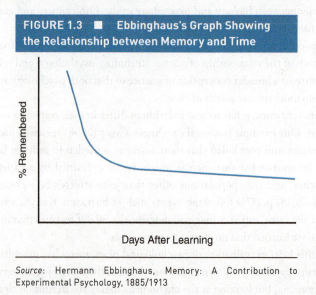

FIGURE 1.3 ■ Ebbinghaus's Graph Showing the Relationship between Memory and Time

Source: Hermann Ebbinghaus, Memory: A Contribution to Experimental Psychology, 1885/1913.

A second example is Shepard and Metzler's (1971) mental rotation research. In a laboratory setting, they projected pairs of geometric stimuli to human participants. While the stimuli were projected in two dimensions, they were designed to convey information in all three dimensions. Participants had to decide quickly whether the two stimuli were alike or different. The stimuli which were alike were presented from 0° up to 180° of rotation from each other in any plane. They discovered a remarkably straightforward relationship between the amount of rotation and

FIGURE 1.4 ■ Shepard and Metzler's Stimuli

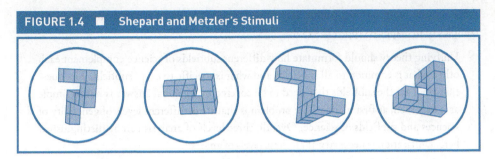

the time it took to decide. As the rotation approached 180°, participants took longer to decide. Moreover, the relationship was linear. Pigeons, too, have been tested for their abilities to mentally rotate objects. Unlike humans, pigeons are able to make accurate mental rotations from various points of view (Köhler et al., 2005). Humans perform mental rotations best while in a normal upright position. Pigeons, on the other hand, perform mental rotations equally well regardless of their spatial relationship to the stimulus. Flying, apparently, affects how pigeons make mental rotations. Thus, results show that different species make mental rotations but not in the same way. Again, while the results of mental rotation experiments are replicable, they are not universal. The species tested makes a difference (Figure 1.4).

UNIFIED PSYCHOLOGY?

Psychology should be a unified way of thinking about the workings of the mind and the behavior of humans and animals. The reality, however, is more complex. As Staats (1991, p. 899) pointed out, "Psychology has developed the prolific character of modern science, without the ability to articulate its knowledge. The result is a great and increasing diversity—many unrelated methods, findings, problems, theoretical languages, schismatic issues, and philosophical positions." Since he wrote those words, the problems he cited have worsened. Since 1997 and in Staat's honor the American Psychological Foundation and the Society for General Psychology (APA Division 1) have sponsored an invited lecture on unifying psychology at the APA's annual convention.

It is difficult to conceive of 21st century psychology as a unified discipline. Still, that has not stopped some psychologists from proposing solutions for making psychology more unified. For instance, Sternberg (2005) believed it is time for psychologists to halt the fragmentation of psychology. He suggested that psychologists could reverse course by measuring psychological phenomena using multiple methods rather than relying on one preferred method, by concentrating more on studying psychological phenomena from a variety of theoretical viewpoints, and by abandoning a reliance on narrow theoretical formulations. Gardner (2005), however, argued that psychology is a young discipline; that it should not be judged against older and more established ones. Furthermore, he pointed out that psychology and other disciplines interact with each other, often absorbing or relinquishing areas of study. Gardner believed that psychology was losing some of its ground to other disciplines. Thus, to him, the unification of psychology is more than an internal affair. Toomela (2007) echoing Vygotsky argued that unification is more complex than it appears (pp. 452–453):

> Unifying theory should formulate how different subfields of science complement each other, what is common to all subfields and what is specific to every subfield. The question what are the subfields that need to be covered by a general answer is not so simple as it may seem at first glance. The problem is that there different levels of generality of sciences and subfields of science. Overall, three levels of analysis can be distinguished here. Unification is necessary at all these levels of analysis.

His first level is a unifying theory for science itself. Here, psychologists must determine what topics are psychological per se and not part of other sciences (e.g., physics, biology, or sociology). For psychology, the second level should demonstrate what its subfields have in common. In other words, why are they part of psychology? The third level acknowledges that subfields can be more finely differentiated. Toomela (p. 454) cited cognitive psychology as divided into "subfields of memory, thinking, attention, perception, emotions, and motivation." Each of those, too, must be worked into an overall picture of unification.

The chapters that follow will look at that ebb and flow that Gardner described. Psychology's changing borders over time echo his analysis. It is easier to see where psychology's borders have been drawn in the past. But it is another thing altogether to predict where the borders will lay in the future. A broader appeal for unified psychology comes from Duntley and Buss (2008, p. 31). They wrote:

> Evolutionary psychology unites the field of psychology with all the other life sciences, including biology, economics, political science, history, political science (sic), legal scholarship, and medicine; it unites humans with all other species, revealing our place in the grand scheme of the natural world.

Chapter 7 will cover evolution and evaluate its value as a unifying concept in psychology.

Mjøset (2001) did not believe that psychologists will ever discover theories describing laws of nature like those of the physical sciences. Instead, he wrote (p. 15), "few social scientists have discussed the term [theory] in a philosophy of science framework. Even fewer have asked whether the term has the same meaning in all social science." Looking at the history of psychology will reveal many examples of its diversity and will trace the emergence of new subfields. Maintaining a vision of a unified psychology throughout may prove difficult. But, by realizing that psychology really exists as an academic discipline that difficulty can be overcome. The fact that psychology is so diverse and complex should make anyone all the more eager to learn and understand its history.

LEARNING OBJECTIVE

6. Identify at least three topics that are purely psychological and not part of another science.

Last Words Before Departing

It's almost time to begin our trip. We will be going to visit the borders between psychology and four other disciplines: philosophy, biology, the computational sciences, and the social sciences. Along the way, we will take side trips deeper into each of those disciplines in order to better understand psychology. Pack your bags, get your shots, and don't lose your passports!

The next chapter will begin four million years ago and end around 2,500 years ago. During that vast span of time, our species evolved from distant hominin ancestors and lived most of that time as hunter–gatherers possessing only stone-age technology. Starting about 50,000 years ago, humans started to look like people today and to develop newer technologies. By 8,000 years ago, many of our ancestors were living in villages and growing domesticated crops. By 4,000 years ago, people were living in cities, making and trading goods, and having enough time to reflect upon the nature of the world. Some of those first thinkers became the first philosophers.

2 PSYCHOLOGY IN PREHISTORY

ZEITGEIST

Camping

Camping is one way to imagine what life was like for humans in the distant past. Of course, even wilderness camping with only a backpack does not come remotely close to duplicating what early human hunter- gatherer groups must have experienced daily. Here are some aspects of 21st century camping along with a partial list of what to bring and then pack into a *vehicle*.

- Tent
- Sleeping bag
- Flashlight
- Cook stove, fuel, matches, dishes and cutlery, and food
- Fishing gear
- Hunting gear
- Extra clothes and rain gear
- Ice chest and ice

Put *gas* in the *vehicle*, drive it down the *road* to a *campsite* in the wilderness and begin to camp. That means picking a *site*, setting up the *tent*, starting a *fire* with *matches*, and making dinner on a portable *cook stove*. Afterwards, it means washing the *dishes*, getting the camp ready for nighttime, and getting into the *sleeping bag* on top of an *air mattress*. In the morning, it means a trip to the *restroom*, preparing breakfast, cleaning up, catching fish with a *rod and reel*, making lunch, cleaning up again, hunting for supper with a *rifle*, preparing supper, and and on and on. After a few days of this, civilization beckons.

Look at all the items italicized in the paragraph above. None of those were available to early hominins unless they made or found similar items themselves. Now imagine camping again, but without the modern conveniences. There are no vehicles, roads, or prepared campsites. As Hildebrand (1999) noted, some places make for better campsites than others; the best ones are on the border between a refuge and a prospect (a place rich in resources). There are no stores and no refrigeration. Shelter, if any, must be made or found. There's no return to civilization either. "Camping" is permanent. Sound like fun?

PREVIEW

This chapter is chock full of ideas which is not surprising given that it covers the longest period of human existence. The tremendous discrepancy between prehistoric and historic *time* is a major feature of human history. Grasping the enormity of our species time on Earth is nearly impossible. Other important ideas are so ingrained that they are difficult to recognize. These include *toolmaking, language*, and *sociality*. Humans have adapted to many different lifestyles as well. *Hunter-gatherers* still exist even as most people now live in *urbanized* settings. *Civilization* has wrought many changes, too, but is all too easily disrupted when its foundations crumble. *Philosophy* is just one of the results of civilization's ability to create surpluses of material goods and time. The earliest philosophers wondered about the *nature of the universe, the origin of life, the reliability of sensory information*, and they coined the first –isms: *materialism, nihilism, monism, dualism,* and *relativism*. The development of *medicine* is another major idea. Medicine began as an *empirical* discipline but eventually lost that characteristic. Hippocratic *humorism* persisted for thousands of years because physicians had become dependent on ancient but unproven ideas.

INTRODUCTION

One of the main purposes of this chapter is to emphasize how little time recorded history occupies within the vast span of natural history. Within those many billions of years, human life spans are less than mere instants. Fortunately, Sagan (1977) created a powerful analogy, the cosmic calendar, to explain how much time has passed since the Big Bang, the primordial explosion that created the universe some 14 billion years ago. In his analogy, Sagan maps time since the Big Bang onto a one-year calendar where January 1 is when the Big Bang happened and January 1 a year later is today. Here are some of his dates:

January 1	____	The Big Bang
September 9	____	The Solar System forms
September 14	____	The Earth forms
September 25	____	Life on Earth begins (no fossil evidence remains for these earliest one-celled organisms)

October 9	_____	Oldest fossils known (bacteria and blue-green algae)
December 16	_____	First worms (fossil evidence of multicellular organisms)
December 19	_____	First fish (first vertebrates)
December 20	_____	Plants begin to colonize surface of Earth
December 21	_____	First insects
December 22	_____	First amphibians
December 23	_____	First reptiles
December 24	_____	First dinosaurs
December 26	_____	First mammals
December 27	_____	First birds
December 28	_____	Dinosaurs extinct
December 29	_____	First primates (our phylogenetic lineage)
December 30	_____	First hominins (human-like organisms)
December 31		
10:30 p.m	_____	First humans
11:00 p.m	_____	Extensive use of stone tools
11:46 p.m	_____	Fire domesticated
11:56 p.m	_____	Last ice age begins
11:58 p.m	_____	Australia settled by sea-traveling peoples
11:59 p.m	_____	European cave paintings created
11:59:20 p.m	_____	Agriculture invented
11:59:35 p.m	_____	First cities built and settled, philosophy begins
11:59:53 p.m	_____	Bronze Age and Trojan War
11:59:54 p.m	_____	Iron Age and biblical Kingdom of Israel
11:59:56 p.m	_____	High point of Roman Empire and birth of Jesus
11:59:57 p.m	_____	Invention of number zero and Moslem conquests
11:59:58 p.m	_____	Crusades and high point of Mayan civilization
11:59:59 p.m	_____	Renaissance, discovery of "New World," rise of science
12:00:01 a.m	_____	Today

Sagan's cosmic calendar clearly illustrated how little time humans have been living on Earth. Although this chapter will cover some four million years of **hominin** existence, that enormous span of years is small in comparison to the life span of the universe and of the planet. Psychology is thus very very young science.

LEARNING OBJECTIVE

1. Calculate the length of each of Sagan's days, hours, and minutes.

EARLY HOMININS

Members of *Homo sapiens,* our own species, are mammals; members of the family *Hominidae,* which includes only four living genera: chimpanzees *(Pan),* humans *(Homo),* gorillas *(Gorilla),* and orangutans *(Pongo).* DNA evidence places chimpanzees as the closest living phylogenetic relatives to humans, sharing about 95% of their DNA (Britten, 2002). Hobolth et al. (2007) dated the divergence of chimpanzees and humans from a common ancestor to a point as early as four million years ago. Anthropological research puts the origin of hominins back further in time, to almost seven million years ago (Zollikofer et al., 2005). Varki and Gagneux (2016) used anthropogeny, the study of the origin of the human species, to analyze a wide variety of differences between humans and great apes. They provided a comprehensive timeline analysis when uniquely human features evolved including: bipedalism, control over fire, cooking, and much larger brains. The rarity of hominin fossils and the wide range of intraspecific variation make more precise dating difficult and subject to change.

The only living hominin species, *Homo sapiens*, has been basically similar in structure and behavior for about 50,000 years or since the "creative explosion" (Pfeiffer, 1982) that began around that time according to archeological evidence. Tools and other artifacts suddenly became more complex and varied, and for the first time were made of materials other than stone (Tattersall, 1999). By 40,000 years ago *Homo sapiens* had populated the entire world. Soon afterward all other hominin species went extinct. However, the whole picture is much more complicated.

One million years ago, an older hominin species, *Homo erectus*, migrated from Africa into Asia and Europe. Around 600,000 years ago, another hominin species, *Homo heidelbergensis*, migrated out of Africa, too. Some members of that species ended up in Europe and evolved into the Neanderthals or *Homo neanderthalensis*. The *Homo heidelbergensis* African populations provided the rootstock for the evolution of *Homo sapiens*. Thus, there were three separate species of hominins that coexisted about 100,000 years ago.

After the creative explosion described above, Homo sapiens' fossil record shows a vastly expanded collection of tools and artifacts, new living habits and ceremonies, and the ability to control fire (Twomey, 2020) and hunt dangerous game successfully. In a relatively short span of geological time, *Homo sapiens* became the only hominin species left on Earth. Why that happened is still unclear. One theory is that the development of the nuclear family was responsible. Another is that cognitive change, especially the development of language, was the key component (Johanson, n.d.). Genetic evidence largely confirms the anthropological picture. Modern humans are amazingly genetically similar to each other. So, modern humans comprise one closely related species that somehow outcompeted and replaced several coexisting species around 30,000 years ago (Li et al., 2008). Varki (2013, p. 29) stated about behaviorally modern humans (BMHs), "despite evidence for cross-fertility with other ancient hominins (including some in Africa), we BMHs remained largely genetically distinct, despite tens of thousands of years of opportunity to mate and mingle into a distinct hybrid species in each locale." Recently, Gabora and Smith (2020) proposed Self-Other Reorganization theory to explain cultural evolution in human history. They analyzed the much older transition (e.g., beginning 2.8 million years ago) from *Australopithicus* to *Homo* and a more recent transition (beginning as early as 200,000 years ago) resulting in behavioral modernity (BM). Better and more types of stone tools, ritualistic burial sites, objects used for personal ornamentation, cave art, improved living spaces with hearths, better and more varied diet, and engraved bone and antler tools are all examples of BM. They concluded (p. 234), "We suggest that the origins of BM be considered an evolutionary transition that culminated in new varieties of information, both within the mind and in artificial memory systems external to it, giving way to new social arrangements, and paving the way for the complex cultural systems in which we are presently immersed." Bipedalism, toolmaking, language, and sociality are some of the characteristics of BM.

BASIC HUMAN CHARACTERISTICS

Bipedalism

All hominins, modern and ancient, walked upright on their hind feet (Harcourt-Smith & Aiello, 2004) while modern apes and monkeys usually move around using all four limbs. Sockol et al. (2007) conducted treadmill studies with modern humans and chimpanzees. They found that human bipedal walking is nearly 75% more efficient than chimpanzee bipedal walking. They speculated (p. 12, 268) that "even if early hominins used a bent-hip, bent-knee form of bipedalism (25), our results suggest that early transitional forms would have reaped some energy savings with minor increases in hip extension and leg length." Rolian et al. (2009) suggested that human feet are an adaptation for long-distance endurance running. Bramble and Lieberman (2004) linked endurance running as a selective advantage for early *Homo* species. Well-conditioned modern !Kung humans are able to run down larger animals (persistence hunting). Glaub and Hall (2017) documented that the !Kung have a strong positive energy return on investment when running down large prey animals. Energy efficiency seems a likely selective advantage of our bipedalism and it frees the forelimbs for other duties such as toolmaking.

Toolmaking

Before Goodall (1971) observations of chimpanzee toolmaking researchers thought that only humans created tools. Since then many animals, especially birds and other primates have been observed making and using simple tools. Nonspecialists would probably mistake the earliest human tools for ordinary rocks. Those earliest rock tools were discovered in Gona, Ethiopia, and have been dated to about two and a half million years ago (Semaw et al., 1997). They have sharp edges made by knocking off flakes from a hand-size rock with another rock (Photo 2.1).

PHOTO 2.1 Gona stone chopper

New, sophisticated Acheulean tools, primarily hand axes and choppers, were made by *Homo erectus*, a million years later. Their usual shape is long, with narrow point at one end and a rounded, hammer-like shape at the other. They persisted in the fossil record for another one and a half million years. The differences between the older and newer tools revealed differences in thinking between the early hominins that produced them. The Acheulean toolmakers selected specific rocks as raw material and had to mentally envision the final product. Acheulean hand axes, regardless of their size or age, exhibit a remarkably consistent height to width ratio *(phi)*, or the golden mean, ~1.6 to 1 (Gowlett, 1984). Hodgson (2020) argued that hand axes were first designed for their utility and later by esthetic symmetry. A modern analogy is the steering wheel. Some of the earliest automobiles used a front-mounted tiller to steer. Once the steering wheel replaced it there was no need to develop another way to steer. All steering wheels work the same way, but many differ esthetically being leather wrapped, wood grained, or with different spoke designs. Similarly, once the Acheulean hand axe was invented, it may have inhibited further functional innovation to it but remained open to esthetic changes.

Broad and fat Levallois tools (first made by *Homo heidelbergensis*) were next step in hominin toolmaking; they were made by first flaking a large piece of rock until it was the approximate shape desired. The last step was to knock the entire, worked piece loose. Levallois tools appear in the fossil record around 300,000 years ago as do wooden ones, spears being the most common (Zimmer, 2005). Around 80,000 years ago newer tools and objects made of materials other than stone appeared in the fossil record, including items with decorative function: beads and other primitive jewelry. Also found were large numbers of sculpted figurines, usually female. One of the oldest known human sculptures was found in Germany; it was a small (2.5" tall) 40,000 year old figurine of a woman with exaggerated physical features (Mellars, 2009). The discovery of these and other objects made by early humans provide evidence of their emerging cognitive capacities (Curry, 2012). When combined with other accomplishments from this period such as cave art and jewelry, it appears the species that produced these objects, *Homo sapiens,* is our own.

Language

Spoken languages are a universal human characteristic. At present, there are over 6,000 languages spoken in the world, but that number is dwindling rapidly (Diamond, 1993). Researchers have correlated linguistic, anthropological, and genetic data to trace the origins of human languages. One discovery was a relatively recent mutation (200,000 to 400,000 years ago) of the FOXP2 gene. This gene is found widely throughout living creatures, from yeast to humans. However, the mutated form is only found in modern humans and *Homo neanderthalensis* (Krause et al., 2007). That has led researchers to believe that the rise of language may have had a genetic basis. Specifically, the FOXP2 gene may be part of a larger complex related to the evolution of language. Enard et al. (2009) altered the FOXP2 gene of mice endogenously, so it had the same genetic structure as the normal human FOXP2 gene. Those mice exhibited lower-pitched vocalizations and specific brain alterations in their basal ganglia. Staes, N., Sherwood, C.C., Wright, K. et al. (2017) found FOXP2 differences in among five ape species. They concluded that the genetic differences were low and that further research might reveal how the gene affects more proximate linguistic mechanisms. Zimmer (2011, pp. 22–24) summarized the gene's effect:

> FOXP2 didn't give us language all on its own. In our brains, it acts more like a foreman, handing out instructions to at least 84 target genes in the developing basal ganglia. Even this full crew of genes explains language only in part, because the ability to form words is just the beginning. Then comes the higher level of complexity: combining words according to rules of grammar to give them meaning.

It is nearly certain that *Homo sapiens* spoke 50,000 years ago, and it is very likely that *Homo neanderthalensis* did also. Many languages show obvious evolutionary relationships with each other while others are nearly devoid of any connection to other languages. Click languages, for instance, are found only in Africa and appear to be among the oldest of languages. In those languages, clicking sounds, formed by using the tongue and lips, have meaning (Greenberg, 1970). Another outlier is the Basque language (Euskara) still spoken in northwest Spain. It is completely unrelated to the Indo-European family of languages spoken in the regions nearby.

In addition, genetic analyses of the Basque population indicate that it, too, is genetically unrelated to its near neighbors. Both the Basque language and its speakers appear to be the descendants of early settlers to the European peninsula (Harding & Sokal, 1988). In general, much of the data emanating from studies of linguistic evolution support independent evidence about early humans gleaned from anthropology and genetics.

Sociality

Another characteristic of *Homo sapiens* is increased levels of social behavior. No one can ever know for sure whether the extinctions of *Homo neanderthalensis* and *Homo erectus* were due to direct (e.g., warfare) or indirect (e.g., natural selection) competition. Some theorists suggest that along with language came an increased capacity for social behavior evidenced by larger-sized bands and mechanisms for minimizing negative effects from contact with other *Homo sapiens* groups. Donald (2020) argued that a collection of interrelated factors: access to procedural memory, metacognitive self-supervision, developmental plasticity, socialization, and mind-sharing (cooperative cognitive work) each contributed to sociality. He concluded (p.294), "It was the emergent properties of those kinds of networks that necessitated the invention of more complex languages, and the elaborate mental life they enabled." The dominant lifestyle of these evolving groups was hunter-gatherer which required a nomadic existence marked by searching for game and plant materials. In these bands, just as in modern hunter-gatherer groups, men did the hunting and women did the gathering.

LEARNING OBJECTIVE

2. Illustrate an example of mindsharing or cooperative cognitive work you have engaged in with another using few if any words.

HUNTER-GATHERERS

Until about 10,000 years ago the nearly universal lifestyle of early hominins revolved around hunting and gathering. That lifestyle also required constant movement from place to place as local resources were depleted. Eals and Silverman (1994) proposed a **hunter-gatherer** hypothesis that claimed that evolving under the conditions required by the hunter-gatherer lifestyle led hominin species to diverge by gender based upon the different skill sets required by that lifestyle; differences, they maintain, that are still manifest today in modern humans. Research since then has supported that hypothesis. Kimura (2004, p. 47) stated:

> Favoring males are these: performance on certain spatial tasks (particularly mental rotation), throwing accuracy and mathematical reasoning tasks; favoring females: verbal memory, and recall of object locations presented in an array.

She added that the effect sizes between these gender differences are large. Other research (Silverman et al., 2007) supported the gender differences found and extended them across seven ethnic groups in 40 countries. Thus, gender differences in thinking are probably relics of the Stone Age and of thousands of years of natural selection for the skills required for the hunter-gatherer lifestyle. Kimura (1992, p. 125) claimed gender differences in cognition exist because "sex differences in cognitive patterns arose because they proved evolutionary advantageous." Furthermore, the adaptive circumstances surrounding those gender differences remained in place for thousands of years. Whether our hunter-gatherer evolutionary heritage is still adaptive today remains open to debate.

Clearly, human cognitive abilities today still reveal the effects of millions of years of living in the hunter-gatherer lifestyle. Thus, studying modern, extant groups of hunter-gatherers is a fruitful way to infer information about early hominins. Modern hunter-gatherer groups apparently remained in the same state as early *Homo sapiens* until recent times. Typically, these living hunter-gatherer groups were "discovered" by more technologically advanced humans, and once discovered, the hunter-gatherers were usually more than happy to avail themselves of modern technology that made their lives more comfortable. They quickly and successfully adopted modern tools and weapons. These modern hunter-gatherers, then, are just as smart and capable as other more technologically advanced humans. They have the cognitive potential to use modern things, but did not independently discover or develop similar technological solutions. At the same time profound lifestyle differences emerged between hunter-gatherers and urbanites.

When prehistoric hunter-gatherers became farmers their health declined. et al. Cordain (1999, p. 384) stated that as people moved from hunter-gathering to farming:

> there was a characteristic reduction in stature [3], an increase in infant mortality [3, 4], a reduction in life span [3, 4, 7], an increased incidence of infectious diseases [3, 4, 7, 8], an increase in iron deficiency anaemia [3, 4, 7, 8], an increased incidence of osteomalacia, porotic hyperostosis and other bone mineral disorders [3, 4,7, 8] and an increase in the number of dental caries and enamel effects.

Similarly, modern humans are affected by the "diseases of civilization," or obesity, coronary heart disease, and type 2 diabetes that are nearly absent in hunter-gatherers (Milton, 2000). The fact is that as human groups, either ancient or modern, moved from hunter-gathering to civilized lifestyles, they saw their health change. That change is called the "discordance hypothesis" (Konner, 2001) and it, attempts to assess the disjunction between those [hunter-gatherer] environments and the ones we live in now (p. 360).

But, adopting a civilized lifestyle has led to lowered infant mortality, increased rates of growth in childhood, and longer life expectancies (Eaton et al., 1988). In Africa today, the health benefits of the diet and lifestyle of modern hunter-gatherers are offset "by relatively high mortality resulting from hunting accidents, falls from honey and fruit trees, snakebites and human conflict" (Dounias & Froment, 2006, p. 224). The bottom line seems to be that humans have changed little physiologically in the last 40,000 years. However, the move from hunter-gathering to farming and then to urbanization has led to large differences in health and well-being in positive and negative directions.

Diamond (1997) argued that Eurasian geography, which is predominantly East-West, plus the domestication of plants and animals already suited to life at those latitudes, promoted the rapid spread of new technologies across Asia and Europe. He contrasted these correlated events in Eurasian cultures to those of cultures living in areas with North–South geographies or with little access to domesticable plants or animals. His conclusion was that Eurasia's head start, combined with a fortuitous set of geographical and ecological circumstances, predisposed peoples living there to first discover, and later use their technologies to carry themselves and their ideas around the world. Morris (2010) echoed Diamond's analysis and extended it into the future. He speculated (p. 33) that, "Geography is…losing meaning. The world is shrinking and the greatest challenges we face—nuclear weapons, climate change, mass migration, epidemics, food and water supply—are all global problems." Relatively unaffected, however, were many contemporary isolated hunter-gatherer groups. Those groups allow scientists to speculate about what human groups must have been like around 50,000 years ago. Konner (2020) examined living hunter-gatherers' diets, mother primacy, parental care, alloparenting, and sibling care by older children. He believed such data contributed to our understanding of ancient hunter-gatherers but agreed that archeological data should remain the primary source for understanding the hunter-gatherer lifestyle.

LEARNING OBJECTIVE

3. Appraise whether the recent use of Zoom or similar electronic tools to teach courses made geography lose its traditional distance barriers.

STONE AGE THINKING

Mithen (1996) divided Stone Age intelligence into three categories: natural history intelligence, technical intelligence, and social intelligence. Natural history intelligence relates to knowledge about world and includes knowing about physical things like tides or biological things like whether a particular animal or plant is dangerous. Technical intelligence relates to knowing how to create and use tools and other artifacts. Finally, social intelligence relates to knowing about how to live with family members and neighbors while also knowing who one's enemies are. Most modern humans probably are less aware of the practical aspects of natural history intelligence (e.g., the yearly path of the sun, which wood burns hottest, or what wild plants are safe to eat) than are hunter-gatherers, either modern or ancient. Most modern humans know much more about technical issues, plus they have much more to learn about technical matters than any hunter-gatherer ever did. Comparing social intelligence between modern and Stone Age humans is probably impossible. The social conditions surrounding hunter-gatherers and modern urban dwellers defy easy comparison. Should they switch places using a time machine the results would surely be disastrous for both.

BORDER WITH COMPUTATIONAL SCIENCE
TIME-FACTORED MARKINGS

Did prehistoric peoples have the ability to track the seasons? Marshack (1972) thought they did; he studied "time factored" markings discovered on prehistoric handheld objects. Time factored meant that the objects had marks on them that corresponded to astronomical events such as the phases of the moon. He claimed that humans who had lived 30,000 years ago had developed nonarithmetical methods for predicting recurrent events such as seasonal migrations of prey animals and biological rhythms such as menstruation. Marshack had his critics, however, "In the 1990s some younger scholars took exception to Marshack's structuralist interpretations, preferring to see more magical and religious motives behind Paleolithic phenomena and decrying Marshack's approach as excessively numerological" (*The Times*, 2005, p. 8).

FARMING, SEDENTISM, AND DOMESTICATION

Today humans could not live without farming. Farmers produce enough food to sustain the entire human population (World Hunger Education Service, 2009). Malnutrition and starvation, then, comes not from the lack of food but from the inability to distribute food where it is needed. Wars, natural disasters, and economic downturns can disrupt existing food distribution networks causing local pockets of malnutrition or starvation. About 10,000 years ago, *Homo sapiens* nearly completely abandoned the hunter gathering lifestyle and adopted farming. The underlying logic behind the adoption of farming is not clear. Modern hunter-gatherers spend less time and effort "working" to sustain themselves than do non-mechanized modern farmers (Stuart, 1997). Also, modern hunter-gatherers water and feed wild plants and plant seasonal gardens. So, why would hunter-gatherers wish to become farmers?

Climate provides a clue. About 18,000 years ago, after the Last Glacial Maximum (LGM), the point of maximum extent of the last Ice Age, global average temperatures slowly rose and peaked about 11,000 years ago. Average temperatures then dropped again for over 1,000 years (the Younger Dryas). For the last 6,000 years, the global average temperature has remained relatively warm and constant. Today, scientists and world leaders worry that the average global temperature may be rising to new record-high levels due to human production of carbon dioxide and other industrial gases, the phenomenon of global warming. Dramatic worldwide temperature swings, regulated by natural cycles, are nothing new, however. They have occurred about every 100,000 years over the last million years. But, those temperature swings were not caused by human technology (Petit et al., 1999). Those naturally occurring climate oscillations may have been partly responsible for moving hunter-gatherers into a new lifestyle, **sedentism**, after the LGM. Holmes (2004) suggested additional reasons for the long and gradual switch to farming: competitive feasting, the new cultivated crops were a kind of luxury good; brewing beer, the grains grown were converted into beer, not eaten; and the new foods sprung a population trap, once people began to farm, they had more children and could not easily return to a hunter-gatherer lifestyle. Morris (2010) emphasized the role of the "lucky latitudes" the parts of the world between 20 and 35 degrees north where farming was easiest and where domesticable animals and plants already existed. Few such lucky areas exist south of the equator. Geography, too, explains much about the origin of farming.

The earliest archeological evidence of sedentism dates from about 11,000 years ago. Alongside the Euphrates River at a village called Abu Hureyra (in northern Syria), people formed one of the first communities based on farming. They built mud houses, hunted migrating gazelles, planted wheat and barley, and domesticated sheep and goats (Moore et al., 2000). The village lasted for thousands of years, although at one point it was abandoned and later reestablished. Also important to sedentism was the domestication of plants and animals.

Domestication is the process of regulating breeding of plants and animals. Domestication has been successful only with a limited number of species. Diamond (1997, p. 132) wrote, "A mere dozen species account for over 80% of the world's annual tonnage of all crops. Those dozen blockbusters are the cereals wheat, corn, rice, barley, and sorghum; the pulse soybean; the roots or tubers potato, manioc, and sweet potato; the sugar sources sugarcane and sugar beet; and the fruit banana." Similarly, only a few species of terrestrial herbivores have been domesticated as well. Diamond stated (p. 159), "Only five species became widespread and important around the world. Those Major Five of mammal domestication are the cow, sheep, goat, pig, and horse." Domestic plants and animals provided more than just food. Flax and cotton provided the raw materials for fabrics. Animals also provided muscle power, wool and hides as fabrics, milk, and organic fertilizer. Early domestication could have been unintentional. In the case of the wild wheats, for example, whose seeds shatter (drop from the plant) easily, early harvesters may have unintentionally altered the reproductive success of genetic variants whose seeds did not shatter by only cutting late maturing plants and perhaps later planting seeds left over from those plants (Mithen, 2004). Eventually, domestication did become intentional: saving some seeds for their desired genetic properties and planting them at the optimal time, selective breeding—allowing animals with desirable genetic characteristics to mate while denying that opportunity to those animals with less desirable genetic traits. Domestication did not require knowledge of genetics. Dogs (15,000 years ago) and cats (9,000 years ago) were domesticated very early and were the only carnivorous species domesticated.

The first continuously inhabited towns date from around 9,000 years ago. Jericho, in Israel, holds the distinction of being the oldest, continuously occupied town in the world. Slowly, most humans abandoned the hunter-gatherer lifestyle as towns and cities grew. Only recently have more people lived in cities than outside of them, the process of urbanization, changing lifestyles even for those who lived outside of towns and cities. Farmers, for example, could sell their surplus crops in urban markets. Urbanization continues to the present day.

BORDER WITH BIOLOGY
ANCIENT PSYCHOSURGERY

Psychosurgery surely seems modern, yet the evidence for trepanning (also called trephination), the intentional opening of a hole in the skull for therapeutic purposes, dates back to about 5,000 years ago. Hundreds of skulls with holes in them have been found in archeological sites around the world. While some of the holes were created after death, many were made while the patient was still alive. The holes in those skulls show signs of post-operative healing (Arnott et al., 2003). No one really knows why the practice of trepanning existed. Modern neurosurgeons cut openings in skulls in order to perform brain surgery, but they repair those holes, unlike their ancient predecessors. Photo 2.2 shows a trepanned skull from ancient Peru.

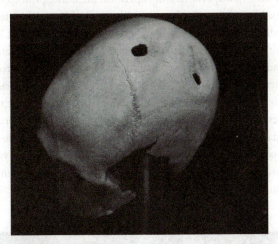

PHOTO 2.2 Trephined skull

Credit: Album / Alamy Stock Photo

LEARNING OBJECTIVE

4. Diagnose why only two carnivores (dogs and cats) were domesticated.

URBANIZATION

Urbanization began about 9,000 years ago in Mesopotamia (modern Iraq). Until very recently, the majority of people in the world lived outside of cities and towns: in villages, or in the countryside. The tipping point came in 2008 when, for the first time, more people lived in cities (UNFPA, 2008). In Europe, 80% of the population lives in cities (Antrop, 2004). In 1950, New York was the world's largest city with a population of 12,463,000 in its metropolitan area (Chandler, 1987). In 2019, Tokyo was the largest city with a population of over 37,426,554 (populationstat.com) in its metropolitan area. In 2019, 21 cities exceeded the 10 million mark (City Mayors Statistics, n.d.) creating high population densities. NASA measures the extent of urbanization by satellite photographs of the Earth taken at night and classifies regions as urban when the population density exceeds 1,000 persons per square mile, as peri-urban when the population density averages 100 persons per square mile, and as nonurban when the density is less than ten persons per mile (Weier, 2002). Mumford (1956) noted that cities first grew out of the agricultural villages of the Neolithic era. The grains grown (wheat, rye, rice, and maize) in various parts of the world where cities first emerged could be stored from year to year creating the first food surpluses. In turn, those surpluses created new specialized occupations, including philosopher (see Chapter 3), which were impossible in hunter-gatherer or village agriculture lifestyles. Mumford speculated that city walls provided new levels of safety for the inhabitants behind them. Also, because of agricultural surpluses and an increased birth rate, there were enough people to successfully defend the walls from outsiders, the first soldiers. He noted (p. 385) that city walls were also metaphors for growth, "Until modern times the extensions of a city's walls marked its growth as surely as does each additional ring of a tree." Other new innovations were reservoirs, sewers, irrigation networks, and paved roads. Cities provided security, but they also provided social continuity including, "a secure base of operations, a seat of law and government, a repository of deeds and contracts, and a marshalling yard for manpower" (p. 387). Cities revolutionized human history and led to the development and growth of the earliest civilizations (Photo 2.3).

PHOTO 2.3 World at night

Credit: iStock/Elen11

CIVILIZATION AND THE BIRTH OF HISTORY

Very few humans today live outside of civilization and its all-encompassing influence: laws, money, records, communications, and occupations. In hunter-gatherer groups there are only a few occupational specializations. In contrast, civilization includes hundreds of occupations. The O*NET OnLine database (US Department of Labor, n.d.) lists almost 1,000 occupations and identifies more than 100 of those as to "bright outlook" occupations including accountants, biostatisticians, and transportation engineers. Additionally, many occupations are labeled as "green" denoting that they are environmentally responsible jobs. Civilization is dynamic with technologies moving from Stone to Bronze, to Iron ages in the past, and to Agrarian, Industrial, and Informational more recently. Modern civilization is moving fitfully toward globalization with universal systems for timekeeping, standardized weights and measures, and worldwide communication. Complete globalization, however, may take centuries and it is possible that forces resisting globalization (e.g., nationalism) may prevent it from ever happening.

LEARNING OBJECTIVE
5. Predict what new technology or device might be a candidate for global standardization.

The First Civilizations

The earliest civilizations developed in Central Asia in an arc ranging from the Russian steppes to Mesopotamia The civilizations traditionally regarded as the oldest, those in Mesopotamia, have not lost their priority. Instead, the research revealed, "a far more complex picture in which dozens of urban centers thrived between Mesopotamia and the Indus, trading commodities and, possibly, adopting each other's technologies, architectures, and ideas" (Lawler, 2007, p. 586). These early civilizations were characterized by urbanization, writing systems, occupational specialization, and monumental architecture (Rudgley, 1999). They also included laws in place of customs, records instead of oral traditions, and, for the first time, schools. Cochran and Harpending (2009) speculated that the changes caused by living in civilizations were so vast that they led to the evolution of new biological and behavioral traits. Living in close proximity with domesticated mammals and with other humans required genetic changes, they argued. Thus, urbanized populations underwent natural selection for immunity to diseases that can leap from animals to humans and for being able to digest milk as adults. Presumably, people who could better withstand the crowding imposed by densely populated urban environments thrived and reproduced more successfully, thus altering many of the basic genetic characteristics of earlier humans. The COVID-19 virus and other communicable diseases spread more easily in urbanized environments (Figure 2.1).

FIGURE 2.1 ■ The Early Sites of Civilization

Other early civilizations developed outside of the central Asian arc. In Eurasia, civilizations arose in Egypt and around the Mediterranean Basin. Further east, civilizations arose in India, China, and Korea. In the New World, civilizations appeared in Mesoamerica and South America. Discussion of these civilizations, however, is outside of the scope of this text. In fact, topics in this text will be limited almost exclusively to the Mediterranean Basin including the Near East and then only to disciplines related to psychology. Once civilizations emerged, the period of prehistory ended. Civilizations created records, and in the process created the raw materials for historians to create history itself.

BORDER WITH SOCIAL SCIENCE
EARLY RELIGIONS

Religious thought and activity also appears to date from after the widespread adoption of sedentism. The presence of grave goods, food and tools buried along with the deceased, is evidence that Stone Age humans believed in the existence of an afterlife. The style and practice of early religious thought and activity differs tremendously from its modern forms. Pettitt (2020) distinguished between mortuary and funerary behaviors in prehistoric humans and proposes an evolutionary continuum eventually leading to the symbolic funerary practices of behaviorally modern humans. Gimbutas (1982) characterized early "Old European" religions as possessing several Goddesses and Gods. In her interpretation, the Goddesses, most notably the Great Goddess, were the most important. Gimbutas maintained that these deities represented a cyclical pattern of birth and rebirth and those, along with natural cycles such as the seasons of the year, emphasized the mystery of female fertility. Archeological evidence supports the rise of religious beliefs. Findings include the remains of temples, figurines (most of which are female), and arrangements of large stones. Gimbutas believed that these older religious traditions were swept away by later arriving groups who replaced them with predominantly male Gods. These new "sky Gods" derived from the sun and moon, required sacrifices of goods and of people, gave rise to the ideas of heaven and hell, and reinforced earlier ideas about the afterlife (Watson, 2005).

BORDER WITH COMPUTATIONAL SCIENCE
EARLY ACCOUNTING

Schmandt-Besserat (1996) wondered why tiny clay tokens were so common in archeological sites from all around the Middle East. She soon realized she had discovered an early accounting system. Each token represented the item in a business transaction. After such transactions, the tokens representing the items traded (e.g., lambs, goats, or sheep) were sealed inside hollow clay tablets to keep an accounting of the transaction. Eventually, the tokens became standardized. A cylinder came to symbolize an animal and an ovoid (egg-shaped token), a jar of oil, for instance. The tokens inside the clay envelopes eventually gave way to marking on clay tablets, one of the earliest forms of writing. Later still, early accountants realized that numerals could be divorced from the object they counted. Thus, they came to see that "three" was different from "three sheep." Numerals could apply to any referent and need not be paired to objects; numerals were abstract.

THE DEPTH OF CIVILIZATION

Civilization seems akin to the thin veneer covering an uglier layer of material underneath. Wars and the aftermath of natural disasters often act like sandpaper and expose our older uncivilized selves. The war in the Balkans in the first half of the 1990s, particularly the 30-month long siege of Sarajevo, stands out as a clear example of civilization breaking down. At the same time, those events demonstrated much about the resilience and adaptability of our species.

In 1984, Sarajevo had successfully hosted the Winter Olympics making the city well known around the world. So, when war broke out in the Balkans in 1991 after the death of Tito, the events that took place in Sarajevo were all the more shocking. The siege of Sarajevo began in April 1992 and lasted until September 1995. The city was surrounded by Serbian and Bosnian forces perched on the mountains surrounding the city and inside many tall buildings. At the beginning of the siege nearly a half million people lived in Sarajevo and because of the relative lack of habitable space were concentrated into a dense urban environment.

Marshall Tito Boulevard, a wide thoroughfare running east-west through the city contained the only trolley line. Soon, that street acquired a new name, one it still carries today, "Sniper Alley." Over 1,200 residents were killed or wounded by snipers during the siege; 60 of the killed were children. Another 60,000 were killed or wounded by artillery bombardments during that same period. Many buildings, some of them historic, also were destroyed or damaged. Soon, the very fabric of civilized life began to rapidly unravel. Some called it urbicide.

Food, fuel, and water became scarce. Schools closed and people moved into their basements. Yet, children still played in the streets, barriers against sniper fire were erected, and signs were posted in the more dangerous locations warning against sniper fire. In short, the lifestyle of Sarajevans acquired a kind of normalcy. Imagine a wife calmly admonishing her husband to watch out for snipers as he went to fetch water. Snipers became another fact of life. It seems that civilization is not that deep. It can be displaced by wars, terrorists, hurricanes, tornados, or other similar dire events. But, people adapt quickly to such changes, not that they like or enjoy them. People also forget the past quickly. Tourists now visit Sniper Alley, and many of the bullet marks have intentionally been left unrepaired. A monument to the victims of the siege in the shape of a large tin can of meat, depicting the kind of food delivered by relief agencies, now stands in Sniper Alley reminding all how quickly civilization can be lost (Photo 2.4).

PHOTO 2.4 Sarajevo Monument

Credit: Associated Press

THE RISE OF PHILOSOPHY

Philosophy and writing were natural partners. For the first time, historians used written records to help convey the story of humankind. Philosophy is part of that story. Because of the great antiquity of those early written records, they may be hard to find, are often undecipherable, and most are irretrievably lost. The nearer to the present, the easier it is to find written records. Philosophy emerged in ancient Greece nearly 3,000 years ago when a small group of thinkers began to wonder if the universe could be explained without resorting to supernatural events or beings. That story will be examined in the next chapter as will be the ideas raised by these philosophers and why those ideas remain important today. All of those philosophers attempted to eliminate supernatural explanations or entities from the pursuit of knowledge. That effort, in effect, defined philosophy itself—it is the love and pursuit of knowledge.

After philosophy defined itself against the supernatural, other questions arose. One set of questions concerned the physical makeup and workings of the universe, natural philosophy. It eventually led to the physical sciences. The search for first principles was a major early question and modern physical sciences have yet to answer it fully. Physicists today still spend millions of dollars every year searching for the primordial constituents of matter. Another early question was the nature of life or what separated living from nonliving things. In other words, what defines living things? The biological sciences grew out of that question. Biologists still struggle with that answer now when they ask questions such as whether viruses are alive or not.

The natural philosophers also struggled with the question of how much to trust sensory data. Indeed, this question has bedeviled intellectual inquiry ever since it was first raised. Early on, philosophers realized that information from the senses was not always reliable. Thus, the problem was to distinguish between reliable and unreliable sensory information. Modern science still struggles with this problem and its methods are, in large part, designed to eliminate or exclude unreliable sensory information. On the other hand, the early rationalist philosophers decided not to trust sensory data at all. They turned their focus from the universe to inside themselves, to their minds.

The dynamism of the universe was another idea explored by these early philosophers. Some argued for change and their philosophical systems reflected that. Others maintained that constancy was a feature of the universe and must be accounted for. Still others sought a compromise between these two extremes and created systems composed of changeless parts that combined and recombined. Modern science reflects that compromise with its laws of conservation on the one hand and its explanations for dynamic processes ranging from evolution to cosmology on the other.

The early philosophers also came up with two long-standing entities that are still very much with us: mind and soul. The mind, in many ways, has become one of the central foci of modern psychology. The soul, too, has survived the long journey from ancient Greece till now. However, the soul is no longer the subject of much psychological inquiry. It is, though, the main subject of nearly every extant religion as is the concept of heaven. Today, in the West at least, the division of mind and soul has become permanent. In ancient Greece, they were still very close to each other.

Many –isms will be examined and defined. Here, a few will be mentioned. Later chapters will cover them more thoroughly. Materialism still remains a powerful idea in modern science. In many ways, it is the Holy Grail of modern science as psychologists search for physical explanations of thought in the brain. Nihilism, monism, and relativism will also be examined. Nihilists, basically, argued that the search for knowledge is impossible, or they argued that even if it were possible, it could not be communicated. So, they asked, "Why bother studying anything?" Monism is more resistant to such easy elimination. Monistic explanations searched for the *one* thing that will explain all of the others. Future chapters will examine a number of plausible monistic formulations (e.g., materialism and idealism) as well as dualistic (two things) and pluralistic (three or more things) formulations.

Relativism, too, is a flourishing hot topic. Culture is a good example. Things that people take for granted as universal may not be so. Triandis related (personal communication, April 1, 1994) how he misinterpreted a simple note in India. He was registered at a hotel and received a note with two words and two boxes. The words were "Vacancy" and "No Vacancy" and the box next to No Vacancy was checked (Figure 2.2). Triandis assumed that his reservation had been canceled and booked another room at an inferior hotel. A couple of days later the manager at the original hotel saw Triandis in the lobby and asked him why he had not checked in yet. Ruffled, Triandis pulled out the note and showed it to him. The manager then said, Yes, we always mark the box that does not apply. He checked in. At the same time, other topics are nearly universal. Perception, for the most part, varies little from person to person around the world. No one with normal vision will argue that the ocean is red. The philosophers raised more questions than they answered. Over time though, the questions kept getting better and some questions did get answered. A look at ancient Greek religion will help set the stage for understanding how philosophy was born.

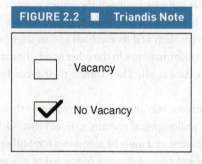

FIGURE 2.2 ■ Triandis Note

☐ Vacancy

☑ No Vacancy

LEARNING OBJECTIVE

6. Demonstrate relativistic thinking where a male might interpret a cultural situation differently from a female.

ANCIENT GREEK RELIGION

Hesiod's *Theogeny* and Homer's *Iliad* and *Odyssey* were the most important original Greek sources relating to the origin and extent of Greek religious thought and activity. Unlike the Judeo-Christian and Islamic religious traditions, Greek religion was polytheistic, local, and included no sacred texts. The Greek gods were numerous, male or female, and immortal.

In Hesiod's account, Chaos was the original god, the primordial and eternal being. Chaos gave birth to Gaia (Earth), Tartaros (the Underworld), and Eros (Desire). Gaia, alone, gave birth to Ouranos (Sky), Ourea (Mountains), and Pontus (Sea). Later, Gaia and Ouranos mated to create the 12 Titans. Ouranos, displeased, hid the Titans in the Earth but Gaia did not want them hidden, so she gave the titan Kronos a sickle with which to castrate his father. When

Kronos threw Ouranos's testicles into the sea, Aphrodite, Goddess of love, emerged fully formed. Kronos now ruled the cosmos (or everything), but learned from a prophecy that one of his children would overthrow him. To prevent that fate, he devoured his children as they were born. Rhea his wife fooled him when she gave birth to Zeus, their last child, by giving him a large rock to swallow instead. Later, and without explanation, Kronos vomited up his five other children. They joined with Zeus in a ten-year war that ended with all of the Titans, save Prometheus, locked in Tartaros, the underworld. Afterwards, Zeus married seven times, lastly with Hera. Athena, Zeus's daughter, was "born" directly from Zeus's head, not from Hera. Angered, Hera too gave birth to a son without sexual intercourse, Hephaestus, the god of fire. Eventually, there were 12 major gods, the Olympians (because they lived on top of Mt. Olympus): Zeus, Hera, Poseidon, Demeter, Ares, Hermes, Hephaestus, Aphrodite, Athena, Artemis, Hestia, and Apollo. Three minor but important gods were Dionysius, Pan, and Hekate. In addition to the gods already mentioned there were also numerous nymphs, gorgons, cyclopedes, river gods, and giants.

The Greek city-states worshiped gods of their own choosing. Athens, for instance, worshiped Athena, while Sparta worshiped Artemis. Worship primarily consisted of blood sacrifice of food animals: sheep, pigs, oxen, horses, or birds. Priests or priestesses accepted and killed the animals, consigning the blood, skin, and bones to the god. The meat was roasted and given to the worshipers. The god's sanctuaries contained an altar for sacrifices and were nearly always outdoors and oriented east (Mikalson, 2004).

The gods themselves were human-like, powerful, and immortal. However, the gods were not *all*-powerful. In the *Iliad,* for example, Apollo could not save Hector from death; fate had already doomed him to die at Achilles' hand. Even the gods were powerless against fate. They fought and plotted among themselves as well, thus giving humans a wide variety of divine examples for their own behavior. Robinson (1981, p. 36) noted, "for almost any form of conduct, a divine example could be found with relative ease." Robinson linked Dionysius and Apollo as examples of emotion and reason, respectively, a distinction that eventually crossed over from mythology into psychology.

It was against this backdrop of Greek religion that the first philosophers began to ply their trade. The birth of that new discipline, philosophy, took place during the Archaic Age (800 to 479 BCE) in Ionia (present day Turkey). Although these new philosophers sought naturalistic explanations for the universe, they did so against the backdrop of these religious ideas. The death of Socrates followed by Plato's seeming reluctance to venture deeply into cosmology and theology testified to the tension between early philosophy and Greek religion (Robinson, 1981). Another early Greek advance was in medicine. Its origins were empirical but, over time, they devolved into received and traditional knowledge. Medicine did not regain its original empirical roots until well into the modern era.

LEARNING OBJECTIVE

7. Interpret why humorism had such a long life in the history of medicine.

GREEK MEDICINE

Greek medicine was another original Greek contribution to civilization. Like philosophy, Greek medicine had shed its early mythological roots. Unlike philosophy, however, medicine evolved into an empirical practice. Alcmaeon was an early writer and teacher of the medical arts. Hippocrates was among the first persons to emphasize the natural nature of disease and firmly reject supernatural explanations for illness. Galen, who lived hundreds of years after Hippocrates, collected and published the corpus of ancient Greek medicine and added his original knowledge to it. Hippocrates's medical writings became the basis of Western medicine for over 1,000 years after they were systematically organized and made popular by Galen nearly 500 years after Hippocrates's death.

Alcmaeon (dates unknown)

No one knows exactly when Alcmaeon lived, but he was probably born sometime between 540 and 510 BCE. He was born in Croton, in *Magna Graecia,* and lived there at the same time as Pythagoras with whom he was likely acquainted. However, he was probably not one of his students or followers. It is not clear whether Alcmaeon was a practicing physician or a naturalistic philosopher. During his lifetime, however, Croton was famous for the skill of its physicians (Photo 2.5).

PHOTO 2.5 Alcmaeon

Alcmaeon wrote one book, *On Nature*, of which only fragments survive. In that book he argued for a naturalistic view of human beings and rejected revelation as a source of knowledge. He proposed several original ideas about humans and animals. Both, he thought, could perceive the world but only humans could take the next step, understanding what they perceived. He placed the mental faculties of both in the brain and made it the home of vision, hearing, taste, and smell. Through dissection, he discovered that the eye had a connection (the optic nerve) with the brain. That discovery led him to infer that the ear, tongue, and nose must also have similar connections. However, there is no evidence that he conducted further dissections to confirm his hypotheses. Also, he never mentioned the sense of touch in his extant writings.

His medical theories were based on the balance or imbalance of opposites. Health, he believed, was related to a balance between factors, while disease was caused by an imbalance or what he called a "monarchy" of one of the factors. Huffman (2008) saw Alcmaeon as influential for three reasons. The first was naming the brain as the seat of intelligence. The second was his empiricism and the third was his argument for the immortality of the soul. Alcmaeon was the first to suggest that the soul was immortal and likely an inspiration for Plato's later thinking about the nature of the soul. He also placed the seat of human faculties in the brain, not the heart. Later, Aristotle (see Chapter 3) moved it back. Panegyres and Panegyres (2016, p. 21) stated:

> The ancient Egyptians maintained that the heart was the place of mind [5]. Some Greek philosophers questioned this view and developed concepts implicating neurological

localisation. Alcmaeon, Praxagoras and Herophilus promoted this cerebrocentric view, which was shared by Hippocrates, only to be later rejected by Aristotle who promoted a cardiocentric model.

The Greek physicians began a tradition that was steeped in empiricism but one that did not survive antiquity. From Alcmaeon on, they observed and collected vast volumes filled with facts about the body and disease. The most famous of these physicians was Hippocrates. His medical discoveries lasted for millennia but the methods he used to find them fell into disuse by the early Middle Ages. Thus, medieval physicians no longer applied empirical methods to medicine either to discover new facts or confirm or reject old ones. Hippocrates himself would have gladly rejected any of his previous findings if they had later been shown to be incorrect. Unlike the medieval physicians, he was a true empiricist.

Hippocrates (460–377 BCE)

Biography

Hippocrates was born on the island of Cos (modern Kos, Greece). His father and grandfather were also physicians. Hippocrates learned medicine but also studied philosophy with Democritus and Gorgias. There are many extant writings attributed to Hippocrates. However, they cannot all be his because they exhibit different writing styles and are often contradictory. Writers after Hippocrates appropriated his name in order to lend credence to their own works. Hippocrates is known as the "father of medicine" because he strongly rejected supernatural explanations of illness and disease; the Hippocratic writings (the Hippocratic Corpus) never mention such causes. Hippocrates lived to an old age, traveled widely throughout Greece, and was well known and respected during his lifetime (Photo 2.6).

PHOTO 2.6 Hippocrates

Contributions

Hippocratic medicine was mostly centered on clinical care and prognosis. Hippocrates recommended that patients be kept clean, treated gently, and brought back to health using natural means. He believed the body could cure itself and that the physician's job was to aid that process. He defined health as a balance of the four humors, internal fluids he believed were vital to well-being. When the humors were out of balance, illness resulted. The four humors were: blood, black bile, yellow bile, and phlegm. The humors, in turn, were linked to the four Greek elements: blood with air, black bile with earth, yellow bile with fire, and phlegm with water. Medical practice from Hippocrates on was dominated by **humorism**, which was not completely discredited until the 19th century. In that system, those with an excess of blood were called sanguine; their personalities and behaviors were hopeful, cheerful, and spirited. Those with too much black bile were melancholic or depressed. Those too full of yellow bile were irritable and grumpy. Those with an excess of phlegm were apathetic and unemotional. Galen and the later Arabic physicians greatly amplified and expanded humorism. Hippocrates was one of the first to diagnose a phobia, describing how a patient, Nicanor, had developed an irrational fear to flute music played at night (Crocq, 2015).

Hippocrates was also well known for his Hippocratic Oath. However, it is not clear that he actually wrote it. Nonetheless, the language of the oath is clear and uncompromising. Physicians should never do harm, administer poison, induce abortions, have sex with their patients, or violate confidences. It is a remarkable document and is the historical basis for modern codes of professional ethics.

Hippocrates's influence on later developments in medicine was paradoxical. Later physicians failed to adopt his empirical methods but held on to the findings Hippocrates and his successors had discovered using those methods. The effect was to halt and reverse the progress of medicine for over 2,000 years. Hippocratic thinking also had little effect on later philosophy. As philosophy became less concerned about the natural world and more concerned about the Platonic Forms, Hippocrates's empirical methods and observations fell into disfavor. By the time that Greek philosophers regained an interest in the natural world, the separation between them and their contemporary medical practitioners was too great to rekindle a synthesis. Robinson (1981, p. 69) stated, "Hippocrates and his followers come closer to the modern spirit of experimental science than perhaps any figure in antiquity." This ancient high water mark of scientific progress would not be regained until the Enlightenment. The knowledge about Hippocrates and of the Hippocratic tradition largely comes from the work of a physician who lived hundreds of years after him, Galen. He not only preserved that knowledge and tradition, but he also added greatly to it.

Galen (129–210 CE)

Biography

Galen was a Greek physician from Pergamum (modern Bergama, Turkey). His father, Nicon, was an architect and educated his son until he was 14. Nicon wished for Galen to become a philosopher. But after a dream, he relented and allowed Galen to study medicine. After completing his medical studies in Pergamum, Galen traveled extensively and studied in Smyrna (modern Izmir, Turkey), Corinth, and Alexandria. He returned to Pergamum and became the physician to gladiators, learning much about human anatomy in the process.

Contributions

Later, he moved to Rome where he soon became famous as a physician, catching the eye of the emperor, Marcus Aurelius, and eventually becoming his personal physician. As a prolific writer, Galen documented his work. Unfortunately, much of it was destroyed in a fire in 191 CE. Enough of his writings survived to cement his position as the most prolific collector of the ancient world's medical knowledge. Much of his extant work is now being translated into English (Singer & van der Ejik, 2019).

Galen, however, was more than a collector of ancient medical lore. He added much to the body of ancient medical knowledge. He dissected animals and was the first to describe how muscles worked in opposing pairs. He severed the nerves of living animals in order to infer their functions. He experimented by tying off the ureters of animals and observing the subsequent swelling of their kidneys. He failed, however, to accurately describe the circulation of blood, believing that arterial and venous flows were independent of each other. Because he could not legally dissect human cadavers, he mistakenly inferred the existence of anatomical structures nonexistent in humans. For example, he thought that humans possessed a *rete mirabile,* a complex vascular network associated with heat exchange in certain animals (e.g., cows, tuna, and some birds). Humans, it turns out, do not possess that anatomical structure. After Galen's death, his discoveries, like those of Hippocrates and Aristotle before him, were canonized by the Roman Church. Thus, his unchallenged ideas about anatomy persisted well into the Enlightenment.

Perhaps because of the early influence of his father, Galen believed that physicians should receive a well-rounded education, especially in philosophy. He also believed that physicians should not enter the profession in order to become rich. Medicine, thus, through the work of Hippocrates and Galen, progressed quickly early on in its history, only to stagnate for over 1,000 years.

SUMMARY

It is nearly impossible to form a clear picture of what humans were like before they began to keep written records. What those prehistoric peoples thought and did cannot be understood using methods requiring living participants. However, as cognitive archeologists and others have shown, inferences about their thinking and behavior can be made by the careful analysis of ancient artifacts, akin to Wundt's *völkerpsychologie* (Kardas & Henley, 2020). That part of Wundt's psychology explored language, myths, customs, and other similar areas in a manner very different from laboratory psychology. Wundt, likely, would find this chapter necessary for a complete understanding of psychology. Biologically, however, the picture is clearer. Most likely, members of the species *Homo sapiens* are more similar to each other than different, at least over the last 50,000 years. Culturally, much has changed over the last 15,000 years. The human species has multiplied exponentially and has transformed much of the Earth through technology and radically changed its demography with most now living in large cities and subject to conditions of crowding scarcely imaginable in the past. Narvaez (2020) urged us to see outside our fishbowl and consider the restraints that civilization has imposed: a foreshortened view of humanity, a negative view of human nature and prehistory, biases against individualism and towards abstraction, and a misunderstanding of human potential. She stated (p. 113), "Understanding where we have been can help us figure out how to move forward." People could learn much about how to live and prosper in partnership with the environment she argued; the San Bushmen, for example, have maintained such a balance with nature for over 150,000 years. People should understand that civilization is very new and it profoundly altered older lifeways. Only some 7,000 years ago did civilizations begin to appear and create surpluses of goods and job specialization. One of those specializations was philosophy, an essential part of any civilization and the mother of nearly every other academic discipline including psychology.

3 GREEK PHILOSOPHY

ZEITGEIST

A Short History of Ancient Greece

The modern country of Greece sits at the southern end of the Balkan Peninsula in south-eastern Europe. Ancient Greece, *Magna Graecia* in Latin, however, comprised a larger area and included Ionia (Anatolia or modern Turkey), the island of Crete, and parts of the Italian peninsula (see Figure 3.1). The geography is dominated by the Aegean Sea, thousands of islands, and a relative shortage of habitable places caused by a mountainous interior. The climate is sunny and warm in the summer and cool and wet in the winter, conducive to growing crops, but with limited arable land. Freezing is rare, and easy access to the sea promoted shipbuilding and maritime trade. The region is in one of Morris's (2010) "lucky latitudes" that band between 20 and 35 north in the Old World that is favorable for farming.

Near the end of the Stone Age, most of the area shown in Figure 3.1 was thinly populated by small groups of newly arriving farmers (Martin, 2000). The Bronze Age arrived around 5,000 years ago and led to the establishment of commerce because the ores required to make bronze; copper and tin were usually not found near each other (Cameron & Neal, 2002). Other new technologies that arose during this period were textiles and pottery.

Around 4,000 years ago, Minoan civilization developed on the island of Crete. It was non-Greek, seemingly peaceful (their palaces were unfortified), and highly organized. Using a script that has yet to be deciphered, Linear A, they kept extensive records on clay tablets and stored large amounts of grain in their palaces. After 1625 BCE, a date linked to the massive eruption of a volcano on the island of Thera (modern Santorini), Minoan civilization gradually began to decline. It was replaced by the Mycenaean culture, warlike Greeks from the mainland. Amateur linguist Michael Ventris deciphered their script, Linear B, enabling modern scholars to read those ancient records (Singh, 1999). The Mycenaean civilization collapsed around 3,200 years ago, plunging Greece into its Dark Age, a period lasted nearly 500 years and saw the loss of writing and a diminution of culture and its artifacts in general (Sansone, 2009). Snodgrass (2001, p. 2) added "a fall in population...loss of certain purely material skills...loss of the art of writing...fall in living standards...a general severance on contacts, commercial and otherwise, with most peoples beyond the Aegean area" as further evidence of a dark age.

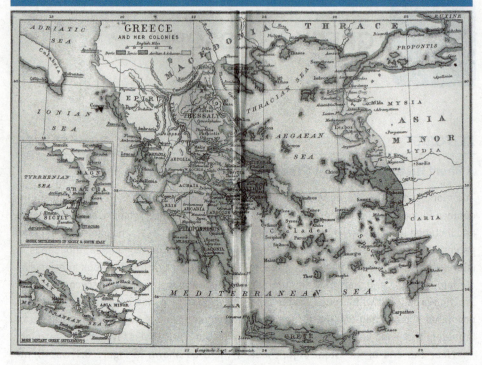

FIGURE 3.1   ■   Ancient Greece

Credit: Colin Waters / Alamy Stock Photo

Greece emerged from its Dark Age about 2,800 years ago and entered the Archaic Period. The well-known system of city-states developed then and Athens and Sparta were the most prominent. Athens, and many other city-states, eventually created democratic systems of government where male citizens, but not females, foreigners, or slaves, could participate in the running of their affairs. Sparta, however, became thoroughly militarized, requiring compulsory military training and service of its male citizens from the ages of 7–60. Renewed prosperity promoted colonization from Greece's Aegean heartland back to Ionia, Italy, Sicily, and North Africa leading to what was later called in Latin, *Magna Graecia,* or Greater Greece.

The Classical Period followed starting about 2,500 years ago. During that period, the Greek city-states united twice to war successfully against the Persians only to war later among themselves. That last war, the Peloponnesian War, ended Athenian democracy and left Sparta ascendant. Phillip of Macedon and his son, Alexander the Great, greatly expanded Greek influence throughout the ancient world. Alexander created a short-lived empire that stretched from Egypt to India (see Figure 3.2). One of the main intellectual consequences of his conquests was spreading Greek ideas and ways of thinking over a wide area, a process called **Hellenization** (*Hellas* is the Greek word for Greece). The first philosophers worked to disentangle reality itself from the supernatural contexts created by the older Greek myths and they provided, for the first time in history, accounts about

FIGURE 3.2 ■ The Macedonian Empire of Alexander the Great

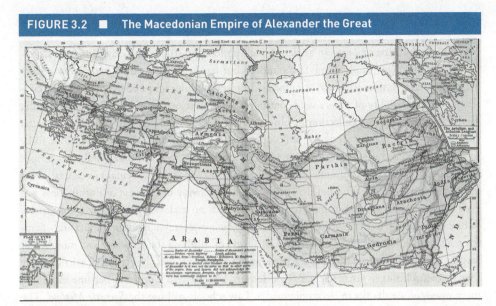

Credit: Classic Image / Alamy Stock Photo

the world and its workings that only relied on observable facts, not on fanciful stories. Greek ideas were carried westward throughout the Mediterranean Basin and eastward into central Asia by Alexander the Great. In 336 BCE, Phillip II, Alexander's father, was assassinated and Alexander became king. He quickly moved to consolidate his position, killing off potential rivals and resecuring Macedon's hold over all of Greece.

Soon after, he led a Greek invasion of Asia. In a campaign lasting three years and ranging from modern Turkey, southward through the Levant, into Egypt, and back eastward into Persia (modern Iran), he defeated the Persian Empire and its king, Darius. While in Egypt in 331 BCE, he founded one of the many cities to bear his name, Alexandria. Soon, it became the intellectual center of the world for hundreds of years. After conquering Persia, Alexander went further eastward, again fighting through Afghanistan as far as the Beas River (modern Hyphasis) on the border of northern India. So far from Greece and exhausted after years of constant fighting, his army refused to march further. Alexander was forced to turn back. Three years later, Alexander died in Babylon after a two-week-long illness at the age of 32. Soon, his empire fell into three large pieces. His body was laid in public view in Alexandria for nearly 500 years where Roman generals, emperors, and others visited it for inspiration.

Alexander spread the Greek ideas far and wide creating a sociocultural amalgam from the many intellectual traditions mixed together by his conquests—a mixture of Greek, Persian, Indian, and Egyptian cultures—and created the world's first experiment in multiculturalism. His conquests exposed him and his fellow Greeks to previously unknown lands, cultures, and languages. This grand mixture of peoples and cultures was the first example of **cosmopolitanism**. Cosmopolitanism eventually spread throughout the Roman world via Cynicism, Stoicism, and Christianity.

PREVIEW

Many ideas that first emerged in ancient Greek philosophy still exist today. *Animistic* thinking continues in the minds of modern children but has been replaced by *materialism* nearly everywhere else. Rationalism retains a prominent place in philosophy and psychology. The conflict over the reliability of *sensory data* continues. Modern science has progressed by imposing methods that assure the collection of observational data is unbiased and reliable. *The mind* continues to be a focus of study for philosophers and scientists and will likely continue to be so for centuries to come. Understanding the relationship between mind and brain has proved to be especially vexing and troublesome (Eccles, 1985). *Love* and *strife* remain as central issues in psychology, sociology, and political science. The discovery of the *void* or nothingness was groundbreaking. Cosmologists have found that there is no such thing as totally empty space, but most of the universe is anything but dense. *Atomism* is central to modern physics and chemistry. *Relativism* has mostly displaced absolutist ways of thinking about culture and morality, at least in scientific contexts. Modern science is anything but *nihilistic* but critics of science argue that there are limits to what science can discover. The modern world has become more and more *cosmopolitan* thanks to electronic media. Law schools still use the *Socratic Method*. The public still debates *relativism* and *absolutism*. Plato's *idealism* is still invoked as an explanatory device. The *observation of nature* has become a scientific enterprise. Doctors and health professionals continue to promote *moderation* as a way to better health. *Cause and effect* are analyzed daily in courtrooms and laboratories. *Inductive, deductive,* and *propositional logic* is thoroughly entrenched in many aspects of modern life. Avoiding determinism and dogmatism are still concerns for thinkers today.

INTRODUCTION

The philosophers were the first thinkers who attempted to explain the world in natural rather than supernatural terms. They wanted to divorce their explanations from magic and superstition and avoid invoking the gods as supernatural agents who intervened in natural processes, including human conduct. Historical knowledge of much of early philosophy is extremely limited because only a very small portion of their original writings survived. Commentaries (or doxographies) by later philosophers also survived, but those may reflect a biased view of their predecessors. Much of what is known about ancient philosophers and their ideas comes from the commentaries of writers who read and wrote about original material now lost to history. Many historians lump all of the philosophers before Socrates into a category called "Pre-Socratic." However, doing so oversimplifies the history of philosophy. Some philosophers so labeled did live before Socrates but others were his contemporaries. Furthermore, much of what is now known about the earliest philosophers comes from the writings of Plato and Aristotle; their treatment of their predecessors may not have been fair and even-handed. Athens after the Peloponnesian War was a far different place than it had been under Pericles during its "Golden Age." The Spartans replaced Athenian-style democracy with an oligarchy, the Thirty Tyrants. These men were Athenians who kept the reins of power firmly in their grasp for

33 years. During that time, they revoked many of the liberties Athenians previously had enjoyed and dispensed with the jury system. They appointed a Council of Five Hundred to take the place of the old system's juries and only permitted 3,000 men to bear arms. Many injustices took place during this period; eventually, the Thirty Tyrants were deposed and democracy restored. That restoration was short-lived as first Phillip and then Alexander conquered and united the former Greek city-states under Macedon. Socrates, too, was caught up in this period of Greek history and, as a young man, fought in the Peloponnesian War. Always outspoken, he refused to kowtow to the newly reestablished Athenian assembly, an action that eventually led to his death. Within this historical context, philosophy was born and came of age. Its earliest thinkers lived in the Ionian city of Miletus.

MILESIAN PHILOSOPHERS

Miletus, around 500 BCE, was a prosperous and ancient city of Ionia known for producing fine fabrics and pottery. In addition, its strong navy allowed it to trade its goods safely throughout *Magna Graecia*. Three philosophers lived and taught in Miletus some 2,500 years ago: Thales, Anaximander, and Anaximenes. The Greek word *philosophos* means lover of wise things. The "wise things" pursued by these thinkers were wide and varied. They included the physical sciences, psychological topics, theology, ethics, and what today we would consider traditional philosophical topics—epistemology and metaphysics. They, for the first time ever recorded, separated the world into two categories, natural and supernatural, and placed a barrier in between them. All three of these philosophers were searching for the first principle (*arche* in Greek) underlying all knowledge. For Thales, the *arche* was water; for Anaximander, it was the *aperion* (a kind of abstract primordial substance), and for Anaximenes, it was air.

Thales (624–546 BCE)

Thales was well known and respected during his lifetime; he was one of the "Seven Sages" of his day and the only philosopher among them. No writings directly attributable to Thales have survived. Aristotle (1999, p. 27), however, wrote, "Thales, too, to judge from what is recorded of his views," which indicates that he had access, since lost, to written materials by or about Thales. Thales was an astronomer. He is often credited with predicting a solar eclipse during a battle between the Medes and the Lydians in 585 BCE. Another astronomical recommendation was that mariners should use the constellation *Ursa Minor* instead of *Ursa Major* as a navigational aid, the former being a more reliable indicator of North.

Thales was a geometer who likely learned that discipline while living in Egypt. Several geometric proofs are attributed to him, including one proving that any triangle inside a semicircle must contain a right angle. Thales spent time in Egypt and probably learned his geometry there. Back in Miletus, Thales trained some of his students, including Pythagoras and Euclid, in geometry. In his philosophy, Thales focused on water as the source of everything else found in the natural world, a natural assumption for an Ionian living in a port city, and who had [does not read correctly without "had" IMHO] seen the Nile's extensive irrigation systems. Water was everywhere and was responsible for life itself. Again, Aristotle (1999, p. 7) was definite when he wrote:

> Thales, the founder of this sort of philosophy, says it is water (for which reason too he declared that the Earth is on water), getting hold of this opinion perhaps from seeing that the nourishment of all things is fluid, and that heat itself comes from it and lives by means of it (and that out of which things come into being is the source of them all). So he got hold of this opinion by this means, and because the seeds of all things have a fluid nature, while water is in turn the source of the nature of all fluid things.

> There are some who think that very ancient thinkers, long before the present age, who gave the first accounts of the Gods had an opinion of this sort about nature. For they made Ocean and Tethys the parents of what comes into being, and made the oath of the Gods be by water, called Styx by them; for what is oldest is most honored, and that by which one swears is the most honored thing. But whether this opinion about nature is something archaic and ancient might perhaps be unclear, but Thales at least is said to have spoken in this way about the first cause.

Note how Aristotle positively contrasts Thales's philosophical views to the older, traditional, prephilosophical accounts of creation.

Thales was an animist—he believed that all objects were alive. Magnetism and static electricity led him to that belief. Lodestones, or natural magnets, were known in ancient times. Thales explained their action on iron objects as resulting from a kind of life force, or **animism**. He explained the attraction of lightweight objects to amber that had been rubbed vigorously in the same way. He inferred from his observations that even physical objects had souls because they could induce motion. Iverson and Jacks (2012) argued that Thales did not actually perform any systematic experiments on electrostatics and that no ancient sources suggest that he did.

Russell (1945, p. 3) wrote, "Philosophy begins with Thales." Thales created the first system of natural philosophy and was the first to attempt a purely physical explanation for the nature of the world. He used water as the source of everything else in the universe and attempted to relate all other observations in terms of their relationship to or origin from water. While he refused to accept supernatural explanations, he did believe that humans, animals, and objects had souls.

Anaximander (611–545 BCE)

Only two short fragments (about 35 words) of Anaximander's writings survive. But, a larger body of commentaries by ancient writers on Anaximander and his ideas still exist. Anaximander knew Thales and had wide interests ranging from astronomy to politics. As an astronomer, he introduced the gnomon, the upright portion of a sundial to Greece. He also created a model of the universe where the Earth was a cylinder floating immobile in space (itself a new concept at the time), surrounded by wheels containing the stars, the moon, and the sun. His model even specified the distances from them to the Earth (using Earth diameters as the units). He was the first to speculate that all of the stars, the moon, and the sun made full circles around the Earth. To him, the Earth had to be a cylinder, because that explained the seeming flatness seen while standing on the surface of it. Figure 3.3 illustrates his model of the Earth in relation to the sun and moon. Anaximander was a geographer and possibly the first to draw a map of the world. That map showed the world as a circle (the top of Earth's cylinder), with Greece as the center of the world.

FIGURE 3.3   ■   Anaximander's Model of the Universe

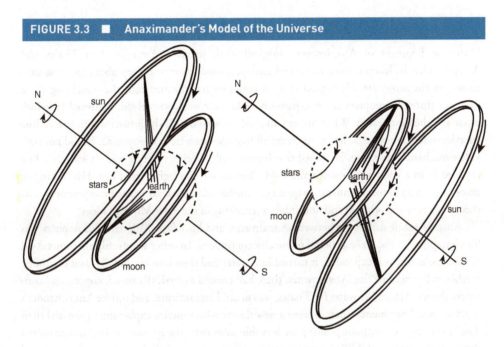

Maps are good evidence of cognition. Their orientation has changed over time with modern paper maps nearly all having North at the top. Gordon (1971) showed how older maps tended to be oriented many ways but nearly always with a four-part division of cardinal directions. Christianity made an eastern orientation important while Islam pointed its believers toward Mecca each linking geography to belief. Today, paper maps are rare thanks to electronic maps that allow users to select how the map is displayed.

Anaximander speculated on human origins and claimed that humans were descended from fish. In philosophy, he diverged from Thales's idea that water was the origin of everything. Anaximander argued that because water was one of the four elements of nature, it could not also serve as the first principle (the ancient Greeks posited four elements: air, earth, fire, and water). Thus, the first principle had to be something other, something limitless and primordial, the *aperion,* the reputed source of the four elements. The *aperion* implied a kind of physical infinity, balancing out the tendency of the other elements to destroy each other. Furthermore, the *aperion* powered nature's cycles: day vs night and the seasons.

Anaximander continued the revolution begun by Thales, but modified the details. The *aperion* was something new in human thinking. It was the first time anyone proposed the existence of an invisible, infinite, yet physical substance in order to explain the workings of the world. Anaximander remained faithful to Thales's natural philosophy in that the *aperion,* too, was a physical thing. It just happened to be a very new and strange kind of thing. Recently, Gregory (2016) cast Anaximander as a protoscientist, one of many contributing to the early development of scientific thought. Gregory saw Anaximander as an observer of nature whose recorded ideas may have been lost even in ancient times.

Anaximenes (585–525 BCE)

Only one fragment of Anaximenes's original work survives. Younger than Thales and Anaximander, he learned from them and later proposed his own theory about the first substance, or the *arche,* air. He argued that air could be transformed into the remaining three elements through compression or expansion. When air was compressed, it turned first into water and then into earth. When air was allowed to expand quickly, it turned into fire. While Anaximander claimed that he could create all four elements from the *aperion,* he did not provide a mechanism to do so. He noted that breath could be either hot or cold. It was hot when expelled from a wide-open mouth and cold when blown through pursed lips. His linking of theory with data in this manner may qualify as the first documented scientific experiment. His theory was new and original and not simply a rehashing of the older Milesian ideas.

Another subtle difference between Anaximenes and his fellow Milesian philosophers was his conception of the *arche* as being physically continuous. In other words, highly compressed air became earth; as it expanded, it turned into water and then into air. Finally, as it expanded further, still it became fire. Anaximenes, then, had created a physically based, cogent, and consistent theory. Air, unlike water for Thales, was neutral and infinite, and unlike Anaximander's *aperion,* real. Anaximenes, then, created a new theory with superior explanatory potential than Thales's theory and without positing an invisible substance, the *aperion,* as in Anaximander's theory. Kalachanis et al. (2015) noted that Anaximander's use of air, his primal substance, and its subsequent conversion into the other Greek elements are, in principle at least, similar to modern physics and its Big Bang theory of the origin of the universe.

Summary of Milesian Philosophy

By attempting to explain the nature of the world and the universe using only physical entities, the Milesian thinkers founded philosophy. Their refusal to inject magical or mystical explanations into their thinking was original. Arguing that their theories make little sense today is missing the point. The search for the *arche* that they began continues today. Scientists in the twenty-first century, too, cannot specify what the original substance was. They can, however, say what it was not. It was not earth, fire, water, or air. Nor was it any modern element. Modern physical theory may be as clueless today about the nature of the first substance that exploded some 14 billion years ago in the Big Bang as the Milesians were about water, the *aperion,* or air. But, the method they created—philosophy—persisted. Philosophy quickly spread across the rest of the Greek world and, ultimately, into our time. Those first philosophers also identified, for the first time, some other questions that continue to puzzle us. One set of questions concerns the origin of the universe. Is the universe eternal? Has it always existed? Or, did it begin at some point? If so, how? If it had a beginning, what came before it? The answers to these ancient questions are still unknown.

LEARNING OBJECTIVE

1. Compare the Milesians choices of primordial substances.

EARLY GROWTH AND DEVELOPMENT OF PHILOSOPHY

As Greece grew and prospered, so, too, did philosophy. The Milesians studied nature. Soon, however, some philosophers began to include humans as a part of nature. More specifically, they began to study the human mind and how it came to understand nature. One of the disciplines that seemed especially apt for understanding the mind was mathematics. Mathematics is logical and rational. Its rules are explicit and unchangeable. It is a creation of the human mind. Might it be possible to describe the universe using mathematics? Pythagoras is remembered for the geometrical theorem named after him, but mathematics was only one of his interests.

Pythagoras (570–490 BCE)

Pythagoras was born on the island of Samos but eventually moved to Croton, a town in *Magna Graecia*. He traveled widely and may have visited Egypt where he probably learned the famous geometrical theorem that bears his name and also picked up the seeds of his later mystical ideas. After he died, his fame grew because of his followers. They promoted and expanded his ideas and created an early quasireligious movement known as Pythagoreanism that redefined the earlier Greek concept of soul and introduced new notions of the afterlife, including reincarnation.

Today, Pythagoras is perhaps the best-remembered figure from this period, especially because of the Pythagorean theorem in geometry. Recall that theorem gives the length of the hypotenuse of right triangles via the formula $a^2 + b^2 = c^2$, where c is the hypotenuse and a and b are the other two sides (see Figure 3.4). Pythagoras probably introduced that theorem to Greece. However, the theorem was already well known in Persia (Burkert, 1972). Less than 200 years after his death, Pythagoreanism thrived, and one part of it was decidedly mathematical. Also, several texts supposedly written by Pythagoras were available. Unfortunately, they were all counterfeits or pseudo-Pythagorean (e.g., later writings claiming to be Pythagoras's own). Pythagoras himself wrote nothing during his lifetime. Much later, in the neoplatonic era, Pythagoras's fame spread even further and some even claimed that he was the source for much of Plato's and Aristotle's thinking (Huffman, 1999). To the ancients, however, he was the leader of a cultlike group who followed the rules for living he had laid down, not a mathematician. Among those rules were not eating beans, not breaking bread, not eating the heart (of animals), not walking on highways, and many more (Russell, 1945).

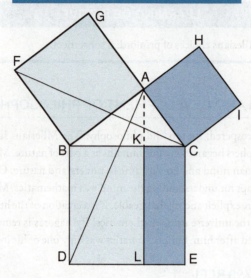

FIGURE 3.4 ■ The Pythagorean Theorem States That for Any Right Triangle $c^2 = a^2 + b^2$

Pythagoras also dabbled in religion and mysticism. It was he who changed the Homeric version of the soul from a kind of shadow into his version, where eternal souls transmigrated after one's death; a form of reincarnation. Xenophanes, in ridicule, told a story about Pythagoras urging a man to stop beating a puppy saying, "stop, don't keep hitting him, since it is the soul of a man who is dear to me, which I recognized when I heard it yelping" (Huffman, 2006, n.p.). He combined the new type of soul he proposed with the concept of life after death. His personality was magnetic and attracted many devoted followers. After he died, some of his followers maintained and expanded his ideas using his name to give them more credence. Zhmud (2016, 2018) thoroughly dissects the history of the Pythagorean and pseudo-Pythagorean traditions and suggests that claims that Pythagoras was a consummate mathematician are overblown.

While the workings of the natural world were the focus of many of the early natural philosophers it was difficult for any of those philosophers to avoid attributing divine origin to physical phenomena such as storms, rainbows, earthquakes, floods, and other natural disasters. Those seemed to be the work of the gods. Xenophanes thought otherwise.

Xenophanes (570–475 BCE)

Xenophanes was born in Colophon, a small town in Ionia, not far from Miletus. Events forced him to leave Colophon, and he traveled to Sicily and eventually to *Magna Graecia*. He lived a long life and probably spent some time in Croton with Pythagoras. All of his writings were in verse and a small number of fragments (less than 50) survive, mostly as quotations by later writers.

Xenophanes was a critic of the older, pantheistic ways of thinking exemplified by Homer and Hesiod and was a pioneering early scientist. In one of his satirical attacks on the Greek gods, he wrote that if horses and cattle could draw or sculpt, they would create gods in their own images. Xenophanes conceived of a higher god, one that was, in the end, unknowable and certainly not similar in appearance to humans. In terms of his natural philosophy, he was close to the Milesians in many ways. His best-known contributions centered on the role of clouds in meteorology. He saw the rainbow as a kind of cloud which was in direct contradiction to earlier, mythological Greek thinking. Xenophanes explicitly attempted to demythologize the earlier ways of thinking and, thus, represented an early bridge from the ancient Greek past to a more naturalistic way of thinking about the world. His scientific ideas may have been too radical for Plato and Aristotle because they did not lead to perfection. However, in many ways, his original naturalistic accounts presaged later scientific thinking (Lesher, 2008). In contrast, his contemporary, Heraclitus, looked for contradictions and changes seeing things differently than most.

Heraclitus (540–475 BCE)

Heraclitus tried to understand complex phenomena as combinations or collections of simpler ones, and investigated the nuances of meaning in new and original ways. For example, rivers were constant yet dynamic at the same time. They were full of water, but the water in the river one day was not the same water that was in the next. He realized that natural philosophy was not an easy subject and that it would take hard work and much study to come to grips with its secrets. van Nispen (2018) reexamines Xenophanes' "precarious" status ascribed to him by Aristotle because of his attacks on the Greek gods and his naivete and describes attempts by Popper and others to rehabilitate his reputation.

Heraclitus was at once, unique, opaque, and polemical. Self-taught, he lived in Ephesus, another Ionian city near Miletus. He never criticized the Milesian philosophers but did criticize Xenophanes and Pythagoras (Zhmud, 2017). Little remains of his original work but it is what characterizes him as an acute observer of contradictions, a proponent of the role of change, and an early cosmologist who saw fire as the universe's basic Greek element. Heraclitus's ideas have been described as dense and difficult. Indeed, he himself warned his readers that they were. Furthermore, the difficulty was not so much in the information he presented, as it was in the ability of his readers or listeners to understand it. He wrote:

> The mind must be properly 'taught,' or equivalently the soul must 'speak the right language': otherwise the evidence presented to the senses, on which all else depends, will not only not be understood, but it will be mistakenly reported *even by the senses themselves* (italics in the original): Bad witnesses are eyes and ears to people, when they have souls that do not speak the right language (B107) (Hussey, 1999, p. 90).

Heraclitus wrote in a style that required readers to figure out for themselves exactly what he was trying to communicate. One message Heraclitus stressed repeatedly was the prevalence of contradictions or opposites in the world.

His keen eye noted many opposites; the same road could, at once, be going uphill or downhill. The traveler determined the direction. Similarly, rivers to him were waters that changed. Where there were no waters, there would be no river. Yet, the river itself was always a river full of water, but never the same water. The oft-repeated quote, "It is not possible to step twice into the same river…" is a later paraphrase by Plutarch and does not really capture Heraclitus's original intent: to identify the river as a changing thing (Graham, 2007). More general was his conception of opposites as unified wholes. Thus, he saw night and day as manifestations of the same thing, not as separate and opposite entities, a new idea for his time. As a cosmologist, he saw fire as the original element but stated that it could change into water, and then water could change into earth. Furthermore, the process was reversible. Heraclitus was influential; if nothing else, he challenged other early thinkers to react to his conceptions. One who did react to him was the Eleatic philosopher Parmenides.

LEARNING OBJECTIVE

2. Discuss Heraclitus' statement about the impossibility of stepping into the same river twice.

ELEATIC PHILOSOPHY

The Milesian philosophers attempted to discover the original substance, or *arche*; they were trying to establish that some physical material—water, the *aperion*, or air—was the source of all other things found in the universe. Today, we would call them **materialists**, meaning that they believed material or physical things held the key to knowledge. However, a later group of philosophers who lived in the *Magna Graecia* town of Elea, modern Velia in Italy, rejected the materialism of the Milesians. Parmenides was the founder of this group, the Eleatics, which also included Zeno of Elea and Melissus. All of them believed that the senses could not be trusted. Instead, the Eleatics wished to view nature as a constant and changeless. Their approach was **rational**, meaning that nature could only be understood through the use of the human mind.

Parmenides (540–470 BCE)

Parmenides was the founder of the Eleatic school and its most influential thinker. His original words, too, have been mostly lost to history. He wrote just one book, a three-part poem, *On Nature,* of which only about 150 lines survive in fragmentary form. In the first part, a young Parmenides is carried to the heavens where an unnamed goddess instructs him in the way of truth (part 2), and later in the way of opinion (part 3). The goddess is only a metaphor and did not provide him with divine revelation. Parmenides proposed a new and different philosophy, one opposed to Milesian materialism and Heraclitus's doctrine of change. He substituted a rational and monistic (e.g., requiring only one principle) philosophy in which reason ruled supreme.

In the second part of the poem, the goddess gave him a short list of qualities that described the cosmos. She said, "it is (a) ungenerated and unperishing, (b) a single whole, (c) unmoving, (d) perfect . . . or bounded . . . or balanced" (Sedley, 1999, p. 118). In the third part of the poem, she explained that earlier philosophers had been too trusting of the information from their senses, while others mistakenly assumed that the cosmos was either easily changeable or boundless. Parmenides offered no solution based on his criticisms but his thinking led to look for solutions. His student, Zeno of Elea, is still famous for his paradoxes. Those showed the disconnections between sensory data and logical thought.

Zeno of Elea (490–430 BCE)

Again, there is little left to history of Zeno's own words. However, Plato, Aristotle, and several other commentators wrote much about Zeno. Only nine of his paradoxes have survived, with the most well known being that of Achilles racing with a tortoise. Zeno sought to defend Parmenides's views about the oneness and unchangeable nature of reality. Paradoxes lead to absurd conclusions. Furthermore, resolving those absurdities seems impossible as well. The logic behind Zeno's paradoxes is *reductio ad absurdum,* a Latin argument that follows logical steps until they reach an obviously absurd consequence. Zeno's other paradoxes concerned motion, density, noise, and infinity (McKirahan, 1999). In the paradox of Achilles (the Trojan War hero) and the tortoise, Zeno gives the tortoise a head start and argues that the swift Achilles could never catch him. The paradox goes like this:

- At the start of the race, the tortoise will be ahead of Achilles.

- When Achilles reaches the point where the tortoise began the race, the tortoise will no longer be there.

- Then, when Achilles reaches the point where the tortoise did start from, the tortoise will have moved on.

- Again (and again, and again…), Zeno argues that the tortoise will always be in front of Achilles, even though Achilles succeeds in reducing the distance between them.

- Finally, Zeno concludes that Achilles can never catch the tortoise.

Zeno argued that there were an infinite number of steps required for Achilles to catch the tortoise. Therefore, he will never catch it. Of course, common sense assures that Achilles *will* catch the tortoise, and that is the paradox. Shouldn't logical, human thinking and observed reality agree? Zeno's paradoxes showed that they did not. His paradoxes so troubled subsequent Greek philosophers that they sought to remove any similar logical inconsistencies in their own theories. Zeno forced them to think more deeply about the nature of physical objects and motion. Furthermore, his use of indirect argumentation was probably a first. Zeno's paradoxes emerged when he argued for the exact opposite of Parmenides's conclusions. The paradoxes resulted in unforeseen and illogical conclusions. Of course, Achilles could catch the tortoise in reality! But why could he not do so logically? Zeno forced later thinkers to reconsider old and cherished assumptions about the physical world. But it took the work of Newton and Leibniz (see Chapter 5) during the seventeenth century to create new meanings for the concepts of motion and infinity.

Melissus (b. 470 BCE)

Melissus was born on Samos, an island off of the Ionian coast. Melissus, a follower of Parmenides wrote in easy-to-follow prose. Both believed that sensory data could not be trusted. Melissus introduced the concept of the void or nothingness. The Atomists would later exploit that concept in their theorizing. Harriman (2018, p. 13) noted:

> Melissus argues for positions that are *prima facie* incompatible with what Parmenides avers in his fragments: Melissus, for example, is committed to the claims that what-is is sempiternal [everlasting] and spatially infinite. Both seem to be in flat contradiction with Parmenides' denial of past and future tenses in B.8.5, his talk of a limit in B.8.30-1 and B.42, and his comparison of what-is to a sphere at B.8.42-4. Strikingly, as well, as many recent interpreters have noticed, Parmenides rejection of plurality, a position universally associated with him in antiquity, receives rather scant support from his fragments. Melissus' commitment to monism, meanwhile is clear from the fragments and uncontested in the secondary literature.

Harriman concluded, however, that Melissus' positions are reinterpretations of Parmenides' position and not direct criticisms. Interestingly, later Greek thinkers including Socrates, Plato, and Aristotle (see below) looked to Melissus as the iconic representative of Eleatic philosophy.

Summary of Eleatic Philosophy

The Eleatics were the first to cast doubt on the reliability of sensory data. Much of their thinking was a response against the natural philosophy of the Milesians. The Eleatics's reliance on reason foreshadowed much of Platonic thinking. The intellectual conflict between the Milesians and the Eleatics foreshadowed subsequent philosophical conflicts. Zeno defended Parmenides's ideas by showing that reason and experience were obviously at odds, while Melissus recast those ideas a more easily understood into prose.

By this point Greek thinkers were locked in an argument over the purposes of philosophy. The key issue was the reliability of sensory data. Dreams and hallucinations alone were enough to cast doubt on all other sensory experiences. Thus, following the lead of the Eleatics, other philosophers began to develop rationalistic systems of philosophy. One question to be answered was what to do with the four elements. One of the first to provide an answer was Empedocles.

LEARNING OBJECTIVE

3. Explain why it is not possible to be penalized for a touchdown in American football and how that is like one of Zeno's paradoxes.

LATER GREEK PHILOSOPHERS

Empedocles (495–435 BCE)

Empedocles was born in Acragas (modern Agrigento) on the island of Sicily. He wrote two long poems (nearly 500 lines survive). He was a defender of democracy, generous to the poor, and a renowned physician. Legend has it that he flung himself into the volcano, Mt. Etna, either to prove he was a god or to make people believe he had ascended into the heavens. If true, the volcano betrayed him by ejecting one of his bronze sandals.

Empedocles formalized the now well-known Greek elements: air, fire, water, and earth. Unlike the earlier Milesians, he did not try to make any of these elements the initial stuff of creation. Empedocles attempted to expand, but not violate, earlier Eleatic ideas, especially those concerning the changelessness of the universe. Thus, he held that the four elements were changeless as well. The compounds they created (e.g., bone and flesh) were temporary and, so, did not violate Parmenides's ideas (Graham, 1999). To the four elements, Empedocles added two forces: love and strife.

Empedocles provided an account of the development of the universe (a cosmogony) in which, initially, all of the elements were united by love and lived in a perfect sphere. Strife then began to swirl and separated the elements from each other. As that process unfolded, animals and humans appeared (a zoogeny). Early on, the parts of animals and humans were first to arise (e.g., arms, heads, legs, and torsos). These combined, and in some cases created fantastical beasts such as oxen with human heads or humans with both male and female features. Eventually, foreshadowing Darwinian natural selection, only the well-formed animals and humans survived. Empedocles provided the first explanation for the process of perception, stating that all objects gave off emanations of themselves and that the sense organs perceived these emanations in a lock-and-key fashion.

Empedocles told of an earlier time when the goddess Aphrodite ruled and love was ascendant. Then, there were no blood sacrifices, humans and animals coexisted, and eating meat was considered cannibalism because he believed in reincarnation. Thus, by eating a cow, one might be eating a reincarnated human being. The world that Empedocles lived in, of course, had been created by strife's ascendancy; there blood sacrifices existed, humans and animals were in conflict, and people ate meat (Parry, 2005). Empedocles attempted to reconcile the earlier naturalistic Milesian accounts of creation with the rationalism of Parmenides.

Another thinker who attempted to reconcile natural philosophy with Parmenides's rationalism was Anaxagoras. He introduced the mind, a force that moved the universe while at the same time rejecting love and strife.

Anaxagoras (500–428 BCE)

Anaxagoras was born in Clazomenae, a city in Ionia. He was the first philosopher to move to Athens, where he lived for 30 years. Pericles (see below), the ruler of Athens at the time, became one of his students. For political reasons, Anaxagoras was arrested for teaching concepts inimical to Greek religion, foreshadowing Socrates's later fate. Through Pericles's influence, he was spared death but exiled to Lampsacus, another Ionian city where he lived out his final years.

Anaxagoras, too, attempted to reconcile the materialism of the Milesians with the rationalism of the Eleatics. He provided a naturalistic explanation for the universe that did not violate Parmenides's injunctions against change and motion. In contrast to Empedocles, Anaxagoras proposed a multiplicity of everlasting elements. Everything contained all of those elements. It was the proportions that determined the appearance of any particular thing. He called this principle "everything in everything." He claimed that any substance could be divided into smaller and smaller parts, or it could always be made larger. But, there was no smallest part of anything, nor was there a largest part of anything. By positing these properties for matter, he remained within Parmenides's rationally derived demands that nothing new could be created, or nothing that already existed could be destroyed.

Anaxagoras created his own version of cosmology. In it, he introduced the mind, a motivating and organizing force. Mind was a substance, too. But unlike all of the other substances, mind was not in everything. In the beginning, all of matter was together, then mind made matter circulate. As matter spun, the heavier parts sank to the middle while the lighter parts moved to the periphery. Slowly, the rotation created the Earth in the center, threw out the sun and stars and set them on fire. The moon was Earthlike and cool, the comets were falling stars, while some dark, cold pieces of matter occasionally moved between the Earth and the sun to cause eclipses. The moon's phases, he correctly discerned, were caused by the reflection of the sun's light. Anaxagoras explained as many physical phenomena as possible and did so using only naturalistic causes. Other philosophers accepted Anaxagoras's explanations of physical phenomena, but his enemies used his reluctance to accept the traditional gods against him during his trial, ultimately leading to his banishment from Athens.

Explaining physical phenomena while tight roping between the Milesian accounts of philosophy, and hewing to Parmenides's insistence of a changeless universe, was a serious challenge for early thinkers. Democritus approached the problem by positing the first atomic theory.

Democritus (460–370 BCE)

Democritus was born in Abdera, a city in the northern province of Thrace. It is impossible to specify whether he, his teacher, Leucippus, or both together should receive the credit for creating atomist theory. However, Democritus extended the theory beyond physics to include epistemological and anthropological conclusions (Taylor, 1999). Most likely, Democritus and his mentor, Leucippus, proposed the first physical theory involving atoms. Naturally, their atomic theory bore little resemblance to the modern atomist physical and chemical theories. The atomic theory of Leucippus and Democritus, like the theories of Empedocles and Anaxagoras earlier, was yet another attempt to resolve the differences between the Milesians and the Eleatics. Parmenides's logically derived assertions that matter could neither be changed nor destroyed were powerful impediments against any materialist theory.

The atomic theory that Leucippus and Democritus proposed posited unchangeable, invisible atoms. Their atoms were, by definition, invisible, eternal, and indestructible. Their atoms could vary in size and shape, and through hooks on their surfaces, attach together to form compounds (Berryman, 2004). The theory also posited empty space, or voids, in between atoms. These voids were in direct contradiction to Eleatic theory but were needed in order to provide a place for the atoms to move. According to atomist theory, the atoms were in constant motion and repelled or attracted each other. The changeable, visible world thus consisted of the interactions of changeless, invisible atoms. The things created by those atoms could arise or decay but the atoms that made them up were eternal.

Democritus attempted to describe perception using *eidola,* or thin ribbons of atoms given off by objects. As these ribbons hit the eyes or ears, they caused those sense organs to perceive the stimuli. Democritus believed that perceptions could be inaccurate, but that action of atoms was understandable and lawful; it just was not perceptible. The truths of nature were the result of atoms and their actions, but perception of visible things could not be directly related to atomic action. Berryman (2004) speculated that Democritus may have developed a radical theory of anthropology. Unlike earlier Greek thinkers, Democritus did not believe that humans were in decline, being the remnants of a long-gone golden age. Instead, he provided a progressive account of human origins much like those of modern anthropologists. Russell (1945, p. 73) concluded that the philosophers up to this point in history "were interested in everything—meteors and eclipses,

Vol.II P.18

DEMOCRITUS.

From a Bust in the Museum at the Vatican

PHOTO 3.1 Democritus

fishes and whirlwinds, religion and morality; with a penetrating intellect they combined the zest of children." After them, he continued, came skepticism, a rejection of sensory data, and a belief that purpose, above all, was the key to scientific knowledge.

LEARNING OBJECTIVE

4. Appraise the need for empty space in Democritus' atomic theory.

In addition, the structure of Greek life, combined with its early form of democracy, made public speaking almost a necessity for any man (women were excluded) who wished to participate in the workings of government. Consequently, a new breed of philosopher emerged, one who specialized in rhetoric, the art of argumentation. Because only humans had the intellectual capacity to argue, these new philosophers concentrated more on psychological issues than on physical ones. The central problem of philosophy shifted from materialism to rhetoric. These new philosophers called themselves Sophists.

SOPHISM

Protagoras (480–411 BCE)

Protagoras, like Democritus, was born in Abdera. He was most famous for teaching rhetoric, the art of arguing in public. At that time rich men often had to defend themselves from lawsuits in front of large tribunals. There were no lawyers, so both accusers and accused had to state their own cases themselves. Presenting the facts of a case and persuading the judges to see them from one's own point of view was important if one wished to retain life and property or to avoid exile. Thus, learning how to speak convincingly was important. Protagoras and others like him taught such skills for a fee, a practice that Plato and Aristotle later condemned. Protagoras began a new philosophical movement called Sophism. Today, that word is pejorative and means to possess the ability to argue cleverly and deviously. Protagoras did argue cleverly, but there is much more to his legacy than that.

One thing that Protagoras taught was the proper and precise use of words. Like modern day grammar sticklers such as Truss (2004), he corrected poets when they misused language. He may have been one of the first to write about grammar. Protagoras is probably most famous for writing: "Man is the measure of all things, of things that are that there are, and of things that are not that they are not" (Russell, 1945, p. 77). Most believe that the fragment says something about the relativity of truth or **relativism**. Think of hot or cold. Often, one person will say she is hot while another, in the same situation, will say he is cold. What is the truth in this situation? This seemingly trivial example carries with it much trouble for philosophies founded on the premise of knowable, universal truths. The very foundations of Greek natural and moral philosophy were at risk. What use would there be for philosophy if everyone had their own version of truth? Lastly, Protagoras was skeptical about the gods themselves, "Concerning the gods, I am not in a position to know either that they exist or that they do not, nor can I know what they look like, for many things prevent my knowing—the subject is obscure, and human life is short" (Woodruff, 1999, p. 306). In this manner, Protagoras limited his philosophy to things he could perceive and excluded from it things that could not be observed for whatever reason. Later Sophists, however, were more radical than Protagoras and excluded much more. They focused nearly exclusively on language. Their ability to argue successfully both sides of any question was legendary. Gradually, Greek philosophy ceased to be a search for truth and became an arena in which the greatest rhetorical skills predominated. Some philosophers, the Nihilists, even went so far as to exclaim that nothing was knowable.

LEARNING OBJECTIVE

5. Illustrate an example of relativism using the dimension of too hot or too cold.

Gorgias (483–375 BCE)

Gorgias was from Leontini, Sicily, where he may have been Empedocles's student. He first came to Athens as an ambassador from Leontini seeking Athenian aid against Syracuse. His oratorical appeals to the Athenians were sensational and achieved their purpose. Athens and Leontini, two democratic city-states, allied. Afterward, Gorgias remained in Athens and began to instruct others in rhetoric. Gorgias's rhetorical skills were legendary. He could take the poorer argument and make it the winner. His speeches rhymed, were full of metaphors and euphemisms, and were overly full of words. Plato so disliked Gorgias and his methods that he wrote a dialogue named *Gorgias* depicting an imaginary conversation between Gorgias and Socrates. In that dialogue, Plato overstated his case against Gorgias's rhetorical methods (Woodruff, 1999).

In one of Gorgias's writings, he attempted to absolve the long-dead Helen of Troy from any guilt for having gone to Troy with to be with Paris, an act that led to the Trojan War. That work was an exercise in rhetoric because the Athenian public had long held Helen culpable. If he could convince that audience that Helen was innocent, then he could convince anybody of anything. Haskins (2018, pp. 252–253) wrote:

> Gorgias' *Encomium of Helen* is a tantalizingly rich text: it is an once a stylistically ostentatious performance piece, an exercise in legal argumentation under the guise of a speech of praise and a far-reaching reflection on the powers and dangers of verbal and visual persuasion.

On Nature, one of his lost works, was more philosophical and an attempt to refute the thinking of Parmenides and the Eleatic school. In that book, he proposed, "for anything you might mention: (1) that it is nothing; (2) that, even if it were something, it would be unknowable; and (3) that, even if it were knowable, it could not be made evident to others" (Woodruff, 1999, p. 305). These three statements parodied (another Sophist technique) Parmenides's proof that matter was eternal and could not be destroyed. Because of these statements, Gorgias is often considered a **nihilist**.

Sophism was a response to the older forms of natural and its effect on philosophy's subsequent development was large as seen in the efforts of Socrates and Plato (see below). That intellectual tension, combined with long periods of war and unrest, explains much about the dominant philosophies that emerged after Sophism in the fourth century BCE. A wider look at the history of Greece at this point is helpful. It was the high point, or "golden age," of ancient Greece.

PERICLES AND ATHENS'S GOLDEN AGE

The life of Pericles (495–429 BCE) partially overlaps Athens's golden age, the period from the end of the Persian Wars (448 BCE) to his death, the period when philosophy matured. The lives of Socrates, Plato, and Aristotle, on the other hand, were mostly lived later, outside of the Golden Age and during the beginning of Athens's decline as a center of power and knowledge. Athens was one of history's first democracies, but the form of its government bore little resemblance to modern democracies. In Athenian democracy only adult (aged 30 and above), native-born males were citizens and could participate vote in the all-male Athenian Assembly.

To expedite state business and to set the agenda, a smaller group of 500, the *boule,* was chosen by a lot yearly. Athenian citizenship was a serious obligation and included jury duty. Athenians were litigious so many disputes required trials. The juries were much larger than modern ones, ranging from 101 to 1,001 citizens, and their verdicts were final. But, the convicted could suggest an alternative sentence; exile over death, for instance.

Women were excluded from public life except in extremely rare cases (e.g., Pericles's mistress Aspasia). Native-born women were considered citizens and could control (but not sell) inherited property. Foreigners were called *metics* and were excluded from public life and could not own land. Aristotle, born near Macedon, was a metic. Slaves abounded, and most were owned by citizens, but a few were property of the state. They had no rights and could be used for sex, beaten, or even killed with impunity. During the Golden Age, the price of slaves had dropped to such a low point that a majority of households owned at least one or two.

In 445 BCE, Pericles was the elected leader of Athens from 445 to 429 BCE. He rebuilt Athens and many of its temples, including the Parthenon, to their greatest glory. He reformed the Assembly by allowing adult male citizens who did not own property to vote. In 431 BCE came the long Peloponnesian War, eventually won by Sparta in 404 BCE ending the Golden Age. Unrest and hardship followed. That new context became the one that Socrates, Plato, and Aristotle lived and worked in. All three built onto the structure of thought created by the earlier philosophers. But, they changed the emphases of earlier philosophies as well. Russell (1945, p. 73) said their philosophies were marked by "an undue emphasis on man as compared with the universe . . . with Socrates, the emphasis on ethics; with Plato, the rejection of the world of sense . . . with Aristotle, the belief in purpose as the fundamental concept of science."

PHOTO 3.2 Pericles

BORDER WITH PHILOSOPHY
MENTAL PROCESSES

The study of mental processes as a psychological phenomenon gained speed as the Sophists emphasized the importance of human thought in philosophy. Since then, the study of mental processes has been a prominent part of philosophy and of psychology. Indeed, the earliest scientific psychologists essentially adopted the same method—introspection—used by the ancient Greeks. The difference between those psychologists and the ancient philosophers was that they used it in an experimental fashion. Later, the behavioral psychologists dispensed with introspective methods altogether. After the computer revolution of the late twentieth century, the scientific study of mental processes again became a legitimate part of modern psychology. If the study of mental processes were a Hollywood plot, it would read: "Psychology finds mental processes, psychology loses mental processes, psychology finds mental processes again."

GREEK PHILOSOPHY'S BIG THREE

In 399 BCE, Socrates stood trial and was narrowly sentenced to death by a jury of 501 citizens for impiety against the gods and for corrupting the youth of Athens. Socrates's refusal to offer exile as an alternative, and asking for a reward for his actions instead, was the final straw. That, along with his lack of remorse, is what led the jury to sentence him to death by a much larger margin than in their original conviction. Following Socrates's death, Plato retired from public life and produced the majority of his now-famous works. Aristotle, Plato's student, eventually rejected much of his mentor's teachings and went on to write extensively as well.

SOCRATES (469–399 BCE)

Socrates was born just outside of Athens and lived there his whole life except during the time of his military service during the Peloponnesian War. His father and he were stonemasons. He served with distinction as a hoplite (a Greek foot soldier) in several battles during the Peloponnesian War and once saved the life of his general, Alcibiades. He returned to Athens and married Xanthippe, whose dowry was large enough for him to no longer have to work as a mason.

Socrates became active in the Assembly and was prominent enough to be lampooned by name in several of Aristophanes's comedies. As a member of the Assembly, he was involved in the decisions that led to military disaster in Sicily. After the war and at risk to his life, he refused to obey the orders of the new despotic rulers when they ordered him to arrest a general associated with the previous and democratic leadership. Only the coincidental overthrow of those despots saved him. The new leaders declared a general amnesty (the first in history). However, a poet named Meletus accused Socrates of crimes subsequent to the declaration of amnesty: impiety (failing to honor the gods) and corruption of the youth of Athens (by teaching them to question their parents). Socrates willingly went to trial and was condemned. He refused to suggest exile over death as a punishment, the traditional practice. In obedience to the laws of Athens, he drank the hemlock and died, surrounded by his friends.

Socrates wrote nothing. Instead, he spoke in what is now called Socratic Method where he acted as if he knew little or nothing about the subject at hand. Then, he would ask a long series of questions designed to reveal how little his listeners knew about the topic. At that point, Socrates would ask another series of questions, all of them now leading to the answer. Those so questioned learned to apply the Socratic method themselves, especially to their parents. Socrates never claimed to be a teacher. In fact, he railed against the Sophists, those self-proclaimed teachers teaching how to use language to gain advantage over others instead of seeking knowledge. Furthermore, the Sophists charged for their services, something Socrates never did.

Socrates was a gadfly, Plato later said, stinging Athenians and making them think. Moreover, he was breeding more gadflies: the young men who followed him around. Descriptions of Socrates were not flattering: he went barefoot and often slept in his clothes, and he was physically ugly and looked nothing like the marble statues extolling the ideal Greek body. Socrates, famously, said "know thyself, an unexamined life is not worth living," and "if I know anything, it is that I know nothing." He was well aware that earlier philosophers were interested in physical explanations of the universe, and he was opposed to the more recent development of relativism and the promotion of rhetoric as a method for seeking knowledge.

More than anything, he was interested in knowing what makes someone virtuous. His answer was that virtue comes from self-examination, and slowly one comes to realize that virtue is knowledge (Penner, 1993). Martinez and Smith (2017) gave a more nuanced interpretation of Socrates' views on virtue. They argued that his aversion to being a victim of injustice was nearly as great as his aversion to doing unjust things. Thus, Socrates changed philosophy in at least two ways. He focused attention on human problems, not physical ones, and he refused to allow the Sophists the easy luxury of their relativism. For him, absolutes such as love, truth, and beauty existed, and it was the philosopher's mission to find and describe them. Plato provided most of what is known about Socrates. Plato, at first, followed his mentor's mission but later in life developed his own original ideas successfully given that later schools of ancient philosophy nearly universally pointed to Socrates, not Plato, as their founder.

Socrates's execution (see Figure 3.5) was an extraordinary event. His refusal to suggest exile as an alternative, along with his willingness to accept the death sentence so coolly, made it all the more memorable. To his students that acceptance of his own death seemed illogical and demonstrated the dangers inherent in public life. Politics had become a deadly business; retreating into a life of contemplation was a safer and adaptive strategy for many including Plato, who turned to philosophy full-time. Whitehead (1978) probably overstated Plato's eventual contribution to philosophy when he wrote (p. 39), "The safest general characterization of the European philosophical tradition is that it consists of a series of footnotes to Plato."

PHOTO 3.3 Socrates

FIGURE 3.5   ■   Jacques Louis David's *Death of Socrates* (1787)

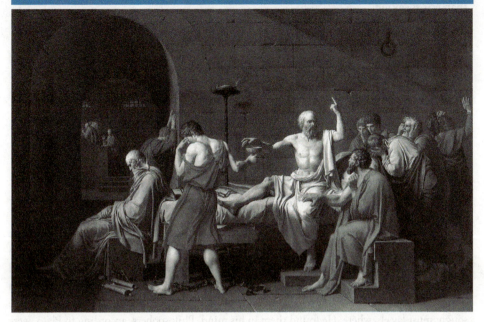

Credit: GL Archive / Alamy Stock Photo

PLATO (429–347 BCE)

The life of Plato is well known, and the number of his writings that survived far exceeds that of any other philosopher discussed thus far in this text. Early in life, he was an adept wrestler and also tried his hand at poetry. Until he met Socrates, Plato seemed destined to become a politician. Afterward, philosophy became his true calling, and he was one of the many young men who followed Socrates around Athens. When Plato was in his early 30s, Socrates was executed. Fearing for his own life, Plato fled to nearby Megara. Most of his life, however, was spent in Athens where he founded his school, the Academy, in 387 BCE in a grove outside of the city. The Academy survived until 529 BCE; the date of its closing is often used to mark the beginning of the Medieval period in Europe.

Plato wrote dialogues that contained his philosophical ideas. Socrates appeared as a literary device in nearly all of them while Plato never did. In the earlier dialogues, Plato seemed content to commit Socrates's ideas to writing. In the middle and later dialogues, however, Plato clearly left Socrates's influence behind and wrote what was in his own mind. The dialogues put the Socratic Method on paper and allowed Plato to reach a much larger audience than Socrates ever had. The dialogues also required readers to think for themselves and not be spoon-fed Platonic philosophy. They had to become engaged participants and figure out the messages for themselves. Most likely, the dialogues were used at the Academy as textbooks are used in college today. In the dialogue *Phaedrus* 275d–275e

(Plato, 1969), Plato had Socrates argue that writing was a less effective teaching method than was speaking:

> Writing, Phaedrus, has this strange quality, and is very like painting; for the creatures of painting stand like living beings, but if one asks them a question, they preserve a solemn silence. And so it is with written words; you might think they spoke as if they had intelligence, but if you question them, wishing to know about their sayings, they always say only one and the same thing. And every word, when once it is written, is bandied about, alike among those who understand and those who have no interest in it, and it knows not to whom to speak or not to speak; when ill-treated or unjustly reviled it always needs its father to help it; for it has no power to protect or help itself.

Presumably, Plato often led and participated in discussions of philosophy at his Academy. Unfortunately, only a few documents testify to those discussions and their nature. Plato's dialogues, nevertheless, tell us much about his ideas.

Plato, like Socrates before him, was searching for truth. Plato was convinced that the Sophists were pushing philosophy toward insignificance because of their belief in relativism. In response, Plato looked for absolute truths. At the same time, he realized that those truths could not be found using the senses. While the senses might provide partial evidence, at best, for a particular truth, nowhere on Earth was there a perfectly knowable truth. Thus, those truths he sought must lay elsewhere. He found them in his mind. Philosophers, according to Plato, were to seek those eternal and abstract truths that lay in their minds.

What were those truths? He called them Forms: Goodness, Beauty, Equality, Bigness, Unity, Sameness, Difference, Change, and Changelessness (Kraut, 2004). Plato considered Goodness as the most important Form. Those Forms only existed in the ideal world of the philosopher's mind. The real world, Plato maintained, was but a shadow cast by those ideal, eternal truths.

In one of his most famous passages, the allegory of the cave from *The Republic,* Socrates (the literary character) asks Glaucon (the name of Plato's older brother) to put himself in the place of some prisoners chained to a wall with an opening to the outside world behind them. However, those prisoners cannot look behind them. They can only see the other wall directly in front of them. Then Socrates asks Glaucon to further imagine the sun shining through the opening and casting shadows on the wall. Socrates asks him to consider that those shadows are the only things those prisoners have ever seen. Suppose, Socrates wonders, that one of those prisoners were to escape and actually see the world and not just the shadows. After seeing the world as it is for the first time, the prisoner returns and describes what he saw to the others. They, of course, would not believe him. They might even think him mad. The goal of philosophy, Plato explains through Socrates, is to see what is casting the shadows.

To Plato, each of the Forms listed earlier existed only in the mind. The Forms (or Ideas) were perfect, and thus, must only exist in the ideal world. Such perfection could not be achieved in the real, physical world. The Forms allowed Plato to answer the tough questions posed by earlier philosophers. On the one hand, the existence and primacy of the Forms made moot the conflict between the Milesians and the Eleatics. It did not matter whether the universe was static or dynamic; that question became irrelevant to Plato. Also, the Forms answered the objections of the Sophists. Their relativism was negated by the ideal absolutism (the Forms) that was above and separated from the perceived world.

In his dialogue *Meno,* Plato had Socrates instruct a slave by engaging him in a dialogue. The slave was uneducated, yet through a series of questions Socrates (as a literary character) enabled the slave to discover and understand the Pythagorean Theorem on his own. Socrates, Plato inferred, did not teach the slave mathematics. Instead, Socrates helped the slave to discover the truth of the theorem that had been hidden inside him all along. Through this method, Plato transformed philosophy and set it on a long path from which it has deviated little ever since. Eventually, Plato expanded philosophy's reach far beyond Socrates's initial and overriding concern with ethics. Plato, of course, did not abandon the study of ethics but he added "metaphysics, epistemology . . . political theory, language, art, love, mathematics, science, and religion" (Kraut, 1993, p. 1) as subjects for philosophy.

Plato believed that humans possessed eternal souls. However, that soul had a separate existence from the body. It was the soul that contained knowledge, thus the search for knowledge had to be directed inward. Plato did not ignore information from the senses, or what he called appearances; he just maintained that such information was incomplete. His reliance on the soul as the source of knowledge made him an **idealist**. Most likely, Pythagoras and his disciples, who had earlier emphasized similar views, especially in mathematics and music, had inspired Plato. Plato divided the soul into three relatively independent parts: rational, appetitive, and passionate. The rational part of the soul concerned itself with the truths of philosophy and was the most important part. The appetitive part of the soul concerned itself with issues of living such as eating and drinking. The appetitive part of the soul could, under certain conditions, override the rational part. Langewiesche (1991) graphically described how drivers stranded in the Sahara desert became so thirsty, that after drinking all of their water, they turned to drinking radiator fluid, and finally (fatally), to drinking gasoline. Their thirst completely overwhelmed their rational knowledge. The passionate part of the soul accounted for emotional behaviors such as love or rage. Emotions, too, could overcome the rational part of the soul. Plato's soul, thus, anticipates many topics that would later be of interest to modern psychology.

In the dialogues *The Republic* and *Laws*, Plato turned his attention to the problems of social behavior and governance. In *The Republic,* Plato proposed his idealized version of the state, and it was anything but democratic. Plato divided the inhabitants of his fictional state into three groups: workers, guardians, and rulers. He linked each of these groups to the divisions of the soul: workers with the appetitive part, guardians with the courageous part, and rulers with the rational part. In *The Republic*, he writes that the state should be ruled by philosopher-kings; only they have the intellectual capacity to rule:

> either philosophers become kings in our states or those whom we now call our kings and rulers take to the pursuit of philosophy seriously and adequately, and there is a conjunction of these two things, political power and philosophic intelligence, while the motley horde of the natures who at present pursue either apart from the other are compulsorily excluded, there can be no cessation of troubles, dear Glaucon, for our states, nor, I fancy, for the human race either (Plato, 1969, p. 509).

Modern political scientists would classify Plato's state as totalitarian because its government would interject itself into nearly every detail of life. The decline of democratic Periclean Athens, the loss of the Peloponnesian War, and the execution of Socrates by the Assembly, taken together, may help explain Plato's concept of governance. In *Laws,* one of Plato's last dialogues, he revisited the issue of governance and made more practical and moderate recommendations. During his visits to Sicily, he acted as advisor to the reigning kings. His inability to convince them to adopt rational methods of governing may have been responsible for his later moderate approach. Annas (2010), however, pointed out that while Plato expected citizens to obey laws slavishly, he also expected them to understand why the laws existed. Thus, the laws themselves were preceded by preambles designed to explain why each law existed. Plato's ideas about religion were also influential. Neoplatonism, essentially an adaptation of Plato's religious ideas that were eventually comingled with Christian doctrine, will be examined in Chapter 4.

Plato transformed philosophy and made it the familiar and recognizable discipline of today. His most famous student, Aristotle, altered much of what he had learned from his teacher, much as Plato himself had earlier done with Socrates's ideas. Unlike Plato, Aristotle was willing to explore the world as experienced through the senses. Like Plato, he further expanded the breadth and reach of philosophy.

PHOTO 3.4 Plato

ARISTOTLE (384–322 BCE)

Aristotle was born in Stagira, a town north of Athens and near Macedon. His father was the physician to the king of Macedon. At the age of 17, Aristotle left Macedon for Athens and soon became a student at Plato's Academy. He remained there until Plato's death in 347 BCE. At that point, he believed he would become the head of the Academy, but Speusippus, Plato's nephew, took its leadership instead. So, Aristotle left Athens for several years, marrying Pythias, his first wife, relatively late in his own life. They lived near the Aegean Sea, and that was when Aristotle developed an interest in the natural world. He classified animals and plants, and his dissections laid the foundations of scientific biology. This period of life ended when Phillip II summoned him back to Macedon to serve as tutor to his son, Alexander. Aristotle served in that position for around three years or until Alexander became king. Aristotle returned to Athens where he founded his own school, the Lyceum. There, in a grove near the temple of Apollo, Aristotle lectured while walking up and down a covered walkway (*a peripatos*). His habit gave rise to the English word "peripatetic" which is still used today to describe Aristotle's philosophy. Neither Plato's Academy nor Aristotle's Lyceum should be thought of as being anything akin to modern universities. However, the subjects discussed at the Lyceum went beyond philosophy and included topics ranging from biology and physics to theology. When Alexander died, Aristotle fled Athens fearing for his life, famously saying the city "must not be allowed to sin twice against philosophy." He moved to Chalcis and died a year later after complaining about a stomach pain.

Nearly nothing remains of Aristotle's early writings composed during his years at the Academy. Those were mostly dialogues, presumably in the style of Plato. Most of his known works seem to have been his original lecture notes, which may account for their terse style. Aristotle was one of the first scholars to collect his own personal library. After his death, it was passed to his student, Theophrastus, who gave the works to his nephew Neleus, who buried them near Scepsis. Two hundred years later, Andronicus, an Aristotelian scholar living in Rome, edited what he could of that collection, and that formed the basis of Aristotle's surviving works known today (Barnes, 1995a). Kenny (2010, p. 77) wrote, "Every detail of this story has been called in question by one or another scholar, but if true it would account for the oblivion that overtook Aristotle's writings between the time of Theophrastus and that of Cicero."

Unlike his mentor Plato, Aristotle took a much wider view on what the subject matter for philosophy should be. Where Plato began with the Forms, Aristotle began with observing nature itself. For Plato, understanding the Forms was the ultimate goal of philosophy. Aristotle, on the other hand, sought to understand nature first and, subsequently, understand the relationship between the observed object to the more general essence behind the object, using reason for a fuller understanding. So, for Aristotle, understanding a cat did not come from thinking about an ideal cat. Instead, it came from observing a great number of cats over a long period. Eventually, that realization would create an inductive mental notion of "cat," Aristotle did not deny the existence of a universal, ideal cat. Unlike Plato however, Aristotle never claimed that anyone, including a philosopher, could ever fully understand the ideal cat—the Platonic Form. To him, the movement from the actual observations of a multitude of particular, real cats to approaching the understanding of the universal concept of "cat" required experience plus intellect. Aristotle maintained that experience, combined with intellect, allowed people to come closer and closer to an understanding of the ideal cat.

LEARNING OBJECTIVE

6. Contrast how Plato and Aristotle might think about cats.

Aristotle approached knowledge via three fronts: practical, productive, and theoretical. Ethics and politics fell under the category of practical. For Aristotle, the guiding principle for an ethical life was true happiness, which he maintained came from a lifetime of rational thought combined with its expression in virtuous behavior. Moral behavior was learned. Aristotle composed a list of virtues and argued that pursuing or engaging in too much or too little of any of them led to problems. Like the older Greek philosophers, Aristotle believed that happiness was found in moderation, not in excess.

The arts were productive. Under the arts, Aristotle included poetry, painting, sculpture, and drama. In all of these, artists created or produced objects or actions that imitated life. For Aristotle, successful imitation of life determined the worth and quality of the arts. In his *Poetics,* Aristotle commented on drama and its importance. His analysis of comedy and tragedy are the oldest known to survive. Although both dramatic forms used the same methods, comedies imitated the positive side of life while tragedies imitated the darker side. The *Poetics* covered painting and sculpture too. Both were another method of imitating nature linked to drama and poetry. He viewed the quality of paintings and sculptures as to how well they imitated life.

BORDER WITH SOCIAL SCIENCE
ARISTOTLE ON POLITICS

Aristotle and Plato differed on the nature of the ideal form of government. In place of Plato's single totalitarian republic, Aristotle described of six types of governments: monarchies, aristocracies, constitutional republics, democracies, oligarchies, and tyrannies. He thought that constitutional republics were the best possible form of government. Again, the two philosophers differed on how to approach knowledge. Plato conceived of his ideal state by looking inside his own mind whereas Aristotle and his students analyzed of 158 Grecian constitutions (only the Athenian one is known); they collected data. Thus they were empiricists and early political scientists.

Under his theoretical category were biology, psychology, physics, and metaphysics. Aristotle studied hundreds of species. Many came from Alexander's game wardens who sent back many exotic specimens for him to study. Aristotle was one of the first to carefully describe the structure and development of many species. His biological studies led him to study psychological topics as well. In *De Anima* (*On the Mind* or *On the Soul*), he investigated psychological topics such as memory, learning, sleep and dreams, sensation and perception, and motivation connecting them to biological explanations. All animals were governed by nutritive, perceptive, and locomotor functions, meaning they had to eat, engage the world with their senses, and move. Humans, along with a few other animals, had an additional function—a rational one. Humans had that function, but so did elephants because he noted that they knew to bow before kings. Aristotle, however, did not experiment as modern scientists do. Instead, he was a skilled and careful observer but stopped short of applying experimental manipulations and measuring their effects.

BORDER WITH BIOLOGY
THE FOUNDING OF BIOLOGY

About 25% of Aristotle's known works deal with biological topics. His biological works included specific methodological recommendations, not just descriptions of biological processes and phenomena. Aristotle wrote a number of works dealing with animals including

History of Animals, Parts of Animals, and *Generation of Animals.* He also wrote a number of shorter works about animals that covered such topics as motion, the senses, breathing, sleep, and aging. His biological writings were very different from his other works in that they were highly cross referenced. Unlike Plato and Socrates, Aristotle believed that studying animals and plants systematically was an important part in the quest for knowledge. He believed that all animals, even the most disgusting ones, had a purpose for existing. After his death, the study of biology lost most of its early momentum and was not regained until the sixteenth century (Lennox, 2006). Albert the Great revived the study of the natural world (see Chapter 4), and biology progressed quickly from then on. Paradoxically, much of that progress in biology only occurred after biologists corrected long-standing and deeply seated misconceptions about nature inherited from Aristotle and other ancient sources.

Aristotle's physics is well known. But much of the early progress in modern science came as scientists like Copernicus, Galileo, and Newton revised or rejected Aristotelian physics. By the late Middle Ages, the Roman Church had elevated Aristotle's ancient physics to nearly the level of Holy Scripture (see Chapter 4). Thus, the church taught Aristotelian beliefs such as: the Earth was the center of the universe, heavier objects fell faster than lighter ones, and projectiles traveled in only straight lines. Not only did the church teach these "facts" but also punished those who dared to contradict them.

Metaphysics, or what Aristotle called Analytics, was the term coined by later editors who, when ordering his works, placed it after physics; metaphysics in Greek literally means "after physics." The irony of that placement is that Aristotle thought of metaphysics as the beginning or base of all theory. Barnes (1995b) described metaphysics by saying it is, "The science of first principles, the study of being *qua* being, theology, the investigation into substance" (p. 69). All of these are relatively easy to understand except for "being *qua* being." Or, in other words, studying existence itself. There, Aristotle's intent was to study things as they were in of themselves. Today, we would call this effort philosophy and its questions philosophical. Thus, questions such as how can we know anything would be called metaphysical. Aristotle's ten categories were also metaphysical, meaning they could be used to describe anything. Those categories were: substance, quality, quantity, relation, place, time, position, state, action, and affection. Read this sentence to see the categories in action:

> One *(quantity)* real *(substance)*, white *(quality)*, horse was standing behind another grey horse *(relation)*, in the barn *(place)*, yesterday *(time)*, near the trough *(position)*, saddled *(state)*, drinking water *(action)*, and enjoying it *(affection)*.

Aristotle's passion for categorization of the real world was another difference between him and Plato.

Aristotle proposed four types of cause and effect. He used the example of a bronze statue to describe them. *Material causes* refer to the substance making up the statue; in this case, bronze. *Formal causes* refer to the fact that the bronze had been made into something by somebody, the sculptor. It was now a statue, not just an equivalent volume of bronze. *Efficient causes* described how the statue was actually made, meaning, the sculptor melted the bronze, poured it into a prepared mold, and later finished it by sanding and polishing. *Final causes* described the goal; in this case the statue itself. It is this last cause, the final cause, which makes Aristotle seem unscientific to modern eyes and ears. The problem is that final causes are circular or **teleological**. Modern science avoids using final causes and substitutes efficient causes. Follow this train of thought: the paper this text was printed on was made in order to teach you psychology because observe, it is teaching you psychology. Does that sentence bother you? Unless you are a twenty-first century Aristotelian, it should. The efficient cause is that this piece of paper was manufactured in order to make a profit for the company that produced it. It was chance, not purpose, that led to these words appearing on this particular page. The fact that you are learning the history of psychology from them should not be interpreted as proof of the paper maker's intent. Final causes died a slow death in science.

Only in logic did Aristotle claim intellectual priority. In all other areas, he acknowledged that he was following in the footsteps of his predecessors. As Smith (1995, p. 27) noted, "he was the first to conceive of a systematic treatment of correct inference itself. As such, Aristotle was the founder of logic." Aristotle's writings on logic are widely scattered throughout his books. He divided logic into two parts: induction and deduction. Induction was discussed above and consists of coming to a conclusion based on repeated observations of an event. However, induction is logically weaker than deduction because it only takes one exception to render a conclusion invalid. Think of cats again. If all the cats you have ever seen had tails, you might believe every cat should have one. But, seeing your first naturally tailless Manx cat destroys that belief. The main form of deductive logic is syllogistic. Syllogisms are composed of three parts: a major premise, a minor premise, and a conclusion. Thus:

All men are mortal. (major premise)

Socrates is a man. (minor premise)

Therefore, Socrates is mortal. (conclusion)

Deductive logic leads to provable conclusions based upon a small number of premises. Aristotle developed deductive logic so completely that it basically stood unchanged until the nineteenth century. His work on logic also influenced his theology. Aristotle's contribution there was his notion of God. The nature of his physical theory demanded an unmoving center and a first mover. His "Unmoved Mover," or God, fit that role. His God was the first essence—perfect, unmovable, and all knowing. Because Aristotle viewed motion as necessary in his physical system and could not logically allow himself to construct a system that moved itself, he needed the Unmoved Mover. He placed the Unmoved Mover in the outermost sphere of the universe, beyond the sphere of the fixed stars (see Figure 3.6).

Aristotle, thus, stands at the beginning of many modern disciplines, including psychology. However, he cannot properly be called a psychologist because of his methodology. While he was an excellent observer, he never developed methods that would have yielded data acceptable to modern psychologists. Also, his insistence on final causes made his thinking incompatible with modern science. Nevertheless, it is safe to say that Aristotle took the first steps toward the eventual rise of science, and with that, the rise of psychology. In between then and now, many events intervened and delayed the onset of modern science.

Still, Aristotle approached becoming a psychologist. He studied a wide variety of topics now considered mainstream psychology and attempted to provide a physiological basis for many of them. Because he did not conduct experiments, he could not demonstrate cause and effect

FIGURE 3.6 ■ Aristotle's Universe

Credit: Getty Images

conclusions. Had he done so, today he might be considered the father of psychology. Johnson (2019, p. 107) highlighted Aristotle's emphasis on zoology and psychology:

> Aristotle stands out from all his predecessors by being the first philosopher to focus on zoology and psychology in his theoretical philosophy, and in so doing he saw a different picture and developed a different theory than his predecessors, who had focused on the natural history of our kosmos and of other possible kosmoi. Aristotle's change of focus was certainly productive for psychology and zoology, but his influence on the history of cosmology was much less successful.

Aristotle's strong belief in final causes also may have prevented him from taking the necessary steps toward becoming a psychologist. Recall

ARISTOTLE

PHOTO 3.5 Aristotle

that his doctrine of final causes assumed that whatever was observed had happened for a reason. Aristotle, apparently, could not envision a statistical universe in which chance played an important role. Following the age of Socrates, Plato, and Aristotle, Greek philosophy branched in several directions. One such branch was Cynicism.

CYNICS

The philosophy of Cynicism begins with Antisthenes, a student of Socrates. The Cynic tradition also owes some debt to the ;Sophists; they were among the first to question authority and convention. While Socrates himself was not a Cynic, he held ideas they later embraced. They admired his pursuit of virtue and indifference to popular opinion. They believed in living a simple, austere life in harmony with nature, and they rejected the trappings of conventional living including the acquisition of wealth, pursuit of fame, or gain of power. The word "cynic" comes from the Greek word for dog and refers to the shamelessness of the Cynic philosophers. Like dogs, they defecated and fornicated in public.

Diogenes, for example, was proud to be called a Cynic and reveled in shocking Athenians by his behavior. The cynics embraced an **ascetic** lifestyle, shunning wealth and power. Crates, for example, gave up his riches to become a Cynic. Hipparchia, his wife, married him despite his poverty and lived with him in the streets of Athens, rejecting the customary life of an Athenian woman. These ancient Cynics should not be confused with the modern use of the word "cynic," which stresses selfishness, faultfinding, and negativity. The ancient Cynics were faultfinders, to be sure, but they were not selfish, and while they were negative about the society they lived in, they lived lives they hoped would inspire others to change their ways. Their form of philosophy lasted for hundreds of years and continues to inspire discussion in philosophical circles today.

Antisthenes (445–365 BCE)

Antisthenes was a student of Gorgias, and later, of Socrates. He was present when Socrates drank the hemlock, and he never forgave those who had passed sentence on his master. Like Socrates, he emphasized the pursuit of virtue as the main goal of life. Antisthenes believed more in action than words, and his life reflected that. He lived an ascetic life and argued that the pursuit of pleasure was dangerous because it led to the loss of individual freedom. Those pleasures eventually would imprison those that sought them. Self-sufficiency, wisdom, and reason were his guiding principles. Scholars debate whether he was the first Cynic or the last Socratic. He quarreled with Plato and might have become Socrates' successor but for his low social class (Meijer, 2017). One thing is clear: he did not hold with Plato's ideal Forms. For Antisthenes, there was a difference between horses and horseness. He claimed to understand the former, but not the latter. His lifestyle was much like that of later Cynics. He lived in the streets, wore and slept in his cloak, and carried a wallet and a staff, all characteristic features of later Cynics. Diogenes of Sinope was probably not his student, and the two may not even have known each other. However, there is no question that Diogenes was a Cynic. He took Antisthenes's ideas and practices to a new, higher level.

Diogenes of Sinope (412–323 BCE)

Diogenes was born in Sinope, a town on the Black Sea, in what is now modern Turkey. He was forced to leave Sinope because of a scandal involving the counterfeiting of currency, a relatively common practice in antiquity and supported by modern archeological evidence (Conn, 2007). He moved to Athens, where he eventually became the archetypical Cynic philosopher exposing the behavior and customs of Greek society as counterfeits. Later in his life, he moved to Corinth and died there. In his honor, the Corinthians erected a marble pillar topped by a dog (Diogenes, 1925).

After his exile to Athens, Diogenes became a philosopher who walked the streets in broad daylight holding a lamp looking for an honest man. Like Socrates, he preferred to lecture rather than write, and attempted to set a good example by living according to reason and virtue. Thus, he chose to live in an abandoned barrel and carry all of his necessities with him, discarding even his bowl as unnecessary after he saw a boy cup his hands to drink. Diogenes believed that humans had lost sight of nature in their desire to live conventionally. He shocked Athenians by eating his food in the marketplace; Athenians shopped for food at the market but only ate at home. When asked where he came from, he replied he was a citizen of the world, a cosmopolitan. He was the first to use that word. That, too, was shocking, because Greeks valued citizenship along with its rights and privileges. As an exile, Diogenes enjoyed neither. Still, he argued that as a stateless exile living in a barrel, begging for his food, and without material possessions, he was happier than those who had everything. Bayram (2015) analyzed modern adoption of attitudes related to world citizenship by respondents in 57 countries. He found (p. 470), "that self-transcendence, self-enhancement (except power), and openness-to-change values, along with generalized trust, lead to the internalization of world citizenship, while conservation values obstruct this self-categorization." Branham and Goulet-Cazé (1996) listed five defining characteristics for Diogenes' cynicism:

- Nature was an ethical model for human behavior;

- Greek society's fundamental values were false;

- Happiness came from asceticism;

- Freedom and self-sufficiency were life's paramount values; and

- Real freedom only came from questioning the status quo.

Diogenes's dogged adherence to his philosophical ideals was widely admired. Alexander the Great once offered him anything he might desire, and Diogenes asked Alexander to move; he was blocking the sun. Alexander replied that were he not Alexander already, he would have wanted to be Diogenes instead. Diogenes also disagreed with Plato's philosophy. After Plato defined man as a "featherless biped," Diogenes plucked a chicken, took it to the Academy, and proclaimed he had found a man. The Academy's definition later changed to a "featherless biped with broad fingernails." Diogenes did not hold with Plato's Forms either. Diogenes once argued that he could see tables and cup, but could not see Plato's Forms of tableness and cupness.

Diogenes lived a long life and impressed his contemporaries with his strict adherence to his views about how life should be led. His life demonstrated that one could be happy by living simply and following reason and not convention. Diogenes inspired others to adopt his simple and austere lifestyle. The Stoics later adopted his views regarding the disconnection between happiness and wealth. So too did the Cynic philosophers Crates and his wife Hipparchia. They lived by Diogenes' maxims.

Crates (365–285 BCE)

Crates was born in Thebes to a wealthy household. When he became a Cynic philosopher, he gave away his fortune. Diogenes (1925) gave several accounts of how he may have disposed of the money. One version has it that he gave the money to a banker, telling him to hold it in trust for his children unless they, too, became philosophers. If they did, they would have no use for the money either! Crates moved to Athens and followed in Diogenes's footsteps and may have been one of his students. He adopted the characteristic clothing and lifestyle of the Cynics: the heavy cloak, a wallet, walking with a staff, and leading an austere existence. Like Diogenes, Crates was respected for his commitment to the Cynic pursuit of a life of virtue. Many opened their doors to him and listened to his counsel. One of his students was Zeno of Citium, the founder of Stoicism. Zeno and the Stoics were profoundly influenced by Cynicism. Relatively late in his life, Crates met, and later married, Hipparchia, the sister of one of his students.

PHOTO 3.6 Crates and Hipparchia

Hipparchia (b. 350 BCE)

Hipparchia was born in Maroneia, a town in Thrace. Her family moved to Athens, and her brother, Metrocles, became a student in the Lyceum under Theophrastus. Metrocles left the Lyceum to study under Crates. Hipparchia, then about 20 years old (half of Crates's age), quickly fell in love with him. Her parents severely disapproved of the match, but, after Hipparchia threatened to kill herself if they did not bless the marriage, they relented. Crates asked for her hand in marriage after taking off his cloak and telling her that what she now gazed at was all he possessed. His lack of money and possessions did not dissuade her and they married. Marriage was not typical among the Cynic philosophers, but theirs was no ordinary Greek marriage. Hipparchia wore the cloak, carried a wallet, and bore a staff. She also participated in discussions as an equal. She shocked Athenian society by not adopting any of the traditional roles assigned to women. However, she and Crates pushed that envelope even further. They dined together, which was another breach of convention. However, Schmitt-Pantel (1999) traces public eating at banquets at ancient Greek banquets. There, she writes that banquet guests (p. 94), "Except for rare occasions, women, children, and slaves were excluded."

Shockingly, they made love in public, thus living out the true doglike nature of Cynicism. Hipparchia bore Crates two children, a girl and a boy. Yet, while pregnant and even afterward, she still participated in philosophical discussions with men. Diogenes (1925) reports that in one such discussion with Theodorus, she bested him with a logical syllogism. He was so incensed that he tore off her cloak in anger, but she just stood there, naked and shameless. Hipparchia broke new ground as a role model, and apparently, was not the only female Cynic, but the names of the other women are lost to history. It is notable that Diogenes (1925) included her as the only woman in his *Lives of the Eminent Philosophers*. Of course, the Cynics were not the only variety of philosopher in Greece after Aristotle. The Stoics, Skeptics, and Epicureans also competed alongside each other and along with Plato's (Academics) and Aristotle's (Peripatetics) successors in the Academy and the Lyceum, respectively.

LEARNING OBJECTIVE

7. Identify some of the hallmarks of an ascetic lifestyle.

STOICS

Stoicism grew out of Cynicism. Zeno of Citium, the first Stoic, originally was Crates's student. Unlike the Cynics, however, Stoics embraced the world and believed that the gods had a plan for its future, but only the most enlightened sages could hope to understand their plan. Stoicism caught on quickly and competed against its Epicurean and Skeptic rivals (see below). By the end of its 500-year history, Stoicism had become the dominant philosophy of the Roman Empire. It was the main form of paganism that Christian thought eventually overcame. Zeno developed Stoicism after a chance encounter with Crates and a brief flirtation with Cynicism.

Zeno of Citium (344–262 BCE)

Zeno was born in the town Citium (modern Larnaca) on the island of Cyprus. He and his father were merchants. After being shipwrecked and while stranded in Athens, Zeno began to study the philosophy of Socrates. While at a bookseller's stall, he asked where he could find someone like Socrates. The book merchant pointed out Crates, who was nearby. Soon after, Zeno became one of his students and, for a while at least, he was a Cynic. Later, Zeno studied with other philosophers including Polemo, then the scholarch (head) of the Academy, and Stilpo, another famous philosopher from Megara. Zeno eventually broke away from Platonic teachings and also redirected his thinking about Cynicism to make it more acceptable to conventional mores. Around 301 BCE, he founded his own school and soon attracted many followers. At first, they were called Zenonians but soon became known as Stoics because they held their outdoor meetings near the marketplace (*agora*), near the painted porch or *stoa*. Stoicism grew quickly and lasted as a viable philosophical system for several hundred years thereafter. Zeno remained in Athens until his death in 262 BCE. He was greatly respected and admired, so much so that Athens offered him citizenship, but he refused because he did not wish to dishonor his native Citium.

Zeno's early version of Stoicism encompassed ethics, physics, and logic. His ethics were similar to Socrates's, and he held that happiness was the goal of life. But unlike the Epicureans, Zeno did not equate pleasure with happiness. Instead, he and later Stoics defined happiness as living in accordance with nature. To them, the standard Greek virtues were unarguably good. Those included moderation, wisdom, and courage. Their physics did not exclude the gods; they believed that the gods interacted with humans and involved themselves in their affairs. Zeno's successor, Cleanthes, revived Heraclitus's physics and saw the world as being part of a continuous cycle ending and restarting in a massive, fiery conflagration. The cycle began with fire, followed by air, water, and earth, only to be consumed by fire again. Later Stoics rejected this model and adopted Aristotle's eternal universe (Sedley, 2003). For the Stoics, truths were revealed by the senses, at least for a well-trained Stoic sage. Such sages could distinguish between dreams or hallucinations and reality.

Stoicism owed much to Cynicism, and Stoicism proved more acceptable to those who did not wish to reject convention. The Stoics's pantheistic approach linked the gods to humans in a rational way. Stoics, because of their belief in a rational universe, were able to maintain inner peace in the face of the world's troubles or personal tragedies. Even when faced with unexpected or tragic events, stoics assumed that reasons for those existed. The modern usage of the adjective "stoical" reflects that attitude. But, Stoicism was much more than the possession of a calm, serene attitude. Stoic philosophers developed new ideas but took care not to criticize or contradict Zeno. Stoicism's third scholarch, Chrysippus, was the Stoic most responsible for crystallizing its philosophy.

Chrysippus (280–207 BCE)

Chrysippus was born in Soli, a city on the island of Cyprus. Little is known of his early life before he moved to Athens. There, he studied with Arcesilaus, who was then scholarch (head) of the Academy. Soon he was attracted to Zeno's Stoicism and studied under Cleanthes, Zeno's successor. After Cleanthes died, Chrysippus became the head of the Stoics. Diogenes (1925) reported that Chrysippus wrote prolifically during his 73 years, producing 500 lines per day and over 700 scrolls. None have survived. Scholars agree that without Chrysippus, Stoicism would have died early (Sellars, 2006).

Chrysippus was a stout defender of Zeno's ideas. He added new and original ideas about logic to Stoicism. Aristotle's logic only barely anticipated Chrysippus's propositional logic. Propositions are statements such as: "George Washington was the first president of the United States" or "3 + 3 = 9." In propositional logic (unlike Aristotelean logic), the propositions are considered to be irreducible. Chrysippus's contribution was to provide rules for combining propositions with logical operators, words such as "and," "or," and "if . . . then." He provided logical rules (today known as truth tables) for combining propositions and determining whether they were then true or false. Thus, for the complex proposition created by two simple propositions joined by the operator "and" to be true, both of the simple propositions had to be true. Whereas if they were joined by the "or" operator, only one needed to be true for the complex proposition to be true. Despite the Stoics's advances in logic, Aristotle's logic dominated until the nineteenth century. Then, because of the work of logicians like Boole, Frege, and Russell, propositional logic became the fundamental bedrock for all of logic.

Chrysippus also provided Stoicism with a way to avoid complete **determinism**. Stoics all agreed that the past was unchangeable. At the same time, however, they wished to avoid promoting a philosophy where the future was inevitably determined by the past. To escape this logical trap, Chrysippus required humans to assent to their futures, their fates. Fate was a complex amalgam of past events and mental dispositions. Bobzien (1999, p. 255) notes, "according to Chrysippus, someone can rightly say 'I was fated to do this,' but could not say 'It was fate which *did* (original italics) that, hence it was not me who did that,' or 'I was forced by fate to do that'." Cleanthes offered the example of a dog tied to a cart. Once the cart began to move, the dog, too, had to move either by walking or being dragged. The dog was fated to move but could choose how to deal with fate. By making humans assent, Chrysippus was able to preserve a deterministic past while at the same time account for rare or unexpected events. Even those events were fated. The future, however, was undetermined. Human actors had to make the decisions required for the future to play itself out. To the Stoics fate was an essential part of human decision-making. Gould (1974) gave an example of a man thinking about starting to smoke for the first time; he wrote (p. 23), "The Stoics…would maintain that the man was already destined either to start smoking or not to start, but to do neither of these apart from deliberation and choice." In other words, his decision was not fully his. Fate would play a role; he was destined to either smoke or not but still had to think and choose nonetheless. Like Cleanthes' dog, fate had already decided whether he would smoke or not but he had to decide for himself to accept what fate had already determined. This stoic position is markedly different from Aristotle's; he would claim that fate played no part and that the choice to smoke was his alone.

LEARNING OBJECTIVE

8. Formulate a propositional logic statement where both propositions must be true.

Later development of Stoicism took place in the Roman Empire with the works of Cicero, Epictetus, and Lucretius, reaching its high water mark with the writings of the emperor Marcus Aurelius. Stoicism became the predominant philosophy of the Mediterranean (e.g., Roman) world during the first several centuries of the Common Era. Interestingly, Tom Wolfe's novel, *A Man in Full* 1998), featured Epictetus's Stoicism and led to a minor modern revival of that ancient philosophy marked by increased book sales of ancient Stoic authors and to people admiring Epictetus' advice for living (New York Times, 1999). The main character, Conrad Hensley, lost his job and his wife and ended up in prison. Wolfe characterizes those as fate. In jail, fate intervened again when he received, by mistake, a copy of Epictecus's *Meditations*. Freed by an earthquake (fate again), he began new life in Atlanta as a practical nurse to a down and out, severely depressed, and suicidal real estate mogul. Henley teaches him that wealth is not the measure of a man and that virtue is its own reward.

Stoicisms' attempts to engage and explain the real world accounted for its success against rival philosophies. Those rival philosophies were a varied lot. Skepticism will be examined first. The Skeptics were fierce rivals of the Stoics, and their main dispute with them centered on the role of the senses. The Skeptics were unwilling to accept, uncritically, the information relayed to them by their eyes and ears.

Skeptics

Skepticism began with Pyrrho but fully bloomed 200 years after his death with two schools: the Pyrrhonists and the Academics (e.g., from Plato's Academy). Both were adamantly opposed to Stoicism and its confident stance towards the truth as revealed by the senses. The existence of detailed sense impressions such as dreams and hallucinations, which had no counterpart in objective reality, caused the Skeptics to reject, or at least suspend, belief about all sensations.

Pyrrho (365–270 BCE)

Pyrrho was born in Elis. In his youth, he was an artist, but later became a philosopher. He studied with Anaxarchus of Abdera and accompanied him to India as one of Alexander's sages. While in India, Pyrrho met some "naked wise men" (Flintoff, 1980) who, according to Diogenes (1925), influenced the future direction of his philosophical thinking. Flintoff noted that Pyrrho introduced the quadrilemma, a distinctive and common form of argumentation in India, back to Greece. Flintoff (p. 92) stated, "But this last brings us on to a still closer connection between Pyrrho's thought and Indian logic… uses that typically Indian mode of argument the so-called quadrilemma…a mode of thinking hitherto without precedent in Greek philosophical…thinking." Quadrilemmas, unlike dilemmas, offer four potential choices instead of two and were commonly used in India to discuss metaphysical issues. Pyrrho brought that mode of thinking to Greece but it did not gain wide acceptance. After his return from India, he lived a widely admired tranquil and ascetic life. Athens made him a citizen; a high honor. Elis, his hometown, even exempted all philosophers from local taxation because of his fame. His system of philosophy, however, had little impact in Greece during his lifetime. But, some 200 years later Pyrrhonism, a type of skepticism, became popular in the Roman Empire.

Because Pyrrho did not write, most of what we know of his philosophy comes from his student, Timon. Pyrrho's skepticism was a response to the **dogmatism** of his contemporaries. He believed they were too willing to accept explanations for natural phenomena. Furthermore, the constant arguing and bickering between rival philosophical camps were proof positive that he was right. So, Pyrrho adopted a new approach, one that involved suspension of belief about natural phenomena. Later commentators parodied his approach, suggesting he was skeptical about everyday phenomena and could not even avoid cliffs or dogs without the help of his followers. Those stories are untrue. Pyrrho and later skeptics accepted the normal appearances of daily existence but did not care to be embroiled in arguing about them. Little bothered Pyrrho's tranquil and unconventional life. Once caught in a storm at sea, he soothed his fellow passengers by pointing out how a pig on board was calmly eating. He was also famous for not wincing during surgery performed without anesthesia, perhaps a skill he learned from the philosophers he met in India. In philosophy, Pyrrho and the later Skeptics preferred to believe that the truth was not yet known and their job was to continue to investigate until it was found; their main goal in life was tranquility. They never discovered any underlying mechanisms explaining the workings of the natural world.

EPICUREANS

Epicurus and his followers stood in stark contrast to other contemporaneous philosophical systems. They were atomists like Democritus and thorough materialists who dismissed any notion of souls living on after death. Still, they saw the Greek gods as role models for human behavior even though they also believed the gods had no interest in human affairs. Living during the turbulent era following the rise and fall of Alexander's empire, Epicurus and his followers sought tranquility (*ataraxia*) instead of wealth or power. The modern word "epicurean" only covers part of the meanings assignable to Epicurean philosophy. That modern word primarily connotes a fondness for good food and drink. Epicurus and his followers did enjoy eating well and partaking in sensual pleasures. But, concentrating on that aspect of Epicurean philosophy misses the larger picture. Epicureanism was at once a physical theory, a kind of psychology, a system of ethics that promoted a lifestyle, and an early account of the evolution of human sociality (Konstan, 2009).

Epicurus (341–270 BCE)

Epicurus was born to Athenian parents who lived on the island of Samos, then a colony of Athens. He moved to Athens when he was 18 to fulfill his military obligation. After the death of Alexander, and while he was still in Athens, his parents were forced to leave Samos. After completing his military service, he rejoined them and learned of Democritus's atomism. He spent some time teaching on the island of Lesbos and in the city of Lampsacus before returning to Athens to stay, around 307 BCE (Konstan, 2009). It was then that he purchased his famous Garden where he and his followers spent most of their time. Epicurus's Garden became another school of Athenian philosophy. It differed from the others notably in that it admitted women and slaves.

Epicurus revived Democritus's atomic theory of matter and made several key changes designed to counter criticisms of it made by Aristotle and others. He reaffirmed the primacy of sensory data, opposing Plato and the Skeptics. Those physical conceptions spilled over into his ethical thinking. He proposed soul atoms; these were responsible for consciousness and the individual's soul. After death, all atoms were recycled. Epicurus argued that souls did not survive death but the atoms that made up the soul did. His psychology was materialistic. Sensations were always faithful representations of the physical world. However, perceptions could either be true or false and had to be checked against reality.

Unlike the Skeptics, the Epicureans trusted their senses but realized that such trust could not be total. Strodach (1963) gave an example of their thinking. He described a Roman who perceived a tower on his daily walks along the Appian Way. One day, he turned toward it, approached it, and examined it closely. The sensation of the tower and its corresponding perception matched. Later, though, his hypothetical Roman decided to (p. 32):

> leave the Appian Way . . . and strike off across country. It is coming up to rain . . . then I see what appears to be another round tower . . . The following week I decide to check on this 'percept that awaits verification' to see whether my impression of the week before was right or wrong. It was wrong. The object turns out to be the sole remaining pier of a ruined aqueduct!

Strodach's Roman speculated about the mismatch between sensation and perception. He eventually attributed it to the rain and low-lying clouds. The atomic films emanating from the tower—the causes of the sensation—had been altered during their passage to his eye. Epicurus also introduced the swerve, an element of chance or uncertainty, to his physical theory. He did so to better describe the match between the action of materialistic atoms and events in the real world. He said that atoms swerved unpredictably from time to time. Those unpredictable movements, he claimed, explained why unexpected outcomes sometimes arose in real life.

Epicurus, however, is most famous for his pursuit of tranquility. The Epicurean response to the tumult and uncertainty of life in Athens during this period was to withdraw from it altogether. Where the Cynics sought to shame Athenians for their behavior by living ascetic lives among them, the Epicureans simply retreated into their Garden. There, they sought to live a happy life among friends while avoiding pain. Epicurus, from his ethical point of view, saw pain as evil and pleasure as good.

PHOTO 3.7 Epicurus

He and his followers, however, were not rampant **hedonists**. Like the other Greek philosophers, they believed in moderation. Epicureans were more interested in avoiding pain than in pursuing pleasure. Epicurus taught that the soul did not survive life; the soul atoms survived, but not the soul. Thus, there was no afterlife, and death was not something to be feared. Similarly, immersing oneself in the world's affairs would lead to a loss of tranquility and that, too, should be avoided. Like the Cynics, Epicureans believed that some desires were unworthy. Among those were fame, power, and the pursuit of money; those could never be fully satisfied. Epicurus and his followers practiced what they preached; they found tranquillity in the Garden. After his death, many saw him as a godlike figure. Later Christian writers denigrated Epicurus and were the ones mostly responsible for casting him and his followers as godless libertines. Epicurus himself, however, believed in the Greek gods. However, he taught that they did not interfere in the ways of the world; they were too busy and disinterested. To Epicurus, however, the gods were real; they just did not interact with the world and the ways of humans. Thus, lightning bolts, storms, and earthquakes all had natural causes. In many ways, Epicurus anticipated later scientific findings. His materialistic viewpoint was unusual for his time. Neuringer and Englert (2017) proposed that there is much in common between Epicurus and B. F. Skinner. They wrote (p. 21), "Both considered human beings to be part of the natural world and both attempted to specify the natural laws relating individuals to their environments. Their common quest was to figure out (and teach) people how to live happy and successful lives."

SUMMARY

Philosophy flourished in ancient Greece. The earliest philosophers, the Milesians, attempted to explain the workings of the natural world. Following them, Pythagoras, Xenophanes, and Heraclitus wrestled with fundamental questions about the soul, gods, and relativism. The Eleatics, led by Parmenides, sought to place philosophy outside of the vagaries of observational data. Thus, they created a system that emphasized constancy and changelessness. Zeno of Elea wrote about paradoxes that arose between ideal thought and reality. Later philosophers attempted to reconcile the physical with the ideal, especially with regard to the four elements. Democritus anticipated modern science when he proposed his version of atomism. Following them came Sophists and Nihilists. The former emphasized language and rhetoric while the latter saw philosophy as a waste of time.

All of the philosophies that followed shared a concern over attaining happiness and living a virtuous life, albeit differently. After Socrates, all philosophies sought to explain happiness in absolute terms rather than in relative ones. Socrates explicitly linked happiness and virtue. Plato, too, was deeply troubled by the moral relativism of the Sophists, disagreeing with their "might is right" point of view. Happiness must be a product of reason, he maintained. For Aristotle, teaching and learning were paramount in achieving happiness and virtue; neither came naturally to society. He believed philosophers had to serve as role models and demonstrate that living an ethical life and striving for moderation in all things were the best.

The Cynics had much in common with Socrates; they believed that society spent far too much time in the pursuit of power, wealth, and fame. They literally took their protests to the streets by living unconventionally and arguing that they were happier and more virtuous in their poverty and shamelessness than the public at large was with their riches and conventionality. They voluntarily disposed of their possessions and shunned luxury. The Stoics were nowhere near as willing to sacrifice the comforts of civilization. They believed that the world was a lawful place, even if only very few could comprehend its laws. For them, the best approach to living happily was to accept things as they were. Whatever happened did so for a reason, to accept their fates, and to live a life of moderation.

The Skeptics had a very different approach to the attainment of happiness. They were unwilling to accept sensory data at face value. Plus, the inability of other philosophies to agree on the simplest of matters convinced them that such arguments were fruitless and a waste of time. They believed the search for happiness and virtue was still ongoing and until that search was complete, tranquility was the key to happiness. The Epicureans were very different in many respects from their contemporaries. They retreated from the world, refusing to participate in politics and the pursuit of wealth and power. For them, happiness was the absence of pain, and the best way to achieve that was to exile themselves to Epicurus's Garden.

LEARNING OBJECTIVE

9. Defend the Epicureans retreat into a garden as a way of achieving tranquility in their lives.

What came next in big history is complicated by the conflict between the secular Greek philosophies and the faith-based doctrines of Judaism, Christianity, and Islam covered in the next chapter. Also, contributing were events such as the closing of Plato's Academy, the fall of the Roman Empire, and the Europe's descent into the Medieval period. Those, compounded by the temporary "loss" of Greek works for nearly 1,000 years eventually led to compromises between philosophy and faith followed, in Europe at least, by a very gradual movement to separate an emerging new natural philosophy (e.g., science) from Christian and Islamic teachings.

4 FROM FAITH TO HUMANISM

ZEITGEIST

Religion

Archeological evidence (Nielsen, 2020) points toward an unbroken line connecting the religious practices of the deep past with those of the present. The Greek philosophers never completely separated their philosophical systems from their religious beliefs. Judaism, ancient even 2,000 years ago, possessed a very different conception about supernatural beings and their interaction with humans. While the Greeks were polytheistic, the Jews were monotheistic. Unlike the Greek philosophers, the Jews were certain about their relationship with their one God. To demonstrate their faith and their covenant with him, they circumcised their male children, observed the Sabbath, built their temple in Jerusalem, ate only proscribed foods, and observed a great many other ritualized practices. Around the year 4 CE, a particularly influential Jew was born: Jesus of Nazareth. The story of Jesus, of course, is well known, thanks to the *New Testament.* Jesus and nearly all of his early followers were Jews. After his death, Christianity emerged thanks to his disciples in Jerusalem and Paul's evangelism. Within 50 years of Jesus's death, Christianity emerged and separated itself from its Jewish origins. By 400 CE, Christianity had become the dominant religion of the Roman Empire and its precepts clashed with Neoplatonic philosophy. The Alexandrine Neoplatonists, recent converts to Christianity, saw their task as reconciling their new faith with the older philosophy. Later, Augustine of Hippo created a new faith-based way of thinking and ended the era dominated by Greek philosophy. The age of faith was now at hand. Judaism and Christianity would soon be followed by another world faith: Islam. Mohamed, Islam's prophet, received the Qur'an from the angel Gabriel and the new faith spread quickly from its origins in Arabia bracketing medieval Europe's East–West axis. By the year 1000 Europe was Christianized having resisted attacks from Asia, Islam, and Vikings. By the 15th century Europe had recovered Greco-Roman knowledge, urbanized, explored outside its boundaries, founded universities, and begun the process of secularization. Christian scholars founded Scholasticism, a logical and comprehensive worldview that did not violate church doctrine but still accounted for worldly truths, especially those derived from Aristotle's works. Contemporaneously, in the Islamic world, secularization all but ceased; Islamic scholars and their universities never attained a similar level of independence and their course of study remained focused on the Qur'an. However,

Dmitrishin (2013, p. 12) argued that the independence of European universities relative to the Islamic ones may be exaggerated:

> The only distinction that seems to distinguish the European university is the already mentioned particularity of its legal status. Unlike other similar institutions, the university was incorporated as a legal body under the medieval law. This peculiarity, however, seems to have little influence on its actual performance compared to that of other similar institutions. Both the university and its peer organizations were subjected to strict controls of their respective socio-political systems.

The two religious worlds each profited as commerce everywhere grew quickly as new maritime technologies made it possible for entrepreneurs to use sea routes to Asia, Africa, and the Americas. As the Renaissance began, Humanism, a new intellectual movement appeared; it promoted people and their accomplishments and slowly separated itself from a singular focus on religion and the divine. The earliest humanists criticized the scholastics, reemphasized the role of language in philosophy, introduced new subjects to the universities, and took advantage of the power of the new printing presses.

PREVIEW

Religion, faith, and *revealed knowledge* lead the list of ideas in this chapter. The three religions discussed—Judaism, Christianity, and Islam—each imposed powerful constraints on believers' behavior and strict limits on their conduct. The development of *medicine* was another major idea. Medicine began as an *empirical* discipline but eventually lost that characteristic. Hippocratic *humorism* persisted for thousands of years because physicians had become dependent on ancient but unproven ideas. *Neoplatonism* grew out of a collection of older traditions in response to *Christianity.* Neoplatonism's emphasis on virtue gave way to Christianity's goal of meeting God in Heaven following a lifetime of trial on Earth. This was a *dualistic* and *transcendental* way of looking at life. Christianity also imposed an antimaterialistic approach to living, but that was difficult to sustain and led to the doctrines of *predestination* and *grace.* Augustine also promoted a *linear,* as opposed to *cyclical,* view of time. The Islamic approach to philosophy was more open than was the Christian approach. Still, Islamic philosophers never promoted ideas explicitly contrary to the Qu'ran. That Islamic scholars could openly read and translate the classic works of antiquity ultimately preserved many of those works for posterity.

Around the midpoint of the medieval period, Christianity had spread throughout most of Europe and provided a new identity: *Christendom.* The age of faith was in full bloom. But the seeds of *secularism* were slowly sprouting. Fed by the rediscovery and translation of ancient texts, Christian scholars struggled to reconcile the works of classic writers such as Plato and Aristotle with *revealed knowledge.* Soon, scholars began to offer logical proofs for the existence of God.

As Christian religious orders for men and women multiplied, *universities* came into being to fill the demand for scholars. Their curricula, the *trivium* and *quadrivium,* eventually led to the establishment of the *liberal arts.* Over centuries, scholastics debated the relationship between religion and acquired knowledge. Gradually, in Christian Europe at least, a gap began to grow between religion and philosophy. Disputes, however, were always resolved in favor of religious *dogma*.

   Biology reemerged as an academic discipline but only in a limited way. The *medical knowledge* gained by Islamic physicians spread as did the more scientific study of *optics*. *Ockham's Razor* provided a way to pare down theoretical explanations. The rise of *Humanism* also led to the creation of new academic disciplines: *anthropology, philology,* and *history*. It also sparked a strongly renewed interest in the study of ancient writers of Latin and Greek works. That, along with the development of the *printing press,* the discovery of *"New" worlds,* a rise in *urbanism,* and a new appreciation for secular *art and music* marked the beginning of the end of the medieval period. Humanism also led to the rise of *moral philosophy*, a direct antecedent to the social sciences.

   The *Black Plague* was a major external shock that, ultimately, opened more doors than it closed. The depopulation it caused shook religious belief and opened new opportunities for survivors. *Astronomy* slowly relinquished its *handmaiden* status to religious beliefs and would soon become the first true science. Its rise was aided by the adoption of *Hindu-Arabic numerals* and a new confidence in *empirical methods*. All of these ideas led to the rise of secularism in Christian Europe. The Islamic world, however, soon lost its early intellectual lead as its scholars were unable to separate religion from philosophy.

INTRODUCTION

This chapter runs in the foreground of the long and continuing conflict between Christianity and Islam. Their conflicts helped shape the future of both faiths and led to the reemergence of philosophy. After a long period of intellectual reflection, Islam proclaimed human attempts to understand the natural world through philosophy as blasphemous. Islam hewed to its founding principles and sought to establish a global society based upon Qur'an. Christianity, too, wished to create its version of a own global society based upon the Bible and the teachings of Jesus. Thus, between the 5th and 13th centuries philosophy, as it is understood today, was forced into hibernation. At the same time, Islam was aggressive and expansionist. Its scholars made much progress and its cities were larger and more livable than those in Europe. In the Islamic universities, the classic Neoplatonist and Aristotelian works never lost to them and were translated from Greek to Syriac, Arabic, and, finally, Latin. Their publication put an end to the "Dark Ages" in Europe and stimulated its slow process toward secularization. Christian scholars reconciled Aristotle's writings with Holy Scripture leading to a renewal of rationalism, empiricism, skepticism, and to the earliest traces of modern science. Outside of scholarship, armed conflict raged between Christianity and Islam for nearly 1,000 years, from the invasion of Spain in 711 CE to the lifting of the siege of Vienna in 1683. Yet, in both cultures, belief in God still reigned supreme and would continue to do so in Europe until the 19th century and to the present day in Islam.

   In both worlds, philosophers studied a wide variety of topics that today would be considered psychological including: common sense, imagination, memory, dreaming, and intelligence. In Europe, these scholars were interested in human intelligence and in the intelligence of God and the angels (Kemp, 1996). Logic was still their dominant methodology and systematic experimentation was still far off in the future. There was no true psychology yet, but there was interest in topics that future psychologists would claim from philosophy and make their own.

NEOPLATONISM

Plato's works continued to exert a profound influence on philosophy long after his death. His Academy continued to operate until 529 CE when the Christian Roman emperor, Justinian, shut it down permanently. Neoplatonism developed slowly and eventually integrated ideas from Plato, Aristotle, Epicurus, and the Jewish religion. Philo of Alexandria, while not a Neoplatonist himself, nevertheless was an important precursor. However, it was Plotinus who gave Neoplatonism its most complete and integrated exposition. Neoplatonism coexisted with the new and expansive Christian doctrine, and, in many ways, was a rear guard defense of the tenets of Greek philosophy. At the same time, it was the last attempt by that philosophy to provide an explanation for living a happy life and earning personal salvation by living in accord to Platonic principles and not by the gift of Christian grace (Wildberg, 2019). By the year 1000 CE philosophies based on religion had almost completely extirpated Neoplatonism and other "pagan" philosophies from the continent of Europe and along the shores of the Mediterranean. The word pagan came from the Latin word *paganus,* meaning country dweller. In Europe, it became a catchall term for non-Christians, Muslims, and polytheists. In Islamic lands it was applied to non-Muslims.

Philo (20 BCE–50 CE)

Biography

Philo was born in Alexandria to a wealthy and noble Jewish family. Philo's education was remarkable in that it included the Jewish and Greek traditions. This combination was important in his later writings as he sought to reconcile those two intellectual traditions. Late in his life, he served as the main Jewish emissary from Alexandria to the Roman emperor, Caligula. That diplomatic mission sought to end attacks by the Greek community on Jews in Alexandria. The mission was unsuccessful and an early harbinger of the later Jewish War of 66–73 CE, which led to the destruction of the Second Temple in Jerusalem.

Contributions

That war also greatly diminished Philo's influence on later Judaism as its scholars rejected his attempts to synthesize the Jewish and Greek traditions. Paradoxically, Philo's influence increased within the growing Christian community as it successfully incorporated both Jewish and Greek ideas into its teachings (Chilton, 2006). From that point on, any reconciliation between Judaism and Christianity was impossible. As Johnson (1988, pp. 144–145) noted:

> The Jews could not concede the divinity of Jesus as God-made-man without repudiating the central tenet of their belief. The Christians could not concede that Jesus was anything less than God without repudiating the essence and purpose of their

movement. If Christ was not God, Christianity was nothing. If Christ was God, then Judaism was false. There could be no compromise on this point. Each faith was thus a threat to the other.

The quarrel was all the more bitter because, while differing on the essential, the two faiths agreed on virtually everything else. The Christians took from Judaism the Pentateuch (including its morals and ethics), the prophets and the wisdom books, and far more of the apocrypha than the Jews themselves were willing to canonize. They took the liturgy, for even the eucharist had Jewish roots.

Later Christian theologians used Philo's writings to create a religion that successfully incorporated parts of Plato's thinking and much of earlier Hebrew theology. Philo's extensive writings on the Jewish law attempted to show the connections between ancient Hebrew traditions and later Greek philosophy. He explicitly combined the Hebrew tradition of hearing the word of God, as revealed by their prophets, with the Greek (and later Roman) idea of *logos,* the belief in a living, rational universe. Hillar (2018) detailed how later Christian thinkers gradually developed that idea into their doctrine of the trinitarian view of God, while at the same time redefining the concept of evil. Philo used Plato's Forms to help create the junction between the two intellectual traditions. He changed the Forms from being universal, ideal, and timeless concepts to manifestations of the mind of God. That being done, he went on to link, allegorically, many parts of the Septuagint version of the Hebrew Bible to Greek philosophy, especially to Stoicism. In doing so, he laid the foundation for later Neoplatonists such as Plotinus.

Plotinus (204–270 CE)

Biography

Plotinus was born in Egypt and moved to Alexandria when he was nearly 30 years old. He first learned philosophy from Ammonius Saccas, a Greek philosopher who lectured near the docks and also worked as a porter. Plotinus studied under Ammonius for 11 years and then attached himself to a military expedition to Persia led by the Roman emperor, Gordian III. That expedition withdrew in failure after Gordian was assassinated by his own troops leaving Plotinus to fend for himself.

Contributions

Eventually, he made his way to Rome where he spent the rest of his life as a philosopher. He became extremely well known and influential. Late in his life, his student, Porphyry, helped organize Plotinus's voluminous lecture notes into nine volumes (the fourth covered psychology), the *Enneads,* and published them along with a biography, thus preserving much of his master's work for posterity. O'Meara (2016) wrote that Plotinus wrote little early in his career but began to put down his thoughts after 254 CE. Porphyry, O'Meara stated (p. 304), "credits himself with stimulating Plotinus to write more, and indeed the treatises which Plotinus then composed gained considerably in extension, depth and freedom of expression." According to Gerson (2008, n.p.), "Plotinus shaped the entire subsequent history of philosophy. Until well into the 19th century, Platonism was in large part understood, appropriated or rejected based on its Plotinean expression."

Plotinus attempted nothing less than a complete synthesis of Greek philosophy. Although he is now remembered and labeled as a Neoplatonist, he also incorporated Aristotelian, Stoic, and Epicurean elements into his philosophical system. His goal was to create a new version of Greek philosophy that would preserve its search for virtue while at the same time offer the hope for personal salvation, thus countering the new and expansionistic Christian teachings. Ultimately, his version of Neoplatonism failed to take root, and instead, the Christian scholars, most notably Augustine of Hippo (see below), reworked Neoplatonism into a version compatible with Christian doctrine.

Plotinus placed everything within a singular, timeless, and abstract entity he called the One or the Good. It was the creator of everything but could not be a thing itself nor could it be studied or understood directly. The Good, he argued, was like a huge basin whose contents overflowed. That overflow created the intellect, or *nous,* which was rational thought and the Platonic Forms. As the Good's emanations flowed further away, they created the soul, which was composed of two parts, one superior to the other. The higher part contained the world soul while the lower part contained individual souls. Furthest away from the Good was matter itself which Plotinus considered the root of evil.

Human happiness, Plotinus maintained, came from contemplation of the intellect. The highest form of happiness came from trying to understand the contents of the intellect or Plato's Forms. Doing so successfully could lead to a state of ecstasy. Porphyry reported that Plotinus himself had fallen into such states only a handful of times. Plotinus realized that nearly all humans had to live in the real world and deal with matter. Leaving the material world behind and moving toward the Good was the path Plotinus sought. True happiness was not to be found in materialism; its rewards were false and perishable. Leaving the material world was a way of returning one's individual soul to the world soul. The highest happiness, however, could not be attained alone. That happiness required the Good to show itself to a seeker as a type of revelation, but only those lucky few who had prepared themselves by turning away from material things and who had spent time contemplating the universal soul and the intellect.

It was an easy step for Christian thinkers to appropriate much of Neoplatonism and to rework it into their own religious framework. Many later Alexandrian Neoplatonist philosophers converted to Christianity and became some of the early church fathers. They laid the groundwork for the union of Neoplatonism and Christianity. At around the same time in Athens, Greek philosophy was approaching its final stage. In 529 CE, after Justinian closed the Academy, some of its members fled eastward to Persia while others moved to Rome. As the tide of Christian thought rose, many of the classic works of Greek philosophy were destroyed as heretical. But, many of the works carried eastward to Baghdad were eventually translated into Arabic from whence they would, hundreds of years later, be translated into Latin.

LEARNING OBJECTIVE

1. Describe the amalgam of philosophical and religious ideas that led to Christianity.

THE RISE OF CHRISTIAN FAITH

The life and work of Augustine, one of the church fathers, brought the classic era of Greek philosophy to a close. In Europe, for nearly 1,000 years after his death (430 CE), the works of Socrates, Plato, Aristotle, and their successors were lost, forgotten, or suppressed. Taking their place was a religiously based way of thinking, Christianity. That religion emphasized a turning away from the world; a life in Heaven after death for some and eternal damnation in Hell for the rest. Christianity's teachings could not be logically inferred. Instead, they were based upon divine revelations from Jesus, his disciples, or self-appointed persons who claimed they had been chosen to reveal messages from God (e.g., the Old Testament prophets and Paul of Tarsus). This new era emphasized the role of the soul as the most important part of personhood and saw a turning away from materialism toward a more introspective philosophy. Interestingly, Augustine was able to start and maintain this new way of thinking through the power of his written words while working as the bishop of Hippo, a small and out-of-the-way see in North Africa.

Augustine of Hippo (354–430 CE)

Biography

Augustine was born in Thagaste, North Africa (modern Souk Ahras, Algeria), to a family of moderate means, but with sufficient money to send him to school. His mother, Monica, was a devout Christian but his father, Patricius, was not. In schools at Madaurus and Carthage, Augustine studied rhetoric and eventually taught the subject in Thagaste and Carthage. At this point in his life he embraced Skepticism because of reading Cicero. After nearly ten years teaching in Carthage, he moved to Rome in order to teach what he hoped would be better students. They were not, and worse still, left him flat when it came time to pay their tuition. After his disappointment in Rome, he moved to Milan to teach rhetoric at the imperial court, a major step up in prestige and visibility. Yet, Augustine's personal life was atypical. He was not married; he had a long time mistress in Africa, one who had borne him a son, Adeodatus. Augustine's mother, now in Milan, arranged a marriage for him, but the bride-to-be was still underage. While waiting for her to reach her majority, he took another mistress and broke off the engagement. During this turbulent time in his life, Augustine began to reconsider his life starting with his religion.

Augustine left the Roman Church, his mother's faith, and became a member of the Manichean sect. Manichaeism was a rapidly spreading religion that had originated in Persia and taught that good, represented by light, and evil, represented by darkness, coexisted in the world and battled for people's souls. It also taught that sin was not a personal fault but, rather, the result of evil. Thus, those who committed sins were not at fault; their actions were beyond their control. The Manicheans also questioned the Christian scriptures, saying they had been falsified. The Roman Church declared Manichaeism a heresy, punishable by death, in 382. While in Rome, Augustine was still a Manichean but was beginning to doubt their teachings. In Milan, he discovered Neoplatonism, most probably through the works of Plotinus. Reading those texts was a pivotal moment in his life. Augustine renounced Manichaeism and converted to Christianity in 387, an event he related in his *Confessions*. He also resolved to live a chaste life from that point on. He and his family left Milan for Africa shortly thereafter. On the way there, his mother died. Not long after, in Africa, so did his son. From that point on, Augustine was fully committed to his newfound work, reconciling Neoplatonism with Christian doctrine. Eventually, he became the bishop of Hippo, a port city on what is today the Algerian coast. From that backwater, he wrote voluminously and almost single-handedly put an end to the era of classical Greek philosophy while at the same time launching a new era, one based on revealed knowledge from God and scripture.

Contributions

Augustine's development of his new Christian philosophy was lifelong and complex. Early after his conversion, he attempted to show how the study of the traditional liberal arts—grammar, logic, rhetoric, geometry, astronomy, and music—were no impediment to Christian philosophers. Later in his life, however, he manifested a less charitable attitude toward those subjects and maintained that faith in God was more important. In his book, *City of God*, he juxtaposed two fictional cities. The earthly city represented the wrong choice made by many as they sought solace and comfort in materialism. The heavenly city, on the other hand, promised salvation and eternal life in Heaven, along with its ultimate reward, the opportunity to know and be with God.

Throughout his life, Augustine never truly separated his theology from his philosophy, which makes understanding his thinking difficult. First and foremost, he put forth understanding the soul and God as the two most important issues in philosophy. At the same time, however, he still believed that humans were primarily governed by reason. In thinking this way, he was close to Neoplatonism, but, there were important differences. For one, Augustine (but not the Neoplatonists) believed the source of the Platonic Forms was God. Thus, in trying to understand the Forms, one was also trying to understand God and perfection. Augustine, however, differed with the Neoplatonists on the issue of souls. Augustine held that each soul was immortal, created, immaterial, and changeable. People were composed of body and soul, but soul was far more important. His conception of the soul led to an explicit **dualism** of soul and matter. With this dualism, Augustine effectively ended Stoic and Epicurean materialism. Recall that the Stoics anticipated modern cognitive psychology by allowing people to assent to their fates and by appealing to individual differences. To them, all observed behavior was lawful, but apparent deviations from lawfulness were due to individual decisions, not chance. The Epicureans also wished to account for all human events but they explained individual deviations via the swerve. They provided an account of socialization in which they explained how humans had moved from a solitary to social existence, invented technologies, and established the rule of law (Konstan, 2009). As Augustine struggled with the problem of human conduct and forced himself to introspect about his own behavior he opened the door to an internal cognitive world that he believed was larger and more important to explaining behavior than was the external world. Thus, he legitimized the use of **phenomenology** and other nonmaterialistic approaches to psychology. Interestingly, 19th century scientific psychology began phenomenologically (see Chapter 6) as the scientific approach to understanding the mind.

In the place of the older philosophies, Augustine substituted a new, religious, and transcendental (e.g., being able to move or transcend from Earth to Heaven) philosophy. That philosophy was loosely based on Neoplatonism plus the teachings of Jesus as codified in the Christian gospels, the letters of Paul of Tarsus, and the writings of other church fathers. Unlike previous philosophies that searched for and promoted virtue and the pursuit of happiness, Augustine's philosophy was more pessimistic. Human virtue was unattainable, and happiness could not be found in life. Instead, the goal of life on Earth was to prepare to know God. Yet, that knowledge required divine illumination of the soul's interior along with the realization that the inner world was more vast and important than the material world.

There were striking differences between this new way of thinking and the older, pagan philosophies, as they were now labeled. One of the most prominent differences was that Augustine saw all humans as equals, a position quite different from nearly all of the Greek philosophers who put men above women and both above slaves. Another difference was that he made people responsible for their own conduct. This was Augustine's doctrine of free will, needed in order to resolve the simultaneous existence of worldly evil and an omniscient God. People had to choose which of Augustine's two cities they were going to live in. The trade-off, of course, was Faustian. Those who chose to live in the earthly city would profit while alive, but suffer eternal damnation in Hell after death. However, those who chose to live in the city of God might suffer while alive, but their reward would be to live in Heaven for all eternity in the presence of God. Nothing could be hidden from an all-knowing God. Thus, one might get away with murder while alive, but not after death. God would rightfully judge murderers and other criminals even if they had escaped human justice while alive. Near the end of his life, Augustine invoked predestination and grace in order to explain how souls ended up in one city or the other. He argued that no human could resist the temptations of the earthly city, thus all were sinners. God's grace or forgiveness alone saved a few, the elect, or those who would live in the heavenly city. That grace was a divine gift, given without merit or the possibility of fathoming the reason it was given. Those outside of God's grace were predestined to eternal damnation without any recourse.

The changes Augustine brought about were massive and long-lasting. Augustine died during the final years of the Roman Empire as Vandals (one of the Germanic tribes that had migrated into Europe) were besieging Hippo in 430 AD. His ideas, however, lived on and grew in importance for nearly 1,000 years. As the Roman Catholic Church solidified its grip on Western Europe, it formalized and promoted Augustine's views. As the Roman Empire fractured, that led to a profound loss of civil central authority; the Church filled that vacuum. In doing so, it emphasized an antimaterial and increasingly antiintellectual stance. The Church knew the *Truth*; it had been revealed to it by God. True happiness was to be found in the afterlife, not on Earth itself. Furthermore, the Church's mission was to convert unbelievers, by force if necessary. Just wars, condoned by Augustine's teachings, were permissible under certain circumstances such as to combat heretical beliefs. Over centuries such thinking led to many attacks on Christian heretics, pogroms against Jews, and crusades against Islam.

Another change Augustine brought about was to the conception of time itself. Recall that the Stoics originally viewed time as an eternal cycle. That cycle, of course, was reinforced by observations of monthly, yearly, and longer natural cycles. Augustinian philosophy, however, could not tolerate such cycles. To do so would be to admit that the life of Jesus was not a unique and transformative event in human history. It was vital that Jesus's birth could only have happened once. Thus, Augustine introduced linearity to the study of history, a trend that continues until the present.

Gradually, the Hellenistic legacy was forgotten. The connection between Neoplatonism and Christian philosophy all but disappeared. Pagan works and customs were suppressed and replaced by Christian orthodoxy. Western Europe had entered its own Dark Age. Elsewhere, however, the Greek traditions continued as in Byzantium, the eastern half of the old Roman Empire, and at Baghdad and Toledo where Moslem scholars continued, mostly unhindered by Islam, to study the classic works and expand their own knowledge. Later events would bring these two religion-based philosophies together, changing them both in nearly opposite ways. Christians became less influenced by religion while Moslems became more so. Thus, a look at Muhammad and the rise of Islam is critical to understanding this chapter of big history.

LEARNING OBJECTIVE

2. Explain how Augustine introduced phenomenology to philosophy.

MUHAMMAD AND THE RISE OF ISLAM

Muhammad was born in Mecca in 570. He was orphaned early in life and raised by his uncle Abu Talib. At the age of 25, Muhammad married an older and rich widow, Khadija. Marrying her elevated his social standing and improved his financial status. It also gave him time to talk to many of the travelers who came through Mecca with the caravans and spend time in nearby caves alone in thought. One night in 610, during the month of Ramadan, Muhammad saw a vision of an angel commanding him to "recite." The vision, who Muhammad later identified as the angel Gabriel, commanded him to recite the verses or suras of what eventually became the Qur'an, the sacred book of Islam. After Mohammad's death the Qur'an was assembled as a written document in Arabic by Muhammad's first two successors. At the time Muhammad was receiving these revelations, Mecca was a prosperous city because of its location astride caravan routes and the many pilgrims who visited the Ka'aba, a building that housed an ancient meteoritic black rock. As Muhammad received more visions he began to preach against the established customs of Mecca, especially those concerning wealth and status. In 622, Muhammad was forced to flee Mecca for the nearby town of Yathrib (since then known as Medina, "the city of the prophet"). In the history of Islam, the move to Medina is called the *Hijira* and it marked the beginning of Islam as well as the starting point of the Islamic calendar. Once in Medina, Muhammad and his few followers gradually forged a makeshift alliance with the local Jewish groups and fought intermittently with the Meccans. The Battle of the Trench (627), the third and last battle between Medina and Mecca, was a complete victory for Muhammad and his followers. Three years later after a series of diplomatic moves, shows of force, and skirmishes, Muhammad entered

Mecca in triumph and destroyed the pagan idols in the Ka'aba. He kept its black stone and made the *Hajj,* or pilgrimage to Mecca, one of the five pillars of Islam. The other four pillars being praying daily five times each day, fasting during the month of Ramadan, giving alms to the poor, and the professing one's faith by saying out loud: There is no God but God, and Muhammad is his prophet. Muhammad died in 632 without designating a successor. Abu Bakr was chosen to succeed Muhammad. Abu Bakr's successors, Umar and Uthman, assembled Muhammad's revelations in written form creating the Qur'an. The Qur'an, along with the *Hadiths* (the sayings of Muhammad), became the guides for Islamic life. Islam spread quickly throughout Arabia and beyond. In less than 200 years after Muhammad's death, Islam had spread from Arabia northward to the gates of Constantinople and westward onto the Iberian Peninsula. Muhammad had unleashed a battle of faiths that would control the dynamics of history until the present day.

ISLAMIC SCHOLARS

As Islam spread northward along the lands bordering the eastern Mediterranean it came into contact with Greek ideas and knowledge that had first been spread by Alexander and later by scholars fleeing the Roman Empire following the closing of the Academy in Athens. By the time of the Islamic conquests those original Greek works had been largely translated into Syriac, a language similar to Aramaic. After the arrival of Islam, and over the course of several hundred years, scholars housed principally in three centers, or caliphates, translated an enormous amount of Greek works into Arabic.

The major caliphate was Baghdad, a city founded in 762 by Al-Mansur, the second caliph of the Abbasid dynasty. Its fifth caliph, Harun Al-Rashid, sponsored "The House of Knowledge" (also called "The House of Wisdom"), a think tank housing scholars from many disciplines and religions. Early on, their main work consisted of translating classical Greek works into Arabic. Later, their successors began to produce new and original knowledge, especially in astronomy, mathematics, and medicine (Dallal, 1999).

The other major center was in Islamic Spain. There, the Umayyad dynasty established its own caliphate. The cities of Toledo and Cordoba became the centers of learning in Spain and were very influential as sources of recovered classical knowledge for Christian Europe because of their relatively tolerant intellectual atmosphere and proximity. In Spain, as in Baghdad (but to a lesser extent), Islamic scholars worked closely with their Jewish and Christian counterparts to produce translations and new works.

The third caliphate, led by the Fatimid dynasty, was in Cairo, a city they founded. The Fatimids were Shi'a Muslims and were exceptionally tolerant of other faiths and sects. They sent their missionaries, the Ismailis, far and wide throughout the Islamic world in an ultimately unsuccessful attempt to reunify with the Sunnis, the other main branch of Islam. So, while most of Europe was mired in its "Dark Ages" and its inhabitants lived in primitive conditions, the Islamic world thrived commercially and intellectually. This period is often labeled as Islam's "Golden Age" (Weller, 2018). One of the earliest of the Islamic scholars was Al-Kindi who produced translations of some of Aristotle's works.

Al-Kindi (800–870)

Biography

Abu Yusuf Ya'quib ibn Ishaq Al-Kindi was known as the "first philosopher" in the Arabic world. He was born in Basra in what is now Iraq. He spent most of his life in Baghdad working as a polymath (e.g., a widely gifted person) intellectual in Harun Al-Rashid's House of Knowledge. He studied a wide variety of topics including: mathematics, metaphysics, ethics, medicine, physics, optics, and astronomy. He also pursued more applied subjects such as perfumery and music (Adamson, 2006a).

Contributions

Al-Kindi is most famous for directing the House of Knowledge's first translation attempts and for first introducing philosophy *(falsafa)* to the Arabic world. His most influential work was *On First Philosophy* in which he wrote:

> We must not be ashamed to admire the truth or to acquire it, from wherever it comes. Even if it should come from far-flung nations and foreign peoples, there is for the student of truth nothing more important than the truth, nor is the truth demeaned or diminished by the one who states or conveys it; no one is demeaned by the truth, rather all are ennobled by it (Adamson, 2006b, n.p.).

Being a devout Muslim, he never placed philosophy over the truth of revelations found in the Qur'an. Instead, he maintained that the truths of philosophy fully supported those of revelation. His approach to metaphysics made understanding God the most important quest. Later Arabic philosophers would disagree with Al-Kindi's approach and place understanding God in a less prominent metaphysical position. Al-Kindi also struggled with Aristotle's conception of an eternal universe. For Al-Kindi, the universe had to have had a beginning and he attempted to prove that the concept of infinity could not exist in the real world.

Al-Kindi's influence on Arabic science and philosophy waned after his death. However, his translation work was instrumental in paving the way for later scholars. D'Ancona (2006, p. 21) gave three trademarks for the *falsafa* begun by Al-Kindi: "(1) philosophy is a systematic whole, whose roots lie in logic and whose peak is rational theology; (2) all the Greek philosophers agree on a limited, but important, set of doctrines concerning the cosmos, the human soul, and the first principle; (3) philosophical truths do not derive from the Qur'an, even if they fit perfectly with it." Al-Kindi's work laid the groundwork for later Arabic scholars and was thus vital in the eventual renewal of knowledge in Christian Europe. Al-Farabi built upon Al-Kindi's work and greatly expanded the scope of Islamic scholarship.

Al-Farabi (872–950)

Biography

Very little is known about the details of the life of Abu Nasr Muhammad Al-Farabi. He was born in Wasij, Turkestan. He spent most of his life in Baghdad where he studied philosophy and other subjects with Yuhanna ibn-Haylan, a Nestorian Christian. From him Al-Farabi learned of the Neoplatonist and Aristotelian traditions still extant in Alexandria.

Contributions

When Al-Farabi created his new curriculum he taught the entirety of Aristotle's logical corpus and added his own original contributions. At that time and to avoid heresy, The Christian church only taught Aristotle's logic to "midway through the Prior Analytics" (Riesman, 2006, p. 65). Later, Aristotle's thinking was gradually incorporated into Christian theology (see further). Although there is little to indicate that Al-Farabi was influential while alive, his work was vital to the development of later Arabic scholarship.

Al-Farabi is best seen as a systematizer of several disparate fields: cosmology, psychology, and education. He was also one of the earliest political scientists because he argued that human happiness, the main goal of life, could not be achieved in isolation. Humans were social animals. His cosmology linked three traditions, those of Aristotle, Plotinus, and Ptolemy. He purposely reframed those ancient theories to make them more palatable to all monotheists. Thus, in the place of Aristotle's Prime Mover, he substituted God. He kept Ptolemy's nine Earth-orbiting bodies but dispensed with the pagan gods (e.g., Mercury, Venus, Mars, Jupiter, Saturn, Uranus, Neptune, and Pluto) that moved them. He modified Plotinus's emanations to create a system that "accounts for nearly every element of Al-Farabi's philosophy and nicely incorporates the astronomical knowledge of his day" (Riesman, 2006, p. 57). His psychology was similar to Aristotle's in that it included a soul with nutritive, sensitive, and appetitive faculties; characteristics humans shared with animals. Humans' souls, however, also had the faculty of reason. However, reason required education to move it from potentiality into actuality. Al-Farabi realized that not all people could be educated to the point of understanding the world completely via the knowledge of logic. Philosophers, of course, could reach such a point through a proper curriculum. The remaining mass of humankind were unable to use that route and had to achieve happiness via the route of prophecy and revelation.

Al-Farabi approached becoming a political scientist and social psychologist when he argued that humans could not achieve happiness through isolating themselves from others. Instead, he identified large (e.g., worldwide), intermediate (e.g., national), and small (e.g., the city-state) levels of human society. Like Plato in *The Republic*, Al-Farabi held that the smallest grouping was the ideal one. Of course, his ideal state was Islamic. Its leaders needed to be educated men who would obey God's laws as well as enforce them. The leaders, similar to Plato's, would be philosophers who would lead by their superior knowledge and virtuous example. Al-Farabi's main contribution was to provide a synthesis of classical knowledge and combine it with new ways of using that knowledge to reach the highest goal: human happiness. In the Arabic tradition, he was known as the "second teacher," that is, second only to Aristotle. The work of Al-Kindi and Al-Farabi was critical to the development of the later and more mature versions of Islamic philosophy. Avicenna and Averroës represented the high point of that intellectual tradition.

Avicenna (980–1037)

Biography

Abu Ali Al-Hussain Ibn Abdallah Ibn Sina, known to the West as Avicenna, grew up in Bukhara in what is now Uzbekistan. His father was governor of a nearby town. He and Avicenna's older brother were members of a secret society, the Brethren of Purity; they believed that self-knowledge would lead to knowledge of God. Avicenna, in his autobiography, reported that as a young child he listened to the discussions that took place in his home between his family and the Fatimid missionaries from Egypt, but claimed that he rejected the conclusions formed at those discussions and did not follow in his father's religious footsteps. Instead, he received a more traditional religious education followed by medical training. Afterward, he taught himself philosophy by closely reading nearly every translated or original Greek text he could find. Because of his skill as a physician he came to the attention of the local prince who made him his personal doctor. The prince also allowed him the privilege of reading the books in his extensive library. By the time he was 18, Avicenna claimed that he had absorbed all the information held in it (Wisnovsky, 2006). His medical writings made him famous in Christian Europe having been translated by the 12th century; they remained standard texts for 500 years. In those he reviewed all previous medical knowledge and added a number of lifestyle factors related to good health: air, bodily movement and repose, sleep and wakefulness, psychic movement and repose, food, drinks, along with evacuation and retention (Choopani & Emtiazy, 2015). His metaphysical writings, however, provoked a severe response by Islamic theologians, especially Abu Hamid al Ghazali.

Contributions

Al Ghazali, too, was well versed in the Arabic translations of Greek texts. In a book called *The Incoherence of the Philosophers,* he disagreed with Avicenna on three main metaphysical points. The first was Avicenna's contention that God and the world were eternal. The second was that God's knowledge was limited, and the third was Avicenna's conclusion that only the soul and not the body was eternal. Al Ghazali also disagreed with Avicenna's mechanism for cause and effect. Despite Al Ghazali's criticisms, Avicenna's thoughts on the relation between philosophy and religion continued to spark debate in the Islamic world well into the 19th century. His "floating man" thought experiment argued for the existence of the soul. It was convincing and powerful. In it, he posited that a fully mature and freshly created human being, deprived of all sensory input and suspended in the air, would yet be cognizant of existence without any physical stimuli and thus have a soul. Griffel (2016) offered that Al Ghazali's writings had the effect of restricting Islamic philosophy by setting religious limits to their work.

In Christian Europe, however, Avicenna's long-term legacy was much less. His main contributions there were in medicine and physiology, not philosophy. He wrote a long and highly influential medical textbook, *The Canon of Medicine.* In it he comprehensively covered nearly the whole breadth of medicine as he knew it. His book listed drugs, diseases, and treatments. It even included sections on what we would now call psychosomatic medicine. *The Canon of Medicine* was translated into Latin in the 12th century and soon became the main textbook for Western medicine. It was reprinted for hundreds of years.

In the area of cognition, he expanded upon Aristotle's five external senses by adding interior senses and locating them in specific areas of the brain. These interior senses were coordinated were the "common senses": imagery, imagination, estimation, instinctive sensing, and memory (Gutas, 2016). The common senses passed along their integrated information to an

"imaginative" faculty, a holdover from Aristotle. Avicenna, however, added additional faculties of mind in animals and humans, going beyond Aristotle's model. These new faculties allowed for imagination in animals and humans and for rational thought in humans alone. He also was one of the first to propose a kind of instinctive faculty, and used it to explain innate behaviors such as fear of predators or attraction to members of the same species.

Avicenna, then, was influential in the eventual rise of Western medicine and physiology. However, his philosophical work failed to take deep root in either the Islamic or Christian worlds. Another Islamic scholar, however, did have a profound effect on Western philosophy. His name was Averroës and his commentaries on Aristotle would prove to be earthshaking to Christian philosophy.

PHOTO 4.1 Avicenna as depicted on an Iranian postage stamp.

Averroës (1126–1198)

Biography

Abu Al-Walid Muhammad ibn Ahmad ibn Muhammad ibn Rushd, known in the West as Averroës, was born in Cordoba in Muslim Spain *(Al-Andalus)*. Averroës was well educated in religion, philosophy, and law. He also was a physician. When he was 40, his colleague Ibn Tufayl asked him to explain the works of Aristotle to the caliph. Averroës accepted the task and that began his career as an Aristotelian commentator. Soon after, the caliph, impressed, appointed him as a judge as well. Averroës held judgeships in Seville and Cordoba and much of his writings concerned Islamic law *(Sharia)*. Eventually, he became the court physician. During this time he wrote voluminously on Aristotle, commenting on all of his works except the *Politics,* which had not yet been translated into Arabic. Many of his commentaries were written in short, intermediate, and long versions with the longer ones tending to be the final definitive versions. Near the end of his life he was exiled for two years, and his books banned and burned because of a rise in Islamic fundamentalism. The bans were lifted and he was restored to Cordoba and died shortly after.

Contributions

Averroës's commentaries were translated into Latin in the early 13th century and his writings had a profound effect on Christian Europe. His writings were less influential within Islam because they were based on logic and rationalism at a time when faith-based arguments were on the rise. Averroës had tried to counter Al Ghazali's critiques of philosophy in a book of his own, *The Incoherence of Incoherence*. In it he repudiated Al Ghazali's three metaphysical arguments. He countered the argument that the universe was not eternal by carefully parsing the Qur'an and saying that if it was not eternal, that put a limit on God's power, which could not be; therefore, God began the world but had existed eternally before creating it. Similarly, for Al Ghazali's second objection, in which philosophers claimed that God could know universals but not particulars (see more on this topic further), Averroës disputed that God thought as humans did. Because God is the cause of knowledge, the human distinction between universal and particulars does not hold for God. For the final objection, that philosophers denied the resurrection of the body, Averroës again turned to the Qur'an, specifically Sura 3:7:

> He sent down to you this scripture, containing straightforward verses— which constitute the essence of the scripture—as well as multiple-meaning or allegorical verses. Those who harbor doubts in their hearts will pursue the multiple-meaning verses to create confusion, and to extricate a certain meaning. None knows the true meaning thereof except GOD and those well-founded in knowledge. They say, "We believe in this—all of it comes from our Lord." Only those who possess intelligence will take heed (Khalifa, n.d.).

For Averroës, that Sura implied there were three kinds of arguments: demonstrative, rhetorical, and dialectical. All could yield the truth, but only the demonstrative arguments could do so provably. For those "well-founded in knowledge" (e.g., philosophers) those methods demonstrated the truth. If there was a discrepancy between the demonstrative methods and the Qur'an, that did not mean that the Qur'an was wrong. Instead, it meant that further work was necessary to bring those multiple-meaning or allegorical verses into agreement with philosophy through further study and interpretation of those less than straightforward sections. Averroës also held that Al-Ghazali's contention that there could be no analysis of cause and effect was wrong, too, saying, "he who repudiates causality actually repudiates reason" (Fakhry, 1999, pp. 269–303). Averroës never contended that the Qur'an was wrong or that there were two ways to truth: philosophy and scripture. Much like Al-Kindi, Averroës believed that philosophy and religion saw the same truth. Nevertheless, his religious writings went largely ignored within Islam. Averroës, like nearly all later philosophers, began to more closely examine the work of pioneers, or engage in exegesis especially on the works of Aristotle because many of his texts had only recently become available in both religious worlds. In contrast, Plato's widely available texts had led to the founding of Neoplatonism and the repurposing of his ideas of soul and the Forms.

Thus, Averroës's philosophical writings were like a bolt of lightning in Christian Europe, illuminating and dangerous. When Averroës's commentaries on Aristotle reached Christian Europe they spread quickly. Very soon he was simply referred to not by name, but as "The Commentator." At the University of Paris, by the end of the 13th century, Averroism had become a movement within Christianity opposed to the more traditional views held by Augustine and other church fathers. While the Averroist's views were not, strictly speaking, those of Averroës, they were inspired by his philosophy. The Christian Church later condemned many of the Averroists's beliefs as heretical. One heresy was the "double truth" which stated that revelation was one path to truth while philosophy was another independent path. Averroës, of course, had never made such a statement. In fact, his position was quite the opposite; both revelation and philosophy pointed toward the same truths. But in the hands of the Averroists, Averroës's exposition of Aristotle had driven a wedge between revelation and the demonstrative methods of philosophy. For the first time since the founding of Christianity the primacy of revelation was being questioned. Secularism had emerged. Averroës, through his commentaries on Aristotle, had unwittingly supplied the match for the slow fuse that would eventually detonate a bomb and lead to the end of an era and the creation of a new one: the Renaissance.

BORDER WITH SOCIAL SCIENCE
LANGUAGE

Arabic, the language of the Qur'an, had become the universal language for ordinary communication, commerce, and scholarly activities throughout the Islamic world. At the same, the main languages in Christian Europe were still Greek and Latin. In the eastern half of the Roman Empire (Byzantium), Greek predominated. In the Western half both Latin and Greek were used, but as the schism between the Roman and Greek churches widened, Greek usage declined. Latin became the leading language for religious and intellectual activity in Western Europe but did not become a common tongue. Instead, vernaculars (e.g., local languages or dialects) gradually replaced Latin among the public and led to the creation of many modern romance languages (e.g., French, Spanish, Italian, and Romanian). Latin, however, did become the universal language for European intellectuals, at least until the 1600s. The fact that European scholars could freely communicate with each other in Latin was a key factor in promoting a revival of cosmopolitanism among scholars in the West. The Islamic scholars use of Arabic was akin to the European scholars use of Latin. Both languages allowed ideas to be easily shared within each world but not so easily between the two worlds.

BORDER WITH SOCIAL SCIENCE
THE ROLE OF WOMEN

Recall from Chapter 3 that traditional Greek views on the role of women in society were very restrictive. Following those traditions, the students and faculty at Plato's Academy were mostly males. However, there were a few women who did attend classes at the Academy when Plato and his successor, Speusippus, were in charge. Two of those women, Lasthenia of Mantinea and Axiothea of Philesia, attended disguised as men, according to Diogenes (1925). Allen (1985) argued that from the time of early Greek philosophers through Plato, men and women were viewed as essentially similar, especially when thinking about them in the ideal. Allen called that way of thinking *sex unity* and it "opened the possibility for women to study philosophy with men" (p. 131). Plato's belief in reincarnation aided the idea of sex unity because his ideal genderless souls could be reincarnated in either male or female bodies. A male being reincarnated into a female body was evidence of having lived a previous life lacking in virtue. But, being reincarnated into a female body was not as bad as being reincarnated into the body of an animal. Aristotle and his Peripatetic successors created a new way of thinking about men and women: *sex polarity*. That view gave the sole responsibility for reproduction to men, the single seed (e.g., sperm) theory. Allen (p. 88) noted that Aristotle "believed that it would be impossible to have an individual soul existing separate from the body. Reincarnation, then, was excluded as a metaphysical possibility." Not surprisingly, there is no record of female students or philosophers in Aristotle's Lyceum. The Cynics included females among their ranks. Hipparchia was the best known of these women but tradition mentions (but does not name) other female Cynic philosophers. The Stoics also allowed women to enter their ranks. The Epicureans admitted men, women, and slaves into their Garden. The picture is fuzzier with the Neoplatonists and beyond. Hypatia of Alexandria, a pagan follower of Plotinus, was an exception to the all-male rule. The date of her death at the hands of a Christian mob in 415 CE has been used as yet another of the many historical markers of the beginning of the Middle Ages. The ancient Jewish tradition regarding the two genders was strict and clear cut. Only Jewish men were allowed to participate in the important rituals and in the intellectual life of the community. In some branches of Judaism, that tradition continues to the present day.

The Christians who emerged from Neoplatonic philosophy were cosmopolitans and preached and practiced equality of all people before God, including women. They also prohibited the long-standing pagan practice of infanticide (usually accomplished by exposure to the elements), which in Athens, at least, was more likely to be the fate of a female child (Stark, 1996). Additionally, Stark noted (p. 95) that most writers "recognized that Christianity was unusually appealing because within the Christian subculture women enjoyed far higher status than did women in the Greco-Roman world at large." Eventually, the near equality of women within Christianity began to disappear after the Roman Catholic Church became the official religion of the Roman Empire and after Augustine's influential consolidation of church doctrine. Female philosophers, always a rarity in antiquity, became rarer still by the end of the Middle Ages. Allen (1985) maintained that *sex neutrality* is the dominant view of modern philosophy and science. In that view, men and women are considered to be essentially the same in intellectual and (most) physical characteristics.

LEARNING OBJECTIVE

3. Discuss how the "lost works" of Greek philosophy were not really lost to Islamic scholars.

CHRISTIAN THEOLOGIANS

During the early part of the Middle Ages, Christian scholars, who were nearly all theologians, had much less access to classical knowledge from Greek, Latin, or other sources, unlike their Islamic contemporaries. Greek was used in Constantinople and many ancient texts were still available there. But in the rest of the Europe, the tumult caused by the successive waves of Asiatic nomads sweeping from east to west made travel dangerous and nearly impossible during the early Middle Ages. In addition, the mounting disagreements between the bishop of Rome (Pope Leo IX) and the patriarch of Constantinople (leader of the Christians in the eastern half of the former Roman Empire) over doctrinal and procedural issues led to a schism between the two branches of Christianity. In 1054, the break between the two branches of Christendom became final with the Pope and patriarch excommunicating (expelling) each other, an action mutually revoked in 1965. The power of excommunication was vast. Being excommunicated meant being exiled and shunned from society. In a society where nearly everyone was Christian, excommunication was the severest penalty short of death. The Western Church became the Roman Catholic Church while the Eastern Church became the Greek Orthodox Church. In western Europe, the Roman Catholic Church worked hard to assure its survival and eventually achieved the authority to approve the selection of sovereigns in Europe and excommunicate them if necessary. In eastern Europe, the Greek Orthodox church gradually lost its territories to Islam until only a small area around Constantinople remained. It, too, was lost in 1453 when Mehmet II captured the city and renamed it Istanbul.

Monasticism was another feature of the early Middle Ages. The first monks were mostly hermits living in Egypt (Dunn, 2017) who had voluntarily withdrawn from society to live ascetic lives and pray. Later, following the lead of Benedict, monks lived communally and followed strict rules governing their behavior; "work and pray" nicely summarizes the 73 chapters of Benedict's Rules. Soon, other monasteries (for men) and nunneries (for women) were founded. In many of them, the work often was intellectual. Many monasteries contained rooms called scriptoria, devoted to the handwritten copying of texts. Most of the texts copied were religious, but some were not. The Irish monks, in particular, because of their distance from the mainland of Europe and thus relatively isolated from invasion, were instrumental in copying texts and preserving them for posterity (Cahill, 1996).

By the year 1000 Europe began to stabilize. By then, most of the invaders had intermarried and converted to Christianity. More and more, translated classical works (from Arabic to Latin) were being carried from Spain into Europe. The earliest works to arrive were Platonic or Neoplatonic. Later, the bulk was Aristotelian. While the Christian thinkers never abandoned their faith, the arrival of these "lost" works led to tension and controversy as European scholars attempted to place the knowledge from these newly arriving materials within the context of Christian doctrine. That process had been completed by the end of the Middle Ages. The works of Aristotle were integrated into Christian theology to form the culmination of medieval thought, Scholasticism. The scholastics attempted to create a logical and comprehensive worldview that did not violate Christian doctrine but could still account for worldly truths. Moral psychology, acts, virtue, and the relationship between them was another focus of Scholasticism (Osborne, 2014). Christian doctrine always held the upper hand in any disputes, however. Those intellectual disputes took place in the universities, institutions chartered primarily to teach and create scholars; theology was the most prestigious subject. The earliest chartered universities appeared after the 11th century, but faculty or students had already organized themselves into guild-like learning communities earlier. The first universities date from 1088 in Italy (Bologna), 1096 in England (Oxford), and 1150 in France (Paris). These early universities shared a common academic structure, attracted a cosmopolitan mix of students and faculty, and secured a relatively high level of academic freedom and autonomy from their early days onward. Later universities adopted the same organization and curricula. Medieval universities were divided into four faculties. The faculty of arts was invariably the largest and offered the beginning courses, or *trivium*, which consisted of grammar, logic, and rhetoric. These courses were followed by geometry, astronomy, arithmetic, and music, or the *quadrivium*. (In the curriculum of modern universities, these "liberal arts" still survive.) Successful completion of these courses earned students a bachelor's or master's degree in arts.

Students could continue their education in the faculties of law, medicine, or theology. Many masters of arts taught courses in the *trivium* or *quadrivium* while they studied for their advanced degrees. By the end of the Middle Ages, law students comprised the largest group of advanced students by far while theology and medical students made up less than 10% of the total enrollment (Kenny & Pinborg, 1982). Much of the success of Scholasticism was due to the founding of universities and their subsequent role in providing a safe haven for learning and studying. Anselm, often considered the first scholastic, felt the need to provide Christians with a logical way to prove God's existence, one beyond simple faith alone.

Anselm of Canterbury (1033–1109)

Biography

Anselm was born in Aosta, a small town in the Alps and now part of modern Italy. While in his early 20s, he wandered for several years until he came to the Benedictine abbey and school at Le Bec (Normandy, France). There he met the head of the school and his first mentor, Lanfranc. Soon after, he was admitted to the Benedictine order and eventually became a scholar and teacher. After he left Le Bec to assume the leadership of another monastery, Anselm began a second career as an administrator. He succeeded Lanfranc at Le Bec, and again in England at Canterbury after Lanfranc's death. He had to wait four years before taking up his bishop's throne (*cathedra* in Latin) at Canterbury because of a dispute between William II, the king of England, and the Pope over who had the right to name bishops. Anselm's tenure as archbishop of Canterbury was so contentious that he was forced into exile twice. Still, he remained a scholar throughout his adult life and wrote many books, most of which dealt with the relationship between reason and theology (Vaughn, 2017). While earlier Christian thinkers were more preoccupied with theology than philosophy, Anselm attempted to use reason as a method to confirm the mysteries of Christian faith. For that reason Anselm is often characterized as the first scholastic thinker.

Contributions

Anselm and his later successors had no doubts about the existence of God and the revealed truths of Holy Scripture. Anselm followed his own motto, "faith seeking understanding" (McInerny, 1970, p. 124). He wished to convince unbelievers that God existed and that such a belief need not rely upon faith alone. But, he maintained that having faith first was a prerequisite for the application of reason. Furthermore, should any article of faith ever be called into question by the methods of reason then faith must prevail.

Anselm is most remembered for his rational arguments for the existence of God. Since Kant (see Chapter 6), such arguments have been labeled as *ontological*. Those arguments, in their simplest form, revolve around demonstrating that if two propositions are self-contradictory, then one must be false. Ontological arguments do not require observation or data collection; logic alone is enough. The first part of Anselm's argument defined existence in the mind and reality. His example was that of a painting before a painter puts it on canvas. Obviously, the idea of the painting was in the artist's mind before its execution. After, the idea of the painting and the painting itself existed, and those together were a stronger version of reality. For example, the idea of flying became much stronger after the Wright brothers actually built an airplane.

In the second part of his proof, Anselm defined God as "that than which nothing greater can be thought." He followed that definition by considering whether there is something greater than his definition of God. He concluded that he could not because if he did his definition of God would be wrong. Therefore God exists. Other contemporary thinkers criticized his proof almost immediately as did later philosophers including Aquinas. Anselm's proof, thus, was not as convincing to others as it was to himself. Later, Abelard demonstrated that the so-called truths of revelation were not so clear or easily understood. However, the controversies surrounding his life negated many of his intellectual contributions.

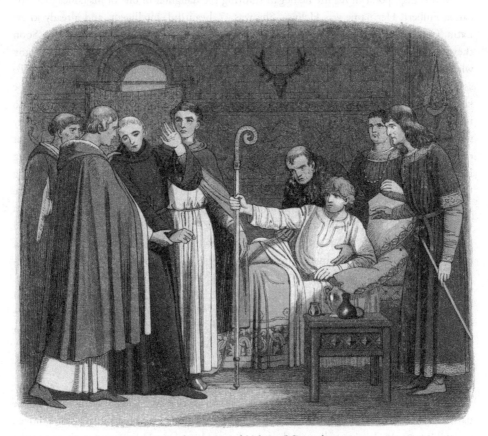

Anselm made archbishop of Canterbury.

PHOTO 4.2 Anselm reluctantly accepts the bishop's crozier of Canterbury from William II.

Peter Abelard (1079–1142)

Biography

Abelard was born in Le Pallet, a small village near Nantes in the French province of Brittany. He could have chosen knighthood and a military career; instead he chose to become an academic. He was an excellent but combative student. He disagreed fiercely with his teachers, so much so that he left his teacher, William of Champeaux, in order to set up his own successful school outside of Paris. However, poor health forced him home for a few years. After he recovered, he returned to Paris and again became Champeaux's student but things were no different between them. Later, he and Abelard debated the concept of universals raising Abelard's prominence as a scholar. He went back to teaching at his own school in Paris and a few years later was invited to teach at the cathedral school at Notre Dame, an extremely prestigious position. There, he became extremely successful as a teacher, and according to his autobiography, "had come to regard myself as the only philosopher remaining in the whole world" (Abelard, 1972, p. 14).

At this high point in his life he began tutoring the daughter of one of his colleagues, the canon Fulbert. Her name was Heloise. She was 17, beautiful, intelligent, and already knew Latin, Greek, and Hebrew. Smitten, Abelard arranged to teach her in Fulbert's home. Soon they became lovers and not long after, Heloise was pregnant. Abelard sent her to Brittany where she gave birth to their son, Astrolabe (named after the astronomical instrument). To assuage her father's anger, Abelard offered to marry Heloise but only if the marriage could be kept secret. Her father agreed but Heloise did not for two reasons. First, she did not wish to impugn his reputation as a teacher, and second, marriage would severely limit his scholarly writing. Nonetheless, they did marry secretly but they did not live together and saw each other only rarely. Her father and family, however, made the marriage public, shaming and angering Heloise to the point where she called them liars and renounced them. At this point, fearing for her safety, Abelard arranged for her to be admitted to the convent at Argenteuil, where she had been educated as a young girl. However, Heloise's family saw Abelard's actions as a means of ridding himself of her. Her father had Abelard attacked at night in his own home and castrated. Orchiectomy, the surgical removal of the testes, has a long history as a legal form of punishment for sex offenders and adulterers and is still legal in many parts of the world including the United States (Gowande, 1997). The love story of Abelard and Heloise is well known. The movie *Stealing Heaven* filmed in 1988 was one of the latest retellings. James (1989, p. C14) called it "a serious telling of the story, suggesting the stateliness and rigidity of the world that the intellectual and sensual Heloise and Abelard resisted." See Moncrieff (1933/2018) to read eight letters between Abelard and Heloise.

Contributions

When he recovered, Abelard resumed teaching at a monastery in St. Denis. His teachings on the nature of the Trinity, however, led to censure and the burning of his books. He left and moved to a wilderness site, hoping to live as a hermit. But, students found him anyway, pitching their tents nearby for the opportunity to hear him teach. The church eventually restored his status as a monk and he returned to Paris to teach again and all seemed as before except that another teacher, Bernard of Clairvaux, accused him of heresy and a tribunal condemned his teachings. Abelard left Paris to appeal directly to the Pope in Rome but stopped instead at the monastery in Cluny. Its abbot, Peter of Cluny, succeeded in lifting the condemnation, and Abelard remained in Cluny teaching until he died a few years later.

Abelard never doubted the truth of revelation. But, he wanted to use logic to make the truths of revelation stronger. During his lifetime, the dominant classical philosophies known were Platonic and Neoplatonic. Some of Aristotle's works were known but the massive flood of translated classical materials from Spain had not yet hit Christian Europe. In particular, Abelard was troubled by the logical concept of universals. He disagreed with the idea that words like "man" or "animal" could be applied to particular men or animals. Instead, he argued that words like those were just names (*nomine* in Latin) and they did not apply to real referents. Moreover, the universality of those words came from the mind and was expressed through language. This new way of thinking was called **nominalism** and it represented a revolution in medieval logic. Nominalism was opposed to **realism**, the idea that universal ideal entities exist. In strict realism, there had to be a real object in the world corresponding to each possible object of thought. While realism was a simple solution it led to all kinds of problems. The main problem being that the same word could apply to both a universal category and to a particular case. Nominalism solved that problem by making the universal category the name given to a large collection of particular cases by the action of the mind.

Abelard, although never certified in theology, a word he coined (Berardino & Studer, 2008), wrote one of the most influential works of medieval theology, the *Sic et Non* (*Yes and No*). In that work, he presented 158 cases where scripture or writings of early church fathers supported or contradicted each case. Unlike previous theological authors, Abelard took no position himself regarding the cases presented. Instead, he left it for readers to make up their own minds. The inspiration for this book came from the conflict between Abelard and Bernard of Clairvaux. Bernard believed that arguments from reason should play no part in the interpretation of scripture. Instead, the revealed truths of scripture should be readily apparent. Abelard's book showed that the truths of scripture were not as clear as many thought. Because Abelard had lived a life of controversy, his ideas were not viewed favorably by many of his contemporaries. However, Abelard's approach to theology was truly revolutionary and inspired the later work of Albert the Great and Thomas Aquinas. One of his students, Peter Lombard, succeeded in transmitting some of his master's ideas to posterity.

PHOTO 4.3 Abelard

Credit: iStock/ZU_09

Peter Lombard (1095–1160)

Biography

Peter Lombard was born in Novara, Italy, to a poor family. A good student, he had the sponsorship of Bernard of Clairvaux, a Cistercian monk, which earned him a place at the University of Bologna. Afterward, he studied at Reims and Paris. Again, his intellectual abilities attracted attention and he was named to the faculty of the Notre Dame's cathedral school. He was a student of Peter Abelard and was profoundly influenced by him.

Contributions

Lombard himself was influential, too, because of his text, *Four Books of Sentences*. That theological text contained biblical passages and commentaries covering nearly all of the religious issues of his day. Generations of later Christian philosophers and their students used Lombard's text well into the 17th century as their introduction to the study of theology. The text was divided into four books. The first book dealt with the existence of God and the nature of the Trinity. The second book covered creation and angels. The topic of the third book was the nature of Jesus, and the last book discussed the sacraments. Lombard's text was designed to put biblical materials and commentaries readily at hand. It was not an original set of ideas nor did it break new ground. However, it usually steered a middle course between controversial religious topics while presenting both sides of issues. Most of the commentaries came from Augustine. Even its organization was Augustinian dividing its topics between the things and signs of immediate reality (Pieper, 1964). Lombard, like Anselm, wished to confirm the truths of faith through the power of rational thought.

Unfortunately for Lombard the great wave of translations of classic texts had not yet hit the shore when he wrote his text. After those translations crashed upon Christendom, Aristotle, not Augustine, became the central focus for Scholasticism. Albert the Great translated the entire body of Aristotle's work, and that was only part of his contribution to knowledge. He also restored the study of the world and nature to prominence. His student Thomas Aquinas also benefited from the new translations of Aristotle. Albert's particular contribution was successfully combining Aristotle's philosophy and Christian doctrine to create a coherent whole, acceptable to the Roman Catholic Church.

LEARNING OBJECTIVE

4. Trace the role of women scholars from the Middle Ages to rise of Humanism.

BORDER WITH SOCIAL SCIENCE
RELIGIOUS VS. CIVIL LAW

The primacy of revealed knowledge, or religion, was central to Islamic and Christian thinking during the Middle Ages. Revelation was also the basis for the dynamics between faith and government. At the start of the Middle Ages in Europe, Christianity was well established throughout the territories that formerly comprised the Roman Empire. However, early Christians did not all hold the same beliefs, arguing over the divinity of Jesus and the Trinity and other doctrinal issues. Islam, too, spread quickly after Mohammad received his revelations. Within a short time after Mohammad's death Islam split into two groups, the Sunnis and the Shias; the *Sharia*, Islamic law, began to develop and evolve. In Islam there never existed a distinction between religion and daily life. Furthermore, every Muslim acknowledged that the *Sharia was* God's will and that it applied to everyone in the community.

In Christian Europe, the Bible and commentaries on it, written by the early church fathers, were the main sources of revealed knowledge. However, Roman law predated the founding of Christianity and persisted afterward so a Christian counterpart to the *Sharia never* evolved. In Western Europe two systems of law developed: civil law for lay matters and canon law for church matters. The popes, in principle, had no legal force over rulers and rulers had no legal force over the church. Popes, however, could and did excommunicate rulers, while rulers could and did depose popes through military force.

Albert the Great (1193–1280)

Biography

Albert the Great *(Albertus Magnus)* was born in the Bavarian town of Lauingen to an aristocratic family. Little is known of his early life until he enrolled at the University of Padua in Italy. His stay there was brief because he was recruited into the newly formed Dominican Order, a group of mendicant monks. The Dominicans and Franciscans, another mendicant order founded at about the same time, represented a new type of Christian religious order (Lindberg, 1992, p. 223):

> The mendicants were committed to an active ministry within an urban setting; this eventually propelled them into the intellectual arena, including the universities, where they became actively involved in all of the great philosophical and theological controversies.

Albert left Padua for Cologne where he finished his early education and then taught at several Dominican schools in Germany. After 12 years of teaching, he was sent to Paris for additional study within the faculty of theology. When he completed his theology degree he remained at Paris as a faculty member, holding one of the chairs reserved for foreign Dominican scholars. While at Paris, he taught his most famous student, Thomas Aquinas. The Dominicans gave Albert a series of administrative posts that required him to travel extensively throughout Germany calling on Dominican houses and missions. The untimely death of Aquinas in 1274 affected Albert deeply. Three years after, he returned to Paris to unsuccessfully defend the teachings of Aquinas at a Church Council. Slowed by age and having lost his prodigious intellectual faculties, he died in Cologne.

Contributions

Despite all of the calls upon his time, Albert wrote extensively on a wide variety of subjects. After leaving Paris to teach at Cologne, he decided to translate the entire Aristotelian corpus into Latin. Twenty years later he had accomplished that task and more, having also translated a host of other classical works. His translations of Aristotle affected his outlook on scholarship. Albert was one of the first Christian European scholars to collect new empirical data. Everywhere he traveled he took note of the natural world. He observed natural phenomena and collected specimens. This was the work that led others to call him "Albert the Great" during his own lifetime. He was not afraid to correct errors he found in Aristotle's natural philosophy or promote empirical methods of learning.

Albert was still a churchman. But, he did not see any conflict between revelation and natural philosophy. He was the first to maintain that theology had no place in natural philosophy. Conversely, natural philosophy had no place in theology either. Albert began the movement that eventually separated theology from philosophy in Christian Europe. His student, Thomas Aquinas, systematized that separation in a manner that stood for over 500 years.

BORDER WITH BIOLOGY
MEDICINE AND OPTICS

During the Middle Ages biology also developed as a borderland for a yet-to-emerge psychology. Two specific biological areas that developed early were medicine and optics. Many of the earliest classical works translated were medical. The entire Islamic medical corpus eventually passed into Christian Europe and formed the basis of medical practice until the 17th century. To be sure, the practice of medicine in Europe during the Middle Ages deserved the adjective "medieval." Physicians routinely bled patients with leeches, prescribed herbs as medicines, and prayed for divine intercession. Women, too, were physicians, especially before the founding of faculties of medicine in the universities. Women also served as midwives and nurses. Later, women who provided medicines or made diagnoses were branded as witches; many paid with their lives by being burned at the stake. The newly minted male doctors from the universities also contributed to the exclusion of women as Ehrenreich and English (2010, p. 31) pointed out:

> The other side of the suppression of witches as healers was the creation of a new male medical profession, under the protection and patronage of the ruling classes. This new European medical profession played an important role in the witch hunts, supporting the witches' persecutors with "medical" reasoning.

Scientific approaches to medicine did not begin until the 17th century.

The study of optics had a long history dating back to the classic era. Ancient extromissive theories of vision held that the eye emitted rays in order to view objects while intromissive theories held that rays entered the eye and were the source of vision (Lindberg, 1992). The Islamic natural philosopher Alhazen was the first to persuasively argue that the eye must be receiving information as light and analyzing it after refracting it through the lens of the eye (Dallal, 1999). Roger Bacon (1214–1292), an English Franciscan friar, added much to the study of optical phenomena including measuring the maximum angle of a rainbow (42°) and experimenting with pinhole images (Hackett, 2007). Bacon was one of the first European thinkers to combine logical analysis with empirical observations and manipulations as a method of study.

These early examples were toeholds for the creation of a larger territory for biology. Medicine would continue to develop slowly and become more scientific. The study of optics first led to progress in physics, not psychology. In the 17th century, Newton systematically explored light experimentally and created a physics of light that held until dramatically altered by Einstein in the early 20th century. The psychological aspects of light—in vision and perception—began to be understood in the middle of the 19th century (see Chapter 7). Biology, thus, carved out a small niche for itself by the end of the Middle Ages.

Thomas Aquinas (1225–1274)

Biography

Thomas Aquinas was born in Roccasecca, near Naples, Italy. His family was from the minor orders of nobility. At age five, they sent Thomas to the nearby Benedictine abbey at Monte Cassino to begin his education. From there Thomas went to the University of Naples where he learned the liberal arts. While at Naples, Thomas decided to become a Dominican friar. When his family learned of this decision they were so opposed to it they locked him up within their castle for two years. They had wanted him to become a Benedictine monk. Thomas's resolve finally overcame their resistance and they let him pursue his vocation. Now a Dominican, the Order sent him to the University of Paris where he studied under Albert the Great, following him to Cologne. Thomas then returned to Paris to complete his studies with the faculty of theology. After receiving his degree in theology he remained at Paris teaching and writing. He left Paris for Italy where he fulfilled duties for Dominicans and Pope Urban IV.

Contributions

Three years later, in 1268, he returned to the University of Paris where a controversy had broken out about the relationship between Aristotelianism and Christian doctrine. That controversy revolved around Averroës's "two truths." Some philosophers at Paris, the Averroists, claimed that the truths of philosophy and theology need not correspond with each other. Aquinas attempted to resolve that crisis through teaching and writing, asserting that they must correspond. Aquinas left Paris in 1272 when the Dominicans allowed him to set up a school in Naples. Shortly after, the new Pope, Gregory X, called him to the Council of Lyon in an attempt to reunite the Roman Catholic and Greek Orthodox churches. Already sick, Aquinas died on the way to the meeting.

That Aquinas accomplished so much during his short life is one testament to his abilities. His writings covered a wide variety of topics, ranging from philosophy, through Biblical commentaries, to metaphysics. In his philosophical writings he was fortunate to live during a time when the remainder of Aristotle's works had been translated. Aquinas also commissioned new translations from a fellow Dominican, William of Moerbeke. Aquinas authored many new commentaries on Aristotle and that work affected his theological thinking. Unlike the Averroists, Aquinas saw no conflict between the truths of revelation and those of philosophy. He refuted their beliefs using philosophy, not theology. He showed through logic that their claim that the universe was eternal did not contradict the biblical revelation of its creation by God. He also disposed of Averroës's claim that there was only one universal intellect in a similar fashion.

Despite his logical bent, it was his metaphysical writings that had the longest lasting effects. For him, philosophy could only go so far in revealing truths. Still, he believed that philosophy and revelation should never disagree. Philosophy, he maintained, could support and confirm revelation as when he used philosophy to demonstrate, in five different ways, the existence of God. But philosophy could not support or confirm some aspects of revelation such as the nature of the Trinity. Some truths had to be accepted on faith. Metaphysics, which for Aquinas was the same as theology or first philosophy, was the ruler of the other sciences because, it and it alone, "seems most intellectual, and accordingly, directive of the others" (McInerny, 1970, p. 318).

Ultimately, Aquinas reconciled Christian faith with the powerful logic of Aristotle. Aquinas did more than meld Christian beliefs with Aristotle's natural philosophy. He changed much about the older ways of looking at the world. For instance, he broadened Augustine's narrower view of the search for knowledge to include any topic, not just those related to faith and salvation. In short, he applied Aristotle's worldview to Christianity. The marriage of Aristotle to revelation, however, did not lead to the birth of science. Instead, it added Aristotle's "facts" to the "truths" of revelation. Thus, the Roman Catholic Church accepted as dogma (undisputable truth) Aristotle's beliefs such as: the Earth was the center of the universe, heavier objects fell faster than lighter ones, and arrows only flew in straight lines. So, Scholasticism after Aquinas became hidebound and stultified. Those later scholars did not act like Aristotle had. Instead, they made his works the secular equivalents of the Bible and refused to question them critically. That critical examination had to wait until after the Renaissance when new ways of thinking emerged and the weight of brute facts broke through. Another necessary piece leading to the new ways of thinking that emerged at the end of the Middle Ages was supplied by William of Ockham. His writings strove to strip away unnecessary layers and keep only the kernel truths. His famous razor has been a part of critical thinking ever since.

William of Ockham (1287–1347)

Biography

William of Ockham (or Occam) was born in the village of Ockham near London. Little is known of his early life before he became a Franciscan friar sometime before his 13th birthday. He was educated in the Franciscan's London house and then went to Oxford where he studied theology. Like all theology students of his day, he wrote a commentary on Lombard's *Four Books of Sentences*. For some reason, he never completed his theology work at Oxford and thus never received a certificate to teach theology. In addition, a colleague thought his commentary on Lombard contained heretical statements so Ockham was called to Avignon, France, where, because of the power of the French kings, the papacy had been moved from Rome.

For more than four years, he wrote, lectured, and appeared when called before the papal court. He was never branded a heretic. But, he was caught up in a conflict between the Pope and the Franciscan Order. The Franciscan's master wished to reaffirm the ruling of an earlier pope stating that neither the order nor its members could own any property. Ockham researched the issue and concluded that the order could choose not to own property without violating scripture or church law (Spade, 2006). Unfortunately for Ockham and the Franciscan's master, that was not the answer the Pope wanted. Ultimately, both were forced to flee Avignon for Munich where they came under the protection of Ludwig of Bavaria, the Holy Roman Emperor. Ockham was excommunicated for leaving Avignon without permission. He died in Munich, apparently a victim of the Black Plague.

Contributions

Most of Ockham's philosophical writing took place in England and France. Thoroughly Aristotelian in his outlook, he nonetheless believed that the state of scholarship after Aquinas was too complex. He revisited the conflict between nominalists and realists arguing that universals (e.g., "humanity") did not exist. Instead, only particulars existed (e.g., more than seven billion humans now alive, not "humanity"). He believed that experience alone led individuals to develop cognitive concepts that were then expressed as words. Ockham was a nominalist and one of the first to place the creation of concepts within the mind itself. Zupko (2018, p. 89) nicely illustrates Ockham's thinking with regard to artifacts:

> For medieval Aristotelians, natural things such as trees and dogs and humans are paradigmatic substances, each having a real essence and constituting something one *per se*, whereas artifacts such as brooms and beds and houses have only a *per accidens* unity, meaning that their formal structure has been imposed upon them by an external agent, the artisan, who reconfigures natural 'raw' materials into something that serves her own contingent purposes.

Ockham, thus, differed from previous scholastic thinkers in that he was willing to allow humans to repurpose the natural world, but not to create new things, a power only allowable to God.

While Ockham never wrote the words attributed to him, "entities should not be multiplied unnecessarily," or what now is called **Ockham's Razor**; his writings showed that he agreed with that saying (Wildner, 1999). Ockham also believed that there were limits to philosophy. Thus, he disagreed with Aquinas that philosophy could prove the existence of God. Theology, for Ockham, was a discipline separate from philosophy. He never doubted God's existence but maintained that belief in God came from faith alone. He, thus, separated theology and philosophy and made a purely **secular** approach to knowledge possible. That approach, however, did not take place quickly or easily. But, for all intents and purposes the Middle Ages were nearing their end.

LEARNING OBJECTIVE

5. Summarize the structure and courses of the medieval university.

THE RISE OF HUMANISM

The **Humanism** that arose in the 14th century and developed for the next 200 years criticized medieval Scholasticism, venerated the finding of newly discovered ancient Roman and Greek texts, emphasized the role of language in knowledge, and adapted itself to the discovery of new lands, peoples, and technologies. This original form of Humanism gave rise or new life to many new academic disciplines (e.g., anthropology, **philology**, and history) before itself disappearing. In contrast, modern humanism and the humanities are the products of that older Humanism and are quite different. The original Humanism was new, original, and a reaction to the medieval world. Modern humanism and the humanities have divorced themselves from the earlier form by becoming more secular, academic, and closely linked to human values and dignity.

Medieval Scholasticism had successfully integrated theology and Aristotelian philosophy. Scholastics had elevated Aristotle over Plato and at the same time had emphasized the more geometrical and logical *quadrivium* over the predominantly linguistic *trivium*. Meanwhile, other non-Scholastic 14th century scholars began to discover and translate then unknown Latin texts. Later, after the fall of Constantinople to the Ottoman Turks in 1453, many Greek scholars fled to Rome and other Italian cities. They brought their Greek texts with them and soon these were translated into Latin and creating a revival of the study of Greek. These two sources of ancient knowledge created a new interest in classic (e.g., pagan) modes of thinking and living. Humanism promoted the written word and revived the *trivium*. At first, humanists emphasized the study of well-written Latin works, especially Cicero's. After, their emphasis shifted to well-written vernacular works where they examined their philological relationships to Latin, Greek, and later Hebrew. Humanists also began to integrate and understand in new ways the interrelations between grammar, rhetoric, dialectics, history, and poetry; those five disciplines made up the principal components of Humanism itself (Kelley, 1991). Unlike the scholastics, humanists saw language, not philosophy, as the main focus of their scholarship.

It is useful to distinguish between the Humanism that began in the 14th century and modern secular humanism. The original humanists were devout Christian believers. While they sought to study, expand, and create humanistic disciplines such as art, architecture, and literature, they never contemplated doing so outside of the Christian tradition. Many modern secular humanists, however, maintain that concepts such as God, Heaven, and Hell do not exist. The ranks of secular humanists include many scientists as well. However, the study of human works, the humanities, is possible within either religious or nonreligious contexts. Christian and Muslim fundamentalists, especially, attempt to include all humanistic studies under the banner of secular humanism. That is unfortunate because the study of the humanities does not automatically assume they are divorced from religious traditions. Ironically, religion itself is a form of humanism. Faria (2015) discussed the roles of secular humanism and religion in the context of bioethics. He concluded (p. 114):

> I prefer individualism, freedom, and humanitarianism, even if stemming from religious precepts, and at last resort, the law of the State; rather than to depend on the secular humanist notions of collectivist utopias and the purportedly intrinsic goodness and capabilities of rational man.

After the invention of the printing press in Germany, Humanism took off like a rocket. The relative ease by which books could be produced, compared to handwritten manuscripts, led to the rapid spread of Humanism from its origins in Italy to the rest of Europe. Soon, printing presses were installed nearly everywhere and vastly facilitated the spread of humanistic ideas.

The discovery of the New World and its inhabitants also spurred the development of Humanism. Having to accommodate the existence of new lands and peoples into the old European mindset proved impossible without a radical change of thinking. Not being Christians, Jews, or Moslems, the peoples encountered by European explorers did not fit neatly into those preexisting European cultural categories. As early as 1512, the Spanish crown issued laws stating that the native inhabitants were human and heathen, but capable of conversion to the Roman Catholic faith. In practice, however, these laws were ineffective in preventing the exploitation or extermination of many non-European peoples.

The growth of cities also contributed to the rise of civic responsibility, another feature of Humanism. Where the Scholastics taught elite students in isolated classrooms, Humanists flocked to cities and attempted to involve themselves in issues of the day and the solving of practical problems. Emulating the ancient Greeks, Humanists rekindled interest in the oratory skills because of how those contributed to success in practical occupations such as law and business. Humanists also revived the works of Plato and the Neoplatonists that had been shunted aside by the Scholastics who preferred Aristotle.

Humanism, then, was a new way of thinking. At the same time it was a throwback to earlier, classical ways of thinking. While humanists emphasized the words, acts, and creations of individual human beings, they did so in a new way from the ancient pagans. Unlike the pagan Greek and Roman writers who mostly separated the religious from the secular, the humanists retained their religious fervor and did not separate Christianity from the pursuit of knowledge. The humanists perceived themselves as believers uncovering the wonders of the natural world that their God had created.

Humanism, in part, led to the Protestant Reformation (see Chapter 5); many of its changes were fueled by printed Bibles in a variety of vernaculars along with the idea that believers could read and interpret the Bible themselves without the aid of priests or other church officials. By itself however, Humanism did little to advance science beyond solidifying its foundations. Most of the scientific revolution came later, during the Enlightenment, although the astronomers had already prepared the ground for science before then (see Chapter 5). Their successful replacement of Ptolemy's geocentric universe with Copernicus's heliocentric universe led others to reconsider traditional thinking in a wide variety of fields including biology, geology, and the social sciences. Art and music also flourished late in the humanistic period. These "fine arts" were another manifestation of Humanism because gifted individuals created art works pleasing to the eye and ear.

Humanists also reanimated interest in moral philosophy (as opposed to natural philosophy or science). Moral philosophy concerned the affairs of people, not things. It was, thus, a precursor to the social sciences, including psychology. As Humanists deemphasized reason, they promoted the roles of emotion and memory in human behavior. Francesco Petrarca is usually acknowledged as the first Humanist and receives most of the credit for igniting that movement.

Petrarch (1304–1374)

Biography

Francesco Petrarca (or Petrarch) was born in Arezzo, Italy, but always considered himself a Florentine. His father had been exiled to Arezzo from Florence following the defeat of his political party. Petrarch and his family later moved to nearby Provence, the site of the Avignon papacy. A gifted student, Petrarch learned Latin quickly and eventually studied law at the University of Bologna. However, he never practiced law; his true love was poetry. He began to collect a personal library and his first book was a copy of Augustine's *City of God*. To support himself he took minor orders, becoming a cleric but not a priest. Thanks to the patronage of the Roman Catholic Church, he always had an income and free time on his hands.

Contributions

He began to write. Early in his life he wrote mostly poetry but near the end he switched to a more rhetorical style and wrote about human conduct; he had become a moral philosopher. His writings were widespread and influential. He was one of the first citizens of a hypothetical nation that later humanists called the Republic of Letters (Kelley, 1991).

In 1345, while at the cathedral in Verona, Italy, Petrarch discovered previously neglected and unknown letters written by the Roman poet, Cicero. He was struck by the eloquence of Cicero's Latin prose and by the sagacity of that ancient's thinking. While a pious Christian, Petrarch believed that the Scholastics, with their reverence for Aristotle, had made the understanding of God too much of an exercise in logic. Petrarch believed that God could be more easily found and understood by simply living life, by being human. In his writings Petrarch introduced new topics, familiar today but new then: alienation, personal autonomy, urbanity, and the usefulness of solitude. His impact was immense and long-lasting. He reintroduced Europeans to ancient and nearly forgotten pagan ideas but did so in a manner acceptable to Christianity. As Trinkaus (1979, p. 135) concluded about Petrarch's influence:

PHOTO 4.4 Petrarch

Credit: iStock/pictore

> Moral philosophy, concerned with affecting the will toward the attainment of goodness, was nonetheless genuine philosophy, though its premises may well have been Protagorean and rhetorical. Such also were the ingredients of Renaissance humanism, which under Petrarch's formation and tutelage vindicated the importance of poetry

and rhetoric as effectors of an intimate bond between reason and emotion, thought and action, intellect and will. Petrarchan humanism became a historical force mobilizing thought and letters against the blind impulsiveness of an illusory popular culture and the elitism of the philosophical schools.

Petrarch had set the stage for the Renaissance, that rebirth of ideas which began in Italy during the 14th century and subsequently spread throughout Europe over the course of several hundred years. In fact, many have called him the father of the Renaissance. Philosophy changed greatly during the Renaissance. Early on, Humanism challenged the medieval interpreters of Aristotle. Those challenges did not go unanswered by as Crick (2019) demonstrated. The polemic exchanges between the two sides created a long- lasting image of Scholasticism, "the scholastic ignoramus who…endures today primarily in the guise of mediated talking heads who provide mechanical rationalizations for material values of corporate culture" (Crick, 2019, p. 180) and, in counterpoint, allowed Petrarch to highlight the virtues of humanistic education. By the end of the Renaissance the rise of science bolstered a new mechanistic view of philosophy.

HUMANISM AND SCIENCE

Philosophy changed greatly during the course of time covered by this chapter. Late medieval philosophy, Scholasticism, had passed its zenith. Humanists such as Marsilio Ficino and his student Giovanni Pico della Mirandola attempted to resurrect Plato's philosophy and make it the central focus of a Neoplatonic revival that connected ancient sources with Christianity. Under the patronage of Cosimo de' Medici in Florence, Ficino translated all of Plato's works and later promoted a hierarchical view of the universe that had God at the top and matter at the bottom. In between was humankind, but elevated to near godlike status, a god on Earth (Robichaud, 2018). In Ficino's view, man was, "master of the natural world and shaper of his own destiny" (McKnight, 1989, p. 64). Howlett (2016, p. 11) saw Ficino as a fusion philosopher:

> He brought ideas together to create something new whilst also attempting to preserve the integrity or character of each of the individual parts. The focus is on complimentarity and compatibility, not on absolute concord. He knows that not everything is the same in each tradition, but in creating a Platonic revival, it is imperative to show, as much as possible, how all the pieces of the jigsaw might fit together for a new coherent view of Plato. This coherent view needed to work within a Christian society. Further it needed to be able to change and renew that Christian society.

By the 17th century, however, the early scientists had forced philosophers to reconsider their revived Neoplatonist views. In their place, natural philosophy was reborn and reenergized but in a mathematical and mechanized form. At the same time, the distinction between natural philosophy and moral philosophy widened and the two branches eventually parted. By the end of the Renaissance, the seeds of modern philosophy and modern science had been sown. Humankind was no longer master of its world or shaper of its destiny. Instead, forces of cosmic proportions within an infinite universe ruled over all matter.

Today, many still see a wide gulf between the humanities and science. Kitcher (2012, p. 24), however, argued, "human inquiry needs a synthesis, in which history and anthropology and literature and art play their parts . . . Many scientists and commentators on science have been led to view the sciences as a value-free zone." He contended that the sciences and the humanities each require generality, precision, and accuracy in their methods. But only a few disciplines, scientific or humanistic, routinely achieved all three criteria. He noted, for example, that ecology is usually precise and accurate but lacks generality. The same pattern holds for history and anthropology too, he maintained. He concluded (p. 25), "Good science depends on contributions from the humanities and the arts." Twenty-first century psychology, too, has a scientific and a humanistic side. The logo of the American Psychological Association captures both sides of the search for knowledge (American Psychological Association, 1991). The right side of the stylized Greek letter *psi* is angular and sharp while the left side is curved and smooth. The logo symbolizes psychology's twin goals of advancing psychology as a science and as a profession (Figure 4.1) (Greenwood, 2017).

FIGURE 4.1 ■ The APA Logo

Credit: B Christopher / Alamy Stock Photo

THE BLACK PLAGUE

The black plague (or bubonic plague), the world's first documented pandemic, struck Europe in 1348. Over the course of the next three years it killed somewhere between a quarter to a third of Europe's population. The plague originated in China several years earlier and spread westward via the Silk Road, the ancient overland commercial link between East and West. Genoese sailors were likely the first to bring it to Europe when they landed in Sicily. From there its progress followed sea lanes, rivers, and roads until all of Europe was affected. The disease was caused by a bacterium, *Yersinia pestis,* which could be transmitted three ways. First and most commonly, it was transmitted by contact with an infected person or animal, or a bite from a flea infected from one of those two sources. Rarely, it could be transmitted through the air or by blood. Nearly everyone infected died during the plague's first waves through Europe and the Mediterranean Basin.

Because of the state of medical knowledge at the time, physicians had no theories to explain how infection proceeded. Onset was sudden and marked by buboes—large swellings in the lymphatic system—that could appear on the neck, armpits, or groin. The buboes grew quickly, were painful, and could burst. After the appearance of buboes, black splotches developed on the skin (the source of the name black death) along with a high fever. Death could occur as quickly as 15 hours or as long a week. A small number of people were immune to the disease.

The initial wave of bubonic plague lasted about four years and affected Christian and Islamic communities equally. Many faithful from both religions saw the plague as a manifestation of God's anger with humankind. Sociologically, the effects were profound. Families and communities were disrupted, and villages and towns were depopulated. The survivors, however, found many opportunities previously closed to them suddenly opened. Out groups were blamed for the plague; thus, Christians blamed Moslems while Moslems, in turn, blamed Christians. Both religions blamed Jews. In Christian Europe many pogroms (assaults on Jews) resulted from such thinking. Unfortunately, the first wave of the plague was not the last. Another wave began in 1356 and subsequent waves continued into the 19th century Schmid et al. (2015) documented recurring climate-driven waves from Asian plague reservoirs and argue that those account for the long history of plague in Europe. The bubonic plague still exists, but antibiotics, public health measures, and the evolution of less virulent strains limit the number of cases to a handful per year around the world today (McEvedy, 1988).

BORDER WITH COMPUTATIONAL SCIENCE
NUMERALS

The introduction and spread of the Hindu-Arabic numerals in Europe changed the European mindset. Those numerals are of ancient origin, were first used in India, spread westward through the Islamic world, entered Christian Europe through Spain, and were widely used in commerce before being adopted for widespread general and academic use by the 17th century (Smith & Karpinski, 1911). Before the use of Hindu-Arabic numerals became common they had to displace the counting board, or abacus. The counting board had long replaced the use of the older Roman numerals in areas where rapid computations were required. The use of Hindu-Arabic numerals was championed by the Italian mathematician, Leonardo of Pisa or Fibonacci (1170–1250), who had learned them as a child in Africa. His book, *Liber Abaci*, provided the common pencil-and-paper algorithms still in use for adding, subtracting, multiplying, and dividing numbers. Nevertheless, it took hundreds of years before the Hindu-Arabic numbers came into nearly universal use. The invention of printing was probably the final impetus for their use and standardization. The use of Hindu-Arabic numerals greatly accelerated the progress of mathematics in Christian Europe. Previously, mathematics was at a more advanced state in the Islamic world.

ASTRONOMY

Islam and Christianity shared an intense interest in astronomy. For both faiths the motivation was religious, not scientific. For Islam, the problem was how to orient mosques and prayers toward Mecca. For Christianity, the problem was how to calculate the date for Easter, the most important date in the liturgical calendar. Both problems required the use of mathematics and astronomical observations. Islamic astronomy was more advanced and their astronomers created instruments such as the **astrolabe** to accurately determine the direction toward Mecca from any point on Earth (Figure 4.2) (Dallal, 1999). Easter, a moveable feast, may fall on any date between March 22 and April 25. Easter is the first Sunday after the first Paschal full moon (i.e., a full moon determined by tables created after the Council of Nicea in 325) after the Spring Equinox. Lindberg (1992, p. 151) called these calculations evidence of the "handmaiden" role of science during the Middle Ages in Christian Europe. In other words, collecting empirical data was fine as long as it had a religious purpose. The use of Hindu-Arabic numerals, the rise of printing, and the collection of astronomical data were all necessary precursors to the rise of science. Advances in astronomy soon led to the earliest conflicts between the theologically based Aristotelian model espoused by the Church and supported by Aquinas's writings and the data and theories of the early European astronomers. The empirical data collected by Copernicus, Galileo, and Kepler, combined with Ockham's Razor, led to a new and radically different worldview (see Chapter 5).

FIGURE 4.2 ■ Astrolabe

LEARNING OBJECTIVE

8. List the necessary precursors to rise of science.

EMPIRICISM

Empiricism, like philosophy, was at a historical low point during much of the Middle Ages. Much of ancient philosophy was empirically based. The earliest natural philosophers used their senses in order to understand the world around them. Plato and the Neoplatonists retreated from empirical methods, and their philosophy centered on discovering an ideal universe within their own minds, largely ignoring the real world around them. Aristotle's philosophy returned empiricism to a prominent position but his influence waned rapidly after his death. The Stoic and Epicurean philosophers resurrected empirical methods, but those two approaches disappeared with the advent of Christianity and the rise of Islam.

Empiricism slowly returned during the Middle Ages to both the Christian and Islamic worlds as the writings of Aristotle became known. The Islamic philosophers despite having had longer and more direct knowledge of Aristotle's writings, could not establish a separate empirically based philosophy because of religious constraints. Consequently, they made progress in more applied and practical realms of knowledge, or topics such as perception or medicine, topics that were not likely to conflict with the teachings of the Qur'an or the *Hadith*.

Until nearly the very end of the Middle Ages, Christian philosophers were caught in a similar situation as the Islamic scholars. Their use of philosophical methods was, at first, limited to independently proving the truths of scripture. All of the Christian philosophers were highly religious and fully believed in the revelations described in the Bible. Scholars like Albert the Great, Thomas Aquinas, and William of Ockham were able to point their minds at new and interesting problems that were far removed from theology. To be sure, theology still dominated intellectual life at the end of the Middle Ages, and the empiricism being applied to examining the real world was primitive. But, the key fact was that empiricism had reemerged onto the intellectual stage. Its future progress, though, would be halting and even dangerous to its practitioners.

SUMMARY

The earliest philosophers were thoroughgoing materialists. Their mission was to explain how, literally, everything in the universe worked. The Greek medical doctors, too, were not only materialists but also empiricists. After Plato, however, much of Greek philosophy became idealistic. After Aristotle's death, Neoplatonic philosophers revived Plato's idealism. They, along with Jewish thinkers and philosophers, were very comfortable with idealist notions such as the Forms and the soul. The rapidly growing Christian movement, too, had little use for materialist philosophy. In Europe, around 600 CE, however, the Christian idealists had won the day, thanks to Augustine's writings. About the same time, Islam arose in Arabia and spread quickly. Its philosophy, too, gave primacy to revealed knowledge. Christianity and Islam soon became locked in a battle of faiths that continues to the present. The so-called Dark Ages were dark precisely because of a near universal repudiation of materialism and empiricism. It would take major events such as large-scale religious conflicts and systematic exploration of the globe, along with the passage of much time, before materialist philosophies could reemerge.

As the Middle Ages ended, the relationship between revelation and philosophy diverged. In Islam, fundamentalism gradually but inexorably, snuffed out any hopes of an independent and secular philosophical tradition. In Christian Europe, Albert the Great and Thomas Aquinas established the independence of philosophy. However, they did not grant philosophy independence. Instead, Aquinas purged Aristotle's works of any and all items that did not conform to Christian doctrine. It would take several hundred more years and much bloodshed and turmoil before a truly independent and secular philosophy arose in Europe. After that happened, the door was wide open for true experimental science to evolve from that philosophy.

The long-term effects of the relationship between religion and philosophy in both cultures were enormous and far-reaching. The world today is still affected by what happened during the Middle Ages. In Europe, philosophy gave rise to science and technology. It also gave rise to materialism and, later, consumerism. In the Islamic world, a long and gradual intellectual decline began, exacerbated by later European colonialism, to be sure. A look at astronomy tells much. Both cultures valued astronomy for its religious value. In Europe astronomical science led to a revolution in thought and to the earliest manifestations of science. Islam's built-in resistance to change prevented a similar move toward science and its empirical methods. As Hetherington (2006, p. xii) pointed out, "Muslim political and cultural stagnation, and consequently relative failure during a period of rapid Western advance, occurred at least in part because that culture did not embrace the Copernican and Newtonian revolutions." Christianity did not embrace those revolutions quickly or willingly either. But eventually its philosophers and later its scientists did. That they were able to do so was the consequence of Aquinas's reconciliation of Aristotle and Christianity. Most likely he would be appalled at the result.

Humanism arose in the 14th century as a response to Scholasticism. Humanists were inspired by the classic writers of the distant past, especially Roman and Greek ones. However, they were also inspired by other ancient traditions including those of the Hebrews and Egyptians. Unlike the scholastics, humanists concentrated on language and its evolution over time. For example, they sought to uncover the original meaning of the *New Testament* by learning Greek and creating new translations, both in Latin and in vernaculars. In the middle of the 15th century, the invention of the printing press gave Humanism a tremendous boost. It created a completely new environment in which books and other material could be printed in enormous quantities. Readers lapped up that flood of printed material creating a revolution still felt today.

5 FROM THE RENAISSANCE TO THE DAWN OF SCIENCE

ZEITGEIST

The Enlightenment

During the years covered in this chapter, the Roman Catholic Church experienced and recovered from a prolonged crisis. Rich and powerful, it had lost sight of its original mission and instead had accumulated an embarrassment of riches and become the home of hedonistic excess. Popes fought in wars, bishops bought their sees, priests kept concubines, and many nunneries were no more than brothels. Martin Luther's defiance of the Pope led to the Protestant Reformation, a long series of religious wars, and later, a vigorous Catholic Counter Reformation that eventually resulted in two Europes: one Roman Catholic and the other Protestant. These religious struggles weakened and transformed traditional views about religion and ultimately led to increased secularism and a decreased role for the papacy in European affairs.

Other large-scale historical events also played a major role. The explorations outside Europe to the Americas and the Indian Ocean led to a long-lasting period of colonialism. Commerce and banking flourished and helped create and expand the middle class while establishing new economic and social roles for companies and corporations. The breaking of the Ottoman's siege of Vienna in 1683 halted the Islamic threat to Central Europe and led to a longer decline of Islam in Eastern Europe. Near the end of the 18th century Enlightenment ideas led to the American and French revolutions.

By 1700, Europe and the world had been transformed. Philosophy evolved into its modern form and science emerged as the final arbiter of empirical knowledge. Psychology's distant origins were also evident by the end of this period as the questions raised by philosophers began to be answered, first by physical scientists and later by social scientists.

LEARNING OBJECTIVE

1. Describe some of the large-scale societal changes that have taken place during the lifetimes of you and your parents.

The French friar, Marin Mersenne (1588–1648), played a critical role as he met and corresponded with nearly every philosopher and scientist of note introducing many of them to one another. Like the "invisible college" (e.g., the informal meetings of early scientists) that had sprung up in England before the chartering of the Royal Society, Mersenne's cell at his monastery in Paris served a similar function. After his death, the impetus provided by his example led to the founding in 1666 of *L'Academie des Sciences*, the French counterpart to the Royal Society (Fauré-Fremiet, 1966). The partial list of those who visited or corresponded with Mersenne reads like a *Who's Who* of the 17th century. It included Galileo, Rene Descartes, Pierre Gassendi, Pierre Fermat, Christiaan Huygens and his father, Thomas Hobbes, Blaise Pascal, and Evangelista Torricelli. Besides being a good host and faithful correspondent, Mersenne was also a theologian and mathematician. He, too, was following Francis Bacon's recommendation that scientists should work collaboratively. However, Mersenne was not a follower of Bacon's empiricist philosophy. Ayers (2006) labels Mersenne a rationalist.

Mersenne helped nurture the early days of the **Enlightenment,** that historical period between the Renaissance and Modernism. Enlightenment thinkers in all areas—science, politics, and the arts—were skeptical about the earlier claims about knowledge coming from religion and metaphysics. The astronomical discoveries that led to the heliocentric model of the universe were early stimuli for a change in worldview. Eventually the Enlightenment broadened beyond astrophysics to include all of science and give rise to new disciplines, including psychology. Enlightenment thinkers believed that the human mind was capable of understanding nature in any of its guises. Usher (2005) included *New Physics* and *New Astronomy* as parts of the *New Philosophy*. He wrote that the New Philosophy (p. 94), "assails the *Old Philosophy* (original italics) whose methodological principles and beliefs stem from the philosophers of ancient Greece and their followers." Something, indeed, was new under the now heliocentric universe.

LEARNING OBJECTIVE

2. Describe how the annual meetings of contemporary scientific societies reflect the interactions between individual scientists that began in Mersenne's cell.

PREVIEW

Many of the ideas covered in this chapter would later be of interest to psychologists. The astronomers in this chapter uncovered *laws* of nature. Those laws applied to the location and movement of planets and stars. Later, psychologists would attempt to find laws of psychophysics and behavior. Furthermore, those laws could be expressed via *mathematics,* another new idea. Gradually, scientists realized that discovering the underlying mathematics for their observations was part and parcel of their jobs. Related to mathematics was the idea of *measurement*. Starting with Brahe scientists realized the importance of precise measurements that would provide the raw data for their theorizing. Precise measurement also required the creation of new and reliable scientific equipment to collect it with. So, Brahe's quadrants and sextants, Galileo's and Newtons's telescopes, and Leeuwenhoek's microscopes ushered in a new appreciation for the importance of creating specialized equipment designed to collect data beyond the power of human senses. Lastly, this era saw the rise of the doctrine of *mechanism,* the idea that everything has a natural cause. All of these 17th-century innovations would carry forward into psychology and become part of its toolkit too.

LEARNING OBJECTIVE

3. Appraise the differences in collecting data with the naked eye to doing so with instruments such as telescopes and microscopes.

The Enlightenment represented a sea change in European thinking about methods of inquiry. The slow-moving separation between theology and philosophy finally split the two disciplines and gave birth to the *new philosophy*. Descartes's *rationalism* sought to explain the natural world by first eliminating doubts about existence itself through his *cogito, ergo sum* exercise. That, combined with his *mind–body* formulation, along with his *interactionist* solution, laid the foundation for future rationalist philosophers. Yet, Descartes (and Berkeley too) were unwilling to totally part with God in their philosophies.

Bacon's philosophy was diametrically different to Descartes's in that he believed in *empiricist* methods. His *idols* were among the first attempts to ensure reliability and validity for sensory observations. Also different was his emphasis on *induction*. His philosophy was bottom-up where Descartes's was top-down. Bacon's separation of science into components of *theoretical* and *applied* has survived to the present day.

Big history in the form of the *English Civil Wars* also played a major role in shaping the future of empirical philosophy. In this case the wars contrasted how the *state of nature* and the *social contract* could suddenly change. That Hobbes and Locke were forced to choose temporary exile because of those wars affected their theorizing. They and most other British philosophers chose a different direction than Descartes while addressing the same problems. Hobbes used *materialism* in order to dispense with the thorny problem of how mind and body affected each other. Locke posited his *tabula rasa* as a powerful empiricist metaphor, but even he understood that it did not explain all behavior. He also promoted the influential doctrine of *associationism*. Berkeley invoked God in his *idealism* in order to deal with otherwise intractable issues surrounding the mind–body problem. Hume removed God from philosophy while searching for more precise ways to understand empiricism. His analyses of *resemblance, continuity,* and *cause and effect* were different and seminal. He reversed the age-old relationship between emotion and rational thought, putting the *passions* first.

LEARNING OBJECTIVE

4. Summarize the major changes in approach to understanding the world caused by the new philosophy.

INTRODUCTION

This chapter covers the time from the end of the Middle Ages to the dawn of science, a period of over 400 years. Looking back upon those centuries, the events, people, and trends seem understandable, and perhaps, inevitable. But for those who lived during that period the changes were probably not so clearly felt or understood. Three major historical events marked this period of history: the Renaissance, the Protestant Reformation, and the Counter Reformation. Another product of this period was the rise of science. Astronomers such as Copernicus, Galileo, Brahe, and Kepler finally and firmly demolished the ancient geocentric (earth-centered) model of the universe and substituted the now familiar **heliocentric** (solar-centered) model. Other sciences and scientists followed. Isaac Newton worked out the physics of light and provided the theoretical explanation for gravity, the force that holds the planets in their orbits. The questions raised by these early scientists remained questions for the first psychologists. Thus, the rise of science during this period provided the foundation for the emergence of scientific psychology during the 19th century. This chapter looks closely at the earliest events that led to the emergence of the new philosophy, as it was called then. We now call it science.

LEARNING OBJECTIVE

5. Modify your thinking about sunrises and sunsets and determine which direction the earth is spinning relative to the sun.

This chapter also looks at philosophy's responses to the empirical research of the early scientists. The new intellectual process, science, inspired by Copernicus and pioneered by Kepler and Newton soon served as a concrete example to others in a variety of disciplines. Philosophers, too, finally began to add to the classic philosophies of Aristotle and Plato. Two new and competing forms of philosophy, empiricism and rationalism, arose. Both had much to say about issues in psychology and in the creation of the discipline of psychology itself. This new philosophy was one of the disciplines from which psychology emerged in the 19th century.

Rene Descartes was the first of the new philosophers. His writings in mathematics, physics, and metaphysics influenced generations of philosophers and scientists and led to the creation of **rationalism** and, later, to its oppositional counterpart, **empiricism**. The two philosophies, however, are not as far apart in practice as they may first seem. The philosophers in this chapter held nuanced views combining both approaches. Descartes was the founder of rationalism and inspired many other philosophers to support his views. At the same time, many empiricist philosophers were equally inspired to argue against his rationalism. The vast majority of the rationalist philosophers lived on the European continent and are often labeled *Continental philosophers,* while the vast majority of empiricist philosophers lived on the British Isles and are usually referred to as *British empiricists.*

LEARNING OBJECTIVE

6. Explain how modern psychology uses empiricism and rationalism to explain human behavior.

THE RENAISSANCE

Humanism (see Chapter 4) helped ignite the historical period known as the Renaissance. The Renaissance began in Florence, Italy, and quickly spread throughout nearly all of Europe. The growth of cities, commerce, and wealthy patrons helped to spread changes in education, art, and architecture. Schools now sought to educate students in the classics and gymnastics seeking to create new "Renaissance men." Artists such as Botticelli, Leonardo, and Michelangelo created paintings and sculptures still revered today. Architects reacted against the medieval Gothic style and built Neo-Classic public buildings along with mansions and villas for successful and newly rich patrons. The invention of the printing press provided new synergy. Suddenly, all kinds of printed matter could be created cheaply and in large quantities. Gutenberg's invention of the printing press with moveable type in 1440 was revolutionary. All at once, the humanist's emphasis on language took on a life of its own as printing presses spread from Germany to every corner of Europe. Bibles were printed, first in Latin and then in nearly every language. Books, journals, and pamphlets appeared sparking a revolution in communication still ongoing. In many ways the rapid appearance and spread of the World Wide Web after 1996 is similar to the appearance of the printing press in the 15th century. However, the Web's effects pale in comparison to the invention of the printing press. Innovations such as multimedia, blogs, and social networking all ride on top of the template provided by the printed page. The printing press was much more transformative than the Web in terms of quantity and type of new material. Very quickly, the press created new classes: authors, and more dramatically, millions of readers. One of the first to exploit the power of the printing press was the quintessential Renaissance man, Erasmus of Rotterdam.

Erasmus (1467–1536)

Biography

Desiderius Erasmus was the name later taken by a Dutch child born out of wedlock to a priest and his concubine, a common household arrangement at that time. Erasmus's parents cared for him and his older brother, including sending them to school, until an outbreak of the plague claimed their parents' lives. The orphaned boys were soon placed in an Augustinian monastery. Throughout his life, Erasmus maintained he had been sent there against his will. Nevertheless, he became a priest and soon found a sponsor in the bishop of Cambrai who needed a secretary well versed in Latin. From an early age, Erasmus showed a special aptitude for Latin and later in life taught himself Greek as well. The bishop allowed

Erasmus to travel to France to study theology at the University of Paris. There, Erasmus developed a lifelong dislike for the Scholastics (see Chapter 4) and their methods. Johnson (1976) wrote that Erasmus claimed he and other students at Paris spent eight weeks debating the relative efficacy of many short versus fewer but longer prayers! He did not receive a degree from Paris. But, while there, he met a British student, Lord Mountjoy, who invited him for a long visit at his rural estate. While in Britain, Erasmus met the theologian John Colet who lectured on the Bible as a literary text. Inspired, Erasmus realized that he must learn Greek in order to understand the literary origins of Scripture because Greek was the original language of the New Testament. He combined Humanism with theology and began to publish works on Christianity. Like Augustine, he believed that the primary form religion should take was inward, toward one's own mind. He thought that the outward manifestations of religious practice, such as attending mass or participating in pilgrimages, had made the practice of religion a series of automatic responses instead of being a guide to living a virtuous life.

Contributions

He returned to Holland and took an academic post at the University of Louvain. There, he found an unpublished manuscript by the Italian humanist Lorenzo Valla that used textual analysis to understand the meaning of the New Testament. Inspired, Erasmus set out to write a new translation of Jerome's Latin Bible using those same methods. After another stay in England he finished his most famous book, *In Praise of Folly*, a biting satire that skewered the Roman Catholic Church, its practices, and its clergy. The book was an instant commercial success and was in print for many years. It made Erasmus famous; he was one of the first media celebrities in history. He moved to Basel, a free Swiss city, in order to work on his translation of the Bible. There, in Johann Froben's print shop, he produced his new Bible. It contained the Greek version on the left side of the page and the corresponding Latin version on the right side. Overnight, it seemed, Erasmus had brought humanist methods to the study of theology.

At this point, Erasmus believed that his work was beginning to heal the abuses of the Roman Catholic Church from within. Unfortunately, he failed to see how deeply entrenched the conservative factions within the Church were. Erasmus attempted to create a trilingual college at Louvain, one that taught Latin, Greek, and Hebrew. The idea was to critically examine older texts in order to trace the historical development of Christian thought. His conservative colleagues at Louvain fought that initiative, arguing that the Bible could be understood without having to examine its past forms or languages. Erasmus also did not count upon the nearly simultaneous emergence of another Augustinian monk, Martin Luther, who was incensed over the corrupt practices of his Church, especially the *sale* of indulgences. Luther's position eventually led to another schism or split among Christians, the Protestant Reformation (see below). However, before that final break occurred Erasmus privately defended Luther against charges of heresy.

Humanists everywhere were torn by the evolving religious dispute and many believed it was the natural outcome of Erasmus's writings. However, Erasmus himself refused to leave his

Church. Eventually, Luther attacked Erasmus in print and there was no hope left for any sort of reconciliation between the new Protestants and the Catholics or between Erasmus and Luther. In his remaining years, Erasmus continued to write extensively. He left Basel after that city became Protestant. As much as he loved living and working there, he could not in good conscience remain as a Catholic in a Protestant city. He moved to nearby Freiburg, still a Catholic city, with much unwanted fanfare. In the last year of his life, he moved back to his beloved Basel, dying there shortly after.

Erasmus's life and works were representative of Humanism. He rose to prominence because of his literary skills despite his illegitimate birth and nearly constant childhood poverty. He was one of the first to take full advantage of the power of the printing press and was the first author to enjoy the benefits of a mass market. He saw clearly the troubles surrounding his Church and worked hard to reform them from within. In the end, he was unsuccessful and witnessed the birth and growth of Protestantism. His writings showed how seamlessly he and his fellow humanists perceived the relationship between God and humans. They sought to understand God through the careful and critical analysis of the texts of the early Church fathers. Erasmus's successful application of Humanism's methods to biblical scholarship began a revolution in theology and finally put an end to the methodology of the medieval scholastics. Morrow (2015) detailed the history of modern biblical scholarship. He concluded (p. 22), "modern biblical studies emerged from the quest for objectivity, in the attempt to create distance between the Bible and the scholar." Luther, however, desired a different solution than did Erasmus. He was neither a scholastic or a humanist (Mattox, 2017). He did not wish to reform the church, he wanted to start anew. He and Erasmus split over original sin, free will, and the depth of God's grace. Luther, more radically, believed that Adam and Eve's original sin was so vile that it could only be forgiven by God's grace, and that the free will to perform good works was not enough to compensate for it.

LEARNING OBJECTIVE

7. Explain the differences between representing knowledge on the printed page vs. doing so on a web page.

THE REFORMATIONS

Martin Luther ignited what later was called the Protestant Reformation. However, his "Lutheran" revolt was only one of several similar actions against the Roman Catholic Church during this period. In the past, the Church had acted quickly and decisively in suppressing similar revolts and had burned at the stake the leaders of those sects. Leo X, the Pope when Luther began his protests, did not act decisively. He was distracted by his building projects in Rome and the need to pay for them. At first, he thought Luther's complaints were just another dispute between Augustinians and Franciscans. Luther also received support and shelter from his prince, Friedrich the Wise, who refused to send Luther to Rome. Had Friedrich given Luther up, the Inquisition would have quickly condemned Luther. Friedrich also wished to stop the flow of money derived from the sale of indulgences from Saxony to Rome.

Luther's use of the printing press, printing in Latin and German, allowed others to learn of his ideas quickly. Thus, what in other circumstances might have been just another failed heresy had the time and opportunity to grow into a new form of Christian religion. Lutheranism was only one of several Protestant denominations that arose during this period. While all were opposed to the Roman Catholic Church, they differed among themselves as to the nature of their specific beliefs. For example, some held that the communion bread and wine truly were Christ's body and blood, while others maintained they were only symbolic of them. Other differences included the marriage of priests and the right to read and interpret the Bible for oneself. Those and other theological issues continue to divide Protestant denominations even today (Johnson et al., 2016). The Roman Catholic Church's response, the Counter Reformation, led to armed conflict, many thousands of deaths, and a permanent division within Christianity. The various Protestant Reformations put an end to unified Western Christendom. That medieval idea was finished. In its place came the first stirrings of modernism.

Martin Luther (1483–1546)

Biography

Martin Luther was born in Eisleben, a town in the Holy Roman Empire. When Luther was born, Germany did not exist. Instead, what is now Germany consisted of a vast number of large and small principalities, duchies, and independent cities. Luther's father, Hans, was a miner and a smelter. Because he wanted to keep his son out of the mines, he sent him to school with the eventual goal of becoming a lawyer. Luther disliked much of what he learned and dropped out of law school. One day, while riding home during a thunderstorm, he was nearly killed by lightning. He prayed to St. Anna, the maternal grandmother of Christ, for deliverance promising he would become a monk if he lived. That is how he became an Augustinian, much against the desires of his family. Luther became an exemplary monk and was sent to study theology at a monastery in Wittenberg. Shortly after, he was appointed to a post in theology at the newly founded university in Wittenberg. He remained there the rest of his life.

Contributions

The precipitating event for Luther's revolt was the sale of indulgences, a long-standing practice in the Roman Catholic Church where by purchasing an indulgence one was guaranteed a place in heaven after death. In 1517, Pope Leo X had declared that indulgences could also be purchased to liberate souls in Purgatory. Leo needed the money in order to complete the new St. Peter's Church in Rome. Indulgences brought in much money to Rome but the money went to opulent building projects while leaving already poor Romans even poorer. Throughout Europe, many pious peasants spent what little money they had to ensure that they and their relatives would have a place in heaven. Luther's Reformation began when parishioners brought indulgences to him so that he could confirm their value and authenticity. He pronounced them worthless.

On October 31, 1517, Luther posted his famous 95 Theses on the church doors at Wittenberg. He printed them in Latin and German and had them widely distributed. Soon, news of them had spread far and wide. Luther had also sent a copy of them to the local bishop, Albrecht, who promptly forwarded them to Rome. Albrecht owed the Pope money for his appointment as a bishop and was going to pay using some of the money collected through the sale of indulgences. Had Leo acted quickly the world might not know the name of Martin Luther. Instead, Leo took his time. He summoned Luther to Rome, but Luther refused to leave Saxony. Had he done so he would have surely been condemned and burned as a heretic. The ruler of Saxony, Friedrich the Wise, successfully lobbied the Pope to have Luther questioned in Germany instead. Leo sent Dominican Cardinal Cajetan to Augsburg to meet with Luther. Their meetings were not productive. In fact, their meeting ended up crystallizing Luther's position on the sacraments while diminishing his objections to indulgences. Luther returned to Wittenberg, still a free man. Wicks (1983, p. 555) decribed Luther's thinking on his way back home:

> The return journey had given Luther time to further assess the two teachings on which Cajetan had charged him with error. Luther was coming to see that indulgences were rather unimportant in comparison with faith in the effect of the sacrament. On the latter point, salvation itself is at stake.

Some months later, at the University of Heidelberg, another theologian, Johann Eck, debated with Luther. Eck skillfully manipulated Luther into a corner. Luther had admitted that Jan Hus, who had been burned as a heretic in 1415, had not really held heretical views. After that admission, Luther could no longer return to the Catholic fold. The Pope soon declared him a heretic and an outlaw. He could literally be arrested or even killed on sight. Again, outside events intervened to save Luther. A new Holy Roman Emperor, Charles V, had been elected. Friedrich persuaded him to allow Luther a public hearing. It took place in 1521, in the city of Worms.

Charles V presided over that meeting, the Diet of Worms. On the first day, when asked if he would recant his collected writings, Luther asked for more time to think. The next day he answered with a short speech. His biographer summarized the speech with the words, "Here I stand; I can do no other." Luther avoided immediate arrest because he possessed a safe conduct pass to and from the meeting. Friedrich protected Luther on his way out of Worms and hid him at Wartburg Castle in Eisenach for eight months. While there, he continued to write and even translated the New Testament into German.

Elsewhere, many throughout the Holy Roman Empire converted Luther's words into action. Monasteries were overrun, church sculptures destroyed, and priests killed. So great was the turmoil and destruction that the Wittenberg city council asked Luther to return and help calm things down. Luther returned to Wittenberg and began to preach again. By now he had thought through many of the changes he wished to see established in the new Lutheran Church. The most radical change was justification by faith. Having reread Paul's letter to the Romans,

Luther preached that God's grace alone leads to salvation. Good works (including indulgences) did nothing to assure salvation. Luther also allowed his clergy to marry and took a wife himself. The Reformation was now inevitable.

Unlike Erasmus, Luther did not consider himself a humanist. However, Luther had received a humanist's education and had taken advantage of the power of his words spread through the new medium of the printed page. The Reformation, though, was inimical to Humanism. Many of the humanists were Roman Catholic clergy, otherwise they could not have been granted faculty status at their universities. Now, some were threatened or killed because of their religion, not their ideas. Luther and other Protestants fell away from the ideal of humanistic free inquiry. In fact, the early Protestants were the first Christian fundamentalists; they hewed to their Bibles as the only source of knowledge and truth. The Roman Catholic Church, too, responded to Luther and Protestantism with a vengeance, launching its Counter Reformation and rolling back through force some of the gains made by Luther and other Protestants.

The Counter Reformation

The Counter Reformation or Catholic Reformation began slowly with calls for a Council to settle the disputes between the Roman Catholic Church and the new Protestant denominations. However, by the time the Council of Trent first met in 1545 it was too late to put the competing forms of western Christianity back together. Instead, the end result was a set of modest reforms: The sale of indulgences was prohibited, bishops were no longer allowed to live outside their sees, priestly celibacy was promoted, and better education was urged for parish priests. Laven (2006, p. 713) writing about the Counter Reformation in Catholic Bavaria stated, "The villagers no longer tolerated concubinage and were suspicious of any dealings between women and priests." The celebration of the mass was standardized and the original seven sacraments were kept. During the rite of communion only bread, not wine, would be offered to communicants. In short, no real concessions were made to the new Protestant denominations.

Additionally, the Roman Catholic Church set up a new mechanism, the *Index of Prohibited Books*. Anyone caught reading or possessing a book on that list could be labeled a heretic. That list was soon to include authors of scientific works such as Copernicus and Descartes. Another mechanism was the establishment of the Roman Inquisition in 1542 by Pope Paul III. Modeled after the earlier Spanish Inquisition, the Roman Inquisition's purpose was to root out heretics. It would soon be used against the natural philosopher Galileo (see below). Bloody religious wars, too, broke out, most famously the Thirty Years' War (1618–1648). By the end of that long war, Europe had coalesced into two major religious camps. On the Catholic side were Spain, Portugal, the Italian peninsula, Austria, Hungary, and Poland. On the Protestant side were England, the Netherlands, Scandinavia, Switzerland, and most of modern Germany. These religious boundaries were destined to last, nearly unchanged, until the present. It was in this environment that scientists first began to discover and publish facts about the universe.

LEARNING OBJECTIVE

8. Compare the current movie rating system (e.g., G, PG, PG-13, R, and X) to the *Index of Prohibited Works.*

THE RISE OF SCIENCE

Recall the importance to all Christians of setting the date for Easter (see Chapter 4). By the 16th century it was obvious that the existing Julian calendar was incorrect. It was about 11 min slow every year. Given that it had been in use for over 1,500 years the cumulative discrepancy had reached 12 days by the middle of the 16th century. Several popes had addressed the problem piecemeal until Pope Gregory XIII finally appointed a commission to solve the problem. The new calendar, the Gregorian Calendar, was put in place in 1582. Moyer (1982) named Christoph Clavius and Luigi Giglio as the astronomers who created the new calendar. One astronomer who earlier had refused to work on the calendar problem was Nicolaus Copernicus, a Polish churchman and astronomer. He refused because he believed better knowledge about the actual motions of the heavenly bodies was needed first. Thus, he spent most of his life working on an alternative theory that might better explain the positions and motions of the sun, the moon, and the six then known planets. His heliocentric model of the universe eventually proved revolutionary and sparked the beginnings of modern science.

Nicolaus Copernicus (1473–1543)

Biography

Copernicus was born in Torun, now part of Poland. Copernicus's parents were well to do and prominent. After Copernicus's father died in 1483, his uncle Lucas Watzenrode cared for him. Copernicus attended several universities: Cracow in Poland and Bologna, Padua, and Ferrara on the Italian peninsula. He received a humanistic education and could read Greek. He also showed an early interest in astronomy and observed the night sky when he could. He returned to Poland in 1510 and remained there the rest of his life.

Contributions

By 1514, Copernicus had privately circulated a few copies of a short manuscript called the *Commentariolus* in Latin or *Little Commentary*. In that document he laid out his initial thoughts on what would eventually become his only major work, *On the Revolutions of the Celestial Spheres*, which was published in 1543 just before his death. The fortuitous visit of a German mathematician and astronomer in 1539, Rheticus, encouraged Copernicus and allowed him to flesh out his ideas. A little later, Rheticus published a short synopsis of Copernicus's heliocentric theory. When Copernicus saw that Rheticus's book had stirred up little controversy he agreed to publish his own longer account. In a preface, Copernicus dedicated his book to Pope Paul III and explained his motives for writing the book, one of which was reform of the liturgical calendar. Unbeknownst to Copernicus, his editor also added an additional unauthorized preface. That preface claimed that the book was just a hypothesis that, "need not be true or even probable" (Wrightsman, 1975, p. 236). Copernicus first saw his published book on his deathbed and was, thus, unable to prevent publication of the unauthorized preface. However, that preface may have prevented an earlier condemnation of his book by the Roman Catholic Church. (The book was placed on the *Index* in 1616.)

In his book, Copernicus switched the positions of the earth and sun, placing the sun at the center of the universe. His apparent reason for doing so was to eliminate Ptolemy's need for equants, hypothetical points he needed to explain the observed changes in speed of the heavenly bodies. Copernicus hoped to create a system that would eliminate the need for such arbitrary concepts and substitute a system that only required spheres and spherical motion (see Figures 5.1 and 5.2). He spent years confirming his measurements and calculations. His heliocentric system did not improve upon the astronomical predictions made by the older,

FIGURE 5.1 ■ Copernicus's Model of the Universe

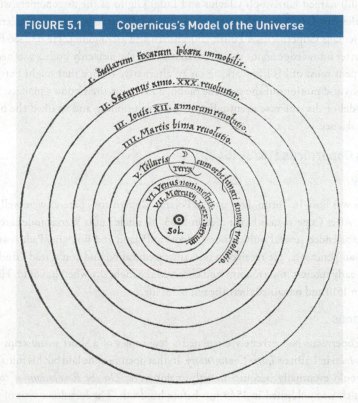

Source: TopFoto/The Image Works

https://en.wikipedia.org/wiki/Copernican_heliocentrism#/media/File:
Copernican_heliocentrism_diagram-2.jpg

FIGURE 5.2 ■ Ptolemy's Model of the Universe

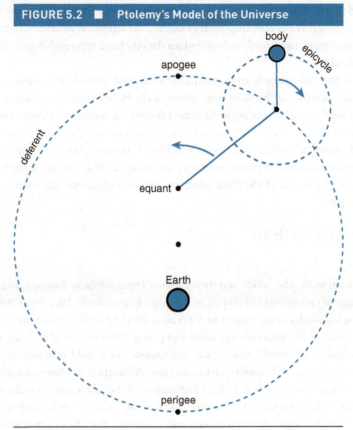

Source: Universal Images Group Limited/Alamy

https://www.sciencephoto.com/media/364122/view/ptolemaic-cosmology

geocentric system. Copernicus's system, however, accounted for nearly all known astronomical observations plus it was a unified system, unlike Ptolemy's older collection of disparate mathematical rules.

Soon, other scientists began to work out the many implications of Copernicus's model. One such implication was not readily grasped. The Ptolemaic and Aristotelian concept of a final, equidistant crystalline sphere of fixed stars was incompatible with the Copernican universe. Astronomers would eventually realize that Copernicus's scheme meant the universe was much larger than previously thought. Another implication was that Aristotle's physics must be wrong because

PHOTO 5.1 Copernicus

Credit: iStock/Graffisimo

he had held that all matter was attracted to the center of the universe, namely the earth. If the earth was no longer the center, then what explained the attraction of objects to it? These and other empirical issues led directly to inquiry into the very basic nature of objects, their motion, and their locations.

Tycho Brahe, another early astronomer, confirmed that new celestial objects could appear in the "eighth heaven," or the outermost sphere of the Ptolemaic universe where that theory located the fixed stars. (According to Ptolemy's theory, the outermost sphere was unchangeable.) Brahe used astronomical instruments (but not telescopes, they had yet to be invented) that he had created himself to measure the locations of stars and planets to a hitherto unheard of high level of precision. When a supernova appeared in 1572, his measurements revealed that it was in the region of the fixed stars, not between the earth and moon, contrary to Ptolemy's theory.

Tycho Brahe (1546–1601)

Biography

Brahe was born in Skaane, which was then a part of Denmark (now Sweden), to a noble family. At the age of two he was kidnapped by his uncle Jørgen. Brahe later wrote that his uncle, "without the knowledge of my parents took me away with him while I was in my earliest youth" (Ferguson, 2002, p. 8). No action was taken and young Tycho remained with his uncle. Brahe attended school and learned Latin, which was unusual for a child of noble birth. After, he attended the University of Copenhagen to study law. While there he observed a predicted total eclipse of the sun. That, combined with his discovery of the tables used to make such predictions, further pushed him toward astronomy. Later, at the University of Leipzig, he lost interest in law but learned to sight stars and planets and discovered that the astronomical tables were wrong in predicting a planetary conjunction he observed. He resolved to construct a new set of tables based upon a more careful and precise observation of the sky. He did not then realize that such a project would consume the majority of his remaining days and not be completed until after his death.

Contributions

Eventually Brahe returned to Denmark. As a nobleman he was a misfit. He was more educated but at the same time had not been to war or conducted diplomatic missions, tasks common to the nobility. He began his project of mapping the sky to a new level of precision. One night in 1572, he observed a new star; one that he knew had not been there the night before. After confirming his observation with others, he realized that he had seen a supernova. Supernovae visible to the naked eye are exceedingly rare; only three have been recorded since 1006. He found that none of the professors at the University of Copenhagen had noticed the new star. Brahe decided to publish his finding. Doing so, however, was not easy. Noblemen did not publish such books; doing so violated the rules of the social order. Nonetheless, he did publish it, and the book made Brahe world famous and led to his most productive years as an astronomer.

Soon after, Fredrick II, the king of Denmark, offered Brahe an island, Hven, along with more than sufficient funds plus the labor of its peasant residents to study astronomy full time. For 21 years Brahe was able to make the most precise measurements of the locations of stars and planets then known using quadrants and sextants of his own design. A quadrant is a pie-shaped 90° section of arc and a sextant is a 60° section. Brahe's largest instruments were enormous, over 15 ft. (4.57 m.) on a side, and they required many men to move them into the proper positions to conduct observations. Brahe also developed procedures for correcting errors due to atmospheric refraction and conducted multiple measurements of the same star or planet in order to assure reliability of measurement. In other words, he was pioneering the use of the basic empirical techniques of science.

The accession of King Christian IV following the death of Fredrick II soon led to the end of Brahe's stay on Hven. Brahe had neglected the care of a church, abused the peasants living on Hven, and underpaid the local pastor (Ferguson, 2002). Christian IV withdrew the generous financial support Brahe had been receiving. Brahe responded by packing up his household and leaving Denmark. Eventually, he settled in Prague after receiving promises of support from the Holy Roman Emperor, Rudolf II. Outside Prague, he set up another observatory. But, Rudolf called him back to Prague where Brahe soon found himself in the role of court mathematician and unofficial advisor. He could no longer continue to collect astronomical data. However, Brahe did employ a younger astronomer, Johannes Kepler, to help work out the mathematical details of a Tychonic model of the universe, one that had the planets circling the sun while the sun and moon circled a still stationary earth (see Figure 5.3). His hybrid system was a less radical modification of Ptolemy's and was, thus, more palatable to astronomers than was Copernicus's.

To understand how Brahe came to employ him requires looking at Kepler's personal history. Kepler, like Brahe, had just suffered a reversal of fortune, but one much more drastic. Kepler had been forced to abandon his academic post because he would not renounce his Lutheran religion. Brahe had issued an invitation to join him in Prague as a collaborator. That invitation eventually enabled Kepler to publish a much stronger version of Copernican theory.

Johannes Kepler (1571–1630)

Biography

Kepler was born to an aristocratic family, but the fortunes of his German Lutheran family were on the decline. He was born premature, a sickly child, and had poor eyesight. However, he showed an aptitude for mathematics early on. After the start of the Reformation in Germany free schools had been established to educate Lutheran children. Kepler attended those schools and then matriculated at the University of Tübingen. There, he intended to study philosophy and theology with the hope of becoming a Lutheran minister. He was also interested in astronomy. His studies with the astronomer Mästlin exposed him to both the Ptolemaic and Copernican theories. Early on he became a convert to Copernicus's ideas. But it was his mathematics that won him a faculty appointment at the University of Graz. At Graz, one of his

FIGURE 5.3 ■ The Tychonic Model of the Universe

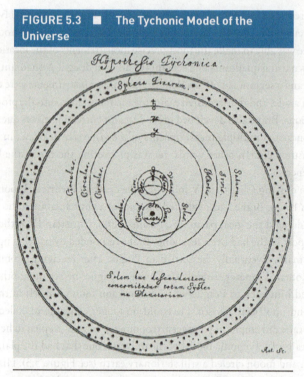

Source: Sheila Terry/Science Source/Photo Researchers

https://upload.wikimedia.org/wikipedia/commons/9/91/Tychonian. png

duties was to prepare astrological horoscopes and calendars, then a normal task for astronomers. Luckily, Kepler predicted a cold winter, an attack by the Turks, and a peasant uprising; all turned out to be true, earning him a raise (Ferguson, 2002).

Contributions

One day in class while lecturing on geometry, Kepler began to think about how different regular shapes could be nested within a circle with just the points touching the circles. He thought that a set of regularly nested shapes might mirror the organization of the universe in a more mathematically pleasing way. However, he quickly realized that nested two-dimensional shapes could be arranged with circumscribed circles in so many ways as to be meaningless. But, when he switched to regular solid three-dimensional shapes, he thought he had uncovered an inherent mathematical pattern explaining the universe. There were only five such solids (cube, dodecahedron, icosahedron, octahedron, and tetrahedron) and if he could nest them appropriately surrounding each with a sphere, he might have a mathematical model of the universe. He thought he had discovered such a model and was pleased with its Platonic simplicity. He disliked Ptolemaic theory because of its complexity, lack of neatness, and dependence on a variety of hypothetical devices (e.g., epicycles, deferents, and equants). He believed that God would not create a universe based upon such an *ad hoc* model.

He published a book detailing the model (see Figure 5.4), the *Mysterium Cosmographicum* (*The Cosmographic Mystery*), but it was not well received. One reason for that poor reception was that Kepler was mixing mathematics and physics. Aristotle had long held that mathematics was part of the liberal arts and that physics was part of natural philosophy. Kepler's attempts to mix the two did not fit the *zeitgeist*. Physicists, from Aristotle on, had not looked for underlying evidence to support or explain their observations. Kepler was one of the first to challenge that ancient divide. Subsequently, mathematics and measurement drove the early rise of science. Still, Kepler realized he needed better astronomical observations along with to prove his case.

FIGURE 5.4 ■ Kepler's Nested Solids Model of the Universe

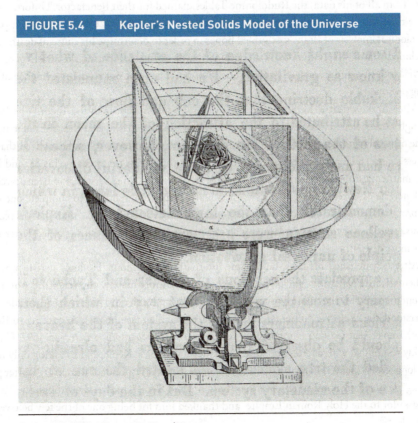

Source: North Wind Picture Archives/Alamy

https://en.wikipedia.org/wiki/Mysterium_Cosmographicum#/media/File:
Kepler-solar-system-1.png

Credit: Chronicle / Alamy Stock Photo

The politics of the Reformation fell heavily on Kepler and his family when the Archduke Ferdinand decided to force all Protestants in Graz to convert to Catholicism. Those who refused were given eight days to leave or be killed. In Kepler's case, because he was the local mathematician, he was allowed to stay while still remaining a Lutheran. However, a year later, even he had to convert or leave town. He looked everywhere for another suitable position but could not find one. Only one invitation came; it was from Tycho Brahe. He needed an assistant at his new observatory near Prague. Brahe was setting up a new astronomical observatory thanks to his new patron, Rudolph II. Kepler arrived there in early 1600 amid the confusion caused by workmen building the new observatory. Brahe soon discovered the depth of Kepler's mathematical talents but did not completely trust him because of a priority dispute about his Tychonic system with Ursus, another astronomer. Moreover, Ursus had published one of Kepler's letters in a book. Brahe needed Kepler, but was not sure of where he stood in the dispute. So, Brahe only gave Kepler the data for the orbit of the planet Mars. In 1601, Brahe relented and decided to collaborate with Kepler to produce a new set of astronomical tables from all of his data, the Rudolphine Tables, named for their benefactor. Unfortunately, Brahe died shortly afterward, apparently of uremia. Kacki et al. (2018) conducted a paleopathological analysis of Brahe's exhumed bones in order to determine his cause of death. They concluded that he likely died from a combination of diffuse idiopathic skeletal hyperostosis (DISH), obesity, and excessive alcohol consumption. They did not find any evidence of him being poisoned.

After Brahe's death, Kepler secured all of Brahe's data and analyzed them. The breakthrough came when he realized that the earth, too, was a planet, and that the orbits of it and all of the other planets were elliptical. That became Kepler's First Law. When he realized that the planets swept equal areas in equal times throughout their orbit that became his Second Law. That mathematical relationship was the kind of Pythagorean simplicity he had been searching for. Later, he discovered his Third Law: the square of the time required to complete one orbit was proportional to the cube of any planet's mean distance from the sun. Again he was pleased because that last law neatly explained why the planets closest to the sun traveled faster than those more distant.

After he published his laws, he became internationally famous. He had, at last, provided mathematical explanations for physical phenomena. Unfortunately, the scientific world was still not prepared for the full import of his ideas. However, Kepler did have one early reader who understood the explosive consequences of his ideas, Galileo (see below). According to Rosen (1966) Kepler sent Galileo two copies of his book *The Cosmographic Mystery* in 1597. Galileo quickly responded with a letter and asked for two more copies. Kepler did so asking only for "a very long letter" (p. 263) in return. Galileo, apparently, never responded. But, in 1610 after publishing his first astronomical observations, he contacted Kepler, indirectly through the Tuscan ambassador to the Holy Roman Empire, and thanked him for being one of the few believers of his work.

Kepler had taken Brahe's precise observations and interpreted them mathematically. His analyses made the Copernican model of the universe the logical choice for rational thinkers. A new way of learning about the universe was emerging and it combined mathematics and physics. Yet the pathway to science was neither straight nor smooth as Galileo was soon to discover. Galileo was an early convert to Copernicus's theory. But, it was not until he created an improved version of a recent invention, the telescope, that he discovered sensational new astronomical facts: The moon had mountains and valleys; there were many more stars than previously thought; and most spectacularly, he found four previously unknown moons circling another planet.

Galileo (1564–1642)

Biography

Galileo was born in Pisa, near Florence, Italy. His father, Vincenzo, was a well-known musician who had also written works on music theory. As a young man, Galileo enrolled in a local monastery, but soon realized that lifestyle was not for him. With his father's help, he left the monastery and enrolled at the University of Pisa to study medicine. Galileo discovered that medicine, too, was not to his liking. He was attracted to mathematics, but never completed his degree at Pisa. Instead, he helped his father with his musical research, learned about the then new technique of perspective painting, and improved upon Archimedes' method of determining specific gravities. That, combined with the efforts of influential friends, won him an appointment as professor of mathematics at Pisa (Sharratt, 1996).

Contributions

At that time, professors of mathematics were at the low end of the academic prestige scale. Galileo's work in mathematics was one of the first steps that elevated that discipline's status, especially in the sciences. At Pisa, he taught mathematics and conducted basic research in local motion, especially the physics of falling bodies. He soon realized that Aristotelian physics was wrong; objects did not fall faster because of their weight. However, there is no evidence that he ever dropped balls of different weights from the Leaning Tower of Pisa in order to see if they hit the ground at the same time.

Several years later, Galileo left Pisa and took up a new position at the University of Padua in the Republic of Venice. It was there that he first heard rumors of a new device, the telescope, which allowed its users to see distant objects. He improved the design, increasing its power, and built a large number of telescopes and gave some to the Doge (ruler) of Venice who soon increased his salary. Galileo began to use his telescope to look at the night skies. Starting on January 7, 1610, he made the most momentous scientific discovery of his life. While looking at Jupiter he saw four other "stars" nearby, invisible to the naked eye. Over the next few nights he continued to observe them and noticed that they had moved. Then, one of them disappeared, only to reappear in a few days. His conclusion was startling; he had discovered moons, not stars. He sent Kepler a copy of his book describing the new moons, and Kepler quickly and enthusiastically responded. The discovery of moons on another planet made Tychonic theory much less likely and supported Copernicus's theory instead.

Soon after, Galileo capitalized on his discovery and engineered a return to Florence as a research professor (meaning he did not have to teach) of mathematics and philosophy for the Grand Duke of Tuscany. By now, he was famous throughout Europe. Biagioli (2007, p. 10) illustrated how completely Galileo's life changed after moving back to Florence:

> Different aspects of Galileo's move from Padua back to Florence have been singled out as emblematic of that transition: from university to court; from a tolerant republic to a pope-dependent absolutist state; from mathematician to philosopher; and from a modest salary and heavy teaching load to a generous paycheck and much free time…the

transition from Padua to Florence was not just between two jobs, two cities, or two titles, but between two different systems of exchange that attached credit and credibility to almost opposite practices.

Soon, however, his new position and his publication of his astronomical works would get him in near fatal trouble with the Inquisition.

The next year he spent a few months in Rome lecturing and visiting with Jesuit astronomers and members of Lyncean Academy, the earliest of the scientific learned societies (Sobel, 1999). Within a few years, however, Jesuits and other ecclesiastical authorities began to question whether Copernicus's theory was heretical. In 1616, Galileo went to Rome to try to defuse the situation. Unwisely, he attempted to argue from a theological point of view. That was a mistake because he was not trained in theology and resulted in his being warned not to "hold or defend" Copernican theory. Shortly after, Copernicus's book was placed on the *Index*. The Roman Catholic Church's attack on Copernicus' system was part of its larger response to the Reformation and was an integral part of the Counter Reformation.

Galileo himself was not suspected of heresy, nor was he in trouble with the Inquisition, yet. Over the next few years he quarreled in print with Jesuit authors over the locations and trajectories of three comets that had appeared in 1618. His last reply particularly offended the Roman Jesuits but not his friend, Pope Urban VII. After visiting with the Pope, Galileo believed that he could safely once again discuss Ptolemaic and Copernican theory in print provided he did so evenhandedly, treated them both as hypotheses, and did not invoke theological explanations. Thus, he began to write the book that led to his condemnation by the Inquisition. All along, however, he received the necessary permissions from the Catholic Church, and the Inquisition even approved the final manuscripts before publication.

BORDER WITH MATHEMATICS
POINT BLANK

It was Galileo who improved on the sector (see Photo 5.2), an early military instrument. The original model required gunnery officers to insert the sector into the barrel of their cannons and then adjust the elevations, exposing them to enemy fire. There were six settings or points between 0 and 45° of elevation on the sector. When the cannon was pointed directly at the target, the sector read 0 or "point blank range." Galileo improved upon the original sector by adding an adjustable foot so that the device could be used at the back of the cannon. He also provided a hinged pivot to make it more portable and added new scales. One of those scales allowed gunners to easily compute the amount of powder needed to fire projectiles made from a variety of materials, especially useful when shooting from newly captured enemy guns (Drake, 1976). Galileo's sector evolved into an early mathematical computing device capable, "of solving all the practical mathematical problems of the day" (p. 113). Galileo's sector was the forerunner to slide rules, mechanical calculators, and today's electronic devices. Science and measurement have been linked ever since.

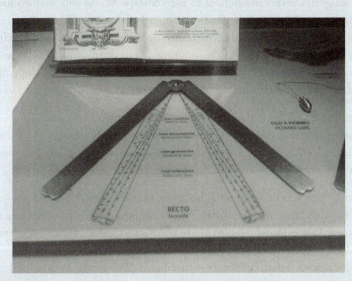

PHOTO 5.2 Galileo's Geometric and Military Sector (photo by the author)

BORDER WITH BIOLOGY
MICROBIOLOGY

The technology of telescopes, when inverted, created the compound (e.g., more than one lens) microscope. In Holland, an amateur scientist, Anthony Leeuwenhoek, crafted a large number of single lens microscopes and used them to discover bacteria, single-celled animals, and blood cells. He reported his findings to the Royal Society where Robert Hooke replicated and confirmed them with a compound microscope of his own design. Hooke's findings were published in 1665 as a book, *Micrographia*, the first major publication of the Royal Society. The book was a commercial success and inspired others to study the world of things too small to see with the naked eye. Once again, new instruments had revealed new facts, this time in biology.

Galileo's book, *Dialogue Concerning the Two Chief World Systems*, was published in 1632, and was an instant success. In it, three companions discussed the relative merits and defects of the Copernican and Ptolemaic models. One character, Salviati, took Galileo's positions; Simplicio took Aristotle's, and Sagredo acted as the host. The action of the book took place over four days of intense discussions at Sagredo's house. Soon, the Inquisition suspended the book, and Galileo was ordered to Rome. The book was obviously a defense of Copernican theory despite its many statements throughout to the contrary. Worse still, Galileo had Simplicio mouth an argument about tides that had come directly from Pope Urban, thus mocking him. Galileo was in deep trouble and had alienated his strongest supporter in the Church.

Galileo was now in the hands of the Inquisition. The warning of 1616 loomed large. His *Dialogue*, in the opinion of the inquisitors, did indeed "hold and defend" Copernican theory. Galileo was forced to recant his errors and to state (in part) that:

> I abjure, curse, and detest the aforesaid errors and heresies, and generally every other error, heresy, and sect whatsoever contrary to the said Holy Church, and I swear that in the future I will never again say or assert, verbally or in writing, anything that might furnish occasion for a similar suspicion regarding me.

His punishment was house arrest at his home near Florence. He could not leave without permission nor could he entertain visitors. The former injunction was upheld generally but the latter was less strictly enforced. Galileo did receive visitors including the Englishmen Thomas Hobbes and John Milton (Sharratt, 1996).

While under house arrest, Galileo wrote and dictated (his eyesight was failing) his last book, *Discourses and Mathematical Demonstrations Relating to Two New Sciences*. It was his *magnum opus* and cemented his place in history as the founder of post-Aristotelian physics and of the new discipline of materials science. In it he covered his life's work including technologies, the physics of motion, the strength of materials, and acceleration. The manuscript had to be smuggled out of Italy and secretly published in Holland, a country outside of the Inquisition's grasp. After his death, the Church prevented the erection of a monument in Florence honoring him because although he had died a good Catholic, he was suspected of heresy. In 1992, Pope John Paul and the Roman Catholic Church finally withdrew the charges of heresy against him.

Galileo, living in Italy, was subject to the full force of the Counter Reformation and the machinery of the Inquisition. In Protestant England, Isaac Newton would take the next steps toward the mathematization of science and toward the further elucidation of the wonders of the natural. His theory of universal gravitation along with his co-discovery of a new kind of mathematics, the calculus, would change physics and science itself forever.

PHOTO 5.3 Galileo

Credit: iStock/traveller1116

Isaac Newton (1643–1727)

Biography

Newton's father, a farmer from Lincolnshire County in England, died three months before his son, Isaac, was born. Newton's mother remarried when he was three years old and left him in the care of his maternal grandmother. Newton attended the local schools and later matriculated at Cambridge's Trinity College. There, his early academic record was unexceptional, but analyses of his personal library suggest that he studied topics beyond those required of beginning students. In his notebooks he recorded reading Descartes and Boyle (Hall, 1948). In addition he also showed himself to be a self-learner (Hall, 1992). In 1665, an outbreak of the plague forced Newton and his fellow students to abandon Cambridge for more than a year. Newton returned home and used the time away profitably thinking and experimenting about the calculus, optical theory, and gravity. Newton's thoughts about gravity were first inspired after he saw an apple fall during that time. Hall (p. 380) concluded his book by writing, "Really, the oddest thing in Newton's life is the fact that the story of the apple, known to everyone, is true."

Contributions

Newton returned to Cambridge a different man. Soon, others came to view him as a student of exceptional ability, especially in math. Newton continued to have wide interests, even to the extent of conducting alchemy experiments. At the age of 26, Newton became the second holder of the Lucasian chair of mathematics at Cambridge, and his first lectures were on optics. The Lucasian chair was endowed in 1663 by Henry Lucas. The first holder was Newton's mentor Isaac Barrow. Newton succeeded him and held the chair until 1702 when he resigned from Cambridge University. Since then, 16 other mathematicians have held the post. Stephen Hawking, a famous theoretical physicist, held the chair from 1980 to 2009. Michael Cates, an expert in the physics of soft matter, is the current holder of the chair.

After building and demonstrating the first reflecting telescope Newton was admitted into the Royal Society. His early years as a member were contentious because of attacks on his optical theories by Robert Hooke, who did not agree with Newton's corpuscular theory of light. So intense were their exchanges that Newton seriously considered giving up scientific work because it was not worth the aggravation. Fortunately for science, their quarrels moderated although they were never truly friendly with each other.

Hooke was working on finding a mechanism to explain Kepler's planetary mechanics and had an idea that the inverse square law might be the key, meaning that the force holding the planets in place decreased as the square of the distance between them and the sun. Hooke wrote Newton about his ideas, but Newton never responded. Later, Edmund Halley, the astronomer (Halley's Comet is named after him), was visiting Newton and asked him what shape a planet's orbit would have if it was under the inverse square law. Newton immediately responded that it would be an ellipse. Halley asked him how he knew and Newton said (Cohen, 1981, p. 169),

"I have calculated it." He immediately but unsuccessfully looked for the calculations, and then offered to recalculate them and send them to him.

That conversation is what brought Newton back into the study of gravity as it related to orbital mechanics. Newton's short response, later published by the Royal Society as *De Motu* (*On Motion*), explained the reason why the planets moved as Kepler had described. (However, Newton never explained what caused gravity itself. The explanation for the phenomenon of gravity is still a hot topic in modern physics.) Within a few years of publishing *De Motu*, Newton published his greatest scientific work, the *Principia Mathematica*. Because it was so heavily mathematical, it was difficult to read. Nevertheless, it was an immediate sensation. In it, Newton more fully explained the reasons behind orbital mechanics. He also presented his three laws of motion. His First Law stated that objects at rest remain at rest, while objects in motion remain in motion provided they are not affected by an external force. His Second Law stated that motion and force are proportional and that the force applied will cause motion in the direction of the force. His Third Law stated that every action has an equal and opposite reaction. Newton's laws of motion have persisted, nearly unaltered, until the present day and are used daily by scientists and engineers. While still an undergraduate at Cambridge, Newton had read Descartes's *Principia Philosophiae*. Hetherington (2006, p. 154) wrote:

> The title page [of Newton's *Principia*] reflects Newton's intent to refute Descartes's philosophical principles, which had appeared under the title of *Principia Philosophiae*. Descartes's title is incorporated in Newton's, and lest readers miss the allusion, set in boldface and larger type. In the third edition, the words *Philosophiae and Principia* were in scarlet color.

Newton was reacting to Descartes's explanation for planetary movement based upon massive interplanetary whirlpools, for which Descartes had provided little, if any, empirical proof. Quite consciously, Newton was attempting to provide a mathematical basis for natural philosophy.

Newton eventually left Cambridge and worked first as warden and later as lord of the Mint. He applied himself to that job as no one had before. Counterfeiting and clipping (cutting bits off coins) were endemic. Newton oversaw the introduction of new techniques of coinage designed to reduce and counter those crimes. After being given police powers, he vigorously prosecuted counterfeiters and clippers (Craig, 1963). Chaloner, one such criminal, ended up being hanged, drawn, and quartered following Newton's second prosecution of him (Hall, 1992).

One controversy that followed Newton for nearly all of his adult life was his claim of priority over the discovery of the calculus. Gottfried Wilhelm Leibniz, a German philosopher and mathematician, also claimed priority. The notation used in modern calculus, however, belongs to Leibniz. Today, most historians agree that both invented the calculus independently. Then, as now, the scientist who first discovers a phenomenon receives the credit for the discovery. Many of the psychological phenomena to be examined in later chapters will reveal such priorities as in the Darwin–Wallace theory of evolution, Young–Helmholtz theory of color vision, and the Bell–Magendie law in physiology. Regardless of priority, Reyes (2004, p. 161) argued that the effects of the discovery of calculus and its infinitesimals ranged far beyond mathematics:

> Newton's and Leibniz's Calculus was the moving-picture stage for mathematicians and scientists; it allowed mathematicians, physicists, astronomers, and countless others to move beyond the study of finites paces and fixed points and into the world of movement, change, and the infinite.

Newton wrote, "If I have seen further it is by standing on the shoulders of giants." Most likely he meant the shoulders of Copernicus, Kepler, Galileo, Halley, and others. Dolnick (2011), however, suggested that Newton's remark was also a jibe against Hooke because he was short and practically a hunchback. Cohen (1994) argued that the effect Newton's physics had on social science is limited to style and metaphor. He labelled attempts by social sciences to emulate Newton as "Newtoniamism" and wrote that social scientists, "never succeeded in producing a satisfactory Newtonian model for a social science on the levels of identity, analogy, or homology (p. 75)" Mjøset (2001) provided four models for social science theorizing and showed how they differed from the natural science models derived from Newton's theorizing. He concluded (p. 15647), that four approaches to social science theorizing existed, "the law-oriented approach focuses on theory testing, the idealizing approach on modeling, the constructivist approach on theory formation, and the critical approach on ethical reflection." Newton's physical "laws" inspired scientists in a wide variety of disciplines, including social science, but creating theories yielding such laws in other disciplines, notably psychology, biology, or economics, has not happened.

Newton, interestingly, wrote more on non-scientific topics than he did on scientific ones. His published and unpublished manuscripts of his reveal a deep interest in religious topics. His unpublished writings were especially concerned with deciphering secrets in Scripture. Newton strongly believed in God and believed that his scientific work had helped uncover the presence of God and his works. Newton never believed that such a perfect physical scheme as the universe could have come to exist without

PHOTO 5.4 Newton

Credit: iStock/GeorgiosArt

God. That being said, Newton's personal beliefs about religion were strongly at variance with Anglican theology. In some of his nonscientific writings it was obvious that he was not a Trinitarian and may even have espoused views that others would have easily labeled heretical (Robinson, 2017).

One thing is clear, Newton bequeathed to the world theories that would keep other scientists occupied up to the present day. Some of those scientists attempted to apply Newtonian analyses to human beings as well. Newton's contemporaries John Locke and Adam Smith were among the first true social scientists. By the 19th century, inspired by Newton and others, psychologists, too, would attempt to search for laws of behavior.

LEARNING OBJECTIVE

9. List the progression of astronomical knowledge and equipment from Brahe to Newton.

BORDER WITH SOCIAL SCIENCE
ARCHEOLOGY, ANTHROPOLOGY, AND POLITICAL SCIENCE

While it is not possible to stretch the origins of psychology back to the Renaissance, it is possible to trace the distant origins of several social sciences back to that period. Rowe (1965) named Ciriaco de' Pizzicolli as the founder of archeology. Pizzicolli was inspired by the humanist's reverence for the past and described his work as, "restoring the dead to life" (p. 10). Rowe also credits Lorenzo Valla as the founder of linguistics and as someone who initiated an interest in cultural differences. The explorations of Africa and the New World heightened that interest; the writings of some Spanish explorers were remarkably objective. Farr (1988) traced the origins of, "the historically inductive study of *realpolitik*" (p. 1178) to Machiavelli while ceding the primacy for the study of practical politics to Aristotle. However, these very early manifestations of social science did not fully bloom into well-developed disciplines until the 19th century. Between the Renaissance and the Enlightenment philosophers battled over the proper approach to the scientific study of the social sciences.

RELIGIOUS INTOLERANCE

In 1600, the Roman Inquisition remanded Giordano Bruno to the secular authorities to be burned as a heretic. Bruno was a Dominican friar who had long been suspected of heretical views. Years before his execution he had fled Italy for France and later to England. McKnight

(1989) argued that Bruno saw Copernicus as a modern-day John the Baptist paving the way for Bruno's "messianic role" (p. 80). Bruno was an advocate of the ancient Egyptian religion and had argued that, "the Egyptian religion was the highest religion given by God" (p. 84). Bruno saw Copernicus more as a messenger reclaiming ancient knowledge than as a scientist and astronomer. After traveling throughout much of Europe, Bruno was invited to Venice by a nobleman, Giovanni Mocenigo, to teach him about memory and invention. Bruno hoped to secure the very same chair in mathematics later offered to Galileo. But, Mocenigo denounced Bruno on multiple charges to the Venetian Inquisition. He was arrested the next day. During the trial, the inquisitors learned that Bruno had once been a friar, that he had met with Protestants, read forbidden books, and had himself written books deemed as heretical. To avoid more trouble with the Inquisition, he confessed his errors and promised to halt such behavior in the future (Finocciaro, 2017). However, the Roman Inquisition then demanded the opportunity to question him as well. After seven years of imprisonment and questioning, the Roman Inquisition branded him a heretic. However, it is not likely that he was condemned because of his advocacy of Copernicanism. More likely, his condemnation and execution was due to his writings that argued against many central tenets of Catholicism. Aquilecchia (2017, p. 6) offered, "Giordano Bruno can legitimately be considered not only as a Renaissance philosopher, but as *the* (original italics) Renaissance philosopher par excellence."

Michael Servetus was burned at the stake in Geneva in 1553 on Calvin's orders. Servetus was a Spanish physician who had published books attacking the Trinity. After seeing the negative reaction caused by his books, he took a pseudonym, Michael Villanovanus and became a translator living in France. However, he could not resist writing Calvin and arguing with him, via correspondence, about the nature of Christianity. Calvin realized that he was corresponding with Servetus and adopted a pseudonym of his own. Calvin kept all of Servetus's letters and confided to others that if Servetus were to come to Geneva, "I will not suffer him to get out alive" (Ozment, 1980, p. 370). The Inquisition caught Servetus in France, but did not have enough evidence to convict him until, somehow, his letters to Calvin mysteriously showed up in France. He was promptly declared a heretic but managed to escape. He crossed the border into Switzerland and appeared in Geneva at one of Calvin's sermons. He was promptly arrested, tried, and burned. (His effigy was also burned by Catholics, *in absentia*, in France (Cattermole, 1997). Thus, intolerance was not solely the property of one version of Christianity. Both Catholics and Protestants were highly intolerant of deviations from their versions of orthodoxy. Thus, throughout most of Europe, philosophy was a dangerous occupation.

LEARNING OBJECTIVE
10. Identify some modern examples of intolerance, religious or otherwise.

THE EARLIEST NEW PHILOSOPHERS

Rene Descartes in France and Francis Bacon in England were among the first to break from Scholasticism and its methods albeit quite differently. Descartes searched for secure, universal knowledge that was independent of sensory observations. Bacon promoted the role of sensory observations and proposed a radical form of empiricism called induction. Both proposed to resolve the problems of classical philosophy, and modern philosophy and psychology are still affected by their competing visions. Descartes received a traditional Scholastic education and was an accomplished mathematician. A series of dreams he had as a young man, however, convinced him to attempt nothing less than a complete revision of all knowledge and the method for obtaining it.

Rene Descartes (1596–1650)

Biography

Rene Descartes was born in La Haye, France (the town was renamed Descartes in his honor in 1967). Many of the men in his family, including his father, were lawyers and they expected him to follow in that tradition. He attended the college at La Fleche where he received a classical education although his teachers were aware of the new scientific discoveries. While Descartes was a student his teachers celebrated the first anniversary of Galileo's discovery of the moons of Jupiter. Nevertheless, the physics taught at La Fleche remained thoroughly Aristotelian. Descartes attended the University of Poitiers where he received a degree in law. After graduation, he served briefly as a soldier, most likely as a military engineer. During that time he met the Dutch mathematician Isaac Beeckman who encouraged Descartes's interest in mathematics. One of the products of that meeting was Descartes's elucidation of the basic principles of analytic geometry.

BORDER WITH COMPUTATIONAL SCIENCE
ANALYTIC GEOMETRY

Legend has it that the inspiration for analytic geometry came to Descartes while he was in bed watching a fly buzz around a room. True or not, modern analytic geometry did not spring fully fledged from Descartes's mind. Instead, he showed that some problems in geometry could be solved algebraically. Later mathematicians developed the now familiar x, y, & z coordinate system using his notation. Although Descartes's analytic geometry was not fully developed, his contribution to mathematics was profoundly important to the later development of the calculus by Newton and Leibniz. Without Descartes's early steps the later mathematization of physics would have been delayed. In the 19th century, the x, y, & z coordinate system was named "Cartesian" in his honor (see Figure 5.5). Interestingly, Descartes never used the full two-dimensional plane. Instead, he restricted himself only to the positive number part; also, he rejected the use of negative numbers (Amadeo, 2018).

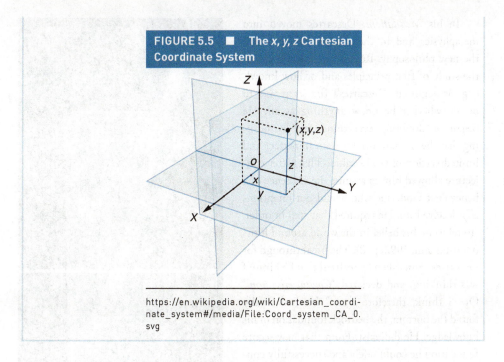

FIGURE 5.5 ■ The *x, y, z* Cartesian Coordinate System

https://en.wikipedia.org/wiki/Cartesian_coordinate_system#/media/File:Coord_system_CA_0.svg

One night, while he was still a soldier, Descartes had three vivid dreams. When he awoke he realized that he had a new mission in life: to completely revise how knowledge was acquired. He began with natural philosophy (physics), a project that took many years. Eventually, he moved to the Netherlands where he spent the longest portion of his life and did the majority of his writing. He withheld publication of his ambitious project titled, *The World,* after he heard of Galileo's condemnation by the Inquisition. In that never published work Descartes placed Copernicus's theory of a moving earth front and center.

Contributions

In 1637 Descartes published his *Discourse on the Method.* In it he outlined the basics of his new system for seeking knowledge and appended three other important works: *Optics, Meteorology,* and *Geometry*; those provided concrete examples of his scientific research. In his research on optics, Descartes explained the phenomenon of refraction. Photo 5.5 shows how a pencil appears to be broken when immersed in a glass of water. Descartes would later use this phenomenon to explain his approach to the proper methods for gathering knowledge. Central to his later thinking was the fact that the immersed object only looked broken; the information presented by the senses was false. However, the mathematically derived rules explaining the phenomenon were true. Physics, Descartes realized, needed a firm metaphysical foundation in order to explain discordant results such as those.

In his *Meditations*, Descartes moved into metaphysics and in the process helped found the new philosophy. Recall that metaphysics is the study of first principles and of how knowledge is acquired. Descartes's first step was to decide whether he knew anything at all. He began by doubting everything and by positing that the human mind was an imperfect and limited version of God's mind. That latter conjecture allowed him to assume the existence of a benevolent God, one who would not intentionally deceive him. He required that step in order, "to reinstate his belief in the world around him" (Cottingham, 1992, p. 8). The breakthrough for Descartes came when he realized that he himself was thinking, and declared *"Cogito, ergo sum."* Or, "I think, therefore I am." He had finally found the bottom, the bedrock foundation of his knowledge. He did exist. From that new secure foundation he could safely and successfully construct his new system of knowledge.

Descartes then moved on to divide the world into two parts. The external, physical part was composed only of matter, and no longer possessed Aristotle's ten qualities (see Chapter 3), which meant that physicists could now legitimately study matter mechanistically by measuring its

PHOTO 5.5 Snell's Law
Credit: Edward Kardas

size, shape, position, and motion. Descartes realized that traditional followers of Aristotle's physics would object and ignore his new approach, so he continued to avoid publishing about controversial topics such as Copernicus's heliocentric model. He was extremely conscious of the danger of being branded a heretic, or worse, an atheist, charges that could be leveled as easily by Catholics or Protestants. The other part of the world was mind. To Descartes, the human mind was not material. Instead, it was an internal, immaterial, and independent entity. The mind could think, imagine, and sense. It operated on ideas and possessed a will that allowed it to seek pleasure or avoid pain. Descartes had defined one of the most persistent of all modern philosophical questions, the mind–body problem.

The Mind–Body Problem

Descartes's division of the world into body and mind was revolutionary. Physics now could concentrate on the body half and only concern itself with the material parts of the universe.

Furthermore, mathematics could explain the workings of the universe beyond all doubt using only the minimum of measurable variables: the size, shape, position, and motion of objects. The mind was where variables such as color, sounds, smells, and tastes originated. Those variables were highly individualized and could not be explained with the same mathematical precision and rigor. In time, many philosophers would refer to size, shape, position, and speed as primary qualities and to color, smells, and tastes as secondary qualities. Descartes was left with the problem of explaining how body and mind interacted.

Descartes's solution to the mind–body problem is called **interactionism**, a type of dualism. He believed that both body and mind existed and that each affected the other. In his *Discourse on methods and meditations,* he wrote (Descartes, 1912/1637, p. 139):

> I here remark, in the first place, that there is a vast difference between mind and body, in respect that body, from its nature, is always divisible, and that mind is entirely indivisible. For in truth, when I consider the mind, that is, when I consider myself in so far only I am a thinking thing, I can distinguish in myself no parts, but I very clearly discern that I am somewhat absolutely one and entire; and although the whole mind seems to be united to the whole body, yet, when a foot, or an arm, or any other part, is cut off, I am conscious that nothing has been taken away from my mind;

The mechanism behind Descartes's interactive dualism was hard to explain. How could an immaterial mind affect a material body and vice versa? Descartes struggled to explain the relationship to his critics but was never completely successful. He claimed that the pineal gland of the brain was the locus where his interactionism occurred. But, his explanations involving animal spirits moving through hollow tubes (e.g., nerves), soon proved inadequate. His theory, was inspired by the moving statues at the royal gardens at St. Germain; they moved because of water pumped in or out of tubes. To explain reflexes mechanistically in both humans and animals he believed that nerves, too, were hollow tubes filled with animal spirits, a liquid (see Figure 5.6). So, when an external stimulus such as a fire heated the spirits, they pushed on the pineal gland, which in turn sent animal spirits down another nerve tube, moving the affected body part. But, he distinguished between humans and animals by assigning a mind only to humans. Animals, he believed, had no minds and behaved exclusively as the result of mechanistic principles. Nearly all of the details of Descartes's physics failed to stand the test of time. For example, Newton's theories of gravitation quickly superseded Descartes vortex theory of planetary and satellite motion (Hetherington, 2006). His mind–body distinction, however, has lasted until the present day. Later philosophers have proposed other solutions to the mind–body problem, including the monistic solutions (e.g., either mind *or* body) of idealism and materialism and the dualistic solutions (e.g., mind *and* body) of epiphenomenalism, occasionalism, parallelism, double aspectism, and pre-established harmony. These solutions will be examined later in this and other chapters.

FIGURE 5.6 ■ Descartes's Reflex Action

Source: Descartes, R. (1664). Traites de l'homme

https://commons.wikimedia.org/wiki/File:Descartes-reflex.JPG

FYI

Descartes and the Reflex

Descartes attempted to explain reflex action using a hydraulic model. He believed that nerves were hollow tubes filled with liquid, animal spirits (see Figure 5.6). When an external stimulus such as the heat from a fire became too intense the spirits pushed on the pineal gland, which in turn sent animal spirits down another nerve tube, moving the affected body part. The moving statues at the royal gardens at St. Germain inspired Descartes's hydraulic model of nerve action. The movement of those statues was caused by water pumped in or out of hydraulic tubes. Descartes sought to explain reflexes mechanistically in both humans and animals. He also distinguished between humans and animals by assigning a mind only to humans. Animals, he believed, had no minds and behaved exclusively as the result of mechanistic principles.

Descartes's Later Life and Legacy

The necessity of nearly constantly defending himself and his ideas eventually led to Descartes leaving the Netherlands. He reluctantly accepted an offer from Queen Christina of Sweden to serve in her court. One reason for his hesitancy was that Sweden was a Protestant country (Descartes remained a lifelong Catholic.). After arriving there, things got worse. For one, he was used to spending mornings in bed. Queen Christina, however, ordered him to give her lessons in philosophy at 5 a.m. In the cold morning air Descartes soon took sick, worsened, and died of pneumonia. He was first buried in Stockholm but later reburied in Paris in the Abbey of St. Germain-des-Pres.

PHOTO 5.6 Descartes

Credit: iStock/CampWillowLake

Descartes's legacy in philosophy was vast. Not only was he the founder of the new philosophy, he also inspired other philosophers to complete and refine his rationalist approach to philosophy or create new philosophies to counter it. Another measure of Descartes's legacy was the fact that the Catholic Church placed all of his books on the *Index*, the list of prohibited works, in 1633 where they remained until the *Index* itself was abolished in 1966. Descartes's discovery of analytical geometry, alone, would have made him a historically prominent mathematician. Descartes himself, however, might have considered his physics his greatest legacy for it was his greatest passion. It is ironic that physics was where his ideas lasted the least amount of time.

BORDER WITH SOCIAL SCIENCE
THE MIND–BODY PROBLEM AND SCIENTIFIC PROGRESS

The synergy between physics, mathematics, and the mind–body problem proved advantageous to physical science. Descartes's separation of body from mind meant that sciences whose subject matters could be studied by measuring the primary qualities only quickly prospered. Thus, first physics and later chemistry developed quickly. Those disciplines could be profitably studied by only examining the physical universe.

Descartes envisioned all of natural philosophy as a tree, with metaphysical roots, a philosophical trunk, and branches of medicine, mechanics, and morals. For Descartes, psychology and the other social sciences would first emerge from moral philosophy. Descartes saw that branch of his tree as being concerned with passions and their control along with methods of directing the will toward good and away from evil. Unlike natural philosophy, moral philosophy required study of both mind and body. Paradoxically, physics and the other "hard" sciences have had a smoother historical path; they have only had to cope with the body, the external and physical half of the mind–body problem. The social sciences, on the other hand, have had to cope with both halves of the problem, a more difficult and bumpy road.

In England, living at about the same time as Descartes, Francis Bacon was planting the first seeds for the philosophy of empiricism. Like Descartes, Bacon wished to put an end to Scholasticism and its methods. Unlike Descartes, however, Bacon firmly believed in the primacy of sensory knowledge. But he also understood that nature could easily deceive naive or unprepared observers. Bacon's main contributions were describing a system by which scientists could avoid making observational errors, classifying the sciences, and proposing ways for scientists to collaborate with each other.

Francis Bacon (1561–1626)

Biography

Bacon was born in London. His father was the Lord Keeper of the Seal, one of the highest political offices in England. Francis Bacon received a classic scholastic education at Cambridge's Trinity College and later became a lawyer at Gray's Inn, one of the four Inns of the Court (law schools) in London. Soon after he traveled throughout Europe with the English ambassador to Paris. Bacon's trip was cut short by the death of his father. His inheritance was small and he was financially troubled throughout his life. He served in Parliament and pursued high office in government unsuccessfully until the accession of James I. Bacon eventually became Lord Keeper of the Seal and later Lord Chancellor, the highest office under the king. Soon after, however, his career in government ended in disgrace following a bribery scandal. He spent his last years writing the works that made him famous. He died of pneumonia perhaps contracted after performing an experiment to see if snow might slow the rotting of a fowl.

Contributions

Bacon was the first to write a book on philosophy in English, *The Advancement of Learning*. In it he separated theology from philosophy and divided the faculties of mind into categories of history, imagination, and reason. Bacon believed that the only proper role for theology was to prove the existence of God. Philosophy's job was to elucidate the wonders of God's creation. Humans had the intellectual ability to do so, but only if they adopted a new way of understanding the world. Bacon revived and expanded the logical method of induction while at the same time diminishing the role of the syllogism, Aristotle's principal method of logical deduction.

Bacon believed that scientists could successfully understand the world through the use of their senses. However, he maintained that scientific facts could only be obtained if sensory information was collected properly. Thus, he discounted reports of phenomena that could not be repeated. He railed against the use of vague or imprecise words such as "moist," the lumping together of different things in the same category (e.g., anything that swam was a fish), and the improper division of similar things into different categories (e.g., ice, water, and steam not being the same substance). He noted that all humans were inherently biased and proposed methods to control for such biases. In his book, the *New Organon*, he explained those biases via four "idols." His idols were not false deities. Instead they were more like false or clouded images. Each idol, if not accounted for, would lead to falsehoods derived from observations. Furthermore, the action of the idols was so subtle as to be nearly unnoticeable or even unconscious.

The four idols were of the Tribe, the Cave, the Market Place, and the Theatre. These idols are surprisingly modern, and have (under different terminology) become part and parcel of the scientific method. The idol of the Tribe refers to errors in perception commonly made by all humans. They include sensory errors, correctable by multiple observers or instrumentation (reliability); jumping to conclusions based upon small samples (small N); and looking to confirm preconceived notions (confirmation bias). The idol of the Cave derives from culture and individual differences. Thus, families, schools, religions, gender, and social class can easily and subtly alter people's perceptions of the same observation (context effects). The idol of the Market Place comes from social interactions and miscommunication; slang and jargon being two prominent examples. Another example was the use of words to describe things that did not exist, such as the *crystalline spheres* of Ptolemaic cosmology. There, the words and reality were completely divorced (jargon). The idol of the Theatre was mainly directed at competing systems of philosophy, especially Scholasticism. Those systems produced theories akin to theatrical productions that required viewers to suspend belief while watching the actions on stage. Such philosophies were based on speculation, small numbers of unsupported observations, or the confounding of theology with philosophy (pseudoscience).

The methodology Bacon proposed to address the problems of biased observation was a new kind of induction. He did not just want scientists to observe the world; he wanted them to do it in a way that would guarantee accurate results or facts. Those facts would then become the reliable databases for all sciences. His next step was to develop tables showing how the facts collected were related to each other. The tables he recommended compiling would establish the presence, absence, or degree of common factors among the large number of observations. In other words, he was looking for a primitive type of correlation. The Pearson product-moment correlation coefficient, *r,* was not developed until the 19th century (see Chapter 7). Strasser (2019) argued that modern scientific databases such as the World Protein Data Bank, GenBank, or Online Mendelian Inheritance in Man where scientists share their findings harken back to the efforts of earlier collectors of specimens. The difference between those older collections and the modern databases is that the latter are much more accessible to the scientific community.

Tellingly, Bacon realized that contradictions of observations were much more logically important than confirmations. Bacon, however, never understood that the scientific practices of his contemporary fellow scientists, who with the exception of Tycho Brahe, were much less systematic and more *ad hoc* (meaning they lacked a comprehensive theoretical backing). Bacon also never proposed a role for the hypothesis, an essential feature of the scientific method. In his utopian novel, the *New Atlantis*, he proposed another idea became an essential feature of modern science, the close collaboration of scientists living and working communally. That idea led, indirectly, to the founding of the Royal Society and the subsequent founding of similar scientific societies such as the American Psychological Association and the Association for Psychological Science.

Bacon was prescient again when he divided science into two categories: theoretical and applied. Physics was theoretical and mechanics was applied. Early on, he saw the intimate relationship between science and technology. Bacon (1960/1620, Book One, p. cxix) wrote:

> Printing, gunpowder, and the compass: These three have changed the whole face and state of things throughout the world; the first in literature, the second in warfare, the third in navigation; whence have followed innumerable changes, in so much that no empire, no sect, nor star seems to have exerted greater power and influence in human affairs than these mechanical discoveries.

Bacon might well have understood and applauded the ever increasing pace of technology in the Internet age. In England, Bacon's ideas fell on fertile ground and inspired generations of philosophers and scientists. His ideas contrasted sharply with those of Descartes and set up a long-running and dynamic conflict between empiricism and rationalism.

THEN AND NOW
APS WIKIPEDIA INITIATIVE

That Baconian ideal has taken a new turn in the 21st century as the Association for Psychological Science (APS), as part of its APS Wikipedia Initiative, has urged its members to:

- Ensure that articles about psychological research and theory are accurate, up-to-date, complete, and written in a style appropriate for the general public
- Ensure that articles are based on independent reliable secondary sources
- Represent scientific controversies and scientific consensus fairly, writing articles in a neutral style
- Improve and review articles to Good Article and Featured Article quality
- Assess psychology-related articles and tag them appropriately when there are problems

APS members may, thus, give away psychology through one of the Internet's most read sources while helping to assure that Wikipedia's articles on psychology are reliable and timely. Marentette (2014) described an assignment she gave her students. They had to achieve 'good article' status from Wikipedia's editors. They succeeded but found that had to learn and hew to Wikipedia's standards of: neutral point of view, verifiable sources, and the avoidance of primary research. Bacon would be proud.

LEARNING OBJECTIVE

11. Differentiate the approaches to understanding the world taken by Descartes and Bacon.

THE ENGLISH CIVIL WARS (1642–1651) AND THEIR CONSEQUENCES

Bacon died before the outbreak of the English Civil Wars that affected England, Ireland, and Scotland nearly simultaneously. The wars altered the lives and fortunes of two empiricists: Thomas Hobbes and John Locke. Both were forced into exile for long periods and the social and political disruption caused by the wars influenced their thoughts and writings. Historians still debate the causes of the wars and their long-term effects. Most agree, however, that issues such as the divine right of kings to rule, religious toleration, and civil rights were central (Braddick, 2008). While the English Civil Wars were brutal and vicious, they paled in comparison to the brutality, viciousness, and extent of the Thirty Years' War (1618–1648) in Europe. Thomas Hobbes and John Locke lived through these events and personally had to grapple with the successive changes in political systems. It is small wonder that their writings were in large measure political as well as philosophical.

LEARNING OBJECTIVE

12. Discuss how the English Civil Wars (e.g., big history) affected the intellectual zeitgeist of Great Britain.

THE BRITISH EMPIRICISTS

Thomas Hobbes (1588–1679)

Biography

Hobbes was born in Malmesbury, England, at the same time as the arrival of the Spanish Armada in 1588. In his autobiography he described his birth with these words, "my mother was filled with such fear that she bore twins, me and together with me fear" (Martinich, 1999, p. 2). His father, Thomas Sr., was a local clergyman who had a bad disposition and not much learning. After a fight with another clergyman, Thomas Sr. fled for London. By the time of that incident, his son had already enrolled in Oxford's Magdalen Hall, thanks to the generosity of his uncle. After graduating from Oxford, he began a lifelong association with a rich and noble family, the Cavendishes. Hobbes's first assignment was as tutor to William Cavendish who was only a few years his junior. Together, they embarked on the first of Hobbes's three **grand tours**. At Oxford, Hobbes had excelled in translation from Latin and Greek. He returned to Europe twice more as a tutor. On his third tour (1634–1636) he met Galileo in Florence, and Pierre Gassendi and Marin Mersenne in Paris. Through Mersenne he learned of Descartes and became one of the commentators to his *Meditations*. At that point, Hobbes was just beginning to develop an interest in philosophy. He later met and corresponded with Descartes but they misunderstood each other and eventually ceased contact (Sorell, 1988).

Contributions

Hobbes disagreed with Descartes over a number of important issues, the most important being Descartes's notion of a separate and incorporeal (existing without a physical substrate) mind. Hobbes was a **materialist**. For him, everything, including God, had to possess a physical existence. Thus, Hobbes was categorically opposed to Descartes's dualism and Descartes's use of God's beneficence as an essential support mechanism for Cartesian philosophy. However, Hobbes agreed with Descartes that philosophy should proceed from rationalistic precepts. Hobbes believed that motions were the cause of everything, including sensations. Thus, in vision, particles of light hit the eye, which in turn caused parts of the brain to move. Those movements of the brain, not the image itself, constituted perception. Like Descartes, and unlike Bacon, Hobbes minimized the importance of sensory experience.

Hobbes's greatest contribution to philosophy, however, lay in his analysis of politics. After his return to England in the years immediately following the Civil Wars he began to write about the relationship between humans and their governments. As a thought experiment, he suggested that prior to the formation of governments humans must have lived in a *state of nature,* a hypothetical primordial state where there were no laws and all, including women, were equal. The state of nature was **relativistic**, chaotic, and even anarchistic; there was no way of distinguishing between good or evil. Hobbes, in his *Leviathan*, famously described life as, "solitary, poor, nasty, brutish, and short." The only right in people had was that of self-preservation, regardless if they were in the state of nature or under a government. The relativism of the state of nature combined with self-preservation led to chaos and a state of constant war as people either retaliated, or worse, preemptively attacked each other.

Hobbes wrote that the only way out to escape the brutality of life and to achieve peace was to voluntarily surrender liberties to an absolute monarch. In turn, the monarch would issue and enforce laws, thus ensuring peace. Under this system, there would be no relativism; all would accede to the monarch's view of good and evil, right and wrong. As long as the monarch kept the governed safe and sound, the agreement would hold. Although Hobbes never used the term, this was the first instance of a **social contract**. John Locke and others would modify and expand that concept greatly. Social contracts are part of the modern *zeitgeist* and have expanded and multiplied since Hobbes's day.

After the Civil Wars broke out, Hobbes, a royalist, felt threatened by Parliament and moved to France where he remained for 11 years. There, he began to write *Leviathan*, his major work. As it was coming into press in London, conditions in England had stabilized sufficiently so he felt safe in returning. *Leviathan*, unlike his earlier works, was fiercely anti-Catholic. He did not wish to remain in France, a country subject to the Inquisition after its publication (Martinich, 1999).

Hobbes spent the rest of his long life in England and renewed his contact with the Cavendish family. He never renounced his views on absolute monarchy but he did provide a mechanism by which former royalists could morally accept the legitimacy of the Parliamentary government. That mechanism, *de facto theory,* held that any government in power that was providing for the public's safety, was legitimate and should be obeyed. Later, the same principle applied to Parliamentarians after the Restoration of Charles II. Hobbes, although pleasant enough in person, was contentious in print and did not like admitting his errors. That attitude prevented him from attaining membership in the newly chartered Royal Society. Compounding that was his belief that experimentation was useless and a waste of money. In the end, he outlived nearly all of his friends and enemies and died peacefully at the Cavendish estate.

Hobbes's contributions were many. He was a scientist, mathematician, and philosopher. His conception of human psychology was limited. He believed that people were motivated more by passion than by reason. His analyses of the social psychology of the governed and the government were original and inspired others to promote alternative theories. He believed that thinking was computation, an idea now prominent in artificial intelligence and cognitive science (see Chapter 13). Like Descartes, Hobbes served as an inspiration or a target for future philosophers. In England, his one time student, John Locke, would turn Hobbes's ideas on their ear and firmly reject his notions about the state of nature, role of government, and character of the social contract. Locke sought to apply the methods of natural science to the understanding of people.

John Locke (1632–1704)

Biography

Locke was born in Wrington, England. His father was a rural lawyer and had fought on the side of Parliament early in the Civil Wars. Locke attended the prestigious Westminster School thanks to the sponsorship of his father's commander, who had become a Member of Parliament. Locke was named a King's Scholar and attended Oxford's Christ Church College. After graduation he stayed on as a faculty member teaching Greek, and later, rhetoric. At Oxford he received the traditional scholastic education but fell in with a group of scientists—John Wilkins, Robert Boyle, and Robert Hooke—all who later became founding members of the Royal Society. They taught him how to study nature and exposed him to their atomic theory. After, Locke read Descartes and Bacon and met Newton; he and Newton became lifelong friends.

Contributions

Locke's life changed dramatically after he met Anthony Ashley-Cooper, Lord Shaftesbury. They became friends and Locke began to work for him as his secretary. Shaftesbury was a member of the Board of Trade, the agency responsible for governing the American colonies. Shaftesbury and Locke drafted the constitution for the Carolina colonies in America; Locke learned much about government from Shaftesbury and later published books on the relationship of the people to their government. Locke also began to work on his most famous work, *An Essay on Human Understanding*, while he was working for Shaftesbury. After Shaftesbury left the government, Locke returned to Oxford and obtained his medical degree. He then visited France for nearly a year and a half. There he visited with French Protestants (the Huguenots) during the time when the Edict of Nantes was still in force. That law provided for religious toleration of Protestants in

Catholic France. Later, and after Locke was no longer in France, Louis XIV would repeal that law and persecute the Huguenots.

Religious problems awaited Locke upon his return to England as well. Shaftesbury had become one of the leaders of a movement to deny James, Charles II's son, from the line of royal succession because James wished to reintroduce Catholicism to England. Parliament's House of Commons voted that measure in but the House of Lords did not, so it failed. Eventually, Charles's son took the throne as James II. Before then, Shaftesbury, and later, Locke, fled for Holland to avoid arrest for treason. Locke spent five years in Holland and finished writing his *Essay on Human Understanding.* He returned to England in 1688 after the Glorious Revolution. From that point on, he was, and continues to be, one of England's most famous thinkers. He again served on the re-established Board of Trade and helped govern the American colonies. Interestingly, much of the language contained in the American Declaration of Independence is Lockean. Many of the founding fathers had read his books.

Locke claimed that the idea for his famous essay came to him one night back when he was working for Shaftesbury. Locke and some friends had been debating long into the night when he realized that he could not answer the questions they were asking him about human knowledge. He decided:

> that before we set ourselves upon inquiries of that nature, it was necessary to examine our own abilities, and see what objects our understandings were, or were not, fitted to deal with (Locke, 1975/1689, p. 7).

In his essay, Locke attempted to bring human understanding into the realm of natural philosophy. Quite consciously, Locke was trying to put together a science of psychology. Ultimately, he failed and was criticized by later philosophers over the inconsistency of some of his ideas. Berkeley and Hume, fellow empiricists, especially questioned some of Locke's assumptions and conclusions. Despite those objections, Locke's essay helped transform England and, later, the world. Ryle (1967, p. 3) emphasized Locke's influence when he wrote:

> If we could fly back in a time-rocket to England in 1700, we could already breathe its air, and we could already converse with our new acquaintances without feeling lost. In the England of, say, 1600, we should gasp like fishes out of water.

Obviously, Locke had helped to completely transform the intellectual landscape of his time. Billig (2008, p. 28), too, argued:

> The idea of Locke as the founder of modern psychology is simultaneously modern and non-modern. The intellectual parent must be distinct from the children. Had Locke been totally modern, he would have been a 'proper psychologist', rather than 'the father of psychology'. Present psychologists will supposedly recognize parts of their own activities in the distant parent's work.

As a proto-psychologist Locke first argued against Descartes's notions of innate knowledge, while admitting for limited forms of pre-existing knowledge such as the existence of God and geometric theorems. But, the rest of knowledge had to be acquired through experience. Here is where he invoked his famous metaphor of the *tabula rasa,* the blank slate (see Figure 5.7). Experience, Locke argued, is like the chalk marks that eventually fill and cover the slate that is our mind. The mind is full of ideas, Locke maintained. Simple ideas come directly from sensation and can be combined by association into complex ideas by reflection and memory. Nowhere, however, did Locke ever provide mechanisms for his theory. Many philosophers after Locke also invoked associationism as a mechanism to explain their own theories. Ivan Pavlov, early in the 20th century, was the first person to provide a successful mechanistic account for associationism through his work on the conditioned reflex and classical conditioning (see Chapter 9).

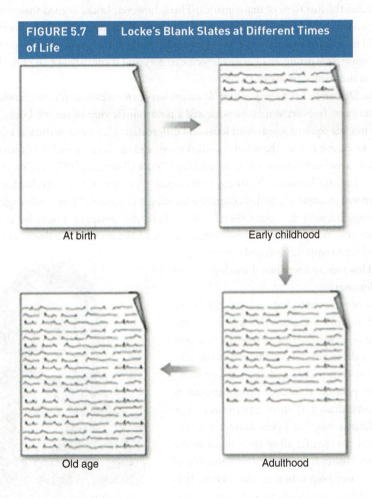

FIGURE 5.7 ■ Locke's Blank Slates at Different Times of Life

At birth

Early childhood

Old age

Adulthood

Locke also discussed the differences between primary and secondary qualities of objects. Primary qualities pertained to properties of objects such as mass, location, movement, texture, and degree of solidity, or qualities that belonged to the objects themselves. Secondary qualities such as color, taste, and smell came from the act of perception and could differ from individual to individual For example, tennis ball containers are marked "optic yellow" but not everyone perceives the balls as yellow. Some will perceive then as green, others as in between green and yellow. Those perceptual differences are what Locke would call a secondary quality. But, no one would perceive a tennis ball as anything other than a sphere. That shape is a Lockean primary quality.

Locke divided knowledge into three categories: intuitive, demonstrative, and sensitive. Intuitive knowledge included knowing of one's own existence as well as God's. Thus Locke, the archetypal empiricist, admitted that some knowledge was pre-existent. Demonstrative knowledge included the theorems of mathematics. There, however, Locke argued that although the theorems existed, they still had to be learned. Once learned, of course, they were unchangeable. So, a child must learn that triangles have three sides and, once learned, accept that definition as a fact. Sensitive learning was Locke's largest category and it consisted of all of the ideas that come to fill the blank slate of our minds.

Unlike Descartes, Locke was willing to accept less-than-certain empirical knowledge from the environment. In other words, he possessed a probabilistic view of reality. Locke looked at language too. He equated words with ideas and differentiated between particular and abstract ideas. Locke examined how the mind classified words and ideas, examined the limits of knowledge, and the relationship between reason and faith. Since Chomsky's (1957) review of Skinner's analysis of language learning, the structure of language and how it is learned has been cited as the best known example of a built-in cognitive learning mechanism. Most psychologists believe that language learning does not follow Locke's *tabula rasa* metaphor. Locke believed he had swept aside the "rubbish" of Scholasticism, countered Descartes's rationalism, and prepared the ground for an empirically based science of psychology. However, in his political writings he was also revolutionary.

When he returned to England in 1689, Locke published another important book, *The Second Treatise of Government.* In it, he set forth a very different understanding from Hobbes of the relationship between people and their government. In Locke's political thinking, people choose to form communities and their government. The main difference was that Locke maintained that people need not transfer all of their rights to the government. Instead, they may transfer some of their rights and keep others to themselves. It is no accident that the American and French revolutions invoked Locke's political thinking. Locke also wrote about religious toleration. He believed that the government should have no say or role in

PHOTO 5.7 Locke

Credit: iStock/denisk0

private religious choice. That, too, became the basis for the doctrine of separation of church and state in the American Constitution.

Locke's writings were a major step forward in the soon-to-emerge science of psychology. He was the first to clearly link the evolving empirical ideas of his time to the possibility of a psychological science. In doing so, he rejected the rationalistic Cartesian model and substituted a radical empiricist model instead. Locke's model, however, would receive criticism from later empiricists and rationalists alike. George Berkeley and David Hume were early empiricist critics. George Berkeley, an Anglican bishop, criticized Locke's division of primary and secondary qualities and provided an idealist alternative to Locke's ideas.

George Berkeley (1685–1753)

Biography

Berkeley was born in Kilkenny, Ireland. He attended Kilkenny College and later Trinity College in Dublin. After, he was ordained as an Anglican churchman and eventually became the bishop of Coyne, Ireland. Berkeley was a scientist; one of his first publications was an analysis of vision. He also attempted to found a new college in Bermuda, a project that was never funded. While waiting for the funds that never arrived, he lived for three years in Newport, Rhode Island. However, his **idealist** (or immaterial) philosophy remains the principal source of his fame. Berkeley used idealism to simultaneously counter Descartes's dualism, Hobbes's materialism, and Locke's version of empiricism. Berkeley wished to prevent philosophy from degenerating into skepticism, or worse, atheism. He saw the materialist accounts of Descartes, Hobbes, and Locke as inevitably leading in that direction.

Many find idealism hard to understand. Idealism posits that all reality: people, buildings, clothes, only exists in the mind. To push that thought further there are several ways that could happen. One is to believe that one's mind is the one creating that ideal reality. That is a very weak explanation. Another explanation would be that there exists a universal conspiracy of minds because people all seem to perceive the same things at the same time. Such a vast conspiracy is, also, a weak explanation for idealism. Bishop Berkeley, however, had a way around both of those weaker explanations. He invoked God's mind as the creator of all that people perceive thus nicely sidestepping the problems with the other explanations.

Contributions

So, how could a rational person justify idealism? Berkeley justified his version of idealism by using God's mind. Everyone simultaneously perceives the consistent but ideal reality created by His mind. Like Descartes, Berkeley required God as an essential component of his philosophy. Thus, Berkeley simultaneously attacked the dualism of Descartes and Locke along with the materialistic monism of Hobbes. Berkeley described his approach as *esse est percipi* (to be is to perceive). His approach to philosophy confounded many of his contemporaries. However, Berkeley insisted that his approach was logical and commonsensical. Most of his criticisms were directed against Locke's empiricism. Specifically, Berkeley disagreed with him over the relationship of ideas to real things. For Berkeley, only ideas were real. Ideas, in turn, could only refer to other ideas. By first denying the existence of anything other than mental constructs, Berkeley could safely deny any relationship between ideas and anything else. Simply stated, there was nothing else.

Berkeley maintained that Locke's primary qualities could not exist. For example, size was no longer a primary quality of an object. Instead, size was simply a perception. Things looked bigger up close and smaller when farther away. Similar logic applied to the other primary qualities of mass, location, movement, texture, and degree of solidity. They all came from the act of perception. Through his emphasis on perception, Berkeley moved philosophy closer to psychology. The earliest scientific psychologists attempted to experimentally determine how perception worked (see Chapter 7). While psychologists have uncovered much about perception since the 19th century, a complete account still remains in the future. Moore et al. (2019) commented on Berkeley's long-term effect on modern psychology:

> Berkeley's impact on the fields of psychology and neuroscience is undeniable. Enacting a simple Google Scholar search beginning in 1879, when the beginning of experimental psychology can be traced to the founding of Wilhelm Wundt's lab in Leipzig, Germany, Berkeley's *An Essay Towards a New Theory of Vision* has been cited in 721 separate works, indicating the impact of his theory from the beginning of experimental psychology to modern times.

In many ways, Berkeley's philosophy anticipated that of David Hume who extended many of Berkeley's ideas, and in the process became the most influential of all the British empiricists. Hume carried the ideas of Locke and Berkeley to their logical conclusions and ended up rejecting metaphysics while placing nearly the whole of his philosophy on the back of perception. Hume's philosophy also minimized the role of rationalism. It was not until after Immanuel Kant's response to Hume that a revised and integrated form of moral philosophy arose and laid the groundwork for creation of the early forms of psychology (see Chapter 6). Hume's system of philosophy inspired Kant's rationalist response much as Descartes's system had done for the earlier empiricist response.

David Hume (1711–1776)

Biography

David Hume was born in Edinburgh, Scotland. He was two years old when his father died. His mother thought him a precocious child; when he was 12 years old he matriculated along with his older brother at the University of Edinburgh. There, he read extensively but did not receive a degree (a common occurrence at the time). After, Hume pursued a short-lived business career as a clerk at a shipping house before deciding to devote himself to philosophy. He wrote his influential, *A Treatise on Human Understanding*, when he was only 26 years old, composing it in France while at the college at La Fleche, the same school attended a century earlier by Mersenne and Descartes.

He returned to England disappointed in the meager reception to his book. Soon after, he traveled to Vienna and Turin as part of an English diplomatic mission. In England he took a post as a librarian, principally to use their resources to write a well-received *History of England*. That book eventually provided him with an income sufficient for him to live independently. He resigned his post at the library after a small scandal over his ordering of books considered inappropriate for the collection. He then attempted to secure an academic position, but his published views on philosophy were radical enough to prevent his hiring. He returned to France on another diplomatic mission. While there, he met many French intellectuals including Denis Diderot, the editor of the first encyclopedia. Hume brought the persecuted Genevan writer, Jean-Jacques Rousseau, back to England and they lived together. Regrettably, Rousseau became depressed and paranoid and eventually suspected Hume of plotting against him. Their friendship ended badly with each publishing their complaints against each other (Zaretsky & Scott, 2009). Hume moved back to Edinburgh where he lived until his death.

Contributions

Hume's philosophy changed little during his lifetime, although his more radical thoughts on religion and God remained mostly unpublished during his lifetime. Hume was committed to two major goals. The first was to rid philosophy of metaphysics and the second was to improve upon the empiricism of Locke and Berkeley. Both of these goals were in the service of creating a science of human nature: a science of psychology. In the end Hume was only partially successful because his radical empiricism left no room for cognition or for innate behaviors. Kant's criticism of Hume led others to a more moderate empiricism and reinstated a role consciousness and pre-existing mental categories in the yet-to-emerge science of psychology.

Hume, like Berkeley, was dissatisfied with Locke's empiricism on several counts. One was Locke's notion that abstract ideas could somehow emerge from a host of specific ones. Another was Locke's separation of perception into primary and secondary qualities. Hume's conclusions, however, were quite different from Berkeley's. Hume's philosophy was materialistic and had no role for God. While agreeing in principle with much of the earlier empiricist agenda, Hume added details that he hoped would strengthen it. He agreed that perception was the major factor in human understanding. He altered the earlier views by adding his own terms and mechanisms. One such addition was the *impression*. Hume's impressions were the direct and vivid results of perception. They were the precursors of ideas. For Hume, ideas were the secondary and dimmer residues of impressions. Ideas, though, retained Locke's distinction of simple and complex, with complex ideas resulting from the combination of simpler ones.

Hume also retained a role for memory similar to Locke's. Hume provided three new mechanisms for the creation of complex ideas: *resemblance, continuity,* and *cause and effect.* The first two were extensions of Locke's principle of association. Much like the later Gestalt psychologists (see Chapter 11), Hume held that events that were similar to each other would be perceived as similar. Likewise, events that followed each other closely in time would also be perceived as belonging together. Hume's explanation of cause and effect was new and different. He gave it the most power and saw it as arising from perception alone when one idea or event always (or nearly always) preceded another idea or event. He rejected any explanations of cause and effect based upon *a priori* knowledge. For Hume, every part of human knowledge had to arise from perception.

Hume also revised the definition of definitions themselves. Definitions, for Hume, were essentially the decomposition of complex ideas, not just the usual restatement of a term using other words. Thus, if one could not decompose a complex idea into its component simple ideas, then that complex idea was erroneous or false. He believed all metaphysical terms fit into the categories of erroneous or false because they, too, could not be reduced to simple ideas.

Morris (2009) described Hume's philosophy as mitigated skepticism. By that he meant that Hume dismissed any talk of ultimate realities not grounded in perception. Mitigated skepticism also included the belief that a science of human nature was possible, but that it had limits. Hume's philosophy was designed to discover those limits and account for the commonplace errors people make. While one's beliefs might be wrong, one's impressions or ideas were never wrong. Morris illustrated by an example: the sounds of water hitting a window. The sounds, or the impressions, are true. The belief that it was raining might not be true, however, if the sounds were made by someone hosing off the window. Regardless, water is still hitting the window; the original impression is true. It is the belief that it is raining that is mistaken. Further perception, however, will lead to the correct belief.

Unlike Descartes, Hume placed rational thought below the passions. For Hume, the passions were innate, unlike impressions. The direct passions such as fear, joy, desire, and aversion came directly from pain or pleasure, good or evil. The source of the indirect passions such as pride, shame, love, or hate was more convoluted but still relatable to pain or pleasure or to good or evil. This reversal of the usual relationship between reason and emotion was new to philosophy, but it had to be so for Hume's philosophy to be consistent. He explained that moral judgments, too, depended upon experience and had to be learned. Those judgments were not the products of reason. Instead, they were the result of the pursuit of pleasure or the avoidance of pain.

Hume argued against Hobbes's use of self-interest to explain social behavior. In its place Hume used benevolence instead. Benevolence was, for Hume, an original part of human nature and it led to justice and social welfare, although in different ways for different societies. Like many of the other new philosophers, Hume's interests encompassed more than just moral philosophy. He wrote about economics, the history of ideas, esthetics, and religion. His views on religion, if nothing else, were consistent with the rest of his philosophy.

PHOTO 5.8 Hume

He viewed religion as irrational and pathological. He leveled his most vehement objections at monotheistic religions because of their intolerance, promotion of irrational beliefs, and corruption of philosophy (Morris, 2009).

Hume's philosophy, then, can be seen as one of the last wedges that finally led to the complete separation of science and religion. Hume's revision of Locke and Berkeley helped lay the foundation for an empirical, materialistic, and behavioral psychology predicated upon the primacy of perception. Such a foundation, however, seemed faulty and incomplete to the rationalists. Immanuel Kant, inspired by Hume, finally synthesized their response, and in the process, helped add innate and cognitive principles to the still incomplete philosophical foundation of psychology (see Chapter 6). Kant's response was the capstone to the philosophy of those who had followed and built upon Descartes's rationalistic philosophy. Their work, described in the next chapter, was also instrumental in creating the science of psychology.

LEARNING OBJECTIVE

13. Assess the contributions of the British empiricists to foundational issues in psychology.

SUMMARY

The Renaissance was the result of many historical forces coinciding. Humanism was one of those but not the only one by far. Other factors contributing to the Renaissance were the growth of cities combined with increases in commerce and population. Wealthy patrons, too, spent their fortunes sponsoring the work of artists and architects. European explorers traveled to all corners of the globe encountering unexpected peoples, animals, and plants. Soon, Europeans spread their ideas, technology, and religions wherever they trod.

Erasmus was one of the first to fully take advantage of the era as it was dawning. He melded Humanism and religion. A devout Roman Catholic, he nevertheless saw and criticized the excesses of his own church. He hoped that his work would help to reform it from within. His efforts, however, did not lead to reform; he had severely underestimated how much the weight of tradition was against him.

Martin Luther, a fellow Augustinian monk, also believed that the Roman Catholic Church had lost its way. The sale of indulgences was the last straw for him and caused him to publicly attack their sale. From the time he posted his *95 Theses* to his excommunication several years later, he wrote prolifically, and in the process gave birth to the Protestant Reformation. Although trained as a humanist, Luther retreated from its principles and based his theology on a close reading of the Bible. Other Protestant reformers followed his lead but, on the whole, the new religions disagreed with each other over doctrine. But, all agreed that they wanted to be free of the Catholic Church. For its own part, the Catholic Church dallied too long in the face of the Protestant revolt. By the time it launched its own Counter Reformation the battle lines between all of the Christian churches had hardened. The period following the Reformations was marked by the long and violent Thirty Years' War that left Europe permanently divided into two parts based on religion.

Almost unnoticed, the first stirrings of science as we now know it began during the 16th century. Astronomy led the way. The ancient Julian calendar was wrong; it was making human timekeeping fall behind the natural seasonal progression of time. Copernicus refused to work on the problem because he believed the basic knowledge required to fix the calendar had to be understood first. He worked alone and gradually developed a new, radical view of the universe. He literally swapped the positions of the earth and sun. The publication of his book caused others to think deeply about his new system. One such early astronomer, Brahe, was fortunate enough to spot one of the rarest of astronomical events, a visible supernova. Furthermore, he possessed the necessary equipment to determine how far away it was. The older Ptolemaic theory put the supernova close to earth. Brahe's observations showed it was much farther away, undermining the older theory. Over the course of the rest of his life, Brahe carefully measured the positions of nearly all the visible stars and planets creating the first scientific database.

Kepler, too, thought about the universe in a different way. He knew of and believed in Copernicus's view of the universe. However, his approach was to discover the mathematical rules behind the intrinsic order that God used to create the universe. Kepler ended up working for Brahe and was able to use the data Brahe had painstakingly collected. Kepler slowly worked out many of the details of the geocentric model that Copernicus had left undone and in the process replaced his circular planetary orbits with elliptical ones and worked out the first laws of planetary motion.

But it was the discoveries of still another astronomer, Galileo, which made the biggest impact. He used a new instrument, the telescope, to discover new facts. The most dramatic of those was the discovery that Jupiter had moons. Galileo's writings in support of Copernican theory led to their suppression by the Roman Catholic Church. Galileo, too, was eventually caught up in the maws of the Inquisition and was forced to recant his views. The Catholic Church viewed such opinions as heretical if they were presented as facts. While under house arrest, Galileo produced his most significant work, one that laid the foundations of classic physics.

In England, a country relatively untouched by the Inquisition, members of the Royal Society met regularly to freely discuss scientific topics and publish the results of their studies. Isaac Newton was admitted to the Royal Society after he demonstrated his invention, the world's first reflecting telescope. Newton first studied the physics of light but nearly quit science because of his disagreements with another member of the Royal Society, Robert Hooke. Later, when asked by Halley about the shape of a planet's orbit if it were to obey the inverse square law, Newton immediately answered that it would be an ellipse, just as shown by Kepler's computations.

Newton's scientific publications were earth shattering. His *Principia Mathematica* opened the door to a new way of thinking about the world. He combined, for the first time, the data from observations with the calculus, a new mathematical description of the forces. Newton's book caused others to think about the world in a new way; the scientific revolution had begun. Very quickly, others would extend the new scientific approach to a wide variety of academic disciplines. In time, psychology, the scientific study of behavior and mental processes, would also take its place in the halls of science

Rene Descartes and Francis Bacon were among the earliest of the new philosophers. Descartes believed he had provided a new way for philosophers to look at the world. His interactionist dualist approach via his clear statement of the mind–body problem liberated natural philosophy from its classic roots. But, his dualism also created problems. The biggest one being: How could a nonmaterial entity, the mind, control the material body? His explanation, reflex action, was too simplistic and physiologically false. Descartes's influence was immense, especially among those who disagreed with him.

Most of those disagreeing with him were British philosophers. Francis Bacon took an opposite approach from Descartes and focused on the problems surrounding the collection of unbiased data, his idols. Bacon divided science into pure and applied domains. Hobbes objected strenuously to Descartes's dualism and proposed a strictly materialist philosophy. In addition, he did seminal work in the area of what today would be considered sociology: the social contract.

Later British philosophers, too, negatively responded to Descartes's new approach. Locke profoundly disagreed with Descartes's ideas about the origin of knowledge. For Locke, nearly all knowledge was learned through experience. He was a radical empiricist who stressed the primacy of perception but still made allowances for primary qualities. Those were part of nature and not learned. Berkeley went further than Locke and proposed a completely idealistic yet empirical philosophy. Berkeley argued that everything was learned and that Locke's primary qualities did not exist. But, Berkeley also left room for God in his philosophy; he needed to, otherwise his theory would not hold. For Berkeley, it was the mind of God that created everything that humans perceived. Hume was the most influential of the British empiricists. He wanted a philosophy free of metaphysics. He disagreed vehemently with Descartes and Berkeley. In Hume's philosophy, there was no room for God. He wanted to explain everything without having to resort to divine interference or aid. His skeptical approach to philosophy added the mechanisms of resemblance, contiguity, and cause and effect, none of which required an *a priori* mental structure such as Descartes's. Unlike his predecessors, Hume had placed emotions above reason, a startling reversal. Emotions and passions were the source of social behavior too. Hume's skepticism also provoked other philosophers to rally against his ideas. Most of those philosophers lived on the continent of Europe. Their approach is the subject of the next chapter.

6 FROM PHILOSOPHY TO SOCIAL SCIENCE

Europe After 1648

After the Peace of Westphalia ended, the Thirty Years War Europe changed. The Dutch Republic became independent, France became the major power on the continent, and the Holy Roman Empire began a slow move towards dissolution into smaller and independent states. In many ways that peace helped shape modern ideas about statehood and the relationships between countries. It also legitimized the simultaneous existence of Protestantism and Catholicism while permitting the practice of both throughout Europe. In addition, the agreements specified principles of international law still in practice including: national sovereignty, the balance of power, and noninterference in the domestic affairs of other sovereign states. At the same time philosophers began to consider other ways to approach Descartes's interactionist solution to the mind–body problem and proposed new ways to look at it. Most opted for solutions that kept philosophy and theology apart. Many began to consider the roles of self-awareness, mathematics, and morality in their formulations. New philosophies appeared too. The Utilitarians analyzed the difference between individual and group goals. The Romantics revolted against the Enlightenment and its drive toward materialism and sought solace in the sensual aspects of life. Social science emerged from this boiling brew giving rise to the new discipline of sociology. By the last quarter of the 19th century the founding of psychology was also at hand.

PREVIEW

Descartes's interactionist solution to the mind–body problem was problematical and led to the creation of other solutions including: *double-aspectism, occasionalism, preestablished harmony,* and *psychophysical parallelism.* Of those, only occasionalism still retained a direct link to God as a causal agent. The remainder, in one way or another, separated any causal connections between mind and body. Some solutions also invoked *determinism* to one degree or another. Some had God determining everything while others only allowed divine intervention at creation. Another important idea was the *nature-nurture* problem. It was at the heart of the conflict between rationalists and empiricists. It remains an important issue in modern psychology. *Representation,* too, is another idea that is of great current interest, especially in cognitive psychology (see Chapter 14). How information is represented in the mind is still not known today. The term, *apperception,* on the other hand, has largely disappeared as a topic in current psychology and has been replaced by perception. *Utilitarian* accounts of behavior have survived into modern psychology but *Romantic* accounts have not. Hegel's *dialectic* flourished as an idea and crossed from philosophy into many other disciplines. Ideas first derived from sociology such as *alienation* and *positivism* crossed over into other subject fields. *Social Darwinism* has fallen far from its original prominent position as an explanatory device but is still invoked by some, especially in political discourse. Herbart's *threshold* or *limen* played an important role in the development of psychophysics and is still a fundamental topic in psychology. Lotze was the first to provide an explicit link between physiology and psychology.

LEARNING OBJECTIVE

1. Summarize the philosophical ideas that led to the emergence of psychology.

INTRODUCTION

Descartes's rationalist philosophy inspired criticism from the British empiricists and the Continental rationalist philosophers. One reason for their criticism was the lack of a mechanism to explain Descartes's interactive dualism. Another was his personalistic approach; his *cogito, ergo sum* assumed that others' personal experience be identical to his. God's role in philosophy was also an issue. Rationalists used a wide variety of approaches to deal with God. Spinoza, for example, adopted a pantheistic approach claiming that nature was God and vice versa. Leibniz sidestepped the problem by invoking separate but simultaneous representations of nature. Malebranche, on the other hand, was more than willing to allow the possibility of divine intervention from time to time. Kant, like the others, believed in God but devised a system that kept his philosophy confined to the real world and declared God to be unknowable through the methods of philosophy. Among the British empiricists, Hume made the biggest break between religion and philosophy (see Chapter 5).

The Continental rationalists disagreed with the British empiricists over the question of the origin of knowledge. The rationalists argued that some portion of human knowledge already existed in the mind and did not require experience. This fundamental difference can still be observed in contemporary psychological theories and is sometimes called the **nature-nurture** question. In its simplest form the nature-nurture question ascribes the source of knowledge to innate, biological factors (e.g., nature) or learned, experiential factors (e.g., nurture). But, while the issue still remains, modern solutions are more nuanced, admit interaction between nature and nurture, and allow for more sources to explain behavior. For example, Seay and Gottfried (1978) proposed three additional "sets" in addition to nature and nurture. Those additional sets were: ontogenetic set, cultural set, and individual set. Ontogenetic set encompasses effects due to maturation and maturation–environment interactions. Cultural set refers to macroenvironmental factors imposed by society. Individual set is a finer grained look at the interactions between (1) individuals and their genetic make-ups and (2) their specific experiences. They argued (p. 31) that:

> Any behavior in an organism is the result of dynamic interaction among the five determinants of behavior described . . . Their action is interdependent, and one determinant can augment, modify, or negate the influence of another. Behavioral determination is always probabilistic . . . The more precisely one can determine the characteristics of the individual organism, the more accurately one can predict and understand that organism's behavior.

These basic differences in approach between the empiricists and the rationalists were evident throughout the history of psychology from its earliest days till now.

FOUR PHILOSOPHERS

Spinoza, Malebranche, Leibniz, and Kant warrant further study because their work influenced the rise of psychology. Baruch Spinoza was the son of Iberian Jews who had immigrated to the Dutch Republic. But, the form of rationalist philosophy he developed angered the Jewish and Christian communities there. Both labeled him an atheist because his philosophical system sought knowledge of God far outside of the traditional ways. Spinoza took Descartes's "clear and distinct ideas" as one of the keys for his own philosophical system but utterly abandoned Descartes's first person approach. Spinoza, although excommunicated by his own religion and viewed as an atheist by Dutch Protestants, nevertheless was allowed to live, write, and publish. He most likely would have been persecuted, or even killed, in nearly any other part of Europe. The Dutch Republic, thus, served as a hothouse for these tender shoots of early rationalist philosophy. The Dutch Republic or what is today the Netherlands achieved its independence from the Kingdom of Spain in 1648 as part of the Peace of Westphalia that ended the Thirty Years War. The city of Amsterdam in the new Dutch Republic soon became the destination of choice for religious refugees from the Iberian Peninsula. Many of those refugees were Jews who had been forcibly converted to Catholicism in Spain or Portugal. In Amsterdam, they were once again able to practice their Jewish religion freely in spite of the predominant Calvinist form of Protestantism practiced there. Because of the long enmity with Spain, the Dutch were actually more tolerant of Jews than they were of Catholics. The religious tolerance in the Dutch Republic was relative and not comparable to the modern use of the word. However, compared to the Inquisition or the beliefs of the more extreme Protestant sects, it was a very tolerant part of Europe for its time. Descartes, famously, had lived most of his life there in order to avoid the Inquisition.

Malebranche's philosophy was one of the few newer philosophies that still had a central role for God. Unlike the other philosophers covered in this chapter, Malebranche did not separate religion from philosophy. His invocation of God's ability to selectively manipulate reality by causing miracles, exceptions to rational rules and logic, made other philosophers uncomfortable. The story of the camel putting his nose under the tent best describes that lack of a barrier between religion and philosophy. If a camel is allowed to keep his nose under a tent then the end result will be the occupants sleeping with the camel. Similarly, allowing one miracle to exist means many others will follow. Philosophy would fall and fail unless any and all miracles were not allowed as explanations.

LEARNING OBJECTIVE

2.   Describe an example of intolerance you have witnessed.

Leibniz's philosophy clearly fit within the rationalist tradition because he argued against Locke's *tabula rasa*, believed that the discovery of knowledge proceeded from universal truths (axioms) and the corollaries derived from them, and held that innate ideas existed. He opposed Descartes's materialism and his interactionist mind–body solution. Leibniz independently discovered the calculus. He also invented the binary notation system for numbers and developed one of the earliest mechanical calculators, improving upon Pascal's design. He demonstrated his calculator to the Royal Society and was made a life member. Later, he helped found the Berlin (later the German) Academy of Sciences and served as its president until he died.

Although Kant's philosophy was not always logically consistent, it nevertheless represented a major breakthrough in the history of philosophy. Singlehandedly, he showed a necessary connection between rationalism and empiricism, peacefully separated philosophy from theology, and provided an innate role for reason in the making of moral decisions. By arguing against Leibniz's version of rationalism Kant showed that pure reason led to illusory and false conclusions. By adding the categories of mind to the sensory observations of the empiricists he created a wider arena for the development of modern science.

Baruch (Benedict) Spinoza (1632–1677)

Biography

Spinoza was born in Amsterdam to a Jewish family that had recently emigrated from Portugal and renounced their earlier forced conversion to Catholicism. Spinoza was an apt student seemingly destined to become a rabbi. However, his exposure to scholastic and early scientific ideas caused him to form and express opinions counter to the orthodox views of Amsterdam's Jewish community. In 1656 that community formally excommunicated him. After, Spinoza changed his name to Benedictus, the Latinized equivalent of Baruch (both names mean "blessed"). The works of Descartes inspired Spinoza to write his first book, *Principles of Cartesian Philosophy*, the only one published under his name during his lifetime. Spinoza's subsequent works were either published anonymously or after his death; all were promptly placed on the *Index*. Spinoza certainly was a rationalist but did not accept much of Descartes's philosophy. Specifically, he rejected Descartes's approach to dualism, his belief in free will, and his compartmentalization of nature. Spinoza spent his life in the Netherlands and eked out a living as a lens grinder. Spinoza died relatively young, perhaps as a result of inhaling the fine glass powder from his lens grinding.

Contributions

By making God the source of everything, Spinoza successfully replaced Descartes's first-person philosophy with one that applied to all people at all times. He turned down several offers of employment during his lifetime including one for the chair of philosophy at the University of Heidelberg. The only restriction it imposed was too much for Spinoza; he was not to disturb the established religion. He graciously turned down that and all other offers. Although he lived a simple and austere life, he corresponded widely and met with some of the leading thinkers of his day including Wilhelm Leibniz and Henry Oldenburg, the Royal Society's first secretary. His letters and posthumously published works reveal his version of rationalist philosophy.

Spinoza's philosophy was radical for its time. Like most rationalists he was convinced that the road to truth was mathematical and did not rely on perception of the real world. Euclid's geometric axioms were the model for his philosophy. Imitating Euclid, he presented his philosophical ideas as axioms, postulates, and proofs. His philosophy equated God and the natural world as one substance. His first step was to prove God's existence ontologically. Recall that ontological arguments for the existence of God rely upon logically demonstrating that two propositions are self-contradictory, meaning that one must be false and the other true (see Chapter 4). Next, he asserted that everything in nature was in God. Furthermore, God was also the cause of everything, making him a **determinist**. He held that understanding God was not only possible but was the highest form of understanding. His conception of God was very different from the traditional Christian and Jewish views. Where those traditions saw God as separate from the world and unknowable, Spinoza saw God as nature itself, one and the same. In addition, Spinoza claimed his version of God was knowable; striving to know God was the ultimate goal of philosophy. Such thinking made others label him an atheist or a pantheist, both serious charges at the time. Spinoza countered by saying that philosophy and religion were separate and independent domains. The path to God, and thus to the truth, could only be found in philosophy. Religion, on the other hand, led to "superstitious behavior and subservience to ecclesiastic authorities" (Nadler, 2008, n.p.).

Spinoza was determined to consider God and nature as a single entity. Everything, from God on down, was a part of nature. Against Descartes's dualism where mind and body were separate yet somehow managed to affect each other, Spinoza provided a dualistic solution where mind and body were instead two separate views of the same substance. One view saw God and nature as ideas whereas the other saw them as things. This solution to the mind–body problem is called **double-aspectism** and it avoids the problem of explaining how mind and body affect each other inherent in Descartes's interactionist solution. A common metaphor for this mind–body solution is the image of the one's face in a mirror. The study of philosophy was thus the study of God and nature, by studying one of those one was also studying the other.

From Descartes, Spinoza took the criterion of "clear and distinct ideas." Those ideas revealed the underlying, axiomatic, and rational composition of the natural world. Spinoza called those ideas *adequate* because they revealed necessary truths about the world, truths that were not revealed simply through observation. Instead, the most that observations could provide were partial understandings or *inadequate* ideas. One reason for their inadequacy was that they might only be true for a given time or place. But adequate ideas, for Spinoza, were true for all time and all places. Like the proofs of geometry, the truths revealed by adequate ideas were true for all eternity.

Human behavior, too, was part of nature and could be studied. Thus, he studied emotions such as love, envy, hate, pride, and jealousy considering them part of nature. He divided the emotions into actions and passions. Actions came from within and were the product of the mind acting upon an adequate idea. Passions came from without and had the power to affect behavior or thinking. Passions always directed people outward attracting or repelling them to people or objects. He defined good as pleasure and evil as pain, with the appropriate passions directing people to the former and repelling them from the latter.

While living a life free of passions was not possible, Spinoza believed that rational thought could moderate the effects of passions. Rational thought could control how passions were evaluated and, ultimately, lead to a virtuous life, or to a life devoted to pursuing knowledge and understanding, the highest understanding being that of knowing God, which, in turn, meant understanding nature as well. Spinoza was not very influential during his lifetime or shortly afterward. However, his philosophy was revived in the 19th century by the Romantic Movement, Marxism, and psychoanalysis. Among the rationalists, however, his philosophy was superseded by that of Leibniz and Kant. Nicolas Malebranche, however, had a very different view of philosophy, occasionalism.

PHOTO 6.1 Spinoza

Credit: iStock/ZU_09

The doctrine of occasionalism is an ancient one in philosophy. It comes in several forms ranging from mild to absolute. All varieties of occasionalism, to some degree, invoke God as a causal agent in the world. Some Islamic philosophers required occasionalism in order to justify the reality of the miracles described in Qu'ran (Fakhry, 1999).

Nicolas Malebranche (1638–1715)

Inspired by Descartes, Malebranche revived a strict form of occasionalism in order to explain how mind could affect body and vice versa. Malebranche, too, was dissatisfied with Descartes's interactionism. Malebranche was a priest who proposed that God was the only causal agent in the universe. Humans and beasts merely provide the *occasion* for God to manifest his power. On rare occasions, Malebranche believed God might cause a miracle, an event unexplainable by ordinary philosophy. Pyle (2003, p. 2) wrote:

Malebranche announces two rules for the guidance of the mind that desires to free itself from such errors and arrive at the truth. Once our minds have been properly purged of vulgar error, Malebranche claims, two great truths will become manifest, opening clear paths into the subjects of metaphysics and epistemology. In metaphysics, we will see clearly that only God can be a true cause, and that what we commonly call 'natural' or 'second' causes are mere *occasions* (original italics) for God to act in accordance with His own self-imposed rules.

The influence of occasionalism was short-lived; it along with classic Cartesian philosophy fell to attacks from empiricists and rationalists. Occasionalism stood as an example of an attempt to maintain alive the ancient link between theology and philosophy.

Gottfried Wilhelm Leibniz (1646–1716)

Biography

Leibniz was only six when his father, a professor of moral philosophy at the University of Leipzig, died. Throughout the rest of his childhood, however, he taught himself, thanks in part to his father's extensive library. He earned his undergraduate degree at the University of Leipzig where scholastic and humanistic influences still ran strong. He earned a doctoral degree in law from the University of Altdorf, but turned down an offer of a faculty position there upon graduation. Instead, he became a lifelong courtier (a bureaucrat), first at Mainz and later at Hanover. While traveling in France and England, he met many of the prominent philosophers of his time including Malebranche, Spinoza, and Christiaan Huygens. From those meetings he developed a strong interest in mathematics and science.

Contributions

Leibniz possessed extraordinary intelligence coupled with interests in a wide variety of fields. In addition to his writings in philosophy, he wrote about topics ranging from the history of the rulers of Hanover to the possibility of reconciling Protestants and Catholics. His output was so extensive that many of his works have yet to be translated and interpreted. Russell (1937, p. 2) noted, "we often find the best statement of his view in short papers . . . [where] we find, as a rule, far less rhetoric and far more logic than in his public manifestoes." Strickland (2006) in his published translations of Leibniz's shorter texts noted (p. 2):

> Much of Leibniz's philosophy was developed in his spare time, through short papers written for himself, book notes, and hasty jottings. In the seventeenth and eighteenth centuries it was common for thinkers to communicate their ideas to others via letters, which were often copied and distributed to other scholars or even published, and Leibniz often disseminated his philosophical ideas this way.

Interestingly, Leibniz's philosophy was severely criticized during his lifetime and shortly after his death, especially by Voltaire, who parodied him as Dr. Pangloss in his play *Candide*. Modern theorists such as Freud and Einstein, however, were much more receptive to his thinking and theorizing. Contemporary cognitive scientists, too, find his views on representation helpful in their work. (See Chapter 14.)

Leibniz proposed a monistic amalgam of materialism and idealism connected by a mind–body solution called **preestablished harmony**. In Leibniz's eyes, God had created two independent worlds. One of those was physical and the other was mental. However, those two worlds never affected each other. Since the beginning of time, each world had always coordinated itself to reflect the other but without one affecting the other. Leibniz wished to avoid the problem inherent in Descartes's interactionist solution, namely how did the mind and body affect each other? In Leibniz's solution they did not. He explained the workings of his mind–body solution using an entity he called the *monad*.

Monads were the constituents of the mental world. They were indivisible, infinite, and they, like mathematical points, did not occupy space. Every person's soul (mind) was a monad. Animal minds, too, were monads, but those could not achieve rational thought. The infinity of monads was hierarchically arranged and each monad could perceive the entire universe, but for the vast majority of monads that perception was confused. God, the top monad, could perceive everything clearly. Memory and self-awareness contributed to a hierarchy of perception. Bare perceptions were those that involved neither memory nor self-awareness and accounted for simple sensory input. Perceptions involved memory and explained how animal minds worked. Unlike Descartes, Leibniz did not believe that animals were automata. **Apperception** occurred in humans when they were aware of their own thoughts. In other words, apperception was self-consciousness.

Monads, in turn, combined to create the physical world, but for Leibniz none of the things in the physical world were substances, in the classic philosophical sense of that word. Instead, physical things were all composites of monads. His doctrine of preestablished harmony meant that the mental world and the physical world were representations of the same thing but from different points of view. Science explained the physical world via efficient causes while philosophy explained the mental world and still preserved Aristotle's final causes.

Thus, Leibniz held that the mental world and the physical world were simultaneously coordinated representations of each other. But, those representations were not fully equivalent. Think of a circle, for example. It can be represented geometrically:

- as a figure,
- algebraically as a formula ($x^2 + y^2 = r^2$),
- algorithmically as a procedure (e.g., fix the point of a compass onto a piece of paper and rotate the end holding the pencil 360°),
- or mentally as an image.

Leibniz was an idealist in that he put reality itself in the mental world. What people perceived as the real world was just the activity of an infinite number of monads. Some of those monads are imperceptible. Leibniz called those monads *petites perceptions* and held that although they were subliminal or imperceptible they could still affect the mind, especially when a large number of them occurred at the same time. Thus, Leibniz argued, people might not hear the sound of a single wave breaking upon the shore but people could hear the roar of the ocean, the summed total of many *petites perceptions* happening at the same time. Freud would later use Leibniz's *petites perceptions* in his discussions of unconscious motivation.

Leibniz's monads were very similar to the premise behind the movie *The Matrix* and its sequels. In those movies, physical reality for nearly everyone consisted of dark imprisonment and attachment to tubes that the conquering machines used to supply themselves with energy. Yet, the imprisoned persons still perceived the world as it was before the machines took over. The machines were manipulating their mental worlds. So, their perceptions reflected their normal human lives: homes, a families, and jobs. But, a few people managed to escape their physical imprisonment and lived in the real world, the dark, dangerous place made by the machines. In these movies, machines have taken over the role that Leibniz had assigned to God. Those machines, not God, created the "matrix" or the ultimate monad. (See Greenberg, 2009, for a longer exposition on the parallels between Leibniz's philosophy and *the Matrix* movies.)

Leibniz's energy was obvious through the sheer volume of his writing. That he accomplished as much in philosophy as he did is even more remarkable given his duties as a courtier. His contributions to mathematics were first rate and he anticipated many of the developments in modern logic. However, his writings on logic were not published until late in the 19th century, after the seminal contributions made by Boole and Frege. Leibniz's main contribution to rationalism was that he inspired Immanuel Kant, the greatest of the modern rationalist philosophers. Kant "interrupted his dogmatic slumber" in order to correct what he saw were the excesses of Leibniz's pure reason and Hume's skepticism. Kant's critical philosophy integrated rationalist and empiricist approaches to knowledge and provided an alternative to hedonistic interpretations of human behavior.

PHOTO 6.2 Leibniz

Credit: iStock/ZU_09

Immanuel Kant (1724–1804)

Biography

Kant was born in Königsberg, East Prussia (modern Kaliningrad). His father was a master harness maker. He and his family were poor and were Pietists, a reform movement within the Lutheran church that believed in hard work, duty, and prayer. Despite his family's poverty, Kant was able to attend a Pietist school and later the University of Königsberg. After, he tutored and lectured for many years, turning down offers elsewhere before accepting a professorship at Königsberg at the age of 46.

Contributions

Kant taught in a wide variety of subjects before specializing in philosophy and was the first to propose the nebular hypothesis for the formation of the solar system. He became a fixture in town because of the popularity of his lectures and the regularity of his schedule. He always woke early, wrote for two hours, gave his morning lectures, had lunch with friends, and then took a solitary walk. He was inspired by the writings of Rousseau and Newton and saw himself as the Copernicus of philosophy. Most divide his writings into two parts, those written before the *Critique of Pure Reason* and those after. That book, along with two others with similar titles, the *Critique of Practical Reason*, and the *Critique of Pure Judgment*, made him internationally famous.

The title of the *Critique of Pure Reason* was directed at Leibniz's rationalist philosophy, but it also attacked Hume's skeptical version of empirical philosophy. Against Leibniz, Kant argued that reason alone could not yield a cogent rationalist philosophy, nor did he believe that Leibniz's monads were required to understand the physical world. Instead, Kant believed that the ordinary objects of experience existed, occupied space, and endured through time themselves as they were. Against Hume, he argued that empirical observations alone could not account for the complexities of human behavior, especially as applied to Hume's account of causality.

Kant believed that the human mind came provided with *a priori* innate organizing principles that enabled it to make sense of experience. He proposed what he termed a transcendental idealism, an already existing synthetic approach to knowledge about the physical world. For Kant, a synthetic approach meant that the innate categories of mind combined with sensory observations to reveal the truths of the physical world. That approach also set limits as to what topics could not be addressed by philosophy. The categories were analytic, meaning they were already present in the mind and did not depend upon experience for their existence. Kant proposed 12 such categories:

- unity, plurality, and totality for the concept of *quantity;*

- reality, negation, and limitation for the concept of *quality;*

- inherence and subsistence, cause and effect, and community for the concept of *relation;*

- and possibility–impossibility, existence–nonexistence, and necessity and contingency for the concept of *modality.*

He derived all of them by deductively working backward until he could go no further. The categories, in other words, represented the very bottom level of conceptual organization. In addition to the categories, Kant proposed two innate intuitions: space and time.

Thus, against the empiricists, Kant argued that humans came into the world already knowing about space and time along with the 12 categories; they did not have to learn them through experience. He held that scientific facts resulted from the combination of observations of the physical world made by a prepared and already organized mind. Kant's philosophy suggested that a unified science was possible with common principles, such as the law of conservation, applicable to all branches of science. Kant's logic dictated that some things—God, immortality of the soul, and freedom—were impossible to know. Those kinds of things were outside of experience and thus could not be approached by his method. However, knowing that they were unapproachable to speculative (e.g., scientific) philosophy was important.

By separating out such topics, Kant solved the "Crisis of the Enlightenment." That crisis had long been brewing and it revolved around the relationship between philosophy and theology that had become more and more acute since the Middle Ages. Descartes, Spinoza, Malebranche, and Leibniz had each felt compelled to include a place for God in their philosophical systems. Locke and Berkeley, too, each had a role for God within their philosophies as well. Hume, eventually, had separated God from his philosophy but in a manner intolerable to most of his contemporaries. Kant's synthetic approach removed the necessity for a place for God in philosophy but kept open a place for worship, reverence, and belief in God. That place, however, was outside of speculative philosophy.

Kant next turned his attention to practical reason. There, he wished to discover similar synthetic *a priori* principles of action based upon reason and not upon passions. Reason, not passions, could provide the marching orders to autonomous and free human agents who could decide whether or not to obey those orders. Kant's aim was to make moral decisions independent of the empirical world. In other words, he wanted to provide a basis for moral behavior that was free of the relativism of hedonistic impulses. Reason, he thought, could provide hypothetical or categorical imperatives. Hypothetical imperatives used the word "if" and were of the form: "If you don't want to get wet stay inside while it is raining." Categorical imperatives, on the other hand, had the word ought in them. You ought always keep your promises would be an example.

Kant posited a top-level categorical imperative that applied to all rational humans, similar to the "Golden Rule" (e.g., "Do unto others as you would have them do unto you."). Categorical imperatives did not require empirical validation. Instead, they validated themselves logically whenever an action led to moral behavior. For example, promise keeping was a categorical imperative because if everyone broke their promises, denying that promises were a universal good, then that would lead to a logical absurdity, the end of promises themselves. Notice that Kant did not believe that all people kept their promises. Instead, he believed that all people *ought* to keep their promises. Furthermore, he was convinced that he had proven the existence of categorical

PHOTO 6.3 Kant

Credit: iStock/Graffisimo

imperatives without having to cross into the empirical world. He had shown that moral behavior was innate and universal. But, people still had to choose to act morally: They had free will. In the *Critique of Practical Reason*, Kant argued that humans were free only when they were not subject to outside forces. Because he believed that everything in the physical world had a cause, he could not locate human freedom there. If he did, then no act made by a human could be truly free. One could always find a cause. Thus, he had to make freedom an idea located outside of the empirical world. Once he placed freedom in that ideal world, humans could contemplate actions and decide, ahead of time, whether or not to carry them out. Varden, H. (2017) argued that he applied the idea of freedom to both men and women while at the same time stressing their essential gender-based differences. In doing so Kant was ahead of his time and *zeitgeist*.

Kant influenced psychology's future as well. Topics such as consciousness and cognition derive directly from Kant. He was also ultimately correct about the futility of introspective methods in psychology, although psychologists would only learn that the hard way, through the failure of those methods (see Chapter 7). Kant did not foresee the eventual development of a scientific psychology, however. It is tempting to speculate that no philosopher of his era could have predicted psychology's future given 21st century psychology's eclectic background.

The 19th century also saw the rise of other philosophies with psychological import on both sides of the English Channel. Sensationalism and Utilitarianism emerged from Empiricism The Romantic Movement arose from Rationalism and dominated the German-speaking world.

LEARNING OBJECTIVE
3. Interpret the differences between the rationalist philosophers' ideas.

OTHER 19TH CENTURY PHILOSOPHIES

Two other philosophical movements preceded psychology's emergence late in the 19th century. One was Utilitarianism. Its proponents were primarily British; the heirs of the British empiricist tradition stretching back to Locke, Berkeley, and Hume. The other movement was Romanticism. Its proponents were mainly German-speaking philosophers who came after Kant and attempted to solve the philosophical problems he had identified, but to their minds, left unsolved.

Utilitarianism

Utilitarianism did not spring up full-grown in the 19th century. Rather, it had a long history going at least as far back as Hobbes, at least in terms of the importance of hedonism to human behavior. However, Utilitarianism distinguished between things that caused pleasure to an individual and things that maximized pleasure for an entire group. The classic definition of Utilitarianism was based in moral philosophy and held that morally correct actions were those that produced the most overall good. Early in Utilitarianism's history its theorists argued that human pleasure was good because it reflected God's beneficent intentions for humankind. After Hume and his attacks on divine influences on human moral judgments, Utilitarianism became distinctly secular. In its simplest forms, Utilitarianism held that pleasure was good and pain was bad. Later forms of Utilitarianism differentiated pleasure into higher and lower categories with intellectual pleasures (writing a history of psychology textbook) being superior to baser ones (playing video games all day). One of the chief problems of Utilitarianism was the conflict between individual and group good. How would a person act when that action was deleterious personally but good for the group? Lazari-Radek and Singer (2017, p. xix) introduced their book on utilitarianism thusly, "Utilitarianism pushes us to examine the boundaries of our moral thinking, and consider the interests of those who we often leave out of our concern. It is not surprising that this style of thinking should sometimes be controversial."

Jeremy Bentham (1748–1832)

Jeremy Bentham was one of the first philosophers to tackle the issue of individual vs. group good but he never truly resolved it. He did, however, supply a list of parameters by which others might judge whether the consequences of an action contributed to the overall betterment of a group. Some of those parameters included intensity (stronger is better), duration (longer is better), certainty (surer is better), purity (unmixed is better), and extent (better for more people). He tried to provide objective ways of measuring the improvement of goodness but, in reality, he kept to more heuristic methods such as rules of thumb and the effects of experience. Bentham's views were somewhat radical for his time because he argued that there were no intrinsically moral behaviors. Every action had to be judged by its utility (e.g., its benefit) to the group in question. Like other utilitarians of his day, Bentham was a social reformer. He sought to change unfair laws and end evil practices such as slavery and discrimination against women. He also maintained that what might be moral today might not be so in the future. Thus, he was a moral relativist.

John Stuart Mill (1806–1873)

John Stuart Mill, perhaps the most influential British philosopher of the 19th century, was a follower of Bentham's. It was Mill who first differentiated Bentham's pleasures into categories of higher and lower, with the intellectual pleasures being the highest. Mill also argued for the importance of internal constraints on morality such as guilt. These internal constraints would prove to be important to psychology later on because they, combined with other concepts such as the unconscious and anxiety, would lead to the founding of psychoanalysis and later to clinical and counseling psychology. In fact, Freud's London library included two volumes written by Mill (Molnar, 2002). In Great Britain the influence of Utilitarianism was strong. When combined with Darwin's theory of evolution it produced a way of thinking that led later scientists to search for answers to questions about the utility of nearly any kind of thing, from the function of animal body parts and shapes to the search for the universal laws of learning. The situation on the German-speaking regions on the continent of Europe was quite different. There, Kant's legacy loomed large but was problematical. He had identified, but not solved, two major philosophical problems: materialism and skepticism.

PHOTO 6.4 J. S. Mill

Credit: iStock/traveller1116

Romanticism

Romanticism was a complex response to many simultaneous and competing social forces and changes that arose at the end of the 18th century. Romanticism affected all of the intellectual aspects of life including literature, art, music, as well as philosophy. It was a response against the Enlightenment and its seemingly inexorable movement toward materialism on the one hand or toward skepticism on the other. Romanticism reacted against reason, reveled in the sensual, and refocused on the individual. In philosophy, the effects of Romanticism were most profound in the German-speaking regions of Europe. At that time Germany did not exist as a separate state. Rather, it was a conglomeration of kingdoms, princedoms, duchies, and free cities, all of which had been part of the Holy Roman Empire (see Figure 6.1). That "empire" was still in existence (it was dissolved in 1806) but was no longer a cohesive or effective governmental unit. The member states were united only by the German language and their politics had become increasingly dominated by its two most powerful states: Prussia and Austria. In addition, the 1648 Peace of Westphalia had legitimized the existing three religions—Catholicism, Lutheranism, and Calvinism—in the regions they had controlled in 1648, but had excluded rights for any other religions (especially Judaism).

Romanticism's early roots lay in Kant's transcendental idealism. He had attempted to solve the Crisis of the Enlightenment by separating topics that were knowable and unknowable. His solution, in the opinion of later philosophers, failed because it left in place the traces of a Cartesian dualism. In addition, large-scale historical events were placing additional burdens upon the Crisis of the Enlightenment, most prominently the American (1776) and French (1789) revolutions. Enlightenment principles had weighed heavily in favor in both of those earth-shattering events. The French Revolution, however, was more influential to Romanticism because of its proximity to Germany and its turn toward political radicalism. Early on, German observers viewed the French Revolution favorably but few were inclined to join it or to extend it

FIGURE 6.1   ■   The Holy Roman Empire in 1789

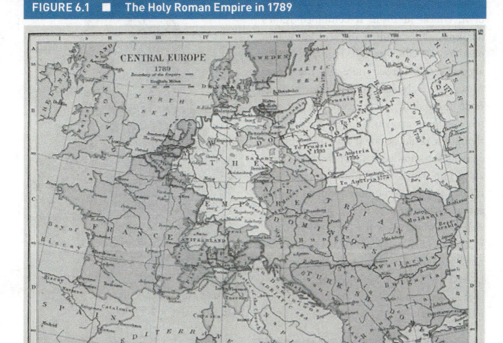

outside of France's borders (Seyhan, 2009). Eventually, the French Revolution's dissolution of the French monarchy, the guillotining of King Louis XVI, and the rise of Napoleon dissolved any hope that the progress made during the Enlightenment could be sustained. But, as Wells (2018) noted:

> Romantics have been accused of dismissing the Enlightenment and reason, even to the point that some academics have put them in binary with each other. Instead of dismissing reason or the Enlightenment, the Romantics saw themselves as inheritors of the Enlightenment, and opened up critiques of previous thought.

Still, many Germans believed that a new philosophical solution was needed. Several such solutions emerged in quick succession culminating in romanticism. One of the first to emerge was the ethical idealism of Johann Gottlieb Fichte.

Johann Gottlieb Fichte (1762–1814)

Fichte was the gifted son of a weaver who worked as a tutor, read Kant, and wrote an analysis of Kant's work that argued that moral law was the only type of revelation compatible with Kant's transcendental idealism (Breazeale, 2006). All that led to an appointment at the University of Jena. Fichte eventually attempted to cure the problems left behind by Kant's transcendental idealism by proposing his own modification of it, ethical idealism. It combined Kant's dualisms, understanding and sensibility, into one idea, the absolute ego. Humans, Fichte argued, each possessed finite egos that strove to reach the absolute ego, but never could reach that point. Fichte never claimed that the world was, actually, an ideal place, but he thought it could be so, at least in principle. Striving for knowledge about the world provided him with a mechanism for explaining history and for accounting for how human action could shape the future, both of which were important goals for later romanticists. Fichte's ethical idealism, "Like a rocket . . . quickly rose to the heights but only to explode in mid air" (Beiser, 2000, p. 31), meaning that Fichte attracted many students but they quickly found flaws in his philosophy.

PHOTO 6.5 Fichte
Credit: iStock/clu

Friedrich Wilhelm Joseph Schelling (1775–1854) and Georg Wilhelm Friedrich Hegel (1770–1831)

Friedrich Wilhelm Joseph Schelling and Georg Wilhelm Friedrich Hegel were two of several German philosophers who quickly seized upon Fichte's ideas as a starting point for their own newer ideas. They believed that Fichte had not yet eliminated Kant's dualism. So they proposed a new and radical solution, absolute idealism. Taking their cue from Leibniz, they redefined matter itself. To them, mind and body became one living Absolute with the human mind and its consciousness at one end and the simplest animal bodies at the other end. In short, all living things were differentiated only by their degree of complexity. Schelling and Hegel eventually disagreed with each other and parted ways. Vater and Wood (2012, p. 4) explained some of the motivations behind the attack on Kantian thought by romanticism:

> Schelling, schooled in Plato's *Timaeus* as well as Kantian critique, sought to expand Kant's fragmentary account of the physical sciences, one based more on the emerging chemistry and biology of the new century than on Kant's Newtonian materialism. And Hegel would take up Kant's systematic leftovers—religion, social philosophy, economics, politics, and history—and fashion them into an account of human reality so bold and sweeping that it dropped the labels "transcendental" or "critical" and proclaimed itself absolute or objective idealism.

Hegel went on to become one of the most influential philosophers of his century, if for nothing else because "virtually every major philosophical movement of the twentieth century—existentialism, Marxism, pragmatism, phenomenology, and analytic philosophy—grew out of reaction against Hegel" (Beiser, 2005, p. 2). Hegel's philosophy, notoriously difficult to read or translate, kept the German idealists' Absolute in place as the unitary goal of all knowledge. It also preserved the historical nature of knowledge along with the fact that individuals were forever limited to their own lifespan. Thus, no mortal could ever hope to realize the goal of knowing everything.

Hegel's longest lasting contribution was his **dialectic**. That concept helped explain the nature of historical change and the provisional status of "truths" within philosophy. Hegel came to the dialectic after noting that the ideas of Heraclitus and Parmenides about change contradicted each other. Plato, however, produced a new synthesis when he reconciled their ideas: some things changed and others did not. Hegel also made **alienation** a central concept in his philosophy. Alienation "is the sudden recognition by mind that it exists apart from the only world in which its own existence becomes possible; a world that is somehow different from the known world in which the mind actually is" (Robinson, 1982, p. 122). The concept of alienation has had a prominent role in psychology and the other social sciences since Hegel first defined it.

PHOTO 6.6 Hegel
Credit: iStock/Graffisimo

Utilitarianism and German idealism were each to play a prominent role in the eventual emergence and development of psychology. At the same time these philosophies were developing, so too, were new branches of science: the social sciences. The earliest of the social sciences was sociology.

LEARNING OBJECTIVE

4. Appraise the responses to rationalism by utilitarianism and romanticism.

THE SOCIAL SCIENCES

A variety of social sciences were emerging in the latter half of the 19th century. These fledging efforts were carving out niches within philosophy, biology, and the computational sciences but were not, at first, seeking to define a common ground that might successfully integrate information from those parent disciplines into new and independent fields of study. Sociology preceded psychology as both readjusted their borders with philosophy, biology, and computational sciences while establishing a new territory: social science. Sociology's founders were Auguste Comte, Emile Durkheim, Karl Marx, and Max Weber. Their writings, although often in marked disagreement, helped found and define sociology. The issues they uncovered and studied legitimized the use of scientific methods in social science. Many of those methods would later also be used by early psychologists. Stepnisky (2019, p. 298) concured:

> Over the last 50 years, Karl Marx, Emile Durkheim, and Max Weber have emerged
> as the core of the classical sociological canon. Each of them conceptualized society in

unique ways that have shaped how sociologists conceive of and study society. Marx, responding to political economists…Durkheim…thought of society as a thing-in-itself that is irreducible to other phenomena…Weber…did not think of society as a thing-in-itself. Rather his approach focused on individual action.

Auguste Comte (1798–1857)

Comte coined the word "sociology" and sought to create a scientific approach to study society based upon positivism. That approach elevated empirical methods as the only source of knowledge. He rejected much of classical philosophy's tenets and even sought to create a secular alternative to human society. In that scheme he divided human history into three periods: theological, metaphysical, and scientific. Naturally, he believed that society had progressed to the last stage.

Emile Durkheim (1858–1917)

Durkheim was inspired by Comte's writings and subscribed to his positivistic outlook. He was the first person to hold an academic appointment in sociology, a department he created at the University of Bordeaux. He published rules for collecting sociological data objectively and analyzing them mathematically. He pointed sociology toward the study of suicide, crime, law, and religion.

Karl Marx (1818–1883)

Like Comte and Durkheim, Marx also wanted to create a secular approach to the study of society, but he rejected positivism. He denied Comte's and Durkheim's positivism and criticized Hegel, eventually substituting a reinterpretation of that philosopher's ideas that now bears his name, Marxism. Specifically, Marx argued that Hegelian philosophy disregarded people while glorifying the state and that philosophy should be about actions not words. Marx hoped that his writings would lead to actual societal change through, if necessary, violent means. In his analysis of 19th century society, the capitalist class was exploiting the working class. After 1917, Marxist ideas were put into action after the creation of a communist government in Russia and, later, in China. The dynamic conflicts between communism and capitalism still cause headline-making tensions around the world.

Max Weber (1864–1920)

Weber disagreed with Comte, Durkheim, and Marx over the goals and methods of sociology. Weber believed in and promoted an antipositivistic approach to social science. His contributions were many and affected not only sociology but also history and economics. His work attempted to analyze the changing historical relationships between individuals, their sense of freedom, religion, and the rise of an increasingly rational, depersonalized, and controlling bureaucracy. The work of these sociologists in explicating the tremendous changes in society that took place near the end of the 19th century naturally focused attention on the individual human beings affected by them. Other social scientists working and writing during that period were more interested in individuals. They were closer to becoming psychologists but they failed to take the final steps to being named psychology's founder. Spencer, Bain, Herbart, and Lotze all approached becoming the first psychologist but narrowly missed receiving that honor.

Herbert Spencer (1820–1903)

Biography

Spencer was born in Derby, England. His father, a schoolmaster and secretary of the Derby Philosophical Society (founded by Erasmus Darwin) and his uncle, a churchman, taught young Herbert early on. However, Spencer was mostly self-taught. Born during the railway boom in England, he first worked as a civil engineer helping build that new infrastructure. Soon, he began to write and his first articles were published mostly in obscure and radical periodicals. He published his first book, *Social Statics*, in 1851, which served to introduce him to many of the leading British intellectuals of the day including Thomas Huxley and George Elliot. Darwin's *Origin of the Species* (1859) was published two years after an essay Spencer had written on progress. However, his ideas and Darwin's were very different.

Contributions

Spencer, unlike Darwin (see Chapter 8), believed that everything—animals, people, and society—progressed in one direction: from simple to complex. His second book, *Principles of Psychology*, first came out in 1855 but sold poorly. But, the 1870 second edition was a major commercial success. It was part of a larger series of texts designed to show the connectedness of all knowledge. Other volumes covered biology, sociology, ethics, and education. They were the works that occupied much of Spencer's later life. He attempted to lay out his idea that all of the natural world, from the microscopic to the most complex human societies, had begun as simple entities and gradually evolved to become more complex. His psychology followed the same path, progressing from simple reflexes and perception to the most complex activities of the human mind, culminating in rational behavior (a point he held that humankind had yet to reach fully).

Like other scientists of his time, Spencer sought to explain the links between psychology and physiology. He was an unabashed Lamarckian, another big difference from Darwin who had taken great pains to construct a system that did not require Lamarck's assumption of gain or loss of acquired characteristics through use or disuse. (However, near the end of his life Darwin felt pressured enough to include Lamarckian ideas in his theory of evolution.) Despite their

MR. HERBERT SPENCER.

PHOTO 6.7 Spencer

Credit: iStock/duncan1890

differences, Darwin's theory provided a tremendous boost to the popularity of Spencer and his ideas. In fact, the famous phrase "survival of the fittest" was Spencer's and not Darwin's. One idea often attributed to Spencer, Social Darwinism, was not really his own. One of the results of 19th century European progress and expansion was the creation of colonial empires by nearly all of the major powers. Social Darwinists justified the vast and real differences in technology, weaponry, and standards of living between themselves and the peoples they subjugated as the result of evolutionary progress and often used Spencer's writings as support for their views. Spencer was one of the most successful authors of his century and did much to raise public awareness about the social sciences. However, he had a contemporary who nearly deserved the title of first psychologist. That man was Alexander Bain.

Alexander Bain (1818–1903)
Biography

Bain was one of five children of a poor Scottish weaver and had to work at the family loom to pay for his rent and schooling (Boring, 1950). He was intellectually gifted and able to attend Marischal College, which had not yet been incorporated into the University of Aberdeen. Boakes (1984, p. 10) wrote:

> As a Scot he was fortunate to live in possibly the only country 150 years ago where a boy from this kind of background could obtain a university education without very much difficulty, providing that he showed intellectual promise.

He distinguished himself academically but was unable to find a faculty position. Instead, he became a freelance writer and made friends with John Stuart Mill to the point of helping him revise his book, *Logic*, in 1842.

Contributions

Bain wrote the first successful textbook in psychology, *The Senses and the Intellect*, in 1855, and followed it up with *The Emotions and the Will* in 1859. For the next 50 years those two books (in frequently revised editions) became the standard texts for teaching psychology in Great Britain and the United States (at least until William James's textbook appeared in 1890). One aspect of Bain's texts became part of nearly every psychology textbook published since, an early chapter linking physiology to psychology. Publication of his texts led, finally, to his appointment to a chair in logic and English at the University of Aberdeen. Because he was not academically prepared to hold such a position he spent much time writing textbooks from which he could teach his courses. But, his true compass was still psychology. One topic that concerned him was the relationship of mind and body. He adopted psychophysical parallelism as a mind–body solution, a modification of Leibniz's preestablished harmony. Because of Mill's influence Bain was firmly within the British associationist tradition. Rosen (2017, p. 39) wrote, "One might depict the relationship between Mill and Bain in terms of a 'double helix' with their intertwined achievements enhancing and enriching the thought of each and of utilitarianism generally."

Thus, his psychology sprang from that philosophical background with its deep roots going back to Locke, Berkeley, and Hume. He adopted their philosophically derived principles: contiguity, similarity, and repetition (or frequency). To these he added something new: *compound association*. He used that concept because it helped explain the complexity behind association. Most ideas were not linked one-to-one with a specific stimulus; instead they were linked to many stimuli, some of which could be quite weak. Consequently, those would have had little chance to elicit ideas by themselves. He also added a concept he called *constructive association* that explained how new ideas arose in the mind.

THEN AND NOW
THE PHYSIOLOGICAL CHAPTER

Over the years I have noticed that many of the students in my introductory psychology sections seem perplexed when they realize they will be studying neurons and the brain close to the beginning of the course. Little do they realize they are following in Bain's footsteps. Contemporary psychology texts universally include at least one chapter on physiological psychology and other chapters related to the border between psychology and biology (e.g., sensation, perception, hormones, evolution, and others). The border between psychology and biology is now well defined.

His most original contribution to early psychology, however, concerned movement. Before Bain, few thinkers had thought to observe and measure movements and to use them as psychological data to understand the workings of the mind. His inspiration came from observations on newborn lambs. He watched as the lambs first struggled to stand on all fours and then move. However, the lambs's "earliest movements were a jumble of side, forward, and backward" (Bain, 1855, p. 412). In a few hours, however, they had learned to walk, run, and nurse. Bain differentiated this type of *spontaneous activity* from reflexive movements. He attempted to explain the motivation behind such spontaneous activities through the *feelings* of pleasure and pain. His explanation was the first statement of trial-and-error learning that was later to become so important in the behavioral theories of Pavlov, Thorndike, and Skinner.

Bain argued that spontaneous behaviors arose and were then associated with the positive or negative consequences that followed

ALEXANDER BAIN

PHOTO 6.8 Bain

those behaviors. Unlike Spencer, Bain had surprisingly little interest in Darwin's theory of evolution. Bain was one of the first persons to devote nearly his whole academic career to the study of psychology. If that is true, why isn't he considered to be the first psychologist? The usual answer is that, unlike Wundt, Bain was a transitional figure, not a revolutionary one. His work could just as easily be seen as the logical culmination of British empiricist philosophy as it could be seen as the first steps in psychology. Also, Bain was not really an experimenter. He did not found a laboratory nor did he train experimentally minded students as did Wundt. Nevertheless, Bain's work represents the beginnings of the fissure that eventually separated philosophy from psychology.

It is now time to cross the English Channel back to the continent to catch up with the psychologically minded philosopher Johann Herbart. He argued for the scientific status of psychology but believed that experimentation on the mind was impossible. He also saw no link between psychology and biology. Despite these views he became an important influence on Fechner and Wundt. Much of Herbart's thinking survives in psychology to the present day.

Johann Friedrich Herbart (1776–1841)

Biography

Herbart was born in Oldenburg, Germany. Due to a childhood accident, his mother, a highly intelligent woman, kept him at home and served as his teacher until he was 12. Herbart was precocious and intelligent as well. He attended the local gymnasium and later graduated from the University of Jena. After graduating he tutored the governor of Interlaken's three boys for three years. During that time he also visited the educational reformer, Pestalozzi, in nearby Switzerland. He began to think about the psychology of education. After quitting his tutoring, he took his PhD degree at the University of Göttingen. There, he studied philosophy and soon developed his own ideas which ran counter to his mentor Fichte and his boyhood idol, Kant. Specifically, he opposed Fichte's idealism and Kant's contention that a science of psychology was impossible. However, he did agree with Kant that experiments on the mind could not be performed. Ironically, he was called to Kant's old chair at Königsberg, vacated because of his death five years before. Herbart remained at Königsberg for 24 years and that was where he wrote his most influential books. He ended his career back at Göttingen. He died young, unexpectedly of stroke, two days after his last lecture.

BORDER WITH SOCIAL SCIENCE
EDUCATIONAL PSYCHOLOGY

Today, educational psychology is nearly its own independent discipline; many universities have separate departments of psychology and educational psychology. Herbart was among the first to think closely about how children learned and how teachers should teach. He set up a separate demonstration school soon after he began teaching at the University of Königsberg. From his experiences there he came up with five rules for teaching:

1. Pick topics and materials that will grab children's interest

2. Teach the topic clearly

3. Ask inductive questions afterward

4. Link the new knowledge taught to what the children already knew

5. Apply the new knowledge in a concrete manner

Herbart's rules were very influential and led to popular acceptance of psychology.

Contributions

Herbart's psychology was to prove influential but it was very different from the others developing around the same time. He argued that his psychology was mathematical, empirical, and scientific. His psychology bordered on philosophy but ignored biology and was not experimental. Influenced by Newton and Leibniz, he substituted ideas for monads and proposed mathematical rules, static and dynamic, for describing how ideas affected each other. Ideas, he argued, preserved themselves and inhibited or promoted other ideas. Ideas, thus, never "died." Instead, some ideas remained in consciousness while others dropped into the unconscious.

One of Herbart's most original contributions was the **threshold or limen**. Later, Ernst Weber and Gustav Fechner made good use that Herbartian concept in their psychophysical research (see Chapter 8). Herbart borrowed Leibniz's notion of apperception and made it an integral part of his psychology through a new and related construct, the apperceptive mass. The apperceptive mass described the sum total of competing ideas at any given time. Some ideas, however, coalesced into readily apperceptible collections of compatible ideas. A geometric example is a triangle. It is any closed two-dimensional figure having three sides. It is an apperceptive mass. On the other hand, a "four-sided triangle" is also a collection of ideas, but one very difficult to apperceive. Thus, while a "three-sided triangle" would be an apperceptive mass, a four-sided triangle would not.

Herbart's reluctance to test his mathematical theories experimentally doomed his approach. The problem was his reluctance to compare introspectively derived results to reality. He was never able to assure himself that the assumptions he made governing the interaction of ideas were true. Nevertheless, Fechner and Wundt separately acknowledged their deep debt to him. Fechner did so in print, writing (Fechner, 1966, p. xxx):

I have intentionally omitted reference to the contrast between the mathematical approach to psychological relations in this work and Herbart's. To Herbart will always belong the credit not only of having been the first to point out the possibility of a mathematical treatment of these matters, but also of having made the first ingenious attempt to carry out such an enterprise; and everyone since Herbart will in this respect have to be second.

Herbart's successor at Göttingen, Hermann Lotze, did much to meld Herbart's psychology with the burgeoning growth of psychophysical research; he helped make a place for psychology distinct from philosophy and biology.

Hermann Lotze (1817–1881)

Biography

Lotze's father was an army surgeon. Shortly after Lotze's birth in Bautzen, Germany, his father was transferred to Zittau where Lotze received his education. After graduating from the local gymnasium, Lotze enrolled at the University of Leipzig. He took a degree in medicine and studied with Ernst Weber and Gustav Fechner. It was Fechner who "inspired Lotze to set to work in the medical sciences, to place them on a firm foundation of hypotheses grounded in the research of the day" (Woodward, 2015, pp. 3-4). After practicing medicine in Zittau for a year, Lotze was back at Leipzig and received PhDs in medicine and philosophy. His feet were in two camps, one in science and the other in the humanities. He even published a volume of poetry. After Herbart died, Lotze was called to fill his chair at Göttingen, a post he held for 37 years or nearly the rest of his life. He died of pneumonia a few months after being persuaded to leave Göttingen for the University of Berlin.

BORDER WITH COMPUTATIONAL SCIENCE
MATHEMATICAL PSYCHOLOGY

Mathematical psychologists are in short supply today (Clay, 2005), but those who remain along with their professional organizations and journals are "keepers of the flame" (Townsend, 2008, p. 275) for the long association between mathematics and psychology. Unlike Herbart, however, today's mathematical psychologists apply their expertise to theorizing and the proper collection of data. Townsend cited signal detection theory, mathematical learning theory, scaling, decision theory, psychophysics, and neural modeling as active areas today related to mathematical psychology. He also noted that "the central advantage psychology has had over other fields in past years has been the relatively heavy component of education in practical statistics and methodology" (p. 276). If anything, Herbart's original vision of the importance of mathematics has been expanded in modern psychology, but there is concern that fewer new students are choosing to become mathematical psychologists.

Contributions

Unlike Herbart, Lotze gravitated more toward philosophy and less toward psychology. In fact, his most significant contributions to psychology came early in his career. Yet, at the same time, psychology was the only course that he lectured on every year of his tenure at Göttingen (Boring, 1950). His book, *Medical Psychology,* was published in 1852 and was the first book ever published to link physiology and psychology. In it, he wrote the first account of Weber's Law (see Chapter 8). He also provided his own account of how the mind perceived physical space; it held that the mind constructed the three dimensions of physical space out of variables that, by themselves, did not provide spatial data. The three variables were intensity, quality, and movement. In some innate way the mind combined them to yield the perception of space. Lotze also contributed to the future of psychology through his students Karl Stumpf and G. E. Müller. He also was close to Franz Brentano.

Lotze was one of the first academics to adopt the modern view of scientists as disinterested observers who carefully weighed all sides of a question. Similarly, he was one of the first to realize the importance of the newly founded scientific journals (Sullivan, 2010). As a philosopher, he helped create a new role for philosophy, separating it from the emerging empirical disciplines and making philosophy the study of problems "independent of the special sciences" (Schnädelbach, 1984, p. 103). Lotze, then, was instrumental in creating two of psychology's borders. He made the border with philosophy clearer and at the same time situated psychology in between philosophy and biology. Unlike the more biologically oriented early psychologists, Lotze saw the border between psychology and biology more distinctly than they did. Later, Wundt (see Chapter 7) acknowledged Lotze and Herbart as his precursors, but carefully selected bits and pieces of their work to incorporate into his own vision of psychology.

LEARNING OBJECTIVE
5. Review the steps to psychology taken by early social scientists.

LEARNING OBJECTIVE
6. Compare and contrast the rationalist philosopher's ideas.

In one way or another, all of the philosophers and psychologists covered in this chapter were not experimentally inclined. Instead, they used the old technique of introspection. For all of them, being trained as philosophers, using introspection was second nature. What was about to happen was that some would start to use introspection experimentally. Those became the first true psychologists.

SUMMARY

Continental rationalists, as a group, disagreed with the British empiricists but they also disagreed among themselves. Spinoza disagreed with Descartes over the nature of God and dualism. Leibniz, too, altered Descartes interactionism using his own dualistic solution, preestablished harmony. Leibniz posited that the universe was made up of infinitesimals, monads, and that those could be viewed from both physical and mental viewpoints simultaneously and independently. Kant, distressed by Leibniz's monads and Hume's version of British empiricism proposed a complex solution, one that separated, once and for all, philosophy from theology. But, unlike Hume, did so in a manner that respected both disciplines. For Kant, questions about God were out of bounds. Kant also revived moral philosophy through his categorical imperative, again, another response to the use of hedonism by the British empiricists.

Other philosophies also blossomed in the 19th century. In England, Utilitarianism arose after the writings of Bentham and John Stuart Mill. In the German-speaking countries, Romanticism flourished culminating with Hegel's dialectic. Social science also made its first appearance with the emergence of sociology. Its founders were Comte, Durkheim, Marx, and Weber.

Two protopsychologists also emerged within social science, Herbert Spencer and Alexander Bain, both of whom wrote textbooks of psychology. Yet neither wore the mantle of being the first psychologist because their approaches were not experimental. Herbart was another early protopsychologist. His approach, too, was not experimental, but he was one of the first to look at an applied area: educational psychology. His work with sensory thresholds helped open the door for psychophysics. Lotze, too, was instrumental as a psychological pioneer. He was the first to publish about Weber's Law and was instrumental in preparing the way for a more scientific approach to psychology.

7 INTROSPECTIVE PSYCHOLOGY

ZEITGEIST

The Scientific Laboratory

Cattell (1928) named the founding of the chemistry *laboratory* at the University of Giessen in 1824 as the first of any in science. Soon other laboratories sprang up to study physics and biology. The founding of Wundt's psychology laboratory in 1879 traditionally marks the beginning of psychology as a discipline and science. Before Wundt, psychological research was largely conducted by solitary individuals. Their work was primarily focused on physiology or sensation and was located close to psychology's border with biology (see Chapter 8). Benjamin (2000, p. 318) noted that one of the most important aspects of the new psychology laboratory was "the community of scholars who conducted collaborative research in pursuit of scientific explanations of mind." Soon after, students from Wundt's laboratory quickly founded other similar laboratories around the world. By 1900, 25 had been founded in the United States, 10 in Germany, and 12 more in ten countries including Japan and China (Harper, 1950).

In the United States, the laboratory and at least one laboratory course became the standard for undergraduate psychology training (Benjamin, 2000). That practice remains a vital part for nearly all undergraduate psychology curricula today. Dunn et al. (2007, p. 654) discussing undergraduate psychology programs stated, "A distinguished program would not only offer individual coursework in scientific methods but would ground all coursework in the scientific foundation of the discipline." Psychology, finally, was at hand having staked its claims to an intellectual territory from the fields of philosophy, mathematics, biology, and social science.

LEARNING OBJECTIVE

1. Analyze how the founding of laboratories was important to early psychology.

PREVIEW

Wundt's psychology was characterized by the advent of the psychology *laboratory* and its equipment. Very quickly other laboratories sprang up around the world. The research at those laboratories was very different than psychological research today. The earliest psychologists concentrated on the scientific study of the mind and *consciousness*. Wundt's research topics included *Voluntarism, apperception, reaction time studies*, and the *creative synthesis*. Titchener, on the other hand, promoted *Structuralism, introspection*, and the *stimulus error. Memory* was the focus for Ebbinghaus. His pioneering work on memory was impressive because of the new methods—*nonsense syllables* and the *savings score*—he applied to study it. Müller and his colleagues extended Ebbinghaus's work using new equipment and stronger experimental methods. Brentano's *act psychology* linked perceivers to the act of perceiving and argued against *systematic experimentation*. Instead, it looked to design and conduct *crucial experiments. Phenomenology* was the focus of Stumpf's work; it anticipated Gestalt psychology's later anti-elementistic stance. The debunking of *Clever Hans's* cognitive powers was a huge step for early psychology and brought it wide attention. The research coming out of the *Würzburg School (imageless thought* and *cognitive set)* demonstrated the problems with introspection as a reliable research method.

INTRODUCTION

Psychology finally made its appearance as a scientific discipline primarily through the work of Wilhelm Wundt. His contributions were central, although as other chapters will show 21st century psychology had many other parents. Wundt was a philosopher who saw the need for a new experimental methodology to study the human mind. His work in psychology emphasized empirical results derived from laboratory experiments. Later in his life he also studied psychological topics that he believed could not be approached by laboratory methods. His definition of psychology had two main parts. One part was lab-based, Voluntarism. It centered on how humans chose to attend to particular stimuli. The other part, *völkerpsychologie* (usually labeled "folk psychology" in English), was unapproachable experimentally and Wundt spent the last years of his life studying its components. His influence upon the new science was magnified by his voluminous written output and the large number of students he trained. Of all of his contributions, however, the psychology laboratory was the one most adopted by others. Only recently have psychologists become reengaged with the topics subsumed under *völkerpsychologie* (Damböck et al., 2020).

Edward B. Titchener was one of Wundt's early students. Titchener was English but spent the majority of his career in the United States. At Cornell University, he modified Wundt's approach and cataloged the many elements of the human mind. Titchener called his approach to psychology Structuralism. He assiduously avoided any attempts to make psychology more applied or to include animal research. While highly influential during his lifetime, his Structuralism all but disappeared following his death.

In Europe Wundt's psychology inspired many others to become psychologists. Georg E. Müller created a laboratory that rivaled Wundt's. The work coming out of that laboratory emphasized psychophysics, vision, and memory. Another contemporary of Wundt's was Franz Brentano. His approach was decidedly different in that he put much less emphasis upon systematic experimentation. Instead, he searched for crucial experiments, ones that were designed to answer a scientific question once and for all. Brentano called his approach Act Psychology. Unlike Wundt, he wrote little and trained only a handful of students, minimizing his ultimate historical influence.

Other European psychologists embraced the experimental method but put it to new uses. Carl Stumpf brought his lifelong interests in music to the psychology laboratory. His early analyses of musical melody contradicted much of the elemental approach to psychology promoted by Wundt and Titchener. Two of Stumpf's students, Wolfgang Köhler and Kurt Koffka, cofounded Gestalt Psychology (along with Max Wertheimer, see Chapter 12). Another German, Oskar Pfungst, demonstrated that the famous horse, Clever Hans, was unable to compute simple mathematical expressions. Hermann Ebbinghaus was inspired to study memory using the new experimental methods of psychology. His work on human memory is still covered in all psychology textbooks. Finally, Oswald Külpe, Wundt's second assistant, broke with him over the issue of imageless thoughts and cognitive sets. Külpe and his colleagues showed that human participants reliably gave similar answers to mental problems but could not introspect as to why they had. Their work was the death nell to the early introspective methods in psychology. How did Wundt and others use introspection?

INTROSPECTION

Introspection, the examination of immediate consciousness, is as old as philosophy itself (Boring, 1953). As psychology emerged from philosophy it was only natural for psychologists to adopt that ancient technique. Over time, some discovered that they and their research subjects could make consistent responses but without being able to introspect about how or why they had made those responses. That led to psychology's first major crisis and eventually doomed introspection as a viable research technique.

Wilhelm Wundt used introspection as one of the data collection tools at his disposal. He also used precisely measured reaction times under a variety of conditions as well as more qualitative methods. His lasting contribution, however, was in creating the psychology laboratory. That innovation of his was widely copied and was his greatest legacy to psychology. He also trained many students who later went on to become early pioneers in psychology. Bunn (2017) reviewed how Wundt became to be hailed as the first psychologist and describes some of his methods and innovations.

LEARNING OBJECTIVE
2. Discuss how introspection became psychology's first methodology.

Wilhelm Wundt (1832–1920)

Biography

Wundt was born near the inland port city of Mannheim, Germany, but his family soon moved to the small town of Heidelsheim. There, his father was a country pastor who died when Wundt was 14. Most of Wundt's early years were lived in solitude, and his early experiences with schooling were traumatic. The assistant pastor his father hired became his unofficial tutor and close companion. That relationship, along with access to his father's extensive library, helped prepare him for university studies. But, Wundt's academic path was rocky. He hated the local **gymnasium** he first attended; he was unprepared to socialize and compete with boys of his own age so he performed poorly.

After his father died, Wundt moved to Heidelberg to live with his uncle; he enrolled in its gymnasium where his academic record was mediocre at best. Upon graduation, he followed his uncle to the University of Tübingen to study medicine. During his year at Tübingen, something finally clicked and he became a successful student. When his uncle was called to teach at the University of Heidelberg one year later, Wundt went with him. At Heidelberg, he graduated in four years and won a prize for his personal research. After graduating, a year-long stint at a woman's hospital convinced him that the practice of medicine was not for him. He successfully applied to become an assistant to Johannes Müller and Emil Du Bois-Reymond in Berlin. A year later he was back at Heidelberg as a docent, the lowest ranking faculty level. Soon, he fell gravely ill and believed he might die. Some months later, after he recovered, he became one of Hermann Helmholtz's assistants. That great scientist was now teaching at Heidelberg too. (See Chapter 8 for details on Helmholtz's career and contributions to science and psychology.)

PHOTO 7.1 Wilhem Wundt

Contributions

Wundt worked for Helmholtz for nearly five years, but the two never truly connected. Wundt kept to himself and worked on problems similar to the ones Helmholtz was also working on at the same time. Diamond (1980, p. 31) speculated that:

> Wundt seems at times to have been deliberately challenging Helmholtz by choosing to work on problems that Helmholtz already had in hand and then thrusting his own unripe solutions forward as if to declare: "Look at me! Acknowledge me as your equal!"

Wundt gradually realized that his interests and Helmholtz's were different. Helmholtz always saw himself as a natural scientist with a mathematical bent. Wundt, on the other hand, was struggling to make a name for himself. It was not until 1862, after he published his 4th book, the *Textbook of Human Physiology*, that he achieved that breakthrough. The book was well received and translated into several languages. Through it he took the first steps toward becoming the preeminent spokesperson for a new discipline, psychology. Wundt combined a number of related subfields: sensory psychophysics, the personal equation, and brain localization as the core of that new discipline. Publishing another book, in philosophy, led to other and more prestigious academic positions in philosophy: first at the University of Zurich and a year later at the University of Leipzig. At Leipzig, he combined his budding experimental prowess with his theoretical interests to create the first laboratory devoted to studying psychology for its own sake. There, he strove to make philosophy a broader field. He saw psychology as a part of philosophy. For him psychology was, on the one hand, a perspective on consciousness that could be tested through experimentation. On the other hand, his folk psychology or *völkerpsychologie* addressed (Kim, 2006, n.p.):

> language, art, myth, and customs . . . objects [that] cannot be investigated in the same way as those of individual 'inner' experience, but require a mode of explanation appropriate to their external, yet non-physical phenomenology.

Thus, Wundt defined psychology as consisting of two parts: one was lab- based, experimental, and nearer to biology and psychophysics, but the other part, *his völkerpsychologie, could not be* studied that way. It was nearer to the social science disciplines of history and anthropology. Wundt believed that part had to be studied by examining how individuals and their conscious experiences developed in social contexts examining the developmental and social processes that led to the creation of individual consciousness. Wundt maintained that his experimental methods would not work in revealing the *völkerpsychologie*. That message was mostly lost to later generations of psychologists. Most of them seized upon Wundt's experimental approach and its laboratory methods and ignored his *völkerpsychologie*. Modern psychologists call Wundt's laboratory approach *first psychology* and call his *völkerpsychologie second psychology*. Cahan and White wrote (1992), p. 227):

> Wundt saw his second psychology as an essential complement to his experimental psychology and this vision would ultimately lead him, in the early 1900s to the writing of a 10-volume survey of ethnographic data about the language, myth, and customs of diverse human cultures.

Araujo (2016) further clarified Wundt's position about science in general, the *völkerpsychologie*, and how the concept of "will" fit into his psychology. He argued that Wundt was more interested in bringing psychology into philosophy than in creating a new science of psychology.

Along psychology's border with biology, Wundt wished to identify and answer distinctly psychological questions and to do so with the apparatus and methods developed by Helmholtz and others. Wundt believed that the consciousness of individual human beings could be studied experimentally. He seized upon reaction time as a reliable measurement of the speed of conscious activity. While he was still working under Helmholtz, he began to measure reaction times under a variety of "complications" or what today might be called experimental conditions. For instance, he discovered that reaction times were slower when participants were required to make discriminations between two stimuli before making a response compared to when responses followed the presentation of only a single stimulus.

In 1879, he took possession of a single room at the University of Leipzig; that room soon housed his personal collection of psychological apparatus and he began to perform purely psychological experiments there, a first, Danziger noted (1980, p. 106):

> The reaction time studies conducted during the first few years of Wundt's laboratory constitute the first historical example of a coherent research program, explicitly directed toward psychological issues and involving a number of interlocking studies

His lab expanded to several rooms and received the designation of a university Institute, meaning it had a budget and official status. He began to attract graduate students in psychology and philosophy. Over time, his role shifted from active experimenter to laboratory supervisor and psychological theorist.

Wundt closely supervised the selection of research projects and met with the teams of students who volunteered to participate in them. Unlike modern psychological experiments, the focus was not on a participant's behavior. Instead, the focus was on self-observation, inner observation, or inner experience, phrases that would later be translated into English under the common term of "introspection." Wundt also required that the members of each team take part in the experiment by playing three roles: participant, experimenter, and observer (Robinson, 2001). The goal of the research was to hold all external conditions constant but one. That one variable was then systematically manipulated. The data were the participant's verbal reports of his introspective experiences as the variable of interest was systematically changed. In Wundt's experiments, the research team was highly trained and knowledgeable about the question under investigation, unlike the naïve participants in most psychology experiments today. Thus, the final introspective reports returned by the participants only came after much practice and familiarity with the equipment. When the experimenters played the role of subject they were not naïve to the design and goals of the experiment. Robinson (2001) described an reaction time experiment conducted by Wundt and two of his earliest students. They measured reaction time differences to simple and complex stimuli. Specifically, participants had to press a key when they saw a white circle, but not press it when they saw a black one. Later, they repeated the experiment, but with 2 and 4 stimuli. Reaction times slowed consistently compared to those for the original, simple stimulus. Wundt published those results and many others in the new journal he founded, *Philosophische Studien*. It became the destination for nearly all of the experimental reports emanating from his lab as well as those from elsewhere. By the 1890s, Wundt had become the world's preeminent psychologist and was attracting students from all corners, including many from the United States.

Wundt saw psychology as a new science, one that fit into a logical sequence after physics, chemistry, and biology (Blumenthal, 2001). Psychology also fit, in Wundt's scheme, before philosophy. So, Wundt's mental map looked like the sequence as follows:

Physics, Chemistry, Biology, **Psychology**, Philosophy

Wundt claimed new ground for his young science. It was to be different than all of the other disciplines in that it studied consciousness itself and not as the derived result of interactions of matter, chemical reactions, or physiological processes. Wundt was certain that the human mind was open to scientific study and was convinced that consciousness was real, natural, and approachable. He realized the enormous difficulty of his task and understood the counterarguments from other scientists and philosophers. For example, some other scientists wished to provide materialistic explanations for psychological phenomena. Wundt resisted those explanations because he thought that consciousness was not a thing such as a lump of matter or the product of a chemical reaction. He saw consciousness as an ever flowing, historical, and developmental process. At the same time, he argued that consciousness could only be studied by trained observers who reflected upon their own consciousness under controlled laboratory conditions. Wundt's laboratory spawned many new psychologists.

By the end of the 19th century, Wundt's new psychological methods and techniques had spread widely. However, Wundt's psychological theories traveled poorly. At heart, Wundt was much more a theorist and manager than an experimenter. His theories focused on the central role of consciousness and a person's ability to actively choose to attend to selective parts of consciousness. Wundt called his theoretical system **Voluntarism** because people chose which parts of their own consciousness they would attend to. He rejected the more mechanical theories of the British empiricists and the prominent role they assigned to associationism. He also rejected the materialist position held by many physiologists who argued that, ultimately, describing and understanding the mechanics of the body would yield the facts of psychology. Thus, Wundt truly represented something new under the sun. He had succeeded in making psychology a new and independent academic discipline. What were the theoretical details behind his definition of psychology?

LEARNING OBJECTIVE

3. Appraise the factors that led to Wundt becoming the first psychologist.

Wundt's Theory of Psychology

The key to understanding how Wundt's theory is to see that he was looking at consciousness, not behavior. Psychology's marriage to behavior as a definitional component comes later in history (see Chapter 10). For Wundt, much of psychology was the scientific study of consciousness. He assumed that consciousness was accessible, and trained observers could reliably report on the content of their own consciousness. This was his *principle of actuality*. It held that consciousness was a process not a thing; it was an ever-changing but continuous flow (Blumenthal, 2001). The sources of consciousness were many. One source came from drives or instincts. These were built-in unconscious motives such as hunger or thirst. These fundamental motives were associated with affective states such as pleasure or displeasure, and with goal seeking or goal avoidance. Furthermore, they could be predictive of the future through learning and memory. Drives, for Wundt, formed the initial raw materials of consciousness.

Some of Wundt's contemporaries saw things differently. They concentrated on movements, not consciousness, and divided the movements (animal and human) into two categories: involuntary and voluntary. Furthermore, they saw a Darwinian progression from the former to the latter. In other words, involuntary movements (e.g., drives or reflexes) were evolutionarily primitive while voluntary movements were derived or evolutionarily advanced. Wundt disagreed and reversed the order, claiming that in many cases of learning, people worked slower at first because they had to choose among a variety of possible movements. Later, when they became more proficient, they could make the movements automatically and without much conscious thought.

THEN AND NOW
AUTOMATICITY

Interestingly, that observation of his survives still in modern psychology as the concept of automaticity. Wundt argued that early in learning, driving a car, for example, people pay more attention to the details of driving such as steering, changing lanes, speeding up, or slowing down. Later, however, drivers accomplish all of those tasks seemingly without thinking. Moreover, they do so while eating a sandwich, toying with the audio, or talking to passengers. That's automaticity.

Consciousness was a response to sensation. For Wundt, sensations caused perceptions. But, those perceptions were general and vague until observers chose to focus on particular aspects of their perceptions through apperception, a voluntary process. Only after apperception had occurred was a movement or verbal response possible.

Wundt's central theoretical concept was the *creative synthesis*. It described how disparate mental events combined to create entirely new and unpredictable cognitions. The creative synthesis, as a metaphor, was derived from the chemical synthesis of elements into compounds. The difference, however, between chemistry and psychology was vast and fundamental. The products of the creative synthesis could not be predicted beforehand. Psychology was not chemistry; the creative synthesis was how the brain reacted to environmental stimuli to produce the myriad number of constantly flowing events in consciousness. It was the brain's reactions to those events that created "the actual psychological qualities known as 'sweet,' 'sour,' 'heavy,' 'dark blue,' 'dazzling crimson,' 'sharp,' 'painful,' or 'meaningful.' To get those qualities you must have a living brain, one that is awake, conscious, and attentive" (Blumenthal, 2001, p. 129).

Wundt's theories were complex and difficult to understand. Furthermore, he changed them over the years. Later, other psychologists, some his students and some not, significantly altered Wundt's theoretical ideas and later passed them off as his. Thus, including Wundt as a member of the movement called Structuralism is incorrect. Structuralism's search for and identification of psychological "elements" was new, different, and decidedly non-Wundtian. Different, too, was how it used introspective methods. (See below.) As psychology blossomed after Wundt, controversies and disagreements arose. Lost in that din was much of Wundt's theorizing. What was kept were the laboratory experimental methods developed by Wundt and his students. As psychology grew and matured it did so as an experimental science, but its new practitioners largely dispensed with the nonexperimental portions that Wundt had elucidated. Wundt had many students; it's time to look at a few of them and how they shaped psychology after leaving Leipzig.

PSYCHOLOGY AFTER WUNDT

Wundt attracted many students to his laboratory at Leipzig with nearly 200 of them earning their PhDs in psychology and philosophy under his supervision. Many of those students were American; their contributions to the early history of psychology will be covered in chapter 9. Subsequently, the early history of psychology after Wundt will be briefly traced through the lives and works of some of his European students. As noted earlier, Wundt's longest lasting influence was through his laboratory methodology and not through his psychological theory.

Edward Bradford Titchener obtained his PhD from Wundt in 1892. He eventually called his approach to psychology Structuralism in contrast to Wundt's Voluntarism. Historians of psychology now distinguish more carefully between these two early "isms" and take pains to show how Titchener altered Wundt's approach to psychology. Generations of psychology students read the influential histories published by Titchener's student, Edwin Boring, and took it as gospel. Blumenthal (2001, p. 125) wrote, "there are today serious reasons for calling the Boring-Titchener account of founding-father Wundt into question." Titchener was not Wundt's clone and representative to America. Instead, he took some of what he learned from Wundt, mixed that with a good portion of British associationism along with some positivistic philosophy to create his own version of introspective psychology: Structuralism.

Edward Bradford Titchener (1867–1927)

Biography

Titchener was born in Chichester, England, in a family whose fortunes had seen better days. Fortunately for him, he was a bright child and earned scholarships to Malvern College, a prep school, and later to Oxford. There, he studied philosophy at first, but later read the third edition of Wundt's *Textbook of Human Physiology* and translated it into English. He visited Wundt in Leipzig shortly thereafter, showing him the translated work, only to discover that Wundt had nearly finished the fourth edition. Nonetheless, Wundt was impressed with Titchener and urged him to go back to Oxford to take a year of biology. Titchener did and returned to Leipzig where he obtained his PhD from Wundt two years later. One of Titchener's fellow students at Leipzig was an American: Frank Angell; they became close friends. After graduating from Leipzig, Titchener could not find a suitable position in Britain, so instead he went to Cornell University in Ithaca, New York, after Angell left there to begin Stanford's first psychology laboratory. Thus, Titchener, a prim and proper English gentleman, was one of the first of Wundt's students to move to the United States. Titchener spent the rest of his life at Cornell, dying suddenly of a brain tumor in 1927 at the age of 60.

Contributions

The **Structuralism** that Titchener developed at Cornell was a marked departure from Wundtian Voluntarism. For one thing, its origins lay in the associationist philosophical tradition that began with Locke and culminated with John Stuart Mill. Thus, Titchener disagreed with Wundt over the most fundamental philosophical precepts. Wundt's psychology was based upon the German idealistic tradition that viewed the mind more holistically and which devalued associationism as an explanatory device. Titchener put much more emphasis upon the role of introspection as a psychological method. Wundt used introspection as well, but used other methods—apperception and the creative synthesis—that Titchener did not. He also disagreed with Wundt over the very definition of psychology, seeing it as an experimental science only. Titchener did not bring Wundt's *völkerpsychologie* with him to Cornell. Both agreed, however, on the importance of establishing psychology as an experimental science. Titchener was more committed to that goal because his definition of psychology was much more narrow and restricted than Wundt's.

PHOTO 7.2 Edward Titchener

Psychology for Titchener was the scientific and experimental study of the human mind. He held no place in psychology for animal behavior, child studies, abnormality, or any other applied area. He believed psychology was too young an enterprise to risk losing it by dabbling in such fringe areas. Titchener wanted to make psychology the academic equivalent of physics. He saw physics, psychology, and biology as the three main sciences. Each was looking at the same data, but interpreting them from its own point of view. Thus, he was instrumental in attempting to create borders for psychology with physics and biology and a home for a thriving independent discipline of psychology. He was only partly successful. "Titchener did succeed . . . in establishing the laboratory as the center of the psychological enterprise, both as central in the educational preparation of psychologists and of the scientific enterprise itself" (Evans, 1991, p. 103).

Titchener's Theory of Psychology

Titchener was a strong proponent for rigorous methods in psychology. To that end he continued to translate German textbooks into English and later wrote his own textbooks and instructor's manuals. Those later works emphasized the necessity for reliable methods of introspection. Wundt and Titchener each believed that introspection could be used to study the mind. Titchener, however, emphasized introspection and highly trained introspectors in his psychology to a much greater degree than did Wundt. For example, Titchener introduced the **stimulus**

error and provided methods for avoiding it while introspecting. To avoid the stimulus error while introspecting, structuralist researchers were only to report their inner states with regard to sensations, images, and affect. For sensations, they could report the quality, intensity, or duration. For vision and touch, they could also report extensity, or the impression that sights and sounds could spread out through space beyond their initial focus. For affect, they could only report pleasantness or unpleasantness, another simplification of Wundt's system. Wundt believed that affect could be broken down into three parts: pleasantness or unpleasantness, excitation or depression, and tension or relaxation. A common classroom object, an eraser, nicely illustrates the stimulus error. None of Titchener's students would dare to call it an eraser while introspecting about their inner states while holding it. Instead, they might note its weight, feel, smell, or even its taste. But, they would never say the word "eraser"; to do so would be to commit the stimulus error because their knowledge of that object as an eraser did not come from introspection but from later learning. Titchener and his students eventually identified over 44,000 elements, with more than 30,000 of those being visual. Obviously, his original project had grown exponentially and he was left with far too many elements to deal with successfully.

Much of the success of Titchener's structuralist approach came from his personality and work habits. He was famously aloof and distant. His wife screened all of his telephone calls, and he never joined the newly formed American Psychological Association or attended any of its meetings, even when they once met in Ithaca, New York (where Cornell University is located). He founded a group called the "Experimental Psychologists" which only admitted *men* who studied the kind of psychology he championed. All others were excluded. After his death, that group continued under a new name, the Society of Experimental Psychologists, which currently has a membership of nearly 300 invited fellows, including women. Titchener awarded 54 PhDs in psychology during his career; 20 of those were to women. Today the story is much different with more than 70% of PhD and PsyD students entering psychology being women (Cynkar, 2007). It is difficult now to imagine a time when women were almost completely excluded from higher education. When Titchener arrived at Cornell in 1892, his first graduate student was a woman: Margaret Floy Washburn. She had studied with James McKeen Cattell at Columbia University, but only as an auditor. At that time, Columbia did not admit female students. Titchener took her on as a graduate student and she completed her dissertation two years later. It was titled: The Effect of Visualization Upon Judgments of Tactual Distance and Direction. Titchener translated it into German and it appeared in Wundt's journal *Philosophische Studien* soon afterward. Washburn went on to have a long and

PHOTO 7.3 Margaret Floy Washburn

distinguished career as an academic psychologist, publishing two books and over 100 articles. However, she spent the majority of her career teaching at women's colleges, notably Vassar. She was paid far less than male professors were. Had she been a man, she would have been offered a position at a research university (Scarborough & Furumoto, 1987), but "the exclusion of women from these positions apparently was not a matter of considering them and rejecting them; rather the idea of hiring women as regular faculty was simply not entertained" (p. 103). Similarly, Titchener, despite being her mentor, never invited her to join the Experimental Psychologists. That group was modeled after the classic British men's club and their meetings were, literally, after dinner smokers. Inviting women to breach such a social barrier was just too much of a break in tradition to entertain back then. Titchener felt having women present at those meetings would inhibit frank discussion(Gall et al., 1996), p 369). For women, much has changed for the better in psychology since 1892, although issues of full parity still remain as the #metoo movement and other similar ones have dramatically revealed.

LEARNING OBJECTIVE

4. Compare the status of women in academic psychology then and now.

After Titchener's unexpected death in 1927, Structuralism all but disappeared from American psychology. It's time to return to Europe to examine how German psychologists reacted to Wundt and his voluntarist approach. While Wundt had many adherents among his former students, he also had some who disagreed with him and his psychology. One of his main critics was Franz Brentano, a charismatic teacher who saw connections between the emerging psychology and philosophy. He believed that Wundt's experimental approach was too focused on the analysis of sensations and, thus, missed the bigger picture. Another critic was Georg Elias Müller, a fellow experimental psychologist who never saw eye to eye with Wundt. Müller was the first psychologist to establish a laboratory that was truly free from philosophy. Over his long career he conducted research in psychophysics, vision, and memory.

LEARNING OBJECTIVE

5. Review the differences between Wundt's and Titchener's theories.

Georg Elias Müller (1850–1934)

Biography

Müller was born in Saxony, now a part of Germany. His father was a teacher and pastor at the local gymnasium, one that emphasized humanistic education. Müller studied history at the University of Leipzig 11 years before Wundt's arrival. He left Leipzig after a year to continue his study of history at the University of Berlin. Fighting in the Franco-Prussian War (1870–1871)

interrupted his studies. After that short war he returned to Leipzig, this time to study philosophy. He soon moved to the University of Göttingen where he received his PhD from Lotze.
His dissertation topic was sensory attention. Müller fell ill after graduating and while recovering read Fechner's *Elements* and corresponded with him. After Lotze left for the University of
Berlin, Müller succeeded him at Göttingen for the next 40 years. The chair Müller took had
been Lotze's for 37 years. Prior to Lotze, Herbart had occupied it for eight years.

Contributions

Once at Göttingen Müller began a productive career in experimental psychology. His output was second only to Wundt's. But, because he was not a self-promoter, published mostly in
German language journals, and trained fewer American students, he was much better known in
Europe than in America. Haupt (2001) suggested that Müller's laboratory facilities were superior to Wundt's in terms of the quality of their equipment. Furthermore, Müller conducted
research himself while Wundt had long ceased to be an active researcher and was, basically,
an administrator. Haupt wrote (p. 246), "Müller had a clear lead over others in the pursuit of
experimentalist attempts to create a rigorous, precise, physicalistic psychology."

Specifically, Müller and his students were active in three main areas of research: psychophysics, vision, and memory. He and his students developed and used new laboratory equipment and instruments made of steel, wood, and brass. These devices spread out to other
laboratories in the period between the founding of Wundt's laboratory and the beginning of
World War I in 1914. This was heyday of "brass instrument psychology." In 1967, the American
Psychological Association hosted an exhibition of many of those early instruments at its 75th
anniversary meeting in Washington, DC (Davis, 1970). Many of those instruments are now
housed at the Archives of American Psychology at the University of Akron. The Psychology
Department at the University of Toronto displays many of those instruments in its museum.
Tošković (2018) established a museum of similar instruments at the University of Belgrade
from a collection there dating from just after World War I. Using such instruments Müller
expanded upon and improved earlier research findings. In psychophysics, Müller improved on
Fechner's methods and conducted new research on lifted weights. In vision, he revised Hering's
opponent-process theory of color vision by proposing a simpler neurological mechanism. In
memory, he and his students confirmed Ebbinghaus's data and updated his methods. One
innovation was the invention of the memory drum, a mechanical device for displaying memory
stimuli to subjects. Müller's group also criticized Ebbinghaus for using himself as a research
participant and adapted his methods for use with naïve participants instead. Müller continued
to be an active researcher till nearly the end of his life. His contributions in the areas of psychophysics and memory crossed the Atlantic and became a large part of American psychology.
However, his work in cognition did not. Behrens (1997, p. 175) noted, "Citations of Müller
peaked in the decade 1950–1959 and diminished thereafter . . . the interpretation can be made
that Müller's direct influence on experimental psychology has essentially vanished." His historical importance, however, was vast. Many of Müller's contemporaries were not experimen-
talists. Franz Brentano, another of Wundt's major critics, was an empirical psychologist, not an
experimentalist.

Franz Brentano (1838–1917)

Biography

Brentano was born in Marienberg on Rhine, Germany, to a family with a strong intellectual tradition. He studied philosophy at the Universities of Berlin, Munich, and Tübingen, where he received his PhD. Shortly after, he was ordained a Catholic priest. He then taught philosophy at the University of Würzburg for seven years. During his time there, the Roman Catholic Church was debating the question of **papal infallibility**. Brentano was opposed to that doctrine and wrote a convincing argument against it, but in 1870 papal infallibility became an official Church doctrine. As a matter of conscience, Brentano felt compelled to resign his academic position because he had obtained it while a priest. A little later, he resigned from the priesthood as well.

Contributions

In 1874, while he was outside the academy, he wrote his most famous book, *Psychology from an Empirical Standpoint*. He argued that psychology was an empirical science and also the basis for the philosophy of logic, ethics, and esthetics (Huemer, 2010). By empirical he did not mean experimental, however. While he agreed that the experimental work in psychophysics was important, he felt that it did not describe psychology fully enough. He called his version *descriptive psychology* and characterized it introspectively. His kind of introspection was strictly personal and intimately linked the act of self-observation to the thing being observed. Thus, his system was also called *Act Psychology*.

In Act Psychology the perceiver and the percept could not be separated. In vision, for instance, it was the act of seeing that was most important, not the object being perceived itself. Brentano also believed that Wundt's emphasis on systematic experimentation was wrongheaded; Wundt was observing the trees but missing the forest. Brentano was in favor of crucial experiments or experiments designed to answer a question once and for all. As history shows, systematic experimentation became the model for research in all of science, including psychology, with only a handful of exceptions. Forsyth (1976, p. 454) writing about theories in social psychology defined a crucial experiment as: "one that will either confirm a given theory or, when two conflicting theories are involved, confirm one while disconfirming the alternative." He went on to argue that crucial experiments are rare not only in psychology but in all science. One of the most famous examples of a crucial experiment in history was Arthur Eddington's 1919 measurement of the gravitational bending of light predicted by Einstein some ten years earlier. Einstein's concept of general relativity held that light did not travel in straight lines, as Newton had argued. Instead, Einstein's theory posited that the gravitational fields of large masses, such as stars, would cause light to bend. Eddington empirically confirmed those predictions and helped pave the way for modern physics, and in the process, made Einstein world famous. Because of the rarity and difficulty of crucial experiments it is no wonder that systematic experimentation has won the day in psychology and all other sciences.

Brentano returned to teaching at the University of Vienna but was again forced to resign because of personal reasons: he wanted to marry but Austrian law prohibited the marriage of former priests. He resigned, crossed the border into German Saxony, married, and returned to Vienna. Unfortunately for him, the university did not take him back. After his wife died, he moved to Florence and eventually remarried. He wrote less and less because of failing eyesight. After the outbreak of World War I, he felt compelled to move to neutral Switzerland because of his pacifism. He died there shortly after. Brentano lost his battles with Wundt. He could not compete with the massive output of experimental studies coming out of Leipzig.

Brentano did, however, have an effect on the early development of psychology. In the writings of his student, Edmund Husserl, descriptive psychology became **phenomenalism**, which had a pronounced effect on the development of 20th century philosophy. Brentano had an indirect effect on the development of psychology as well through the work of his students who included Christian von Ehrenfels and Sigmund Freud. Another student, Carl Stumpf, combined his lifelong love of music and his training in philosophy to study the psychology of music and sound. Stumpf brought the study of phenomenology into psychology.

Carl Stumpf (1848–1936)

Biography

Stumpf was born in Bavaria. His father was the court physician. His maternal grandfather, also a doctor, lived in the same household. His grandfather taught him Latin and other subjects from an early age. When he was seven, Stumpf learned to play the violin, beginning a lifelong love of music. After attending two gymnasiums, he enrolled in the nearby University of Würzburg. Because he could not study music there he chose esthetics, which soon led him to philosophy.

Contributions

At Würzburg, he fell under the influence of Franz Brentano. Because of Brentano's low academic rank he could not supervise PhD students, so he sent Stumpf to get his PhD in philosophy from Lotze at the University of Göttingen. After, Stumpf returned to Würzburg for additional study with Brentano, then returned to Göttingen to teach for a few years. When Brentano resigned because of his difficulties with the Roman Catholic Church, Stumpf with Brentano's support and blessing, succeeded him at Würzburg.

Stumpf soon realized that he could combine his interests in music and psychology. He moved on to several other academic appointments (Prague, Halle, and Munich) before he was called to be chair at the University of Berlin, arguably the most important department of psychology in Germany. He knew or had worked with many prominent early psychologists including Ewald Hering, Ernst Mach, Hermann Helmholtz, and Hermann Ebbinghaus. William James (see Chapter 9) visited him at Prague and they became lifelong friends and correspondents. While at Munich, he fell into a nasty and never resolved controversy with Wundt over Stumpf's musically based research methodology. By 1890 psychology had grown to the point where there were many universities teaching experimental psychology. Along with Ebbinghaus and others, Stumpf helped found a new journal, the *Journal of Psychology and Physiology of the Sense Organs* to disseminate the results emerging from schools other than those from Wundt's lab at Leipzig. Stumpf remained at Berlin until his death, eventually becoming its rector (e.g., chancellor or president). He published heavily, but

PHOTO 7.4 Carl Stumpf
Credit: Getty Images

mostly related to his interest in music and psychology. He helped popularize the role of phenomenology in European psychology. Eventually, and through his students, Wolfgang Köhler and Kurt Koffka, Gestalt psychology became popular in Europe, but was much less influential in the United States. (See Chapter 12) By the time Stumpf moved to Berlin, fewer American students were matriculating at German universities because new psychology laboratories had been founded in the United States. One consequence of the worldwide success of psychology was that Wundt's lab, because of its early infusion of American students, became the model for American psychology, especially in terms of methodology. By 1890, American graduate students tended to receive their training at home. Psychology's window to Germany had closed and that led to a divergence of ideas about psychology between Europe and the United States. On both continents, however, laboratory psychology reigned supreme.

Unlike Wundt, Stumpf viewed psychology more broadly and was instrumental in setting up an institute in Berlin to study child psychology. He also created an archive to store phonograph recordings of primitive music from around the world. Indirectly, he contributed to progress in animal psychology. He arranged for Köhler to be the director of a research station at the island of Tenerife. It was there that Köhler conducted his famous experiments on chimpanzees and discovered insight learning. (Köhler's animal research is covered in Chapter 12.) Stumpf was also directly involved in the famous case of the horse "Clever Hans."

CLEVER HANS AND HIS EFFECT ON PSYCHOLOGY

In 1904, Stumpf was asked to head a special commission to investigate whether a horse, Clever Hans (see Photo 7.5), could actually perform all of the advanced mental tasks his trainer and owner, Wilhelm von Osten, claimed. Hans had been observed to add, subtract, multiply, divide, take square roots, tell time, and much more. The horse indicated his answers by tapping his hoof. For example, when shown a card with the numbers:

$$2 + 3 =$$

Hans would tap five times. He usually got the correct answer. His owner claimed that it was the way he had taught Hans that had made the difference. The Kaiser appointed a 13- person special commission that included a cavalry officer, circus owner, director of the Berlin Zoo, veterinarian, magician, and others. The commission, after studying the owner and his horse, concluded no trickery was involved and that von Osten's instructional methods must account for the horse's remarkable performance. Just to be sure, however, they left one of Stumpf's students, Oskar Pfungst, behind to conduct a more thorough investigation.

Pfungst (1911) described his patient and thorough investigations on Hans and his owner. He discovered that Hans could answer correctly even when others were asking the questions. When he had von Osten ask questions to which he himself did not know the answer, Hans's performance dropped to the level of chance. When he looked more closely at von Osten as he asked the questions (ones that von Osten knew the answer to) he noticed that von Osten was giving the horse nearly imperceptible cues for when to start and stop tapping his hoof. By the time he was finished studying Hans, Pfungst, just through subtle facial and bodily movements,

PHOTO 7.5 Herr von Osten and his Horse, Clever Hans

could make the horse start and stop tapping. Apparently, von Osten did not realize he was making such movements.

So, Hans was intelligent, in a way. He was intelligent enough to learn to pair the signs that his trainer was giving him with hoof tapping. Pfungst showed the world that Hans was not as smart as a human being and in the process helped demonstrate the utility of the new science of psychology.

LEARNING OBJECTIVE

7. Review Clever Hans's effect on early psychology.

In many ways, Stumpf was instrumental in giving German psychology a new direction and an alternative to Wundt. He helped propagate many of the ideas of his mentor, Brentano, especially his emphasis on Act Psychology and the need for the careful description of phenomena before proceeding with experimentation and causal explanation. His work with music was original and provided an antielementistic alternative to Wundt's and Titchener's psychologies. Stumpf argued that melody was much more than one musical note followed by another. The melody itself was the cognitive unit regardless of how it was reproduced even if it was different than the original tune. Once, I was listening to elevator music when I suddenly recalled the tune. It was *Eleanor Rigby*, a Beatles song. How had I recognized it? Stumpf had the answer: I recognized the melody. That all other musical variables from the original version had changed—the instruments, tempo, and lack of lyrics—did not matter. The elements, in this case the notes, were not the stimuli. Rather, it was how those notes hung together phenomenologically that led to my eventual recognition of the lyrics of that familiar tune: "Eleanor Rigby picks up the rice in the church where a wedding has been . . . "

Stumpf's work, however, had little influence on American psychology because fewer Americans studied in Germany. Hermann Ebbinghaus was unique in early psychology in that he single-handedly created a new subfield, the study of memory, practically overnight. His research on memory opened the door to the experimental study of *higher mental processes*, topics that Wundt and Titchener believed were scientifically unapproachable.

Hermann Ebbinghaus (1850–1909)

Biography

Ebbinghaus was born near Bonn, Germany. His father was a merchant. Ebbinghaus attended the local gymnasium before enrolling at the University of Bonn to study philology and history. He also studied at the University of Halle and the University of Berlin. After the outbreak of the Franco-Prussian War (1870–1871), he joined the army and served as a lieutenant. When he left the army, he returned to Bonn and earned his PhD in philosophy. He spent the next seven years traveling in France and England supporting himself by tutoring. During that period he found a used copy of Fechner's *Psychophysics*. Fechner's work in sensation and perception (See Chapter 8). It inspired Ebbinghaus to use the methods in that book and to modify them to study memory.

Contributions

No one before him had attempted to experiment on memory. Before Ebbinghaus began his experiments on memory, that topic was firmly within the grasp of philosophy. To study memory he created new techniques for experimentally manipulating items to remember and new ways of measuring them. The nonsense syllable was the key to the new technique. It was a consonant–vowel–consonant combination that was not a word. He realized early on that he needed items to place into memory with which he had little or no previous experience. Among the examples he used (in German, naturally) were: ZAT, BOK, and SID (Boring, 1950, p. 388), nonsense syllables that would work in English as well. Ebbinghaus wished to study memory in its purest form, that is, without linking it to items already stored in the mind due to experience. He proceeded to memorize thousands of lists randomly made up from the 2,300 nonsense syllables he had created. To measure his own memory (he was the only participant), he measured the time it took him to learn a particular list for the first time, and later, after a predetermined interval (enough time to forget the list), measure the time it took him to relearn it. In each instance, the criterion of learning was reciting the list without any errors. He discovered that it always took him less time to learn the list on the second trial. He called the results a *savings score* because he was saving time when he learned the list the second time. From his data, he constructed a graph showing that the interval between the first trial and the second trial was the most important feature. That graph, now known as Ebbinghaus's curve of forgetting (see Figure 7.1), has stood the test of time and been replicated countless times. He also discovered other facts about memory including that the savings score improved with the number of repetitions made on the first trial and when practice was distributed over time (Schacter, 2001).

Neisser and Hyman (2000, p. xiii) refer to Ebbinghaus's approach to as "the high road" to the study of memory. He was trying to study memory in its purest form. In contrast, the "low road" to memory is studying it in natural contexts, for example, answering questions such as, where did I leave the car keys? In those contexts, the importance of previous experience becomes paramount. In practice, however, it is impossible to study memory in its pure form.

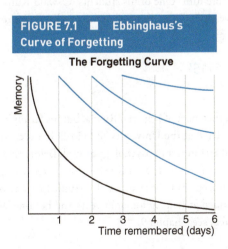

FIGURE 7.1 ■ Ebbinghaus's Curve of Forgetting

The Forgetting Curve

Memory

Time remembered (days)

Research has revealed that nonsense syllables, too, carry meaning. But, it is possible to choose nonsense syllables that have been shown to carry less meaning than others (Hull, 1933b).

Ebbinghaus had begun his memory research during the time he was on his own. He continued it after being hired to teach at the University of Berlin in 1880. There, he carefully replicated his earlier experiments and finally published them five years later as a book, his first publication other than his PhD thesis. That book, *Über das Gedächtnis* (*Concerning Memory*) catapulted him to instant fame. Paradoxically, he never published any other research in memory afterward. Ebbinghaus moved on to other topics and left the working out of memory details to others, notably G. E. Müller and his coworkers. Schacter (2001, p. 143) listed seven topics that emanated from other laboratories based upon Ebbinghaus's pioneering work: "repetition effects, the curve of forgetting, stimulus attributes and presentation modality, individual differences, interference and inhibition, methods of learning, and recognition and affect." That this list sounds modern is testament to Ebbinghaus's breakthrough.

His later career, however, was not like most of the other early psychologists. He did not publish as extensively as his contemporaries and that probably cost him his chance to advance at the University of Berlin. That chair went to Carl Stumpf instead. Ebbinghaus moved to the University of Breslau and later to the University of Halle. He died of pneumonia suddenly in 1909. He did, however, perform several other important services for early psychology. One was helping found the second European journal of psychology, the *Journal of Psychology and Physiology of the Sense Organs* to provide an alternative outlet for psychological research. Ebbinghaus also wrote two influential textbooks that were praised for their readability and scientific content. One of them opened with the now famous and oft quoted line, "Psychology has a long past, but only a short history."

He was an early worker in the development of psychological tests for children. Like Brentano, he did not supervise many PhD theses, so he left little intellectual legacy behind other than his first and monumental work in memory. That, though, was more than enough. More than anyone else of his time he opened doors to areas of psychology that no one else had even imagined existed before him. One of his students, Oswald Külpe, presided over a group of researchers at the University of Würzburg whose research led to the first major crisis in the young science of psychology.

Oswald Külpe (1862–1915)

Biography

Külpe was born in Latvia, then part of Imperial Russia, but his family's language and traditions were German. He matriculated at the University of Leipzig in order to study history but after meeting Wundt developed an interest in psychology as well. Before finally selecting psychology as his life's work he studied at several other universities before returning to Leipzig to complete his PhD under Wundt. During his time away he also studied psychology under G. E. Müller at Göttingen. Külpe remained at Leipzig for eight years and became Wundt's second assistant (after James McKeen Cattell, see Chapter 9).

Contributions

Slowly, Külpe began to form his own ideas about psychology. Influenced by Ebbinghaus's research on memory, he wondered if thinking itself might be accessible to introspective research. Wundt, however, believed that thinking and memory were beyond the reach of experimental psychology and were topics only accessible through his own *völkerpsychologie*. Külpe was called to Würzburg shortly thereafter; it was there that he and his faculty began to investigate the psychology of thought.

   In the early years of the 20th century, the psychologists at Würzburg developed an interest in what people were thinking about while they introspected. More precisely, they were interested in what happened in between the presentation of a stimulus and the formation of introspectable mental content. The answer surprised them. They discovered that participants could introspect reliably but they could not say how or why they did so. Their first experiments were timed word associations where the stimulus might be the word "fire." Participants were asked to say the first thing that entered their minds (e.g., "house") but then when asked why they had completed the word association in that way they could not say why. The Würzburg researchers believed they had discovered that introspectively unknowable thoughts existed. Eventually, they called these imageless thoughts. Later research by James Watt and Narziss Ach provided even stronger support for imageless thinking. Watt discovered what he called in German the *Einstellung* or task instructions. Later, Ach defined the idea more tightly and labeled it *Zielverstellung* or determining tendency (Elliot & Fryer, 2008). In modern psychology that concept is now known as *cognitive set*. Take a look at the examples that follow:

   Complete the following simple sums:

$5 + 4 =$	$7 + 2 =$	$4 + 3 =$	$6 + 2 =$	$8 + 2 =$

   What number are you now thinking of when you see:

5	2

You should have said "7" when you saw the 5 and 2 next to each other. But suppose you had seen this stimulus instead:

   Complete the following simple subtractions:

$5 - 4 =$	$7 - 2 =$	$4 - 3 =$	$6 - 2 =$	$8 - 2 =$

   What number are you thinking of when you see:

5	2

   Most likely you would say "3." What if the numbers in the box were multiplied? Then the "correct" answer would be 10. Of course, there is no correct answer. Ach argued that the preconditions to the problem, the operands (+, -, or ×) caused participants to either add, subtract, or multiply the next pair of numbers presented. Furthermore, the participants could not say why they had done so. Ach called his technique systematic self-observation and claimed that it demonstrated imageless thought.

Karl Bühler developed further techniques asking questions such as: "Was the theorem of Pythagoras known in the Middle Ages?" When he posed such questions to the graduate students and professors who served as participants, they too, could not introspectively account for all of their thinking. They reported some aspects of their thinking as having no sensory properties but, nevertheless, still being in consciousness as a kind of vague awareness.

Wundt and Titchener were profoundly opposed to the idea of imageless thought. Wundt saw it as a case of poorly conducted experimentation while Titchener saw it as a classic example of the stimulus error. The main issue, however, was not imageless thought as was introspection itself. The premise of the new science of psychology had been that contents of the mind were analyzable through introspection. The imageless thought controversy, as it came to be called, brought that assumption into question. If psychology was to be a science it must have a method that all of its practitioners could agree upon. The imageless thought controversy caused them to doubt each other's data. Angell (1911, p. 322) demonstrated the depth of the controversy when he wrote:

I find the doctrine of imageless thought open to suspicion on the following points: . . . the method . . . is at least not wholly satisfactory in meeting the demands of ordinary experimental procedure . . . imageless thought seems . . . to be a sporadic and occasional phenomenon . . . it seems almost impossible to describe it, save in negative terms.

The controversy itself died down after Külpe moved to the University of Bonn and then to the University of Munich. Despite their intellectual disputes, Külpe and Wundt remained on friendly terms personally. The "Würzburg School" of psychology faded away but the problems it had brought up did not. Thomas (2010, n.p.) summed it up nicely, "The irresolvable dispute contributed significantly to a growing sense of intellectual crisis within psychology, leading to a deep loss of confidence in the scientific value of introspection." It took some time, however, before psychologists completely dispensed with introspection.

LEARNING OBJECTIVE

8. Illustrate how introspectors could not explain the source of their own thoughts.

SUMMARY

In this chapter, psychology finally becomes an academic discipline. Wundt's influence was enormous. Trained as a philosopher, he made himself into an experimental psychologist. He and his many students published original research and created new academic territory for themselves and others. His system, Voluntarism, put a person's conscious choice front and center. Titchener, his student, significantly altered Wundt's system and created Structuralism, a single-minded approach dedicated to uncovering the elements of the mind. After Titchener died, his system has little further influence on psychology as a whole.

In Europe and the United States, meanwhile, psychology prospered and grew. But, what developed the most was the laboratory tradition begun by Wundt. Müller's lab actually outshone Wundt's. Brentano offered an alternative, Act Psychology, to the experimental psychology of Wundt and others. Brentano's Act Psychology emphasized the importance of the person in the process of perception. His work inspired later progress in phenomenology and after, in Gestalt psychology (see Chapter 12). His student Stumpf widened the scope of psychology by examining the perception of music and melody, both of which were instrumental in the later founding of Gestalt psychology by two of his students along with Max Wertheimer. Stumpf was also the head of the commission that examined the horse, Clever Hans. That investigation, conducted by Pfungst, popularized psychology worldwide.

Ebbinghaus widened psychology's scope when he experimentally investigated human memory. He developed techniques and discovered data still in use today. His work showed how psychology could be applied to areas previously thought to be unreachable by experimental investigation. Külpe, too, expanded psychology's reach into thinking and cognition. The research emanating from his laboratory helped doom introspection as a research tool. Soon, psychology faced its first crisis: How to collect data without using introspection. One answer came from biology, another of the disciplines along psychology's borders. Another answer came from across the Atlantic in the United States and Canada. The path psychology took in North America was markedly different than its European parent. Those new paths are covered in Chapters 8 and 10.

8 BIOLOGICAL PSYCHOLOGY

History of Biology

Aristotle was one of the first to study living things systematically. His descriptions of animals and plants stood as authoritative for centuries. Hippocratic humoral tradition in medicine lasted, nearly unaltered, into the 18th century. Medicine was always linked to biology but its early practitioners were held in lower esteem compared to philosophers or theologians. By the 19th century, however, biology became a scientific and empirical science following in the earlier footsteps of physics and chemistry. The invention of the microscope revealed a previously unknown living universe beneath the threshold of vision. The discovery of gigantic fossilized bones helped destroy the older idea that the living things present on earth had existed unaltered since the beginning of time. Geologists gradually added more and more years to the age of the earth, moving its age from a few thousand years to a few billion. By the end of the 19th century, the science of biology had been completely transformed.

Darwin's evolutionary theory provided a profound unifying and explanatory structure for many previously difficult to explain phenomena. Gregor Mendel's research in genetics, although ignored until its rediscovery in the 20th century, provided some of the missing pieces required to explain how evolution worked at the molecular level leading to biology's *modern synthesis*, the union of evolutionary and genetic theories in the early 20th century. Watson and Crick's model of the DNA molecule in 1953 (aided by Rosalind Franklin's crystallographic images) launched a new era in biology during the latter half of the century as researchers began to delve more deeply into the machinery of life itself.

Modern biology is a relatively young science, another child of the Newtonian revolution, but unlike physicists and chemists, biologists study living things. Those living things change over time, exhibit far greater variability, and resist easy theoretical explanations of their underlying mechanisms compared to the objects of study of physics and chemistry (Kagan, 2009).

PREVIEW

The scientific study of biology was marked by many breakthroughs. Nearly all of them related to the elucidation of the machinery of the body. Starting with Harvey's description of the *circulation of blood*, biologists went on to describe *spinal cord organization*, how sense organs worked as *transducers*, the speed of the *nerve impulse*, and the mechanisms of *color vision*. The theory of *evolution* provided biology with a conceptual backbone. It helped to reconcile older speculations about *speciation, geological time, taxonomy*, and *continental drift*. Later, the rediscovery of *genetics* combined with *natural selection* led to biology's *modern synthesis*. Older concepts such as *vitalism* and *Lamarckism* fell to the weight of empirical data as did *phrenology*. *Psychophysics* became psychology's first subdiscipline as researchers identified individual differences in the perception of *time, color*, and many more variables. *Absolute and relative thresholds* were discovered, and new methods were developed to study perception: *limits, constant stimuli*, and *adjustment*. Psychologists began to study animal thinking and behavior as well, leading to *comparative psychology*. Galton took the first steps in the study of *psychometrics, eugenics, forensic psychology*, and *statistics*.

INTRODUCTION

This chapter tells the story of how biologists inspired philosophers and other scholars to link the study of the mind to the study of physiology and study their interaction. In the process, they gave rise to biological psychology. The border between biology and the newly emerging science of psychology was beginning to be drawn.

By the 17th century, European scientists had begun to apply scientific methodology to the study of living things, especially in the area of human physiology. Harvey's pioneering study of the circulation of blood was a spectacular early example. Soon after, the invention of the microscope and new treatments such as smallpox inoculations enabled biological scientists to study physiological processes better, and gave them the hope that they could successfully combat disease.

By the 19th century, scientific biology was well established. Biologists were systematically collecting and classifying living things. Just after mid-century, Charles Darwin's evolutionary theory provided biology with its principal explanatory theory: evolution. Although substantially modified since then it remains at the core of modern biological theorizing. Dobzhansky (1973, p. 125) would later write, "Nothing in biology makes sense except in the light of evolution."

At around the same time, other biologists were making deep inroads in the understanding of human physiology. By the end of that century, some philosophers began to use biological methods in order to better understand how the human mind worked. Their **psychophysiologi-cal** research created the first inklings of an empirical psychology. Over the course of the 19th century, biologists experimentally worked out some of the mechanisms of the nervous system. Discovering, for example, the organization of the spinal cord, how the sensory organs communicate with the brain, and how fast nerve impulses travel. Ernst Weber and Gustav Fechner pushed psychophysics further by independently discovering the first psychophysical laws. Weber's JND (just noticeable difference) and Fechner's new methods linked physiology to sensory psychology. George Romanes and C. Lloyd Morgan helped found comparative psychology, the study of animal behavior, and placed human psychology along a naturally occurring Darwinian continuum. Francis Galton contributed much to psychology by the end of the 19th century. His groundbreaking psychological studies included anthropomorphic measurements, descriptions of genius, the use of fingerprints for identification, and the use of the normal curve and statistics to describe human populations.

Biology's late but rapid ascent as an empirical science began with a 72-page book written by William Harvey. That book, *The Motion of the Heart and Blood in Animals*, marked the beginning of modern biology.

William Harvey (1578–1657)

Biography

William Harvey was born into a family of merchants in Folkestone, England. Always a good student, he attended King's School and then studied medicine at Cambridge University, and later, Caius College. After, he went to Padua, at the time considered one of Europe's best medical schools, to continue his studies. Galileo taught mathematics at Padua when Harvey was a student, but there is no record of whether they ever met or knew each other. Harvey's mentor at Padua was Girolamo Fabrizio (Fabricius) who had begun to study how blood circulated in the body. Fabrizio's research undermined Galen's older ideas about blood and how it moved through the body.

Contributions

After completing his studies at Padua, Harvey returned to England and began a long career in medicine. He held a lifelong position at St. Bartholomew's Hospital in London and served as personal physician to Kings James I and Charles I. But, he suffered the loss of prestige, power, and money for having been a loyal royalist during the English Civil Wars. After the wars, widowed and without property, he lived with his brothers until his death. It was his earlier work as a lecturer and researcher for the College of Physicians, however, which made him famous. Using only a magnifying glass along with a large number of empirical tests, he was able to demonstrate that the heart was a muscle that pumped large volumes of blood into the lungs and then received them back in a continuous and closed fashion. Later scientists, aided by microscopes, confirmed his predictions, discovering the tiny capillaries whose existence Harvey had inferred but could not directly observe.

Harvey combined close observation with empirical tests. By observing the slower beating hearts of reptiles and dying mammals, he was the first to observe that the heartbeat was composed of two phases: *systolic* (when the heart contracts) and *diastolic* (when the heart relaxes and expands). His experiments also showed that the heart was a muscle. By estimating the enormous volume of blood pumped over time, he proved that the body only contained a relatively small amount of blood but circulated it continuously. He also demonstrated that arterial blood (blood pumped out of the heart) and venous blood (blood returning to the heart) were the same substance. He named the pulmonary artery, the artery that connects from the right ventricle of the heart to the lungs. Similarly, he named the pulmonary vein; the vein through which blood flows back from the lungs into the left auricle of the heart.

While others before him had speculated that blood circulated throughout the body in a closed loop, Harvey adapted the newer empirical methods of science and applied them to biology. His research provided one of the first steps toward modern biological science. Bolli (2019, p. 1301) noted:

> Harvey started doing experiments when he addressed the second part of the problem: how does blood go from the heart to the tissues and, then, how does it return to the heart? That's when, for the first time, he used measurements—or quantitative evidence. The introduction of quantitative evidence in physiology was one of Harvey's fundamental contributions to medicine. He was the first person to actually use measurements in studies of physiology.

However, it would still require some 200 more years before biology could be considered to be truly scientific. Some of the earliest signs of psychology itself came shortly afterward. Early psychologists linked discoveries about the machinery of the body to correlated cognitive processes. But, before that linkage occurred, many preliminary questions in biology itself had to be answered. The answers to nearly all of those biological questions fell neatly into place following the publication of Darwin's *Origin of the Species* in 1859.

LEARNING OBJECTIVE

2. Appraise how Harvey's methods led to a new view of an old problem, the circulation of blood in the body.

BIOLOGY BEFORE DARWIN

Biology's development during the period between Harvey's research and the publication of Darwin's theory can only be described as slow and fitful. There were several reasons for that. One was the age of the earth itself. By analyzing biblical dates, scholars estimated that world to be somewhere around 6,000 years old. One churchman even calculated the very day of divine creation: Sunday, October 23, 4004 BCE! Gradually, geologists began to realize that the planet was much older than that. Modern geologists now estimate the age of the earth to be around 4–5 billion years old. However, it took many years before scientists who lived during the 19th century could accept so distant a date.

Another issue was the immutability of species. Most early biologists assumed that species never changed; they believed that the species they observed around them had been present since the beginning of the world. The discovery of large numbers of extinct fossilized animals and plants combined with evidence confirming the ever lengthening age of the earth prompted a reevaluation of the species concept; some species had gone extinct and newer species had somehow arisen. More remarkably, the fossils themselves proved to be reliable indicators of the passage of geological time. The worldwide distribution of extinct fossilized life was extremely uniform and could be used to date the age of the rocks they had been found in.

Some mysteries remained unsolved well into the 20th century, however. One was that the continents themselves had slowly been on the move throughout earth's history (Hurley, 1968). So, not only had species changed over time, so had the face of the earth itself. By looking at all of the available evidence, geological and biological, seeming inconsistencies such as similar fossils being discovered in now remote locales slowly faded away. In the distant past, those fossils had been deposited near each other. Continental drift, taking place over millions of years, had separated them. Biologists, inspired by Linné's (1964) book *Systema Naturae*, began the process of classifying living things into related groups, the now familiar **taxonomy** of kingdom, phylum, class, order, family, genus, and species. Generations of biology students have learned to recall the sequence of Linnaeus's system with the familiar acrostic: **K**ing **P**hillip **C**ame **O**ver **F**rom **G**ermany **S**ober. Thus, the effort to classify species began long before Darwin ever published his own ideas about evolutionary relationships between species. Darwin's ideas about evolution formed only after many others had already considered the notion of species change including some Islamic scientists. Arguing against only Western ideas existing in biology and evolution Malik et al. (2017, p. 16) wrote:

> We briefly summarised the evolutionary ideas of eight of the most renowned Muslim scholars between the eighth and fourteenth century, showing that these theories were proposed in a continuum of time during the Islamic Golden Age, well before Charles Darwin's time. All eight Muslim scholars suggested that humans underwent some type of phenotypic evolution. Some of them specifically wrote about similarities between humans and apes/monkeys, in many cases stating that humans derived from an ape/monkey ancestor. This is in complete contrast with the view, defended nowadays by most Muslims and Christian creationists, that humans did not undergo evolution, specifically from apes/monkeys.

They concluded that Islamic scientists during the Golden Age of Islam anticipated Darwin's theory of evolution only to see such ideas swept away in the 20th century due to Eurocentrism and the reaffirmation of Islamic fundamentalism.

DARWIN'S INFLUENCE ON BIOLOGY AND PSYCHOLOGY

Charles Darwin's book, *The Origin of the Species* (1859), was "'one long argument' . . . for evolution and natural selection" (Brown, 2007, p. 68). Darwin had provided biology with its principal theoretical backbone, the evolution of organisms by means of natural selection. Of course, it took time before biologists and other scientists came to accept his conclusions. One reason for that lag was the state of biology before Darwin.

By the end of the 18th century, biologists struggled to interpret the new evidence accumulating yearly. Some argued that the close fit between organism and environment could only result from divine design. Others countered that organisms changed but did so in order to better match the requirements of their unique environments. Lamarck famously argued that species changed according to their own efforts during their lifetimes and then somehow passed those improvements onto their offspring. For example, he held that as ancestral giraffes stretched their necks more and more over many generations in order to eat higher and higher vegetation they somehow passed those successive neck stretchings from parent to offspring. Embryologists discovered the process of differentiation: early embryonic forms of many obviously divergent species closely resembled each other. But, as they developed, they diverged sharply from each other until they closely resembled their adult forms.

Darwin was well aware of the current state of knowledge about nature, physical and biological, before he ever set foot on the HMS Beagle. After he returned to England nearly five years later, he was still far from ready to set down any coherent thoughts about evolution. The idea for natural selection did not come to him until after he had read Thomas Malthus's essay on how the external limiters (e.g., wars and famines) to unchecked human population growth. Darwin quickly realized that all animals and plants, too, were subject to similar limits. Competition, or what he termed natural selection, was the key to organismic evolution. How he gradually arrived at that conclusion is the next topic.

LEARNING OBJECTIVE

3. Briefly review the state of biology before Darwin.

Charles Darwin (1809–1882)

Biography

Darwin was born in Shrewsbury, England. His father was a physician. His grandfather, Erasmus Darwin, was an early naturalist whose work anticipated evolutionary theory. Charles Darwin showed little early promise as a scholar. He attended the University of Edinburgh hoping to study medicine only to leave after two terms. He could not stand to observe the grisly operations. Anesthesia was not yet part of medical practice, so patients screamed in pain during their surgeries. Darwin then went to Christ's College, Cambridge, intending to become a minister. There, he was still not much of a student but developed a close relationship with a botanist, John Stevens Henslow. After Darwin graduated, Henslow helped arrange a place for him on the HMS Beagle, a small naval ship about to map the coastlines of South America and make soundings for depth charts. The Beagle's captain, Robert FitzRoy, was looking for a gentleman to accompany him on the voyage to serve as a naturalist and companion. The previous captain had committed suicide on its last mission, apparently due to loneliness combined with the strain of command. The rules and regulations of the Royal Navy prohibited captains from engaging in any personal interactions with officers and crew. Because naval captains were the supreme authorities on their vessels, the British Admiralty believed that any personal relationships would undermine discipline. Darwin (or any other civilian) was exempt from that regulation. In fact, Darwin and FitzRoy were amiable dinner companions throughout the Beagle's years at sea.

At first, Darwin's father objected to the trip, believing that his son had already wasted enough of his life, but relented after Charles's maternal grandfather, Josiah Wedgewood, recommended the trip. The Beagle left England in 1831 and did not return until 1836. During that time it sailed to South America, the Galapagos Islands, New Zealand, Australia, South Africa, and back to South America before setting for home (see Figure 8.1). Darwin collected thousands of specimens of animals and plants during the voyage and shipped them back to England whenever the Beagle made port. It is a myth, however, that Darwin came to some grand revelation about his theory of evolution during the trip, or that he realized the importance of his Galapagos Islands specimens at the time (Waller, 2002).

FIGURE 8.1 ■ The Voyage of the HMS Beagle

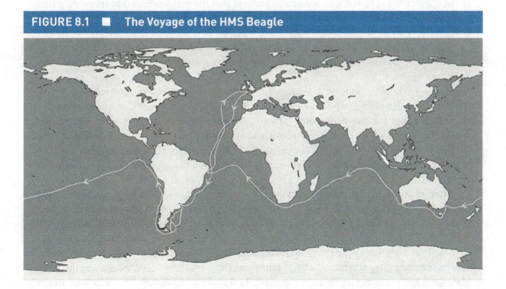

Contributions

Once back in England, Darwin struggled to make sense of his observations. He believed that species changed over time but could not come up with a mechanism that was neither God given (e.g., creationist) or directive (e.g., one that led inevitably toward humans as the pinnacle of evolution). After reading Malthus, however, the mechanism did come to him; he called it **natural selection**. Malthus had argued that human populations could grow much more quickly than could their food supply. Thus, people had to compete with each other in order to stay alive. Darwin applied the same logic to all creatures when he wrote, "This preservation, during the battle for life, of varieties which possess any advantage in structure, constitution, or instinct, I have called Natural Selection" (Darwin, 1868, p. 6). In a stroke, Darwin had discovered a mechanism for how species could change over time that did not depend on a creator. Furthermore, the method was random, not directed. Changes in animals and plants happened via some mechanism yet unknown to Darwin. But, if those changes turned out to confer an advantage to their possessor, no matter how slight, then it would outcompete others of the same species. After he had thought up natural selection, he saw that it explained much in biology. The only other thing natural selection required was time; at least 300 million years, Darwin estimated.

THEN AND NOW

Evolutionary Theory, Creationism, and Intelligent Design

It might seem logical after reading the account of the origin and rise of Darwin's theory that it must be nearly universally accepted by now. But that is not the case. Substantial opposition to evolutionary theory does exist, especially in the United States. More than fifty years before Darwin published *The Origin of the Species*, the English theologian William Paley had made a case for creationism, using his now-famous watch analogy. He argued that if one found a watch in the forest, one would not assume that the many pieces that made it up had come together by chance. Instead, one would assume the existence of a designer, someone who had conceived of and assembled those pieces into a working mechanism. By extension, Paley argued that all animals and plants had been similarly created and that God was their designer. Darwin's theory provided a new, noncreationist, and nondirected alternative to Paley's approach.

By the early 20th century, American fundamentalist Protestants revived their Young Earth Creationist theory. Hewing closely to a literal interpretation of Christian Scripture, they denied that the earth was older than 6,000 years or that humans were descended from other species. The climax of that early skeptical approach to evolution peaked at the famous "Scopes Monkey Trial" in Tennessee in 1925. John Scopes, a teacher, was tried for teaching evolution, a violation of Tennessee law at that time. Scopes was convicted and fined $100.

After, other states considered passing similar laws, but only Arkansas and Mississippi succeeded. In 1968, the United States Supreme Court invalidated the Arkansas law, writing that it had only been enacted to protect a particular religious view (e.g., Christianity), a violation of the First Amendment. That decision forced opponents of evolution to adopt different tactics. They began to argue that evolution was only a theory. Instead of attempting to outlaw its teaching, they wanted it to be taught alongside "creation-science," a discipline they claimed was an alternative scientific account to Darwinian evolution. The Supreme Court eventually ruled that creation-science, too, was based upon religion and not a science; they prohibited curricula that taught otherwise.

The most recent chapter in this story, Intelligent Design (ID), revives Paley's watch metaphor. Those promoting ID argue that a "designer" created all living organisms on earth. That designer, some believe, was divine, but others believe that it need not have been; it could have been an extraterrestrial alien. The ID "tent" is a large one and houses a wide variety of opinions about whom or what was the designer. All of those under that tent, however, share an intense dislike of evolutionary theory and its implications. One thing that ID proponents lack is hard scientific evidence to back up their theories. Modern evolutionary theorists, on the other hand, contend that natural selection, along with other biological findings, "including gene transfer, symbiosis, chromosomal rearrangement, and the action of regulator genes . . . fits the evidence just fine" (Scott, 2002, p. 79). At least one thing is clear: opponents to evolutionary theory will not likely ever be convinced by appeals to rational or scientific argument. The battle between them and evolutionists will rage on for many years to come.

Darwin was in no great hurry to publish his theory. For one thing, he realized that its publication would cause much criticism. So, he anticipated many possible attacks against his ideas by conducting detailed research on barnacles, investigating how breeders altered the morphology and behavior of domestic pigeons, and reading extensively. He hoped eventually to publish a massive tome while answering all possible objections. Unfortunately for Darwin, the arrival of a letter written by a younger biologist, Alfred Russel Wallace, changed those plans. The letter asked Darwin to evaluate Wallace's own independent ideas about organismic evolution. The letter shocked Darwin, for he immediately realized that he could lose scientific priority to Wallace. The ideas in the letter were nearly identical to his. He showed the letter to his scientist friends, Lyell and Hooker. Their solution was to invite Darwin and Wallace to present jointly summaries of their theories at a meeting of the Linnean Society in 1858. That way both would share priority. The meeting took place; others read the papers, neither Darwin nor Wallace attended the meeting (Boakes, 1984). Immediately afterward, little public notice ensued.

Over the course of the next few months, Darwin worked feverishly to put together a shorter version of the big book he had planned to write. That book, published in 1859, was *The Origin of Species by Means of Natural Selection*. It forever changed biology and, eventually, came to have a major impact on early psychology as well. The book was an instant success; the first printing of 1,250 copies sold out in one day. From that point on, Darwin's life changed too. Many biologists and scientists quickly accepted his conclusions. However, many did not. One who did not was Lord Kelvin, the most prominent physicist of the time (for one thing, he had discovered the Second Law of Thermodynamics). Kelvin had calculated the age of the earth based on the assumption that it had cooled from molten rock to its present state. The age he calculated was far less than Darwin's 300 million years. This was a serious problem for the successful operation of natural selection, and was only removed after the discovery of radioactivity in the late 19th century. Kelvin's calculations had not taken into account the fact that radioactivity added heat to the earth. Another objection raised by many was the problem of complexity. How could an organ as complex as an eye have evolved from the minute changes Darwin had proposed? Darwin answered that question by pointing out there were many different kinds of light-gathering organs in the animal kingdom, ranging from simple to complex. Thus, he argued, the eyes of mammals were highly evolved and had originated from earlier and simpler precursors.

The issue of how the changes of natural selection were passed on from generation to generation was also incomplete.

PHOTO 8.1 Charles Darwin

The emergence of genetics and its subsequent synthesis with evolutionary theory still lay in the future. Darwin himself waffled over Lamarck's idea of acquired characteristics. By the last edition of his book he had reintroduced Lamarck's idea as another possible evolutionary mechanism. Fortunately for Darwin, others, including Thomas Huxley (known as "Darwin's Bulldog") took up the fight to preserve, promote, and revise his theory.

After biology's modern synthesis, the union of genetics and evolution, and after much research filling in gaps in data, evolution came to hold the central position in biology that it continues to occupy today. Evolution, however, was only one of the advances in biology important to the emergence of psychology. Also playing major roles were two other new biological areas of study: neuroanatomy, the study of the structure and organization of the brain and nervous system, and psychophysics, the study of the relationship between physical stimuli and their detection and interpretation by the conscious and unconscious mind.

LEARNING OBJECTIVE

4. Discuss the role of multiple sources of evidence from geology and physics contributed to the acceptance of evolutionary theory.

NEUROANATOMY

Scientific interest in neuroanatomical topics began to rise in the early days of the 19th century. Two neuroanatomical categories: the organization of the brain and spinal cord, along with the relationship of the senses to the brain, led directly to active present day areas of research in physiological psychology. However, another 19th century category, phrenology, did not.

Phrenology

Phrenology arose from the research of Franz Joseph Gall (1758–1828), an anatomist who specialized in the structure of the head and brain. Gall was interested in physiognomy, the study of the relationship between the face and body and a person's behavior. In 1810, he published a major text on anatomy and physiology and began to lecture extensively throughout Europe. His student Johann Spurzheim (1758–1828) coined the term "phrenology" and became the principal propagandist for spreading it throughout Europe and North America. Phrenology was based upon a small number of fundamental assumptions. One was that the brain was the organ of the mind. Another was that the mind was organized into faculties, and as those faculties changed through experience they would cause the skull to change shape. In other words, a phrenologist could infer the affective and intellectual faculties of persons via a careful examination of the bumps on their skulls. Thanks to Spurzheim's efforts, phrenology quickly became popular with the public. Boring (1950, p. 57) noted that phrenology "was born in Edinburgh in 1823 and died in Philadelphia only in 1911. Phrenology had flourished for a century!"

As a serious scientific approach to neuroanatomy, however, phrenology was found wanting even though many otherwise respectable scientists supported it. As a theory, phrenology was plausible. But, as a body of empirically based results it was not. The bottom line was that the brain does not change in shape or size with experience, thus it does not cause the skull to change shape either. Still, phrenology did exert a tremendous effect on physiology as a whole. It popularized the idea that the brain controlled behavior and that different parts of the brain were responsible for specific functions. That change in the *zeitgeist* made it easier for other researchers to promote their empirically based theories of neuroanatomy. Phrenology's popularity made it easier for people to accept new ideas about the organization of the brain and spinal cord, the functional relationships between the senses and the brain, and the relative slowness of nervous transmission.

The Organization of the Spinal Cord

Early in the 19th century, two researchers, the Sir Charles Bell (1774–1842) of England and François Magendie (1783–1855) of France, independently discovered the organization of the spinal cord by conducting experiments on animals. The resulting Bell–Magendie Law stated that the role of the neural fibers that exit the spinal cord on its ventral side is to communicate commands from the brain and spinal cord to the body. That law further stated that the role of the neural fibers that enter the spinal cord on its dorsal side is to communicate information coming from the senses to the brain and spinal cord. Their discovery of the spinal cords organization took place early in the 19th century. In the last third of that same century, Gustav Fritsch (1838–1927) and Edvard Hitzig (1838–1907) experimentally demonstrated that specific regions in the cortex were responsible for motor movements, and that the cortex was "a topographically organized representation of the body in the brain" (Gross, 2007, p. 320). By applying experimental methods to the study of living things, biologists were finally beginning to understand the intricate mechanisms of the body.

Communication Between the Senses and the Brain

Another important physiological discovery was Johannes Müller's (1801–1858) Law of Specific Nerve Energies. That law stated that what is perceived comes from the action of nerves and not from the physical objects that stimulate sense organs. The Law of Specific Nerve Energies implied that the mind is aware only of its own activity and not of the physical world itself. Müller published one of the first comprehensive texts, the *Handbook of Physiology*, on the relationship between the physical world and the mental activity it stimulated. It was soon translated into other languages and became influential.

He argued that it was the action of nerves terminating at specific locations of the brain that caused people to perceive things. Thus, when the eyes sent neural signals to the brain they were visually perceived in the brain after the signals arrived. However, blows to the head could also cause someone to "see stars" (phosphenes) even though the eye was never involved and there was no corresponding visual stimulus. One of his students even suggested that if the nerves linking the eye and ear to the brain were switched, then people could "see" with their ears and "hear" with their eyes. What Müller had actually discovered was that all of the sense organs were organic **transducers**. They took in a physical stimulus such as light or sound and then transformed it into neural activity. In other words, the sense organs all spoke the same "language" and the brain could understand it regardless of whether it originated from the eye, the ear, or any other sense organ. Müller's ideas were seminal. Rachlin (2005, p. 43) wrote:

> According to Müller our minds have access only to this nervous energy. From this energy, plus whatever innate tendencies our minds possess (according to Müller, the Kantian categories: space, time, moral sense, and so forth), they must construct the world. How they manage this construction became the business of all of psychology for the next hundred years and of non-behavioristic psychology even up to today.

Additionally, Müller was a **vitalist**. He believed that living things possessed a "life force" of their own. That life force was an unknown substance that made them different from inanimate objects; it somehow conferred life. One consequence of Müller's vitalist beliefs was that he assumed nerve impulses traveled extremely fast and could not possibly be measured. One of his students, Hermann Helmholtz, took severe exception to Müller's vitalism. Along with his fellow students, he searched for strictly physical and nonvitalist explanations for biological processes. Around mid-century, Helmholtz succeeded in measuring the speed of nerve impulses, discovering they were actually quite slow (e.g., averaging around 60 mph). He went on to discover many other basic facts about the workings of the body. He was one of the most important scientists of the 19th century.

PHOTO 8.2 Johannes Müller

Hermann Helmholtz (1821–1894)

Biography

Helmholtz was the son of the headmaster of the Potsdam Gymnasium, a newly established type of school for Prussian boys that emphasized a classical curriculum. There, Helmholtz absorbed Kant's philosophy along with Fichte's "nature philosophy," a highly subjective view of science that emphasized the primacy of philosophical thinking over the collection and analysis of empirical data. Later in his career many of Helmholtz's scientific contributions would help overturn nature philosophy. After graduating from the gymnasium, Helmholtz wanted to study physics, but because of his family's inability to financially support him, entered medical school instead. Medical education in Prussia was free to men who pledged to spend five years as army doctors following completion of their studies.

Contributions

At the Friedrich Wilhelm Medical Institute in Berlin, he studied under Johannes Müller. However, Helmholtz and his fellow students soon secretly rebelled against Müller's vitalist views. Some of them founded the Berlin Physical Society in response; Helmholtz soon joined that group. That society was dedicated toward providing strictly physical explanations for biological phenomena. Helmholtz and three others prepared a document for an "alliance" stating their mechanistic views with each of them signing it using a drop of their own blood (Coren, 2003). Cahan (2018, p. 62) described their views as:

> The "alliance" referred to in the oath that du Bois-Reymond and Brüke had taken in 1842 to explain all organic phenomena in terms of physical and chemical forces, using physical, chemical, and mathematical methods or instruments and avoiding the use of the vague, *"Lebenskraft"* (life force) as an explanatory term. They sought to understand living phenomena as material matter in mechanical motion.

After graduating from medical school, Helmholtz was assigned to an army post in nearby Potsdam. His duties were minimal and he was able to conduct his own research there and, while on leave, in Berlin. His research gained him some attention and an early release from his army commitment.

In 1847, very early in his academic career, he published one of his most important findings, a pamphlet on the conservation of energy. In it, he clearly explained and mathematically demonstrated that heat and energy were equivalent and that neither was ever destroyed. That relationship is now called the First Law of Thermodynamics. Helmholtz's elucidation of that law did much to finally bury vitalist approaches to biology.

LEARNING OBJECTIVE

5. Survey the accumulation of scientific facts that led to the demise of vitalism as a theory in biology.

The reception by other scientists to that law was mixed at first. Younger scientists, in general, approved, whereas older scientists did not. Thus, the discovery of conservation of energy did not, at first, make Helmholtz famous. Two of his subsequent discoveries did so, however. The first of those was his measurement of the speed of the nerve impulse and the second was his development of the ophthalmoscope, an instrument that permitted him and others to see into the living human eye clearly for the first time. Soon after, he published the *Handbook of Physiological Optics*. In that book, he combined his deep knowledge of physics with his interest in physiology. His goal was to trace completely the route taken by nerve signals as they pass from the eye to the brain. Helmholtz was unaware of the complexity of the task he had set for himself. That question remains not fully answered today.

Another of his important contributions to the physiology of vision was his theory of color perception. He amplified the earlier ideas of Thomas Young (1773–1829) to create the now familiar Young–Helmholtz trichromatic theory of color vision. That theory holds that humans perceive color because of the simultaneous activity of three different types of visual receptors, the cones of the eye. The Young–Helmholtz theory maintains that the activity of millions of cones—tuned to red, green, or blue—make color vision possible. Helmholtz also studied the physics of sound and physiology of the ear. His interest in physical phenomena preceded his research in the physiology of hearing. Once again, he developed instruments to aid him in his physiological research. In the case of hearing, he developed the "Helmholtz resonator," a device that could isolate the prime tone of a sound. The small end of the resonator was coated with wax (to provide a good seal) and inserted into the ear. The larger end was also open. Each resonator was tuned to a specific tone. When a complex sound was presented, the wearer could identify the particular prime tone because it could be heard clearly. All other tones were muffled. Later, he built more advanced and adjustable electric resonators that could be tuned to any specific pure tone. Helmholtz pioneered the study of psychoacoustics. His student, Heinrich Hertz (1857–1894), extended Helmholtz's early steps beyond sound and into the study of radio waves and other oscillating phenomena.

Helmholtz also published many articles on physical and mathematical topics including vortex motion, hydrodynamics, and non-Euclidean geometry, or geometries that allow parallel lines in space to touch. When Helmholtz realized that those non-Euclidean geometries existed and they were just as logically consistent as Euclidean geometry, he finally broke with Kant's nativist conception of space. (Recall that Kant believed that humans did not need to learn about space, time, or causality. That knowledge, he maintained, was already present at birth.) Helmholtz came to believe that humans learned about the nature of space through experience. The fact that other geometries existed was the clincher for him. How could Kant be correct if more than one type of space existed? Helmholtz finished his years as the Director of the Institute of Physics at the University of Berlin where he laid the earliest foundations of 20th century modern physics. While Helmholtz was uncovering the workings of the eyes and ears, two other scientists were doing similar work on the workings of the skin senses: touch, hot, cold, and pain.

PSYCHOPHYSICS

Naive Ideas About Sensation and Perception

By early 19th century, astronomers realized that they must correct for previously unknown and large systematic errors in their observations. Astronomers used the "eye and ear" method to measure the time of the transits of moving stars across their stationary telescopes. They had assumed that all observers were consistent in their timing of the transits. Friedrich Bessel (1784–1846), an astronomer from Königsberg, was the first to realize there was a discrepancy between observers and that it was involuntary. He had read old reports from the Greenwich Observatory about how an assistant there, David Kinnebrook, had been relieved of his duties in 1796 because his observations did not match those of his supervisor, Nevil Maskelyne. Kinnebrook had been consistently 0.8 seconds slower than Maskelyne at timing the same transits. After being warned of the difference, Kinnebrook's observations became even more inconsistent.

Eventually, Maskelyne fired Kinnebrook. Bessel noticed the consistent difference in their transit times and wondered whether any two astronomers, especially experienced ones, would show similar differences. So, Bessel compared himself to other astronomers of equal reputation and discovered that the discrepancies between he and they were even larger than those between Maskelyne and Kinnebrook. Again, the differences were remarkably consistent. That led Bessel to develop the personal equation, a correction factor between observers. Unfortunately, the personal equation only provided a relative correction between two observers, not an absolute correction between all observers and the actual astronomical event. Thus, astronomers began to search for new methods and equipment for conducting reliable observations. The solution came with the development of the chronograph, a clock linked to a pen-and-paper recording device. Astronomers, then, were among the first to realize that the observations each made were not the same.

Early psychologists, too, became interested and, "after 1880 . . . professional astronomers realized that the question of the psycho-physical basis for personal error had been taken out of their hands . . . a new science had come into existence; the science of experimental psychology" (Duncombe, 1945, p. 13).

Similarly, a tragic train crash in Sweden led to the realization that color blindness was more common than previously believed. A railway employee had caused the crash by misreading a colored signal. Subsequently, Frithiof Holmgren (1831–1897), a Swedish physiologist and former student of Helmholtz, devised a color blindness test and administered it to Swedish railway employees and discovered that nearly 5% of them were color blind. Holmgren's test was portable, easy to administer, and soon in use around the world by railway companies. Once again, scientists had demonstrated that traditional assumptions about human perception were in error. Not everyone saw colors in the same way. By the end of the 19th century, research in psychophysics had overturned many of those older and naive assumptions about the similarity and consistency of human perception. Today, the psychology of individual differences is well established and many psychological variables vary along the normal curve.

Scientific Psychophysics

Psychophysics is one of psychology's oldest areas and it is still an active field of contemporary research. Two German scientists, Ernst Weber and Gustav Fechner, were among the first to experiment systematically in that subfield of psychology. Weber was trained as a physician and held a post at the University of Leipzig for 50 years. He published extensively in all facets of medicine but it was his research on the relationship between physical stimuli and human perception that helped give rise to the science of psychophysics. Weber discovered a relatively consistent lawful relationship between a given level of physical stimulation and the necessary difference in stimulation required for someone to report that they had sensed the difference. That amount turned out to vary according to intensity of the physical stimulus first presented. If it was small, then only a small additional amount was sufficient. But if it was large, then a larger amount was needed. That discovery was the foundation of psychophysics. Here was a way for scientists to apply physical methods to the study of human sensory physiology.

But, it was Fechner who put psychophysics on the map when he published his *Elements of Psychophysics* in 1860. In that book, he cited many examples of psychophysical research, but more importantly, he provided methods for conducting such research, methods that are still used today. Ehrenstein and Ehrenstein (1999, p. 1213) list some of the tasks of the psychophysicist:

> The problem is . . . how to describe and investigate individual percepts so that they can be communicated and shared by others . . . The basic principle is to use the physical stimuli as a reference system . . . An investigation might begin with a simple question such as, 'Can you hear the tone?' That is, the task may be one of *detection*.

They go on to list several more psychophysical tasks including identification, discrimination, thresholds, reaction time, and comparative psychophysics. They concluded that the field of psychophysics may yet "emerge as a discipline in its own right" (p. 1237). The historical importance of psychophysics is that it marked the first self-conscious attempt to create a scientific psychology, one that attempted to measure psychological variables as precisely as had been the physical variables of physics and chemistry.

Ernst Weber and the JND

Biography

Ernst Weber was born in Wittenberg, Germany. He attended the prestigious Prince's Academy and later Wittenberg University, where he obtained his medical degree. In 1821, he joined the faculty of the University of Leipzig where he spent the rest of his long career.

Contributions

Weber was among the very earliest to pursue psychophysics experimentally. Most of his research concerned differences in sensitivity to physical stimuli. Early on, he noticed that sensitivity varied consistently as a function of the original stimulus applied. If the original stimulus was small, then people could detect a difference in a comparison stimulus even if there was just a little measurable difference between the two stimuli. But, if the original stimulus was large, then a much larger comparison stimulus was needed for a difference to be noted. Weber called this variable the JND (just noticeable difference).

After much experimentation, he noticed that he could predict just how much more or less a new physical stimulus had to be for someone to notice the change. He also noted that each sensory modality followed the same pattern, but that the sensitivities were not the same. People were more sensitive to brightness than they were to loudness, for example. Nevertheless, the same mathematical relationship held, the change in intensity of the stimulus divided by the intensity of the original stimulus was a constant, or:

$$\Delta I/I = k$$

where ΔI represented the measurable change, I the original stimulus, and k the constant for a particular modality. Fechner, realizing that Weber's work preceded his (see further), would later call this discovery *Weber's Law*. The value k later became known as the *Weber Fraction*.

Subsequent research showed that the Weber Fraction only held for midrange physical stimulus values but not for extreme ones.

Weber concentrated on the skin senses: pressure, hot, and cold. One of his main discoveries was the two-point threshold. By using a simple geometric compass he was able to demonstrate that certain parts of the body were much more sensitive than others. The most sensitive areas were the fingertips, lips, and face. On those areas of the body the two-point threshold was very small (2–6 mm), meaning that blindfolded subjects could reliably discriminate whether they were being touched with either one or two points. However, on areas such as the calf, the two-point threshold was large (45 mm). Special calipers to measure the two-point threshold are commonly used to demonstrate this phenomenon to students. Weber also pioneered the study of lifted weights. Using objects that looked identical but did not weigh the same, he asked his subjects to tell him which object weighed more. Once again he discovered that the more the objects weighed then the difference in their weights had to be larger in order to tell the difference. Weber's research showed that human abilities could be successfully investigated and understood using the same methods that had already yielded so many fruitful results in the physical sciences.

Until recently, retailers were selling slightly lower wattage incandescent light bulbs and touting them as a way to save energy. They were taking advantage of the Weber fraction for brightness, 0.079 (Teghtsoonian, 1971). Thus, applying the formula $\Delta I/I = 0.079$ yields JND wattages of approximately 92, 69, 56, and 37 for the traditional wattages of 100, 75, 60, and 40, respectively. Consumers buying those lower wattages would save a little energy and not be able to perceive any difference in brightness. Now, however, the incandescent bulb itself is largely history, thanks to new federal regulations (e.g., in the United States: the Clean Energy Act of 2007). The only exceptions include special purpose bulbs such as appliance lamps, black lights, colored lights, and a few others. New technologies for lighting include CFL bulbs and LED bulbs. Those lights convert more energy into light than do incandescent bulbs. They last longer but cost more to buy initially.

Yet, Weber's contribution was only a small first step. Gustav Fechner took the next large leap when he took Weber's JND and made it the unit of measurement for sensation. Then, after devising new methods (all still used today) for measuring sensation and conducting many experiments, he proposed the first psychophysical law; the one he termed Weber's Law, but now is known as the Weber–Fechner Law. That relationship between measured sensation and corresponding known amounts of physical stimulation served psychologists well until replaced in the mid-20th century by S. S. Stevens's (1961) Power Law.

PHOTO 8.3 Ernst Weber

Gustav Fechner (1801–1887)

Biography

Fechner was born in a small village in southeastern Germany. Due to his father's early death, his uncle raised him from the age of five. When Fechner was 16, he matriculated at the University of Leipzig, the very same year that Weber began to teach there. Fechner studied medicine but lost interest in the subject after graduating. He published (anonymously) the first of his 14 satirical papers under the pen name of Dr. Mises, soon afterward. Those writings were his way of safely criticizing the deficiencies of nature philosophy (Beiser, 2020).

Contributions

Short of money and interested in the sciences, he began a massive effort to translate two French science textbooks into German. That work paid off and he joined the faculty at Leipzig in the department of physics and soon began to publish original research in the area of electricity. He worked himself so hard that he had a severe physical breakdown. He nearly went blind because of looking at the sun directly through colored lenses. He resigned his position and literally dropped out of sight for three years.

Unexpectedly, he recovered, but in the interim had decided to become a philosopher. His overwhelming concern was to demonstrate the unity of mind and body. His philosophical arguments on that point were never persuasive and had he not turned to psychophysics he might have been just another mediocre philosopher. But, on October 22, 1850, he was inspired, while lying in bed, to develop a scientific program designed to make, "the relative increase of bodily energy the measure of the increase of the corresponding mental intensity" (Boring, 1950, p. 280).

Over the next ten years he once again worked tirelessly, but this time in the area of psychophysics. The result was his *Elements of Psychophysics*. In that book, he set out the first full set of methods and corresponding data for what became psychology's first subject area. Building on the earlier psychophysical work of Müller and Weber along with Herbart's and Leibniz's earlier work on sensory thresholds, Fechner proposed nothing less than a science that would reveal the functional relationships between body and mind.

Fechner began his program by taking Weber's JND and making it the indirect measurement for sensation. He mathematically transformed Weber's equation from

$$\Delta I / I = k$$

to:

$$S = k \, \log I$$

where S was the magnitude of the sensation, k was a constant specific to the modality of the sensation, and I was the measured intensity of the physical stimulus. Fechner's equation was mathematically equivalent to Weber's and assumed equal spacing between JNDs. Fechner conceived of two separate, but related, types of psychophysics. His *outer psychophysics* was what his equation measured. It was the relationship between the mind and stimulus. His *inner psychophysics* was the relationship between the stimulus and the subsequent activity of the nervous system. He realized that inner psychophysics was a much more difficult problem and, indeed, that has proven to be the case. To research outer psychophysics, he developed three psychophysical methods: limits, constant stimuli, and adjustment. Each of these methods is still in use today in modern psychology although they have been supplemented by an ever-increasing array of more sophisticated techniques. Fechner's methods are especially useful for the analysis of absolute and relative thresholds.

In the case of absolute thresholds, the problem is to determine the least amount of sensation that a person can detect. The problem for the relative threshold is to detect the smallest difference in sensation (or to determine the JND). For determination of thresholds the three methods yield similar data. Fechner realized, however, that he needed to control for variations due to individual differences and chance variables. So, he introduced the use of averages to balance out those differences. He also collected data from many trials for each person. In the method of limits, he showed his research subjects two stimuli. For relative threshold determination one stimulus was always the same, while the other was more or less intense. The subject's task was to say which one was more intense.

In the method of constant stimuli, Fechner randomly presented stimuli chosen from a small set. He also always presented a standard and invariant stimulus. Again, the task was to decide whether the single stimulus chosen from the set was more or less intense than the standard. In the method of adjustment, the research subject could turn a dial or knob to make changes to one stimulus. The other stimulus available never changed. The task here was to make the adjustable stimulus match the unchanging standard stimulus. These methods were just as easily used to determine the absolute threshold. There, the task was to tell whether a stimulus was present or not.

Why is Fechner not hailed as the first psychologist? One answer is that after publishing his *Elements of Psychophysics* he lost interest in the area. Others, notably Helmholtz and Wundt, latched onto Fechner's methods and used them to delve more deeply into psychological research. After pioneering psychophysics, Fechner turned to the scientific study of esthetics, an area of psychology that is still methodologically difficult (Graesser et al., 1996). Fechner unsuccessfully attempted to apply statistical methods to settle a dispute between two German cities, Dresden and Darmstadt, over the authenticity of two paintings of the Madonna by Hans Holbein the Younger. Taking advantage of a public showing of both paintings, Fechner conducted the first public opinion poll ever, asking the 11,842 visitors to judge which of the two paintings was more beautiful. Unfortunately, only 113 of the visitors answered the poll and most of them failed to follow the instructions (Livio, 2002). Since then, opinion polls have become ubiquitous in psychology. If not the first psychologist, Fechner was certainly the first to put psychology on a scientific footing. Woodward (2018, pp. 14-15) summarizes Fechner's contributions to psychophysics, philosophy, and esthetics:

> Fechner wrote in a time before the emergence of psychology as a discipline and a profession. (1) He offered a quantitative theory of pleasure as a computational principle in

action, directed toward the goal of stability or equilibrium. (2) Bodies and minds are collections of phenomena in Fechner's phenomenalism. Mental changes are a function of bodily changes, but not vice versa, an asymmetric relationship. Double-aspect theory can be seen as relating clusters of body phenomena and mental phenomena. Is their relation functional or causal? (3) Fechner's psychological parallelism contributed a widely-accepted meme to nineteenth-century philosophical and psychological thought. (4) Scholars have anchored his psychophysics in sensitivity, expanded it to a psychophysical worldview, and drawn lessons for memory from the inner psychophysics. (5) Fechner's experimental aesthetics drew on judgments of beautiful objects by naïve subjects, taking into consideration the proportions of the object as well as the feelings of the subject.

PHOTO 8.4 Gustav Fechner

At the same time psychophysics was emerging, another biological discipline was arising too. Inspired by Darwin, that field was animal psychology. One of its first practitioners was the English scientist, George Romanes.

LEARNING OBJECTIVE

6. Demonstrate how and why psychophysics was the first truly scientific subfield of psychology.

ANIMAL INTELLIGENCE AND COMPARATIVE PSYCHOLOGY

One of the main controversies inspired by the Darwin–Wallace theory of evolution was the issue of **continuity**. The theory of evolution made human beings just another species rather than the final, perfect product of Aristotle's scale of nature. The adoption of continuity by scientists late in the 19th century opened up the door to the study of animal psychology. Darwin himself had pioneered that subfield following the publication of his 1872 book, *The Expression of Emotions in Man and Animals*. George Romanes, a younger follower of Darwin, popularized the idea of studying animal intelligence through his books on the subject. C. Lloyd Morgan, in turn, followed Romanes and revised much of his work through careful observation along with a much more thorough and skeptical approach to the field. Unlike Romanes, Morgan discounted nearly completely the anecdotal reports from untrained observers to which Romanes had become enamored of late in his life and career. Romanes, for example, had bought a monkey for his sister to raise. When the monkey learned how to unscrew a bolt, Romanes inferred that it had learned the mechanical principles behind threaded screws. Morgan, while not doubting that the animal could indeed screw and unscrew bolts, interpreted the monkey's behavior more cautiously; it had learned that turning the bolt one way or another led to a predictable outcome. Morgan went on to suggest what he called his canon (Morgan, 1894, p. 53):

> In no case may we interpret an action as the outcome of the exercise of a higher psychical faculty, if it can be interpreted as the outcome of the exercise of one which stands lower in the psychological scale.

Morgan intended for his canon to put animal psychology on a par with human psychology by providing a rule for interpreting animal minds scientifically (Costall, 1993). Morgan did not wish to disallow comparison between human and animal intelligences. In fact, he believed that such comparisons were legitimate; they just had to be made carefully (Karin-D'Arcy, 2005). However, a completely different result ensued. The comparison of animal intelligence and human intelligence disappeared as a psychological topic until its revival late in the 20th century. Thus, *comparative psychology* was part of early psychology that grew out of its border with biology. Today, the situation is not much different for the subfield. While comparative psychology reappeared within psychology, it has gradually become a rarer course in the psychology curriculum. Abramson (2018, p. 3) in an article supporting comparative psychology's importance in the face of generalized neglect by the rest of psychology stated:

> In my view, there is no psychology as important as comparative psychology. The skills and perspective of a comparative psychologist would make them a highly valued member of any research team. Comparative psychology should be taught not only at the college level but in high school as well.

Remarkably modern psychology has all but ignored a pioneer in the study of animal cognition, Charles H. Turner. He was an African American psychologist who conducted experimental research in animal cognition on insects, birds, and reptiles. Despite publishing important research results including three articles in *Science*, only a handful of his contemporaries were aware of his contributions. Today, in his honor, the Animal Behavior Society gives an annual travel award to members of underrepresented groups (Dona & Chittka, 2020).

But, as Dewsbury (2000) noted, the scientific study of animals, their minds, and their behavior soon gave way—more practical approach to an applied human psychology. The origins of that still-dominant approach lie in the seminal work of Darwin's half cousin, Francis Galton.

PHOTO 8.5 Charles Henry Turner

LEARNING OBJECTIVE
7. Reflect on the history of comparative psychology. Why do you believe there has been such resistance to studying the psychology of animals?

PSYCHOMETRICS

Francis Galton (1822–1911)

Biography

Francis Galton was born in Birmingham, England. His grandfather was Erasmus Darwin; thus, he was a cousin to Charles Darwin. Francis was the youngest of seven surviving children. He later wrote that his sister, Adele, age 12 when he was born, successfully "begged hard to be allowed to consider me her sole ward" (Galton, 1908/1974, p. 13). Galton prospered under her tutelage. He could read before he turned three. After he started school he quickly mastered Latin and Greek. His parents sent him to school in France for a period, ostensibly to learn fluent French, but he never did. He profoundly disliked the school and its harsh discipline. Soon after, his parents recalled him to England and he continued his schooling there. At the age of 16, he began medical training at the Birmingham General Hospital. That was followed shortly after by more medical training at King's College in London. He interrupted his medical training to pursue a degree in mathematics at Cambridge at the recommendation of his cousin Charles. Before starting at Cambridge, he took the first of many long voyages, touring Eastern Europe and ending up in Istanbul. He returned to Cambridge, completed his degree in mathematics, and briefly returned to medicine, but when his father died shortly thereafter, he claimed his substantial inheritance and began to travel in earnest. His first claim to fame came after two trips to Africa. The book he wrote on his travels earned him a gold medal from the Royal Geographic Society. But that was only the beginning of his many scientific achievements.

Contributions

When Charles Darwin published *The Origin of the Species*, it changed Galton's life and led him to formulate a theory of human intelligence that was based upon heredity. His book, *Hereditary Genius* (1869), was written after he had sent questionnaires to members of the Royal Society. Those questionnaires were designed to uncover relationships between family kinship and worldly success. Galton believed he had shown that intelligence was inherited. He coined the phrase "nature vs. nurture" and argued that human intelligence was mostly due to the nature side of that dichotomy. He next turned to the study of mental associations. Using himself as a subject, he attempted to analyze his thoughts as he took the same stroll along Pall Mall, a street in London. From those carefully repeated walks he came to realize that much of the operation of his mind was hidden from him, below the level of consciousness.

He turned to the study of mental imagery and discovered that people exhibited a wide range of variation in the ability to visualize images. Some people hardly reported any such ability while others reported such vivid imagery that it was nearly indistinguishable from reality. In 1884, Galton set up a laboratory at the London International Health Exhibition. There, he collected data from over 9,000 people; each paid a small fee for the privilege. He measured 17 physical and mental human characteristics including height, weight, grip strength, visual acuity, reaction time, and hearing. That rich database led him to discover that many of the measurements he had made were normally distributed.

BORDER WITH MATHEMATICS
PROBABILITY AND STATISTICS

The 19th century was a fertile period for the development of probability and statistics (Verduin, n.d.). Friedrich Gauss demonstrated the utility of the normal distribution for predicting observational errors. Adolphe Quetelet described the "average man" for the first time. Francis Galton originated the quartile, or the division of a group into four equally sized smaller groups. Karl Pearson built upon Galton's concept of regression to introduce the correlation coefficient. Later, he developed the chi-square statistic. So, many of the familiar statistical tools and concepts so vital to psychology had their origin during this period.

At that point, however, hardly any of the statistical techniques familiar to modern psychologists existed. Galton was one of the first to develop those techniques. He was responsible (along with Karl Pearson) for developing the correlation coefficient, the regression line, regression to the mean, the median, and percentiles. Simply put, he was obsessed with trying to measure anything and everything. Interestingly, he never finished analyzing all of the data he had collected from his anthropometric studies. The dataset was too vast, and he lacked the tools (e.g., computers) and necessary statistical techniques. Johnson et al. (1985) analyzed the data from nearly 7,000 participants of Galton's laboratory and described them using modern statistical methods. They found the data reliable and exhibiting similar patterns of human development to more recently collected datasets. Interestingly, they also noted that the pace of human maturation was slower in Galton's era. Galton, thus, was the father of psychometrics, one of psychology's largest applied fields.

Galton was a pioneer in other fields beside psychology. He was the first meteorologist. He organized the collection of weather data from over 300 observers from weather stations spanning most of the European continent. Those observers collected data three times a day for an entire month. From those data Galton constructed the first weather maps and discovered anticyclones, the counterclockwise movement of air around areas of low pressure. Later, he promoted the use of fingerprints as a method of identifying people, especially criminals. Others had previously suggested and used fingerprints as a method for identifying criminals. However, Galton was the first to closely study and classify fingerprints. He developed methods to quickly determine whether a particular fingerprint was identical to another. His estimate that the odds of the fingerprints of two unrelated individuals being exactly alike was, "1 to about sixty-four thousand millions" (Stigler, 1999, p. 135). Galton's fingerprint research was one of the direct sources of yet another modern applied area of psychology: forensics.

THEN AND NOW
PSYCHOMETRICS

Galton's pioneering efforts in the measurement of human abilities evolved into one of psychology's largest applied areas: psychometrics. The first breakthroughs came through the work of Alfred Binet, Theodore Simon, and later, Lewis Terman. Their work with measuring the IQ of children led the way toward additional IQ tests for adults and preschoolers designed by David Wechsler. Today the testing industry produces thousands of psychological tests for uses including marital satisfaction, personality, attitudes, neuropsychology, and many more. Most students now are accustomed to taking professionally designed standardized tests.

LEARNING OBJECTIVE

8. Recall your experiences with psychometrics; what standardized tests have you taken?

Near the end of his career, Galton searched for the genetic mechanisms behind inheritance but failed to find them. He did, however, coin another word: "eugenics." For Galton (1904, p. 1), eugenics was "the science which deals with all influences that improve the inborn qualities of a race; also with those that develop them to the utmost advantage." He, however, failed to grasp the importance of learned and environmental variables in psychology. Similar to many other thinkers of the Victorian Age, he assumed that Europeans were genetically superior to all others in the world. Before he died he witnessed the widespread adoption of his ideas and methods. Of all of his contemporaries including—Darwin, Wallace, and Huxley—only he was knighted. Much of his version of psychology, mathematical

PHOTO 8.6 Francis Galton

Credit: iStock/RockingStock

and hereditarian, has persisted, albeit in modified form, until today. The ideas of his evolutionist colleagues were to lay dormant for several decades (Boakes, 1984). Before those ideas could arise again in the form of Behaviorism, a truly original and introspectively based psychology had to arise and run its course (see Chapter 10). Before that, however, another form of introspective psychology was on psychology's stage: Functionalism.

SUMMARY

Biology possesses another old, long, and deep border with psychology. Progress in biology was slow and fitful despite its ancient origins in Greek medicine and the work of Aristotle. Harvey was the first modern biologist, but even his pioneering work was not appreciated until long after his death. Slowly, biology became a science following the work of Linnaeus. But, it was Darwin who set biology on its current course. After his voyage on the HMS Beagle, and inspired by Malthus's essay, Darwin slowly put together the pieces that became evolutionary theory. Spurred on by Wallace's letter, Darwin hurriedly published the *Origin of the Species* and completely altered biology and later, psychology. By the 20th century, biologists used Darwin's theory to explain many of the mysteries of their discipline. They were aided by the modern synthesis of biology, which combined Darwin's work with Mendel's. During the 19th century, much progress also took place in neuroanatomy, specifically in the areas of understanding the action of the spinal cord and how the senses communicated with the brain. Helmholtz, especially, contributed much to the understanding of both areas with his research on the speed of nerve conduction and perception. Another area with rapid progress in the 19th century was psychophysics. There, Weber and Fechner measured physical stimuli (e.g., touch and vision) and their corresponding effects on perception. Each independently developed the first psychophysical laws along with research methods still used today. Two other areas near biology also developed in psychology during the late 19th century: comparative psychology and psychometrics. Comparative psychology extended the discipline into the animal kingdom and helped lay the groundwork for Behaviorism. Galton, nearly singlehandedly, developed psychometrics, which is now one of the largest areas of 21st century psychology.

9 FUNCTIONAL PSYCHOLOGY

ZEITGEIST

American Universities Before Daniel Coit Gilman

Before the founding of Johns Hopkins University in 1876, nearly all American colleges and universities were teaching institutions. Research, as it is now known and practiced, took place outside of academe, but was not extensive or financially well supported. At the same time in Europe, three predominant university models existed: British, French, and German. Daniel Coit Gilman (1831–1908), the founding president of Johns Hopkins University, took the German model, altered it slightly, and nearly single-handedly changed the historical path of the American university. Most nineteenth-century American colleges and universities were originally chartered as seminaries. Their faculty taught a wide variety of courses and had little time left for other scholarly pursuits. The state of medical education, too, was just short of scandalous. Students were admitted with no previous higher-level academic preparation, and there was hardly any science to be had or learned in the medical curriculum. Gilman's work in California and at Johns Hopkins changed both types of institutions. He took the German university as his model but made several key changes. One change was to require that students have adequate academic preparation prior to beginning advanced (e.g., graduate school) studies. In order to recruit graduate students, he offered the first **fellowships**. Those fellowships were enormously successful in attracting well-qualified students to Hopkins. Reisz (2018, p. 35) noted, "Johns Hopkins became the first American university founded explicitly as an organization dedicated to higher education and advanced scientific research and was also the first to grant doctoral degrees in different scientific domains."

Another change Gilman instituted was to create the now familiar academic department headed by a chair and housed in a school or college headed by a dean. Departmental faculty, now to be specialists in their fields, did not teach outside of their academic areas. Gilman's first hires were mostly natural scientists. He hired psychologist G. Stanley Hall (see below) later. His reorganization of the American university was spectacularly successful and widely imitated, so much so that it is nearly impossible to find other models in the United States today. Less imitated, however, was his policy toward women. In his inaugural address at Johns Hopkins, he said (Johns Hopkins University, n.d.):

> That they are not among the wise, who depreciate the intellectual capacity of women, and they are not among the prudent, who would deny to women the best opportunities for education and culture.

Despite his words, it would still be many years before women were routinely admitted to American colleges and universities (including Johns Hopkins). Nevertheless, Gilman's new plan revolutionized American higher education and paved the way for the rapid growth of psychology and other academic disciplines in the United States in the late nineteenth and early twentieth centuries.

PREVIEW

The rise of the *research university* was instrumental to progress in science and psychology. It provided a home for the newly established psychological laboratories. *Fellowships* for graduate students, too, ensured a steady supply of qualified applicants. Opposition to Structuralism (see Chapter 7) was the main cause for the rise of *Functionalism*. Its definition of psychology was broader and included applied areas such as *clinical psychology, forensics, educational psychology, emotion*, along with *child* and *adolescent psychology*. It also embraced the study of the animal *mind*. Closely associated with Functionalism was philosophical *Pragmatism*. The *1908 meeting at Clark University* introduced psychologists from Europe and North America to each other while popularizing the newly emerging psychoanalytic approach (see Chapter 13). Functionalists in the United States began to study and promote new ideas such as *mental tests, statistics courses, the adaptive act*, and *learning*. Thorndike, especially, was instrumental in positing the *law of effect, S-R psychology*, and *learning curves*. Woodworth led a rearguard action for Functionalism with his *dynamic psychology*. In the end, though, Behaviorism (see Chapter 10) erased much of the Functionalism's legacy to psychology.

INTRODUCTION

In this chapter, the story of psychology in North America unfolds. In the middle of the nineteenth century, psychology was nearly unknown in the United States. One man, William James, changed that by teaching the first psychology course taught in the United States. Soon, many others brought psychology back with them following their studies in Europe. Americans such as G. Stanley Hall and James McKeen Cattell traveled to Germany to study with Wilhelm Wundt and learn about the new psychology.

Following their return to North America they quickly established psychology laboratories in the Wundtian model. Surprisingly, the psychology that emerged from those labs was, for the most part, different from the psychology they had learned in Europe. For one thing, many of these new psychologists left their labs and brought psychology into the schools, workplaces, and mental asylums. They also began to work on the psychology of the animal mind. At the same time the colleges and universities were changing too. Following the lead of Germany, American schools reorganized their curricula, faculty, administrations, and missions. Research and training of future generations of researchers became one of their top priorities. By the third decade of the twentieth century, psychology had become primarily an American enterprise. Three schools of psychology: Structuralism, Functionalism, and Behaviorism vied with each other over the very definition of the discipline. This chapter tells the story of the beginning of that exciting era.

At around the same time that Gilman was reforming American higher education, William James was laying the foundation for psychology to occupy a large portion of the new educational structure Gilman and others were building. Like Gilman at Hopkins, James's efforts did much to elevate Harvard to the high position of eminence it holds today.

LEARNING OBJECTIVE

1. Consider the effect of American universities adopting the German model on the rise of psychology in the late nineteenth century.

William James (1842–1910)

Biography

William James was the first of five children born into what became a prominent and close family. His younger brother was Henry James Jr., the novelist. Their father, Henry Sr., was a wealthy man who moved his family nearly constantly around New England and Europe. Thus, William James attended schools in Europe in Geneva, Paris, and Boulogne-sur-Mer, France, usually in short stints. He became fluent in German and French. At the age of 16 and back in Newport, Rhode Island, he studied painting with William Hunt while attempting to pursue a career in art (see Figure 9.1), a choice contrary to his father's wishes. His study of art was briefly interrupted by another year-long stay in Geneva, but resumed upon his family's return to Newport. James, of his own volition, finally abandoned painting as a potential career in 1861 when he enrolled at the Lawrence Scientific School, a part of Harvard University. James's father believed that none of his children should attend any college, but may have struck a deal with his son to keep him from fulfilling his 90-day enlistment in the Newport Artillery Company, thus keeping him out of the American Civil War (Richardson, 2006). At Lawrence, he met a young chemistry professor, Charles Eliot, who later became Harvard's president and a major influence on James's career.

FIGURE 9.1 ■ William James, Self-portrait (1866)

Contributions

In 1864, James enrolled in Harvard's medical school but did not complete his degree until after five years of discontinuous study. An early interruption occurred when he accompanied the famous naturalist, Louis Agassiz, on a scientific expedition to the Amazon River. He took sick while on the expedition and spent another year in Europe attempting to recover his health and took time to study at the University of Berlin with Hermann Helmholtz. James's health was a lifelong problem and concern to him. After receiving his medical degree he again fell ill, suffering from depression. He never practiced medicine, nor had, he up to this point in his life, ever held any paying job. Eliot, by now Harvard's president (and James's neighbor), offered him his first employment—teaching comparative anatomy and physiology for one term. James accepted the position; from that point on Harvard and him were yoked for life.

Eliot reappointed James, who accepted the position, but only after spending another year in Europe. James took to teaching easily; his constant travels along with the many prominent people he had met were natural assets in the classroom. When he returned to Harvard in 1874, he taught comparative anatomy, but also taught for the first time in the United States a graduate course in psychology. The following year James taught a new course, physiological psychology, setting up a small teaching lab for the course. Thus, he and Wundt were each performing psychology experiments, the first in the world, at about the same time. James had convinced Eliot that the physiological psychology course belonged at Harvard and that it should be positioned between offerings from the departments of biology and philosophy. James based his course on several new and converging scientific disciplines: evolution, psychophysics, and archeology. Throughout his life, James sought to include data from as many disciplines as possible under the umbrella of psychology. For example, in his later years he explored the nature of religious thought and often attended séances in order to investigate the possibility of paranormal psychology.

When first teaching physiological psychology James used Spencer's textbook. He soon realized, however, that he needed to write his own textbook. He believed it would take him two years to write his text, *Principles of Psychology*, but it took him 12 long years. When it finally appeared it firmly established him as the principal spokesperson for American psychology. Much happened to James and American psychology during those 12 years. For one, he married Alice Howe Gibbens. That change in status required both of them to adapt to each other, but they eventually settled into a mutually agreeable domesticity. Her presence also seemed to moderate the number and frequency of the assaults on his health.

James took another trip to Europe some eight years before *Principles of Psychology* appeared. It was during that trip that he met many early European psychologists including Ewald Hering, Carl Stumpf, Ernst Mach, Jean-Martin Charcot, and Wilhelm Wundt. When he returned to Harvard, he taught courses in psychology and philosophy. In 1889, he became Harvard's first professor of psychology, but was still a member of the department of philosophy. By then, psychology departments were being founded at many North American universities (see Figure 9.2), mostly by Wundt's students and other European psychologists. James convinced Eliot that Harvard, too, needed a professor of psychology in order to keep up with the times. Eliot agreed and appointed James. In addition to his teaching duties, James also continued to run Harvard's

FIGURE 9.2 ■ Early North American Psychology Laboratories

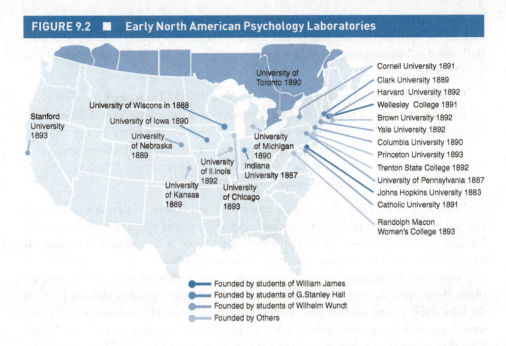

University of Toronto 1890

University of Wiscons in 1888
University of Iowa 1890
University of Nebraska 1889
University of Il.inois 1892
University of Kansas 1889
University of Chicago 1893
Indiana University 1887
University of Michigan 1890
Stanford University 1893

Cornell University 1891
Clark University 1889
Harvard University 1892
Wellesley College 1891
Brown University 1892
Yale University 1892
Columbia University 1890
Princeton University 1893
Trenton State College 1892
University of Pennsylvania 1887
Johns Hopkins University 1883
Catholic University 1891
Randolph Macon Women's College 1893

— Founded by students of William James
— Founded by students of G.Stanley Hall
— Founded by students of Wilhelm Wundt
— Founded by Others

psychology laboratory. Many of the empirical results from James's laboratory research eventually were published in his *Principles of Psychology*. Interestingly, Harvard did not establish a department of psychology until 1934. When Hugo Münsterberg (see below) succeeded James as director of the Harvard psychology laboratory, James voluntarily reverted to being a professor of philosophy. He did so in order to give Münsterberg the freedom to run things his own way without interference from another "psychologist."

The Principles of Psychology and the Psychology: Briefer Course

When James's text finally appeared in 1890, it was praised and criticized. It sold well. James quickly revised the text into a shorter version, designed specifically for students: *Psychology: Briefer Course.* That much shorter text sold even more briskly.

Readers then and now often refer to books by the author's name. So it was with *The Principles of Psychology* and *Psychology: Briefer Course.* James's first textbook ran well over 1,000 pages while the revised text had some 400 pages. Thus, students called the earlier, longer one the "James" and the later, shorter one the "Jimmy." Ross (1991) listed the following nine contributions from James's texts to psychology, which continue to be recognized today (p. 24). Those contributions were: space perception, the James-Lange theory of emotion, the importance of instinct, the preeminence of habit, the use of psychopathology to explain normal behavior, an early version of self-psychology, a model of memory that anticipated the Atkinson-Shiffrin information processing view (see Chapter 13), understanding the importance of physiological inhibition, and his overt attempts to understand vague, transitory, or mystical states. By the time *The Principles of Psychology* appeared, it was in competition with texts newer than Spencer's.

While there was much praise for the style and content of James's text, there was also criticism. Wundt, for one, dismissed it as literature, not science. James's student, G. Stanley Hall, called it "impressionistic," and an anonymous reviewer for the journal *Science* (1890, p. 207) wrote:

> It is not, and makes no pretence of being, a systematic work. The topics most liberally treated are such as the perception of space, perception of time, perception of "things," perception of reality, the stream of thought, association, attention, imagination, self-consciousness, the emotions, the will, necessary truths; though the more concrete problems of the functions of the brain, habit, discrimination and comparison, memory, instinct and hypnotism are by no means slighted.

In the long run, though, James's texts endured the test of time. His prose remains readable and lively, and most of the topics he covered are still part and parcel of psychology today. Unknowingly, many still use words or phrases first coined by James and used in his text. He was the first to use the following: "hegelism, time-line, pluralism . . . the bitch-goddess success, stream of consciousness . . . moral equivalent of war, healthy-minded, and live-option." (Richardson, 2006, p. 306). In his own time, *The Principles of Psychology* elevated James to the lofty status among psychologists that he still enjoys today. The completion of the two texts, however, had a perverse effect on James's professional life and interest in psychology. After their publication, he became more and more interested in philosophy. He, along with his Harvard friend and colleague, Charles Sanders Peirce, turned their efforts toward developing **Pragmatism**, a new approach to philosophy. James, it seems, was content to leave further progress in psychology to others. James's fame as a psychologist, however, lasted to the end of his life. In 1905 he happened to be in Rome and decided on the spur of the moment to attend the Fifth International Congress of Psychology meeting there. Nubiola (2011, p. 4) related this incident taken from James's correspondence:

> He went to the conference hall to register, "and when I gave my name," he told Alice, "the lady who was taking them almost fainted, saying that all Italy loved me, or words to that effect." His effusive admirer called in one of the officers of the congress, who, just as impressed, implored James to give a talk at one of the general meetings. "So I'm in for it again," James admitted with delight, "having no power to resist flattery."

Even after having left psychology, James was still highly regarded around the world as a psychologist.

Jamesian Psychology

A comprehensive system of Jamesian psychology never really existed. Furthermore, James never had any formal training in psychology. Instead, he cobbled together a psychology derived from his training and interests in biology, psychophysics, experimental psychology, archeology, religion, mysticism, and even parapsychology. Those interests along with his extensive travels and his ability to read and speak German and French made him the ideal ambassador to bring psychology to America. His wide view of what the discipline of psychology should ultimately include contrasted severely with the narrower and more strictly experimental views of most American psychologists who received their training in Europe. Indeed, by the end of James's life, the historical phase where American students sought training in psychology abroad had all but ended. American students were studying at home, in laboratories and departments that were busily at work creating a distinctly American brand of psychology: **Functionalism**. James, strictly speaking, was a functionalist but he did not participate heavily in the later development of that school of thought. By the time the functionalist school was in full bloom, James had already turned his attention toward philosophy. Yet it will pay dividends to look at James's psychology a little more deeply before looking at the development of the discipline under his successors.

James came to his kind of functional psychology early when he was reading Darwin's *Origin of the Species*. Darwin equated animal structures with biological functions, and consequently, with their survival. Similarly, James thought that the same type of functional relationship might hold between mental events and the survival of organisms. Such an approach, however, required introspection as a method and James embraced introspection as necessary for a complete psychology. Much like Wundt, James saw the necessity and potential for the new experimental methods in psychology, but believed that they could not provide the answers to all of the questions he was interested in. James also believed that consciousness was functional and adaptive. Furthermore, it could not be studied in isolation. Instead, it had to be studied as part of an ever expanding "stream of consciousness," one that changed constantly and could be pushed in new directions through the action of the self via the will.

Thus, James helped give rise to a new kind of psychology, one based on **phenomenology**. That underlying philosophy served as the midwife for many new areas of psychology, including, "Freud's psychodynamic theories . . . personality research; social, clinical, and child psychology; abnormal psychology; and educational and school psychology" (Pajares, 2003, p. 48).

After writing *The Principles of Psychology*, James reviewed the newly emerging French psychology that was studying subconscious thought and psychopathology. He corresponded with Pierre Janet, one of Freud's teachers. James wrote the first review of Freud's work to appear in the United States and met with Freud and Jung during their visit to America in 1908. James practiced what he preached; the establishment of a complete psychology, one that included experimental methods as well as yet-to-be developed methods for studying topics unapproachable by experimentation. Psychology's path in America after James did not follow James's model. Instead, American psychologists, by and large, stuck to experimental methods alone and began to use those methods on animals as well as humans. By the third decade of the twentieth century, American psychology bore little resemblance to James's model.

By 1891, James was spending up to four hours a day in the Harvard psychology laboratory supervising as many as 80 students. He complained about having to spend that much time there, and often characterized lab work as boring, although much of the material in his texts had come from his own, original work in that laboratory. That year, Eliot allowed James to recruit a replacement for himself in the Harvard psychological laboratory. James successfully recruited a younger German psychologist, Hugo Münsterberg, whom he had first met in Paris at the First International Conference of Physiological Psychology three years earlier. Münsterberg accepted a three-year probationary appointment. Although he returned to Germany after his initial stay at Harvard, he returned a few years later and remained there until his premature death in 1916.

Hugo Münsterberg (1863–1916)

Biography

Münsterberg was born in Danzig, Germany (now Gdansk, Poland). He attended the local gymnasium and had wide interests, including music and poetry. He became a more serious student after his mother died when he was 12 years old. He attended the University of Geneva briefly, then moved to Leipzig intending to pursue a degree and career in medicine. After hearing Wundt lecture, Münsterberg switched to psychology.

Contributions

Three years later, after receiving his PhD under Wundt, he completed his medical degree at the University of Heidelberg. He then secured a faculty appointment at the University of Freiburg. There, using his own money, he set up a small psychology laboratory and began to experiment in psychophysics. Titchener and Müller, however, criticized his work saying that it deviated too far from Wundtian principles. Münsterberg did not emphasize emotion enough for them. James, though, found his work appealing and was impressed with Münsterberg following their meeting in Paris. Three years later, James convinced him to leave Germany and take over the Harvard psychology laboratory. Münsterberg agreed to come to Harvard on a three-year trial basis, much to James's pleasure. That was when James dropped his title of professor of psychology and reverted to professor of philosophy. After Münsterberg's three years were up, he returned to Germany for two years. Once again, James and Eliot were successful in getting Münsterberg to return to Harvard, this time for good.

THEN AND NOW
THE PHYSIOLOGY OF EMOTION

The study of emotion has a long history, given its pivotal role in human behavior. James and Lange, independently, proposed the first scientific theory of emotion late in the nineteenth century. In their theory, today known as the James-Lange theory of emotion, an environmental event started the emotional reaction. That event was followed by a cognitive appraisal of the situation, and then in turn by the physiological responses associated with emotion (e.g., trembling, sweating, rapid heartbeat, and other similar ones). Or, in James's (1894) famous words, "I see the bear, run, and then am afraid." Two other major theories of emotion followed the James-Lange theory, the Cannon-Bard theory and the Schachter-Singer theory. Research evidence has not supported the Cannon-Bard theory's argument that the components comprising emotional responses are independent of each other. The Schachter-Singer theory posited that all physiological emotional responses are the same. Therefore, the interpretation of a particular emotion depended more upon a cognitive evaluation of the situation than anything else. Thus, they contended that any proper theory of emotion must evaluate the environmental context surrounding it. Kalat and Shiota (2012, p. 25) asked, "Isn't it about time we decided who was right? We contend that the James-Lange theory is more or less correct, if described in modern terms . . . The data indicate that a least some emotional appraisal is quick, preceding the physiological changes and observable behavior." Once again, James appears to anticipate modern research. The study of emotion is yet another old area of psychological interest receiving revived attention.

Early on, James had noticed Münsterberg's seemingly limitless capacity for work. At Harvard, Münsterberg continued to work at a frenetic pace. However, he soon abandoned the line of experimental research he had pursued in Europe. In its place, he began to work in more practical and applied areas. One of those areas was clinical psychology. Münsterberg conducted some of the earliest examples of clinical research. He did not charge his patients and only met with them if he found their cases interesting. Israel Goldiamond (personal communication) operationally defined research and therapy. Research, he said, was when you paid the participant. Therapy is when the participant paid you. By those definitions, Münsterberg was doing research and not therapy.

Therapy, however, was only one of his applied interests. Another was forensic psychology, the study of human behavior as it relates to crime and its punishment. Münsterberg's 1908 book, *On the Witness Stand*, pioneered the development of that area of applied psychology. Münsterberg also was among the first to examine the relationship of psychology to the workplace. He founded yet another applied field, industrial psychology (now called industrial-organizational psychology or I/O psychology). There, he investigated hiring, improving worker efficiency, and advertising. Münsterberg's greatest contribution to psychology was founding the area of applied psychology. As noted in Chapter 1, the area of applied psychology employs the vast majority of psychologists today.

BORDER WITH SOCIAL SCIENCE
EYEWITNESS TESTIMONY

Münsterberg was the first psychologist to research the fallibility of eyewitness testimony and the coerced extraction of confessions. But, his research had little influence on how police interrogated witnesses following crimes or on how they interrogated suspects. It was not until after the dogged efforts of Elizabeth Loftus (1979) that psychological research actually led to changes in police practices in interviewing witnesses (Wells et al., 2006) and minimizing the possibility of false confessions due to coercion (Napier & Adams, 2002).

Despite his significant contributions, Münsterberg is today relatively unknown. The main reasons for that were his activities before and during World War I. He kept his German citizenship, never becoming a naturalized American citizen. In 1910, before the War, he attempted to strengthen the relationship between Germany and the United States by serving as the director of the American Institute in Berlin. After the war began, relations between the two countries deteriorated quickly due to Germany's invasion of the neutral countries of Luxembourg, Belgium, and Holland, done in order to bypass French-fortified positions. British propaganda about the violation of neutrality successfully mobilized anti-German sentiments in the United States. Münsterberg, by then a well-known public figure, never ceased to justify the German cause in the war. That led to death threats, accusations of being a spy, and rumors of him being in the employ of the German government. Fouka (2019, p. 407) described the change in the public's attitudes toward German-Americans after 1915:

> Public opinion against Germans in the country first started to shift after the sinking of the ocean liner RMS Lusitania by a German U-boat in 1915, which resulted in the death of hundreds of American passengers. With the entry of the US in the war in 1917, this opinion shift turned into full-blown hostility.

Horak (2019) argued that Münsterberg's Jewish heritage was another complicating factor in his life; he provided many examples of the anti-Semitic *zeitgeist* at Harvard and within the American academic community at large during the early years of the twentieth century.

One day, while lecturing at neighboring Radcliffe, Münsterberg collapsed and died in front of his students. Most likely, the stress of the war and his defense of his native land contributed to his sudden passing. Münsterberg was the last of the major European talent imports in the young history of American psychology (although the rise of the Nazis in Germany after 1933 led to a second wave of European psychologists coming to the United States, see Chapters 1 & 12).

In the late nineteenth century and early twentieth century, Americans who had gone to Europe for their training made up the bulk of the next generation of psychologists. When they returned home, they founded laboratories and conducted research in two new and distinctly different schools of psychology: Functionalism and Behaviorism. Before those schools fully emerged, however, there were psychologists already at work who did not neatly fit into those yet-to-emerge schools of thought. One of those was G. Stanley Hall.

LEARNING OBJECTIVE

2. Interpret the importance of Münsterberg's emphasis on applied psychology to the role and position of applied psychology today.

Granville Stanley Hall (1844–1924)

Biography

G. Stanley Hall was born in Ashfield, Massachusetts, and did not want to become a farmer like his father. Instead, he decided to become a minister and attended seminary for a short time. After, he returned home where he taught school. His father purchased a draft exemption for him, which kept him out of the American Civil War, something that gnawed at Hall for the rest of his life. He felt guilty for not serving in the war. The history of American psychology might have been quite different had either Hall or James fallen during that war. In 1863, Hall enrolled at Williams College and proved himself an excellent student. He was attracted early on to philosophy and the theory of evolution. Both would serve as lifelong guides to him; Darwin's theory especially so. After graduating, he attended the Union Theological Seminary. There, his earlier attraction to philosophy affected his future prospects as a minister. So much so, that his trial sermon moved one listener to pray for Hall's soul! Henry Ward Beecher, the famous abolitionist preacher, advised him to study philosophy in Germany instead of going into the ministry.

Contributions

Hall traveled to Germany to study and stayed three years, studying philosophy and physiology first at the University of Bonn, and later at the University of Berlin. Out of funds, he returned to the United States and served as the pastor of a rural church in Pennsylvania for less than three months. He then moved to Antioch College in Ohio, where he taught English and philosophy. While there, he read Wundt's 1874 book *Physiological Psychology*. After reading it, he determined to return to Germany to obtain his PhD in psychology under Wundt. But, he could not afford to go. Instead, he accepted an offer from Harvard's president, Charles Eliot, to teach English and pursue graduate study under William James. Hall became the first American to obtain a PhD for a dissertation in psychology; it was titled "The Muscular Perception of Space." Much of the research was conducted in Henry Pickering Bowditch's physiological laboratory at Harvard. After obtaining his PhD, Hall went to Germany again, and after a brief sojourn in Berlin went to Leipzig to become Wundt's first American student. While at Leipzig, Hall roomed next door to Fechner and studied psychology and physiology. Wundt did not make a strong impression on Hall, except when it came to the importance of the laboratory to the young science. Hall was never a committed believer in introspection, and after he returned to the United States, he lost his personal enthusiasm for laboratory work as well.

When Hall came back home he had no position or prospects. But, after hearing him give a talk to the National Education Association, Eliot again hired Hall, this time to give a series of Saturday classes on the problems of education. Those classes proved highly popular and led to an invitation to lecture, part-time, at the Johns Hopkins University. Hall's lectures there, too, were successful, and he was invited to join their faculty. The next year, he founded what he claimed was the first psychology laboratory in the United States, much to James's consternation. In truth, however, Hall founded his laboratory in order to conduct research while James had created his, originally, to teach physiological psychology.

The problem was deeper than simple priority, however. James and Hall had different visions about psychology. At this point in his career, Hall was "focused, in his psychological work, entirely on laboratory experiments and German-style research" (Richardson, 2006, p. 281). At the same time, James was still struggling to finish his text with its emphasis on topics that were difficult to approach experimentally. Their relationship was always complex, and they often argued and reconciled. In the short run, Hall's approach was more successful, especially in the founding of university-based psychological laboratories. In the long run, however, James's vision of the future of psychology was the more prescient one.

Hall, though, began to move away from laboratory-based psychology, leaving it to others, but never doubting its fundamental importance to psychology. He, however, became more interested in broader topics such as child, and later, adolescent psychology. He left Johns Hopkins when he was offered the presidency of a new school, Clark University, in Worcester, Massachusetts. There, he attempted to improve on Gilman's graduate school model. A few years after taking on the presidency at Clark, Hall founded his second journal, *Pedagogical Seminary* (later renamed the *Journal of Genetic Psychology*), which highlighted his new interest in the psychology of children. He was among the first to emphasize the relationships between development, evolution, and adaptation. Much of Hall's research was accomplished through questionnaires, an approach he used extensively. Young (2018, p. 478) wrote:

> Between 1894 and 1915, Hall and his extended network of students and associates distributed more that 200 different questionnaires, on a plethora of topics, many of them related to child study (Hall, 1924).

He followed up his interest by publishing his most important work in 1904, *Adolescence*. That book created adolescent psychology as a new subdiscipline of developmental psychology and also caused him difficulty when he began to research adolescent sexuality. He was too far ahead of his time for that topic. As Chilman (1979, p. 23) noted:

> The topic of human sexuality has been difficult to study. It has been traditionally shrouded in secrecy and surrounded with prohibitions and resultant anxiety. Only in the past 30 years or so, since Kinsey's tradition-shattering research, has it been possible to study *adult* (added italics) sex behaviors and attitudes in any extensive way . . . The whole subject of childhood sexuality, from which adolescent sexuality springs, has hardly been touched, other than through clinical observations. Thus, adequate understanding of this subject will continue to be limited until more systematic research can be undertaken.

Hall's colleagues, including Thorndike and Angell, were aghast at his inclusion of sexuality in the study of adolescence (Boakes, 1984). Hall eventually moved on to other topics, including the psychology of religion and aging. He even wrote a book in 1917, titled *Jesus, the Christ, in the Light of Psychology*, but it was not well received. Hall was elected twice as president of the American Psychological Association, the organization he led as first president after helping found the organization in his own living room in 1892. He died in 1924, during his second presidency.

LEARNING OBJECTIVE

3. Discuss why Hall's research into adolescent sexuality was so jarring to other psychologists.

Hall's Influence on American Psychology

Hall's mind was always at work looking for new ways to make psychology more prominent in the academy and the real world. He and his students were responsible for founding laboratories at Clark University, Indiana University, the University of Wisconsin, and the University of Iowa (Benjamin, 2000). While he was at Clark University, he oversaw the awarding of 81 PhDs in psychology. Despite that large number, his students were not members of a school of thought. Hall's wide diversity of interests militated against the founding of a school. But, such a large number of students did mean that Hall was in large part responsible for much of the growth of American psychology during this period. Many of his students went on to become famous psychologists themselves. James McKeen Cattell, John Dewey, Henry Goddard, and Lewis Terman were among his many students. Hall, like James, had read Freud's early books and articles. For the twentieth anniversary celebration of the founding of Clark University, Hall invited Freud and Jung to Clark. He also invited Wundt, who declined because of his advanced age and a personal conflict, the University of Leipzig was celebrating its 500th anniversary that year. The meeting at Clark was a tremendous success and cracked open psychology's door for the eventual admittance of abnormal and clinical psychology, two of the discipline's largest subfields today. Those invited comprised a *Who's Who* of psychology, although with notable exceptions. "There was no one whatsoever from Chicago. Animal psychologists were also notable for their absence" (Boakes, 1984, p. 165). Hall, almost single-handedly, increased the size and influence of psychology during his lifetime.

It is nearly obligatory when writing about Hall to list the many things he was the first to accomplish. If nothing else, it serves as a good way to study about him and his life.

- First American PhD with a psychological topic,

- Wundt's first American student,

- First research laboratory in the United States (at Johns Hopkins),

- Founded the *American Journal of Psychology*, the first one in the United States,

- Founded the American Psychological Association and served as its first president,

- First president of Clark University, and

- Granted first PhD to an African American: Francis Cecil Sumner (1920).

However, it was one of Wundt's students, James McKeen Cattell, who led the tremendous expansion of American psychology in the last decade of the nineteenth century and the first two decades of the twentieth century. Cattell, too, set up new laboratories; he reintroduced Galton's ideas and methods to America, and, through his many journal editorships, worked to include psychology within the larger structure of American science.

PHOTO 9.1 G. Stanley Hall

PHOTO 9.2 Freud, Hall, and Jung (the three men in the front row) at Clark University (1909)

Credit: Getty Images

James McKeen Cattell (1860–1944)

Biography

Cattell was born in Easton, Pennsylvania, into a well-to-do family. His father was a professor of ancient languages at Lafayette College and later became its president. Cattell enrolled at his father's school and was academically successful, earning BA and MA degrees. He then went to Germany to study philosophy, first at Göttingen with Lotze, and then at Leipzig with Wundt. A paper he wrote on philosophy earned him a fellowship at Johns Hopkins. He stayed there one year, but lost his fellowship because of his irascible personality and a personal conflict with Gilman. Interestingly, his fellowship then went to John Dewey (see below). Sokal (2016) examined Cattell's early but brief career at Johns Hopkins and pointed to his lifelong arrogance. However, Sokal (2016, p. 14) also noted the importance of Cattell's early research to later psychology:

> Even in the mid-1880s, the emphasis of these experiments on the behavioral (rather than the introspective) nature of a subject's reactions certainly helped shape the concerns of experimental psychology for several decades (Danziger, 1990; Sokal, 2010).

Cattell returned to Germany and again studied with Wundt for three years, receiving his PhD in 1886. Legend has it that he announced to Wundt that he would become his first assistant. Leading Wundt to declare Cattell as "typically American" or *"ganz Amerikanisch"* in German (Blumenthal, 1980). Wundt probably never suspected how correct he was in that characterization, for Cattell would eventually do much to differentiate American psychology from its Wundtian origins. But that was in the future. While at Leipzig, Cattell worked on several reaction time studies and did much to improve the laboratory equipment used to conduct those types of studies.

Contributions

Cattell returned to the United States and taught psychology for a year at Bryn Mawr and the University of Pennsylvania. He crossed the Atlantic again and taught for a year at Cambridge University, where he met and worked with Francis Galton. Their brief association was pivotal, for it caused Cattell to think about the role of statistics in psychology and later, to conduct research along Galtonian lines. While at Cambridge, he founded their psychology lab. He left Cambridge for the University of Pennsylvania and founded their psychology lab. He left Penn for Columbia University where he spent the next 26 years. In 1917, he was fired for his alleged disloyalty to the United States. He had written letters to Congress urging the United States to not require conscripts to engage in combat in the war in Europe. In truth though, his dismissal from Columbia had been long in coming because of his constant bickering with administrators over issues surrounding academic freedom and faculty governance (Godin, 2007).

BORDER WITH COMPUTATIONAL SCIENCE
STATISTICS

Psychology majors today realize that their curricula will nearly always include at least one course in statistics. Cattell was the first to offer that course in the United States, and such courses have been an integral part of psychology curricula ever since.

Cattell spent the rest of his long life outside of academe. Most of his influence on psychology and science came from his editorship of journals. He helped found and edit the journal *Psychological Review*, started in order to provide an alternative to Hall's *American Journal of Psychology*. Cattell, James, and others believed that Hall's journal was too slanted toward his view of psychology and that he published the work of his students preferentially. Cattell bought and edited other journals, most notably *Science*. He rescued that journal from bankruptcy and served as its editor for 50 years. Today, *Science* is probably the world's top journal devoted to scientific studies of all types, including psychology. Cattell worked all his life to ensure a place for psychology in the halls of science and on the pages of *Science*.

Cattell also founded the directory, *American Men of Science*, in 1906. Despite the title, women scientists were not excluded from the directory. The second edition, published in 1910, listed 19 women (out of 5,500 total entries). In 1971, the name was changed to *American Men and Women of Science*. It is still published today. Cattell's inspiration for publishing his directory was Galton's 1874 book, *British Men of Science*. Both men believed that eminent intellects were on the decline in society. Galton attributed the decline to heredity because his statistics showed that eminent men sired fewer children. Cattell, on the other hand, argued that the lack of environmental opportunity (good schools, primarily) was the main cause for the decline. Unlike Galton, he believed the decline could be reversed by providing educational opportunities for qualified students. In 1910, Cattell analyzed the change in eminence rankings from the first edition (1906) of *American Men of Science* and correlated them with the institutions they originated from to obtain the first listing of eminent departments of psychology. As ever, he wished to use those data to illustrate where students could best hone their skills, and to point out where better schools were needed. Since then, such lists have become commonplace. The National Research Council published a similar list in 2010 for graduate departments of psychology. Here are the top ten schools on both lists shown side by side along with their NRC ranks today:

Cattell 1910	NRC 2010
1. Columbia University (16.5)	1 Stanford University
2. Harvard University (6)	3.5 University of Michigan (tie)
3. Clark University (51.5)	3.5 Yale University (tie)
4. Cornell University (14.5)	3.5 UCLA (tie)

Cattell 1910	NRC 2010
5. University of Chicago (21.5)	3.5 University of Illinois (tie)
6. University of Iowa (35)	6 Harvard University
7. Wellesley College (not ranked)	7 University of Minnesota-Twin Cities
8. Wisconsin University (14.5)	9.5 University of Pennsylvania (tie)
9. Stanford University (1)	9.5 University of California-Berkeley (tie)
10. Indiana University (21.5)	9.5 University of California-San Diego (tie)
	9.5 Carnegie Mellon University (tie)

Note that only Stanford and Harvard are on both lists.

Cattell's methods for measuring scientific productivity and performance have been modified since his day. Xie (2011) decried those new methods: number of publications, citations, patents and metrics such as Hirsch's *h* index. He added (n.p), "There doesn't appear to be a good solution that will work across all scientific disciplines. We know that none of the measurable factors effectively paint a complete picture of a researcher's success." (Godin, 2007, p. 719) suggested, "Money devoted to R&D [research and development] is now the preferred statistic." Cattell's directory, however, was another pioneering use of statistics intended to promote the growth of science and psychology.

LEARNING OBJECTIVE

4. Critique modern methods of judging scientific productivity.

Cattell was the first to use the words "mental test." When he returned from Cambridge, he attempted to measure and correlate the academic performance of Columbia students on a wide variety of measurements. The measurements he used were very much like those Galton had used earlier in his own research. Cattell measured things such as hand strength, the two-point threshold, pain sensitivity, and reaction times. Unfortunately, the data he collected yielded extremely low correlations between items or with other measures of academic success. So, he abandoned this line of research. Soon after, Binet and others, using more complex cognitive tasks, successfully launched the testing movement in psychology.

In 1921, Cattell and two other Columbia colleagues began the Psychological Corporation. The idea behind that new company was to enlist psychologists as consultants to industry and education. Initially, the company was not successful. By the 1940s, however, it did become financially successful, but as a publisher of psychological tests, not as a consulting organization. One of Cattell's students at Columbia Edward Lee Thorndike began his psychology career studying animal learning using chicks, and later, cats and dogs. He was one of the first to study learning. Later, he turned his attention to the study of children and psychological testing. By the end of his long career, he was universally acknowledged as "the dean" of American psychology (Boring, 1950, p. 566).

Edward Lee Thorndike (1874–1949)

Biography

Thorndike was born in Lowell, Massachusetts. His father was a Methodist minister who ran a strictly religious household. Thorndike attended Wellesley College where he promptly left his religious upbringing behind. There he read James's *Principles of Psychology* and was inspired to enroll at Harvard to study psychology. Münsterberg was back in Germany when Thorndike arrived at Harvard, so he took his courses from James. He also began the animal research that was to make him famous. Originally, he had planned to conduct research on children, but was unable to get his project approved. So, he decided to look at maze learning in newly hatched chicks. He was inspired by the earlier observations of Romanes and Morgan. Thorndike wanted to explore learning more thoroughly and do so experimentally. He had to conduct the research with chicks in the basement of William James's house because his landlady would not allow him to keep chicks in his apartment. The results he obtained were promising; his chicks did seem to run his simple mazes (constructed out of old textbooks) more quickly with experience. He was living hand to mouth at Harvard, however, so when Cattell offered him a fellowship at Columbia he moved there, taking a few of his best chicks with him.

Contributions

At Columbia, he finally secured laboratory space in the attic of Schermerhorn Hall, then and now the home of the psychology department. In that attic he began a new series of experiments designed to look more carefully at the problem of learning. He built a series of puzzle boxes from which either cats or dogs could only escape by learning to operate the mechanism. Some boxes required the animal to step on a treadle, others required them to pull on a loop, and still others required a sequence of steps. He kept his animals hungry and allowed them to eat once they had escaped from the puzzle box. Years later, his son (Thorndike, 1991, p. 145) wrote about his father's mechanical ability, "if you look at pictures of the equipment that he used in his original animal experiments you realize that they would have shamed Rube Goldberg." (Rube Goldberg (1883–1970) was an American cartoonist who drew incredibly convoluted and inane machines designed to accomplish simple tasks with great difficulty.) Nevertheless and despite their primitiveness, Thorndike's puzzle boxes yielded extraordinary and original results. He noticed that cats first attempted a large number of fruitless actions in their attempts to escape. Gradually, those actions disappeared. Nearly always, cats made a chance discovery of the action that operated the escape mechanism. When he returned the cats that had discovered the trick for escaping from a particular puzzle box, they exited the box more and more quickly. In other words, their latency decreased. A cat that had been returned to the puzzle box many times escaped almost as soon as it was put in. From his latency data, Thorndike constructed the first **learning curves**. Those curves highlighted behaviors and not ideas as the basic data for psychology.

5. Explain how many writers in the popular media reverse the meaning of "steep learning curve."

Unwittingly perhaps, Thorndike laid the groundwork for Behaviorism, psychology's next school of thought. He continued his animal experiments for a few years and discovered that once a particular cat or dog learned to escape one of his puzzle boxes, they could again escape it even when placed there after a long time. Furthermore, the behaviors that failed to lead to escape never returned. He thought of the behaviors that led to escape as being "stamped in" and those that did not as being "stamped out." He also investigated whether his animals could profit by instruction. They did not. He was surprised to discover that his cats and dogs learned to escape no faster when their paws were moved by him to make the requisite response. His major contributions however were his laws of learning, the most important of which was his *law of effect* (Thorndike, 1911, p. 244):

> Of several responses made to the same situation, those which are accompanied or closely followed by satisfaction to the animal will, other things being equal, be more firmly connected with the situation, so that, when it recurs, they will be more likely to recur; those which are accompanied or closely followed by discomfort to the animal will, other things being equal, have their connections with that situation weakened, so that, when it recurs, they will be less likely to occur. The greater the satisfaction or discomfort, the greater the strengthening or weakening of the bond.

Another law Thorndike proposed was the *law of exercise*. That law stated that learning would last longer when animals were exposed to more instances of a stimulus (the puzzle box) and a response (escaping). As Robinson (1981, p. 409) pointed out, "There is little in either of these "laws" that could not be gleaned from Locke, or Hume or Bentham or, for that matter, Aristotle . . . The difference . . . is that the laws in Thorndike's case are supported by experimental findings." Again, Thorndike was anticipating Behaviorism. His S-R (stimulus-response) connections would become one of the mainstays of later behavioral psychology (see Chapter 10). Thorndike also worked with a number of monkeys. For them, he made the puzzle boxes so they would have to open them in order to obtain some food. He discovered that their learning curves were much steeper, meaning they learned faster. He abandoned that line of research because of the difficulty of handling them; had he continued he might have discovered that monkeys learn differently than do cats and dogs. When Cattell suggested that he begin to work with children, Thorndike left animal work behind for over 30 years. His work with children led to tremendous success in the applied areas of testing and educational psychology.

After he left Columbia as a student, he worked for a year at the College for Women of Western Reserve College (now Case Western Reserve University) in Ohio. He returned to Columbia, but not to the psychology department. Instead, he became a member of their Teachers College, a position he held until he retired in 1939 (although he continued to work until his death ten years later). Thorndike and Woodworth (1901) conducted an influential study on transfer of training from one domain of human learning to another (e.g., from Latin to math). Their results showed no such transfer took place, and their work led to radical revisions in school curricula. Similarly, Thorndike approached the design of children's dictionaries. Before his analysis of them, those dictionaries were simply abridged versions of adult's dictionaries. Working with Clarence Barnhart, they created new children's dictionaries where the words used to define terms were all simpler than the term itself and where pictures were used extensively along with sentences designed to illustrate the meaning of terms.

Thorndike also was one of the first successful developers of tests. He was so successful that he was one of the first psychologists to make a substantial income from his work outside of academe. He applied his statistical methods to vocational guidance and academic success too. That work yielded low correlations for workers followed over a nine-year period, but higher correlations for students who reached college (Thorndike, 1991). Thorndike remained active until his death in 1949. He lived to see psychology grow from its American infancy until its post-World War II boom years.

In 2020, the Board of Trustees of Teachers College, Columbia University voted, unanimously, to take Thorndike's name off of one of its buildings. In an announcement from the president and trustees, they stated: "While Thorndike's work was hugely influential on modern educational ideas and practices, he was also a proponent of eugenics, and held racist, sexist, and antisemitic ideas." They added that Teachers College was not erasing Thorndike's name from its history, and that the former building plaque would be moved elsewhere on campus. The college's history, they added, should be faced with honesty, bravery, and with humanity.

It's now time to look more closely at the Functionalist School that emerged from the work of the early pioneers in psychology. That school of thought had two major centers, one being the newly founded (1892) University of Chicago and the other Columbia University.

PHOTO 9.3 Edward Lee Thorndike

THE UNIVERSITY OF CHICAGO (1892)

The oil baron John D. Rockefeller wished to create a "Harvard" of the Midwest in the city of Chicago. He hired William Rainey Harper to be the first president of the University of Chicago. Working with civic leaders, churchmen, and businessmen (including Marshall Fields, owner of the department store of the same name), Rockefeller and Harper opened the school for classes in 1892. Although both were Baptists, their new school was nonsectarian by design.

The University of Chicago admitted women and minorities from its founding. Rainey had even hired nine women as faculty. On the psychology faculty roll was June Etta Downey, listed as "Second Assistant in Psychology," one of Chicago's lowest faculty ranks. (Chicago had ranks of: reader, lecturer, docent, assistant, associate, instructor, assistant professor, professor, and head professor.) Years later, Downey returned to her native Wyoming and became head of the department of psychology and philosophy at the University of Wyoming. She was a prominent psychologist and was elected to the American Psychological Association's Council and named a fellow of the American Association for the Advancement of Science.

Thanks to Rockefeller's deep pockets, Rainey had lured prominent faculty from around the country to work at Chicago for higher wages and the promise of being part of a community of scholars. For his social science division, he had "raided" the faculty and graduate students of Clark University, much to G. Stanley Hall's great and permanent displeasure. Chicago was the first American university to house an independent sociology department.

But, its psychology department was still housed within the department of philosophy, which in turn was divided into three subareas: psychology, education, and philosophy. John Dewey was the head of the philosophy department. Psychology had a total of seven faculty including Dewey. James Rowland Angell was hired in 1894 and John B. Watson in 1903. The University of Chicago grew quickly and soon became an academic powerhouse, especially in psychology. Functionalist psychology slowly emerged from the University of Chicago and Columbia University as psychologists at both universities responded to Titchener's (1898) criticisms of their research. It was Titchener who first called them "functionalists." He argued that while questions about biological and psychological function were useful and ultimately necessary, asking them before the structure of the mind was fully understood as premature and would lead to misleading results. McConnell and Fiore (2017, p. 263), comparing Functionalism's view of Descartes's version of the mind–body problem wrote:

> The functional psychology of the late nineteenth century was a notable departure [from Descartes], couching psychology within the context of the environment. For John Dewey, Harvey Carr, James Rowland Angell, and others, behavior was adaptive. There was a clear Darwinian influence, suggesting that psychology was properly the study of cognitive and behavioral processes that were selected for by evolutionary pressure. The strongest possible statement of this view might be that the evolution of consciousness itself subserves the need of adapting to the environment. Such a view requires a mind that exists within and is acted upon by the natural environment. It follows, then, that mind must be materialized and embodied. It should be emphasized that the place in which this mind is embodied is not the Cartesian notion of space, but rather it is the natural environment—more specifically, it is the ecological niche of the perceiving animal, that is, the place in which it evolved.

Historically and in the longer scheme, Functionalism never had the chance to fully develop and embrace its founding principles. Behaviorism, early on at least, (see Chapter 10) fundamentally altered Functionalism's dualistic approach by dispensing with dealing with mental events entirely.

FUNCTIONALISM

Chicago Functionalism

John Dewey (1859–1952)

Biography

Dewey was born in Burlington, Vermont, where he attended the local public school, and later, the University of Vermont. After graduating, he taught high school in Oil City, Pennsylvania, for three years while also reading and studying philosophy on his own. An essay he wrote won him a fellowship at Johns Hopkins (Cattell's, see above). There, he studied with G. Stanley Hall and the idealist philosopher, Sylvester Morris, who introduced him to Hegelian philosophy. After receiving his PhD from Hopkins, Dewey taught at the University of Michigan for a total of ten years. His stay at Michigan was briefly interrupted by a six-month term at the University of Minnesota. When he returned to Michigan, however, it was as chair. Consequently, he was able to hire George Herbert Mead and James Hayden Tufts, both of whom would become long-term collaborators. Tufts left for the University of Chicago and soon convinced President Harper to hire Dewey. Dewey, once at Chicago, again hired Mead and also James Rowland Angell.

Contributions

Over the next ten years, the seeds of functional psychology sprouted and grew at Chicago. Dewey (1896) is usually credited as the founder of Functionalism following the publication of his article, "The Reflex Arc Concept in Psychology," published in *Psychological Review*. That article took the prevailing analysis of the reflex arc to task. Specifically, Dewey wrote that the arc was really a circle. Furthermore, there was no plausible distinction between the components of the arc, namely stimuli and movements. Instead, those were only noticeable when reflexes went amiss. Otherwise they were simply coordinated actions that when sufficiently practiced went virtually unnoticed. One implication of Dewey's article was that psychology needed what today would be called an ecological approach. As Manicas (2002, p. 287) noted:

> If Dewey is correct, we need to be talking about an intact organism with a brain, including, ultimately, an organism with a mind in Dewey's sense, acting in an environment.

Dewey argued for a psychology where mind, brain, and purpose interacted and where an evolutionary mechanism selected the functional outcomes. Such a model appealed to his pragmatist philosophy and made him an early social activist. One concrete example of his activism was the laboratory school he founded at Chicago, the first of its kind. At that school, his graduate students could watch and observe teachers in action as they taught their classes. Eventually a dispute with President Rainey over the laboratory school led Dewey to resign from Chicago and move to Columbia University. Much like James earlier, Dewey abandoned psychology for philosophy after he arrived at Columbia.

THEN AND NOW
DEWEY AND THE MIND

The functional approach to the mind persists in modern psychology, meaning that Dewey's approach still resonates. His definition of Functionalism through the definition of the reflex arc (see above) still holds. Organisms are more than brains and nervous systems. They are, instead, brains and nervous systems and minds operating in an everchanging environment governed by evolutionary rules. Dewey argued that simply studying one of those parts without the others was wrong. Boyles and Garrison (2017) support Dewey's analysis and gave it a name, the mereological fallacy, the study of part whole relations, they added (p. 113):

> The mereological fallacy arises from confusing the properties of a necessary subfunction with the properties that derive from the unity of the whole functional coordination. Cognitive neuroscientists and their votaries commit some version of the mereological fallacy when they confuse a part (e.g., the brain) with the larger whole involved in mental functioning. Humans are a psychophysical union. We may say of human beings that they reason, emote, consider, and self-reflect. We may not say of the human brain the same things.

Later, (p. 128) they concluded:

> Having a human mind requires having a human brain functioning in a human body continually transacting with its physical, biological, sociocultural environment. Lacking any of these, we lose mental capacity. Where is the mind? We argue that the question is misplaced, as it were, and indicative of the very problem Dewey helps us solve. The answer to the question, nonetheless, is: wherever intentional functioning occurs. *The mind is a complex distributed biological-sociocultural function that is not simply located anywhere and, therefore, is not completely in the possession of any one (person, place or thing); it occurs wherever it has consequences.* (original italics)

So, Dewey's Functionalism may, in fact, yet persist in modern psychology. The answers to many interesting questions may still require current researchers to adopt his approach.

Dewey, as a member of the department of philosophy at Columbia's Teacher's College, became an internationally known expert in educational psychology. He and his wife traveled and lived around the world visiting school systems and consulting in Japan, China, Mexico, Turkey, and the Soviet Union (Barone, 1996). Dewey, like other functionalists, put much stock in a psychology that extended far outside the laboratory and into applied settings. Today, his influence on educational psychology is still heavily felt. Dewey "retired" in 1930 but remained active until his death. Among his legacies are teacher's unions, the American Association of University Professors, and the New School for Social Research. His colleague, James Rowland Angell, took up where Dewey left off after leaving Chicago and

PHOTO 9.4 John Dewey

gave Functionalism its clearest definition, contrasting it to Titchener's Structuralism. From that point on, James Rowland Angell became the leader of Chicago Functionalism.

James Rowland Angell (1869–1949)

Biography

Like Dewey, Angell was born in Burlington, Vermont. His father was president of the University of Vermont and a few years later became president of the University of Michigan. Angell grew up in Ann Arbor, Michigan, and went to school and college there. He graduated from the University of Michigan and then went to Harvard to study with James. He made the customary trip to Germany to study with Wundt, only to discover that he had no spaces left in his lab. So, Angell studied first in Berlin and then at Halle. He completed a thesis there, but before it could be accepted, he had to rewrite it in better German, which he never did because he would have missed out on a position at the University of Minnesota. So, he never finished his PhD degree. He stayed at the University of Minnesota briefly until Dewey hired him to teach experimental psychology at Chicago. Later, he became the first person to head Chicago's new department of psychology.

Contributions

In 1906, he was elected president of the American Psychological Association. His presidential speech (Angell, 1907) remains one of the best descriptions of functional psychology ever written. Contrasting Functionalism to Titchener's version of Structuralism, he gave the following three ways to define functional psychology. First, it is the psychology of mental operations, not the description of mental elements. Second, it is the psychology of the utility of consciousness. Third, it is psychophysics itself. Or, in his own words (pp. 85–86):

> If we now bring together the several conceptions of which mention has been made it will be easy to show them converging upon a common point. We have to consider (1) functionalism conceived as the psychology of mental operations in contrast to the psychology of mental elements; or, expressed otherwise, the psychology of the how and why of consciousness as distinguished from the psychology of the what of consciousness. We have (2) the functionalism which deals with the problem of mind conceived as primarily engaged in mediating between the environment and the needs of the organism. This is the psychology of the fundamental utilities of consciousness; (3) and lastly we have functionalism described as psychophysical psychology, that is the psychology which constantly recognizes and insists upon the essential significance of the mind-body relationship for any just and comprehensive appreciation of mental life itself.

Also prominent in his statement of Functionalism were animal, developmental, and clinical psychology. The first point linked psychology to biology and to evolutionary theory. The second linked it to the processes of change while the final one linked it to deviancy. The contrast to Structuralism was stark and dramatic. Functional psychology had set for itself a much wider scope compared to Structuralism. Yet, even Angell admitted that Functionalism was not a school or even a movement. It was, he said (Angell, 1907 p. 61), "little more than a point of view, a program, an ambition." Remarkably, modern psychology reflects Angell's definition nicely, as Dewsbury (2003, p. 62) noted, "Like the functionalist approach, today's psychology is broad and inclusive, rooted in biology, and both behavioral and cognitive."

During the pre-World War I years, Angell became more and more an administrator at Chicago. During the war, he worked with Walter Dill Scott and the US Army on personnel classification. After the war, he quickly assumed three important positions successively: Chair of the National Research Council (1919), president of the Carnegie Corporation (1920), and president of Yale University (1922–1937). At Yale, he helped strengthen its psychology department and implemented many changes, leading Yale's department to the high position it continues to hold today. With his moves away from academic psychology, the leadership of the functionalist school passed to Harvey Carr at Chicago.

Harvey Carr (1873–1954)

Biography

Carr was born on an Indiana farm and attended nearby DePauw College until he suffered a severe illness. After recuperating for a year and working on the family farm for another year, he decided to teach school. That experience, he later wrote (Carr, 1961, p. 70), "was primarily responsible for my later specialization in psychology and for the educational slant to my psychological interests." Teaching, he discovered, was much harder than it looked. He decided to go back to school, but did not wish to return to DePauw, so he enrolled at the University of Colorado. There, he became a psychologist because of a chance meeting with Arthur Allin, the psychology professor. Allin had received his PhD from Berlin and had spent a year at Clark with G. Stanley Hall, but was not an experimental psychologist. Carr graduated from Colorado with a master's degree and went to Chicago on a fellowship.

Contributions

At Chicago, he soon fell under the spell of Angell and became an experimental psychologist. After Dewey left for Columbia, John B. Watson was hired. Carr studied under Watson conducting experiments using Titchener's laboratory manual and later wrote (Carr, 1961, p. 76), "Watson as an instructor evinced no hesitation in expressing his opinion of the futility of this material. He was objective-minded, both by training and temperament, and the appearance of his Behaviorism was no surprise to those who knew him well." Carr was unable to obtain a teaching position in psychology following his graduation from Chicago and eventually took a job teaching high school in Texas. Later, he held jobs at a normal school in Michigan and the Pratt Institute in New York. In 1908, after Watson left Chicago for Johns Hopkins, Carr took his place. He remained at Chicago until his retirement in 1938. After Angell left Chicago, Carr became the main spokesman for functional psychology.

Unlike Angell, who had become an administrator, Carr, over the course of his career as a research psychologist, was competing against two other viewpoints in psychology. The first was Titchener's Structuralism and the second was Watson's Behaviorism. Functionalism won the contest with Structuralism, but was soon overwhelmed by Behaviorism. At least, that's how the story looks from today's vantage point. The "victory" over Structuralism was obvious because the functionalist ideas about animal psychology, mental testing, educational psychology, child psychology, and psychopathology carried the day. From Carr's point of view it was difficult for him and his fellow functionalists to yet see the size of the behaviorist tsunami. In his textbook (Carr, 1925, p. 1), he was still defining psychology using the older (e.g., nonbehaviorist) terminology:

> Psychology is primarily concerned with the study of mental activity. This term is the generic name for such activities as perception, memory, imagination, reasoning, feelings, judgment, and will. The essential features of these various activities can hardly be characterized by a single term, for the mind does various things from time to time. Stated in comprehensive terms, we may say that mental activity is concerned with the acquisition, fixation, retention, organization, and evaluation of experiences, and their subsequent utilization in the guidance of conduct. The type of conduct that reflects mental activity may be termed adaptive or adjustive behavior.

Behaviorism displaced Functionalism for many reasons, but not because psychologists such as Carr changed sides or decided to alter radically their long-established views. Carr was willing to dispense with introspection but he was never willing to let go of the mind, be it human or animal. He also proposed new mechanisms to counter the behaviorists' single-minded obsession against mentalism. The most prominent of those mechanisms was the adaptive act, which involved three components: a motivating stimulus, a sensory stimulus, and an activity. The adaptive act was designed to explain the interrelatedness of all three components. Thus, a motivating stimulus aroused an activity, and the sensory stimulus directed it toward a particular goal. Imagine seeing the same animal in the wild vs seeing it in the zoo. One day while I was guiding a zoo tour, word went out that the black panther was loose. While getting a bath in a squeeze cage, the soapy panther had slipped out through the bars. The character of the tour and the behavior of the teachers and children immediately changed. They no longer wished to see the panther! Carr would have noted that the loose panther now aroused a very different adaptive response.

Carr was the last of the functionalists in Chicago. The other center of Functionalism was at Columbia University. Dewey, its father, had moved on to pragmatic philosophy and to social activism. Cattell and Thorndike were functionalists, too, at least in terms of their applied orientations toward psychology. Robert S. Woodworth never abandoned his early functionalist orientation and tried to keep the tradition alive with his dynamic psychology.

LEARNING OBJECTIVE

6. If Behaviorism had not existed imagine what the growth and development of Functionalism might have led to.

Columbia Functionalism

Robert Sessions Woodworth (1869–1962)

Biography

Woodworth grew up in New England and was the first child of his father's third wife. Although he had eight half-brothers and sisters, because of his living arrangements he considered himself "as an oldest child" and thought that his early personality had been shaped by "the neighborhood rather than the home" (Woodworth, 1930, p. 359). He attended Amherst and majored in math. During his senior year, he took his first psychology course, but it was not until he read William James and G. Stanley Hall that he decided to study the subject.

Contributions

He enrolled at Harvard and studied philosophy under Josiah Royce and psychology under James. He helped James with some dream research. While at Harvard he became interested in two problems—motivation and mind–body—which remained lifelong interests of his. He finally decided to pursue psychology exclusively and accepted a fellowship at Columbia University from Cattell. He received his PhD from Columbia in 1899. From Cattell, he also developed an interest in mental testing and the assessment of individual differences. He spent a year in Liverpool to study with Charles Scott Sherrington, the famous English physiologist. Cattell brought Woodworth to Columbia that same year, and he spent the rest of his long career there.

At Columbia, Woodworth researched a wide variety of areas including anthropometry, thinking, time perception, motor control, and kinesthetic imagery. That last topic required him to use introspection. Unlike the behaviorists, Woodworth was always willing to use a variety of methodologies other than experimentation in order to solve the problem at hand. The preface to the second edition of his *Experimental Psychology* (Woodworth & Schlosberg, 1954, p. vii) summed up his approach to psychological research:

> We have tried to maintain an eclectic approach throughout the book . . . our approach should be called "functional," with a definite preference for objective data but no taboo against material obtained through introspection if it helps the psychologist to understand what the organism is doing in relation to the environment.

His text was the first ever to use the terms so familiar to psychology students today: *independent variable* and *dependent variable*. Winston (1990) detailed how Woodworth's (and psychology's) definition of experiments changed over time, gradually excluding mental testing from the definition of experimental research. Winston concluded (p. 398), however:

> Woodworth would not have accepted these restrictive implications. His *Dynamic Psychology* (1918) and *Dynamics of Behavior* (1958) emphasized motivation and drives, and he literally put the "O" in the S-O-R model of behavior. He was the consummate eclectic, and it is very unlikely that he changed his textbooks as part of a plan to restrict how people did research.

Probably the best way to view Woodworth and his approach to psychology is to recall how his life fit into the *zeitgeist* of his times. He lived during the time when Functionalism was battling against Structuralism while at the same time Behaviorism was being born. Woodworth always wished a middle road for psychology, one that was not dogmatic or exclusionary. So, he argued just as vociferously against Titchener as he did against Watson. He saw those two as "bogey men" saying, "I always rebelled at any such epistemological table of commandments" (Woodworth, 1930, p. 376). Specifically, he was against Titchener and his insistence on sensations and against Watson and his prohibition of introspection.

Woodworth's solution was **dynamic psychology**, best described as an eclectic mixture of methodologies that included experimentation, introspection, comparative psychology, and mental testing. It also included a reformulation of Thorndike's S-R psychology (which was adopted by Watson and the behaviorists, see Chapters 10 and 11) to S-O-R, where the "O" stood for "organism." By putting the organism in between the stimulus and response, Woodworth hoped to account for all of the psychologically interesting variables that might appear, especially motivation. Like Carr, he preferred the word activity over the word behavior because he believed that Watson had preempted the use of the latter word and made it too narrow in meaning. In his textbook (Woodworth, 1921, p. 25), he stated why behavior was too narrow a word:

> As to "behavior," it would be a very suitable term, if only it had not become so closely identified with the "behavioristic movement" in psychology, which urges that consciousness should be entirely left out of psychology, or at least disregarded. "Behavior psychology," as the term would be understood to-day, means a part of the subject and not the whole.

In a footnote on the same page he added, "A series of waggish critics has evolved the following: "First psychology lost its soul, then it lost its mind, then it lost consciousness; it still has behavior, of a kind."" That saying nicely summarized the history of psychology up to his day.

Woodworth never fully developed his S-O-R psychology, but his efforts were similar to Tolman's S-S psychology (see Chapter 11) which was more fully fleshed out. Woodworth retired, for the first time in 1945, but came back to teach, and finally retired at the age of 89. He was the first recipient of the American Psychological Foundation's Gold Medal for psychology in 1956. His career was a monument to eclectic thinking in psychology and the field today, in many ways, reflects his orientation.

LEARNING OBJECTIVE

7. Appraise the differences between James's functionalism and that of the later functionalists.

FUNCTIONALISM AS PHOENIX

Carr was correct when he said Functionalism was not yet a school of thought. More than anything else, functionalists were struggling with the very definition of psychology itself. They were profoundly unsatisfied with Titchener's Structuralism and Watson's Behaviorism. Their search for a solution, however, came to an abrupt end once Behaviorism came on the scene. For the next 30 years, nearly all American psychologists would devote their time and energy to create a positivistic and nonmental science of behavior. But, the behaviorists could not repress forever the questions originally asked by functionalists. In more recent times, and aided by the information processing metaphor, those questions have risen up once again from the ashes of Functionalism (see Chapter 14). The next chapter looks at the first part of that story, the rise of Behaviorism.

SUMMARY

Much changed in the United States following the Civil War. Johns Hopkins University, led by Daniel Coit Gilman, helped set the model for nearly all colleges and universities currently operating in the country today. Gilman implemented a revised version of the German model research university.

At around the same time, William James brought psychology to Harvard from Europe. After he published his textbooks, he became the face of American psychology. His successor, Hugo Münsterberg, emphasized applied psychology by conducting research in clinical, forensic, and industrial psychology. G. Stanley Hall was another American pioneer. His many firsts defined his career. Through his leadership of Clark University, the training of many graduate students, and the founding of the American Psychological Association, he left a permanent imprint.

James McKeen Cattell helped differentiate American psychology from its European cousin. He founded journals and conducted research along Galtonian lines. Edward Lee Thorndike was third only to James and Hall during this period. His early animal research set the stage for Behaviorism. His later contributions centered on animal learning, educational psychology and testing.

Functionalism itself was a short-lived school of thought centered at two universities: Chicago and Columbia. Chicago functionalists included John Dewey, the founder (who later moved to Columbia), James Rowland Angell, and Harvey Carr.

At Columbia, in addition to Thorndike and Dewey, was Robert Sessions Woodworth. His dynamic psychology along with his textbook in experimental psychology was influential past the midpoint of the twentieth century.

10 BEHAVIORISM

Russia from 1860 to 1917

Compared to the rest of Europe, Russia was an enigma. While it had an enormous population and immense natural resources, it was ruled by a despotic monarch, the czar. In addition, the Russian Orthodox Church held a near monopoly on accepted religious practices. Xenophobia (fear of outsiders and their influence) was practically official policy. Foreign travel for Russians was highly restricted for the same reasons. Czar Nicholas I (1796–1855) feared his power might diminish should he allow Western ideas to seep into Russian culture. Despite these restrictions, a scientific renaissance nevertheless slowly took hold, almost like a weed growing in the crack of a sidewalk.

The accession to the throne of Czar Alexander II in 1855, following Nicholas' death, nourished the growth of science in Russia. Alexander wished to modernize Russia. His major act of reform was to liberate the serfs in 1861. Previously, they were bound to the land and the landowners in a quasi-medieval system. Alexander had inherited the Crimean War (1853–1856) from Nicholas I; following Russia's crushing defeat, he modernized the army and created new governmental administrative units that were more responsive to his wishes. In the area of science, he allowed students to once again study abroad and permitted universities to adopt the new German model (see Chapter 9). Unfortunately for Russian science these liberal tendencies did not last long.

A new education minister, Count Tolstoy, imposed a new curriculum, one that emphasized the Greek and Roman classics. At the same time, he reenergized the review and censorship of scientific publications written by Russian authors. In addition, he required all science students to work on experimental projects with their professors because he believed that idle students would devote their free time toward creating political troubles. The unintended consequence of that rule was that he created a cadre of experienced graduate students while at the same time making researchers more productive because they now had free labor (Boakes, 1984).

Czar Alexander II was assassinated in 1881. His son, Alexander III, returned to the despotic ways of old and resumed the practice of shutting off Russia from the West. His son, Nicholas II, was the last czar, and following another crushing military defeat—this time to Japan in the Russo-Japanese War (1904–1905)—found himself and Russia beleaguered by revolutionary thought and action. Peasant revolts and demonstrations in the streets followed. From 1905 to 1917 Russia was in a nearly perpetual state of political and social agitation. It was in this climate that three physiologists, Ivan Sechenov, Ivan Pavlov, and Vladimir Bekhterev, took the first steps toward what would prove to be a physiologically based psychology, one that would for the first time provide a convincing mechanism for associationism. Mackintosh (2003, p. 178) noted:

> The history of associationism, as of all good, and some not so good, ideas can be traced back to ancient Greek philosophy. But, it was Pavlov's discovery of the conditioned reflex that made the scientific study of associationism or associative learning possible . . . Pavlov's experimental paradigm set the standard for what is required for the experimental analysis of associative learning, and virtually all the advances that have been made since 1965 in our understanding of associative learning, even if they have not relied on salivating dogs, have been based on procedures closely modeled on those he developed.

LEARNING OBJECTIVE

1. Appraise how Russia's rulers created an on again, off again environment for scientific progress in the late 19th century.

PREVIEW

Pavlov's discovery of *classical conditioning*, although mostly unknown at the time in the United States, along with his objective methods eventually paved the way for Behaviorism's later success. Watson's *Behaviorism* synergized several extant movements in psychology: *physiological psychology, comparative psychology, testing, applied psychology*, and *clinical psychology* because all were interested in behavior, not in mental states. Several of those areas saw little difference in the methods necessary to study human or *animal behavior*. Combining classical conditioning with psychophysics, for instance, allowed researchers to investigate the *sensory capacities of animals* for the first time and to answer age- old questions such as: Do dogs see color? (See below.)

Behaviorism eventually moved into more applied areas as well. Research with *Little Albert* demonstrated that fears could be learned, and later research showed they could be *extinguished* too. Work in that area has blossomed into the modern subfields of *behavioral medicine* and *wellness* as therapists attempt to deal with the effects of posttraumatic stress disorder (*PTSD*) and the *stresses* of life in the 21st century. Business was yet another area to take advantage of the behavioral approach, leading to research in *marketing* and the power of *advertising. Hereditarian* theories competed with *environmental* ones as psychologists debated the existence, extent, and nature of *instincts*. The first inklings of widespread technological change date from the rise of *radio* and the subsequent forms of *media* created since.

INTRODUCTION

This chapter details some of the multiple sources that led to the eventual demise of introspective psychology. One influential source came from Russia via the work of physiologists Ivan Sechenov, Ivan Pavlov, and Vladimir Bekhterev. Pavlov's discovery of classical conditioning re-energized older associative models of psychology derived from British empiricist philosophy. Another source was American comparative psychology. Early researchers such as Jacques Loeb and Herbert Spencer Jennings were followed by a number of influential psychologists whose main emphasis was the study of animal behavior. Some of them still saw animals as convenient models for studying comparative cognition in the tradition of C. Lloyd Morgan and George Romanes (see Chapter 8). Others, however, began to study animals for their own sake and gradually relinquished ideas about studying the animal mind. Instead, they began to use only objective methods.

Of these, John B. Watson was the most prominent. In 1913, he launched a new school of psychology, Behaviorism, which intentionally rejected mentalistic approaches to psychology and emphasized that all psychology should be based on objective methods only. While Watson's ideas were groundbreaking, it took over a decade before psychologists as a whole began to join his new school in significant numbers.

William McDougall, an English psychologist whose later career was spent in the United States, debated Watson on radio in 1924. McDougall had his own version of Behaviorism. His approach retained a role for introspection and emphasized instinctive behavior, albeit with a definition different from that of earlier psychologists such as Herbert Spencer. Watson's brand of Behaviorism eventually evolved into Neobehaviorism, the topic of the next chapter.

RUSSIAN PSYCHOLOGY

Russian psychology was inspired by discoveries in physiology made during the latter half of the 19th century. The most important early contribution was Sechenov's realization of the importance of physiological inhibition. Previous physiological accounts of behavior had depended solely on reflex activation and that had been insufficient in explaining the complexity of animal and human behavior. Sechenov also promoted the use of animal models for understanding human behavior while, at the same time, arguing against the use of introspective methods. His work inspired the next generation of Russian physiologists, especially Pavlov and Bekhterev. Their research strongly linked physiology to behavior and led to a materialist and objective approach to psychology very unlike contemporary models elsewhere on the continent of Europe or in the United States. Because of Russia's self-isolation, the relative rarity of English translations of Russian scientific results, and the great distance between Russia and the United States (compounded by the slowness of rail and steamship travel), American psychologists knew little about Russian psychology until about ten years into the 20th century (Wight, 1993).

Ivan Sechenov (1829–1905)

Biography

Had Sechenov lived earlier or later in history, his life would have been totally different. Because he could travel abroad to complete his education, thanks to the brief opening of a window to the West, he was able to study with some of the leading physiologists of his day. But his early life was hard. At ten years of age, he lost his father, a Russian nobleman. After, a German governess taught him German and French, laying the necessary foundation for his future eminence (Kichigina, 2009). At the age of 14, he entered the Military Engineering School where he enjoyed the scientific aspects of his training, but not the military ones. Because of his obvious dislike of all things military, he was assigned to Kiev, an undesirable Russian army outpost. There, he met and fell in love with a young and newly-widowed Polish woman who impressed him with her love of science and devotion to the idea of female equality. But, when she abruptly married a fellow engineer, Sechenov quit the army and returned to Moscow to study medicine. He now saw his life's path clearly: he wanted to study medicine. However, at the University of Moscow, he developed distaste for clinical work but began a lifelong love affair with physiology.

Contributions

At that time, Russian students did not have access to the latest physiological texts, but knew through rumor and hearsay that the current state of physiology was far more advanced at other European universities. The death of Czar Nicholas I led to a brief period during which Russian students were permitted to travel abroad. Thanks to that and a timely inheritance, Sechenov left Russia and traveled in Europe for six years. During that time, he met or studied with Hermann Helmholtz and Emil Du Bois-Reymond. Both were students of Johannes Müller and pioneers in applying the methods of physical science to biology. Du Bois-Reymond's earliest research was on electric fishes. Later, he created the field of electrophysiology. While outside of Russia, Sechenov conducted his own physiological research and discovered that reflexes could be inhibited via direct stimulation of some parts of the forebrain (the thalamus) but not others (the cerebral cortex). That discovery broadened the understanding of reflex action and demonstrated that the CNS played a role in the control of reflexes. Stuart et al. (2014) described the details and importance of his research on inhibition in physiology. They also discussed his female trainees, Maria Alexandrovna Bokova and Nadezhda P. Suslova, who became the first two licensed female clinicians in Russia. Sechenov later married Bokova.

He returned to Russia as one of the world's leading researchers in physiology and accepted a position at Military Medical Academy in St. Petersburg. Once again, he was at the right place at the right time. His article (later published in book form in 1866 titled *Reflexes of the Brain*) was published just before Count Tolstoy's restrictions on universities were put in place. That book would prove to be influential to later Russian physiologists, especially Pavlov. Sechenov himself did not personally follow up on the issues he identified as important to the connection between physiology and psychology. But the direction he provided was a blueprint for later Russian physiologists. In his book, Sechenov argued that all behaviors had a cause and that the cause was always external and physical, not psychic or mental. In a later article: *Who Must Investigate the Problems of Psychology and How*, published in 1870, he argued that for psychology to become a science it had to quit looking for universal theories derived from introspective accounts, and instead, concentrate upon uncovering facts that could be verified. Naturally, he held that physiology would be the portal to such a psychology. Additionally, he argued that because human psychology was so complex the natural starting place for his kind of psychology was with simpler animal models. In 2000, Eric Kandel shared the Nobel Prize for Physiology and Medicine for his research with the sea slug, *Aplysia californica*. Castellucci and Kandel (1976) traced the neural mechanisms behind sensitization, a simple nonassociative form of learning. Moroz (2011) described the sea slug's behavioral repertoire:

> *Aplysia* can develop both non-associative and associative forms of long-term memory, following all fundamental learning paradigms (habituation, sensitization, classical and operant conditioning). *Aplysia* can remember a repetitively trained gill-withdrawal response for more than two to three weeks — impressive given its short life cycle (about one year). Importantly, the cellular and molecular mechanisms of long-term plasticity in *Aplysia* have many parallels in humans, suggesting profound evolutionary conservation of elementary events underlying learning and memory.

That *Aplysia* does this with only 20,000 neurons is remarkable and supports Sechenov's early vision of the relationship between physiology and behavior. Naturally, scaling this relationship up to the level of the human brain with its 100 billion neurons will take decades or even centuries of work.

Sechenov, thus, left an important legacy to the Russian physiologists who followed him. He had put in place all of the pieces they would need to discover the first empirical connections between physiology and psychology. Pavlov never met Sechenov but had read his works while still a student. Pavlov spent his early career in the single-minded pursuit of the physiology of digestion. But, once he and his collaborators discovered the link between physiology and behavior, the famous conditional reflex, they pursued it just as avidly and, in the process, provided the necessary physiological mechanisms to support Watson's Behaviorism.

Ivan Pavlov (1849–1936)

Biography

Ivan Pavlov, the son of a Russian Orthodox priest, was born and raised in the small peasant village of Ryazan. As a youngster, Pavlov expected to follow his father into the priesthood. Pavlov was forced to enter school later than normal because of a bad fall. His uncle, an abbot, cared for him for two years at a nearby monastery while he was recovering. The abbot's example of hard work and perseverance stuck with Pavlov. Pavlov attended the local church school, which was relatively immune from Count Tolstoy's campaign against science education in the state-supported schools. Thus, he received a well-rounded education. Pavlov matriculated at St. Peterburg University the same year that Sechenov resigned. Ilya Cyon was Sechenov's successor and he quickly established a reputation as tough teacher. Pavlov, however, prospered under him and stayed an additional year in order to complete a research project on the pancreas, one that won him a gold medal and a scholarship. Pavlov had long been interested in the physiology of digestion; his training at St. Petersburg further focused him on the goal of elucidating all of the physiological aspects of that complex process. Cyon arranged a postdoctoral assistantship for Pavlov but it never materialized because Cyon left Russia for France. Instead, Pavlov took another assistantship, this one in veterinary medicine. The components of his later career were lining themselves up.

Soon after, Pavlov met Sergei Botkin, another Russian physiologist of Sechenov's generation. He and Sechenov had been classmates in Du Bois-Reymond's laboratory in Germany. Botkin had revolutionized the study of physiology in Russia and because he was so busy needed someone to supervise the graduate students in his animal laboratory. Pavlov got that job and, thanks to Count Tolstoy's policies, had many graduate students to supervise. They all needed hands-on research experience in order to graduate. Pavlov successfully managed the laboratory and its students, gaining valuable experience in supervising research in the process. While he was working for Botkin, Pavlov married. His new wife, Seraphima Vasilievna Karchevskaya, was totally devoted to him allowing him to spend nearly all of his time at the laboratory. The only things she required of him were that he never drink alcohol and that he leave the laboratory and socialize during the weekends. Pavlov was only too happy to agree and developed a near monastic and rigid work routine.

In order to improve his surgical skills, he took leave from his work in Russia to spend two years in Germany studying with Carl Ludwig. After he returned, he won another gold medal for his own research and completed his medical training. An appointment at the Military Medical School in St. Petersburg followed which finally took him and his family out of the near-poverty conditions under which they had been living. He also was named director of the Physiology Department of the newly founded Institute of Behavioral Medicine, modeled after the Pasteur Institute in France and funded by a rich Russian patron. Pavlov now held two appointments, one at the Military Medical School and one at the new institute. Finally, he possessed all of the facilities and funds required to conduct his research in digestion.

Contributions

For seven years he and his students (who included women and Jews, both unusual in Czarist Russia) worked out the details of the digestive process using living dogs. Unlike other researchers, Pavlov developed physiological techniques that allowed him to collect data on how dogs digested their food in real time. His student, Yekaterina Shumova-Simonovskaya, pioneered the surgical creation of gastric pouches, or flaps designed to catch food swallowed before it reached the stomach (sham feeding), and the successful insertion of tubes (fistulas) into the various glands of the digestive system (Hill, 2019). Slowly but surely, he and his coworkers became internationally known, and in 1904 he won the Nobel Prize for Physiology and Medicine, the first Russian to receive a Nobel Prize.

Beginning in 1897, however, and following an interesting discovery, the direction of the laboratory's research became behavioral. Windholz (1989) identified Pavlov's students and their contributions. One of them, Ivan Tolochinov, first noticed that dogs began to salivate to non-food cues that they were learning to anticipate food when it was paired with a neutral stimulus. The evidence was that the dogs began to salivate to stimuli such as color and odor alone. All that was required was the close pairing in time of such neutral stimuli followed by a food stimulus. Very quickly, Pavlov shifted his laboratory's research direction to study this new **Pavlovian conditioning** process. The question of how to theoretically account for it caused dissention between him and one of his students. After some thought and many arguments Pavlov rejected any explanations for conditioning that involved introspective elements. In his Nobel lecture Pavlov (1904) said as follows:

> We decided to take an entirely objective point of view also towards the psychical phenomena in our experiments with animals. Above all, we tried to discipline sternly our way of thinking and our words and ignored completely the mental state of the animal; we restricted our work to careful observation and exact formulation of the influence exerted by distant objects on the secretion of the salivary glands. The results were according to our expectations: the observable relations between external phenomena and variations in the activity of glands could be systematically analyzed; they appeared to be determined by laws, because they could be reproduced at will.

BORDER WITH BIOLOGY
PHYSIOLOGY AND BEHAVIOR

The border between biology and psychology had first been created with the rise of psychophysics. However, the work of the Russian physiologists expanded the exchange of ideas across that border. While Pavlov never considered himself to be a psychologist, he was quite willing to explore the connections between physiology and behavior. The genius of Pavlov was to realize that he and his associates had discovered something new in classical conditioning and to redirect their research efforts nearly completely from digestion to conditioning.

Note the use of the word "we" previously. Pavlov was one of the first researchers to embody and practice "big science" (Hill, 2019), meaning the establishment of a large and cooperative group of researchers working together to solve related scientific questions. More recent examples of big science include the Manhattan Project of World War II, The Human Genome Project, and efforts to combat HIV/AIDS. The COVID-19 pandemic has mobilized another worldwide big science mobilization to understand and, hopefully, defeat that virus.

3. Explain how Pavlov created the world's first "big science" project.

Pavlov was convinced that the only way to approach an understanding of psychology was through the elucidation of underlying physiological laws. He and his students soon discovered other now familiar conditioning phenomena: extinction, generalization, and spontaneous recovery (Windholz, 1989). These phenomena, too, seemed to rise to the level of scientific laws. Plus, they could be investigated in the laboratory without requiring any recourse to consciousness or introspection. By 1930, Pavlovian conditioning was well known to American psychologists. Behaviorists, especially, found conditioning to be a powerful way to explain the acquisition of new responses so they emphasized the study of learning as a new central focus for psychology in the United States (see Chapter 11). Interestingly, Pavlov and his group were more interested in how conditioning could be inhibited or suppressed. Most likely that interest derived from the long history of the study of physiological inhibition begun by Sechenov. In Pavlov's laboratory, research concentrated on the conditioning of autonomic responses such as digestion, and nearly always, surgery of some type was required. Another Russian scientist, however, emphasized the conditioning of voluntary responses. He realized that Pavlov's discoveries could be generalized to responses other than salivation. His name was Vladimir Bekhterev.

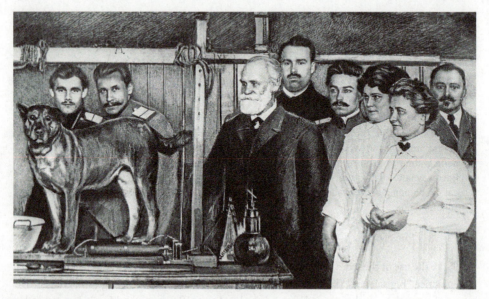

PHOTO 10.1 Ivan Pavlov

Credit: RIA Novosti/Science Source

Vladimir Bekhterev (1857–1927)

Biography

Vladimir Bekhterev was born in Sarali, Russia. His father was the town's police officer. At the age of 16, he matriculated at the Military Medical Academy in St. Petersburg. Compared to Pavlov, Bekhterev's interests were broader and more applied. Following a mental breakdown and subsequent recovery during his third year at school, he decided to specialize in psychiatry and mental illness (Akimenko, 2007). His dissertation was titled: "The Experience of a Clinical Study of Body Temperature in Some Forms of Mental Illness." He wrote extensively throughout his career and always seemed to be working on papers for publication even while lying in bed or riding in a taxi. Three years after completing his dissertation he won a travel fellowship. He spent a year away from Russia and studied with German scientists Carl Ludwig, Emil Du Bois-Reymond, Paul Flechsig, and Wilhelm Wundt. From there he went to France to meet with J. M. Charcot and ended his tour in Vienna visiting Thomas Meynert. When he returned to Russia it was to head the department of psychiatry at the University of Kazan. He stayed there eight years or until he was called to St. Petersburg as head of the Department of Psychic and Nervous Diseases and as director of the Clinic of Mental Diseases. His research at Kazan and early on at St. Petersburg was in neuroanatomy and brain localization. His reputation was immense; one contemporary said of him, "There are only two persons who know the anatomy of the brain perfectly—God and Bekhterev" (Akimenko, 2007, p. 103).

Contributions

Soon Bekhterev, too, became world famous. In 1907, he founded the Psychoneurological Institute, which is still in place today and named after him. His major book, Objective Psychology, was written in 1910. In it, he incorporated Pavlov's conditioning model, but instead of using autonomic responses such as salivation, he emphasized voluntary movements in response to external stimulation. One of those was leg flexion in dogs following an electric shock to the foot. Thus, he demonstrated that Pavlovian conditioning applied to voluntary behaviors as well. Furthermore, he noted that his methodology did not require researchers to perform surgery (e.g., inserting fistulas) into animals. After 1917, as Bechterev began to research infants and young children, he renamed his "objective psychology" as "reflexology" believing, in contrast to Pavlov, that those inherited conditional reflexes gradually built up secondary reflexes in response to environmental conditions (Byford, 2016).

Pavlov and Bekhterev were intense competitors with each other and their personal relations were unfriendly. Pavlov and his coworkers successfully attacked the work coming out of Bekhterev's laboratory as sloppy and poorly controlled. One issue they quarreled over was color vision in dogs. Neither laboratory ever successfully presented strong scientific evidence sufficient to answer that question, but Pavlov's reputation prevailed and for many years psychologists believed that dogs could not see colors.

One of the leading uses of the physiological techniques developed by Pavlov and Bekhterev was to investigate the sensory capacities of animals. By establishing a perceptual standard through conditioning (e.g., a wavelength, tone, or other physical stimulus), researchers could then systematically vary the stimulus and observe any changes in the animal's behavior. While neither researcher could resolve the question of whether dogs saw color or not, modern psychology has successfully answered that old question. Dogs can see color, but in a way different from how humans do. According to Neitz et al. (1989) dogs can see color but they are dichromats, not trichromats like humans and other primates. They concluded (p. 124):

> that dogs should be capable of making color discriminations between stimuli whose predominant spectral energies lie, respectively, to the long and short sides of 480 nm.

So, the answer to the old question is now known. Neitz, Geist, and Jacobs used techniques derived from the kind of research first begun by Pavlov and Bekhterev to answer the very same question they had struggled with years earlier.

LEARNING OBJECTIVE

4. Demonstrate how classical conditioning made it possible to "ask" animals questions about their sensory capacities.

After his conflicts with Pavlov, Bekhterev's research career declined. But, he still maintained his administrative duties and moved more into clinical psychology. He was sympathetic to the 1917 Russian Revolution and served on the local political council or soviet. His death in 1927 was sudden and mysterious. It came after a psychiatric consultation with Stalin in which Bekhterev diagnosed him as paranoid. Bekhterev was never seen again. Antonov-Ovseyenko (1981) suggested that Stalin had him poisoned and cremated. Later, Stalin ordered all of his works suppressed and had his son killed. In retrospect, Bekhterev must be viewed, along with Pavlov, as pioneer in the nascent behaviorist movement. There is no evidence that he knew of Watson's work or vice versa. The Russian physiologists represented an independent thread in the fabric that was to become Behaviorism.

Pavlov continued to work until his death. Unlike Bekhterev, he did not support the 1917 Revolution and the communist system that emerged from it. Lenin, however, saw in Pavlov the opportunity to advertise to the world how communism supported scientific work. Thus, he ordered that Pavlov and his laboratory continue to receive support and funding. In 1923, Pavlov visited the United States and gave several lectures. The timing of that visit was fortuitous for the promotion of Watson's Behaviorism. Pavlov's data, combined with Watsons ideas, eventually led to a powerful theoretical and practical synergy. The Russian physiologists argued for and sought objective methods to study psychology while rejecting consciousness and introspection. They used animal models for human behavior and, most of all, provided behavioral psychology with one of its first strong methodologies: classical conditioning. Since then many have used classical conditioning to create a sense of anticipation. In the movie *Jaws* Stephen Spielberg used the now familiar eerie theme music to prepare the audience for their eventual first view of the shark late in the movie. The music was the conditioned stimulus and, at first, the audience had no reaction to it. But, as Spielberg paired the music with shark attacks without actually showing the shark the audience began to anticipate those attacks and felt fearful even when no attack was followed by the music. He classically conditioned the audience; the music now scared them.

Timing is everything, it seems. Edwin B. Twitmyer, while a graduate student at the University of Pennsylvania, discovered classical conditioning and reported on it about one year before Pavlov. Twitmyer was investigating the patellar (knee-jerk) reflex when he accidentally discovered that he could condition his subjects to perform the reflex without physical contact. They would exhibit the reflex to a tone if he first sounded the tone and then hit their knee. After, when he only sounded the tone they would involuntarily exhibit the reflex. He reported his results in his dissertation in 1902 and at the American Psychological Association meeting of 1904. But few other psychologists took notice. American psychology at that time was simply unprepared to understand the significance of Twitmyer's results. When Pavlov's reports appeared some years later, American psychology had changed sufficiently and was ready to accept objective data about behavior.

THEN AND NOW
CLASSICAL CONDITIONING

There have been many new discoveries in classical conditioning since Pavlov first described it. Pavlov explained the process in terms of contiguity in time, meaning that the temporal relationship between the previously neutral stimulus (the conditioned stimulus) and the stimulus that caused a physiological reaction (the unconditioned stimulus) was the key to understanding the process. As Todes (2014) explained, Pavlov hardly ever used a bell as the conditioned stimulus, instead (p. 1), "(h)e most frequently employed a metronome, a harmonium, a buzzer, and electrical shock)." The conditioned stimulus had to precede the unconditioned stimulus, and there was a limit to how much time (about 0 to 15 seconds) could pass between them before conditioning failed.

Robert Rescorla (1968) demonstrated that simple temporal contiguity was not enough to cause classical conditioning. His research showed that the conditioned stimulus would not cause classical conditioning even when paired with the unconditioned stimulus unless the conditioned stimulus reliably predicted the occurrence of the unconditioned stimulus. He systematically varied the predictability of a sound signal (the conditioned stimulus) and a shock (the unconditioned stimulus) in rats. Some groups were always shocked after the sound signal and never shocked without the warning of the signal. Other groups were shocked after a sound signal or shocked without warning in various combinations of predictability. Conditioned rats would freeze their movements, anticipating the shock. Rats that were subjected to equal likelihoods of shocks with a sound warning or shocked without warning never froze.

So, the subsequent Rescorla-Wagner model of classical conditioning derived from his experiments added correlation to Pavlov's temporal contiguity. Modern explanations of classical conditioning require that the conditioned stimulus and the unconditioned stimulus be close in time and that the conditioned stimulus reliably predict the unconditioned stimulus. Like Pavlov's theory, modern conditioning theory still does not require appeals to consciousness or introspective accounts.

AMERICAN PSYCHOLOGY AT THE TURN OF THE 20TH CENTURY

As the 20th century dawned American psychology was a mixed bag. William James and G. Stanley Hall were still living and influential. E. B. Titchener at Cornell promoted his structuralist view of psychology. The functionalists at Chicago and Columbia were opposed to Structuralism, but their alternative was little different from it. Animal research was beginning to become more prominent but its main proponents differed over its goals. Some viewed that research as a way towards understanding the minds of animals. Others saw animals as interesting in their own right and believed that animal consciousness was a subject unapproachable to scientific methods. As in Russia, the latter view came to dominate the new subfield of com-parative psychology. At Chicago, the German physiologist, Jacques Loeb, conducted studies on animal tropisms, or forced movements. For instance, he cataloged how different animals reacted to physical stimuli such as light (phototropisms) or gravity (geotropisms). Loeb believed that animals were essentially passive until faced with specific environmental stimuli. Then, they would react to those in a stereotyped manner. He described many examples of such behavior in a wide variety of species. Consider, for instance, how to use positive phototropism to induce a common housefly to leave a room. Flies are positively phototropic, meaning they are attracted to light. Turn off all of the lights, the computer monitors, and any other light sources; draw the window shades, but leave the door open. More often than not, the fly will orient to the only light left in the room that coming in from the hall through the door. When it flies out, quickly close the door and make that fly someone else's problem.

In 1906 at Johns Hopkins, another comparative psychologist, H. S. Jennings (1906), published an important book, *The Behavior of the Lower Organisms*. In contrast to Loeb, Jennings believed that even the behavior of so-called "simple" organisms (e.g., paramecia or sea anemones) was highly variable and that they responded differently to the same physical stimuli depending upon their internal state. For example, an anemone that had recently eaten would react differently to food items than would one that had not. Soon, other psychologists began to more closely investigate how animals acquired new behaviors.

One psychologist, Robert M. Yerkes, set out to compare how different animals might learn. Using new and original apparatus, he looked at learning in many species from crabs to apes. Yerkes obtained his PhD from Harvard and after graduating stayed on as a faculty member. He ran the animal laboratory there. At that time, there were relatively few American researchers specializing in comparative psychology. Yerkes's position at Harvard was especially tenuous in that neither his chair, Münsterberg, nor the incoming president favored animal research. In fact, both warned him that to further advance in his career there he needed to turn to educational psychology. It was in that context that Yerkes might have felt compelled to demonstrate to them and to American psychology, in general, the importance of Pavlov's work by writing an article detailing the importance of classical conditioning (Yerkes & Morgulis, 1909). Interestingly, Yerkes himself did not apply Pavlovian thinking to his own research.

Yerkes's friend and extramural collaborator, John B. Watson, however, eventually adopted classical conditioning methods into his own research. Watson was another early comparative psychologist. Unlike other animal researchers, Watson saw early on that the same methods they were using to study animals could also be used to study humans. The big step necessary was to quit focusing on human consciousness and the use of introspective methods. At first, Watson was the only person bold enough to consider such a radical reorientation of psychology. Behaviorism had arrived on the scene.

John Broadus Watson (1878–1958)

Biography

John B. Watson was born into a large family in the tiny town of Traveler's Rest, South Carolina. His mother was deeply religious and gave him his middle name in honor of a famous Baptist minister from nearby Greenville, John Albert Broadus. Brewer (1991, p. 171) wrote, "As a youngster, Watson was called Broadus and not John B." Watson's father did not share his wife's religious faith; he was a brawler and a heavy drinker.

Watson matured early and easily learned and enjoyed working with his hands. He went to several country schools before his mother moved the family to nearby Greenville because of its better schools. Watson was never an outstanding student even while attending Furman University, the local Baptist college. He spent five years there, graduating with a master's degree. An oversight—turning in his exam incorrectly during his senior year—led to a failing grade and the need for a fifth year. The psychology professor, Gordon B. Moore, had warned the class exactly how he wanted the exams returned. They were not to be turned in "backward." After graduating from Furman, Watson taught school in South Carolina for a year before enrolling at the University of Chicago in 1900. Three years later, he received his PhD in psychology, Chicago's first doctorate in the new discipline (Benjamin, 2009). James Rowland Angell and H. H. Donaldson, a neurologist, jointly supervised his thesis on the learning ability of albino rats at various ages. Following the style of animal research at the time, Watson inferred what his rats might have been thinking while he subjected them to his experimental manipulations. Soon, he would cease to analyze his experiments in that introspective manner.

Contributions

After graduating from Chicago, he stayed on as a faculty member. During Watson's tenure at Chicago (1900–1908) he was surrounded by an eclectic and exciting group of academic stars including John Dewey (although Watson later claimed he never understood anything Dewey ever told him), George Herbert Mead, the sociologist, and Jacques Loeb, the biologist. Watson himself ran the psychology department's animal laboratory; his research concentrated on elucidating the sensory capacities of animals, especially their vision. He also conducted naturalistic observation and field experiments with the sea birds that nested in the Dry Tortugas Islands (located about 70 miles from Key West, Florida) with Karl Lashley, then a student at Chicago. Soon after, however, James Mark Baldwin persuaded Watson to leave Chicago for Johns Hopkins. Baldwin had been hired to revive the study of psychology at Hopkins, which had lain dormant since G. Stanley Hall's departure. Baldwin had previously founded the psychology laboratories at the University of Toronto and Princeton University. He saw Watson as an energetic up and coming researcher who could help put Hopkins back on psychology's map.

Watson was reluctant to leave Chicago, but a promotion to full professor and the near doubling of his salary tipped the scales in Hopkins's favor.

Ironically, only weeks after Watson's arrival, Baldwin was forced to resign. He had been arrested during a raid at a brothel. But, he had given the police a false name and thus prevented an immediate scandal. Two reporters had recognized him but did not publish any stories mentioning him by name. Later, however, when he was invited to join the Baltimore School Board, news of his earlier arrest leaked out. To limit the scandal, the president of Hopkins forced him to resign immediately. Baldwin did so and moved to Mexico, his contributions to academic psychology effectively ending. Before leaving, he made Watson chair of the department and editor of the journal *Psychological Review*. Baldwin's personal troubles became Watson's gain. He, at an inordinately young age, had suddenly acquired great power and influence at Hopkins and within psychology itself. Brewer (1991, p. 177) quoted from a letter that Watson wrote to Furman University students in 1950:

> A few weeks after I began work at Johns Hopkins, Prof. James Mark Baldwin came into my office and said, "I am resigning and leaving now for the University of Mexico. You are the new editor of the *Psychological Review*." . . . I was about as well prepared to undertake this work as I was to swim the English Channel.

At colleges and universities, influence and prestige to faculty largely comes from publication of articles and books. Thus, the editors of scholarly journals and publishing houses can easily become gatekeepers of new ideas, allowing some into print while excluding others. Typically, academic journal editorships fall to established scholars who are well respected by their peers. In Watson's case though, the editorship of the most prestigious journal in psychology fell to him only through Baldwin's personal problems. But, Watson proved to be a competent and hard-working editor; that position also allowed him later to spread more easily his radical views about psychology and its problems.

Watson's years at Hopkins were productive. He published a textbook, *Behavior: An Introduction to Comparative Psychology* (Watson, 1914) and expanded upon his earlier research with animals. He was also elected president of the American Psychological Association in 1915. All of these accomplishments followed his famous speech at Columbia University in 1913. That speech and its subsequent publication (Watson, 1913) in *Psychological Review* pitted his Behaviorism against two of the original schools of thought in psychology: Structuralism and Functionalism.

Behaviorism

Behaviorism was not original to Watson. Earlier trends in psychology—animal psychology, testing, applied psychology, and clinical psychology—had already demonstrated the utility of focusing on behavior while either minimizing or ignoring consciousness and introspective reports. Animal researchers had laid an impressive foundation by emphasizing the relationship between environmental events and behavior (Loeb, 1911) and the behavioral complexity of the minutest of creatures (Jennings, 1906). Pavlov's research on conditioning was also instrumental because it provided a mechanism to explain how associationism worked. (Thorndike's,

1898) pioneering experiments with puzzle boxes were also highly influential. Galtonian style testing was also well underway, although the results had not yet panned out in terms of predicting future success in school or on the job. Applied psychology was making headway in education and reforming classroom practice. In clinical psychology, James had long led the effort to include psychopathology and its treatment as part of psychology. The Johns Hopkins Hospital psychiatrist Adolph Meyer, who would later become instrumental in Watson's career, while still in New York had "turned the state's insane asylums into modern mental hospitals" (Boakes, 1984, p. 168). Watson's contribution was to meld these disparate streams into one and to propose a radically new approach for psychology, one which severed it nearly completely from its past. In short, he argued for a completely new psychology, one that dispensed with introspection and consciousness in a single stroke. He called his approach **Behaviorism**.

Watson delivered his famous speech at Columbia University. He argued that psychology "has failed signally . . . to make its place in the world as an undisputed natural science" (Watson, 1913, p. 163). He claimed that neither Structuralism nor Functionalism had made much progress in advancing psychology because both were wedded to consciousness, albeit in different ways, and neither could provide a coherent scientific account of the discipline. He wished to "never use the terms consciousness, mental states, mind, content, introspectively verifiable, imagery" (p. 166) again. In their place he proposed the study of behaviors only. He noted that there was already a history of success of such research using animals (p. 176):

> Psychology, as the behaviorist views it, is a purely objective, experimental branch of natural science which needs introspection as little as do the sciences of chemistry and physics. It is granted that the behavior of animals can be investigated without the appeal to consciousness . . . The position is taken here that the behavior of man and the behavior of animals must be considered on the same plane; as being equally essential to a general understanding of behavior. It can dispense with consciousness in a psychological sense.

He also warned, "Should human psychologists fail to look with favor upon our overtures and refuse to modify their position, the behaviorists will be driven to using human beings as subjects and to employ methods of investigation which are exactly comparable to those now employed in animal work" (p. 159). In short, Watson was rejecting the methodology of the structuralists and functionalists, although his greatest fire was reserved for the latter, "I have done my best to understand the difference between functional psychology and structural psychology. Instead of clarity, confusion grows upon me" (p. 165).

Watson was not entirely negative, however. He cited examples within human psychology where the behavioral approach had already led to success. Specifically, he mentioned educational psychology, psychopharmacology (but did not use that yet-to-be-invented term), advertising, forensics, and testing. He favored the adoption of uniform experimental procedures, writing, "The man and the animal should be placed as nearly as possible under the same experimental conditions" (p. 171). He hoped that, eventually, nearly all of the "really essential" problems of psychology would be approachable through Behaviorism. Twenty years later, most American psychologists were following his lead (see Chapter 11). By and large they were not converted structuralists or functionalists. Instead, they were younger scientists attracted to Watson's ideas.

However, the idea that Watson initiated a sudden change in how psychologists conducted their business is wrong. It took a while because neither structuralism nor functionalism would die easily (Samelson, 1981).

In 1917, the United States entered World War I and many psychologists were called into the United States Army to help with the war effort. While psychologists such as Robert M. Yerkes worked to solve the problems surrounding the mobilization and subsequent classification of recruits, Watson's expertise lay elsewhere. Eventually, he, too, was drafted and served in the Signal Corps. By and large, however, he found his wartime experiences exasperating. He especially chafed being under the command of army officers he thought were incompetent and rebelled against their decision-making. For that he was nearly court-martialed. Fortunately for him, however, the war ended and he once again returned to Hopkins.

PHOTO 10.2 John B. Watson

Over the course of ten years (1914–1924) the Johns Hopkins University had moved from its original downtown location to the uptown neighborhood where it now stands. After the move, the psychology department ended up with less laboratory space. So, when Adolph Meyer offered Watson some space in the newly built Phipps Clinic at the Johns Hopkins Hospital, he eagerly accepted it. Watson, apparently following his own advice, was beginning to research human psychology. At first, he wanted to study psychopathology, but Meyer thought Watson lacked the necessary clinical experience. Instead, Watson began to study the newborn babies at the nearby Harriet Lane Home for Invalid Children near the Phipps Clinic "where Watson's Infant Laboratory was housed. A corridor connected the two buildings, which allowed the baby to be brought into the laboratory without exposing him to the winter air" (Beck et al., 2009). One of those babies, of course, was Little Albert. Watson's research with him became the high point of his career as well as the beginning of the end of it.

When Watson resumed work at the Phipps Clinic following the war, he and his students became interested in studying emotional behavior in humans. At first, they could only identify three instinctive emotions (e.g., unlearned behaviors): fear, rage, and love. After further work though, they began to realize that the repertoire of unlearned behavior (e.g., reflexes) in babies was much larger than they had originally supposed. They also discovered that many of those behaviors, such as the strong grasp reflex, disappeared with advancing age. Another finding was that some infants were afraid of stimuli such as white laboratory rats, dogs, or masks while others were not. Such observations led them to hypothesize that children exhibiting such fears must have learned **conditioned emotional responses** (Watson & Rayner, 1920) during the course of their "early home life" (p. 1). To test their hypotheses, they selected "Albert B.," today known as Little Albert who was healthy from birth and one of the best developed youngsters . . . He was on the whole stolid and unemotional. His stability was one of the principal reasons for using him as a subject in this test (p. 2). Later they wrote (original italics) *At no time did this infant ever show fear in any situation* (p. 3).

Their stated goals were to determine whether they could condition him to be afraid of a white rat, whether the fear would transfer to other objects, what effect time might have on conditioned emotional responses, and if emotional responses could be removed following their acquisition. Watson and Rayner used a loud noise sounded from behind the infant in order to cause a fear response. "The sound was that made by striking a hammer upon a suspended steel bar four feet in length and three-fourths of an inch in diameter" (Watson & Rayner, 1920, p. 2). In the experiment, the bar was struck as soon as Albert touched the white rat. After only two trials Albert showed a fear response. A week later, Albert was subjected to five more trials. At the end of those and when presented with the rat alone (original italics):

> *The instant the rat was shown the baby began to cry. Almost instantly he turned sharply to the left, fell over on left side, raised himself on all fours and began to crawl away so rapidly that he was caught with difficulty before reaching the edge of the table (p. 6).*

Albert showed fear of the white rat that had not scared him previously. Five days later, they showed him a rabbit. Again, he showed fear and burst into tears. He also showed fear (but not as much) to a white seal fur coat and to cotton wool. The conditioned emotional response transferred. Watson and Rayner waited a month to see if Albert's fears disappeared over time. They did not. The researchers never had a chance to attempt to decondition or extinguish Albert's fears as he left the hospital to go home. A few years later one of Watsons students, Mary Cover Jones (1924) was the first to demonstrate that it was possible to extinguish conditional emotional responses.

PHOTO 10.3   Rosalie Rayner and Little Albert

THEN AND NOW
LITTLE ALBERT

Watson and Rayner's research is cited and described in nearly every general psychology textbook. Often, the exact details are glossed over or misrepresented. Cornwell et al. (1980), p. 216) noted that "many of Albert's observed fear responses were stimulated not by a conditioned stimulus object but by the removal of his thumb from his mouth." Harris (1979) listed several failures to replicate Watson and Rayner's results and many others have pointed out how unusual it is in psychology for a study involving only one subject (Albert) to have achieved such wide prominence and notoriety. Replicating the study now is out of the question because of ethical constraints on research. Such ethical standards did not yet exist in 1920. Watson, too, helped popularize his account by republishing it in his subsequent books and by filming the original research, probably a first for psychology. Today, it is well accepted that people and animals can acquire fear responses through conditioning. Furthermore, the extinction of those fears is possible through a variety of techniques derived from behavioral theory (e.g., counterconditioning and flooding). Watson, Rayner, and Little Albert are likely to continue to appear in future psychology textbooks if nothing else to illustrate the scientific highwater mark of Watson's career.

Watson and Rosalie Rayner soon became more than collaborators in research. They fell in love and eventually married. The problem was that Watson was already married when their romance sprouted and grew. Watson's marital problems with his wife, Mary Ickes, had developed long before his liaison with Rayner. Both women came from prominent families and both had originally been students of his; Ickes at Chicago and Rayner at Hopkins. Watson's marriage to Ickes might have ended in a mutually agreed upon divorce except for two circumstances. The first was that Ickes managed to steal some of the love letters Watson had written to Rayner. The theft took place at the house of Rosalie Rayner's parents during a dinner party (the Watsons and the Rayners were friends). Ickes excused herself to the bathroom feigning discomfort and instead found the letters in Rosalie Rayner's room. The second was that she later showed the letters to her brother, an attorney.

Before long portions of the letters were published in the newspapers. One letter read in part, "every cell I have is yours, individually and collectively. My total reactions are positive and towards you. So likewise each and every heart reaction. I can't be any more yours than I am even if a surgical operation made us one" (Buckley, 1994, p. 24). The letters caused a scandal but they also revealed Watson's nearly total commitment to his behaviorist tenets. Watson (1928) later revealed a similar commitment in a book on childcare when he argued that children should be treated like little adults and never be kissed or hugged. Moreover, Watson refused to be discreet in his relationship with Rayner while he was still married. Although their affair was no secret to some of his friends and colleagues, it rapidly developed into a major scandal, one mostly unanticipated by Watson himself. The president of Johns Hopkins asked for Watson's immediate resignation. Soon, he and Ickes divorced. Less than a week after the final divorce decree, he married Rayner. However, his career in academic psychology had come to an abrupt end.

Watson's Career after Hopkins

Watson felt adrift immediately after his dismissal from Hopkins. Few of his former colleagues came to his support and there was no possibility of his obtaining another academic position. Stanley Resor, head of the J. Walter Thompson advertising agency, decided to take a chance on hiring Watson, and using his behaviorist methods, bring a scientific approach to the manipulation of consumer behavior through advertising. Before hiring Watson, he sent him to Mississippi to investigate the rubber boot market. At that time, very few of the roads in Mississippi or other nearby states were paved, so rubber boots were practically a necessity.

After hiring Watson, Resor put him through the agency's internal training process so that Watson could learn all the aspects of the advertising business from working as a clerk at Macy's to writing and editing copy to actually running an account. Resor saw Watson's role at J. Walter Thompson as "ambassador-at-large" (Kreshel, 1990, p. 52). Watson became a vice-president of the agency four years after being hired and earned a salary astronomically higher ($70,000 per year equivalent to about $910,000 today) than anything possible at that time in an academic setting. Watson directly managed accounts such as Baker's Chocolate and Coconut, Johnson and Johnson Baby Powder, and Pond's extract. He also brought his earlier ideas about the biological primacy of love, rage, and fear to advertising. He saw his job as the attempt to stimulate one of those basic impulses through advertising.

His position at J. Walter Thompson, while not leaving him much time to pursue original research, did allow him the opportunity to spread his ideas about Behaviorism to a new audience: business leaders. He also had time to write popular books and articles on a wide variety of topics, including "childrearing, sex, marriage, the role of women, how to succeed in business" (Kreshel, 1990, pp. 55–56) just to name a few. His audiences: business people and the public avidly harkened to his ideas. It is likely that Watson's vision of Behaviorism spread more quickly into the culture through his popular writings than it would have had he remained at a university. At any rate, the academic community continued to shun him and would do so until late in his life, when the American Psychological Association awarded him its second Gold Medal for lifetime achievement in 1957. Watson eventually left J. Walter Thompson to become vice-president at another agency. After his retirement, he lived a spartan existence on Long Island, his wife Rosalie having died young.

In addition to founding Behaviorism, Watson also contributed much to the establishment of applied psychology. That his success in doing the latter only came after his involuntary separation from academic psychology is telling. He helped move psychology away from philosophy toward biology and, later in his life, opened a conduit between psychology and the business world. After Watson, and on the academic side of psychology, Behaviorism slowly but inexorably became the leading school of thought in American psychology. The path to its eventual dominance of American psychology was not smooth. Birnbaum (1955) analyzed Behaviorism's appeal to the newly emerging mass markets and how Watson's late career expertise in advertising helped him sell Behaviorism to the public. Watson published several books, wrote many articles in the popular press, made movies, and spoke to countless groups to promote his ideas. But, Birnbaum also detailed how members of the intelligentsia opposed Watson. They included religious leaders and theologians, philosophers, newspaper columnists, and academics. Probably the most vociferous early critic of Watson was fellow psychologist, William McDougall, who, too, called his own brand of psychology Behaviorism. In theory and practice, however, the two were far apart.

William McDougall (1871–1938)

Biography

William McDougall was born in the north of England into the family of a wealthy industrialist. At the age of 14, he enrolled at the University of Manchester where he became interested in philosophy. He took a second degree at Cambridge and followed that with medical school. Like many others of his generation, he read James's textbook and decided to become a psychologist. After participating on a scientific expedition to the Far East, he spent a year honing his physiological skills with G. E. Müller in Germany.

Contributions

McDougall struggled to find a full-time psychology teaching position, finally ending up at Oxford University. He published a book, *An Introduction to Social Psychology,* in 1908, but its title probably should have been something like *Instincts and the Primary Tendencies of the Human Mind*. The book largely set the stage for what was to be the major focus of McDougall's career: instincts. McDougall (1926, p. 30) defined instincts as:

> an inherited or innate psycho-physical disposition which determines its possessor to perceive, and to pay attention to, objects of a certain class, to experience an emotional excitement of a particular quality upon perceiving such an object, and to act in regard to it in a particular manner, or, at least, to experience an impulse to such action.

McDougall was not the first to study instincts or make them important components of psychology. He believed that previous definitions of instincts by other animal researchers such as Washburn, Jennings, and Morgan were inconsistent and incomplete because they only focused on inborn patterns and tendencies. McDougall's definition of instinct added emotion and goal directedness to the earlier definitions. For him, an instinct always included three components: a behavior, an emotion, and a goal. Both animals and humans possessed instincts, but human instincts could be modified or inhibited by culture or habit. He proposed seven basic instincts and associated emotions:

Instinct	Emotion
flight	fear
repulsion	disgust
curiosity	wonder
pugnacity	anger
self-abasement	subjection
self-assertion	elation
parental	tender emotion

Living in post-Victorian England, McDougall was reluctant, at first, to add sexual behavior as an instinct. But, after Freud popularized his own ideas about the importance of the id (see Chapter 13) as the instinctual source behind the personality, McDougall, too, added mating to his list of instincts and associated it with the emotion of lust.

LEARNING OBJECTIVE

6. Predict how future psychologists might deal with the issue of instincts.

After World War I broke out, McDougall joined the British Army and helped treat soldiers for shell shock (an early name for PTSD). When the war ended, he accepted the position of chair of psychology at Harvard University. Before leaving Europe forever, he met with Carl Jung (see Chapter 13) who psychoanalyzed him. McDougall was never fully comfortable in the United States. His hereditarianism ran counter to the prevailing environmentalism first promoted by functional psychology and later radicalized by Watson and Skinner. In addition, McDougall was a Lamarckian and conducted research attempting to demonstrate that successive generations of white rats would inherit increased abilities in a discrimination task. That position, too, was in opposition to the Darwinism espoused by most other psychologists of the time.

At nearly the same time as Watson, McDougall (1912) wrote a book defining psychology as the study of behavior. His book, however, preserved an important role for introspection and free will in psychology. He criticized Watson's form of Behaviorism throughout the latter stages of his career. At one point, he and Watson even staged a live radio debate, later known as "The Battle of Behaviorism." McDougall left Harvard for Duke University where he remained for the rest of his life. At Duke (and much like William James before him) he became interested in parapsychological topics such as mental telepathy. In time, psychologists would come to appreciate that the views of McDougall and Watson each held grains of truth within them. Before such reconciliation could take place, a newer form of Behaviorism, Neobehaviorism, took the stage and held it firmly for nearly four decades (see Chapter 11).

The Battle of Behaviorism

On the night of February 5, 1924, a crowd of around 1,000 people gathered at the Psychology Club of Washington, DC, to hear John B. Watson and William McDougall debate over the nature and definition of Behaviorism. The debate was broadcast as well over a new medium: radio. Today it is difficult to imagine a world without telecommunications. That technology began in the 19th century with the invention of the telegraph, the telephone, and wireless radio broadcasting. Of those three seminal technologies, broadcast radio probably had the most impact. The earliest licensed broadcast stations in the United States date from 1920. Thus, the Watson–McDougall debate on live radio in 1924 was another first for the interaction of psychology and technology (e.g., recall Watson's filming of Little Albert as another early use of available technology). As new and exciting as today's telecommunications breakthroughs might seem—think of cell phones and tablet computing—they are still only incremental additions to an already existing telecommunications technology. When broadcast radio first appeared, it was radically new and different. It is hard to imagine some new technology today that would seem so different to us as radio seemed to the public back then.

Both debaters considered themselves worthy of the label "behaviorist" but their respective definitions were quite different. Watson wished to rid psychology of all mentalistic terms and only use objective methods. McDougall studied the behavior of animals and humans, but was not willing to part with the analysis of consciousness through introspection. A contemporary observer (Skinner, 1929, p. 254) commenting on the debate following its publication as a book (Watson & McDougall, 1929) observed:

each of the debaters is launching some of their arguments against a straw man. Watson, for example, does not deny the existence of consciousness as such, but he does deny that it can be studied objectively. McDougall in turn seems to believe that a dualistic position is the only way out . . . Instead of debating two kinds of behaviorisms . . . would not more be accomplished if the discussion were to center about what postulates should be set up by our psychologists as a basis for their science?

At the end of the debate the audience judged McDougall the winner by a small margin. But, by the time their book was published, popular opinion had swayed more strongly toward Watson's position. Within psychology itself, Behaviorism was also solidifying its hold. Near the end of their book (p. 94), McDougall remarked, "in America the tide of Behaviorism seems to flow increasingly." Later (p. 95) he continued, "Dr. Watson knows that if you wish to sell your wares, you must assert very loudly, plainly, and frequently that they are the best on the market." Watson may have narrowly won the debate, but his ideas quickly won the hearts and minds of nearly all American psychologists.

Yet, the Neobehaviorism that followed was not monolithic. While its practitioners agreed that studying behavior objectively was key, they disagreed over many other issues. A look at three of the most prominent neobehaviorists, Edward Tolman, Clark Hull, and B. F. Skinner will illustrate those agreements and disagreements (see Chapter 11). In Europe, another school was emerging: Gestalt psychology (see Chapter 12). Its followers, too, were dissatisfied by structuralism and its emphasis upon mental elements. They also proposed a radical solution, disregarding those elements and looking at relationships instead. Because of the rise of Hitler and the eventual breakout of World War II, Behaviorism and Gestalt psychologists would become strange bedmates during the 1930s and beyond.

BORDER WITH PHILOSOPHY
SEALING THE BORDER?

Behaviorism effectively sealed the porous border that had long existed between psychology and philosophy. As long as psychology defined itself introspectively, its border with philosophy allowed the free passage of ideas in both directions. More importantly, Behaviorism eventually led to another solidifying distinction between the disciplines: experimentation. Behaviorists promoted the design and conduct of experiments that did not require introspective analysis. In a way, behaviorists took psychology out of its armchairs and into its newly founded laboratories. But, as mentioned earlier (see Chapter 1) Knobe and other philosophers have pushed for a new approach in philosophy, experimental philosophy or X-phi. In an interview (Roberts & Knobe, 2016, p. 15), Knobe defined experimental philosophy thusly:

> Experimental philosophy is an interdisciplinary field at the intersection of philosophy and psychology. Very roughly, the field aims to make progress on the kinds of questions traditionally associated with philosophy using the kinds of methods traditionally associated with psychology.

Mallon (2016, p. 437) adds, "experimental philosophy is...quickly becoming larger still, blurring the disciplinary boundaries between psychology and neuroscience with consequences that have yet to reveal themselves." It seems that the border between psychology and philosophy is now being renegotiated.

SUMMARY

By the turn of the 20th century, Russian psychologists had made important advances in physiological psychology. Pavlov's work on the conditioned reflex was the most important of those. Gradually, news of those findings filtered back to the United States.

At that point in history, American psychology was in flux as Structuralism, Functionalism, applied psychology, and animal research all vied for attention. Behaviorism began in 1913 with Watson's speech. His radical position gained adherents slowly, but picked up steam after Pavlov's conditioning research became well known. Watson's academic career, however, was short-lived after a scandal involving him and his research assistant, Rosalie Rayner. Just prior to the scandal, they had conducted important research with an infant, Little Albert. After the scandal, Watson worked for advertising agencies, lectured and wrote, and promoted applied psychology using his Behaviorism.

William McDougall also called himself a behaviorist, but his approach was very different from Watson's. McDougall was British, a Lamarckian, and a hereditarian. He put much stock in the role of instincts in behavior. Watson and McDougall debated on the radio in "The Battle of Behaviorism." Watson's position gradually strengthened and was taken over by Neobehaviorism.

11 NEOBEHAVIORISM

The United States From 1914 to 1941

When Watson first proposed Behaviorism in 1913 as a way of making psychology more scientific, the United States was beginning to experience rapid technological and social changes. Still, the country was far from becoming the world power it is today. America's entry into World War I in 1917 was a watershed moment. The US Army, for instance, grew to more than five times its prewar size. For the first time, psychologists played a pivotal role in selecting and assigning troops to specialized roles. With the country a full partner in the war on the Allied side, President Wilson felt confident enough to propose his Fourteen Points in a speech to Congress delivered ten months before Germany's surrender; it was an idealistic framework for the peace to follow. The points included an end to secret alliances, full freedom of the seas, the lifting of trade barriers, better treatment of native colonial populations, specific readjustments of territory to prewar conditions, and the establishment of the League of Nations. Thus, the United States found itself in a new position relative to the victorious allies, that of a peer nation. Because of the Fourteen Points, Germany expected a just set of peace terms when it agreed to the Armistice on November 11, 1918. Unfortunately, Wilson's Fourteen Points had not been discussed with or agreed upon with France and Great Britain, the other Allies. The subsequent Treaty of Versailles in 1919 imposed severe conditions on Germany including the loss of territory and colonies. It also imposed a burdensome war debt or reparations for having begun the war.

Socially, much changed in the United States following World War I. For women, the changes were most dramatic. Women filled the workplace as men were drafted or volunteered for military service. The *Seattle Union Record* (1918, p. 1) newspaper reported:

> There has been a sudden influx of women into such unusual occupations as bank clerks, ticket sellers, elevator operator, chauffeur, street car conductor, railroad trackwalker, section hand, locomotive wiper and oiler, locomotive dispatcher, block operator, draw bridge attendant, and employment in machine shops, steel mills, powder and ammunition factories, airplane works, boot blacking and farming.

That women could hold occupations such as these was unheard of before the war. After the war, American women successfully completed a long battle for the right to vote. The 19th Amendment to the Constitution guaranteeing "The right of citizens of the United States to vote shall not be denied or abridged by the United States or by any State on account of sex," was ratified in 1919.

Another major social change was the passage and ratification of the 18th Amendment, "the manufacture, sale, or transportation of intoxicating liquors within, the importation thereof into, or the exportation thereof from the United States and all territory subject to the jurisdiction thereof for beverage purposes is hereby prohibited." The 18th Amendment was the result of a long campaign against alcohol consumption, mostly on moral grounds. In the end, the Amendment backfired as it encouraged an underground economy devoted to alcohol, the development of organized crime, and disrespect for the law. Prohibition ended in 1933 with the passage of the 21st Amendment, the only amendment in the US Constitution to repeal another.

Technologically, much changed too. World War I saw the advent of the mechanized army with trucks beginning to displace mules and horses (although that process was not complete until the end of World War II). Airplanes went from being toys for the rich to utilitarian tools as airmail and passenger service were born. The biggest technological change, however, was the popularization of the automobile along with the subsequent development of roads and highways.

The Roaring Twenties were nearly ten years of continuous change socially and technologically, marked by worldwide economic prosperity. The stock market crash of 1929 put a sudden stop to that period and led the Great Depression, a worldwide time of economic shrinkage and personal loss of fortune for most. In the United States, unemployment levels rose dramatically, many former farm families were forced to leave their land for jobs in cities, and spending power dropped precipitously. The election of Franklin D. Roosevelt along with his New Deal plan helped mitigate some of the economic pain after 1933, but full recovery did not occur until the start of World War II.

LEARNING OBJECTIVE

1. Discuss how World War I led to major social changes in the United States during and after the war.

PREVIEW

A slow-moving *neobehaviorist* movement gradually emerged from Watson's ideas (see Chapter 10). Neobehaviorism promoted the use of *animal models* for studying learning and freely extrapolated results from *rats, monkeys*, and *pigeons* to humans. Tolman's *Purposive Behaviorism* posited *expectancies* and *cognitive maps* in humans and rats. He and Hull used *mazes* extensively to investigate learning. Although their methods were similar, the ends each sought were different. Tolman's *S-S* approach saw animals as goal directed. Hull did not. He saw his animals as automatically responding to the variables that controlled learning in a straight *S-R* fashion. Their theories differed too. Hull looked for a *hypothethico-deductive* approach that would ultimately yield a universal theory of learning. Tolman's theory was never fully developed. Mostly, he concentrated on disproving Hullian theory without offering a palatable cognitive alternative.

Behaviorism evolved into two types of Neobehaviorism: *mediational* and *radical*. Mediational versions such as Tolman's and Hull's permitted the existence of unobservable or *intervening variables* as long as they could be *operationally defined*, a borrowing from modern physics. Radical Behaviorism dispensed with any type of unobservable variables, labeling them as *mentalistic*, and instead adopted a selectionist methodology where the survival of a particular behavior depended on the consequences that followed it. *Reinforcers* selected for survival of behaviors while *punishers* selected for their extinction.

Skinner's Radical Behaviorism survived to the present, mostly as a self-isolated subfield of psychology. Its proponents often label themselves as behavior analysts or applied behavior analysts. Nevertheless, its accomplishments have been many starting with the *operant chamber (Skinner Box)* and the *cumulative recorder. Applied behavior analysis* moved Radical Behaviorism out of the laboratory and into homes, classroom, businesses, and hospitals. Its discoveries of *schedules of reinforcement, the partial reinforcement extinction effect,* and *shaping* are covered in all introductory psychology texts. Less influential have been Skinner's contributions to the study of *language acquisition* and his *utopian* desire to transform the world for the better using Radical Behaviorism.

LEARNING OBJECTIVE

2. Assess the scientific and practical contributions made by Radical Behaviorism.

INTRODUCTION

From 1918 on psychology changed. The functionalist attacks on structuralist psychology had left the field open for a new definition, something other than the introspective study of the parts of the mind. At the same time, most psychologists on both sides of the Atlantic began to see themselves more as scientists and less as philosophers. So, any redefinition of psychology had to put it firmly on the side of science. In Europe, two new forms of psychology emerged and both saw themselves as sciences closely linked to biology and psychophysics. They were Wertheimer's Gestalt psychology (see Chapter 12) and Freud's Psychodynamic psychology (see Chapter 13). Both developed in Europe after World War I and only began to affect American psychology in the 1930s.

In the United States, Neobehaviorism grew out of Watson's Behaviorism. Neobehaviorism concentrated on understanding learned behaviors, used animal models, and practically eliminated from psychology any references to mental life. Influenced by the success of physics, some neobehaviorists attempted to construct overarching theories that would explain all learning through the action of measurable variables. Others would turn to analyses of goals and intentions along with looking at how variables related to each other. Still others would move even closer to evolutionary biology and develop systems where behaviors competed for survival through their consequences. By the beginning of World War II, American psychology was dominated by neobehaviorists, nearly all of whom used either rats or pigeons as their research subjects within a laboratory context.

The public image of American psychology also changed. Psychologists were people who wore lab coats, ran experiments with rats, and then generalized their findings to humans. Most American psychologists saw themselves as behavioral scientists pursuing the yet unknown laws governing learning. Neobehaviorist approaches would dominate psychology in the United States well into the 1970s. Today, it is difficult to spot the fossilized remains of that era save in one place, Skinner's Radical Behaviorism. Nearly all the rest of the Neobehaviorism has passed from the current scene or has been absorbed into mainstream psychology. Hullian theory, for example, is virtually unknown to modern psychology students despite having been, during its time, the central core of the discipline. For the most part, Neobehaviorism has become of historical interest only.

Modern Behaviorism, the psychology that emerged from Neobehaviorism, comes in several forms. Nearly all psychologists today are behaviorists in that they agree that the definition of psychology must include understanding behavior and that the scientific method will yield reproducible results. Watson's conception of Behaviorism was the original form. He argued that psychology should only concern itself with overt behaviors. Neobehaviorists saw his definition as overly confining and thus introduced Mediational Behaviorism, which allowed for unobservable stimuli and responses so long as they could be operationally defined. Tolman, Hull, and Woodworth's approaches all fit the definition of Behaviorism. Skinner's Radical Behaviorism is quite different from the approaches above. While it retained Watson's goal of prediction and control of behavior, it rejected practically everything else found in previous behaviorist and neobehaviorist formulations. Radical Behaviorism sees psychology as a part of biology, argues that all other behaviorist approaches are dualistic, insists upon environmental causation only, and completely cleanses psychology of any mentalistic conceptions. Students, thus, must be aware that the words "Behaviorism" and "Neobehaviorism" carry more than one meaning. So, most modern psychologists hue to a position called Methodological Behaviorism. Moore (2013) defined Methodological Behaviorism as possessing two original features: observable stimuli and behaviors and formal theory testing.

LEARNING OBJECTIVE

3. Describe the types of Behaviorism that existed in the past and compare to the types that currently exist.

THREE NEOBEHAVIORISTS

After Watson's manifesto, American psychologists struggled to incorporate Behaviorism into psychology. One of the main problems was that Watson's extreme stance so closely linked physiology to psychology that it was difficult to imagine or to discover underlying biological methods for many behaviors. Watson's "revolution" proceeded slowly and did not possess the suddenness of change typically associated with that word. But, by around 1930, a change in psychology away from introspection toward a more moderate form of Behaviorism had occurred. The term Neobehaviorism distinguished this new approach from Watson's original position. Neobehaviorism, however, was not a single movement. The earliest neobehaviorist, Edward Tolman, was one of the first to use albino laboratory rats extensively as models for human learning. He also introduced the use of intervening variables to psychology. Those variables were hypothetical and unseen, but they were operationally defined, making them objective and measurable unlike the older introspective variables. In Tolman's theory, the intervening variables were cognitive and assumed to have causal power over behavior.

Tolman's theories were too close to introspective psychology for Clark Hull. His Neobehaviorism sought to emulate Newton's physics by discovering objective variables that underlay behavior. Hull dispensed with cognition entirely and created a complex theoretical system designed with a minimal number of assumptions. He, too, adopted intervening variables, but anchored them in the physical world. His intervening variables were tied to stimuli and responses, not to cognitive states. Seeking to make psychology more like physics, the dominant model of twentieth century science, Hull created a theoretical structure that attempted to assess the causal relations between stimuli and responses based upon a mathematical relationship between underlying intervening variables.

Skinner, also a neobehaviorist, rejected the two preceding formulations. In their place he proposed Radical Behaviorism, which borrowed from Darwinian selection at three separate levels: phylogenetic, individual, and cultural. Skinner defined psychology as a science of behavior. For him, biology was psychology's nearest neighbor. He used operant conditioning to explain much (but not all) of the behavior of organisms. He also wrote extensively about how cultures operate to select long-standing practices through the action of verbal communities. Most telling, however, was his environmental determinism along with his overarching definition of the environment. For him, the environment extended "inside the skin," a move that displaced any cognitive components and any arguments for free will or individual autonomy. Of these three neobehaviorist approaches, only Skinner's survives to the present day (although it includes only a relatively small proportion of contemporary psychologists).

NEOBEHAVIORISM

As Samelson (1981, p. 420) noted, "Looking for the sources of behaviorism's powerful appeal to American psychologists, we found more often criticisms or partial acceptance . . . What I had not realized at the outset was that the victory of behaviorism took so much longer in coming about." Contrary to received tradition, Watson's Behaviorism was not an overnight success by any means. By 1930, however, a new form, Neobehaviorism, had come to dominate American psychology and would continue to do so for over the next 30 years. Psychologists, slowly but inexorably, were abandoning the study of consciousness through introspection. However, Watson's brand of Behaviorism failed to satisfy many. Few psychologists wished for a return to introspective methods, but fewer still had successfully transformed Watson's extreme approach into a coherent theoretical substitute.

One of the first neobehaviorists was Edward Tolman. After arriving at the University of California at Berkeley in 1918, he began to teach a course in comparative psychology and conduct research in learning. He quickly discovered that neither Thorndike's nor Watson's approaches to learning satisfied him. Soon he developed his own theoretical approach: Purposive Behaviorism. His version emphasized goal-seeking behavior and assumed that learning and performance were different from each other.

Edward Chace Tolman (1886–1959)

Biography

Edward Tolman was born in West Newton, near Boston. His family was wealthy, but espoused simple values derived from their Quaker heritage. Tolman graduated from the Massachusetts Institute of Technology. After, influenced by working with Yerkes and having read James, he decided to pursue graduate study of psychology at Harvard. There he noticed a disjoint between his lecture and laboratory classes. In the laboratory, his teachers used objective methods while in class they still lectured about introspection. Tolman was an early convert to Watson's Behaviorism and later reported personal relief at being able to leave introspection behind. Unlike many American psychologists of his generation, Tolman went to Europe to study. He spent a year in Germany studying with the Gestalt psychologist Kurt Koffka (see Chapter 12). Tolman was one of the few American psychologists to incorporate theoretical explanations from Gestalt psychology into Behaviorism. In 1918, he began to teach at the University of California at Berkeley, where he remained throughout his long career. Late in his career, at the height of McCarthyism, Tolman refused to sign a loyalty oath to the state of California and was fired along with 30 other faculty. The oath required faculty to state they were not members of the communist party. In a lawsuit that followed, he successfully defended his position and the law was struck down. He was rehired in 1952 and retired two years later. Similarly, when I became a graduate teaching assistant in 1976, I had to sign a loyalty oath to the state of Louisiana. Unlike in California, the Louisiana loyalty oath continues to be required of all state employees.

Contributions

Tolman began a research program that quickly added many new concepts to the emerging neobehaviorist school. He wanted to divorce psychology from its close dependence on physiology while at the same time seeking a better theoretical structure for Neobehaviorism. One of his first contributions was to redefine behavior itself into two categories: molecular and molar. Molecular behaviors were closely linked to physiology (e.g., muscle contractions or glandular secretions). Molar behaviors, on the other hand, were of a larger scale. Examples of molar behaviors included maze learning (whether running it, swimming it, or wading through it) and driving home from work (regardless of the route taken). Interestingly, Tolman argued that molar behaviors could be studied themselves without reference to any underlying physiological mechanisms. Tolman's approach was a far cry from Watson's earlier appeal for a tight linkage between behavior and physiology.

Tolman popularized the use of the white rat in psychology. Using mazes of varying types, he and his students discovered a number of cognitively based phenomena including expectancies and cognitive maps. His student, Tinklepaugh (1928), using a delayed reaction task, demonstrated that monkeys reacted negatively when they were shown a banana being hidden under a cup, but discovering that lettuce had been substituted there in their absence. As a control, Tinklepaugh had also left the lettuce hidden and untouched in other trials. Here is his description of the monkey's reactions (p. 229) during the control (a) and experimental conditions (b):

(a) Subject rushes to proper cup and picks it up. Seizes lettuce. Rushes away with lettuce in mouth, paying no attention to other cup or to setting. Time, 3–4 seconds.

(b) Subject rushes to proper cup and picks it up. Extends hand toward lettuce. Stops. Looks around on floor. Looks in, under, around cup. Glances at other cup. Looks back at screen. Looks under and around self. Looks and shrieks at any observer present. Walks away, leaving lettuce untouched on floor. Time, 10–33 seconds.

He and Tolman interpreted these results as evidence that the monkey expected lettuce in the control condition and received it, but expected a banana in the experimental condition and received lettuce instead. They interpreted the monkey's different reaction in each case as behavioral evidence of different cognitive states. Tolman believed he had demonstrated **expectancy** in a nonhuman animal.

One of Tolman's most famous contributions was the cognitive map, a concept he derived from Gestalt psychology. In a series of experiments, Tolman and his coworkers demonstrated that rats learned the spatial relationships between themselves and a food item. After learning an initial forced roundabout relationship in a maze between themselves and food located in a specific place, rats would successfully choose a new path in a different maze but one in which the food was in the same place it had been in the previous maze. That new path, usually, was a direct line to the food item. To Tolman, that indicated that the rats knew where the food was located in a cognitive map that they carried in their heads. He wrote describing one of his studies (FIgure 11.1) (Tolman, 1948, p. 204):

the rats in this experiment had learned not only to run rapidly down the original roundabout route but also, when this was blocked and radiating paths presented, to select one pointing rather directly towards the point where the food had been.

Many students possess detailed and accurate cognitive maps of their preferred routes to class or nearby stores. But, their cognitive maps for places they seldom visit are more fuzzy and inaccurate. Tolman would have argued that people's cognitive maps developed with experience. The more experience they had with a route or location, the better their map, he thought. Carroll

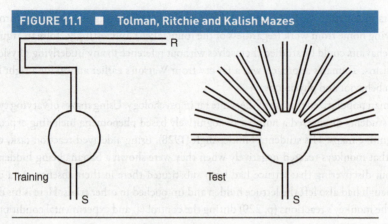

Source: From: Tolman, E. C., Ritchie, B. F., & Kalish, D. (1946). Studies in spatial learning. I. Orientation and the short cut. *Journal of Experimental Psychology, 36*, 13–24.

(2017) argued that Tolman's research on cognitive maps, although using only observable behaviors, has led to the now burgeoning field of cognitive neuroscience. He wrote (p. 216):

> Tolman demonstrated how the methods of the behaviorist could be used to study more complex and interesting psychological phenomena. Psychologists' recognition of the potential of his approach to pursue long-neglected topics—coupled with events in artificial intelligence, linguistics, and neuroscience—played a central role in the resurgence of interest in cognitive processes in the latter half of the twentieth century.

The emergence and growth of cognitive psychology and Tolman's role in the development of that subfield of psychology are examined in Chapter 14.

Another famous concept of Tolman's was latent learning. That line of research led to his distinction between learning and performance. Following earlier work in his laboratory, Tolman and Honzik (1930) decided to investigate whether learning required a reinforcer (food, in this case). They trained three groups of rats in the same complex maze using the average number of errors per trial as the criterion for learning. Those errors should drop over time, exhibiting a classic learning curve. One group, the control (HNR), was never fed. Another group was always fed (HR), and the final group (HNR-R) was only fed after the 11th day of training. If learning required a food reinforcer, then that last group should begin learning the maze only after commencing to eat on the 11th day (see Figure 11.2).

That is not what happened. Instead, once the last group began to be fed, their errors dropped precipitously. Tolman and Honzik interpreted these data by saying that those rats had already learned the maze, but that it took the presence of food in the goal box for them to perform or demonstrate their learning. They called the phenomenon latent learning because the learning, they argued, had already taken place. They argued that the new presence of the food reinforcer now changed the situation, causing their errors to go down accordingly. In their theorizing, reinforcement was not necessary for learning.

Tolman created a viable neobehaviorist alternative to Watson's earlier scheme. To do so, Tolman endowed his rats (and, by extension, people) with **intervening variables** or variables

FIGURE 11.2 ■ Tolman and Honzik's (1930) Latent Learning Data

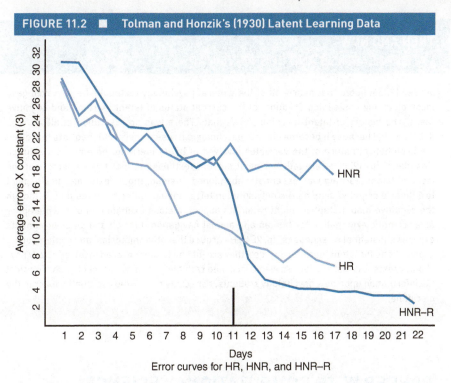

Error curves for HR, HNR, and HNR–R

that lay between a physical stimulus and an observable behavior. Those intervening variables were the actual cause of the behavior, but were unobservable. Yet, they were still amenable to experimental analysis via the doctrine of **operationism** that had come to psychology via physics. One of the best examples of a psychological intervening variable is hunger. To an old-time introspective psychologist, hunger would be an aspect of consciousness, a kind of feeling. However, no one could estimate or compare degrees of hunger made by different hungry people using introspective methods. Tolman (and nearly all psychologists since) operationalized hunger by providing descriptions of how to obtain hunger, namely by withholding food. Thus, a rat that had not eaten for 12 h was hungrier than one that had not eaten for 6 h. Operational definitions allowed neobehaviorists to describe internal states without using the methods of traditional introspection.

Tolman created a liberal compromise between the introspective methods of the past and Watson's extreme behaviorist position. In place of S-R theory, he introduced S-S (stimulus-stimulus) theory. Learning, for Tolman, was all about the relationships between stimuli, not the response to a given stimulus. His position, however, was too close to the older kind of psychology for many psychologists. Clark Hull, in particular, became Tolman's main theoretical rival. Hull, too, sought to remedy the problems of Watson's Behaviorism. His solution was to keep Watson's central idea intact; behavior could be controlled and predicted without using any reference to cognitive concepts such as expectancies or cognitive maps. He tried to explain learning via a complex and ambitious overarching theory full of mechanistic variables.

THEN AND NOW
LATENT LEARNING AND COGNITIVE MAPS

Jensen (2006) noted that nearly all of the general psychology textbooks he surveyed gave incomplete and misleading accounts of the current status of latent learning and cognitive maps. The history of latent learning shows that "There was no resolution at all . . . The debate ended because it became clear to psychological researchers and theorists that given the hypothetical nature of the variables involved in latent learning, no empirical solution was likely" (p. 195). He argued that most current textbooks do not tell students that the issue of latent learning was essentially abandoned. Instead, those texts uncritically point to Tolman's cognitive map as the only solution left standing. Later he notes that "although the cognitive map metaphor might retain its appeal, a close examination of the metaphor as a scientific explanation for human and animal navigation through spatial environments exposes substantial weaknesses" (p. 204). He argued that other historical and contemporary explanations for latent learning do exist; they are just no longer covered in introductory psychology texts. Ultimately, Jensen was concerned with the pervasive effect of such historical misinformation upon new psychology students, especially those who eventually major in the discipline.

BORDER WITH COMPUTATIONAL SCIENCE
MODERN PHYSICS

The many discoveries in modern physics leading up to the development of the atomic bomb also required the use of operationism. For instance, the many subatomic particles created by bombarding the nuclei of atoms were first described as intervening variables. Many experiments were run to determine if those unseen particles actually existed. Those particles that followed the paths predicted by atomic theory were deemed to exist despite never actually being observed themselves. The rise of modern physics occurred at around the same time as the emergence of Neobehaviorism and influenced it markedly. In psychology, the intervening variables that predicted particular behaviors were also viewed as real despite being unobservable. Percy Bridgman, a physicist and the author of an influential book, *The Logic of Modern Physics* (1928), was partly responsible for leading psychologists to imitate physicists. During the twentieth century, physics was the quintessential model for how any science should operate, and most psychologists aspired to make their science resemble it.

LEARNING OBJECTIVE

4. Explain the logic behind Tolman's use of intervening variables.

Clark Hull (1884–1952)

Biography

Clark Hull was born near Akron, New York, but spent most of his boyhood in Michigan. He attended the academy associated with Alma College before enrolling at the University of Wisconsin. In his 20s, he contracted typhoid fever and polio, illnesses that left him with lifelong disabilities including a withered leg. Gifted with mechanical ability, he designed and made his own leg brace to compensate. Later, he designed an automated correlation calculating machine (Hull, 1925) to aid his work on aptitude testing. After holding a series of jobs, he returned to Wisconsin and received a PhD in psychology in 1918. He remained there until 1929, when he moved to Yale's Institute of Human Relations as a research professor. Before arriving at Yale, his research was eclectic and included books on aptitude testing (Hull, 1928) and hypnosis and suggestibility (Hull, 1933a). He also was interested in concept formation and verbal learning.

Contributions

Hull's interests turned strictly to rat learning after arriving at Yale. He spent the rest of his career providing an alternative to Tolman's line of research while providing a synthetic theory that combined aspects of Thorndike's law of effect and Pavlovian conditioning. Like Tolman, Hull believed that much could be learned about human behavior by running laboratory experiments using the white rat. Although his theory was extremely influential during his lifetime, it is of only historical interest today. Nevertheless, any history of psychology that neglects or omits it is incomplete. Additionally, failure to understand Hull and his influence makes it difficult to see properly how subsequent attempts to understand learning developed.

Hull wished to make psychology as scientific an enterprise as physics. His two models were Newton's *Principia* and Euclid's *Elements*. From both, he adopted the **hypothetico-deductive system** and the tight logic of inferred theorems constructed from a minimal set of *a priori* postulates and definitions. He believed that psychology would advance only when theory and observations were closely linked. Then, those types of investigations would yield "facts of intrinsic importance" while "indicating the truth or falsity of the theoretical system from which the phenomena were originally deduced" (Hull, 1935, p. 493). Later (pp. 512–513) he wrote:

> Scientific theory in its best sense consists of the strict logical deduction from definite postulates of what should be observed under specified conditions. If the deductions are lacking or are logically invalid, there is no theory; if the deductions involve conditions of observation which are impossible of attainment, the theory is metaphysical rather than scientific; and if the deduced phenomenon is not observed when the conditions are fulfilled, the theory is false.

Systematically, he set out to do for psychology what Newton had done for physics and Euclid had done for geometry. He used Thorndike's law of effect and Pavlov's analysis of classical conditioning as a starting point. He retained Watson's S-R model but added intervening variables. He anchored his intervening variables, via operational definitions, to both the S side and the R side of the S-R formulation, something he claimed other theorists failed to do. In two major books (Hull, 1943, 1952), he specified the details of his system. True to his advice, the later book incorporated theoretical changes forced by the accumulation of new experimental data. His system was dynamic, designed to change in the face of unexpected new data. In explicit contrast to Tolman's approach, Hull wanted to explain learning through the interaction of stimulus variables and intervening variables only. Purposive behavior had no place in his system. Ultimately, his system failed to explain learning. But, while he was alive, his system inspired a large number of psychologists to pursue his vision of a mechanistic explanation for learning. It is worthwhile to briefly examine some of Hull's variables and how they interacted.

Hull's System

Hull's system was complex. Marx and Hillix (1963, p. 247) described its final form as including:

> ...a total of eighteen postulates and twelve corollaries was produced. In accordance with the hypothetico-deductive procedure that Hull intended to follow, these primary principles were to be used deductively to predict secondary principles, such as "goal gradient and latent learning".

The basic structure of the system consisted of three (see Figure 11.3) types of variables: stimulus, organismic or intervening, and response. The four stimulus variables were measurable. They were the number of reinforced trials, stimulus deprivation level, stimulus intensity, and size of the reinforcer.

FIGURE 11.3 ■ Hull's System

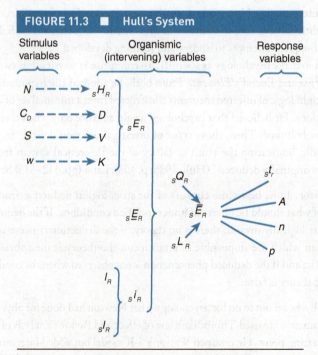

Source: Marx, M. H., & Hillix, W. A. (1963). *Systems and theory in psychology.* New York: McGraw-Hill.

Each of these, in turn, was connected to a corresponding intervening variable, habit strength $_sH_r$, drive D, stimulus intensity dynamism V, and incentive K, respectively. Together, those four variables accounted for acquisition of a learned response, its maintenance, or its decline. Their mathematical relationship was multiplicative; thus should any one of them drop to zero then the product of all of them would be zero as well. Other intervening variables accounted for extinction and spontaneous recovery: reactive inhibition I_r and conditioned inhibition $_sI_r$; individual differences, oscillation $_sO_r$; and consistency of learned response, threshold $_sL_r$.

The mathematical equation of the intervening variables just mentioned equaled yet another one: overall or net reaction potential $_s\bar{E}_r$. The response variables, too, were measurable. They were response latency $_st_r$, amplitude A, number of responses until extinction n, and response probability p. These last variables, naturally enough, were the ones measured as the rats interacted with the laboratory apparatus under various experimental conditions. Here are all of the intervening variables and their mathematical relationships in the final version of Hull's equation:

$$_s\bar{E}_r = (_sH_r \times D \times V \times K) - I_r - _sI_r - _sL_r + / - _sO_r$$

LEARNING OBJECTIVE

5. Demonstrate what happens in Hull's equation when H, D, V, or K have a zero value.

The biggest change between the final version and previous versions was the addition of incentive *(K)*. Hull added incentive because of experiments by Crespi (1942) that demonstrated that rats ran faster when the food reward in the goal box was made larger and slower when it was made smaller.

Hull was an S-R theorist. He believed that learning was strengthened by repetition (through habit strength) and that reinforcement was related to the satisfaction of internal drive states such as hunger and thirst. In other words, reinforcement was a biological drive and as it was satisfied, it played less of a role in predicting behavior. But, later as it renewed itself as a drive, its role grew again. Think of hunger as an example. Food only acts as a reinforcer when hunger is high. Extinction was accounted for by the rapid accumulation of reactive inhibition following unreinforced trials. Spontaneous recovery occurred because reactive inhibition was only temporary. Criticism of Hullian formulations led to further patchwork and repair of the theory. After Hull's death in 1952, interest by others dropped considerably. His most prominent student, Kenneth Spence, carried on Hull's tradition but very quickly dropped his support for the drive reduction view of reinforcement and was much less concerned about maintaining the formal structure Hull had created. Eleanor Gibson, too, was one of Hull's students. She came to him after being rejected as a potential graduate student by Yerkes; he rejected any female student (Rodkey, 2010). Her dissertation was couched in Hullian terminology although her underlying views were more functional. Later in her career she carved out a research career at Cornell University because Smith College, where her husband James Gibson worked, would not allow the hiring of married couples. At Cornell, she and Richard Walk developed the visual cliff apparatus, at first working with rats and eventually with human infants. She eventually was hired as a professor at Cornell and received the National Medal of Science in 1992, an award rarely given to psychologists.

PHOTO 11.1 Eleanor Gibson

PHOTO 11.2 Visual Cliff Apparatus

Credit: History Science Images/Alamy Stock Photo

PHOTO 11.3 Clark Hull (center)

Credit: Len Collection/Alamy Stock Photo

As Hull's star waned, another neobehaviorist movement was gathering steam. Skinner's Radical Behaviorism would prove to be the most tenacious version of Neobehaviorism, one that still thrives at present. Radical Behaviorism was opposed to all forms of mentalism including other neobehaviorist approaches that used intervening variables.

B. F. Skinner (1904–1990)

Biography

Fred Skinner, as his friends called him, was born in Susquehanna, Pennsylvania. His father was a lawyer. His mother was a homemaker who kept close watch on her two sons. (Skinner's brother died of an accident at the age of 16.) Early on, Skinner exhibited a knack for solving problems using mechanical devices, a skill that would play a crucial role in his later research. He was a good student and attended Hamilton College where he majored in English. His goal then was to be a writer. After he graduated, he attempted to write short fiction, but was unsuccessful. In his autobiography (1970, p. 7), he wrote, "I had failed as a writer, because I had nothing important to say, but I could not accept that explanation." After reading Russell's (1927) *An Outline of Philosophy*, that, along with Watson's and Pavlov's works, he became a behaviorist, although the Radical Behaviorism he created later would be much different than anything he had learned at school.

He went to Harvard to study psychology and received his PhD in 1931; he remained there five more years as a fellow. A discussion with the philosopher Alfred North Whitehead at a fellow's dinner proved seminal to Skinner's later theorizing. Whitehead challenged Skinner to demonstrate that studying language scientifically was possible. Skinner's response, however, was long delayed. It came in the form of a book (Skinner, 1957), *Verbal Behavior*, a work he considered to have been his most important contribution to psychology. Following his years as a fellow, Skinner first worked at the University of Minnesota for nine years followed by three years as chair at the University of Indiana. In 1948, he returned to Harvard where he remained an active faculty member until his retirement in 1974. However, he continued to work and publish there as professor emeritus until his very last days of life. His final public appearance was at the American Psychological Association's 1990 meeting just days before his death. There, he reaffirmed his commitment to Radical Behaviorism in the face of the "cognitive revolution" which had swept through psychology during his lifetime. In his speech, delivered before an overflow crowd in a large hall at the convention, he proclaimed, "Cognitive science is the creation science of psychology, as it struggles to maintain the position of a mind or self" (Skinner, 1990, p. 1209). What legacy to psychology, exactly, did Skinner leave with his Radical Behaviorism?

Contributions

During World War II, Skinner engineered an apparatus for pigeons housed inside bombs. The pigeons could guide the bomb to the target by pecking at a display. The device worked but was never operationally deployed. After the war, Skinner made an Air Crib in which he and his wife, Yvonne, raised their second daughter. He made the Air Crib (see Photo 11.4) for their second child, Deborah, partly to keep her warm in the Minnesota weather without having to bundle her with layers of clothing. Skinner attempted to market the device, but it never caught on, especially following an article in the *Ladies' Home Journal* magazine (Skinner, 1945) that described it as an experiment in child rearing. Urban legends circulated that Deborah had either gone crazy or committed suicide. Those legends were untrue; she was a well-adjusted child and a successful adult (Joyce & Faye, 2010).

PHOTO 11.4 The Air Crib
Credit: Sam Falk/Science Source

Skinner invented two pieces of laboratory apparatus that were instrumental in the development of Radical Behaviorism. One was the operant conditioning chamber or Skinner Box. The other was the cumulative recorder. He constructed Skinner boxes suitable for rats and pigeons. In rat chambers the response was usually a lever press while in pigeon chambers the response was a peck on a target disk (see Photos 11.5 and 11.6). A small bit of food or water served as the reinforcer. The chamber itself was the discriminative stimulus, but other discriminative stimuli (e.g., lights or tones) could be added. The dependent variable in a Skinner Box was the rate of response (number of responses over time) which was measured by the cumulative recorder. The Skinner Box made the discovery of schedules of reinforcement and shaping possible (see below).

PHOTO 11.5 Rat Operant Chamber
Credit: Walter Dawn/Science Source

PHOTO 11.6 Pigeon Operant Chamber

Credit: PR INC./Science Source

BORDER WITH BIOLOGY
RADICAL BEHAVIORISM

As far as radical behaviorists are concerned, no border exists between psychology and biology. In fact, they consider Radical Behaviorism to be a part of biological science. Borrowing the mechanism of selection from evolutionary theory, they argue that it operates at three levels. The first level is Darwin's natural selection that selects organisms whose genes allow them to reproduce and become more numerous. Innate behaviors come from this level. The second level is operant conditioning that selects organisms' emitted behaviors (or operants) through the action of the environment. Those selected behaviors also "reproduce" and become more numerous. Learned behaviors in animals and humans come from this level. The final level is cultural where humans' verbal responses (also considered to be operants) are selected through the action of the linguistic communities people live in. The verbal responses selected by the linguistic community a person lives in also become more numerous. Culturally based behaviors in humans come from this level.

Radical Behaviorism interprets each type of selection at its own level with each possessing its own time frame. So, phylogenetically based innate behaviors evolved over millions of years. Learned behaviors in animals and humans develop over the course of the lifetimes of individual species members. Culturally based behaviors also evolve over long periods, from as little as several lifetimes to thousands of years. In terms of theory, radical behaviorists confine themselves to the last two levels but take pains to demonstrate that at all three levels either genes, behaviors, or verbal behaviors are being selected mechanistically according to environmental consequences operating at their respective levels.

Radical Behaviorism

Radical Behaviorism is, by design and intent, completely different from Watson's Behaviorism and other neobehaviorist formulations. Radical Behaviorism, however, preserved Watson's definition of psychology, the prediction and control of behavior, but it rejected other neobehaviorist theories because of their use of intervening variables; those were rejected because they were mentalistic and because they assumed dualism (which is mentalistic as well). At the same time, Radical Behaviorism was not S-R psychology either. Instead, it explained learned behavior through selection by consequences. Thus, operant conditioning occurs when a response is followed by a reinforcer causing that response to be emitted more often. Organisms also learn the environmental occasions when reinforcement is likely. Skinner diagrammed the relationship as follows:

$$S^D \rightarrow R \rightarrow S^R$$

where the S^D is the discriminative stimulus, R is the emitted response, and S^R is the reinforcer. In the laboratory, specifying the three terms above is relatively easy. Outside of the laboratory, the search for discriminative stimuli and reinforcers is more difficult, but still quite possible. The standard traffic light makes a good example of the two types of discriminative stimuli. The green light serves as an S^D because it signals that continuing to drive through the intersection is OK (or, more technically, a long history exists between the green light, pressing the accelerator, and the reinforcement of continuing to move). The red light, however, is an S^Δ or a discriminative stimulus that signals that proceeding through the intersection is not OK. Running that red light might lead to any number of negative consequences up to and including death.

A branch of Radical Behaviorism, applied behavior analysis, specializes in searching for and understanding how operants or discriminative stimuli are at work in natural situations. Some applied behavior analysts work in clinical areas of psychology and use their knowledge to alter patients' environments in ways that lead to positive outcomes to health or adjustment. Behavior modification is one of the techniques used by applied behavior analysts. It consists of imposing new and consistent environmental contingencies in real world situations such as classrooms. Nearly every elementary and secondary teacher in the United States is at least aware of behavior modification and many use it to manage their classrooms effectively and efficiently.

BORDER WITH SOCIAL SCIENCE
TOKEN ECONOMIES IN THE CLASSROOM

Token economies, a type of applied behavior analysis, have been created for a wide variety of natural situations. All varieties are similar in that they use tokens (e.g., arbitrary items such as poker chips or stickers) as conditioned reinforcers. The tokens may be cashed in for primary reinforcers such as food according to published schedules.

A classroom token economy is a form of contingency management where students may earn tokens for following explicit, behaviorally based classroom rules. Little and Akin-Little (2008) revealed that 73% of teachers surveyed had created their own set of classroom rules. Maggin et al. (2011) reviewed 24 studies of classroom token economies and concluded (p. 22), "students generally respond to these types of interventions" but that "practitioners need to be aware that the use of token economies in schools and classrooms likely requires careful oversight and systematic protocols for delivering generalized conditioned and secondary reinforcement." They also called for more rigorous research that better reported student characteristics and contexts in which token economies are designed and delivered. Despite the fact that managing behavioral contingencies in the real world is more difficult than doing so in the laboratory, many teachers do so successfully every day.

Understanding Skinner

DeBell and Harless (1992) examined common misunderstandings about Skinner using a short quiz they administered to psychology students and faculty. They identified five common misperceptions or myths (p. 68):

a) the role of physiology and genetics in behavior,

b) the extent to which all behavior can be conditioned,

c) the uniqueness of the individual,

d) the use of punishment in controlling behavior, and

e) the existence of internal states.

Their quiz had 14 questions, half of which were filler questions about Skinner that did not relate to the myths above; the other half addressed the five myths. Their results showed that Skinner believed that genetics did play an important role in behavior (Myth a), that punishment and negative reinforcement were different processes (Myth b), that individuals were unique and using group statistics was not helpful (Myth c), that positive reinforcement was a better way to influence behavior than was punishment (Myth d), and that he believed consciousness existed (Myth e). Interestingly, even psychology faculty missed more than half of the myth questions. Advanced undergraduates missed nearly all of them!

LEARNING OBJECTIVE

6. Judge why so many students and faculty misunderstand Skinner's position and fall victim to the five myths.

Skinner understood that physiology and genetics played an important role in behavior and that innate behaviors existed. Innate behaviors were the result of natural selection. However, the conditions that originally led to their selection could change, albeit slowly, as the environment changed. When it changed, so did its selection pressures. Organisms either adapted or went extinct. Also, behaviors that were adaptive at one point in phylogenetic history might become maladaptive at a later point; the flight or flight response in humans is one example. In the distant past it served an obvious adaptive purpose; it led to escape from danger. But, in the modern, industrialized world it had become maladaptive as it contributed to increased levels of hypertension and risk of heart attacks.

Skinner never claimed that all behavior was modifiable by operant conditioning; contingencies at the phylogenetic level or the cultural level might prevent it. However, operant conditioning was the major mechanism operating during a person's life. Over the course of a person's lifetime the environment would select behaviors that were followed by reinforcement and extinguish those that were not.

Skinner believed in human uniqueness and maintained that, except in the case of identical twins, all persons had been uniquely shaped by genetics, their environments, and the cultures they lived in. His research strategy reflected that belief. He conducted research on only a few organisms at a time and eschewed the use of large groups and the concomitant reliance upon statistical analysis. Instead, he argued for visual inspection of large amounts of data collected from only a few individuals. One of his innovations was the N = 1 research design where a single individual animal or human is subjected to successive experimental manipulations (see Kennedy, 2004, for more information on single case designs). One of the most common N = 1 designs is the ABA design. In it, the organism is observed in its environment without altering any behavioral contingencies. The purpose of that is to determine a **baseline** or control. This is the A part of the ABA design. Next, the experimenter alters a contingency (this is the B part) and looks for a change in the rate of responding. This step is the **intervention**. If a change occurs then the next step is to remove the contingency and observe whether the rate of responding returns to the baseline rate. These steps may be repeated (e.g., ABABABAB . . .) and if the rate of responding consistently changes, then the researcher may infer that the intervention was causally responsible for the change in behavior. The ABA design is often used in applied behavior analysis to discover interventions that will change people's behaviors. For Skinner, then, each individual and each situation were unique. He believed introducing large group designs and analyzing them statistically only confused understanding.

Skinner also differentiated strongly between reinforcement and punishment. Although both are similar structurally, but in opposite directions, they are quite dissimilar in their long-term effects. Reinforcement follows a response and strengthens it, and punishment follows a response and suppresses it. But, the structural similarity ends there. Skinner (1953) offered three reasons why punishments should not be administered: they only work temporarily, they create conditioned stimuli that lead to negative emotional reactions, and they reinforce escape from the conditioned situation in the future. He wrote (pp. 192–193):

> Civilized man has made some progress in turning from punishment to alternative forms
> of control . . . But we are still a long way from exploiting the alternatives, and we are not
> likely to make any real advance so long as our information about punishment and the

alternatives to punishment remains at the level of casual observation. As a consistent picture of the extremely complex consequences of punishment emerges from analytical research, we may gain the confidence and skill needed to design alternative procedures in the clinic, in education, in industry, in politics, and in other practical fields.

Skinner's view on internal states is probably the most startling example of his way of thinking about Behaviorism. He rejected any idea that a separate mental world exists. At the same time, however, he made possible an analysis of the environment inside the skin. Each person is affected only by the environment, but that environment consists of two parts: a public one potentially accessible to all and a private one accessible only to one's self. So, as of right now, nearly eight billion human private environments exist, one inside each person alive today. Skinner described the private world as:

> part of the universe enclosed within the organism's own skin . . . With respect to each individual, in other words, a small part of the universe is *private* (original italics). We need not suppose that events which take place within an organism's skin have special properties for that reason" (Skinner, 1953, p. 257).

Moore (2001, p. 237) added, "(1) private events are behavioral in character, and (2) they can contribute to discriminative control over behavior." More simply put, Radical Behaviorism eliminates "mind" and in its place substitutes "private behavior." But, Skinner's standing among psychologists is due more to the results of his research than to the theory behind it.

Long-term Successes of Radical Behaviorism

Skinner deserves his position as the most eminent psychologist of the twentieth century (Haggbloom et al., 2002) because of his long-lasting contributions to the discipline. Of his many contributions, a few stand out above the others. Already mentioned are the operant conditioning chamber and the cumulative recorder. Those two enabled the discovery of schedules of reinforcement, the partial reinforcement extinction effect, and shaping. Another long-term contribution was his desire to apply psychology toward the betterment of the world. Or, to put it in radical behaviorist terms, to reshape the environment in such a way as to improve nearly every aspect of human behavior. In this last respect, Skinner was very much a utopian who believed that psychology, properly conceived and applied, could improve the world.

Skinner first described four basic schedules of reinforcement in addition to the original one, continuous reinforcement, where a lab animal received a reinforcer every time it made the operant response. He termed the new ones intermittent schedules to distinguish them from continuous reinforcement. The intermittent schedules delivered reinforcers on the basis of time (interval schedules) or number of responses (ratio schedules). In addition, each type could be delivered reliably (fixed) or randomly (variable) leading to four different schedules: fixed interval (FI), variable interval (VI), fixed ratio (FR), and variable ratio (VR). Each schedule was associated with a consistently different pattern of responding that came from the schedule itself.

Skinner (1953, p. 99) noted of behavior under intermittent schedules, "Usually, such behavior is remarkably stable and shows great resistance to extinction." One of Skinner's most startling discoveries was the partial reinforcement extinction effect or PREE. It is counterintuitive and makes a wonderful rejoinder to those who argue that psychological research simply validates common sense. The PREE is seen in organisms under intermittent reinforcement. Compared to organisms under continuous reinforcement, those under intermittent reinforcement take much longer to extinguish; they also achieve higher response rates. When students are asked "Will an organism work harder and longer when you give it a food reward every time it makes the correct response or when it gets a food reward every tenth time?" they, more often than not will select the first alternative. Hochman and Erev (2013) examined the apparent inconsistency of the PREE in laboratory vs field situations:

> As was suggested by Nevin and Grace (2000), our results demonstrate that the effect of the reinforcement schedule is highly sensitive to the evaluation criteria. In many cases, partial reinforcement has a small positive effect on selecting the promoted alternative during extinction, and a larger negative effect on this behavior during training. This sensitivity can explain the apparent inconsistency between laboratory and field studies of partial reinforcements: Most laboratory studies have focused on the positive effect of partial reinforcements during extinction, whereas most field studies have focused on the fact that the overall effect of partial reinforcement tends to be negative.

Put more simply, learning under a partial schedule may take more time and effort but when (and if) the learning criterion is reached, extinction will take longer under a partial schedule than it would under a continuous one.

The four basic schedules displayed very different cumulative recordings as displayed in Figure 11.4. The steeper the recording is, the faster the response rate. FR and VR schedules can achieve high rates of responding while the VI schedule never does. Also, note the characteristic differences in the shapes of the curves. The FI schedule is scalloped because organisms slow down immediately after receiving a reinforcer and speed up just prior to its delivery. The FR schedule shows post reinforcement pauses after each reinforcer is delivered.

Outside of the laboratory, schedule effects are easily observed as well. Slot machines pay off following a variable ratio schedule, and players continue to insert money and pull the handles for long periods. Remuneration for most jobs follows a fixed interval schedule (e.g., getting a paycheck once a week). Workers in those jobs work the hardest just prior to receiving their checks, but their work rates drop off dramatically afterward. Wise managers, thus, pay their employees late on Friday afternoon. Some jobs, though, pay according to a fixed ratio schedule (piecework). Those workers achieve higher levels of production and earn more than workers paid on a fixed interval basis. Reinforcement schedules can exert powerful contingencies on behavior.

Shaping was another of Skinner's discoveries. He described operant conditioning as a process similar to a sculptor shaping a lump of clay. Operant responses, he argued, are not "discrete units of behavior" (Skinner, 1953, p. 91); rather they are the end products of a process he called shaping (see Photo 11.7). Here is how he described the shaping of a pigeon to peck at a particular location on the wall of its enclosure (p. 92):

FIGURE 11.4 ■ Intermittent Schedules of Reinforcement

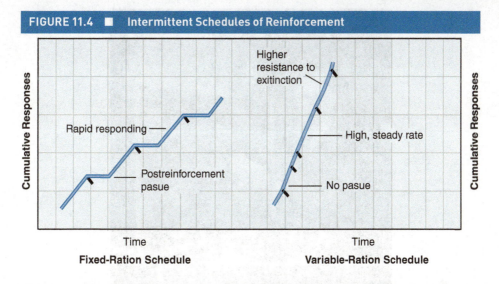

Fixed-Ration Schedule

Variable-Ration Schedule

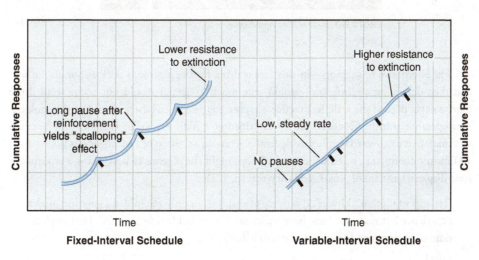

Fixed-Interval Schedule

Variable-Interval Schedule

To get the pigeon to peck the spot as quickly as possible we proceed as follows: We first give the bird food when it turns slightly in the direction of the spot from any part of the cage. This increases the frequency of such behavior. We then withhold reinforcement until a slight movement is made toward the spot. This again alters the general distribution of behavior without producing a new unit. We continue by reinforcing positions successively closer to the spot, then by reinforcing only when the head is moved slightly forward, and finally only when the beak actually makes contact with the spot. We may reach this final response in a remarkably short time. A hungry bird, well adapted to the situation and to the food tray, can usually be brought to respond in this way in two to three minutes.

PHOTO 11.7 Skinner Shaping a Pigeon

Credit: Sam Falk/Science Source

The alternative to shaping—in this case waiting for the pigeon to peck a spot on the wall and then delivering a reinforcer—would take much longer. It would not occur at all if the pigeon never pecked the wall. In practice, shaping has proven to be a powerful way of molding new operants quickly. Goddard (2018) described how Skinner, Keller Breland, and Norman Guttman first discovered shaping using feral pigeons on a rooftop of a Minneapolis flour mill in 1943 while conducting wartime research. They taught the pigeons to bowl using a repurposed food dispenser and small pins. Goddard wrote (p. 421):

> It is important that Skinner's discovery of shaping not only resembled a genuine eureka experience but may also have been influential in emboldening Skinner's later applications of operant conditioning to human behaviors...

Goddard went on to argue that Skinner's discovery of shaping was fundamental to his later application of Radical Behaviorism to selectionist accounts of personality change, implicit theories of intelligence, skill learning, and language.

Skinner's utopian visions appear most prominently in his books *Walden Two* (1948) and *Beyond Freedom and Dignity* (1971). In the latter work, especially, he argued that society can be improved, but only if people are willing to give up belief in free will and personal autonomy as causal factors. In their place, Skinner proposed that people could arrange environmental contingencies in such a way as to promote a better world. He understood the difficulties he would have in promoting his solution. Freedom and dignity were the last preserves of "autonomous men" and they blocked the path to a scientific understanding of how the environment could be changed in order to promote good behavior:

Freedom and dignity illustrate the difficulty. They are the possessions of the autonomous man of traditional theory, and they are essential to practices in which a person is held responsible for his conduct and given credit for his achievements. A scientific analysis shifts both the responsibility and the achievement to the environment. It also raises questions concerning "values." Who will use a technology and to what ends? Until these issues are resolved, a technology of behavior will continue to be rejected, and with it possibly the only way to solve our problems (Skinner, 1971, p. 25).

In place of traditional views on causation (e.g., free will and personal autonomy), Skinner (1981) urged that science accept a new conception for the source of behavior. That conception was his triad of selection by consequences found at the levels of natural selection, operant conditioning, and culture. He concluded (p. 504), "So long as we cling to the view that a person is an initiating doer, actor, or causer of behavior, we shall probably continue to neglect the conditions which must be changed if we are to solve our problems." Skinner's hopes have yet to be realized. Moreover, while radical behaviorists continue to research and apply their results to practical situations, psychology itself has moved in another direction, away from Radical Behaviorism. The radical behaviorists, themselves, have explored that phenomenon.

Radical Behaviorism Today

Radical Behaviorism and the rest of psychology are uneasy partners at best. On the one hand, all psychologists recognize Skinner as one of a small handful of eminent twentieth century researchers and theorists. But on the other hand, the research and practice of Radical Behaviorism and nearly all of the rest of psychology hardly ever overlap or affect each other.

This situation was dramatically illustrated by Morris et al. (2005) when they described how an earlier article (Morris et al., 2004) they had written about Skinner and how much of his research incorporated biology had been rejected by five nonbehavior analytic journals. Ultimately, they published it in *The Behavior Analyst*, and then had to respond to inquiries about why they had published it there, in a place where the "readership was already aware of Skinner's views and that the paper should have appeared in a journal whose readers had more to gain" (Morris et al., 2005, p. 169). Their reply was simple: their article had been rejected by five other generalist journals. They observed that behavior analysis had become isolated from the rest of psychology for a variety of reasons. In addition, Skinner's views on what he

PHOTO 11.8 B. F. Skinner
Credit: Getty Images

termed the science of behavior are often unknown or distorted by mainstream psychology faculty and students.

Of all of the neobehaviorist approaches, only his remains vital today. But that vitality is only seen in a relatively small and remote corner of psychology's garden. As Segal and Lachman (1972, pp. 53–54) noted:

> After World War II . . . major formal and theoretical advances outside psychology in finite mathematics, computer technology, information theory, and philosophy of science . . . gave rise to procedures and ideas applicable to formulations in competition with the behaviorist approaches. Problems within S-R behaviorism which were generally conceived to be empirically resolvable proved to be intractable. The strong neobehaviorist positions have weakened so considerably in the face of this competition that neobehaviorism can hardly be identified. Thus, the justification for the domination of psychology by neobehaviorism has eroded, as has the domination itself.

THE TREND TOWARD COGNITIVISM

The simple Hollywood plot line for psychology might read, "Psychology finds mind, psychology loses mind, psychology finds mind again." Two of the neobehaviorists in this chapter fit the first two scenes of that script. Hull and Skinner wished to create a mindless psychology. Tolman tried to "find mind again" but mostly skirted around the issue of mind. In fairness, however, he did not have the full benefit of the computer model that emerged after World War II. Also, the *zeitgeist* he lived in punished references to mentalism. All three of these neobehaviorist approaches relied heavily upon the use of animal subjects as models for human behavior. In fact, psychologists of the neobehaviorist era were often characterized as "rat runners," an apt characterization.

Students may wonder if modern Behaviorism is passé or even dead. Roediger (2004) argued otherwise. He provided scenarios designed to illustrate Behaviorism's role in today's psychology. In the first one, he speculated that cognitive psychology represented a kind of intellectual revolution that attracted graduate students away from behaviorist's animal labs and towards new cognitive research problems. In his second scenario, he wondered if the problems behaviorists were attacking had become too focused and had missed the bigger picture. The third scenario offered that there was nothing wrong with modern Behaviorism with its adherents numbering some 12,000 psychologists working on animal and human research problems. For his fourth scenario, he leaned on Tulving's observation that there are now two separate psychologies, one that studies behavior and the other that studies mind. Both views only overlap slightly and, like humpty dumpty, may never become whole again. In his final scenario, he offered that maybe the behaviorists had won the war and managed to convert all psychologists to Behaviorism. In the end, he leaves the decision of Behaviorism's health and prognosis for others to decide.

With the exception of Radical Behaviorism, most of contemporary psychology has been dominated by a new cognitive paradigm, one derived from the sources outside of Neobehaviorism. Cognitive psychology's road to its current dominant position has been rough and rocky (see

Chapter 14). The next Chapter 12 details the beginnings of that long journey as it examines the rise of Gestalt psychology and its subsequent fate. Jenkins (1976) provided a comprehensive review of entire behaviorist and neobehaviorist era and subsequent research by Spence, Estes, Rescorla and Wagner, and Seligman. The interactions between those later theorists and the conflicting interpretations of data by cognitive psychologists are covered in Chapter 14.

THEN AND NOW
RATS IN PSYCHOLOGY

Lockard (1968, p. 734) noted that "the albino rat . . . occupied the laboratory as the result of a chance chain of circumstances." Watson was one of the first beneficiaries having received his rats from a colony established earlier at Chicago. Tolman, Hull, and Skinner all used albino rats in their research. Tolman even went so far as to dedicate his book, *Purposive Behavior in Animals and Men* (1932), to the "white rat." At midcentury, comparative psychologist Frank Beach documented just how pervasive the use of the albino white rat or *Rattus norvegicus* had become. He wrote (Beach, 1950, p. 119):

> one cannot escape the conclusion that psychologists . . . have tended to concentrate upon one animal species and one type of behavior in that species. Perhaps it would be appropriate to change the title of our journal to read "The Journal of Rat Learning."

The behavior in question was learning and his analysis of journal articles demonstrated that studies of conditioning and learning had exceeded all other topics in every year but one during the period spanning from 1927 to 1948. What has happened since then?

The short answer is that both the number of animal species studied has increased and that the topics studied are wider too. In addition, the studies using white rats have declined precipitously. Shettleworth (2009, p. 215) wrote, "the classic criticisms of Beach and others regarding undue focus on a small number of species do not apply to contemporary research on comparative cognition . . . the range of problems being studied is also much broader than in the past." Psychology has moved away from its once dominant animal model and today continues to study human behavior and a much broader range of animals, both for their own sake as well as to shed light on human behavior.

SUMMARY

Neobehaviorism gradually replaced Watson's Behaviorism. Two of its principal theorists, Tolman and Hull, created systems no longer part of modern psychology. B.F. Skinner's system, Radical Behaviorism, is still a part of modern psychology, albeit a small part.

Tolman created Purposive Behaviorism, a system that sought cognitive relationships between stimuli and between stimuli and responses. He believed that animals (he popularized the use of albino rats in psychology) and humans were goal directed. He also believed that analyzing the cognitive maps inside the heads of organisms was possible. Tolman was one of the few American psychologists who had spent time in Europe studying the Gestalt movement.

Hull, unlike Tolman, attempted to create an overarching system similar to those of Newton and Euclid. Furthermore, he believed that by seeking for and identifying the proper variables he could explain learning mechanistically. He, too, worked with rats nearly exclusively near the end of his career. Ultimately, his system remained incomplete, and following his death disappeared from psychology.

Skinner's Radical Behaviorism was closer to biology than anything else. Using Darwinian logic, he believed that the environment selected consequences for organisms. The twist was that he defined the environment differently. For him, the environment contained two parts: a public part and a private part. Moreover, the same rules applied in both. Skinner was an environmental determinist who believed that much of psychology outside of his Radical Behaviorism was wrong or misguided.

12 GESTALT PSYCHOLOGY

ZEITGEIST

A Short History of Modern Germany

The history of Gestalt psychology is intimately connected to the history of modern Germany. Unlike France and Britain, Germany only emerged as a modern unified nation state in the late 19th century following the Franco-Prussian war (1870–1871). The new German Empire was a constitutional monarchy with the Kaiser (emperor) at its head. The first Kaiser, Wilhelm I, had Otto von Bismarck as his chancellor; he worked to make Germany a nation capable of competing militarily and economically with Britain and France. Through rapid industrialization and urbanization Germany quickly achieved those goals.

Following the death of Wilhelm I in 1888, the new Kaiser, Wilhelm II, relieved Bismarck of his duties and set a new course seeking to expand German influence beyond Europe. That meant becoming a colonial power. Wilhelm II expanded the German military and stirred up a diplomatic crisis with France over Morocco prior to World War I. Complicated defensive alliances with Austria–Hungary contributed to Germany's entry into the World War I. All sides expected a short war; after four years of trench warfare on the Western Front, the entry of the United States into the war, and a successful naval blockade by Britain, Germany was forced into an armistice by November 1918. After, the Kaiser abdicated and a German republic was proclaimed. Almost immediately, revolution broke out in Germany with one side trying to duplicate the success of the Russian Bolsheviks and the other attempting to restore the old order. Nearly a year later and mostly because of army intervention, the revolution ended having changed little politically or socially. The 1919 Treaty of Versailles ending the war imposed stiff penalties on Germany: the loss of all of its overseas colonies and portions of its European territory. Plus, it demanded enormous monetary reparations for having started the war.

The next 14 years, the Weimar Republic, were tumultuous. Hyperinflation hit hard in 1923, raising the prices of ordinary products such as bread and butter from a few marks to billions of marks. The value of money dropped so quickly that people rushed to buy goods as soon as they were paid their salaries and before prices went up again later in the day. Many lost everything they owned. The establishment of a new currency ended the inflationary cycle but the wounds were long-lasting. Paradoxically, the next few years led to a German renaissance in the arts and sciences. Berlin became a cosmopolitan world capital hosting a new kind of *avant garde* experiment in social mores. During this period new plays and cinema thrived, German scientists won Nobel Prizes, the Bauhaus school of architecture evolved, and the cabaret emerged as a popular form of entertainment. It was the German version of the Roaring Twenties. The worldwide stock market crash of 1929 hit Germany hard. The last years of the Weimar Republic saw increased factionalism, fighting in the streets between armed groups, and political intransigence. In this atmosphere, Adolph Hitler and his Nazi party grew quickly by appealing to a mythical German past and promising an end to chaos.

The Weimar Republic ceased to exist in January 1933 when Hitler was named chancellor. His Nazi party quickly moved to squash all opposition. German Jews were targeted early, including world-class scientists such as Albert Einstein. German psychology and science, which up to this point was arguably the best in the world, came to an abrupt near halt. Scientists, artists, performers, and authors left Germany; many ended up in the United States (see Chapter 1).

Gestalt psychology was deeply affected by its forced expulsion from Germany. The history of psychology, itself, was brutally altered by the events following Hitler's accession to power. Toomela (2007a) argued that those events led to the abandonment of the methods and goals of pre-World War II German–Austrian psychology and that since then (p. 10, original italics), "*modern mainstream psychology can be understood as a direct continuation of pre-WWII North American psychology.*" Meaning that psychology today would be much different had Gestalt psychology continued to flourish in a Europe without Nazism. Many of its findings remain in modern mainstream psychology, but no one can say what the history of psychology would have been otherwise.

LEARNING OBJECTIVE

1. Imagine how modern psychology might look today had Hitler not come to power and where American Neobehaviorism had to interact with German gestalt psychology on equal terms.

PREVIEW

The antecedents to Gestalt psychology mostly centered around the phenomenon of *melody* and attempts to explain it. Ehrenfel's concept of *gestalt quality* presaged the later definition of a *gestalt*. Other early work included Mach's explanation of the *Doppler Effect* and his discovery of *Mach Bands*. Wertheimer's description of the *phi phenomenon* put Gestalt psychology on the map as did his elucidation of the *Gestalt principles of perception*. From the beginning, Gestalt psychologists considered themselves as scientists attempting to discover causal relationships between gestalts and underlying physiological mechanisms. They also borrowed freely from physics appropriating concepts such as *force fields, isomorphism,* and *field theory.* Wertheimer's early research on *mathematical thinking* was an example of *cross-cultural psychology*.

Gestalt psychology was broad in its approach going beyond perception to include learning (human and animal), thinking, and social psychology. Köhler's research on *insight learning* and *transposition*, Zeigarnik's work on *memory*, Wertheimer's book on *thinking*, and Lewin's and Asch's *social psychological studies* all testified to the breadth of Gestalt psychology. Gestalt psychology lives on in 21st century psychology; one just has to know where to look.

INTRODUCTION

This chapter details the rise of Gestalt psychology, which developed and grew primarily in Germany at about the same time as Behaviorism and Neobehaviorism were coming into ascendance in the United States. The earliest glimmers of Gestalt psychology came in the late 19th century as Ernst Mach and Christian von Ehrenfels struggled to understand sensation and perception. Both realized that musical melodies persisted despite radical alterations in tempo, key, or instrument. Ehrenfels coined the phrase "*Gestaltqualitäten*" or Gestalt Quality in an attempt to capture the phenomenon of melody which was not just a collection of elemental notes strung together in time. Instead, melody was a gestalt, a thing in and of itself. Ehrenfels's idea was influential but incomplete.

His student, Max Wertheimer, was the first to expand upon the still evolving idea that a melody could be psychologically real and irreducible to more fundamental units (see further). The breakthrough for Gestalt psychology came when he later discovered the phi phenomenon, or the apparent movement of a spot between two rapidly flashing light sources. Fortuitously, Wertheimer found himself in the company of two younger researchers: Wolfgang Köhler and Kurt Koffka. Together, the three of them became the founders of Gestalt psychology. In Germany from 1912 to 1933, Gestalt psychology grew quickly and threatened to become a viable alternative to American behavioral psychology. But, history intervened in the form of Adolph Hitler and the rise of Nazi Germany. All three of the founders and many of their students fled Germany, most of them at peril of their lives. The move to the United States stalled the further growth of Gestalt psychology. Few American behaviorists were congenial to their ideas and theories. Furthermore, the displaced Gestalt psychologists were mostly unable to regain the traction and momentum they had enjoyed in Germany. They trained few new students, and two of them, Wertheimer and Koffka, died young.

Despite those obstacles, a second generation of Gestalt psychologists emerged. Two social psychologists, Kurt Lewin and Solomon Asch, influenced American psychology greatly. Lewin extended gestalt ideas into social psychology and personality. Asch conducted groundbreaking research in perception and conformity. Rock and Palmer (1990) argued that Gestalt psychology has succeeded in becoming a major part of 21st century psychology in the areas of perception, learning, and cognition. Indeed, Gestalt psychology and its ideas are still inspiring research in psychology today.

Wherever a naturally occurring and energy-efficient phenomenon or process exists that seems irreducible to simpler constituent parts, researchers should suspect that a **gestalt** exists. What are gestalts? The simplest answer is that they are coherent wholes, but that is too simple a definition. For the most part, gestalts are already present in the environment, either as percepts, solutions to problems, or ways of social interaction. The Gestalt psychologists saw themselves as explorers, discoverers, and chroniclers of gestalts. The best way to understand their approach and what they meant by a gestalt is to examine the history leading to Gestalt psychology.

LEARNING OBJECTIVE
2. Recall a time when you personally discovered a gestalt.

ANTECEDENTS TO GESTALT PSYCHOLOGY

The earliest origins of Gestalt psychology occur in the 1860s in German-speaking Europe. By then, physics was no longer the only dominant science. Biology, bolstered by Darwin's theory of evolution, and psychology, because of Fechner's psychophysics, had become the new scientific triumvirate. Ernst Mach, himself a young scientist at the time, later wrote:

> Physics, physiology, and psychology are indestructibly connected, such that each one of these sciences can only be successful in combination with the others, and yet each one of them is an auxiliary science to the other two (Quoted in Heidelberger, 2004, p. 160).

Mach lived a life immersed in all three of those academic disciplines, contributing original work in physics, psychology, and biology. While he is most remembered today for his contributions to physics, it is a mistake to neglect his work in biology and psychology. In physics, he explained the reasons behind the **Doppler Effect** using simple apparatus. Mach demonstrated that the Doppler Effect was not an illusion. Instead, it was a physical phenomenon. As a noisy object approached an observer, the sound waves from it arrived faster, raising their pitch because their own speed was added to the speed of the moving object. After, as the object passed by the observer and receded, the sound waves arrived more slowly, lowering their pitch because the object creating them was moving away. Mach, thus, demonstrated a physical cause for a psychophysical phenomenon.

LEARNING OBJECTIVE
3. Explain why the Doppler Effect is not an auditory illusion.

Mach is most famous for the physical concept that bears his name: Mach numbers. The development of bullets that could travel faster than sound was the impetus for that research. Using high-speed photographic techniques he developed, Mach explained how objects that exceeded the speed of sound caused the now familiar sonic boom.

Mach used evolutionary theory to explain the development of science itself. He was one of the first scientists to write about science as a way of thinking. For him, science was the culmination of a long natural history of cognition that began with simple animal behaviors such as reflexes and perception. The evolution of memory was a major milestone in the process. After, came everyday thinking, followed by scientific thought. Mach considered evolution as necessary for any adequate scientific description of the world. He believed that "the purpose of science is to give the most economical description of nature as possible" (Pojman, 2009, np).

Mach also heavily influenced psychology and may be considered to be one of the earliest Gestalt psychologists. His analysis of **Mach Bands** (see Figure 12.1) led to a new conception of the relationship between sensations and perceptions. Much like Kant before him, he argued that the sense organs themselves preprocessed sensations before sending them to the brain. In other words, the eyes, ears, and other sense organs did not simply send unaltered sensory information to the brain for analysis. Instead, the sense organs first interpreted stimuli, altered them, and then sent that information to the brain for further processing. In the case of the Mach Bands, the preprocessing he discovered was later explained by the physiological process of lateral inhibition, where the sensors inside the eye pay more attention to areas of contrast than they do to areas of constancy. The Mach Bands are illusory because they are artifacts of the perceptual process, not true representations of stimuli. Thus, early on in the history of what was to become Gestalt psychology, an explicit connection was sought between sensation and physiology.

Mach argued that observers did not have direct access to the external world. Instead, the observers themselves, along with their perceptual processes, created an experiential version of the real world. He argued further that it was the relations between stimuli that were most important to perception, not the stimuli themselves. Any other interpretation, he argued, would lead to chaos. Much like Wertheimer later, Mach seized upon music and melody as powerful examples. He was one of the first to realize that melody depended upon the tonal relationship of notes, not upon the notes themselves. Mach's notions were seminal to later Gestalt theorists. Christian von Ehrenfels took Mach's ideas and coined a new term—form qualities or *Gestaltqualitäten*. With that, the Gestalt psychology genie was truly out of the bottle.

Christian von Ehrenfels's (1890) article *"Über 'Gestaltqualitäten'"* (On "Gestalt Qualities") was the most influential early article on Gestalt psychology. In it he refined Mach's early ideas. Where Mach saw a gestalt such as a melody as the unitary perception of two things, the notes over a time span, Ehrenfels saw the melody as *the* gestalt itself. Thus, Ehrenfels created a completely new psychological entity, the gestalt, which could be analyzed on its own without having to worry about analyzing its component parts. Wertheimer studied with Ehrenfels and later cited his article as one of the main inspirations to the founding of Gestalt psychology. However, there were other sources of inspiration floating in the *zeitgeist* as well. One of those was William James's approach to psychology; another was the discovery of physical force fields and their effects.

William James had long opposed Wundtian elementism. In its place he had substituted his stream of consciousness approach (see Chapter 9). James strongly resisted any attempt to study consciousness by any means that involved its analysis into constituent parts. Such attempts, he believed, would destroy the phenomena themselves. Carl Stumpf (see Chapter 7), who maintained a lifelong personal relationship with James, passed on Jamesian ideas to his students Kurt Koffka and Wolfgang Köhler. They, together with Max Wertheimer, provided the final impetus for the founding of Gestalt psychology.

FIGURE 12.1 ■ Mach Bands

Ever since Newton, psychologists and other scientists had looked toward physics for inspiration. The first Gestalt psychologists were no exception. Köhler, especially, was drawn to the latest findings in physics through his studies under the famous physicist Max Planck. Much of Köhler's research late in his life was devoted to finding an isomorphic (point-to-point) relationship between the outside world and the brain (he never found it). Einstein and Wertheimer were personal friends for most of their adult lives and often discussed the relationships between physics and psychology. The discovery of force fields (e.g., magnetism and electricity) late in the 19th century was of prime importance to the gestaltists (see Figure 12.2). The fact that magnetism and electricity exhibited a

FIGURE 12.2 ■ Iron Fillings Reveal the Field Surrounding the Poles of a Magnetic Force Field

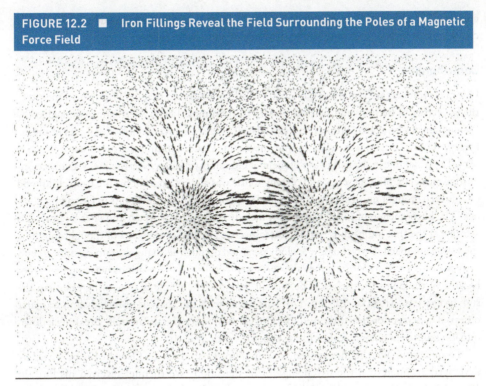

Credit: iStock/Stephan Hoerold

higher-order and predictable patterns gave Gestalt psychologists the hope that they might discover similar patterns in the brain. Thus, the convergence of several factors: the discovery of the gestalt itself, a widespread reaction against Wundtian elementism, and new data from physics helped set the stage for Gestalt psychology to emerge during the early part of the 20th century. The universally acknowledged founder of Gestalt psychology was Max Wertheimer whose analysis of the thinking of the Vedda tribe from Sri Lanka marked the first instance of full-blown Gestalt psychology.

THE FIRST GENERATION OF GESTALT PSYCHOLOGISTS

Max Wertheimer (1880–1943)

Biography

Max Wertheimer was born in Prague where his father ran a successful business college. The Wertheimer family lived comfortably while simultaneously straddling two cultures, Jewish and German. Later, Max Wertheimer's Jewish ancestry would put him and his family at risk of their lives and force them to emigrate first to Czechoslovakia and then to the United States to escape Nazism. Wertheimer's father groomed his other son, Walter, to succeed him as director of the business college. Max, on the other hand, resisted his father's wishes and obtained a more traditional education. After attending a Catholic grammar school and a local gymnasium, he enrolled at the University of Prague to study law. In addition, he took a wide variety of other courses and after two years switched to the study of philosophy and psychology.

Contributions

One of his teachers at Prague was Christian von Ehrenfels. From Prague, Wertheimer moved to the University of Berlin where he studied with Carl Stumpf. There, Wertheimer worked in the Phonogram Archives that Stumpf had established. Those archives collected samples of music, preserved on wax cylinders, from around the world. Understanding the psychology of music played a pivotal role in the early development of Gestalt psychology. Wertheimer was an accomplished musician. Singing songs and playing music was always a part of his life from childhood on. He even brought musical instruments to class in order to illustrate points in Gestalt psychology. The phenomenon of the persistence of melody first noted by Mach and later by Ehrenfels was one of the first indications that the introspective analysis of elements of thought might be the wrong approach to psychology. Melody persisted despite the changes in notes, musical key, or type of instrument. Musical melodies persisted because of the relations between notes, not because of the notes themselves. The Gestalt maxim, "the whole is something else than the sum of its parts," (Koffka, 1935, p. 176) first began with the analysis of melody and was later observed in perception, learning, and thinking. A melody is a gestalt; a whole. Breaking it down into its component notes reveals nothing about the melody itself.

From Berlin, Wertheimer moved to Würzburg to study with Oswald Külpe where he developed an interest in the psychology of lie detection. Wertheimer received his PhD in 1904; the topic was "Experimental investigations of diagnosis on the facts of a case." He published several other articles on forensic topics soon after. A dispute with Carl Jung (see Chapter 13) over who had first published research about methodologies of lie detection soured Wertheimer's interest in the topic. Despite possessing a PhD, he could not yet teach in a German university or supervise graduate students. Like all other European PhD graduates of his day he had to complete yet another thesis (the habilitation thesis) in order to secure a university position. He spent time visiting and studying at various universities before settling down in Vienna. There, he worked with experts who were studying the effects of brain lesions on speech, the aphasias. Following that work, he did ethnographic research on the music of the Vedda nation of Sri Lanka. Their songs had been recorded on wax cylinders and preserved at the Phonogram Archives in Berlin. Another early research project concerned the mathematical thinking of non-European peoples. Unlike many of his contemporaries, he did not assume that Aboriginal peoples possessed inferior or primitive modes of thinking. This research was his first to use the gestalt point of view explicitly. King and Wertheimer (2005, p. 96) remarked:

> The entire article is imbued with the Gestalt mode. It appears to be the first extensive instance of this kind of approach, and is unmistakably a product of Gestalt-theoretical thinking, a way of thinking that was clearly hinted at in the 1910 paper on the music of the Veddas . . . the paper makes it clear that the early Gestalt mode of approaching issues occurred in cognition, the psychology of thinking, and "Völkerspsychologie."

Wertheimer's next research area, apparent motion, made him famous and qualified him to teach and supervise graduate research. The research on apparent motion, later called the phi phenomenon, was not the first example of Gestalt psychology. It was, however, the datum that caused others to take notice of Gestalt psychology for the first time.

The Phi Phenomenon

No one knows exactly what Wertheimer observed in 1910 through the train window as he was traveling from Vienna to begin a vacation. One version (Hunt, 2007) stated that he noticed that the more distant telegraph poles, houses, and hilltops along the route seemed to be speeding along with the train. He realized the "movement" he was observing had to be somehow coming from his brain. To an observer outside the train, all of those stimuli would appear stationary. Regardless of what the inspiration was, it caused him to stop at the next station, Frankfurt, and buy a common toy available at the time—a zoetrope or stroboscope. The rapidly spinning slits made the slightly different images on the inside of the toy appear to move. He quickly dropped his vacation plans and went to the University of Frankfurt where one of his former teachers, Friedrich Schumann, was working. He made laboratory space available to Wertheimer along with a tachistoscope of his own design. That instrument allowed its users to present stimuli under accurate timing conditions far beyond those of the toy zoetrope. Schumann also volunteered two of his graduate students, Wolfgang Köhler and Kurt Koffka, as research subjects. This lucky confluence of people and events marked the beginning of Gestalt psychology as a new movement in psychology.

But, what exactly had Wertheimer found and why was it so important? Steinman et al. (2000), while teaching about Gestalt psychology, found that their students were "skeptical about Wertheimer's publication launching a revolution in perception" (p. 2257). Those students already knew that motion pictures and nickelodeons had preceded the discovery of the phi phenomenon, so they wondered what was so new and unusual about it in 1912. The authors concluded that psychology textbook authors failed to describe the phi phenomenon correctly. Furthermore, they inferred that Boring (1942) had reversed the definitions of the phi phenomenon and its complementary partner, optimal movement (the beta phenomenon):

> He [Boring] got only one thing wrong. Namely, the φ-phenomenon is observed near simultaneity and not near successivity . . . The φ-phenomenon is not observed when the switching speed is increased from successivity towards optimal movement (β). This rather mysterious error in Boring's influential book probably led to the confusion about Wertheimer's revolutionary phenomenon that is evident in most contemporary textbooks (Steinman et al., 2000, p. 2259).

Simply put, the phi phenomenon is *not* the apparent movement of an object to and fro caused by displaying two similar visual stimuli (e.g., dots or lines) alternately in a darkened room. Instead, the phi phenomenon that Wertheimer and his subjects observed was the movement of a spot between the two stimuli that occurred when the stimuli were presented nearly simultaneously. Such spots were not real; they were created by the brain. Furthermore, observers saw both stimuli and the moving spot at all times.

Wertheimer's article on the phi phenomenon, while groundbreaking, provided only the sparsest description of the phenomenon itself. His lectures and other verbal communication were much more influential in spreading the finding. Wertheimer was always at his best while speaking and often confessed that he had trouble writing about his ideas. Also, he allowed his ideas to sit, unpublished, for years before finally putting them on paper. Students who heard his lectures, both in Germany and later in the United States, fell into two distinct camps. They either became avid disciples or were completely lost. Wertheimer published the least of the three original gestalt psychologists but was always considered to be the fountainhead of the movement. For example, Koffka (1935, pp. 53–54) wrote:

> Wertheimer had just completed his experiments on the perception of motion in which Köhler and I had served as the chief observers . . . on that afternoon he said something which impressed me more than anything else, and that was his idea about the function of a physiological theory in psychology, the relation between consciousness and the underlying physiological processes, or in our new terminology, between the behavioural and the physiological field. To state it in these new terms, however, is not quite fair, because this very statement was only made possible by Wertheimer's idea; before, nobody thought of a physiological or, for that matter, of a behavioural *field*. [original italics]

Wertheimer's discovery of the phi phenomenon was more than the simple elucidation of a new finding. He sought to explain the physiological basis for it and ruled out, experimentally, older explanations that argued that eye movements were the cause. The physiological mechanism he proposed—short circuits in the cortex—has not stood the test of time. Indeed, modern psychology has yet to provide a universally accepted physiological explanation for the phi phenomenon. From the beginning, Gestalt psychologists saw themselves as experimenters and posited a causal relationship between the molar phenomena they studied and yet-to-be discovered neural mechanisms. Further, their vision for Gestalt psychology went far beyond the area of perception alone. The Gestalt psychologists were proposing a complete reworking of the entire psychological enterprise. Wertheimer, late in his career, was more interested in the gestalt analysis of thinking and problem-solving. Still, the impact of Gestalt psychology on the study of perception was immense. Wertheimer's (1923) early research was especially so.

Gestalt Principles of Perception

Gestalt psychology developed quickly following the discovery of the phi phenomenon. During World War I, Wertheimer and other psychologists were drafted into the German army. There, Wertheimer performed various research projects including one with Erich von Hornbostel (Volmar, 2014) in which they developed an instrument capable of precisely determining the direction from the user to a noise source (e.g., the discharge of a cannon). In 1916, Wertheimer moved back to the University of Berlin as an instructor. Quickly, Berlin became the nerve center of Gestalt psychology. In addition to Wertheimer, its Institute of Psychology, led by Köhler, included Hornbostel and Kurt Lewin as faculty. One of its legacies to psychology was Wertheimer's (1923) principles of gestalt perception which still grace the pages of every general psychology textbook today (see Figure 12.3).

FIGURE 12.3 ■ The Gestalt Laws of Perceptual Organization

These drawings have different interpretations. Most people report seeing one interpretation and then the other but never both simultaneously.

Wertheimer (1923) summarized gestalt principles of perception naming proximity, similarity, common fate, set, direction, closure, good curve, figure-ground, and past experience as the main ones. He also argued that for past experience:

> Some of our apprehensions are determined in this way. Often arbitrary material can be arranged in arbitrary form and, after sufficient drill, made habitual . . . And yet, despite its plausibility, the doctrine of past experience brushes aside the real problems of apprehension much too easily (p. 86).

Thus, he acknowledged the role of experience in perception but believed it accounted for only a small piece of the puzzle. Today, modern psychology texts (e.g., Weiten, 2010) typically focus on a shorter list of Gestalt principles. Weiten's text lists figure-ground, proximity, closure, similarity, simplicity, and continuity. It is tempting to limit Gestalt psychology's effect on psychology to perception only, but that is a mistake.

As Rock and Palmer (1990, p. 61) pointed out when they wrote about the long-term influence of Gestalt psychology:

> The list of major perceptual phenomena they elucidated—grouping, figure-ground organization, frames of reference, figural goodness, and apparent motion . . . is impressive. Although it is logically possible that these discoveries could have been made independently of their methods and theoretical beliefs, it seems unlikely. The Gestalt attack against Structuralism was devastatingly effective. In addition, the Gestaltists were victorious over the Behaviorists in their clash regarding the nature of learning, thinking and social psychology.

LEARNING OBJECTIVE

4. Defend the importance of including the gestalt principles of perception in 21st century general psychology textbooks.

From these perceptual beginnings, Gestalt psychology branched out to affect psychology as a whole. The history of Gestalt psychology, however, is intimately tied to political events in Germany following World War I. The rise of Adolph Hitler in 1933 altered the life courses of Wertheimer and many other Gestalt psychologists. Because many of them were Jewish, Wertheimer and nearly all of his colleagues were forced to leave Germany. Had they stayed they would have, doubtlessly, fallen into the hands of the Gestapo and been killed in the concentration camps.

Wertheimer's Later Career

At the University of Berlin, Wertheimer began to turn his interests away from perception and toward the psychology of thinking. As always, he was slow in turning his ideas into print. His magnum opus on the subject, *Productive Thinking* (Wertheimer, 1945), was not published until after his death. As Gestalt psychology achieved worldwide prominence in the 1920s, all three of its founders were invited to appointments in the United States. Only Wertheimer declined. His negotiations with Harvard University were protracted and ultimately failed. One reason for his not accepting the American offer was that he was also in negotiations with his old school, the University of Frankfurt. When offered a chairmanship there along with the rank of full professor, he accepted. After he arrived, Frankfurt rapidly became a center for research in the social sciences. Theologian Paul Tillich taught there, as did psychologists Theodor Adorno, Erich Fromm, and philosopher Herbert Marcuse.

But, the Nazi storm clouds were growing. After Hitler was named chancellor of Germany in 1933, change came quickly. Sooner than most, Wertheimer realized that his days in Germany were numbered. He had never listened to Hitler speak on the radio, but after doing so, Wertheimer and his family left Germany the next day (King & Wertheimer, 2005). Soon after, he accepted an offer to teach at the newly formed New School for Social Research in New York City where he taught until his death. Because Koffka and Köhler had published far more than he had and because they had been in the United States longer, they had become the public faces for Gestalt psychology. However, they both always acknowledged Wertheimer as the founder of Gestalt psychology. Once in the United States, Wertheimer was quickly and cordially accepted into the American Psychological Association and the Society of Experimental Psychologists. He taught his first courses at the New School for Social Research in German, but soon began to lecture in thickly accented English. He was on friendly personal terms with Boring and Hull although they did not agree with his version of psychology. He supervised many graduate student theses, most of which dealt with thinking and not perception. His new emphasis on thinking led him to finally produce a book on the topic, *Productive Thinking* (1945). He began to write the book in 1935. He finished it just before his death eight years later and it was published posthumously. The book is short; it is only 224 pages long. Its first five chapters covered problem-solving using mostly geometric and mathematical examples. The last two chapters described how Galileo and Einstein arrived at their historic discoveries. Throughout, the focus was on elegant as opposed to "ugly" solutions. Commenting on his examples, he concluded:

> We found factors and operations at work—essential to thinking—which had not been realized by the traditional approaches, or had even been neglected by them. The very

nature of these operations, e.g., of grouping, of centering, of reorganization . . . is alien to the gist of the traditional approaches . . . the features and operations described are of a characteristic nature: they are not piecemeal, they are related to the whole-characteristics, they function with reference to such characteristics (pp. 189–190).

To Wertheimer, Gestalt psychology could encompass nearly any aspect of human or animal behavior. The key was not to break down natural processes artificially; instead it was to look for an organic whole, a gestalt, and examine it concretely, functionally, and experimentally. His colleague, Wolfgang Köhler, was the first Gestalt psychologist to study animal learning. His research on insight learning in apes challenged existing views of learning as a trial and error process.

PHOTO 12.1 Max Wertheimer

Wolfgang Köhler (1887–1967)

Biography

Wolfgang Köhler was born in Reval, Estonia (modern Tallinn), where his father ran a German school. Köhler returned to Germany when he was six. Academics were stressed in his family; all five of his brothers and sisters were well educated. Köhler himself attended three universities: Tübingen, Bonn, and Berlin. Although he loved physics and studied at Berlin under Max Planck, the famous physicist, Köhler's research and PhD degree were in psychology. He was teaching at Frankfurt when Wertheimer conducted his phi phenomenon research and served as one of the original participants.

Contributions

Köhler was immediately attracted to Gestalt psychology. After Koffka's arrival at Frankfurt, all three engaged in long conversations about their new approach to psychology. Soon after, however, Köhler was appointed by Stumpf as the second director of the newly established Primate Station on the island of Tenerife off the west coast of Africa. The station had been established so that "the behavior of the chimpanzee, gorilla, orangutan, and gibbon would be studied and compared, permitting a better evaluation of these animals on an evolutionary scale" (Teuber, 1994, p. 552). Tenerife was picked because of its relatively constant temperate weather and its nearness to Cameroon, then a German colony and a place where apes could be captured in the wild and then transported to Tenerife for study under more controlled conditions. The apes had preceded the arrival of the first director, Eugen Teuber. Upon his arrival he quickly found and developed a site, hired an animal keeper, and began filmed observational studies. Teuber's research focused on the animal's emotional behavior and their communication abilities. However, once Köhler arrived, he and Teuber began studying the apes' cognitive abilities. Working together, they set up a fruit basket that was suspended in the air by means of a rope and pulley. At the end of the rope, a large ring hooked onto a tree limb held the fruit in place.

Köhler hoped that the apes would examine the rigging of the basket and simply unhook the ring and get the fruit. That never happened. Instead, a chimpanzee named Sultan learned to dislodge the fruit from the basket by vigorously shaking the rope and causing the fruit to fall to the ground. Köhler realized that his initial experiment was too complicated. After Teuber left for home and because Köhler believed he, too, only had a year to conduct his research, he quickly went to work. He could not foresee or imagine that he would end up staying on Tenerife for nearly six years. The outbreak of World War I in August 1914 was the event that led to his long sojourn on the island.

Following the failure of the fruit basket experiment, Köhler devised simpler tests for his animals. He provided them with wooden crates that they could move and stack. Later, he hung a banana out of reach from the netting that formed the roof of the animal enclosure. Sultan, eventually judged the smartest of the station's apes, solved the problem in about five minutes. But, his solution was unlike any previously described example of animal learning. Unlike Thorndike's cats, for instance, Sultan showed no evidence of trial-and-error learning. Instead, he first attempted to retrieve the banana by jumping up for it. When that failed, he quit trying for a short period. Then, he stood up, grabbed a box, and placed it *directly* under the banana. Now, he was close enough to jump up and grab it. From that point on, getting the banana was accomplished in the same way. Köhler named this type of learning as **insight learning**. It was characterized by the sudden appearance of a solution after a period of quiescence. Köhler interpreted Sultan's solution in gestalt terms. He believed that Sultan had reorganized the problem cognitively. The ape had somehow realized that putting the box right under the banana was the solution. Köhler devised other similar tests including hanging the banana higher so that boxes had to be stacked upon each other in order to retrieve the banana (see Photo 12.2), tests involving the use of sticks to retrieve food items, and detour tasks. He also compared the behavior of his apes to that of dogs, chickens, and a young child. (See more information on insight learning in Chapter 14.)

PHOTO 12.2 One of Köhler's Chimpanzees Stacking Boxes

Credit: Science Photo Library/Science Source

LEARNING OBJECTIVE

5. Identify how Sultan created a new gestalt when he solved the banana problem.

Another test he used demonstrated the phenomenon of **transposition**. He used chickens first and chimpanzees later. The chickens first learned to discriminate between two gray boxes, learning to choose the lighter shade. Next, Köhler tested them with the original light gray box and a newer one colored an even lighter gray. The chickens now chose the new lighter shade. Chimpanzees showed the same pattern; for the apes the stimuli varied in size not in color. Köhler concluded that both species had learned a *relationship* because neither picked the original training stimulus. Thus, he used Gestalt psychology to interpret his animal learning experiments. He believed he had demonstrated that his apes had exhibited intelligent behavior, a radical concept at the time. Remarkably while war raged in Europe, he wrote up his results and had them published while still at Tenerife. His book, *The Mentality of the Apes*, was published in German in 1917 and in English a few years later (Köhler, 1925). Although the book made him world famous, he mostly left animal research behind after his return to Germany.

Was there another reason for Köhler to stay at Tenerife so long? Ley (1990) researched Köhler's life on Tenerife. He discovered that Tenerife had been a strategic location for German naval and that German spies operated on Tenerife and other nearly islands. While he uncovered no direct evidence linking Köhler to those espionage operations, he found that Köhler knew the German spies, and that he may have housed a hidden radio set on the property of the Primate Station. Most likely, Köhler was *not* sent to Tenerife as a spy. Teuber (1994) disputed the account in Ley's book and he responded to her criticisms. Ley's book, if nothing else, provided intimate glimpses at Köhler's life and times, including details of his personal life largely unavailable elsewhere. For example, according to his second wife Lili (Ley, 1990, p. 202), who, in response to why Köhler had agreed to go to Tenerife, told him:

> She smiled fondly as she told me that Wolfgang was an "adventurous romantic"; it was the adventure that led him to accept the post . . . Mrs. Köhler explained that Americans don't understand people like Wolfgang, people who have two sides to their personalities—a public self and a private self. Americans are usually one way or the other. That is, an American who is a serious-minded scholar would be a serious-minded scholar all of the time; there would not be another side to his personality. Thus, many Americans may never have thought that Wolfgang was ever anything but a serious scholar. They certainly would not have guessed that he was an "adventurous romantic."

Interestingly, Köhler hardly ever spoke about his years at Tenerife afterward. Ley also discovered that his closest colleagues were still in awe of him and his accomplishments long after his death. Of course, whether or not he was a spy on Tenerife had no impact on his career as a psychologist.

Köhler's appointment to the chairmanship of the Psychological Institute of the University of Berlin, succeeding Stumpf, soon after his return from Tenerife surprised many because he was so young. Soon, he had put together what was perhaps the best collection of psychologists in the world at that time. Henle (1978) listed many of the faculty who worked at Berlin before Hitler came to power. Among the faculty she named: Kurt Lewin, Karl Duncker, Hedwig von Restorff, and Otto von Lauenstein. She wrote (p. 944):

The institute attracted students from many countries; and the ideas of Gestalt psychology were respected and were spreading in Germany and in other countries. It is possible that our science would be different today if that institute had been able to continue its work.

Before he finally resigned from Berlin, Köhler traveled twice to the United States. In the mid-1920s he taught at Clark University and in the mid-1930s at Harvard. After his time at Harvard he returned to Germany. Unlike Wertheimer and Koffka, who were Jews, Köhler was a Protestant. So, he did not need to flee Germany for religious reasons as they had. Nevertheless, when James Franck, a Jewish physicist at the University of Berlin, was fired, Köhler wrote an article protesting it. It was "the last anti-Nazi article to be published openly in Germany under the Nazi regime" (Henle, 1978, p. 940). Köhler fully expected the Nazis to arrest him and waited up all night (when the Nazis usually made such arrests) playing chamber music with friends. The Nazis never came for him. He resigned while still in the United States after discovering that personnel changes were being made at the Institute without his being consulted. He returned to Germany to settle his affairs and then accepted a faculty position at Swarthmore College in Pennsylvania where he remained for the rest of his career. In the United States, his research centered on the connection between cognition and physiology. He was particularly attracted to **field theory** and attempted to discover a connection between the electrical activity of the nervous system and behavior. Those experiments, however, did not find any such connection. After the end of World War II, he traveled back to Germany from time to time and taught courses at the Free University of Berlin, completing, partially at least, a kind of life circle. The third original Gestalt psychologist, Kurt Koffka, was the first to move to the United States and the first to describe Gestalt psychology to an English-speaking audience.

PHOTO 12.3 Wolfgang Köhler

Credit: Album/Alamy Stock Photo

Kurt Koffka (1886–1941)

Biography

Koffka was born in Berlin. His father and many of his relatives were lawyers. However, one of his uncles was a biologist and influenced him not to follow in the family's legal tradition. After graduating from a Berlin gymnasium, Koffka spent a year studying at the University of Edinburgh in Scotland. Unlike Wertheimer and Köhler, Koffka learned English early in life. He received his PhD from the University of Berlin; his dissertation topic concerned the teaching of rhythms. From Berlin, he first went to Würzburg and then to Frankfurt to work with Friedrich Schumann. Koffka and Köhler were his assistants. Koffka would later say that his early career in psychophysics had prepared him to accept Wertheimer's Gestalt psychology (Harrower-Erickson, 1942). Koffka soon moved to the nearby University of Giessen. He and his students published many experimental studies during that period. Tolman visited Koffka twice and was one of the first Americans to get a first-hand look at the emerging Gestalt school.

Contributions

Koffka's (1922) article in the *Psychological Bulletin* was the first concrete exposition of Gestalt psychology in English. Early on he wrote (p. 532):

> I shall try first of all to make my American readers understand what the theory purports to be. So far there exists no general presentation of the theory which marshals all of the facts upon which it rests; indeed, the general field of psychology has not, as yet, been treated from this point of view.

However, Koffka failed to live up to those words. Most of his article discussed perceptual research done by gestalt psychologists and left the long-term impression that Gestalt psychology was primarily concerned with perception. He was correct, however, in stating that the ideas behind Gestalt psychology had yet to be presented in print. Both he and Köhler would later publish books that better explained their new movement.

Koffka was the first of the three Gestaltists to move to the United States. After brief stints at Cornell and Wisconsin, he accepted a research professorship at Smith College. His contract allowed him five years without teaching duties or expectation of publication. An expedition to Uzbekistan to study people who had recently experienced widespread levels of social change led to his contracting a fever and being bedridden. During his long illness he drafted the first chapter of his book *The Principles of Gestalt Psychology* (Koffka, 1935). His book, however, proved to be difficult to read and did little to further the cause of Gestalt psychology in the United States. It did, however, extend the scope of Gestalt psychology beyond the study of perception. He argued that from the fundamental question of perception, "Why do things look as they do?" (p. 680) logically followed necessary structures: the perceptual field, the realization that behavior requires an environment, an ego, memory, learning, and social intercourse:

PHOTO 12.4 Kurt Koffka

Credit: Album/Alamy Stock Photo

> We have followed the principles of organization as they become manifest under diverse conditions, starting from the simplest and proceeding to those of higher and higher complexity . . . A gestalt is therefore a product of organization, organization the process that leads to a gestalt . . . organization as a category is diametrically opposed to mere juxtaposition or random distribution (pp. 682–683).

Following its publication he turned to other areas of interest: the humanities and ethics. He realized that those areas, too, were candidates for research by psychologists.

Near the end of his life and just prior to the outbreak of World War II, Koffka spent a year at Oxford University working with brain-injured patients. A book he had planned to write, *Human Behavior and its Modification by Brain Injuries*, never appeared in print due to his early death from heart disease (Harrower-Erickson, 1942). Thus, by 1943 two of the three original Gestalt psychologists had died. Despite being displaced and forced to emigrate they, nevertheless, managed to train students who were, to an extent, successful in further spreading Gestalt ideas to social psychology. Kurt Lewin and Solomon Asch would contribute mightily to the founding and early development of experimental social psychology.

THE SECOND GENERATION OF GESTALT PSYCHOLOGISTS

King and Wertheimer (2005) documented the growth of Gestalt psychology in Germany after World War I by looking at a "second generation" (p. 163) of Gestalt psychologists, primarily students of Wertheimer, Köhler, and Koffka. While space does not permit mention of all of those students, two deserve further treatment here. Kurt Lewin, easily the most prominent researcher of the second generation, was not a student of any of the three founders of Gestalt psychology. Instead, he completed his PhD under Stumpf at Berlin just prior to Köhler's arrival there. Another student was Solomon Asch, who studied under Wertheimer in the United States after completing his doctoral studies at Columbia University. After Wertheimer died, Asch took over his position at the New School of Social Research for a few years. Lewin and Asch eventually became prominent American social psychologists. They expanded Gestalt theory into new areas of psychology beyond perception and learning. Lewin applied it to personality and social dynamics, while Asch examined topics such as field dependence and independence, impression formation, and conformity.

Kurt Lewin (1890–1947)

Biography

When Lewin was born in Mogilno, it was a small village in Prussia (now Poland). He and his family were Jews during an era when anti-Semitism was rampant. Jews could not own land or serve as army officers (Lewin, 1998). When he was 15 his family moved to Berlin. He proved to be an excellent student, and after completing his preparatory studies, he eventually enrolled at the University of Berlin, hoping to become a medical doctor. Soon, however, he decided to study philosophy and psychology under Carl Stumpf. When World War I broke out he enlisted in the German Army. Wounded, he recovered and returned to Berlin as a faculty member where he became interested in Gestalt psychology.

Contributions

Before arriving at Berlin and while convalescing from his wounds, he wrote an article (Lewin, 1917/2009) presaging some of his later theoretical thinking. In it he argued that the same objects change markedly in the mind of observers depending whether they are home during peacetime or on the battlefield at war. A soldier might tear down a house for firewood whereas a peacetime neighbor would not:

> That which lies within the combat zone belongs to the soldier as his rightful property . . . Even something as barbaric as the burning of floors, doors, and furniture is utterly incomparable to similar treatment of house furniture under peacetime conditions (p. 205).

These early observations of his would be later fleshed out in gestalt fashion. He would eventually combine the environment, motivations, and tensions as all contributing to an ever-changing complex gestalt, the life space. Once established at Berlin, he quickly began to publish articles and train graduate students. One of his students, Bluma Zeigarnik, discovered the phenomenon that bears her name, the **Zeigarnik Effect**. After noticing that waiters in a restaurant seemed to forget patron's orders after they had served them, she conducted experimental research along those lines. She had people work on several types of tasks such as stringing beads or naming objects beginning with a particular letter. Then, she interrupted them on half of the tasks. Later, she asked them what they had been doing and discovered that they were extremely more likely to remember tasks that had not completed compared to those that had. Soon, because of the research produced by Lewin and his students, he was

PHOTO 12.5 Bluma Zeigarnik

internationally known and had become nearly as prominent a gestalt theorist as Wertheimer, Köhler, or Koffka.

In 1933, Lewin served as a visiting professor at Stanford University. He was about to return home when Hitler came to power. Köhler, concerned about Lewin's safety in Germany as a Jew (despite his war record), won him an extension of his leave. During that time, Lewin was able to secure a faculty appointment at Cornell in the Department of Home Economics. He and his family moved to the United States as yet another set of refugees from Hitler's Germany. From Cornell, he moved to the University of Iowa, where he made many original contributions to the psychology of personality, the study of leadership, and group dynamics.

From Gestalt theory, Lewin adapted field theory and applied it to personality. In his conception of personality, behavior was a function of a person and environment. He provided a simple equation:

$$B = f(P, E)$$

which simply restated those words mathematically. Each person, though, was different from any other person (including identical twins) because no one lived in the same environment. His "life space" was a dynamic representation of his personality theory. As people moved through life they added interests and abilities. As they developed, their life spaces became more and more complex. He applied field theory toward a variety of personality variables: needs, abilities, and barriers. He also saw personality as a kind of locomotion through the environment. Later, he would use this framework to change people's ideas and move them from prejudice to tolerance, for instance. He called his approach **Topological Psychology.** From early on in his career, Lewin was interested in applying psychology to the world outside the lab. Kihlstrom (2019, p. 4) later redefined Lewin's life space thusly, returning it to Koffka's definition of gestalt psychology:

> In the spirit of Lewin's pseudomathematics, the proper formulation of Lewin's Grand Truism is not $B=f(P, E)$ or $B=f(P + E)$ but rather $B=f(PxE)$: the whole is greater than the sum of its parts.

Ash (1995, p. 274) noted:

> From his early essay on Taylorism to this talk to teachers during the Depression, Lewin's aim remained consistent—to humanize social practice in the factory and the school as well as in the laboratory . . . He clearly made the ideological and social power dimensions of this issue more explicit than anyone else in the Berlin school.

After World War II started, Lewin applied his research on leadership toward the training of American servicemen. Just before the United States entered the war, he had completed research on leadership styles (Lewin et al., 1939). Working with 10-year-old boys, they simulated three different kinds of leadership styles: autocratic, democratic, and laissez-faire. They found that the boys responded very differently depending on how they were being led. When led in an autocratic style, the boys were lethargic and docile. When led in a democratic style, they were friendly and playful with each other. The boys led in a laissez-faire style were more aggressive with each other and less likely to cooperate or engage in constructive activities. The results of that study were used to select candidates for espionage for the Office of Strategic Services (which became the CIA after the war).

Lewin left Iowa for MIT in order to found the Research Center for Group Dynamics. Inspired by his personal experience with Nazism, he investigated whether people could change ingrained beliefs and attitudes. During an early session with government employees, he discovered that immediate feedback helped reduce prejudice. He also found that established attitudes could be "unfrozen," changed, and then frozen again as new changed ones. Soon after founding the Group Dynamics Center, Lewin unexpectedly died from a heart attack. Yet, during his

PHOTO 12.6 Kurt Lewin

Credit: INTERFOTO/Alamy Stock Photo

short but eventful life, he was able to bring gestalt ideas to the fields of personality and social dynamics. Ash (1992, p. 204) summarized Lewin's career in the United States:

> Nearly alone among the leading émigré psychologists, Kurt Lewin succeeded in creating both a successful career for himself and a "school" of followers in America through his skillful use of the growing network of private, semiprivate, and public funding agencies that formed the transition from an academic discipline to a science-based profession. His field-theoretical ideas on the problems of minority groups played an important part ... in American social psychology.

Solomon Asch, himself another émigré, conducted fundamental and groundbreaking research in social psychology using Gestalt psychology as his guiding light.

Solomon Asch (1907–1996)

Biography

Asch was born in Poland. His family emigrated to the United States when he was in his teens. He attended the City University of New York and did his graduate work at Columbia University. His interest in psychology came relatively late in his academic career; at first he wanted to become an anthropologist. At Columbia, he worked under Woodworth for his master's degree and H. E. Garrett for his PhD. His psychological training was quite conventional for an American psychologist of his era. His dissertation was on the similarity of shapes of learning curves.

PHOTO 12.7 Solomon Asch

Credit: INTERFOTO/Alamy Stock Photo

Contributions

He began to teach at Brooklyn College and shortly after met Wertheimer in New York City. Wertheimer profoundly influenced Asch and he, in turn, was the force behind the publication of Wertheimer's book, *Productive Thinking* (King & Wertheimer, 2005). After Wertheimer died, Asch took his place at the New School for a few years. Later, he moved to Swarthmore for many years and there worked with Köhler. He moved to Rutgers and then to the University of Pennsylvania. Over his long career he conducted a number of important experiments, nearly all of which emphasized a gestalt point of view.

Early on, Witkin and Asch (1948) collaborated on a series of experiments designed to test how people responded to changes in their frame of reference. Using a new procedure, the rod-and-frame test, they discovered that people responded in either of two ways. Some people oriented the rod visually, parallel to the vertical side of the frame even when the frame was tilted. Others oriented the rod in an upright position using gravitational cues, disregarding the visual cues provided by the frame. They labeled people who used visual cues to orient the rod as *field dependent* and people who used gravitational cues as *field independent.* Rock (1992, p. 405) wrote:

> Witkin was particularly interested in these differences [field dependence and independence], so at this point he and Asch parted company . . . Witkin sought to correlate these differences with differences in other perceptual tasks . . . This work was among the first investigations of what came to be called *cognitive styles* [original italics]. Asch and Witkin's experiments were clearly attempts to quantify, experimentally, a gestalt concept, the frame of reference.

Asch was more of a social psychologist than anything else. He conducted studies on impression formation (Asch, 1946) and suggestibility (Asch, 1948). He also published a well-received text in social psychology (Asch, 1952). But, his most famous studies dealt with the relationship between conformity and independence. Asch (1955) summarized those studies. Dissatisfied with previous theoretical accounts of opinion change, Asch created a simple yet powerful experiment. He arranged for male college students to report about an easy-to-discriminate perceptual task (see Figure 12.4). Not surprisingly, the control group made the correct discrimination almost 100% of the time. In the experimental situation, however, there was only one participant. All of the other people in the room were confederates of the experimenter. That lone participant had to make his decision after all the others had already done so. There were 18 trials; in 12 of them all of the confederates gave the wrong answer. The results were remarkable. Fully, 25% of the participants refused to go along with the majority and consistently picked the right answer. But, some 37% consistently went along with the majority giving the wrong answer. In other words, they yielded to the social pressure created by the experimental situation. Nearly all social psychology texts review this experiment. But Friend et al. (1990, p. 39) maintained that "textbooks have frequently given very one-sided readings of the basic quantitative results, without pointing out how different was (and is) Asch's own interpretation." They argued that many social psychology textbooks overemphasized the conformity aspects of the studies and underreported that many of the participants stood fast even under great social pressure to doubt the visual stimuli in front of them.

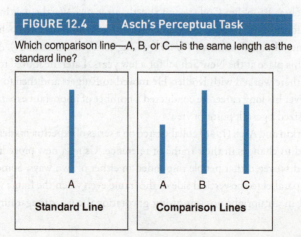

FIGURE 12.4   ■   Asch's Perceptual Task

Which comparison line—A, B, or C—is the same length as the standard line?

A

Standard Line

A   B   C

Comparison Lines

Asch (1952, p. 132) pointed toward his view of such social pressure in the laboratory situation he had created:

> The clash of views generates events of far-reaching importance. I am induced to take up a particular standpoint, to view my own action as another views it or as the action of another person, and, conversely, to view another's action as my own. Now, I have within me two standpoints, my own and that of the other; both are now part of my way of thinking. In this way the limitations of my individual thinking are transcended by including the thoughts of others. I am now open to more alternatives than my own unaided comprehension would make possible. *Disagreements, when their causes are intelligible, can enrich and strengthen, rather than injure, our sense of objectivity* [italics added].

Asch, then, had experimentally created an unusual and complex gestalt in his laboratory. He forced his participants to reconsider their most basic assumptions about their own perceptual abilities by subjecting them to social pressure. He was pleased to find that many of his participants stuck to their guns in the face of nearly overwhelming social pressure. At the same time, he was concerned about those who had yielded. But, both sets of participants had reorganized their thinking. Asch (1955, p. 35) concluded:

> That we have found the tendency to conformity in our society so strong that reasonably intelligent and well-meaning young people are willing to call white black is a matter of concern . . . Yet anyone inclined to draw too pessimistic conclusions from this report would do well to remind himself that the capacities for independence are not to be underestimated . . . those who participated in this challenging experiment agreed nearly without exception that independence was preferable to conformity.

LEARNING OBJECTIVE

6. Assess the results of Asch's conformity experiment.

Will Gestalt psychology rise again? No, that is not likely. The holistic philosophy that supported it in Europe found few inroads in America. Thus, Gestalt psychology never took root in the soil of the American atomistic and reductionist philosophical garden. The better question is: How much of 21st century psychology still includes findings from Gestalt psychology? A careful examination will reveal that much of Gestalt psychology remains, but is no longer called by its original name.

BORDER WITH BIOLOGY
THE MOON ILLUSION

Since the earliest humans first gazed at the rising full moon they (and we) perceived the moon as much larger as it rose against the horizon. Later, when the same moon approached its zenith it was perceived as much smaller. This phenomenon is a true illusion. Simply covering the moon at both positions with a fingernail will prove that as will taking photos. Those photos will show that the moon is the same size at the horizon and at its zenith. Many researchers have proposed explanations for the illusion but none of those have fully explained the illusion. Dyches (2021) noted that the moon at the horizon tends to have an orange or yellow hue because the light from the moon at that point must travel a longer path through the atmosphere stripping away the blue wavelengths. When the moon is at its zenith, however, those blue wavelengths are visible yielding the perception of a white moon. He pointed to a variety of possible explanations for the moon illusion including relative size, foreground objects, and the Ponzo Illusion. Ultimately, however, neither he nor a long list of earlier scientists have yet to fully explain the moon illusion. His advice is simply to enjoy the difference between the two moons.

THEN AND NOW
GESTALT THEORY

Gestalt psychology began by proposing a new way to understand sensations and perceptions. Wertheimer's discovery of the phi phenomenon was the principal originating event. Within a short span of years, Gestalt psychology began to provide new explanations for learning and thinking. In the United States, Lewin and Asch extended Gestalt ideas into social psychology, group dynamics, and conformity. For a variety of reasons: displacement from Germany, resistance from Neobehaviorism, the premature deaths of Wertheimer and Koffka, and the small number of graduate students produced, Gestalt psychology all but faded away. Yet, many of its principal ideas live on in modern psychology. Wertheimer's principles of gestalt perception and Köhler's insight learning are prominent examples. Koontz and Gunderman (2008) argued that radiologists must practice gestalt perceptual principles daily as they make diagnoses based upon radiographic images. More recently, Wang et al. (2018) proposed using deep learning techniques based on gestalt psychological principles to detect breast masses in mammograms. Similarly, Wertheimer (1999) pointed out that a long-standing gestalt finding—contour salience or how edges of stimuli are perceived—is now being explained via mathematical algorithms. Sharps and Wertheimer (2000) urged psychologists to heed Gestalt psychology's perspective and take domain specificity into account in their theoretical formulations. They also emphasized the importance of "interchanges between organisms and surroundings as determinants of behavior" (p. 315). Guberman (2016) reviewed gestalt theory and its search for a neurophysiological basis for its findings and argued (p. 235):

> Before we thought that perception starts with sensations and finishes with Gestalt – the pure product of mind. Now we see that (at least in communication tasks) the percept is embodied in our physical body. The perception will change dramatically if our body changes.

Gestalt psychology is yet present in the 21st century and is still developing theoretically and being applied in new areas, especially in Artificial Intelligence (AI). Guberman (2018) reviewed AI's early dismissal of psychophysical research and its embrace of logic as a model of human thinking. Only recently, he noted, have psychology and AI rediscovered Wertheimer's fundamental notion of the gestalt, one presaged by the analysis of melody by Ehrenfels and Mach, supported by neurological research of brain-damaged victims, by the discovery of mirror neurons, and by incorporating the motoric elements of speech and handwriting perception. What emerged is a (p. 10) "rearranged Gestalt theory [21] on the basis of a single principle, equipped with well-defined notions, and covering all Gestalt phenomena - just as Wertheimer wanted it to be." Pizlo (2008, p. 28) writing about the rediscovery of gestalt principles in AI and machine vision noted, "Unfortunately, the Gestalt psychologists did not elaborate on the relation between shape perception and figureground organization. This oversight probably explains why they did not do much to advance the study of shape perception." Later (p. 60), he wrote:

> In short, we perceive the 3D world as 3D, rather than as 2D, not because the 3D interpretation is simpler, which it may very well be, at least on some occasions, but because it is a smart thing to do. [original italics] This claim spells out the main difference between the Gestalt and the cognitive approach to perception.

Gestalt principles are still being used profitably in modern psychology and in computer science.

WHAT IS GESTALT PSYCHOLOGY?

Arnheim (1986, p. 823) summarized gestalt theory thusly:

> Gestalt theory is concerned primarily with the complex dynamics of organization in field situations, be they physical or psychological. This dynamics is not fully described by the tendency toward simple, regular, symmetrical structure but requires acknowledgement of a countertendency that meets tension reduction with tension enhancement. The countertendency articulates physical and psychological units or objects in interaction with the equilibrating force . . . gestalt psychologists . . . were very much concerned from the beginning with the biological, cognitive, and aesthetic reward of gestalt processes, namely the creation of well-functioning, stable, and clarifying patterns in nature, science, and art—a perfection difficult or impossible to obtain otherwise.

Gestalts, thus, exist everywhere. They can be simple ones such as the perception of a triangle. They can be cognitive such as when a new solution suddenly emerges following a period of thought. Think of insight learning, transposition, or perceptual set. They can be social such as when what others do forces people to reconsider their own cherished ideas or beliefs. In all cases, however, the gestalts involved are integrated wholes and relationships between stimuli that cannot be understood by examining their constituent parts in isolation. They can only be understood *in toto*, or as gestalts.

A good way to end this chapter is to consider one of Wertheimer's favorite problems (King & Wertheimer, 2005, pp. 390–391):

> A hunter sees a bear one mile due south of where the hunter is standing. He aims a gun at the bear, shoots, and misses. The hunter next walks the one mile due south to where the bear was when the shot was fired, then walks one mile due east, then one mile due north—and ends up standing at exactly the same place from which the gun was shot . . . What color was the bear? (See answer below.)

7. Support the idea that gestalt psychology encompassed more than just the study of sensation and perception.

SUMMARY

The history of Gestalt psychology is inextricably linked with the history of Germany in the early 20th century. Gestalt psychology, however, did not spring up fully formed. William James's stream of consciousness and Stumpf's research on music had already argued against Wundtian elementism. The work of Ernst Mach and Christian von Ehrenfels in the 19th century was foundational. Both of them were struck by the persistence of musical melodies and each attempted to provide theoretical explanations as to why melodies could not be decomposed meaningfully into individual notes. Ehrenfels's *Gestaltqualitäten* inspired Wertheimer to investigate and, later, to found Gestalt psychology properly.

Max Wertheimer conducted the first research explicitly judged as Gestalt psychology when he examined the mathematical thinking of the Veddas. But it was his research of the phi phenomenon and the Gestalt principles of perception that caused others to first notice the emergence of a new school of psychology. Wertheimer, along with Wolfgang Köhler and Kurt Koffka, formed the initial nucleus of Gestalt psychology.

Köhler became famous for his research on insight learning and transposition in apes. Later, he chaired the psychology department at the University of Berlin, the most important center of Gestalt psychology. The rise of Hitler and Nazism put an end to Gestalt psychology in Europe and most of its researchers emigrated, many to the United States. While still in Germany, Koffka taught at the University of Giessen. Tolman visited him there twice and served as an early conduit of gestalt ideas to American psychology. Koffka moved to the United States and wrote the first book about Gestalt psychology to be printed in English. Unfortunately it was a difficult read. That work and an earlier article he wrote left the mistaken impression that Gestalt psychology only applied to perceptual psychology. That impression still lingers today.

Wertheimer and Koffka died prematurely, limiting their potential long-term effect on psychology. Nevertheless, a newer generation of Gestalt psychologists did emerge. Kurt Lewin had been a colleague of Köhler and Wertheimer at Berlin. After Hitler became chancellor, Lewin chose to remain in the United States where he had served as a visiting faculty member at Stanford. Because he was Jewish it was not safe for him to return home. Lewin became a prominent social psychologist. But, he, too, died an early death. He pioneered topological psychology, researched leadership, and attempted to find ways to reduce prejudice.

Solomon Asch emigrated to the United States from Poland. He was trained in the behaviorist model but fell under the influence of Wertheimer. Asch, too, was a social psychologist. He conducted research on impression formation, suggestibility, and opinion change. His textbook on social psychology was well received. His most famous research was on opinion change. He arranged a laboratory situation in which a naïve subject was subjected, at times, to intense social pressure to conform to an obviously incorrect decision on a perceptual task made by several other strangers.

In many ways, Gestalt findings persist in 21st century psychology. The phi phenomenon and the Gestalt principles of perception are covered in every general psychology textbook. Current research in cognition acknowledges its debt to Gestalt psychology. For example, Morgan et al. (2019) analyzed the role that expectations played in melody comparing gestalt ideas to modern statistical learning theories. They concluded (p. 31):

> Our finding that both statistical learning and Gestalt-like principles influence melodic expectations raises a new question: what sort of cognitive process might combine these two types of knowledge in determining melodic expectations? Broadly speaking, we envision two possible types of answers: in one case, statistical learning and Gestalt-like principles operate independently, and then their predictions are combined. In the other case, these two types of principles might in fact emerge from a single system.

Thus, gestalt psychology still influences modern cognitive psychology. The unanswerable question always is: What would psychology be like today had Gestalt psychology been allowed to flourish in its European home?

Oh, what about Wertheimer's bear? It was white. (Hint: there is only one spot on the world where the conditions in the problem could take place. The gestalt, of course, ties that spot to the bear.)

ZEITGEIST

The Nineteenth Century

Historical change accelerated during the nineteenth century. Technology led the way as horses gave way to railways; candles to gaslights followed by electric lights. The telegraph and Morse code transformed communication. News could travel far faster than before and reach a telegraph office anywhere in the world. The telephone added voice communication on its own global network. The industrial revolution spurred people into urban areas to work in the new factories forcing those cities to provide the basic human necessities to a much larger population. In time, those new workers struggled for political power with many coming under the sway of socialist, nationalist, or anarchist movements.

Nowhere were those struggles more evident than in Vienna. There, following a mid-century revolution, a humiliating military defeat, the establishment of a constitutional government, and a reduction of the privileges of the ancient aristocracy, a nascent liberal democracy took root. But, Vienna was a latecomer to the political changes that had already taken place in other European capitals. Catching up to the rest of Europe in a hurry led to prosperity and growth, but did so on shaky foundations. The emerging Austrian bourgeoisie never replaced or coopted the aristocracy. Instead, that emerging middle class depended upon the beneficence of the emperor and lent him their loyal support. At the same time, the working classes were becoming more powerful, more nationalistic, and anti-Semitic. The ancient city walls and fortifications were torn down in the last half of the century and a broad, circular street was created; the *Ringstrasse*. It surrounded the old city and became the new focal point for development in the city. A massive building campaign soon filled the street with magnificent public and private buildings. The *Ringstrasse* effectively isolated the old city from the new suburbs, and in the process, created a new urban center where museums, theatres, cafes, and salons proliferated.

Such was Vienna when Sigmund Freud first arrived there as a young child. But by the time he was a college student, much had changed. Vienna by then was pulling itself apart:

> Until the nineties the contending political forces had been the classic ones: liberal versus conservative. But now the lower social strata generated the strength to contest the power of the older elites. Out of the working class sprang socialism; out of the lower middle class and peasantry arouse both virulent nationalism and Christian Socialism. The fall of Vienna to Karl Lueger's anti-Semites in the elections of 1895 was a stunning blow to the bearers of liberal culture, Jew and Gentile. The forces of racial prejudice and national hatred, which they had thought dispelled by the light of reason and the rule of law, re-emerged in terrifying force as the "century of progress" breathed its last (Schorske, 1980, p. 185).

Fin de siècle (end of the century) was the French phrase applied to this era. To many it seemed that the world had turned upside down. The promise of technology had turned hollow. The Enlightenment had a dark side as evidenced by the French Revolution and the changes it had caused. Science itself was not immune to doubt. The study of physiology had turned out to be much more difficult than anticipated. Psychology, psychiatry, and neurology had emerged as new sciences but their progress had been halting. In that vacuum, spiritualism had made a revival and even distinguished psychologists such as William James and C. G. Jung participated in séances as interested observers. More importantly, there had been an increase in "nervous disorders" and the attempt to classify and treat them. Neurasthenia (nervous exhaustion) and hysteria (conversion reactions) were diagnosed more often while the search for biomedical causes for those diseases came up empty. Therapies and cures were sought, especially hypnosis. The end of the century was proving to be a difficult time for psychology; it needed explorers of the troubled mind. Building on older approaches to psychopathology, Freud successfully led a new movement that primarily sought to identify and cure specific psychopathologies by exploring the unconscious minds of his patients. He found everlasting fame because of his efforts and inspired others to join him; many did so but some later disagreed with him founding their own theories for psychopathology and its treatment.

LEARNING OBJECTIVE

1. Discuss the European public's loss of optimism at the end of the nineteenth century and how it provided a fertile ground for Freud's theorizing.

PREVIEW

This chapter contains many ideas that are still current in psychology, the scientific study of *psychopathology* being the most prominent. As the world became more urban and industrialized, scientists noticed the rise of new and abnormal conditions such as hysteria and neurasthenia.

Thus, *treatment* or *therapy* for those conditions became a part of a new applied clinical psychology. The achievement of *insight* into their personal problems by sufferers, guided by therapists, was new.

Freud, Jung, and Adler each developed therapeutic techniques based upon their own theoretical models of personality. For Freud, the personality was driven by the *instincts* of sex *(id)* and aggression *(thanatos)*. But, those instincts were (usually) under the control of the *ego* and the *superego* and the conflicts of the personality were mostly hidden in the *unconscious*. Jung expanded Freud's unconscious by adding the *collective unconscious* as the primordial source of much of human motivation. The collective unconscious contained universal symbols interpretable by those who took the time to study and understand them. Jung added new dimensions to his model of personality that sought to explain much about human behavior including our public faces (the *persona*) and our bisexual natures (the *anima* and *animus*). Adler was very uncomfortable with how Freud and Jung emphasized the unconscious and with how they partitioned the parts of the personality. Instead, he emphasized a <u>holistic theory</u> that looked at *feelings of inferiority* and how people overcame them. His individual psychology emphasized *lifestyle* and *personal goals* and stressed the uniqueness of individuals. All three pioneered *insight therapies* that are still practiced today. They also inspired other models of therapy based on psychological theories quite different from their own (e.g., behavioral and humanistic theories).

Karen Horney and Anna Freud were among the many women attracted to psychotherapy. Perhaps inspired by her own childhood experiences, Horney believed that *basic anxiety* was generated in people by the environment, not internal conflict. Early in her career, she distanced herself from Freudian theory, especially its emphasis on *penis envy* in the Electra Complex. In response, she proposed *womb envy* as a mechanism for the Oedipus Complex. Neurotic personalities developed because of *neurotic needs*. Her thinking about the development of neurotic needs evolved from a list of twelve needs to *moving toward people, moving away from people,* and *moving against people*. Later still, she described those needs in terms of *compliance, aggression*, and *detachment*. She explained neurosis as a mismatch between the *ideal self* and the *real self*. Therapy, thus, consisted of helping patients develop more realistic ideas about their ideal selves.

Anna Freud went from being Freud's daughter to becoming his indispensable helpmate and companion in his old age. Along the way, he subjected her to analysis; later she became an analyst herself (without ever attending a university), refined and altered his ideas, and in her old age became the face of psychiatry. She clarified Freud's ideas about *defense mechanisms*, putting them into their now-familiar form. Her early work with children helped open the area of *child therapy*. She was the first to use *children's drawings* as a way to explore their unconscious personalities. Later, she developed the area of *adolescent therapy*, pointing out that it needed to be different because adolescents did not seek therapy on their own. Parents brought them in, thus changing the nature of the therapeutic encounter. During World War II, she continued her work with children, eventually inspiring others to see the importance of *attachment* between caretakers and children. During her final years, she worked to change laws governing the custody of children. Her theoretical emphasis centered more on the role of the ego and the importance of *mothering*.

INTRODUCTION

The practice of psychotherapy today is much different from that described in this chapter. For one thing, the ethical standards now in place were nonexistent then. Therapists back then could have multiple relationships with their patients. They might not only provide therapy but could be friends or lovers too. Today's models for therapy were yet to be developed. Recall from Chapter 1 how the Boulder Model only emerged in the mid-twentieth century and was followed 24 years later by the Vail Model. Freud, Jung, Adler, Horney, and Anna Freud each created brand new models for psychotherapy built upon tenuous scientific foundations. All but Anna Freud were trained as medical doctors and all felt the need to attack psychopathology from a psychological point of view. For Freud, that meant creating a theory primarily based upon a premise of infantile sexuality. For Jung, it meant discovering ancient and hidden manifestations of human evolution buried deep in the collective unconscious. For Adler, it meant focusing on the social factors found in the family and early life that needed to be overcome by everyone in their own unique way. All three constructed theories of personality along with insight therapies designed to help those with personality problems. Horney rejected Freud's use of penis envy to explain the Oedipus Complex and proposed womb envy as an alternative. Anna Freud, although the keeper of her father's flame, nonetheless changed his theories where she believed she had to; she disagreed with him over the importance of mothering in development.

Today, the *Diagnostic and Statistical Manual (DSM-5)* of the American Psychiatric Association classifies psychopathology along five axes: Clinical Syndromes (Axis I), Developmental and Personality Disorders (Axis II), Physical Conditions (Axis III), Severity of Psychosocial Stressors (Axis IV), and Highest Level of Functioning (Axis V). *The DSM-5* is designed "to move away from a classification that focused on reliability while inadvertently sacrificing validity toward a classification that is far more clinically useful than that of the DSM-IV and far more open to validation" (Bernstein, 2011, pp. 7–29). Thus, the work begun on psychopathology by those covered in this chapter continues to the present day.

In those early years of psychotherapy, the classification of mental disorders was far less advanced. The main classifications used were neuroses and psychoses. The effects of neuroses could range from annoying to debilitating, but the personalities of sufferers did not disintegrate. Psychoses, on the other hand, were more serious and usually led to personality disintegration along with the need for hospitalization. The terms "neurosis" and "psychosis" are no longer used as descriptors of personality because they are not specific enough. However, they are still commonly used by laypersons to describe abnormal behavior.

LEARNING OBJECTIVE

2. Review the five axes of the DSM-5.

HISTORICAL BACKGROUND

The historical roots of psychopathology are ancient. The idea of people being possessed by demons has a long history and persists to the present (e.g., "The devil made me do it"). During the late Middle Ages, demonic possession was seen as a real phenomenon. Unfortunately, that meant many of them were tortured or killed. Today people exhibiting such symptoms would be labeled psychopathological and treated using modern methods.

Another historical approach to psychopathology was isolation of sufferers in asylums. The Bethlem Royal Hospital (founded in 1247) in London began using this method in the fourteenth century. By the seventeenth century, it had moved into a large building designed by Robert Hooke. Until 1770, the hospital allowed visitors to view the inmates as a form of entertainment. Hogarth's last painting in his series "*The Rake's Progress*" (see Figure 13.1) shows Rakewell as an inmate ignoring his well-dressed female visitor.

FIGURE 13.1 ■ Hogarth's last painting from A Rake's Progress showing Bedlam

Credit: World History Archive/Alamy Stock Photo

By the eighteenth century, however, belief in that model began to change. In France, Pussin and Pinel successfully removed chains and straitjackets from their insane asylum inmates and saw them improve, giving rise to a new era in the treatment of psychopathology. During the nineteenth century, attitudes toward victims of psychopathology changed and the medical model dominated. Still, as Europe became more industrialized, the number of sufferers increased; asylums and mental hospitals could not handle the overflow of patients. So, any treatment that could cure mental patients would be a godsend. The *zeitgeist* was ready for someone such as Sigmund Freud.

LEARNING OBJECTIVE

3. Appraise the approaches to mental health and therapy before Freud.

FREUD'S PSYCHOANALYSIS

Sigmund Freud (1856–1939)

Biography

Sigmund Freud was born in Freiburg, Moravia (modern Pribor, Czech Republic), the first child of Jewish parents. His father, Jacob, worked in the wool business, but economic circumstances three years after Sigmund's birth forced him and his family to move to Vienna. Sigmund Freud lived there from that time until his forced exile to London in 1938 to escape the Nazis. In his writings, Freud often alluded to his happy childhood in Freiburg, especially his early close relationship with his mother, Amalia. The birth of his sister, Anna, altered young Sigmund's relationship with his mother, he later recalled. That, along with the unusual family structure he lived in—his father was 20 years older than his mother and had two sons from an earlier marriage living with the family—may have contributed to some of Freud's later theorizing about the effects of early

PHOTO 13.1 Sigmund Freud
Credit: Getty Images

experience on personality. After the family arrived in Vienna, they lived thriftily. His mother gave birth to four more sisters followed by a brother, Alexander. Anna Freud later wrote that ten-year-old Sigmund suggested that name at a family council in honor of Alexander the Great (Gay, 1988).

Freud held the role of first child tightly even to the extent of having his own room despite the family's bleak economic circumstances. He was first in his class at the gymnasium, read widely in German, English, French, and Spanish, and developed a lifelong interest in the classics and archeology. Despite his humanist inclinations, he enrolled in the medical school of the University of Vienna although he never felt any strong inclination to become a physician. During his eight years of medical training, he took a wide variety of courses including some from Franz Brentano. He also tried his hand at research in biology. His first publication followed his dissection of hundreds of eels in an attempt to assess whether they were hermaphroditic. After he received his medical degree, he went to work for several years in the lab of Ernst Brücke, an eminent physiologist. There, Freud developed his scientific skills and came to possess a positivist attitude toward science. Brücke, citing the better economic prospects in medicine, urged him to leave the lab and open his own medical practice. That meant obtaining clinical training in the medical specialties at a hospital. Freud did so and developed an interest in neurology. He won a travel grant to Paris to study with one of the most prominent neurologists of his era, Jean-Martin Charcot.

BORDER WITH BIOLOGY
FREUD'S INSTINCTS

Perhaps because of his early biological research, Freud nearly always preserved a link between his personality theory and biology. The most obvious linkage was between personality and the instincts of sex and aggression. Freud, at first, emphasized the connection between sexuality and personality using the libido. Later, he added another connection, thanatos, to explain what he believed to be the human propensity toward violence. Interestingly, movies and television shows follow his model, emphasizing romance, violent action, or both.

Contributions

Charcot was just beginning his research on hysteria at the time Freud arrived in Paris. For Charcot, hysteria was a catchall diagnosis that included (Noland, 1999, p. 14):

> paralysis, anesthesia, difficulty in walking and standing, tunnel vision, and hysterogenic points on the body (points that, if pressed, either started or stopped a seizure). He also described male as well as female hysteria . . . and contributed to the death of the old idea that hysteria was connected to the uterus . . . and hence that only women could have hysteria. For Charcot hysteria was a disease not of the uterus but of the central nervous system.

One of the most interesting aspects of hysteria was that there seemed to be no connection between its symptoms and its underlying physiology. For instance, a very common form was glove hysteria, now known as a type of conversion reaction. In that condition, patients reported either paralysis or loss of feeling in the wrist or hand. Ali et al. (2015) described the symptoms:

> Conversion anesthesia may occur anywhere, but it is most common on the extremities. One may see a typical "glove and stocking" distribution; however, unlike the "glove and stocking" distribution that may occur in a polyneuropathy, the areas of conversion anesthesia have a very precise and sharp boundary, often located at a joint.

But, such symptoms could not be explained physiologically; the patients themselves were causing their own symptoms. Charcot believed that a physiological cause for hysteria existed; it just had not yet been discovered. He also was experimenting with hypnosis as a cure for hysteria. Freud adopted hypnosis early on as a treatment for hysteria, but soon abandoned it for the "talking cure," the name given to the approach used by Josef Breuer, another physician, on one of his early patients Anna O. The study and treatment of hysteria would become Freud's avenue to fame.

Freud returned to Vienna and began to treat patients complaining of hysteria and other similar conditions using hypnosis. Together, Freud and Breuer tackled the case of Anna O, one that exhibited many of the classic symptoms of hysteria: paralysis, anesthesias, headaches, and even the inability to speak in German from time to time. Once Breuer began to hypnotize her and then ask her to recollect traumatic memories from her past, she began to improve. Freud never treated Anna O., but he and Breuer discussed her case extensively. Eventually, Freud persuaded Breuer to publish the case along with several others. That book, *Studies on Hysteria* (Breuer & Freud, 1895), marked the beginning of psychoanalysis and caused others to take notice of Freud and his methods. He and Breuer, however, soon grew apart. Throughout his life, Freud split from many of his former colleagues and collaborators. Kramer (2006, pp. 61–62) described a meeting on the street between Freud and Breuer many years later, "There was always a vengeful quality to Freud's ruptures with men he had relied on. In Breuer's old age, he happened upon Freud in the street and opened his arms in greeting, Freud pretended not to see him."

Freud soon began to develop new techniques to cure his patients' symptoms along with theoretical concepts designed to explain their origin. He also abandoned hypnotism as a technique, substituting free association in its place. It was early on in his career that Freud also employed his famous couch while he sat facing away from his patient. He also began to develop two important concepts related to free association: resistance and transference. He noted that when patients began to speak less freely about a topic, he assumed that was because they were nearing the source of their problem. Paradoxically, patients seemed more reluctant to free association the closer they came to what Freud considered the root of their problem. Thus, he believed that resistance was a good sign of progress in therapy. He also noticed that patients seemed to transfer their problems from the actual source (e.g., another person) to the therapist, often seeing the therapist as the source of the ideas that distressed them. Again, Freud saw transference as a normal and necessary part of the therapeutic process.

Imagine yourself spending 50 min in a room with someone you barely know, someone who refuses to engage in normal conversation with you. Such was the original design behind Freudian psychoanalysis. Because Freud failed to provide the normal and usual responses of conversation, patients eventually began to talk without expecting verbal responses in return. That one-sided patient monologue was free association. Freud met with his patients much more often than do modern therapists (sometimes daily for years on end) so patients soon became accustomed to the routine Freud expected from them. After they left, Freud would make notes and begin to form ideas about the patient's mental illness.

LEARNING OBJECTIVE

4. Compare and contrast Freud's technique of free association to a normal hour of conversation with a friend.

Early in his medical career, Freud wrote an article praising the beneficial effects of cocaine. Freud himself used cocaine afterward for several years (it was not a controlled substance at the time). Only after publishing his article did he realize the addictive qualities of the drug. In fact, he was unsuccessful in helping a friend get off of cocaine. His friend developed a lifelong addiction instead. Inspired by Freud's article, a medical use for cocaine was found by another physician, Carl Koller. His research demonstrated that cocaine could be used as an anesthetic during eye surgery. Koller's research on cocaine made him famous while Freud's research hounded his reputation as a scientist for many years.

Over the next 10 years, Freud published several groundbreaking books related to psychoanalysis: *The Interpretation of Dreams* (1900), *The Psychopathology of Everyday Life* (1901), and *Jokes and Their Relation to the Unconscious* and *Three Essays on the Theories of Sexuality* (both in 1905). These books laid down many of the basic tenets of psychoanalysis, including the role of unconscious motivation, the overarching importance of childhood sexuality, and dream analysis. The books also made him famous, so much so that other physicians and scientists began to seek him out. Psychoanalysis quickly evolved into a movement, and many men and women began to meet weekly with Freud in order to discuss cases and share their experiences.

During Freud's first years of meeting with patients, he was struck by how often they all seemed to recall incidents of seduction by adults from their childhood years. In his early theorizing, he argued that such incidents were responsible for the problems his patients were exhibiting. Later, however, he pulled back from that extreme position disbelieving that such high levels of child molestation could possibly exist. In the place of actual molestation, Freud substituted a central role in his theorizing for childhood sexuality as a biologically based instinct. In other words, he began to believe that his patients' problems were still sexually based, but only symbolically (at least for the majority of his patients). Much of his later theorizing, especially the Oedipus Complex (see below) was based upon the premise that children possessed unconscious sexual motivations from a very early age.

In 1909, G. Stanley Hall invited Freud and Carl Jung to speak at Clark University and to receive honorary degrees. Jung, at the time, was first among the many of Freud's disciples (their permanent break was still in the future). At Clark, Freud gave five lectures (all in German) on psychoanalysis covering "hysteria and the psychoanalytic method, the idea that mental illness could arise for a person's early experience, the importance of dreams and unconscious mental, infantile sexuality and the nature of transference" (Hoffman, 2009, p. A21). Many prominent American scientists, including the anthropologist Franz Boas and psychologist William James, attended the lectures. After the lectures, Freud, Jung, and Sandor Ferenczi, another of Freud's followers, visited the Adirondack summer camp of James Jackson Putnam, an American psychoanalyst. From there they visited Niagara Falls and hiked wilderness trails. It was to be Freud's only visit to America. He returned to Vienna energized by his visit and feeling that his ideas had been accepted saying, "In Europe I felt as though I were despised; but over there I found myself received by the foremost men as an equal" (quoted in Gay, 1989, p. 32). In contrast, however, he also believed that the United States was far more primitive and decidedly less urbane than Vienna.

After his return from the United States, Freud turned his energies toward making psychoanalysis a worldwide movement. His early informal meetings with the Wednesday Psychological Society in Vienna morphed into the more formal Vienna Psychoanalytical Society. Soon, similar groups formed in cities all over Europe and North America. The International Psychoanalytic Association (IPA) was formed in 1908 and began to hold meetings (congresses) on a regular basis. At their second congress in Nuremberg, Carl Jung was elected president and its offices were relocated to Zurich where Jung lived and worked. Freud was agreeable to both Jung being president and the move to Zurich because he wanted to internationalize the movement and make it appear less Jewish. Alfred Adler's resignation, the growing hostility between Jung and Freud, and World War I caused organizational chaos. In response, a few of Freud's most faithful followers secretly formed "the Committee," and they all agreed to hold fast to Freud's ideas regarding psychoanalysis. The IPA grew slowly during the interwar period. After World War II, it grew more quickly and held a congress in Vienna for the first time in 1971, a meeting highlighted by the first return of Anna Freud to her homeland since 1938. Today, the IPA has more than 12,000 members from all over the world.

THEN AND NOW
DREAMS

Freud's analysis of dreams began when he undertook his own psychoanalysis following the death of his father in 1896. Fitfully and haltingly, he tackled his own symptoms (one was that he hated to travel) through the analysis of his own dreams. It was during this time that he first realized the importance of the unconscious and began to work out the details of the Oedipus Complex. Eventually, Freud came to believe that the unconscious generated dreams and that *"A dream is a (disguised) fulfilment of a (suppressed or repressed) wish"* (Freud, 1900/1923, p. 183, original italics). The interpretation of dreams became a major focus of his therapeutic work. But, dreams could not be interpreted in terms of their face content or what Freud called their manifest content. Instead, interpretation depended on teasing out the latent (or symbolic) content, much of which was sexual. Thus, Freud provided a long list for translating dreams from their manifest content to their latent content. Here are some examples:

Manifest Content	Latent Content
King and Queen	Father and Mother
Any long object	A penis, a man
Any container	A vagina, a woman
Climbing stairs	Engaging in sexual intercourse
Balconies	Breasts
Taking a trip	Death or dying

Freud described dreams as the "royal road to the unconscious."

Modern dream research has not supported much of Freud's theorizing, especially his idea of latent content. Schwartz (2000) argued that modern dream research and theorizing is remarkably similar to that of the nineteenth century scientists who worked before Freud's theories of dreaming disrupted that continuity. Domhoff (2019) defended his neurocognitive theory of dreams and compared and contrasted it with Freud's and three other modern competing theories: activation-synthesis, memory-consolidation, and threat simulation theories. Today, dreaming is studied via brain imaging techniques, cerebral dysfunctions, and brain lesions that affect recall of dreams. Very few contemporary psychologists still support Freud's theory of dreaming.

Freud remained in Vienna writing and seeing patients until 1938. Hitler's takeover of Austria that year provoked a crisis. Reluctantly, Freud agreed to leave Vienna. After worldwide pressure on the Nazis along with the payment of a considerable ransom, they allowed him and his daughter, Anna, to leave Austria for London. By the time Freud arrived in London, he suffered from an advanced oral cancer and he was in much pain. Yet, he continued to write and publish until the very end of his life. Finally, when the pain was too much, his personal physician, by prearrangement, gave him a fatal dose of morphine to end his suffering.

Freud's Main Ideas

Freud's main ideas can be summarized into three separate categories: the structure of mental life, the development of the personality, and the defense mechanisms. Freud wished to put the roots of personality in biology so he first posited the **id** as the home of the libido or the instinctual sex drive. Later, he felt forced to add another instinct to explain human aggression. He called that thanatos or the death instinct. The id and thanatos were present at birth and only gradually brought under control by the two other parts of the personality, the **ego** and the **superego**. The ego developed in childhood through experience and was under control of the reality principle. Thus, one difference between infants and children was that the latter could begin to control their ids because of their stronger egos. The superego developed with social experience and was composed of two parts: the conscience and the ego-ideal. From the conscience came knowledge of right and wrong or morality. The ego-ideal, on the other hand, was a kind of inner model of oneself created from experience with others. For instance, statements by adults such as: "Good boys do not hit their sisters" or "Nice girls keep their clothes clean" could, over time, contribute to the construction of individual ego-ideals.

The personality, then, consisted of those three components: id, ego, and super-ego. Only the ego was visible to others; it was on the surface. Freud (1923/1960, p. 15) wrote, "It is easy to see that the ego is part of the id which has been modified by the direct influence of the external world." The id and the superego operated internally, with the id pressuring the personality to satisfy its innate urges. At the same time, the superego acted as a brake on the system, resisting much of the id's pressure.

The picture above is complicated, however, by which parts of the mind are conscious or unconscious. To Freud, the unconscious parts were the largest and included all of the id and parts of the ego. The conscious part was the smallest and lay at the top of the ego near the surface in Freud's topological model. In between the conscious and unconscious parts was the preconscious. According to his model, some parts of the unconscious were repressed and could not be brought into the preconscious. Other parts of the unconscious, though, could be moved into the preconscious. Once an item was in the preconscious, it was readily accessible to the conscious. Thus, mental life was an amalgam of unconscious, preconscious, and conscious ideas. The id, the ego, and the superego completed the complex picture.

Although Freud never worked with children, he nevertheless created psychoanalysis as a developmental stage theory. The stages developed in conjunction with the id, ego, and super-ego, and children's personalities and behaviors changed accordingly as they passed through the four stages. The stages were associated with the pleasures derived from the control over various parts of the body as children matured and grew. Imagine two hungry children, one older than the other. The younger one, a two-year-old wants a cookie and asks her mother for one while she is speaking on the phone. Instead of receiving a cookie, her mom puts her in time out. Now imagine the other child, a five-year-old. She waits until her mother finishes speaking on the phone before asking for a cookie. She gets a cookie. Freud might have argued that each child possessed the same level of hunger or the same amount of id energy. But, the younger child was unable to suppress her id and consequently ended up not getting a cookie. The older child, however, realized from experience that if she asked her mother for a cookie while she was speaking on the phone, then no cookie would be forthcoming. That child, Freud might say, already possessed the reality principle, knowing that interrupting her mother while she was on the phone would not get her a cookie.

The first stage was the oral stage. It lasted from birth through the first year of life. Freud called it the oral stage because children used their mouths to derive pleasure. The evolutionary implications of the oral stage were obvious. Human children, being mammals, had to find, latch onto, and suck from their mother's nipples. The second stage was the anal stage. It lasted from ages one to three and involved the control of elimination of urine and feces. The next stage was the phallic stage. It lasted from ages three to six and was the most important of the stages because, according to Freud, it included the Oedipus Complex for boys and the Electra

Complex for girls. From ages six until puberty, Freud posited his latency stage, where there was no clear indicator as in the earlier stages. During the latency stage, boys and girls avoided each other, played in same sex groups, and saw the other gender as alien. Freud's last stage, the genital stage, emerged after puberty and marked the successful end of normal psychosexual development. In this stage, boys and girls quickly developed an interest in each other. Biologically, this stage was key toward the maintenance of the human species over time.

Once Freud abandoned his idea that all of his patients had been seduced by adults while children, he still needed a way to resolve the dynamics of childhood sexuality. Inspired by the play *Oedipus Rex*, Freud adapted it to his purposes. His Oedipus Complex applied to boys. When they were old enough to realize the difference between men and women, they also assumed that females (such as a sister, perhaps) had lost *their* penises in a battle with their father. He had ripped them off. Freud's name for this presumed belief was castration anxiety. The formerly stable family unit was now under threat, as both the boy and father desired the same woman: the child's mother and the father's wife. Furthermore, the father was much larger and more powerful than the son. Freud believed that sons abandoned their mother and identified with their fathers, thus resolving the crisis created by the Oedipus Complex. Following the resolution, it was quickly and deeply buried in the unconscious. After its resolution, boys began to take the first steps toward manhood.

But, for girls, Freud's story, the Electra Complex (but named by Jung), was less convincing. During their phallic stage, girls, too, learned the difference between the sexes. Freud now argued that they felt what he called penis envy. The resolution of the Electra Complex was less clear cut as well. Girls already identified with their mothers because of their long association since birth, but the lack of a penis prevented them from consummating their childhood id desires for her. Instead, they began their own heterosexual journey, seeking their lost penis first in their fathers and later in their husband. Freud believed they finally satisfied their penis envy while giving birth. As in the case of boys, girls too totally repressed this episode in their psychosexual development.

Anxiety and its resolution were a major part of Freudian theory. Freud linked anxiety to the ego, id, and superego. Reality anxiety was not imagined; it came from threats to life and limb from external events. So, facing a mugger pointing a gun is a good example of reality anxiety. The mugger is real, the gun is real, and death or injury may be imminent. Neurotic anxiety came from the id and was the fear of doing something sexual or violent at the wrong time or place. So, striking a boss after being fired is a good example of neurotic anxiety. There, the id broke through the ego's defenses and caused even more trouble than simply being fired. Finally, moral anxiety came from the superego. There, a forbidden action occurred, having extramarital sex with a neighbor, for example. The superego was insufficiently strong to hold back the id's pressure. But, guilt now followed (instead of pleasure) and feelings of worthlessness and shame might arise.

Interestingly, Freud (Breuer & Freud, 1895, p. 305) told his patients that he was happy with his therapeutic results "if we succeed in transforming your hysterical misery into common unhappiness." To that end, much of his therapy centered on discovering how his patients were dealing with their anxieties. Patients did not realize exactly how they coped with their problems. Freud proposed that they did so via defense mechanisms, or unconscious methods they employed unknowingly that helped them allay or disguise their anxieties. However, it was Freud's daughter, Anna, who formalized the definitions shown below (Freud, 1946).

Defense mechanisms operate unconsciously and they distort reality in a way that reduces anxiety. *Repression* does so by putting the anxiety-arousing item into the unconscious, thus hiding it from the ego. But in Freudian theory, simply placing the item in the unconscious does not mean that it is gone. It can still slip into consciousness during dreams, slips of the tongue, or in humor. One goal of psychoanalysis was to uncover those repressed items and confront them.

Denial is another defense mechanism in which reality is distorted in order to reduce anxiety. Denial is refusing to see or admit the truth of a situation. Parents, often, are in denial about their children. They may, unconsciously, believe that their children are smarter, better behaved, or more moral than they actually are. For parents to think otherwise might raise their levels of anxiety to a point too high for them to handle.

Projection is another common defense mechanism. It consists of blaming others or blaming things instead of blaming oneself. People who project reduce their anxiety because they hardly ever blame themselves for anything. Imagine playing doubles tennis with a poor partner. But, that partner refuses to admit a lack of tennis skill. Instead, missed shots or net balls are blamed on the wind, falling leaves, or distractions from other players or spectators.

Rationalization reduces anxiety by substituting a socially acceptable reason for one that is socially unacceptable. So, failing a class because of being lazy might arouse high levels of anxiety. But, failing the class because of exhaustion is less anxiety arousing.

Intellectualization is a defense mechanism where emotion is actively suppressed and knowledge is sought instead. It is as if cold hard facts are substituted for an emotional reaction. So, faced with a life-threatening illness, a patient may turn to the Internet and devour all of the information available online about the disease. Doing that may prove to be less anxiety arousing than facing the reality of imminent death.

Regression is retreating developmentally to an earlier way of coping with anxiety. Typical expressions of regression might include crying, throwing a tantrum, or refusing to continue an activity. The volatile professional tennis player Ilie Nastase regressed once during a match following what he thought was a bad call by the chair umpire. His opponent was serving, so Nastase stood to receive serve but held his racquet under his arm and allowed the serves to come in without returning them. Regression is often childish.

Reaction formation is one of the better-known defense mechanisms. In reaction, formation people unconsciously express the exact opposite of their true feelings. Doing otherwise would arouse too much anxiety. Consider the young teacher whose first job might be at a tough, inner city school where students are violent and gang activity is rife. He might say, "I love my job" and really mean it. Because to admit to himself that he wasted four years in college to take a dangerous and low-paying job might be too anxiety provoking. Also think of all of the movies where the stars first "hate" each other. It's almost cliché to realize that they will marry by the end of the film.

Displacement is another well-known defense mechanism. Here, the superego prevails, warning off (again unconsciously) the ego from engaging in some forbidden activity such as having an affair or beating up the boss. Instead, that energy is redirected into a more socially acceptable behavior. Engaging in hobbies or playing musical instruments being classic examples.

Compensation is another defense mechanism in which a substitution takes place unconsciously. Here the issue is a perceived deficit, perhaps physical or intellectual, and is compensated for by becoming skilled in another area. The most famous example (and most likely highly exaggerated) was Napoleon's lack of stature. He compensated by attempting to conquer the whole of Europe!

As noted, Freud was highly influential, but he was also highly protective of his theory and ideas. The "committee" attempted to shield him from the day-to-day effort required to keep his ideas "pure." Many of the people initially drawn to Freud and his ideas either later distanced themselves from him or were rebuffed by him. But, their ideas, too, became part of psychotherapy.

JUNG'S ANALYTICAL PSYCHOLOGY

C. G. Jung (1875–1961)

Biography

Christened Karl Gustav by his parents, Jung changed the spelling to Carl while at college. Later in his life he was universally known as C. G. He was born in Kesswil, Switzerland, to a relatively poor family. He was the fourth child born to his parents but the first to survive infancy. His father, Paul, was a minister in the Swiss Reformed Church at Laufen near the Rheinfall, the highest waterfall in Europe. His mother Emilie was hospitalized for several years early in Jung's life, so he was looked after by two other women. His father, too, spent much time with him. He nearly always answered Carl's questions with a call to faith, an answer Carl could not accept. He wanted to know the scientific answer. After his father transferred to another parish near Basel, his mother's health improved, and she gave birth to a girl, Trudi. Jung attended a gymnasium in Basel where

PHOTO 13.2 C. G. Jung

Credit: Getty Images

he was an excellent student but rough and uncultured compared to his urban peers. Once, a teacher accused him of plagiarizing an essay because it was so well written. The work was Jung's but the charge stuck. Another time, a fellow student pushed Jung to the curb causing him to faint. He began to have fainting spells from then on, so many that he had to leave school for many months. After overhearing his parents despair about his condition, he decided to conquer it through the force of his will. He finished his years at the gymnasium successfully and went on to the University of Basel to study medicine. In doing so, he was following the footsteps of his grandfather and namesake, a famous medical doctor.

Contributions

Jung prospered at Basel. Shortly after beginning his studies, Jung's father died leaving the family in dire financial straits. Jung secured a loan from a relative and managed to support his mother and sister while completing his studies. He soon decided to specialize in psychiatry. His dissertation, "On the psychology and pathology of so-called occult phenomena," was inspired by the séances conducted by his cousin, Helly Preiswerk. Upon graduation, he obtained a position as a psychiatrist at the Burghölzi Mental Hospital in Zurich. There he worked for ten years with Eugen Bleuler, one of the pioneers of psychotherapy who coined the term "schizophrenia."

At Burghölzi, Jung treated schizophrenics and began to listen closely to their wild rantings and attempted to understand them. He adapted the Word Association Test and used it as a method to investigate the minds of his patients. Jung used the test as a quantitative measure of resistance by precisely measuring the time it took for patients to respond to each word. He assumed that responses to words that took longer indicated unconscious resistance to that topic. The results he obtained brought him his first measure of fame as a psychiatrist.

Jung had read Breuer and Freud's (1895) book soon after its publication. A few years later, he reread it and began a correspondence with Freud. Soon, they were writing each other regularly with Freud nearly always answering letters promptly and Jung not. Jung regularly began his letters with an apology for not answering sooner. Their letters indicated from the beginning that their respective views on psychopathology and therapy were not entirely congruent. Nevertheless, they continued to write each other and on March 3, 1907, they finally met face to face in Vienna.

Jung walked into Freud's house at 1 p.m. and did not leave until 2 a.m. the next morning; both were surprised that 13 h had passed seemingly unnoticed. Delighted as they were to have found each other as kindred spirits in the study of personality they realized from the onset that they were not in complete agreement with each other. For one thing, Jung was decidedly uncomfortable with Freud's position on infantile sexuality. Freud, right from the start, saw himself as the father figure in their relationship. In Jung, he quickly perceived, lay the future of Freudian psychoanalysis. Jung was younger, already well known professionally, and most importantly, not Jewish. Because of all of those qualities Freud believed that Jung could become his successor and take psychoanalysis to a much larger audience.

Consequently, Freud laid new responsibilities on Jung including organizing the first meeting of the Congress for Freudian Psychology and taking on the editorship of a new journal devoted to psychoanalysis. The new relationship between Jung and Freud put a severe strain on Jung's relationship with Bleuler, and he soon asked Jung to resign. Jung did and began a private practice in Zurich. Shortly after, he and Freud went to the United States at G. Stanley Hall's invitation. Hall had invited both of them independently, but Freud and his theory were the biggest beneficiaries of the trip. Of course, at that time Jung had not yet begun to differentiate his ideas sharply from Freud's. Jung relished his visit to New York. Bair (2003, p. 163) wrote,

> He and Freud saw the United States from differing points of view. Jung was wildly enthusiastic about American culture and eager to experience every aspect of it in order to better understand its vastly diversified population. Freud had little interest in the American people or their country except to impose his theory on it.

Freud would only visit the United States once during his lifetime. Jung, however, returned four more times, all before the onset of World War II.

Jung's friendship with Freud quickly disintegrated over the next several years following their trip to the United States. The final nail in that coffin came when Jung published a book that added a new twist to Freud's thinking about the unconscious. That new idea was the **collective unconscious**, a concept that would prove central to Jung's later theorizing. The idea for the collective unconscious had been brewing in Jung's mind since his childhood. It became more prominent to him after Freud analyzed one of his dreams during their trip to the United States. In that dream, Jung found himself in a house he assumed was his own. As he descended deeper into the lower levels of the house, he found himself in a basement full of pottery shards and skulls. He interpreted those as the remains of an ancient culture. Freud tried to get him to identify whose skulls they were so that Jung could identify his death wishes against the people represented by the skulls. Jung, however, rejected Freud's attempted interpretation and stuck to his original idea, that he was seeing evidence of the collective unconscious. From that point on, his theory and Freud's diverged greatly. Jung and Freud broke completely from each other soon afterward. After 1913, they never communicated again. The shock of the break and its accompanying changes were distressful to Jung. Although he never ceased his practice or his teaching, he ventured near psychosis as he pursued the nature of the collective unconscious within his dreams and visions.

Jung began to keep secret and detailed journals of his mental experiences, the *Black Books* and later the *Red Book*. Jung called those years his confrontation with the unconscious. From then on, he began to seek confirmation that the dream experiences he had were derived from the collective unconscious and that the symbols he had dreamt of were found universally. In trips to the United States, Africa, and India, he visited with locals and confirmed his ideas about the collective unconscious. Later, he began to collect and study ancient texts on alchemy in order to link them with his ideas about the collective unconscious as well. Jung, more so than anyone before or since, successfully broadened the study of personality beyond the borders of psychology itself. He studied those myths, religions, and occult practices (such as alchemy) in order to discover commonalities between them and psychology. He did so, however, as a scientist, always answering his critics by noting that the important issue was not whether he believed in the topics he was studying, but that the symbols those topics shared were manifested in the collective unconscious. Near the end of his life, he even began to study extraterrestrial beings and flying saucers. Again, he never argued for their physical reality. Instead, he argued that those beliefs came from the collective unconscious combined with the anxieties generated by the atomic age.

The years preceding World War II were controversial for Jung. He held the presidency of the International Society for Psychotherapy starting in 1933, the year Hitler seized power in Germany. Over the next few years, as it became clear that the Nazis sought complete control over German science, including psychiatry, Jung found himself in an extremely uncomfortable position. The Nazis had publicly burned Freud's books and "conformed" German science by expelling all Jews from German scientific societies. Jung, however, secretly rewrote the bylaws of the International Society for Psychotherapy so that individuals (Jews, especially) could join without first having to be members of their national societies. He also arranged for the last meeting of the International Society before World War II to take place in England and not Germany. He did that so Jewish members could attend and participate. However, it is still an open question to historians about Jung's motivations and behavior in the late 1930s. Valiunas (2011, pp. 114–115) noted:

> Richard Hayman's *A Life of Jung* (1999) is appropriately unsparing about Jung's political follies. Deidre Bair's *Jung: A Biography* (2003), on the other hand, gestures toward even-handed comprehensiveness but settles into apologetics . . . Still, it must be acknowledged that Jung recognized the monstrous in Nazism even as he was heralding the movement. The essay "Wotan," which appeared in a Swiss journal in March 1936 . . . opens with a catalogue of horrors, the "veritable witches' Sabbath" that followed the Great War.

Once World War II began, Switzerland managed to remain neutral although there were widespread worries early during the war that Germany would attempt to annex the German-speaking cantons. Isolated by the war, Jung continued to practice therapy and write. In 1944, while taking a walk, he fell and broke his leg. While recuperating, he suffered a heart attack and became comatose. In his last book (Jung, 1965, p. 289) he wrote:

> At the beginning of 1944 I broke my foot, and this misadventure was followed by a heart attack. In a state of unconsciousness I experienced deliriums and visions which must have begun when I hung on the edge of death . . . It seemed to me that I was high up in space. Far below my feet lay Ceylon [Sri Lanka], and in the distance ahead of me the subcontinent of India.

Despite his advancing age and failing health, Jung continued to write productively until the very end of his life. His legacy, analytical psychology, never achieved the prominence of Freud's psychoanalysis. Jung, however, did inspire many others to explore and investigate his claims of universal symbols. In fact, he coined the now familiar phrases "New Age" and "Age of Aquarius." McCabe (2018) detailed little known indirect and direct correspondence that took place between 1945 and 1961 between Jung and Bill Miller, founder of Alcoholics Anonymous. The intermediary of those indirect letters was Margarita Luttichau, Jung's student and a protégé of Bill Wilson. Although Jung was generally opposed to group therapy, he found merit in the work of Alcoholics Anonymous.

Jung's Main Ideas

As noted above, the main construct in Jung's complex theory of the personality (or psyche as he termed it) was the collective unconscious. He added other components as well: the persona, anima and animus, and the shadow. He introduced the terms extraversion and introversion as well. His theory was the first to assume development throughout the lifespan. He promoted a typology of personality with eight different types. It's a mistake to think of Jung's theory as simply a modification of Freud's. The two are quite different even though both introspectively examine the unconscious.

For Jung the scientist, the psyche had to obey the rules of physical science, especially the law of conservation of energy. Furthermore, obeying those laws implied that normal personalities were balanced or in equilibrium. It followed logically that abnormal personalities were unbalanced and that the role of the psychotherapist was to analyze and then suggest ways to restore the balance. Jung was quite different in his approach to therapy. Where Freud put his *patients* on the couch and interacted with them minimally, Jung and his **analysands** sat facing each other in comfortable chairs, sometimes knee-to-knee. Moreover, Jung spoke throughout the session, very often speaking more and about himself than the analysands spoke about themselves and their problems. Where Freud's patients engaged in free associationistic monologues, Jung's patients engaged in active dialogues with him. The goal of Jungian therapy was to attain individuation, a state where all of the various parts of the personality can find "their fullest degree of differentiation, development, and exposure" (Hall & Lindsey, 1970, p. 101).

The collective unconscious was home to a large number of **archetypes** or templates for behavior that Jung believed were found universally in everyone's collective unconscious. They came, Jung believed, from the collective experience of humankind over the long evolutionary history of the species. Some archetypes were even older than that and came from animal ancestors (e.g., eating, surviving, and reproducing). The archetypes, being unconscious, only revealed themselves during dreams, visions, humor, or slips of the tongue. Jung, following his break with Freud, had forced himself to face and discover these archetypes primarily through dream analysis. He realized their universality after visiting with native peoples in Africa, the United States, and India. Later, he turned to ancient alchemy texts and deduced that the medieval alchemists had earlier discovered archetypes in their own work. Jung believed there were many archetypes but that some were more common than others. They included: the hero, birth and rebirth, death, the old wise man, the earth mother, the devil, and God.

Jung's theory of the personality was complex. It included the personal unconscious, which was very similar to Freud's, and the collective unconscious. The **persona** was inspired by the masks used by ancient Greek actors. To Jung, everyone had a mask or a persona that they exhibited to the world. The persona was the public face of the personality. Children and young people developed their personas under the influence of social pressure, especially pressure to conform. In the second half of life, Jung argued that older people were more able to show their egos publicly and no longer needed to hide their true selves behind a mask. Think of older men and women who fearlessly speak their minds in public. In contrast, think of those whose jobs require them to interact with the public. Jobs in sales, daycare, or government agencies often require employees to cover up their true feelings about their customers, parents, or recipients of benefits. Those who are the best in those jobs can adopt their personas sincerely and convincingly. The personas of others in those occupations are sometimes easy to see through. Meeting such people outside of their job setting may be shocking. There, they may drop those masks and reveal their true personalities.

Jung also believed that men and women each possessed archetypes that expressed the thoughts and feelings of the opposite sex. Thus, the male psyche had an **anima** while the female psyche had an **animus**. These archetypes, derived from the evolutionary past, helped both sexes understand each other better. However, each could also impede understanding if the archetypes were too discrepant from actuality. Thus, a man whose anima projected women as homebound mothers and housewives might have great marital difficulties if he married a woman who did not fit that archetype. Similarly, a woman whose animus projected men as caring and giving caretakers of their children might not understand why her husband worked late and weekends at the office. Jung's anima and animus were novel aspects to the personality; he assumed that sex roles were more complicated than previously thought.

The psyche also contained the **shadow**. Like a real shadow, it followed the ego around constantly. The shadow archetype represented hidden motives and desires (it is Jung's counterpart to the Freudian id). In twentieth century parlance, the shadow is much like "the dark side of the force" made popular by the *Star Wars* movies. That series of films nicely illustrated many Jungian archetypes including: the Jedi Knight as the *hero*, Ben Kenobi as the *wise old man*, and Princess Leia as the *maiden*. Luke Skywalker was on the *quest*. The shadow was where one's true desires and feelings were located. Often, those feelings and desires were such that saying them out loud or acting upon them might cause real trouble (e.g., as in sexual harassment). Thus, the shadow was a protective structure for the normal personality. If the shadow tool over the psyche incarceration or commitment to a mental health facility could easily be the result.

Jung also was the first to use the terms extraversion and introversion, and they have been part of descriptions of personality ever since. In Jung's system, they balanced each other, so those who exhibited extraversions (e.g., through the ego) would, inside, be introverted; they would possess an introverted personal unconscious. Jung added four functions to the personality as well. He termed thinking and feeling as rational functions. The other two, sensation and intuition, he called irrational. By combining the functions to the attitudes of extraversion and introversion, he created a theory of psychological types with eight separate categories. Jung never argued that the types dominated a person's personality. For him they were more like loose-fitting clothing. Furthermore, each visible type (the superior type) was paired with another complementary one (the inferior one). The Meyers-Briggs Type Indicator (MBTI) was a test later developed based on those Jungian types.

Jung's eight personality types were:

- Extraverted Sensation: People with this type tend to be thrill-seekers.

- Introverted Sensation: People with this type notice details that others miss.

- Extraverted Thinking: People with this type are good problem solvers.

- Introverted Thinking: People with this type love abstract theories and ideas.

- Extraverted Feeling: People with this type are easy to get along with.

- Introverted Feeling: People with this type silently live up to their rigid standards.

- Extraverted Intuitive: People with this type envision future possibilities easily.

- Intraverted Intuitive: People with this type treat their own ideas as real.

Randall et al. (2017) in a meta-analysis of the MBTI concluded that the test gave useful data when used on college populations. They wrote:

> The populations in six of the seven studies were college-age students in various academic programs; thus, interpretations of the tool are perhaps more applicable to this population than to others. Given this, we have a relatively good degree of confidence that we can generalize the findings from this systematic review of the literature in our university classrooms.

Jung, like Freud, used dreams extensively in his therapy. But, unlike Freud, who used particular dreams mostly as starting points for free association, Jung stuck more closely to the dream itself, mining it for all of the evidence possible. Jung also distinguished between "big" dreams and "little" ones, attaching more importance to the former. He also paid more attention to repetitive dreams or serial dreams. Those he considered more important as well. Here are some examples of the repetitive dreams I have experienced over the years. When I was younger I often dreamt that I had to cross a bridge, another archetype. Only, in my dreams the bridge was always under construction. The only way across was to walk or crawl along the girders that eventually would hold the roadway. More often than not, the bridge was long, high, and crossed a broad expanse of water. All of those dream features connected nicely to Jung's notion of the first and second half of life. The main mission for the young, Jung maintained, was to learn, raise a family, and develop some degree of financial comfort. All of those are frightening prospects. Today, my most repetitive dreams concern a country house I lived in with my wife and young children some years ago. Home is another archetype. That house sat on five acres ten miles outside of town and was surrounded by woods and pasture. The nearest neighbors were about a half-mile away. There's a big difference in dreaming about crossing a dangerous bridge compared to dreaming about living in an idyllic home. Jung might argue that the home archetype represents the place to which we all hope to return following our life's adventures.

Again, it is a mistake to think of Jung's analytic personality theory as a simple extension and modification of Freud's psychoanalytic theory. Jung made the collective unconscious the central core of his theory. Freud's theory possessed no similar structure. Jung also rejected, from the beginning, Freud's primacy of infantile sexuality as the dominant source of energy for the personality. Both, however, always considered themselves as scientists who were plumbing the depths of the unconscious mind through introspective means. Their reliance on introspection, their own and that of their patients, was one source of discomfort for psychologists who had already rejected introspection as a reliable method for psychological research. Jung's introspections, especially, were difficult for others to fathom because they ranged so widely into ancient and universal mythology. Freud also inspired another reaction to his theorizing from Alfred Adler. He was another of Freud's early followers and the first to defect from psychoanalysis. He called his approach to personality individual psychology.

ADLER'S INDIVIDUAL PSYCHOLOGY

Alfred Adler (1870–1937)

Biography

Adler was born in Vienna to middle-class Jewish parents. His father was a grain merchant. Adler was a sickly child who suffered from rickets. When he was four-years old, he nearly died of pneumonia and overheard his doctor tell his parents that he would not live. He did survive and vowed to become a better doctor than the one who had treated him. He struggled physically and academically during his school years. At one point, a teacher suggested that he become an apprentice cobbler because he had failed his mathematics course (Lundin, 1989). He persisted, passed the course, and went on to become an ophthalmologist after completing his studies at the University of Vienna. He later changed his medical interests and became a psychiatrist.

Contributions

In 1902, Freud invited Adler to join his Wednesday night meetings of the Vienna Psychoanalytic Society. Interestingly, although Adler was familiar with Freud's early writings and had even defended them in print, he was not one of Freud's students or disciples. In addition and unlike the rest of the members of the Wednesday group Adler had never undergone psychoanalysis. Nevertheless, he rose to the presidency of the group and edited its journal. By 1911, however, his ideas and Freud's had diverged so far from each other that a break was unavoidable. The break came after Adler published his own views on psychoanalysis. He resigned from the group and gave up editorship of the journal. Several other members also resigned at the same time. Together, they and Adler set up a competing psychoanalytic group, the Society for Individual Psychology, and began publishing their own psychoanalytic journal.

PHOTO 13.3 Alfred Adler

The reasons for Adler's break from Freud included acute discomfort with Freud's emphasis on the primacy of sex as a human motive and disagreement with his division of the personality into id, ego, and superego. Instead, Adler saw the personality as a unitary structure. He believed that all individuals were unique and, thus, had to be understood as the interactive outcomes of a multiplicity of factors, especially social ones. So, Adler soon brought new social features to his individual psychology such as the effect of birth order, social interest, activity, and striving for superiority. As was the case in Jung's analytical psychology, Adler's individual psychology was much more than a casual tweaking of Freudian psychoanalysis. Although Adler's and Freud's systems originated from common interests they diverged widely soon thereafter.

After the break with Freud, Adler published extensively. His interests branched out into new applied areas such as education. He was a social activist and promoted the equality of women, another major difference between him and Freud. Although he had converted to Christianity he still feared Nazi persecution because of his Jewish family history. So, he emigrated to the United States where he taught first at Columbia University and later at the Long Island College of Medicine. He died of a heart attack two years later while lecturing in Scotland. His approach to psychopathology and its treatment still is practiced today. Bettner (2020) cited how Adler's ideas combined optimism, striving to improve, the role of family dynamics, individual courage, and the founding of child guidance centers all bear witness to the ongoing influence of individual psychology.

Adler's Main Ideas

Adler's approach to personality and psychotherapy focused on human uniqueness, the interaction of people with their environment, feelings of inferiority, and pursuit of short-term and long-term personal goals. Unlike Freud or Jung, Adler viewed the personality as a unitary construct, describing it as the flower that bloomed from the union of its germ cells. That flower, like the personality, was a unity, not a collection of independent parts. Adlerian therapy closely resembled Jung's in its treatment of patients as equals, but differed in its goals. Where Jung and Freud looked to the unconscious in one way or another, Adler concentrated on the present, the "here and now."

Adler called his approach "individual psychology" intentionally. He believed that every human was unique and that it was a mistake to view a person otherwise. While he did not discount the influence of biology on the personality, his early medical practice had shown him that many patients with "organ inferiority" (e.g., those with poor eyes or ears) overcame their physical deficits through practice of force of will. He transferred that idea into psychiatry later and called it **compensation**. Just as he had overcome his own childhood physical problems, so had his patients overcome their psychological ones. Unlike Freud's version of compensation, Adler did not believe it needed to be unconscious. It could be conscious or unconscious.

Adler put much stock in how people related to their social environments, beginning with the *family constellation* where children first interact with their mothers and later with other family members. He recalled how he felt "dethroned" following the birth of a younger brother. He had to cope with the loss of his mother's attention as she spent more time caring for the new baby. Later, as a psychologist, he studied the effects of birth order categorizing children as first-born, middle child, last born, and only child. He noted that first-borns tended to be leaders, middle children were more competitive, and that last-borns were more likely to be spoiled by their parents and develop into problem children. More recently, the study of birth-order effects has spawned much research and controversy.

THEN AND NOW
BIRTH ORDER EFFECTS

Since Adler first described birth-order effects much research effort has been devoted toward confirming or disconfirming the idea that first-borns enjoy advantages over later-borns. Currently, research suggests that in a number of measures, especially academic success and income, birth order effects are real. First-borns do better in school and earn more money than their later-born siblings. But, that is not the end of the story. The next question is what causes the birth-order effect. That question has yet to be adequately resolved although there are a number of competing theories. The parental time dilution theory argued that first-borns get to spend more quality time with their parents than do later-borns. Zajonc's confluence model identified several factors as important in explaining birth-order effects: first borns receive more parental attention, are exposed to adult language earlier and more often, and as younger siblings are born, become their teachers. The model also argued that the overall intellectual milieu of the family declined as more children are born. Related to the confluence model is the "no one left to teach" theory. It explained the poorer academic performance of last-borns by the fact that those children do not get to learn by tutoring younger siblings. Regardless of the theory, severe methodological problems remain. Birth order is not the only variable of interest. Gender, too, plays an important role. In a two-child family, there are four possible birth orders: boy–girl, boy–boy, girl–boy, and girl–girl. Most studies fail to distinguish between those types of two-child families. The spacing of children by birth order also can affect the results as when a two-child family consists of children born far apart in time. In such cases the second child may be treated more like a first child. Also, parents change, too, and may become more adept at caregiving as they rear additional children. Economic factors can also play a role as family income tends to rise over the course of a marriage. So, Adler's original conception about birth order still inspires much research. Rohrer et al. (2017) reviewed such recent research and conducted their own large scale study on 11 narrow personality measures coming from a large database, the German Socio-Economic Panel, they wrote (p. 1822), "that allows for both between- and within-family analyses of birth-order effect." Only one of those measures, self-reported intellect, showed a significant statistical difference between first- and later-borns, a result that confirmed other research on that measure. They concluded (p. 1827):

Taken together, our analyses indicated that there were no statistically significant birth-order effects across various model specifications on locus of control, negative and positive reciprocity, life satisfaction, interpersonal trust, risk taking, patience, impulsivity, and political orientation. By contrast, our analyses showed that the small effect of birth order on self-reported intellect, which had already been reported for the present sample (Rohrer et al., 2015), was robust across a wide range of possible specifications, which demonstrates that specification-curve analysis is sensitive enough to detect small effects, even on a single-item measure.

Thus, the overall picture on birth-order and its effects is still unclear and will likely occupy the attention of psychologists for years to come.

Adler placed much importance on schools and education as social factors in the development of personality. Always believing that prevention was preferable to therapy, he founded many child guidance centers in Vienna. He also believed that a person's style of life was already established by the age of five, so it was important to work with children while they were young and still malleable. All people possessed feelings of inferiority, Adler thought. Mere possession of such feelings, however, was not abnormal. Instead, feelings of inferiority were actually the main source of energy in the personality. People strove to overcome their feelings of inferiority through conscious and unconscious goal setting. His **inferiority complex**, however, was an abnormal feature of the personality. People who possessed an inferiority complex felt discouraged and lacked hope for the future. Some overcompensated by lashing out against others violently. In either manifestation, they required therapy.

Adler's approach was teleological, meaning that he believed the future was more important than the past because everyone had short-term and long-term goals. Furthermore, although the past and the present were important, they did not determine the direction of action. Instead, the past and the present worked together with goals to determine future action. In Adler's psychology, the individual chose the goal and that choice was the principal determinant of action or behavior. For example, suppose a college student was studying for a test when a roommate suggested they play a video game. If the student declined, then the goal directing behavior was obvious. Studying was more important. Sometimes, Adler allowed for hidden goals, or goals about which a person was unaware. Freud or Jung might have called those types of goals "unconscious." Adler, in contrast, did not. Some goals might be completely fictional (e.g., to grow up to play shortstop for the New York Yankees), but they would still work as goals. Thus, a child with such a goal might buy a baseball mitt and spend hours throwing and fielding a baseball bouncing off of a wall. For that child the fictional goal would explain the long hours of practice. Similarly, everyone, Adler argued, had their own fictional goals: all men and women are created equal, crime does not pay, or honesty is the best policy. None of those statements are objectively true. Some people are smarter than others. Some criminals succeed and do not pay the consequences. Being honest might ruin a friendship. Yet, for most people those fictional goals determined the actions they took.

Beyond these goals lay a final goal, one that was usually unknown either partly or totally. This final goal was subjective and different for everyone. It eventually answers the question of: Who am I? Most college students pursue their degrees in this way. They know that they need high GPAs and admission test scores. They know they need to attend class, complete their assignments, and take tests. Many change their majors at least once in response to changing goals. Some even graduate without really knowing what their life's work will be. But, nearly all will have some kind of internal fictional final goal (to become a famous surgeon, to raise happy children, or to win the lottery and never have to work again). The exceptions, those who do not have final goals are candidates for therapy. Adlerian therapy might help them identify who they are and what they want from life.

Adlerian therapy, while still seeking personal insight, was quite different from the Freudian or Jungian models. Mosak and Maniacci (2011, p. 84) listed six goals of Adlerian therapy:

1. The fostering of social interest.

2. The decrease of inferiority feelings, the overcoming of discouragement, and the recognition and utilization of one's resources.

3. Changes in the person's life-style—that is, in her or his perceptions and goals. The therapeutic goal, as we have noted, involves transforming big errors into little ones (as with automobiles, some need a tune-up and others require a major overhaul).

4. Changing faulty motivation that underlies even acceptable behavior, or changing values.

5. Encouraging the individual to recognize equality among people (Dreikurs, 1971).

6. Helping the person to become a contributing human being.

LEARNING OBJECTIVE

7. List the ways that Adler's therapy differed from Freud's.

Unlike Freud, Adler sought to develop a personal relationship with his patients. Similarly to Jung, Adler sat with his patients face to face on chairs that were of the same size and shape and equally comfortable. Adler encouraged the development of feelings of equality between patients and himself. During therapy, Adler tried to discover where patients fit in their families. He probed them for their earliest memories as well, believing that those memories revealed much about their style of life. He asked them about their families, occupation, hobbies, interests, and other personal or cultural values. Following that, he would list their *basic mistakes* about life. Mosak and Maniacci (2011, p. 87) listed "overgeneralization . . . false or impossible goals of security . . . misperceptions of life and life's demands . . . minimization or denial of one's worth . . . family values" as basic mistakes about living that therapists should identify and correct through interpretation.

I often ask students to share their earliest memories. Many students cannot recall events in their lives that took place when they were less than five years old. A small minority claim to remember events when they were two years old or even younger. One of my earliest memories dates from when I was three or four. My father and I were sitting on the stairway landing halfway upstairs looking out a window at *Nevado del Ruiz*, a distant Andean peak that was only visible from Bogota in clear weather (see Photo 13.4). From that memory, Adler might have inferred the existence of an early and close relationship between my father and I. He would have been correct.

PHOTO 13.4 Nevado del Ruiz as seen from Bogota, Colombia

Credit: Getty Images

In Adlerian therapy, the therapist was free to suggest interpretations about patients' problems. But, Adlerians did not emphasize patients' pasts or use free association. Dreams were interpreted but in a manner much different than the way Freud or Jung might do so. Adler did not believe in universal symbols nor did he think that dreams required decoding because of a censor in the preconscious. Adler did classify dreams and interpret their meanings though. He listed several common dreams and what they meant. So, dreams about falling might represent a loss of some kind. Dreams about flying, on the other hand, might suggest victory over obstacles. Dreams of being chased could indicate feelings of inferiority. True to his vision of individual psychology, Adler believed that dreams had to be interpreted *in toto* and not as single dreams. Thus, he would interpret a person's dreams over a long period and not look at only individual dreams. Moreover, Adler saw dreams as functional, as ways of solving future problems. To Adler, not remembering dreams was a sign of mental health.

Adler's individual psychology influenced many other later models of personality and psychotherapy. Ellenberger (1970, p. 645) wrote, "It would not be easy to find another author from which so much has been borrowed from all sides without acknowledgment than Adler." Others have suggested that the traditional category of Neo-Freudian psychotherapy ought toreally be called Neo-Adlerian.

TWO FEMALE ANALYSTS

Karen Horney (1885–1952)

Biography

Karen Horney was born in Hamburg, Germany. Her father was a ship's captain; consequently he was away from home for long periods. Horney was much more attached to her mother, who supported her educational ambitions. She was fortunate in that she was born at the point where German universities had begun to admit women into their medical schools. She graduated from the University of Berlin; several years later she began to teach at the local institute for psychoanalysis. Ten years later, after divorcing her husband, she moved to Chicago to become associate director of the Chicago Institute for Psychoanalysis. In 1934, she moved to New York City to teach at its Psychoanalytic Institute. Because of negative reactions from colleagues in response to her critiques of Freudian theory she resigned that position and founded a competing organization, the American Institute of Psychoanalysis. Quinn's (2019) biography illustrated how deep a rift Horney caused among Freudian theorists of the New York Psychoanalytic Society and how Horney eventually felt compelled to start her own group.

Contributions

Horney disagreed with Freud's emphasis on sexuality, his assertion that aggression was innate, and the importance of the id in the personality structure. Most of all, she disagreed with his use of penis envy to explain the female personality. Because of that she rejected his explanation of the Oedipus Complex and, instead, argued that social factors in early childhood within the family (e.g., maternal overprotection or paternal rejection) were responsible for how children developed. In the same vein, she believed that Freud's developmental stages were not universal. She was among the first psychoanalysts to promote a feminist psychology. In place of Freud's penis envy she proposed womb envy, arguing that men realize they cannot give birth and thus are biologically excluded from life's most creative activity.

Her own theory accepted parts of Freudian theory, especially unconscious motivation and the role of the psyche in initiating behavior. Her most original contribution was basic anxiety. She described it (Horney, 1945, p. 41) as:

> The feeling a child has of being isolated and helpless in a potentially hostile world. A wide range of adverse factors in the environment can produce this insecurity in a child: direct or indirect

PHOTO 13.5 Karen Horney

Credit: Getty Images

domination, indifference, erratic behavior, lack of respect for the child's individual needs, lack of real guidance, disparaging attitudes, too much admiration or the absence of it, lack of reliable warmth, having to take sides in parental disagreements, too much or too little responsibility, overprotection, isolation from other children, injustice, discrimination, unkept promises, hostile atmosphere, and so on and so on.

Thus, Horney adopted a social basis for her personality theory. Conditions such as those described above could lead to the development of a neurotic personality. In her later theorizing, she identified ten neurotic needs. Later, she collapsed those under three headings. Under *moving toward people* were the needs of affection, approval, and for a partner. Under *moving away from people* were the needs for power, social recognition, personal achievement, self-admiration, and a need to exploit others. Under *moving against people* were needs for perfection, self-sufficiency, and restriction of life practices. Later still she collapsed the needs even further into the categories of compliance, aggression, and detachment, each of which represented a coping strategy for neurotic anxiety. Unlike Freud, Horney believed these categories developed through experience and were not innate characteristics.

Horney's theories included comparison between the *real self* and the *ideal self*. The real self is an accurate and honest assessment of the personality. The ideal self reflects potential life outcomes. A neurotic might create an unrealistic ideal self in order to combat threats to self-esteem. At the same time, creating such an ideal self impedes understanding of one's true self. Horney's therapy in such cases was directed at making patients understand that they themselves had created their false ideal selves. This was a far cry from "Freud's stance of scientific and moral neutrality towards neurosis . . . She therefore urged people to become aware of this conflict so as to become true to themselves" (Sayers, 1991, p. 136). While Horney was moving away from Freud, his daughter Anna was extending his theories into childhood.

Anna Freud (1895–1982)

Biography

Anna Freud was the last of Freud's children. (Note to reader: To avoid confusion I will use "Anna Freud" and "Freud" for Sigmund Freud in this section.) She later described her childhood as unhappy. As a child she was competitive with her sister Sophie. Anna Freud eventually became her father's constant companion and was allowed to sit and watch while he conversed with visitors in his study. She attended the Cottage Lyceum, a school not designed to prepare students for university studies. She never attended a university. Later in life she proudly displayed the honorary degrees she had received, "perhaps out of regret at never having had a university education" (Sayers, 1991, p. 182).

Contributions

Freud began to psychoanalyze her when she was 23 years old, a practice that would be ethically forbidden today. Two years later, she presented her first paper to the Vienna Psychoanalytic Society and became a lay analyst. The topic of her paper, "The Relation of Beating Fantasies to a Daydream," supposedly was about a clinical case but in reality was autobiographical. In her paper she supported her father's ideas about females and the Oedipus Complex.

After becoming an analyst, Anna Freud began a private practice of her own. Her office was opposite to Freud's, and they shared the same waiting room. She began to see children as patients, something Freud never did, although he approved of the idea. In her therapy with children she used dream and daydream analysis as well as interpreting children's drawings. She believed that children were unable to free associate as well as adults. Thus, they could not be analyzed by examining their resistances. One of her main contributions to psychoanalysis during this period was clarifying the defense mechanisms. In the long run, that work began a new direction in Freudian theory, one that more closely examined the ego instead of the id.

PHOTO 13.6 Anna Freud

As Freud's health deteriorated, Anna Freud became more and more attached to him, becoming his main helpmate. At the same time, the *zeitgeist* in Austria had changed markedly becoming pro-Nazi. In 1938, Germany effectively annexed Austria putting the Freuds in deadly peril. The Gestapo interviewed Anna Freud and frightened her. Shortly after, she and her father left Austria for London. They left all four of Freud's sisters behind in Vienna only to discover after World War II that all had died in Nazi concentration camps. Anna Freud's response to an interview question about that news was, "They [the Nazis] wanted their apartments" (Young-Bruehl, 2008, p. 280). No one in the family had envisioned that such harm would come to four elderly Jewish ladies.

Freud died in England about a year after his arrival, (soon after World War II broke out). Anna Freud became the director of the Hampstead War Nursery where she provided care to children displaced by the war. Her experiences there caused her to rethink her previous ideas about psychoanalysis. Young children separated from their mothers suffered more than those whose mothers stayed with them. In addition, the mother's behavior also made a big difference. Children modeled their mothers during bomb attacks, for instance. Children whose mothers were calm remained calm themselves while those whose mothers were anxious also showed anxiety. These observations led her to revise Freudian theory to emphasize the role of mothering, a distinct departure. After the war, she advised physicians about the dangers of hospitalizing young children without having their mothers with them. Her work led directly to that of John Bowlby, and later, Mary Ainsworth; both demonstrated the importance of attachment in children under three years old. Ludwig-Körner (2017) detailed Anna Freud's work at the Hampstead War Nurseries in London during and after World War II. Ludwig-Körner interviewed five of the women staff of the nursery who had been trained by Anna Freud as observers of the children housed there, she wrote (p. 133), "Not only did she teach them how to observe the children, but she also observed them (the staff) in order to convey to them a psychoanalytic perspective on the children."

LEARNING OBJECTIVE

8. Interpret how Anna Freud's work at the Hampstead War Nurseries affected how hospitals changed their handling of children's long-term stays.

Anna remained in London for the rest of her life but traveled frequently to the United States. Working with colleagues at Yale University she profoundly influenced American and British laws dealing with children. She argued that child custody decisions in the case of divorce or death of parents should be made quickly in order to minimize damage to the child. She recommended that the "psychological parent" be given custody over a biological parent in cases where it was obvious such a decision was in the best interests of the child. She urged psychoanalysts not to become substitute mothers for their child patients, arguing that doing so was impossible and would lead to interminable analysis.

Anna Freud became the face of psychoanalysis in the United States following World War II. She preserved much of her father's theoretical structure but also changed it where she deemed it necessary. Like other psychoanalysts of her era she placed more importance on the ego and upon the role of the mother in child development, especially during the earliest years of life. She also opened up the area of adolescent psychoanalysis. There, she noted that therapists had to treat those patients differently because they did not seek therapy themselves; they were brought in by others. Again, this was yet another departure from how Freud handled patients. Up to the end, she kept her father's theory alive but was not afraid to change it where she believed it needed change.

PSYCHIATRY AND THE MOVIES

Gabbard and Gabbard (1999) documented the close relationship between film and psychiatry. They noted that the first movie to feature a psychiatrist was made in 1906. Since then more than 500 commercially released films have included psychiatrists in their plots. Gabbard (2001) argued that movies about psychiatrists reflected the *zeitgeist*. One example is Joaquin Phoenix's portrayal of the role of Arthur in the 2019 film *Joker*. Driscoll and Husain (2019), both medical doctors, critiqued the portrayal of Arthur, calling it a misrepresentation of mental illness:

> Arthur's supposed loss of grip on reality is suggested by a peppering of nods to psychotic symptoms: delusional ideas of a grandiose nature ("I am an undiscovered comedic genius") and hallucinations of his neighbour—which are confirmed by his eventual admission to a psychiatric institution. This restoration of order via Arkham Asylum affirms the overarching inference of the film: Arthur's descent into violence and destruction is triggered by his mental deterioration. The result of this is to—disappointingly—remove Arthur's agency and divert attention from a potentially more stimulating conversation about wealth inequality and its responsibility for societal collapse.

Still, Gabbard showed that psychiatrists can be portrayed in many different ways and for many different reasons. In films and on television shows they might serve as expository aids, heroes, villains, or lovers. Gabbard and Gabbard (1999, p. xix) wonder "if more psychiatrists are represented in American movies than are surgeons or practitioners of any other medical specialty." If so, that demonstrates how deeply the ideas championed by the Freuds, Jung, Adler, and Horney have penetrated into world consciousness.

SUMMARY

The period from the late nineteenth century to the beginning of World War I, I marked the end of an extraordinary time of change in Europe. Urbanization and industrialization were only the tip of the iceberg. Social changes loomed large, too, as the old order sped to its unexpected crash with modernity in World War I. After the war, monarchies became rare and aristocrats all but disappeared. Science, along with its technologies, grew and inspired its practitioners to include all human activity under its wings. Psychology, too, had been born and, following an initial burst of successes, had experienced its first growing pains. By 1913 it was a mixture of Wundtian Voluntarism, Titchenerian Structuralism, American Functionalism, incipient Behaviorism and nascent Gestalt psychology. But very little psychological progress had yet been made in understanding personality in its normal or abnormal manifestations.

So, when Freud and his theories emerged at the turn of the twentieth century many took notice. His theories provided a new way to understand psychology. His model of the personality, stages of development, dream analysis, and the role of the unconscious were original and earth shattering. So, it was no wonder that he quickly attracted followers. Two of them, C. G. Jung and Alfred Adler, however, soon rejected much of Freud's ideas and went on to develop their own theories of personality and therapy. Many, though, remained Freud's devoted followers and acknowledged his leadership.

Jung, from the beginning of his relationship with Freud, disagreed with his emphasis on infantile sexuality. When Jung revealed his concept of the collective unconscious to Freud, that ended their collaboration forever. Jung used the collective unconscious as the mainstay of his theories adding the persona, anima, animus, shadow, archetypes, and more to create a very different theory of the personality. Jung's therapy, too, was different. He did not use free association; he sat facing his analysands, he talked, and he analyzed dreams differently.

Adler's association with Freud predated Jung's and his exit from Freud's circle came before Jung's. Adler, too, disagreed with Freud over the importance of infantile sexuality. But, he also disagreed with Freud and Jung over the basic structure of the personality. Adler believed that the personality could not be chopped up into competing component parts. Instead, he supported a unitary view of the personality, one that emphasized the role of social factors in the development of the personality and argued that they played their role early in life. His view of personality stressed the overarching role of feelings of inferiority and how people could overcome them. His therapy, too, differed markedly from Freud's. Adler sought to foster social interest, decrease inferiority feelings, change styles of life, and turn people toward socially productive interests.

Karen Horney also reacted negatively to Freud's theories. She proposed *womb envy* as a counterweight to his *penis envy*. She argued against Freud's instinctive drives of sex and violence. In their place she substituted a theory in which the environment was the main cause of anxiety and believed that patients could analyze themselves.

Anna Freud was among the first to provide psychoanalytic therapy to children. Her wartime work with children convinced her that her father had been wrong about the role that mothers play in child development. Later she urged lawmakers to put the needs of children first when it came to issues of custody.

These psychologists laid the foundation for what today constitute two of the discipline's largest fields: personality and psychopathology. Indeed, nearly every undergraduate psychology major on being asked the question, "What is your major?" nearly always next hears a statement such as, "Oh, you are going to analyze me." That public perception is testament to the influence exerted on psychology by Freud, his followers, and his opponents.

14 COGNITIVE PSYCHOLOGY: REVOLUTION OR EVOLUTION?

ZEITGEIST

World War II

World War II indirectly stimulated the rebirth of a new kind of cognitive psychology. Among the causes of the war were expansionist agendas by Hitler in Germany and Tojo in Japan. In 1937 Hitler annexed Austria and the Czechoslovakia's Sudetenland and Japan invaded China. The war broke out on September 1, 1939 after Germany's invasion of Poland; Britain and France declared war on Germany in response. The Soviet Union, having signed a non-aggression pact with Germany, invaded eastern Poland, adding to its territory. In 1940 Germany invaded Belgium and France and very soon forced their surrender. Britain's troops on the continent were evacuated at Dunkirk with the loss of nearly all of their heavy equipment. Later in 1940, Germany and Britain fought the aerial Battle of Britain; that British victory prevented an invasion across the English Channel.

Despite these events antiwar sentiment in the United States still ran high and president Franklin Roosevelt could only use indirect measures such as the Lend-Lease program to provide needed assistance to Britain. The Japanese surprise attack on Pearl Harbor on December 7, 1941 flooded away American antiwar qualms and galvanized public sentiment toward punishing Japan. But, most Americans still wished to keep the country out of another European war. Hitler made that desire moot when he declared war on the United States a few days after Pearl Harbor. Roosevelt and Pentagon military planners directed most of the American war effort toward keeping Britain in the war and eventually defeating Hitler in Europe. The United States Navy and Marine Corps along with some Army units would fight Japan on the islands in the Pacific until Hitler was defeated. After, all efforts by the United States and its allies (principally Britain and the Soviet Union, now an ally following Hitler's invasion of their country in 1941) focused on Japan. It took nearly four years to defeat Germany and to ready the plan to invade Japan. Only the use of atomic bombs on Hiroshima and Nagasaki ended the war quickly and prevented the invasion of Japan and a prolonged war.

After Pearl Harbor many American men rushed to enlist in the armed forces. American psychologists were ready for them, thanks to the earlier efforts of the American Psychological Association and the American Association for Applied Psychology. Their 1939 joint meeting took place only three days after Germany invaded Poland. The psychologists planned to create methods for evaluating recruits anticipating the United States' eventual entry into the war. Based on World War I's effects on soldiers, one of their main concerns was "shell shock" or what is today diagnosed as posttraumatic stress disorder (PTSD). But, they were also concerned about how to select apt recruits for specialized skills such as airplane piloting, navigating, and bombing. The tests they developed did predict successful completion of the training courses but did not predict actual success in combat (National Research Council, 1991) Nevertheless, after the war those kinds of tests became the basis for a new and widespread testing movement within psychology. Thus, the war planted some of the first seeds of what would become modern cognitive psychology. Among those seeds were the first digital computers along with advances in cryptanalysis and coding and new models of cognition based on advances in computer science. Other seeds included new ways of studying memory, the analysis of human problem-solving, a new paradigm in understanding language, and renewed effort in understanding the links between cognition and neurophysiology in humans and other animals. After the war these areas grew into a new and different conception of cognition, one that did not depend on introspective accounts or the positing of an incorporeal mind.

BORDER WITH SOCIAL SCIENCE
STANDARDIZED TESTS

Although standardized testing dates from imperial China some 18 centuries ago (Himelfarb, 2019), the modern form began in the 19th century. Francis Galton, Alfred Binet, Theodore Simon, Lewis Terman, James McKeen Cattell, Robert M. Yerkes, and Edward Lee Thorndike all developed tests from the late 1800s to World War I. But the modern testing movement was a product of the post-World War II era. Lemann (1995) describes the growth and development of the use of standardized tests in the United States. He noted the importance of the early years of the Cold War and the beginning of the Korean War as important factors in the rise of the testing movement. The scientists who had emigrated from Europe had been the ones mostly responsible for the success of the Manhattan Project and the creation of the atomic bomb. As the Cold War opened, American politicians and educational leaders were concerned about maintaining a pipeline of American scientists, educated in the United States, to serve the nation with their brains and not their brawn. Thus, the Selective Service System, the government agency in charge of the draft, began to offer deferments to college students from military service. In 1957, the Soviet Union launched the first earth-orbiting satellite, Sputnik. That event strongly reinforced the idea that the United States needed more scientists marking the beginning of interest in promoting STEM (science, technology, engineering, and mathematics) careers.

Today, American students are subjected to standardized tests throughout their careers in the K-12 grades and beyond. College admission, still in large part and despite moves by many universities to drop the SAT and ACT tests in response to the COVID-19 pandemic, depends on test scores and high school GPA. Beyond the traditional baccalaureate degree lie more standardized tests: the GRE (Graduate Record Exam), the MCAT (Medical College Admissions Test), the LSAT (Law School Admissions Test), just to name a few.

The bottom line is that universities, businesses, and governments want to have some method by which they can select students and employees rationally and efficiently. Unfortunately, human cognitive abilities are still beyond the reach of such tests and only give partial results as to who will become the top students or the best employees. Cognitive psychology has yet to reach that point and it may never do so. Time will tell.

PREVIEW

After World War II *digital computers* were slowly integrated into business and later into daily life. The *codebreaking* breakthroughs during the war led to the creation of *software* to run on the rapidly evolving computer *hardware* and led to a more sophisticated understanding and use of *information*. A new way of looking at cognition evolved redefining old terms such as *memory* and *problem-solving*, the *information processing model*. In that model, *algorithms* and *heuristics* were repurposed as concrete methods for researching cognitive topics. *Language*, too, became a topic of intense interest to psychologists. The ancient goal of understanding cognition through its underlying *neurophysiology* also saw breakthroughs in human and *animal cognition*.

INTRODUCTION

The Slow Move to Cognitivism

The first psychologists were cognitivists too, but their methods were reliant on introspective reports. By the early part of the 20th century it was clear that such methods were faulty (see Chapter 6). As a result, Watson's Behaviorism and later Neobehaviorism came to dominate American psychology during the last half of the 20th century (see Chapters 9 and 10). But, that domination was never complete. Greenwood (1999) argued that Neobehaviorism and the emerging modern cognitive psychology did not really compete with each other or claim exclusive control of psychology. Behaviorists (from here on in this chapter "Behaviorism" will be used as a term encompassing all of its forms), for the most part, used operational definitions as a tool to understand behavior but overstated the importance of conditioning and were too strict in their prohibitions against any type of mental construct. Meanwhile, new topics such as sensory registers, types of memory, and heuristics were explored by the earliest modern cognitive psychologists. Behaviorists and Cognitivists shared a passion for experimental data collection, its analysis, and interpretation but their goals were different. Behaviorists interpreted their results in the light of S-R theory while Cognitivists interpreted theirs as evidence of cognitive processes (Carroll, 2017). By the mid 1950s psychologists began to craft theories of cognition in the areas of memory, problem-solving, and language. Many of those were based on the model provided by computers using such terms as inputs, outputs, and storage. Miller (2003) described the cognitive revolution as a counterrevolution. He wrote (p. 142):

> Whatever we called it, the cognitive counter-revolution in psychology brought back the mind into experimental psychology. I think it important to remember that the mind had never disappeared from social or clinical psychology.

Regardless if it was an evolution or a counterrevolution, the mind was back as a topic in experimental psychology. The new cognitive psychology was not a revolution in the usual sense as a rapid change over a short time period. Plus, it did not intend to replace Behaviorism. There was no rapid conversion from Behaviorism to Cognitivism. The mind was back in psychology but the pace was evolutionary not revolutionary. Still, it was a revolution in terms of its approach to some of psychology's new questions:

- Is the brain a kind of computer?
- What was memory and how did it affect behavior?
- How did people solve problems?
- What was language and how was it acquired?
- What are the physiological underpinnings of cognition?

Those five areas, the computer model, memory, problem-solving, language, and neurophysiology became the doors by which cognition re-entered psychology. But, those new areas, their methods, and their theories did not displace Behaviorism. Rather, they became a parallel part of a larger and evolving psychology.

COMPUTERS AND PSYCHOLOGY

The first digital computer in the world was the Atanasoff-Berry computer, a nonprogrammable machine built at Iowa State University. It foreshadowed later and more advanced programmable World War II computers such as Colossus were used by American and British codebreakers to decode the German Enigma code machine. That work was known as the Ultra Secret and its decrypts were very highly classified. In the Pacific theater, American code breakers had already decrypted the Japanese diplomatic code before the war and had begun to solve the Japanese Navy's code, JN-25. In May 1942 Navy codebreakers anticipated the Japanese plans to attack Midway Island. Convinced by his codebreakers, Admiral Nimitz sent his three remaining aircraft carriers to intercept the Japanese fleet off Midway Island. The resulting battle was a United States victory, one of its first and a turning point in the war. But other than in codebreaking, electronic computers did not play any other important roles during the war.

After the war, however, computers played an important part in nearly all phases of life, including psychology. There, the electronic computer served as a concrete metaphor for cognition. Its programs or software could be thought of as the equivalent of thoughts and

PHOTO 14.1 Colossus Computer in 1945

Credit: Getty Images

plans; its hardware could be considered analogous to the brain. Software and hardware could be exploited experimentally and eventually led to the founding of the field of Artificial Intelligence (AI), the attempt to create intelligent machines. Unlike psychology's earlier introspective attempts to understand human cognition the software in the computer model operationalized thinking. In other words, there was now a concrete way to think of the mind in terms that could be studied experimentally. Human thinking could be thought of as a complicated kind of computer code operating in an extremely powerful biological computer, the brain. Furthermore, such a model offered researchers new ways to consider animal cognition too. Animals possessed their own software operating in simpler brains. Karl von Frisch's (1967) experiments with honeybees could be explained as relatively simple software codes operating in a small computer, the bee's brain. Bees could communicate the type of flowers and the distance and direction to find them. Thinking, redefined in this manner, mapped nicely onto the Darwinian model of evolution.

The digital computer itself also took up space on psychology's expanded stage. In the hands of researchers such as Allen Newell and Herbert Simon (1956) they brought psychology closer to the AI paradigm. AI studied cognition itself as a subject and later led to the creation of a semi-independent discipline, Cognitive Science. Nuñez et al. (2019) contended that (p. 788):

Indeed, bibliometrically, affiliation and publication patterns in the flagship journal of the *Cognitive Science Society* show that the field has been essentially absorbed by psychology, and the journal does not directly contribute to advances in brain research, or to many (if any) advances in anthropology or philosophy. In general, (cognitive) neuroscientists choose to publish outside of cognitive science journals.

Today, the cognitive revolution in psychology has essentially reabsorbed many of cognitive science's original disciplines (philosophy, linguistics, anthropology, and neuroscience). The two other original disciplines, psychology and computer science, have also diverged from each other as well. That is the situation at present. How did psychology move into cognition in its modern form? One of the keys to that change was the study of memory.

THEN AND NOW
A WORLD WITHOUT COMPUTERS

The word "computer" originally referred to a person who could add, subtract, multiply, and divide numbers. Later, devices such as the abacus were invented to help those human computers do a faster and better job in obtaining mathematical results. Pascal created the first successful mechanical calculator in 1642. Many improvements followed and mechanical calculators persisted well into the 20th century. When I first started graduate school in 1973, the chair of the department was proud to show us first-year grad students the calculator room. There sat a dozen Monroe rotary calculators (see Photo 14.2). The chair sternly warned us never to make the calculators divide by zero. Doing so would cause them to attempt to find infinity!

PHOTO 14.2 Monroe Calculator

Credit: Getty Images

Later in our graduate careers we filled large pieces of paper with the preliminary calculations necessary to achieve the final statistical results of our experiments. But change was afoot. Hewlett-Packard and Texas Instruments led the way when they introduced handheld digital calculators (see Photo 14.3) that could compute square roots and other necessary mathematical functions. Soon after, the personal computer came on the scene and, behind it, came the first software statistical programs.

PHOTO 14.3 Texas Instruments SR 10

Credit: Chris Wilson/Alamy Stock Photo

The computer age had arrived and the old mechanical calculators were junked. Today's grad students analyze their experimental results using sophisticated computer software such as: R, MATLAB, SPSS, or any of the many such offerings. Odds are those students have no idea about mechanical calculators, large sheets of paper, and computing intermediate results.

MEMORY

The study of memory is ancient and goes back to Plato and Aristotle at least. But, memory as a psychological topic dates to the last quarter of the 19th century. Wundt, for instance, believed memory was a subject beyond the reach of laboratory study. As noted in Chapter 6, Hermann Ebbinghaus, nearly singlehandedly, brought memory into psychology and it has remained there since. Recall that Ebbinghaus studied memory using himself as his only subject and invented the nonsense syllable or consonant–vowel–consonant (CVC) combination in order to study memory in what he considered its purest form. He wanted to study memory under ideal laboratory conditions and his work set the stage for much of subsequent research in memory. His methods were original and have survived the test of time. His work later led to a large body of laboratory-based research in human memory, verbal learning. That research will be covered in the following. Before doing so, however, attention must be paid to another pioneer in memory research Frederic Bartlett whose research began in the 1930s. Roediger and Yamashiro (2019) described that British psychologist's contributions as anthropological in contrast to Ebbinghaus' laboratory approach. Bartlett was more interested in the errors people made while trying to remember and he also analyzed how people used meaning to help them remember. Bartlett, thus, was more interested in memory in natural contexts. He sought to discover the process by which people reframed and reconstructed memories. He was less interested in verbatim recall and more interested in recall of the meaning of the complex stories he posed to his respondents. The most famous of those stories was his "War of the Ghosts" (Bartlett, 1932). In that story (see below) he asked his respondents to read it and later to retell it. For Bartlett, memory was more than simple recall. He contended that people reconstructed their memories from own experiences and recombined those with the new materials they learned. He was one of the first to use **schemas** as an explanation for memory and thinking. In his book he had his British students read the "War of the Ghosts" story and then retell it later. He found (Deese, 1967, p. 223) that "Cambridge undergraduates, when they repeated the story, tried to make it conform to their own language habits and to things with which they were familiar." For instance, many students substituted "fishing" for "hunting seals" and boats for canoes presumably because those were more familiar experiences and terms for them. Bartlett found that the longer the interval between reading the story and repeating it the less detail was recalled. However, the meanings and experiences (recruitment, war party, arrows, and fighting) in the story were preserved in the retellings. Here is the original story (Bartlett, 1932, p. 65):

One night two young men from Egulac went down to the river to hunt seals and while they were there it became foggy and calm. Then they heard war-cries, and they thought: "Maybe this is a war-party." They escaped to the shore, and hid behind a log. Now canoes came up, and they heard the noise of paddles, and saw one canoe coming up to them. There were five men in the canoe, and they said:

"What do you think? We wish to take you along. We are going up the river to make war on the people."

One of the young men said, "I have no arrows."

"Arrows are in the canoe," they said.

"I will not go along. I might be killed. My relatives do not know where I have gone. But you," he said, turning to the other, "may go with them."

So one of the young men went, but the other returned home.

And the warriors went on up the river to a town on the other side of Kalama. The people came down to the water and they began to fight, and many were killed. But presently the young man heard one of the warriors say, "Quick, let us go home: that Indian has been hit." Now he thought: "Oh, they are ghosts." He did not feel sick, but they said he had been shot.

So the canoes went back to Egulac and the young man went ashore to his house and made a fire. And he told everybody and said: "Behold I accompanied the ghosts, and we went to fight. Many of our fellows were killed, and many of those who attacked us were killed. They said I was hit, and I did not feel sick."

He told it all, and then he became quiet. When the sun rose he fell down. Something black came out of his mouth. His face became contorted. The people jumped up and cried.

He was dead.

Bartlett's work was seminal in the area of memory in natural contexts and led to the distinction between *surface structure* (the actual words) and *deep structure* (the meaning) in subsequent memory research. His work, however, lay dormant for many years until revived by Neisser (1967) and others in the 1970s. Before that happened many Behaviorists gradually began to study memory in the laboratory. They studied memory in humans under the banner of verbal learning.

LEARNING OBJECTIVE
1. Describe the deep structure of Bartlett's Egulac story.

Verbal Learning

The study of memory in the verbal learning tradition goes back to (Calkins's 1894), a method later known as paired associates, a technique she developed near the end of the 19th century. By contrast, Ebbighaus's methods were termed serial or learning one thing after another. The power of the paired associates method was that respondent's memory could be assessed independently of the order of original learning. Paired associates consisted of a combination of a cue item and a response item. The paired items could be words, nonsense syllables, or even graphic items. To illustrate the difference between serial and paired associates here is a serial list of words:

$$\text{Boy} \rightarrow \text{Horse} \rightarrow \text{Mother} \rightarrow \text{House} \rightarrow \text{Car} \rightarrow \text{Lamp} \rightarrow \text{Ball}$$

Respondents would learn the list and then attempt to repeat it. Note that except for the first and last items on the list all of the other items serve as cue and response. For example, "horse" is the response to "boy" and the cue for mother. Almost invariably three things became evident.

The first item and the last item were recalled more easily than the items in the middle of the list. Primacy was the term assigned to the ease of remembering the first item, recency was assigned to the ease of remembering the last item, and the difficulty of remembering items in the middle of the list was labeled the serial position effect. In the paired associate task, respondents might learn a paired list (A-B) such as the one shown in Table 14.1.

TABLE 14.1 ■ Sample Paired Associate List	
Cue Item (A)	Response Item (B)
Rug	Boy
Blue	Horse
Dog	Mother
Highway	House
Doll	Car
Bed	Lamp
Bowl	Ball

The first item (A) was the cue and the second paired item (B) was the response. Notice that, unlike the serial method, the cues and the responses do not overlap. Researchers could then give any of the cue items in any order to a respondent and expect the correct answer. (So, the answer to "bed" would be "lamp.") Over the years, the technique of paired associates was used in a wide variety of ways to investigate human verbal memory. Serial techniques were used too as were free recall items. In free recall, respondents were shown a list of words or an array of items for a period. After, they were asked to recall as many items as possible. Verbal learning researchers used these methods to create a large body of knowledge related to human memory and to its opposite, forgetting.

The earliest theories of forgetting simply assumed that the passage of time caused forgetting. Eventually, memories rotted away so they were classified as decay theories. But, subsequent research showed that model to be too simple and simply wrong. Many memories persisted, some over very long periods. Verbal learning researchers created interference theory to explain forgetting. They posited two types of interference: retroactive and proactive. In retroactive interference, the learning of new material interfered with the memory of older and previously learned material. In proactive interference, the opposite occurred. Previously learned material interfered with the learning of new material. Interference theory nicely explained the primacy, recency, and the serial position effect. In the case of primacy, there was no or little proactive interference. In the case of recency, there was no or little retroactive interference, and for the items in the middle both types of interference affected those items.

The paired associate technique was widely used to demonstrate both types of interference in the lab. In the Figure 14.1 the letter A designates the cue items and the letter B designates the response items. C designates the new response items to be learned to the original A cue list. E is the experimental group and C is the control group. Notice that the control group only learns the A-C list and thus has little or no proactive interference. In the experimental group the A-B list interferes proactively with the learning of the A-C list (meaning it takes longer for that group to learn the A-C list).

FIGURE 14.1 ■ Proactive Interference

Proactive Interference

E	A-B	A-C	A-C
C		A-C	A-C

The setup for retroactive interference is similar (see Figure 14.2)

To demonstrate retroactive interference researchers would first have both groups learn the same list of paired associates, A-B. Then, the experimental group would learn another list, A-C. Both would be tested on the A-B list. The group that had to learn the A-C list had more difficulty in recalling the A-B list.

FIGURE 14.2 ■ Retroactive interference

Retroactive Interference

E	A-B	A-C	A-B
C	A-B		A-B

Eventually, interference theory was supplemented by data showing that respondents in laboratory settings could learn material more easily when either they or the researcher organized the material in some way. Miller (1956) in his influential article showed that people had a limited capacity for holding items in short-term memory (STM) (see more about memory's stages below) and that organizing items in some way made remembering easier. He called those larger units chunks and noted that words are chunks of phonemes. Sentences, of course, are chunks of words and paragraphs are chunks of sentences. Most people could easily remember seven items (words, numbers, and syllables) but had trouble remembering more than nine. Miller's work set the stage for a move to a new way to study memory, information processing.

LEARNING OBJECTIVE

2. Memorize the paired associate list in Table 14.1 by putting the cue words on one side of a 3×5 card and the response words on the other. How many trials did it take you to learn the list without making any errors?

Information Processing

Miller's article presaged a shift to information processing psychology, a shift marked by reliance on the computer model of cognition. After World War II computers gradually moved from being room-sized machines to being pocket-sized. By 1980 the personal computer had become available to the public and eventually transformed society. Today, nearly everyone carries around a general purpose computer with them all day long, the smartphone. In the face of this process it was logical for psychologists to incorporate the terms of computing into their theorizing about cognition. Thus, words such as software, hardware, storage, memory, retrieval, and coding came into common usage. Before that, however, two psychologists had already formalized such thinking into psychology, the Atkinson-Shiffrin model of memory (Atkinson & Shiffrin, 1968). They proposed three stages of human memory: the sensory register, STM, and LTM. In their model all perceptions entered the visual and auditory sensory registers, but most of those were quickly lost. Those that remained passed into short-term memory for a period of seconds to minutes. Finally, what remained of the original perceptions were encoded into long-term memory where they could remain from hours to years (including a lifetime). The study of memory moved from being a thing to being a process.

The first step in the process was input from sensation into one of the sensory registers. Fairly quickly, psychologists realized that the visual (or iconic) sensory register and the auditory sensory (or echoic) register operated differently. Sperling (1960) showed that the contents in the visual sensory register only lasted a few fractions of a second before they disappeared. However, the contents of the auditory sensory register lasted as long as four seconds. Still, nearly all of the sensory input received by either register was lost. The STM was the next step and it was researched extensively. Psychologists found that STM lasted less than 30 seconds unless a person made an effort (termed rehearsal) to keep the item in STM. Mentally repeating the item to oneself was one example of rehearsal. Forcing respondents to carry out distractor tasks such as counting backwards out loud by threes from 100 eliminated rehearsal. The final step in Atkinson and Shiffrin's original model was LTM. The length of LTM could be as short as a few hours or as long as a lifetime. Additionally, LTM seemingly possessed unlimited capacity. Retrieval was the process by which people accessed and reported the contents of their LTMs. In summary, the information processing model in its simplest form contained three processes: input, storage, and retrieval that acted as kinds of filters for sensory input. The sensory registers accepted that input, losing most of it. What was left went into STM, where again most of that was lost too. Finally, the remainder was stored in LTM. Some items in LTM could be easily retrieved but others depended on the respondent finding the right cue at the right time. Such data led to the notion of retrieval failure, meaning that the memory existed in LTM but the person could not retrieve it automatically or reliably. Countless students have experienced retrieval failure during a test only to remember an answer later, perhaps as soon as leaving the building where they had been tested.

Subsequent modifications to the information processing model included Craik and Lockhart's (1972) levels of processing model. They proposed that the effort people expended in memorizing items made a difference in subsequent recall. Items that underwent shallow processing (e.g., counting the number of letter Es in a list of words) would lead to less recall while items that were processed more deeply (e.g., deciding whether a word was pleasant or unpleasant) would lead to higher levels of recall. Both types were compared to people in control groups who were told to memorize the same lists but not given any further instructions. Tulving (1972) proposed a distinction between episodic and semantic LTMs. Episodic memories were autobiographical and time-tagged. They included the events in one's life such as high-school graduation, marriage, or the loss of a loved one. Semantic memories were akin to knowledge. So knowing that the capital of the country Burkina Faso was Ouagadougou might be an arcane bit of semantic memory. Notice that in this model all the knowledge in one's head was once a bit of episodic memory. For example, nearly everyone knows that $3 \times 7 = 21$ (a semantic memory) but very few would remember the instant they first learned that mathematical fact (an episodic memory). Baddeley and Hitch (1974) added details to STM including a phonological loop that helped listeners understand the sounds of language and visuospatial sketchpad that aided the understanding of images or when people pointed or made faces. Tulving (1983) proposed the encoding specificity principle where retrieval from LTM was more likely when people were in the same state or physical context as they were when they encoded the information in the first place. The information processing approach and its modifications led to much research on human memory and eventually led psychologists to consider memory as a series of processes instead of kind of mental construct. Problem-solving was another simultaneous approach to a revived cognitive psychology.

LEARNING OBJECTIVE

3. Indicate which of the following capitals are already in your semantic memory by giving their countries: Ouagadougou, Kabul, Brazzaville, Stockholm, Ottawa, Montevideo.

PROBLEM-SOLVING

Mental Set or *Einstellung*

Problem-solving too was explored using new nonmentalistic approaches. Abraham Luchins, an American Gestalt psychologist used the metaphor of water jars to pose problems and to analyze the results. He was interested in setting up a mental set or *Einstellung* (see Chapter 8) by allowing participants to solve a series of problems using hypothetical water jars labeled *a, b,* and *c*. He posed a series of problems involving where jars held different quantities of water and asked his respondents to come up with a procedure to obtain a given quantity of water (Luchins, 1942) The first problem was a demonstration and could be solved by the formula: $a - 3b$ (See Table 14.2). The next five problems were presented so that a solution worked out early in the process, $b - a - 2c$ would work for all five. The next four problems could be solved using the same equation, but they could also be solved much more simply ($a - c$ for Jars 7 and 9, and $a + c$ for Jar 8 and 10). Most participants adhered to the original and longer tried-and-true method they had learned and failed to perceive the easier solution, thus demonstrating the mental set or

Einstellung effect. A final problem had to be solved in a completely new way. Using today's computer terminology, Luchins was analyzing the **algorithms** used by his respondents. Note that he could use their solutions to the problems he posed to analyze their thinking without needing to ask them about their thinking.

Here are Luchins' Original Problems

How would you use the three jars with the indicated capacities to measure out the desired among of water?

TABLE 14.2 ■ Luchins Water Jar Problems (Luchins, 1942)				
Problem	Jar A	Jar B	Jar C	Desired
1	29	3		20
2	21	127	3	100
3	14	163	25	99
4	18	43	10	5
5	9	42	6	21
6	20	59	4	31
7	23	49	3	20
8	15	39	3	18
9	28	76	3	25
10	18	48	4	22
11	14	36	8	6

Insight Learning

As described in Chapter 11, Wolfgang Köhler discovered the phenomenon of insight learning while interned on the island of Tenerife during World War I. Working with chimpanzees he found that some of them were capable of linking two pieces of knowledge together suddenly after originally failing to solve the problem. He termed that quiescent period an impasse, meaning that the chimpanzees seemed to have given up on solving the problem. The chimpanzee, Sultan, for example, before he learned to move boxes directly under the bananas that Köhler had hung in the animal enclosure had demonstrated an impasse; he appeared to have given up on reaching the bananas. Suddenly, Sultan moved the box immediately under the bananas. (Note that unlike Thorndike's cats Sultan did not exhibit a gradual learning curve. Sultan put the box directly under the bananas.) Köhler interpreted Sultan's successful solution in the light of gestalt psychology. Sultan had reinterpreted the two separate situations, the hanging banana and the boxes in the enclosure into a new and related gestalt. Subsequently, gestalt psychologists argued that the suddenness of insight learning meant it was different from S-R learning. The quick solutions seen inferred that cognitive processes were taking place during the impasse's interim between problem perception and solution. Ash et al. (2012) conducted experiments using undergraduates to study insight as a problem-solving phenomenon using puzzles and arithmetic problems. They wrote (pp. 6-7, original italics), "very little modern research has been conducted to investigate the core concept of sudden *insight learning*, which was actually the primary phenomenon of interest to the Gestalt psychologists." They asked undergraduates to solve four puzzles and four mathematical problems after their participants initially rated the problem's components as to their importance in solving the problem. After, the participants worked two practice problems (one puzzle and one mathematical problem) and were coached in thinking aloud while attempting to solve the problems. Finally, the participants completed eight problems, four puzzles, and four mathematical problems. They were allowed four minutes to complete each problem. Impasses were 2.77 times more likely for the puzzles than for the mathematical problems but many participants solved both types of problems without an impasse. A week later, participants once again attempted to solve the same problems. For the puzzles, the results were clear (p. 19), "the re-solution effects observed on the puzzle problems solved with impasse were not simply due to re-exposure to the problems." They added (p. 22), this emphasis on internal representation is what motivated the resurgence of interest in cognitive psychology in response to the Behaviorist theories of the late 1950s. Ash et al. saw the research program of Newell and Simon (1972) and its emphasis on problem spaces and representation as the flip side of Gestalt psychology, one that studied problem-solving representations (such as those of Luchins and Ash et al.) but did not closely examine how those representations became internalized. Exactly what are representations and how do they fit into problem-solving?

Representations

Roitblatt (1982, p. 353) defined representations as "a remnant of previous experience that allows that experience to affect later behavior." For him, representations contained five parts: a domain, specific content, a code, a medium, and were dynamic. The domain was the subject matter of the representation. For example, the domain of this book is psychology, not baseball. Consider the question: "What should I do on oh and two?" What domain does it come from? Knowing its answers depends on knowing its domain, baseball. The words oh and two refer to the count facing a batter (no balls and two strikes). For the batter, the answer is swing on any pitch that might be a strike. (For those unfamiliar with baseball batters get three strikes per batting attempt; it is embarrassing to strike out without attempting a swing at a pitch that could be a strike.) For the pitcher, the answer is, throw a pitch that is hard to hit but that could be a strike. (For a pitcher to throw an easy-to-hit pitch to a batter with two strikes risks letting that batter off the hook.) For anyone not familiar with the domain baseball any such questions would be difficult if not impossible to answer. Knowledge of the domain is an essential part of any representation.

The contents of a representation were its descriptive features. Many convenience stores in the United States have a vertical strip near the door with the numbers 4, 5, and 6 printed on it. Should someone rob the store employees watch as the perpetrator exits the store. That strip allows them to estimate the height (in feet) of the robber. Later, when describing the robber they can reliably tell the police how tall the robber was. They can, of course, add other descriptors such as clothing, hair, and eye color. Every representation will have descriptive contents. Think of cats. They might have coats describable as: tabby, calico, piebald, short-haired, or long-haired.

The code of a representation is how the information is conveyed to others. The words of a language, written or spoken, are ubiquitous examples of such a code. The 6,000 or so languages in the world are each unique codes. Making sense of a representation described in an unfamiliar language is practically impossible. *Nyní přestaňte číst.* Did you follow the instructions of the last sentence? It said, "Stop reading now." But, it was in Czech. Slang, too, can be a kind of restricted code. Some readers might not agree that this is a "crunk" book, for example. (The slang word crunk has a variety of meanings ranging from a type of rap music to feeling good. Here, it means the book is a good read.) Codes can occur in any of the perceptual modalities. Asking someone to smell the two-week old milk would be an example of an olfactory code leading to a decision to drink the milk or throw it away. Icons are visual examples of codes. The design of easily understandable iconic signs in public places is an applied science. In 1974 the United States Department of Transportation (DOT) working with the American Institute of Graphic Arts created visual icons for use in airports and other public places. The idea was to convey content in pictures instead of words and to have that content be understandable to people from all around the world. Eventually, 50 such icons were created. Figure 14.3 shows a sampling of those icons. Can you interpret them correctly?

FIGURE 14.3 ■ DOT Icons

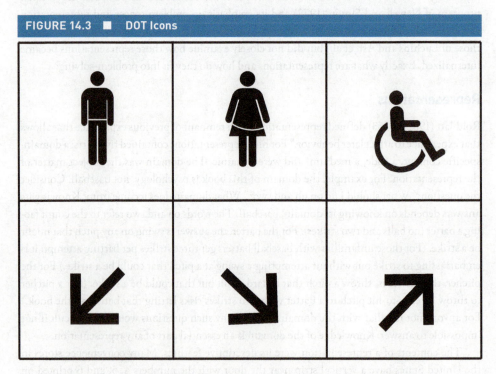

The medium of a representation can vary widely. This book is using a paper and ink medium, but it could also be represented as pixels on a computer screen. Computer media have changed rapidly since the 1980s. Data and programs were once stored on 5.25" floppy disks, then on 3.5" disks, later on CD-ROMs and DVDs. Today, hardly any modern computers have the necessary hardware to read those media. Any information stored on such vintage media is essentially lost. Other examples of media include movie film and the magnetic tapes of DVRs. Both of those media might contain the same information but each requires the appropriate hardware to display it. Now consider the problem preserving a medium over long periods of historical time, say 10,000 years. How might people today represent DANGER to people 100 centuries from now? Weichselbraun (2018) reviewed the film *Containment* that speculated about how difficult it will be to warn humans in the distant future about the deadly buried nuclear waste substances. What medium could possibly last thousands of years and still convey the message, "Stay Away?"

Representations change over time; they are dynamic. The poem *Beowulf* was written in Old English between 600 and 1100 CE and is not understandable by those who can read modern English. Here are the last lines from that epic poem in Old English: (Anomymous, nd).

Swa begnornodon Geata leode

hlafordes hryre, heorðgeneatas,

cwædon þæt he wære wyruldcyninga

manna mildust ond monðwærust,

leodum liðost ond lofgeornost.

Here are the same lines in modern English (Tinker, 1912, p. 142).

So the Geatish people, companions of his hearth, mourned the fall of their lord; said that he was mighty king, the mildest and kindest of men, most gracious to his people, and most desirous of praise.

Try picking out the modern meanings of those Old English words. Slang, too, is dynamic. In the 1920s "cat's meow" might mean the same as today's "lit." Both words referring to good times or enjoyment. Cultures, too, change; they are dynamic (Kashima, 2014). He suggested that cultures change via importation from other cultures, invention within a culture, ideas selected in or out of a culture, and via random processes (cultural drift). Questions about cultural dynamics include the nature and prevalence of a culture or how cultural changes come about. In other words, the dynamism of representations is an inherent feature so expecting a representation to stay constant is a mistake.

How and when did representations come to be part of cognitive psychology? One answer is they came via computer programming. Programmers needed to represent information digitally, to convert it into the ones and zeros that computers use. The earliest successful computers, the mainframes, were designed to handle the needs of business. So, representing profit or loss was easily done; the representation was arithmetical. In 1956, however, psychologists Allen Newell and Herbert Simon created Logic Theorist, a computer program that did what accomplished mathematicians did, which solved mathematical proofs on its own.

Logic Theorist

Newell and Simon (1956) published Logic Theorist. That program successfully created proofs for 38 of the 52 theorems in Whitehead and Russell's (1910) groundbreaking book on mathematics. Gugerty (2006, pp. 882–883) paradoxically described Logic Theorist as an AI program and as a simulation of human cognition:

> In an article in the *Psychological Review* in 1958, Newell, Shaw and Simon pointed out that the elementary information processes in the Logic Theorist were not modeled after human thinking, and that the model was not shaped by fitting to quantitative human data. Also, the branching control structure and the list-based knowledge representation of the Logic Theorist were later determined to be psychologically implausible. These considerations support the conclusion that the Logic Theorist does not simulate human cognitive processes, and therefore, given its intelligent behavior, is an AI program.
>
> On the other hand, the higher-level information processes in the Logic Theorist – the methods instantiating the four heuristics – were explicitly modeled after the introspective protocols of Simon and Newell themselves. Newell and Simon explicitly claim that heuristics are a good way to model the quick but error-prone nature of human problem solving, and they used heuristics to model other kinds of problems solving (e.g., chess) around this time. In their 1958 *Psychological Review* article, Newell et al. point out a number of other similarities in how people and the Logic Theorist solve logic problems – e.g., both generate subgoals, and both learn from previously solved problems. These considerations suggest that in terms of higher-level information processes such as heuristics, subgoaling, and learning, the Logic Theorist was a simulation of human cognition.

That dichotomous description pointed to a fork in the road in the history of cognitive psychology. The AI branch eventually led to today's explosion of "intelligent" computers, the increasing use of algorithms, and machine learning. The psychological side addressed human problem-solving in new ways focusing on "learning, concept formation, short-term memory phenomena, perception, and language behavior." (Simon & Newell, 1971, p. 148) Simon and Newell viewed their work as another facet of information processing psychology, one that added to the discipline's knowledge base and not one that competed with Behaviorism. They introduced terms, based upon well-defined processes, to explain human problem-solving: heuristics, problem spaces, and operators. Those, along with representation, provided a new way to look at human problem-solving.

Simon and Newell noted (1971, p. 154), "There are many "trick" problems…where selection of the correct problem space permits the problem to be solved without any search whatsoever." Restructuring is an operator that permits such a solution in many problems. In other words, restructuring involves choosing another different problem space, one that yields a quick solution without search. Look at this classic problem: How are these numbers arranged?:

$$8, 5, 4, 9, 1, 7, 6, 3, 2, 0$$

Nearly everyone will begin to look for a mathematical rule, but there is no such simple rule. Now look at these numbers:

Eight, Five, Four, Nine, One, Seven, Six, Three, Two, Zero

What is different? Now look again:

Eight, **Fi**ve, **Fo**ur, **N**ine, **O**ne, **Se**ven, **Si**x, **Th**ree, **Tw**o, **Z**ero

Have you made the switch yet? Have you changed the problem space from mathematics to English? The numbers are arranged alphabetically in English.

Heuristics

Newell and Simon programmed four principal heuristics (Gugerty, 2006) into Logic Theorist: substitution, detachment, chaining forward, and chaining backward. Gugerty (p. 881) wrote, "Newell had learned about the importance of heuristics in problem solving from the mathematician George Polya. Simon and Newell discovered potential heuristics by noticing and recording their own mental processes while working on proofs." Heuristics are problem-solving strategies that, unlike algorithms, do not guarantee a solution. They are akin to "rules of thumb" and are usually based on experience and trial-and-error. The heuristics in Logic Theorist were useful in theorem proving and were similar to how humans solve logical problems and mathematical expressions. How did Simon and Newell (1971) redefine human problem-solving? They saw the task environment of a problem as a god's eye view of the problem, or the problem maker's view. The problem space, on the other hand, was the constructed view of the problem solver. Once created, the problem space included the present state, the final desired goal state, and the operators that allowed the problem solver to move successfully through the problem space to the final desired state. That movement, they argued, was constrained by the fact that humans are serial processors, possess limited but quick STMs, and have essentially infinite but slow LTMs. Those inherent limits prevent parallel processing approaches or lengthy searches of large problem spaces; modern AI systems, of course, have no such limitations. Operators are cognitive tools, such as analogy, induction, or metacognitive process (Burns & Vollemeyer, 2000). Problem solvers applied heuristics in order to move through the problem space to a solution. The means-ends heuristic looks for the differences between the current problem state and the final desired solution. Subgoaling is where problem solvers breakdown the problem into a set of smaller interrelated problems. Working backwards is when problem solvers mentally place themselves at the final desired state and then look back from there to determine the steps necessary for a solution. Analogies, too, are prominent heuristic methods. Being able to see the analogical relationships between previous problems and the current one will often yield a solution.

Think of the following problem: getting from Magnolia, Arkansas to Little Rock. The distance between those two locations is 136 miles (219 kilometers). That distance is the basis for a means-ends analysis solution. The problem, stated in terms of that heuristic, is simply to reduce that distance to zero. If the two cities were islands on the hypothetical Sea of Arkansas, then sailing a heading of 30 would be sufficient. But, there is no sea so roads must be used. That solution requires a vehicle. If one is available so much the better. If not, one has to be obtained. It could be rented, borrowed, or stolen (not recommended). Once obtained, it must be fueled and a route mapped out. Once those preliminary steps are completed, arrival in Little Rock could be two hours and fifteen minutes away. All of those steps are examples of subgoaling or breaking the problem into smaller and related problems: obtaining a vehicle, fueling it, selecting a route, obeying the speed limits, and finding the destination. Suppose the trip to Little Rock is a medical emergency and the goal is to get to a trauma center within an hour. Now roads and vehicles no longer suffice as operators, they are not fast enough. The operator may now be a medical helicopter. It could cover the distance in an hour or less (but at much greater expense).

The working backwards heuristic also helps with this problem. Suppose the final goal is to be in Little Rock at 5 p.m. and it is 7 a.m. on that day. Here is a likely scenario for working backwards:

- Goal: Be in Little Rock by 5:00 p.m. today—Time = 5:00 p.m. (with 15 minutes to spare)

- Driving time: 150 minutes—Time = 4:45 p.m.

- Leave for Little Rock—Time = 2:15

- Fueling time: Fifteen minutes—Time = 2:15 p.m.

- Drive to gas station: Fifteen minutes—Time = 2:00 p.m.

- Leave home for gas station: Time = 1:45 p.m.

- Go home, have lunch, change clothes: 105 minutes—Time = 1:45 p.m.

- Office hours: 135 minutes—Time = Noon

- Teach class: Sixty minutes—Time = 9:45 a.m.

- Go to work: Fifteen minutes—Time = 8:45 a.m.

- Get showered and dressed: Sixty minutes—Time = 8:30 a.m.

- Have breakfast: Thirty minutes—Time = 7:30 a.m.

- Wake up: Time = 7:00 a.m.

Analogy is another useful heuristic. In this example the necessary operators to solve the problem have already been learned: drive on the right side of the road, red traffic lights mean stop and green lights mean go, do not exceed the posted speed limits, on superhighways only use the left lane to pass, leave three seconds worth of distance from the vehicle in front, and many more. These operators came from experience. Student drivers do not drive on Interstate highways on their first day behind the wheel. Instead, they start their driving lessons in a safe location such as a large, empty parking lot. They slowly progress to driving on lightly traveled streets and work their way up to fast highways. Could a person make it to Little Rock without knowing how to drive? Yes, but someone else would have to drive. Imagine solving this problem in Great Britain instead of the United States. There, one part of previous driving experience would be useless; driving on the right side of the road is not allowed there. A new operator would need to be learned, and fast!

Are humans rational decision-makers? Do they weigh the objective data about problems to make decisions? What kind of heuristics do humans use to make decisions? These kinds of questions emerged from the research on problem-solving. It turns out that under certain conditions humans make decisions using heuristics that, "sometimes lead to severe and systematic errors." (Tversky & Kahneman, 1974, p. 1124).

Biased Judgments

Tversky and Kahneman (1974) described three heuristics people commonly use: representativeness, availability, and adjustment and anchoring. They demonstrated that the quick and facile use of those heuristics often led to biased judgments. In representativeness heuristic "probabilities are evaluated by the degree to which A is representative of B" (p. 1124). When using the representativeness heuristic people misjudged probabilities, sample sizes, chance factors, predictability, and statistical regression. Thus, Tversky's and Kahneman's participants were more likely to judge the person in the following description as a librarian than as a farmer, salesman, airline pilot, or physician. "Steve is very shy and withdrawn, invariably helpful, but with little interest in people, or in the world of reality. A meek and tidy soul, he has a need for order and structure, and a passion for detail." (p. 1124).

In the availability heuristic participants judged probabilities of events on factors such as the ease to which they could be brought to mind, their salience, abstractness vs. concreteness, and imaginability. The adjustment and anchoring heuristic is a bias toward initial values (the anchor). When two groups of high school students were asked to estimate in five seconds the product of:

$$8 \times 7 \times 6 \times 5 \times 4 \times 3 \times 2 \times 1$$

or the product of:

$$1 \times 2 \times 3 \times 4 \times 5 \times 6 \times 7 \times 8$$

their answers differed widely. The ascending group's average estimate was 2,250 while the descending group's estimate was 512. (The actual answer is 40,320.) The students did not have enough time to multiply all of the numbers and underestimated the product. The anchors in this case (the starting numbers of each sequence) played a strong role in the difference of the two estimates. Tversky and Kahneman concluded (p. 1131), "These heuristics are highly economical and usually effective, but they lead to systematic and predictable errors. A better understanding of these heuristics and of the biases to which they lead could improve judgments and decisions in situations of uncertainty." While algorithms and heuristics contribute much to the understanding of human cognition, the elephant in the room is language, a universal feature in all human groups.

LEARNING OBJECTIVE
5. Estimate the number of death per year due to shark attack or bee sting. What heuristic would predict a higher number for shark attacks?

LANGUAGE

The study of language or linguistics has a long history. Plato and Aristotle each wrote about rhetoric, a predecessor of linguistics (see Chapter 3). Also, recall how Renaissance philology, especially the study of ancient Roman texts, led to humanism (see Chapter 4). By the early 20th century, linguistics was an established social science. The study of language was another player in the emergence of cognitive psychology.

Origins of Language

The distant origins of language are an unsolved mystery. Donald (2020, p. 287) noted, "In a word, the language mechanism is bound up with culture." He argued that two preconditions preceded the evolution of language: a capacity to refine a wide variety of skills via practice and rehearsal and creation of long-lasting materials (e.g., stone tools) that required transmission from generation to generation to ensure preservation of the techniques required for their making. He argued that as humans became more skilled in the manufacture and use of tools and other material goods they needed to communicate more effectively about them. Mimesis, an embodied analogical representation such as those still seen in displays of grief and celebration, preceded language and evolved into voco-mimesis, the use of nonword signals. Merlin argued that language evolved slowly (p. 294):

> Thus, at least three very basic brain properties – voluntary access to procedural memory, improved metacognitive self-supervision, and greater developmental plasticity - were prominent among the modifications that the primate brain needed to evolve, before the preconditions needed for the genesis of language and symbolic invention were in place.

These, along with other cognitive adaptations related to socialization and mindsharing, were necessary for the emergence of the highly variable knowledge networks unique to modern humans. It was the emergent properties of those kinds of networks that necessitated the invention of more complex languages, and the elaborate imaginative mental life they enabled.

The relatively recent mutation (200,000–400,000 years before present) of the FOXP2 gene points to a genetic component to the evolution of language. The mutated form of the gene has been found in modern humans and Neanderthals (Krause et al., 2007). Zimmer (2011, pp. 22–24) summarized the role of the gene:

> FOXP2 didn't give us language all on its own. In our brains, it acts more like a foreman, handing out instructions to at least 84 target genes in the developing basal ganglia. Even this full crew of genes explains language only in part, because the ability to form words is just the beginning. Then comes the higher level of complexity: combining words according to rules of grammar to give them meaning.

Fisher (2019) called the FOXP2 (p. R67), "one piece of an extremely elaborate puzzle." Truer words have seldom been spoken. The evolution of language remains a mystery.

Language in Psychology

Noam Chomsky's book *Syntactic Structures* (1957) played a key role in making language a psychological topic. In that book he proposed that linguists should study a language's grammar first. He used the sentence, "Colorless green ideas sleep furiously." As an example of an English sentence that is grammatically correct but meaningless and unlikely to ever be uttered. Chomsky's view of language did much to change the direction of linguistics by putting syntax at the forefront over morphology (the study of words) and phonology (the sounds of language). Chomsky's (1959) critique of Skinner's book *Verbal Behavior* (1957) contrasted his approach to language as a process involving (p. 47), "data-handling or "hypothesis-formulating" ability of unknown character and complexity" to Skinner's reinforcement-based individual learning approach. Skinner, himself, never responded to Chomsky's critiques, but MacCorquodale (1970) did so. He focused on three aspects of Chomsky's critique: verbal behavior was an untested hypothesis, Skinner's use of technical terms were paraphrases of more traditional treatments of verbal behavior and the complex nature of speech. MacCorquodale (p. 98) writing about Chomsky's revolution notes:

> So far there have been no telling engagements in the revolution. The declaration of war has been unilateral, probably because the behaviorist cannot clearly recognize why he should defend himself. He has not hurt anyone; he has not preempted the verbal territory by applying his methods to verbal behavior…"

One fruitful area in the study of language has been how children come to learn language, the process of language acquisition.

Language Acquisition

In the 21st century more nuanced and well researched views of language and its acquisition have emerged. Kuhl (2000, p. 11856) lists six tenets of language acquisition:

- infants initially parse the basic units of speech allowing them to acquire higher-order units created by their combinations;

- the developmental process is not a selectionist one in which innately specified options are selected on the basis of experience;

- rather, a perceptual learning process, unrelated to Skinnerian learning, commences with exposure to language, during which infants detect patterns, exploit statistical properties, and are perceptually altered by that experience;

- vocal imitation links speech perception and production early, and auditory, visual, and motor information are coregistered for speech categories;

- adults addressing infants unconsciously alter their speech to match infants' learning strategies, and this is instrumental in supporting infants' initial mapping of speech; and

- the critical period for language is influenced not only by time but also by the neural commitment that results from experience.

Infants, thus, are sophisticated learners of language who are already learning language *in utero*. Moreover, that learning reshapes the brain and warps the brain's perceptual processes. Animals share some aspects of these features of learning (categorical learning), but not others (the perceptual magnet effect). The alteration of the brain by language learning helps explain why second language learning in adults is difficult for them but not for children. Adults who learn a second language must depend on separate brain regions for those languages while children who learn two languages early in life do not (Kim et al., 1997). The study of language acquisition continues to be a complex and fertile area for cognitive psychology.

LEARNING OBJECTIVE
6. Imagine what human cognition would be like without language.

NEUROPHYSIOLOGY AND COGNITION

One of psychology's long-term goals has been to understand the biological underpinnings of behavior. Aristotle linked body and soul (recall that in Latin the word *anima* may be translated as either soul or mind) tightly together and both, working together, were responsible for nearly all human functions. Descartes, in the 17th century, separated body and soul and provided his interactionist solution of the mind–body problem. His conception of humans as biological machines possessing both a mind and a body was revolutionary. He proposed that the link between those two separate parts was the pineal gland because it was not a paired brain structure. Berhouma (2013) analyzed whether Descartes knew of contradictory contemporary physiological evidence against his views about the pineal gland and concluded (p. 1670), "Descartes' neuroanatomical errors were intentional and do not result from Descartes' lack of knowledge. It seems that Descartes adapted his original neurophysiological concept to his metaphysical dualistic theory." Physiological explanations of behavior were rekindled in the late 19th century with the discovery of the neuron and the synapse, restimulating the search for links between neurophysiology and behavior. The next step was to describe how the 100 billion neurons in the human body form brains and peripheral nervous systems; that description is still a long distance away.

After World War II, theorists oriented toward psychobiology attempted to link behavior to biological processes. Karl Lashley's efforts to find the engram (1950) and Donald Hebb's (1949) cell assemblies were early examples of that type of research. Neither fully succeeded in finding causal links between the nervous system and behavior but they opened the door to later researchers including Nobel Physiology and Medicine Prize winners Roger Sperry and Eric Kandel.

Roger Sperry won the 1981 Nobel Prize (shared with David Hubel and Torsten Wiesel) for his research on "split-brain" human epileptic patients. Those surgeries, called corpus callosotomies, the severing of the corpus callosum, were treatments of last resort to inhibit grand mal epileptic episodes from crossing from one side of the brain to the other. Sperry recruited 11 such patients and discovered new findings about brain lateralization. After the surgery, one result was that patients could only name objects flashed on a screen that went to their right visual field. Gazzaniga (2014, p. 18094), then Sperry's graduate student recalled his excitement at the results from the first patient he ever tested:

> A circle is flashed to the right of fixation, allowing his left brain to see it. His right hand rises from the table and points to where the circle has been on the screen. We do this for a number of trials where the flashed circle appears on one side of the screen or the other. It doesn't matter. When the circle is to the right of fixation, the right hand, controlled by the left hemisphere, points to it. When the circle is to the left of fixation, it is the left hand, controlled by the right hemisphere, that points to it. One hand or the other will point to the correct place on the screen. That means that each hemisphere does see a circle when it is in the opposite visual field, and each, separate from the other, could guide the arm/hand it controlled, to make a response. Only the left hemisphere, however, can talk about it. I can barely contain myself. Oh, the sweetness of discovery.

The patient could only verbally respond to stimuli sent to his left visual field (e.g., from the right eye). But, when the stimulus was presented to the right visual field he could not respond but he pointed to the location where the stimulus had been with his left hand. Blindfolded patients could name objects in their right hands but not in their left hands. Interestingly, they could use those objects correctly but still could not name them. For example, a comb placed in the left hand of a blindfolded patient would elicit no verbal response. But, when asked to use it, they combed their hair (and still could not name the object). These were the results that eventually led to Sperry's Nobel Prize.

Eric Kandel won the Nobel Prize for Physiology and Medicine in 2000 (shared with Arvid Carlsson and Paul Greengard) for his research on the sea slug, *Aplysia californica*, (Castellucci & Kandel, 1976). Kandel and his coworkers showed that simple learned responses (habituation, sensitization, and dishabituation) were controlled by specific sensory and motor neurons. In other words, they were able to link behaviors to biological processes. That research led to insights about learning in animals with relative few brain cells (20,000 in *Aplysia* and 300,000 in *Drosophila*, the fruit fly), that the hip-

PHOTO 14.4 Roger Sperry

pocampus contains a cognitive map, how STMs convert to long-term, that increases in synaptic strength lead to memory formation, while synaptic depression provides a parallel mechanism for memory storage (Kandel, 2009). Such pure psychological research has been paralleled by similar research in artificial intelligence (AI).

On the AI side one goal is to build a brain, a biological neural network, in their parlance, but using computers. In AI, thus, the search is for an "artificial neural network" (ANN). The ANN goal is similar to what Feynman, the physicist, had written on the blackboard at his classroom at Caltech, "What I cannot create, I do not understand." Hiesinger (2021) has attempted to link neurobiology (his field), AI, developmental biology, and robotics together by pursuing each's notion of the concept of information. Prior to writing the book he created a workshop with ten seminars attempting to bring developmental neurobiologists and AI researchers together. He found that the discussions in the seminars were useful but (p. 11):

> As I kept on going back to my own discussions and tried to distill their meaning in writing, it turned out all too easy to lose their natural flow of logic and the associations that come with different perspectives. So I decided to present the discussions themselves. And as any discussion is only as good as the discussants, I invented four entirely fictional scientists to do all of the hard work and present all of the difficulty problems in ten dialogs. The participants are a developmental geneticist, a neuroscientist, a robotics engineer, and an AI researcher.

The participants in those fields define and view information differently. The goal of his workshop was to enable better communication among these fields because they are all working on the same problems related to cognition, be that in living things or constructed devices. While Hiesinger indicated, (p. 37) "this seminar series is not about the applications of AI" much has been learned about the interaction of neurophysiology and neural engineering.

Since the advent of the transistor in the 1950s scientists and engineers have forged a link between neurophysiology and neural engineering creating successful devices such as cochlear implants, cardiac pacemakers, and many other similar devices. Prochazka (2017, p. 1302) attributed the success of such devices to "the development of materials, miniaturization, computerization, wireless communication surgery, and, last but not least, to the understanding of the underlying neurophysiological mechanisms." Thus, there is benefit to science from the applied side too.

ANIMAL COGNITION

Bräuer et al. (2020) reviewed the field of animal cognition and concluded that in the past researchers had been too anthropomorphic and had neglected to take (p. 2) "the biological context of behaviors" into account. They complained that all too often researchers assumed that one general and overall form of cognition was sufficient to explain all cases. While many researchers still consider humans as possessing the ultimate form of cognition, Bräuer et al. provide many counterexamples where animals outperform humans including the ability of many birds to classify objects and remember cached locations of food over long periods. They point to how researchers failed to use the proper sensory modality when testing for animal cognition. They cite the paucity of studies in dog behavior that assess that species's (p. 12) "most relevant sense," olfaction. Researchers, however, should take care to consider animal cognition in its own context to avoid anthropomorphic interpretations and be aware that they are not studying a general form cognition but rather are studying a wide variety of cognitions in a Darwinian sense. Bräuer et al. (p. 29) argued that considering each case by itself:

> allows us to reveal the evolutionary, developmental, and environmental conditions that foster the growth of certain unique abilities in the young of a species, or the convergence of skills shared among species.

Modern psychology animal cognition, too, is an active area of research and has re-emerged phoenix-like from Romanes's overtly anthropomorphic origins and it near-banishment by classical Behaviorism.

SUMMARY

The scientific study of the mind was the impetus that first led to the founding of psychology by Wundt. That early form of cognition foundered because of methodological problems and led to Watson's founding of Behaviorism, a slow-moving movement that eventually came to dominate much of American psychology well into the 1970s. But, as Miller (2003) noted, the mind had remained alive within social and clinical psychology. World War II helped revive interest in cognition through the need to rapidly assess and select personnel for the specialized tasks of warfare. After the war, that effort led to a massive revival of psychological testing in a wide variety of arenas including education and job placement. The work of codebreakers using the earliest digital computers also led to their introduction to the civilian world after the war was over. The rise of ransomware has demonstrated how completely the digital computer and its networks have come to dominate the current scene.

The study of memory was not a part of psychology's initial list of topics. It only gained prominence after Ebbinghaus published the results of the research he had painstakingly collected from himself using his new savings method. His results are still valid and appear in every general psychology text today. Bartlett was another early memory researcher but his goal was different from Ebbinghaus's. Bartlett looked for the errors his students made after reading stories he presented. He found that the longer the interval between reading and testing the worse was their recall of story details, or the surface structure. Plus, his students tended to change unfamiliar topics to more familiar ones. But, nearly all of his students recalled the meaning of the story, its deep structure.

Ebbighaus's methods were quickly adopted and modified and led to an interest in verbal learning by many psychologists. Calkins developed the paired associate method and it was used extensively in laboratory settings to study memory because it avoided the problems of serial methods. Recall methods were used too, as participants attempted to remember as many verbal of physical items following a brief presentation. Theories of forgetting were also part of the verbal learning movement. The earliest decay theories yielded to interference theories and later to theories that factored in biological constraints or the benefits of organization to memory. Miller's "magic number 7" and Atkinson and Shiffrin's information processing theory were examples of each, respectively. Later modifications included Craik and Lockhart's levels of processing model, Tulving's distinction between episodic and semantic memories, and Baddeley and Hitch's working memory. The verbal learning researchers changed the idea of memory as a thing to memory as a process.

Luchins's water jar experiments demonstrated how once a solution was found to a problem it tended to persist even when a simpler solution was available. Köhler's insight learning showed how some problems were solved after an impasse and the linking of two separate gestalts together into one. The use and acceptance of representations also aided problem- solving. Being able to switch from a representation that inhibited the finding of a solution to another where the solution was clearer aided problem- solving. Roitblatt's elucidation of the components of a representation: domain, content, code, medium, and dynamism made it easier to understand how representations played a role in problem-solving. Newell and Simon's Logic Theorist computer program demonstrated that computers, too, could be made to solve difficult problems through the use of formal logic and heuristics working together. Their definition of problems as consisting of a problem space, an initial set of conditions, a final desired goal, and operators to move through the problem space to the final goal has been widely adopted. While heuristics have proved helpful to problem-solving, Kahneman and Tversky demonstrated how some heuristics led to biased judgments.

Language is an ubiquitous human phenomenon but one whose origins are lost in time. Biologically, the FOXP2 gene has been implicated in the evolution of language but many argue that human sociality also played a large role. In the 1970s Chomsky brought language into psychology as a major topic. Many studies have demonstrated the remarkably consistent process of language acquisition in children and in adults learning a second language.

The chapter concludes with a look at the relationship of neurophysiology and cognition. This old problem was revitalized in the late 20th century by Lashley's search for the engram and Hebb's idea of cell assemblies. Sperry's discovery of the "split brain" won him a Nobel Prize and showed in new detail the organization of the human brain. Kandel also won a Nobel Prize for his work on *Aplysia*, the sea slug. He demonstrated the neurobiology of many types of learning. Hiesinger, a neurobiologist, attempted to bring neuroscientists, developmental geneticists, robotics engineers, and AI researchers together to better understand how information is handled by all of those disciplines and to have them better communicate about it among each other. Prochazka noted the many successes of applied devices such as cochlear implants and cardiac pacemakers. He pointed out how the transistor and integrated circuits have made it possible to make daily life better through engineering. Bräuer argued that the cognition of nonhuman animals is another worthwhile area for future study. He believed that researchers should become less anthropomorphic and should take animal ecology into better account in the future.

REFERENCES

Abelard, P. (1972). *The story of my misfortunes* (H. A. Bellows, Trans.). McMillan.

Abramson, C. I. (2018). Let us bring comparative psychology back. *International Journal of Comparative Psychology*, *31*, 1–15.

Adamson, P. (2006a). Al-Kindi and the reception of Greek philosophy. In P. Adamson & R. C. Taylor (Eds.), *The Cambridge-companion to Arabic philosophy* (pp. 32–51). Cambridge University Press.

Adamson, P. (2006b). *Al-Kindi. Stanford Encyclopedia of Philosophy.* http://plato.stanford.edu/entries/al-kindi

Akimenko, M. A. (2007). Vladimir Mikhailovich Bekhterev. *Journal of the History of the Neurosciences*, *16*, 100–109.

Ali, S., Jabeen, S., Pate, R. J., Shahid, M., Chinala, S., Nathani, M., & Shah, R. (2015). Conversion disorder-mind versus body: A review. *Innovations in Clinical Neuroscience*, *12*, 27–33.

Allen, P. (1985). *The concept of woman.* Eden Press.

Amadeo, M. (2018). Textbooks revealing the development of a concept-the case of the number line in the analytic geometry (1708–1829). *ZDM Mathematics Education*, *50*, 907–920.

American Psychological Association (Author). (1991). APA's new logo 'radiates warmth'. *APA Monitor*, 6–7.

Angell, J. R. (1907). The province of functional psychology. *Psychological Review*, *14*, 61–91.

Angell, J. R. (1911). Imageless thought. *Psychological Review*, *18*, 295–322.

Annas, J. (2010). Virtue and law in Plato. In C. Bobonich (Ed.), *Plato's laws: A critical guide* (pp. 74–91). Cambridge University Press.

Anonymous. (1890). Review of the book: *The principles of psychology* by William James. *Science*, *10*, 207–208.

Anonymous. (n.d.). *Beowulf.* https://www.poetryfoundation.org/poems/43521/beowulf-old-english-version

Antonov-Ovseyenko, A. (1981). *The time of Stalin.* Harper & Row.

Antrop, M. (2004). Landscape change and the urbanization process in Europe. *Landscape and Urban Planning*, *67*, 9–26.

Aquilecchia, G. (2017). Giordano Bruno as philosopher of the renaissance. In H. Gatti (Ed.), *Giordano Bruno: Philosopher of the Renaissance* (pp. 3–16). Routledge.

Araujo, S. d. F. (2016). *Wundt and the philosophical foundations of psychology: A reappraisal.* Springer International Publishing.

Aristotle. (1975). *On the soul* (W. S. Hett, Trans.). Harvard University Press.

Aristotle. (1999). *Aristotle's metaphysics* (J. Sachs, Trans.). Green Lion Press.

Arnheim, R. (1986). The two faces of Gestalt psychology. *American Psychologist*, *41*, 820–824.

Arnott, R., Finger, S., & Smith, C. U. M. (2003). *Trepanation: History, discovery, theory*. Psychology Press.

Asce, S. E. (1946). Forming impressions of personality. *Journal of Abnormal and Social Psychology, 41*, 258–290.

Asch, S. E. (1948). The doctrine of suggestion, prestige, and imitation in social psychology. *Psychological Review, 55*, 250–276.

Asch, S. E. (1952). *Social psychology*. Prentice-Hall.

Asch, S. E. (1955). Opinions and social pressure. *Scientific American, 193*, 31–35.

Ash, I. K., Jee, B. D., & Wiley, J. (2012). Investigating insight as sudden learning. *The Journal of Problem Solving, 4*, 1–27.

Ash, M. G. (1992). Cultural contexts and scientific change in psychology: Kurt Lewin in Iowa. *American Psychologist, 47*, 198–207.

Ash, M. G. (1995). *Gestalt psychology in German culture*. Cambridge University Press.

Atkinson, R. C., & Shiffrin, R. M. (1968). Human memory: A proposed system and its control processes. In K. W. Spence & J. T. Spence (Eds.), *The psychology of learning and motivation* (pp. 89–195). Academic Press. 2.

Ayers, M. (2006). Was Berkeley an empiricist or a rationalist? *The Cambridge companion to Berkeley*, (pp. 34–62). Cambridge University Press.

Bacon, F. (1960/1620). *The new organon*. Bobbs-Merrill.

Baddeley, A. D., & Hitch, G. (1974). Working memory. *Psychology of Learning and Motivation, 8*, 47–89.

Bain, A. (1855). *The senses and the intellect* (3rd ed.). D. Appleton and Company.

Bair, D. (2003). *Jung: A biography*, Little, Brown and Company.

Baker, D. B., & Benjamin, L. T. (2000). The affirmation of the scientist-practitioner. *American Psychologist, 55*, 241–247.

Barnes, J. (1995a). Life and work. In J. Barnes (Ed.), *The Cambridge companion to Aristotle* (pp. 1–26). Cambridge University Press.

Barnes, J. (1995b). Metaphysics. In J. Barnes (Ed.), *The Cambridge companion to Aristotle* (pp. 66–108). Cambridge University Press.

Barone, D. F. (1996). John Dewey: Psychologist, reformer, philosopher. In G. A. Kimble, C. A. Boneau, & M. Wertheimer (Eds.), *Portraits of pioneers in psychology* (Vol. 2, pp. 47–61). American Psychological Association.

Bartlett, F. (1932). *Remembering: A study in experimental and social psychology*. Cambridge.

Bayram, A. B. (2015). What drives modern Diogenes? Individual values and cosmopolitan allegiance. *European Journal of International Relations, 21*, 451–479.

Beach, F. A. (1950). The snark was a boojum. *American Psychologist, 5*, 115–224.

Beck, H. P., Levinson, S., & Irons, G. (2009). Finding Little Albert. *American Psychologist, 64*, 605–614.

Behrens, P. J. (1997). G. E. Müller: The third pillar of experimental psychology. In W. G. -Bringmann, H. E. Lück, R. Miller, & C. E. Early (Eds.), *A pictorial history of psychology* (pp. 171–176). Quintessence Publishing Co, Inc.

Beiser, F. C. (2000). The Enlightenment and idealism. In K. Ameriks (Ed.). *The Cambridge companion to German idealism* (pp. 18–36). Cambridge University Press.

Beiser, F. C. (2005). *Hegel*. Routledge.

Beiser, Frederick C. (2020). *Gustav Theodor Fechner. The Stanford Encyclopedia of Philosophy*. https://plato.stanford.edu/archives/spr2020/entries/fechner/

Benjamin, L. T., Jr. (2000). The psychology laboratory at the turn of the 20th century. *American Psychologist*, *55*, 318–321.

Benjamin, L. T., Jr. (2009). *A history of psychology* (3rd ed.). Blackwell Publishing.

Berardino, A., & Studer, B (Eds.). (2008). *History of theology*. Liturgical Press.

Berhouma, M. (2013). Beyond the pineal gland assumption: A neuronantomical appraisal of dualism in Descartes' philosophy. *Clinical Neurology and Neurosurgery*, *115*, 1661–1670.

Bernstein, C. A. (2011). Meta-structure in the *DSM-5* process. *Psychiatric News*, *5*, 7–29.

Berryman, S. (2004). *Democritus. Stanford Encyclopedia of Philosophy*. http://plato.stanford.edu/entries/heraclitus/

Bettner, B. L. (2020). Are Alfred Adler and Rudolf Dreikurs relevant for parents today? *The Journal of Individual Psychology*, *76*, 70–78.

Biagioli, M. (2007). *Galileo's instruments of credit: Telescopes, images, secrecy*. University of Chicago Press.

Billig, M. (2008). *The hidden roots of critical psychology: Understanding the impact of Locke, Shaftesbury and Reid*. SAGE.

Birnbaum, L. C. (1955). Behaviorism in the 1920's. *American Quarterly*, *7*, 15–30.

Blumenthal, A. L. (1980). Wilhelm Wundt and early American psychology: A clash of cultures. In R. W. Rieber (Ed.), *Wilhelm Wundt and the making of a scientific psychology* (pp. 117–135). Plenum Press.

Blumenthal, A. L. (2001). A Wundt primer. In R.W. Rieber & D.K. Robinson (Eds.), *Wilhelm Wundt in history: The making of a scientific psychology* (pp. 121–144). Kluwer/Plenum.

Boakes, R. (1984). *From Darwin to behaviourism*. Cambridge University Press.

Bobzien, S. (1999). *Determinism and freedom in Stoic philosophy*. Oxford University Press.

Bolli, R. (2019). William Harvey and the discovery of the circulation of the blood: Part II. *Circulation Research*, *124*, 1300–1302.

Boring, E. G. (1942). *Sensation and perception in the history of experimental psychology*. Appleton-Century-Crofts, Inc.

Boring, E. G. (1950). *A history of experimental psychology* (2nd ed.). Appleton-Century-Crofts, Inc.

Boring, E. G. (1953). A history of introspection. *Psychological Bulletin*, *50*, 169–189.

Boyles, D., & Garrison, J. (2017). The mind is not the brain: John Dewey, neuroscience, and avoiding the mereological fallacy. *Dewey Studies*, *1*, 111–130.

Braddick, M. (2008). God's fury, *England's fire: A new history of the English Civil Wars*. Penguin.

Bramble, D. M., & Lieberman, D. E. (2004). Endurance running and the evolution of *Homo*. *Nature*, *432*, 345–352.

Branham, R. B., & Goulet-Cazé, M. O (Eds.). (1996). *The Cynics: The Cynic movement in antiquity and its legacy*. University of California Press.

Bräuer, J., Hanus, D., Pika, S., Gray, R., & Uomini, N. (2020). Old and new approaches to animal cognition: There is not "one cognition," *Journal of Intelligence*, *8*, 28.

Breazeale, D. (2006). *Johann-Gottlieb Fichte. Stanford encyclopedia of philosophy.* http://plato.-stanford.edu/entries/johann-fichte/, Retrieved December 19, 2010, from

Breuer, J., & Freud, S. (1895). *Studies in hysteria.* Beacon Hill Press.

Brewer, C. L. (1991). Perspectives on John B. Watson. In G. A. Kimble, M. Wertheimer, & C. L. White (Eds.), *Portraits of pioneers in psychology* (Vol. 1, pp. 171–186). Lawrence Erlbaum.

Bridgman, P. W. (1928). *The logic of modern physics.* The Macmillan Company.

Britten, R. J. (2002). Divergence between samples of chimpanzee and human DNA sequences is 5% counting indels. *Proceedings National Academy Science, 99,* 13633–13635.

Brown, B. (2007). *Evolution: A historical perspective.* Greenwood Press.

Buckley, K. W. (1994). Misbehaviorism: The case of John B. Watson's dismissal from Johns Hopkins University. In J. T. Todd & E. K. Morris (Eds.), *Modern perspectives on John B. Watson and classical behaviorism* (pp. 19–36). Greenwood Press.

Bunn, G. (2017). Wilhelm Wundt and the emergence of scientific psychology. *Psychology Review, 22,* 10–12.

Burkert, W. (1972). *Lore and science in ancient pythagoreanism.* Harvard University Press.

Burns, B. D., & Vollemeyer, R. (2000). Problem solving: Phenomena in search of a thesis. *Proceedings of the Annual Meeting of the Cognitive Science Society, 22,* 627–632.

Byford, A. (2016). V. M. Bechterev in Russian child science, 1900s-1920s: "Objective psychology"/"reflexology" as a scientific movement. *Journal of the History of the Behavioral Sciences, 52,* 99–123.

Cahan, E. D. (2018). *Helmholtz: A life in science.* University of Chicago Press.

Cahan, E. D., & White, S. H. (1992). Proposals for a second psychology. *American Psychologist, 47,* 224–235.

Cahill, T. (1996). *How the Irish saved civilization.* Anchor.

Calkins, M. W. (1894). Association I. *Psychological Review, 1,* 476–484.

Cameron, R., & Neal, L. (2002). *A concise economic history of the world* (4th ed.). Oxford University Press.

Carr, H. A. (1925). *Psychology: A study of mental activity.* Longmans, Green.

Carr, H. A. (1961). Harvey A. Carr. In C. Murchinson (Ed.), *A history of psychology in autobiography* (Vol. 6, pp. 69–82). Prentice-Hall.

Carroll, D. W. (2017). *Purpose and cognition: Edward Tolman and the transformation of American psychology.* Cambridge University Press.

Castellucci, V., & Kandel, E. R. (1976). Presynaptic facilitation as a mechanism for behavioral sensitization in *Aplysia. Science, 4270,* 1176–1178.

Cattell, J. M. (1905). A biographical directory of American men of science. *Science, 21,* 899.

Cattell, J. M. (1928). Early psychological laboratories. *Science, 67,* 543–548.

Cattermole, G. N. (1997). Michael Servetus: Physician, Socinian, and victim. *Journal of the Royal Society of Medicine, 90,* 640–644.

Chandler, T. (1987). *Four thousand years of urban growth.* St. David's University Press.

Chen, Y., Farzan, R., Kraut, R., YechehZaare, & Zhang, A. F. (2019). *Motivating expert contributions to public goods: A personalized field experiment on Wikipedia 1*. Retrieved on December 19, 2019 from https://www.semanticscholar.org/paper/Motivating-Expert-Contributions-to-Public-Goods-%3A-A-Chen-Farzan/da8374e0d0546599d1a019f31f591f6a581d0bba

Chilman, C. S. (1979). *Adolescent sexuality in a changing American society*. U.S. Department of Health, Education, and Welfare.

Chilton, B. (2006). Christianity: What it is and how it has interacted with western civilization. In J. Neusner (Ed.), *Religious foundations of western civilization*, (pp. 71–104). Abingdon Press.

Chomsky, N. (1957). *Syntactic structures*. Mouton.

Chomsky, N. (1959). A Review of B. F. Skinner's Verbal Behavior. *Language*, *35*, 26–58.

Choopani, R., & Emtiazy, M. (2015). The concept of lifestyle factors, based on the teaching of Avicenna (Ibn Sina). *International Journal of Preventive Medicine*, *6*, 30–37.

City Mayors Statistics. (n.d.). *The world's largest cities and urban areas in 2019. City Mayors Statistics*, http://www.citymayors.com/statistics/largest-cities-population-125.html

Clay, R. (2005). Too few in quantitative psychology. *Monitor on Psychology*, *36*, 26.

Cochran, G., & Harpending, H. (2009). *The 10,000 year explosion*. Basic Books.

Cohen, I. B. (1981). Newton's discovery of gravity. *Scientific American*, *244*(3), 166–179.

Cohen, I. B. (1994). Newton and the social sciences, with special reference to economics, or, the case of the missing paradigm. In P. Mirowski (Ed.), *Natural images in economic thought* (pp. 55–90). Cambridge University Press.

Commission of the Status of Women. (2008). *Report on the fifty-second session*. United Nations. (Economic and Social Council Supplement No. 7)

Conn, R., IV. (2007). *Prevalence and profitability: The counterfeit coins of archaic and classical Greece* [Unpublished master's thesis], Florida State University.http://etd.lib.fsu.edu/theses/available/etd-11132007-101625/unrestricted/Conn.pdf

Cordain, L., Miller, J., & Mann, N. (1999). Scant evidence of periodic starvation among hunter-gatherers. *Diabetologica*, *42*, 383–384.

Coren, S. (2003). Sensation and perception. In D. K. Freedheim (Ed.), *Handbook of psychology* (Vol. 1, pp. 85–108). John Wiley & Sons.

Cornwell, D., Hobbs, S., & Prytula, R. (1980). Little Albert rides again. *American Psychologist*, *35*, 216–217.

Costall, A. (1993). How Lloyd Morgan's canon backfired. *Journal of the History of the Behavioral Sciences*, *29*, 113–122.

Cottingham, J. (1992). Introduction. In J. Cottingham (Ed.), *The Cambridge companion to Descartes* (pp. 1–20). Cambridge University Press.

Cottrell, W. D. (2005). Moving driverless transit into the mainstream: Research issues and challenges. *Public Transportation*, 69–76.

Couzin-Frankel, J. (2018). The roots of resilience. *Science*, *359*, 970–971.

Craig, J. (1963). Newton and the counterfeiters. *Notes and Records of the Royal Society of London*, *18*, 136–145.

Craik, F. I. M., & Lockhart, R. S. (1972). Levels of processing: A framework for memory research. *Journal of Verbal Learning and Verbal Behavior, 11*, 671–684.

Crespi, L. P. (1942). Quantitative variation of incentive and performance in the white rat. *American Journal of Psychology, 55*, 467–517.

Crick, N. (2019). Invectives against ignoramuses: Petrarch and the defense of humanist eloquence. *Review of Communication, 19*, 178–193.

Crocq, M. A. (2015). A history of anxiety: From Hippocrates to DSM. *Dialogues in Clinical Neuroscience, 17*, 319–325.

Crust, L. (2008). A review and conceptual re-examination of mental toughness: Implications for future researchers. *Personality and Individual Differences, 45*, 576–583.

Curry, A. (2012). *The cave art debate. Smithsonian.com.* https://www.smithsonianmag.com/history/the-cave-art-debate-100617099/.

Cynkar, A. (2007). The changing gender composition of psychology. *Monitor on Psychology, 38*, 46.

Dallal, A. (1999). Science, medicine, and technology. In J. L. Esposito (Ed.), *The Oxford history of Islam* (pp. 155–213). Oxford University Press.

Damböck, C., Feest, U., & Kusch, M. (2020). Descriptive psychology and *völkerpsychologie*—In the contexts of historicism, relativism, and naturalism. *The Journal of the International Society for the History of Philosophy of Science, 10, 226–233*.

D'Ancona, C. (2006). Greek into Arabic: Neoplatonism in transition. In P. Adamson & R. C. Taylor (Eds.), *The Cambridge companion to Arabic philosophy* (pp. 10–31). Cambridge University Press.

D'Antoni, P. (Producer)., & Yates, P. (Director). (1968). *Bullitt* [Motion picture]. Warner Brothers/Seven Arts.

Danziger, K. (1980). Wundt's theory of behavior and volition. In R. W. Rieber (Ed.), *Wilhelm Wundt and the making of a scientific psychology* (pp. 89–116). Plenum Press.

Danziger, K. (1990). *Constructing the subject: Historical origins of psychological research (Cambridge studies in the history of psychology)*, Cambridge: Cambridge University Press, doi:10.1017/CBO9780511524059

Darwin, C. R. (1868). *The variation of animals and plants under domestication* (Vol. 1). John Murray.

Dautenhahn, Katherine E. (2018). *An empirical examination of doctoral training models in clinical psychology in the United States*, 494. *Loma Linda University Electronic Theses, Dissertations & Projects*. http://scholarsrepository.llu.edu/etd/494

Davis, R. C. (1970). The brass age of psychology. *Technology and Culture, 11*, 604–612.

DeBell, C. S., & Harless, D. K. (1992). B. F. Skinner: Myth and misperception. *Teaching of Psychology, 19*, 68–73.

Deese, J. (1967). *General psychology*. Allyn and Bacon].

Descartes, R. (1912/1637). *Discourse on method*. J. M. Dent.

Dewey, J. (1896). The reflex arc concept in psychology. *Psychological Review, 3*, 357–370.

Dewsbury, D. A. (2000). Issues in comparative psychology at the dawn of the 20th century. *American Psychologist, 55*, 750–753.

Dewsbury, D. A. (2003). James Rowland Angell: Born administrator. In G. A. Kimble & M. Wertheimer (Eds.). *Portraits of Pioneers in Psychology* (Vol. 5, pp. 57–71). American Psychological Association.

Diamond, J. (1993). Speaking with a single tongue. *Discover, 14*, 78–85.

Diamond, J. (1997). *Guns, germs, and steel*. W. W. Norton.

Diamond, S. (1980). Wundt before Leipzig. In R. W. Rieber (Ed.), *Wilhelm Wundt and the making of a scientific psychology* (pp. 3–70). Plenum Press.

Diogenes. (1925). *Lives of eminent philosophers*. (R. D. Hicks, Trans.). Harvard University Press.

Dmitrishin, A. (2013). Deconstructing distinctions: The European university in comparative historical perspective. *UPF Journal of World History, 5*, 1–18.

Dobzhansky, T. (1973). Nothing in biology makes sense except in the light of evolution. *The American Biology Teacher, 35*, 125–129.

Dolnick, E. (2011). *The clockwork universe*. HarperCollins.

Domhoff, G. W. (2019). The neurocognitive theory of dreams at age 20: An assessment and a comparison with four other theories of dreaming. *Dreaming, 29*, 265–302.

Dona, H. S. G., & Chittka, L. (2020). Charles H. Turner, pioneer in animal cognition. *Science, 370*, 530–531.

Donald, M. (2020). Key cognitive preconditions for the evolution of language. In T. B. Henley, M. J. Rossano, & E. P. Kardas. (Eds.), *Handbook of cognitive archeology: Psychology in prehistory* (pp. 287–295). Routledge.

Dounias, E., & Froment, A. (2006). When forest-based hunter-gatherers become sedentary: Consequences for diet and health. *Unasylva, 57*, 26–33.

Drake, S. (1976). Galileo and the first mechanical computing device. *Scientific American, 234*, 104–113.

Dreikurs, R. (1971). *Social equality: The challenge of today*. Adler School of Professional Psychology.

Driscoll, A., & Husain, M. (2019, October 21). Why *Joker's* depiction of mental illness is dangerously misinformed. *The Guardian*. https://www.theguardian.com/film/2019/oct/21/joker-mental-illness-joaquin-phoenix-dangerous-misinformed

Duncombe, R. L. (1945). The personal equation in astronomy. *Popular Astronomy, 53*, 2–13.

Dunn, D. S., McCarthy, M. A., Baker, S., Halonen, J. S., & Hill, W. H. (2007). Quality benchmarks in undergraduate psychology programs. *American Psychologist, 62*, 650–670.

Dunn, M. (2017). Monasticism/asceticism. In Toom. T (Ed.), *Augustine in context* (pp. 169–171). Cambridge University Press.

Duntley, J. D., & Buss, D. M. (2008). Evolutionary psychology is a metatheory for psychology. *Psychological Inquiry, 19*, 30–34.

Dyches, P. (2021). *Moon illusion: Why does the moon look so big sometimes?* https://solarsystem.nasa.gov/news/1191/the-moon-illusion-why-does-the-moon-look-so-big-sometimes/

Eals, M., & Silverman, I. (1994). The hunter-gatherer theory of spatial sex differences: Proximate factors mediating the female advantage in recall of object arrays. *Ethology & Sociobiology, 15*, 95–105.

Eaton, S. B., Konner, M., & Shostak, M. (1988). Stone agers in the fast lane: Chronic degenerative diseases in evolutionary perspective. *The American Journal of Medicine, 84*, 730–749.

Ebbinghaus, H. (1908). *Psychology: An elementary textbook*. Heath.

Ebbinghaus, H. (1913). *Memory; a contribution to experimental psychology*, Teachers College, Columbia University.

Eccles, J. (1985). *Mind and brain: The many-faceted problems*, (2nd ed.). Paragon House Publishers.

Ehrenfels, C. von. (1890). Über 'Gestaltqualitäten.'*Vierteljahrsscrift fur. Wissenschaftliche Philosophie*, *14*, 249–292.

Ehrenreich, B., & English, D. (2010). *Witches, midwives, and nurses* (2nd ed.). Feminist Press at the City University of New York.

Ehrenstein, W. H., & Ehrenstein, A. (1999). Psychophysical methods. In R. H. S. Carpenter & J. G. Robson (Eds.), *Vision Research: A Practical Guide to Laboratory Methods* (pp. 1211–1241). Oxford University Press.

Ellenberger, H. F. (1970). *The discovery of the unconscious*. Basic Books.

Elliot, A. J., & Fryer, J. W. (2008). The goal construct in psychology. In J. Y. Shah, W. L. Gardner, (Eds.), *Handbook of motivation science* (pp. 235–250). Guilford Press.

Enard, W., Gehre, S., Hammerschmidt, K., Hölter, S. M., Blass, T., & Somel, M. (2009). A humanized version of Foxp2 affects cortico-basal ganglia circuits in mice. *Cell*, *137*, 961–971. doi:10.1016/j.cell.2009.03.041

Evans, R. B. (1991). E. B. Titchener on scientific psychology and technology. In G. A. Kimble, M. Wertheimer, & C. White (Eds.), *Portraits of pioneers in psychology* (pp. 88–103). American Psychological Association.

Fakhry, M. (1999). Philosophy and theology. In J. L. Esposito (Ed.), *The Oxford history of Islam* (pp. 269–303). Oxford University Press.

Faria, M. A. (2015). Religious morality (and secular humanism) in Western civilization as precursors to medical ethics: A historic perspective. *Surgical Neurology International*, *6*, 105–116.

Farr, J. (1988). The history of political science. *American Journal of Political Science*, *32*, 1175–1195.

Fauré-Fremiet, E. (1966). Les origines de L'academie des sciences de Paris. *Notes and Records of the Royal Society of London*, *21*, 20–31.

Fechner, G. (1966). *Elements of psychophysics* (H. E. Adler, Trans.). (Vol. 1). Holt, Rinehart and Winston, Inc.

Ferguson, K. (2002). *Tycho and Kepler*. Walker Publishing Company.

Finocciaro, M. A. (2016). Philosophy versus religion and science versus religion: The trials of Bruno and Galileo. In H. Gatti (Ed.), *Giordano Bruno: Philosopher of the Renaissance* (pp. 51–96). Routledge.

Fisher, S. E. (2019). Human genetics: The evolving story of *FOXP2*. *Current Biology*, *2*, R65–R67.

Flintoff, E. (1980). Pyrrho and India. *Phronesis*, *25*, 88–108.

Forsyth, D. R. (1976). Crucial experiments and social psychological inquiry. *Personality and Social Psychology Bulletin*, *2*, 454–459.

Fouka, V. (2019). How do immigrants respond to discrimination? The case of Germans in the US during World War I. *American Political Science Review*, *113*, 405–422.

Freud, A. (1946). *The ego and mechanisms of defense*. International Universities Press.

Freud, S. (1900/1923). *The interpretation of dreams*. Basic Books.

Freud, S. (1923/1960). *The ego and the id*. Norton.

Friedlander, S. (1997). *Nazi Germany and the Jews: The years of persecution, 1933–1939*. HarperCollins.

Friend, R., Rafferty, Y., & Bramel, D. (1990). A puzzling misinterpretation of the Asch 'conformity' study. *European Journal of Social Psychology, 20*, 29–44.

Gabbard, G. O. (2001). *Psychoanalysis and film.* Karnac.

Gabbard, G. O., & Gabbard, K. (1999). *Psychiatry and the cinema* (2nd ed.). American Psychiatric Press.

Gabora, L., & Smith, C. M. (2020). Exploring the psychological basis for transitions in the archeological record. In T. B. Henley, M. J. Rossano, & E. P. Kardas (Eds.), *Handbook of cognitive archeology: Psychology in prehistory* (pp. 220–240). Routledge.

Gall, S., Beins, B., & Feldman, A. J. (1996). *The Gale encyclopedia of psychology.* Gale.

Galton, F. (1869/1978). *Hereditary genius.* St. Martin's Press.

Galton, F. (1904). Eugenics: Its definition, scope and aims. *The American Journal of Sociology, 10*, 1–6.

Galton, F. (1908/1974). *Memories of my life.* AMS Press.

Gardner, H. (2005). Scientific psychology: Should we bury it or praise it? In R. J. Sternberg (Ed.), *Unity in psychology: Possibility or pipedream?* (pp. 77–90). American Psychological Association.

Gay, P. (1988). *Freud: A life for our time.* W. W. Norton & Company.

Gay, P. (1989). *The Freud reader.* W. W. Norton.

Gazzaniga, M. S. (2014). The split-brain: Rooting consciousness in biology. *PNAS, 111*, 18093–18094.

Gerson, L. (2008). *Plotinus. Stanford Encyclopedia of Philosophy.* http://plato.stanford.edu/entries/plotinus/

Gilbert, M. (2004). *The First World War.* Routledge.

Gimbutas, M. (1982). *The goddesses and gods of old Europe.* University of California Press.

Glaub, M., & Hall, C. A. S. (2017). Evolutionary implications of persistence hunting: An examination of energy return on investment for !Kung hunting. *Human Ecology, 45*, 393–401.

Goddard, M. J. (2018). Extending B. F. Skinner's selection by consequences to personality change, implicit theories of intelligence, skill learning, and language. *Review of General Psychology, 22*, 421–426.

Godin, B. (2007). From eugenics to scientometrics: Galton, Cattell, and men of science. *Social Studies of Science, 37*, 691–728.

Goldstein, M., & Goldstein, I. F. (1978). *How we know: An explanation of the scientific process.* Plenum Press.

Goodall, J. V. (1971). *In the shadow of man.* Houghton Mifflin.

Gordon, B. L. (1971). Sacred directions: Orientation, and the top of the map. *History of Religions, 10*, 211–227.

Gould, J. B. (1974). The Stoic conception of fate. *Journal of the History of Ideas, 35*, 17–32.

Gowande, A. (1997). *The unkindest cut, Slate.* https://slate.com/technology/1997/07/the-unkindest-cut.html

Gowlett, J. A. J. (1984). *Ascent to civilization: The archeology of early man.* William Collins.

Graesser, A. C., Person, N., & Johnston, G. S. (1996). Three obstacles in empirical research on aesthetic and literary comprehension. In R. J. Kreuz & M. S. MacNealy (Eds.), *Empirical approaches to literature and aesthetics* (pp. 3–22). Ablex.

Graham, D. W. (1999). Empedocles and Anaxagoras. In A. A. Long (Ed.), *The Cambridge companion to early Greek philosophy* (pp. 159–180). Cambridge University Press.

Graham, D. W. (2007). *Heraclitus. Stanford Encyclopedia of Philosophy.* http://plato.stanford.edu/entries/heraclitus/

Gray, P. (2008). The value of Psychology 101 in liberal arts education: A psychocentric theory of the university. *Observer, 21,* 29–32.

Green, C. D., & Martin, S. M. (2017). Historical impact in psychology differs between demographic groups. *New Ideas in Psychology, 47,* 24–32.

Greenberg, J. H. (1970). *The languages of Africa.* Indiana University.

Greenberg, S. (2009). *Matrix and monadology: Leibnizian themes and The Matrix.* https://mobilave303.com/archive/phil-matrix/monadology-leibnizian-themes/

Greenwood, J. D. (1999). Understanding the "cognitive revolution" in psychology. *Journal of the History of the Behavioral Sciences, 35,* 1–22.

Greenwood, J. D. (2017). The long and winding road: 125 years of the American Psychological Association. *Behavioral Scientist,* https://behavioralscientist.org/long-winding-road-125-years-american-psychological-association/

Greenwood, J. D. (2020). On two foundational principles of the Berlin School of Gestalt psychology. *Review of General Psychology, 24,* 284–294.

Gregory, A. (2016). *Anaximander: A re-assessment.* Bloomsbury Academic.

Griffel, F. (2016). *Al-Ghazali. The Stanford Encyclopedia of Philosophy,* https://plato.stanford.edu/archives/win2016/entries/al-ghazali/

Gross, C. G. (2007). The discovery of the motor cortex and its background. *Journal of the History of the Neurosciences, 16,* 320–331.

Guberman, S. (2016). Gestalt psychology, mirror neurons, and the body-mind problem. *Gestalt Theory, 38,* 217–238.

Guberman, S. (2018). Gestalt theory of cognition and "solid" sciences: Physics, mathematics, and artificial intelligence. *Journal of Psychiatry and Cognitive Behaviour, 3,* 1–10.

Gugerty, L. (2006). Newell and Simon's logic theorist: Historical background and impact on cognitive modeling. *Proceedings of the Human Factors and Ergonomics Society Annual Meeting, 9,* 880–884.

Gutas, D. (2016). *Ibn Sina [Avicenna]. The Stanford Encyclopedia of Philosophy.* https://plato.stanford.edu/archives/fall2016/entries/ibn-sina/.

Hackett, J. (2007). *Roger Bacon. Stanford Encyclopedia of Philosophy.* http://plato.stanford.edu/entries/roger-bacon

Haggbloom, S. J., Warnick, R., Warnick, J., Jones, V. K., Yarbrough, G. L., & Russell, T. M. (2002). The 100 most eminent psychologists of the 20th century. *Review of General Psychology, 6,* 139–152.

Hall, A. R. (1948). Sir Isaac Newton's note-book. *The Cambridge Historical Journal, 9,* 239–250.

Hall, A. R. (1992). *Isaac Newton: Adventurer in thought.* Cambridge University Press.

Hall, C. S., & Lindsey, G. (1970). *Theories of personality* (2nd ed.). John Wiley & Sons.

Harcourt-Smith, W. E. H., & Aiello, L. C. (2004). Fossils, feet and the evolution of human bipedal locomotion. *Journal of Anatomy, 204,* 403–416.

Harding, R. M., & Sokal, R. R. (1988). Classification of the European language families by genetic distance. *Population Biology, 85,* 9370–9372.

Harper, R. S. (1950). The first psychological laboratory. *Isis*, *41*, 158–161.

Harriman, B. (2018). *Melissus and Eleatic monism*. Cambridge University Press.

Harris, B. (1979). Whatever happened to Little Albert? *American Psychologist*, *34*, 151–160.

Harrower-Erickson, M. R. (1942). Kurt Koffka: 1886–1941. *The American Journal of Psychology*, *55*, 278–281.

Haskins, E. C. (2018). Reimagining Helen of Troy: Gorgias and Isocrates on seeing and being seen. In A. Kampakoglou & A. Novokhatko (Eds.), *Gaze, vision, and visuality in ancient Greek literature* (pp. 245–270). Walter de Gruyter.

Haupt, E. J. (2001). Laboratories for experimental psychology: Göttingen's ascendancy over Leipzig in the 1890s. In R. W. Rieber & D. K. Robinson (Eds.), *Wilhelm Wundt in history: The making of a scientific psychology* (pp. 205–250). Kluwer/Plenum.

Hayman, R. (1999). *A life of Jung*, Bloomsbury.

Hebb, D. O. (1949). *The organization of behavior; a neuropsychological theory*. Wiley.

Heidelberger, M. (2004). *Nature from within: Gustav Theodor Fechner and his psychophysical worldview* (C. Klohr, Trans.). Pittsburgh University Press.

Henle, M. (1978). One man against the Nazis: Wolfgang Köhler. *American Psychologist*, *33*, 939–944.

Henley, T. B., Rossano, M. J., & Kardas, E. P (Eds.). (2020). *Handbook of cognitive archeology: Psychology in prehistory*. Routledge.

Hetherington, N. S. (2006). *Planetary motions*. Greenwood Press.

Hiesinger, P. R. (2021). *The self-assembling brain: How neural networks grow smarter*. Princeton University Press.

Hildebrand, G. (1999). *Origins of architectural pleasure*. University of California Press.

Hill, D. B. (2019). Androcentrism and the great man narrative in psychology textbooks: The case of Ivan Pavlov. *Journal of Research in Gender Studies*, *9*, 9–37.

Hillar, M. (2018). Philo of Alexandria. In T. Angier C. Meister & C. Taliaferro (Eds.), *The history of evil in antiquity*, (pp. 213–223). Taylor & Francis.

Himelfarb, I. (2019). A primer on standardized testing: History, measurement, classical test theory, item response theory, and equating. *Journal of Chiropractic Education*, *33*, 151–163.

Hobolth, A., Christensen, O. F., Mailund, T., & Schierup, M. H. (2007). Genomic relationships and speciation times of human, chimpanzee, and gorilla inferred from a coalescent hidden Markov model. *PLoS Genetics*, *3*, 294–304.

Hochman, G., & Erov, I. (2013). The partial-reinforcement extinction effect and the contingent-sampling hypothesis. *Psychonomic Bulletin & Review*, *20*, 1336–1342.

Hodgson, D. (2020). The cognitive mechanisms deriving from the Acheulean handaxe that gave rise to symmetry, form and pattern recognition. In T. B. Henley, M. J. Rossano, M, & E. P. Kardas. (Eds.), *Handbook of cognitive archeology: Psychology in prehistory* (pp. 241–260). Routledge.

Hoffman, L. (2009, August 29). Freud's Adirondack vacation. *New York Times*, A21.

Holmes, B. (2004). Manna or millstone. *New Scientist*, *183*, 29–31.

Horak, J.C. (2019). Hugo Münsterberg: A German Jew (?) in America. In R. Steinmetz (Ed.), *A treasure trove, friend of the photoplay - visionary - spy?: New trans-disciplinary approaches to Hugo Münsterberg's life and oeuvre* (pp. 215–238). Leipziger Universitätsverlag.

Horney, K. (1945). *Our inner conflicts*. W. W. Norton.

Howlett, S. (2016). *Marsilio Ficino and his world*. New York.

Huemer, W. (2010). *Franz Brentano. Stanford Encyclopedia of Philosophy*. http://plato.stanford.edu/entries/brentano/

Huffman, C. A. (1999). The Pythagorean tradition. In A. A. Long (Ed.), *The Cambridge companion to early Greek philosophy* (pp. 66–87). Cambridge University Press.

Huffman, C. A. (2006). *Pythagoras. Stanford Encyclopedia of Philosophy*. http://plato.stanford.edu/entries/pythagoras/

Huffman, C. A. (2008). *Alcmaeon. Stanford Encyclopedia of Philosophy*. http://plato.stanford.edu/entries/alcmaeon/

Hull, C. L. (1925). An automatic correlation calculating machine. *Journal of the American Statistical Association, 20*, 522–531.

Hull, C. L. (1928). *Aptitude testing*. World.

Hull, C. L. (1933a). *Hypnosis and suggestibility: An experimental approach*. Appleton-Century.

Hull, C. L. (1933b). The meaningfulness of 320 selected nonsense syllables. *The American Journal of Psychology, 45*, 730–734.

Hull, C. L. (1935). The conflicting psychologies of learning—a way out. *Psychological Review, 42*, 491–516.

Hull, C. L. (1943). *Principles of behavior*. Appleton-Century-Crofts.

Hull, C. L. (1952). *A behavior system*. Yale University Press.

Hunt, M. (2007). *The story of psychology*. Anchor Books.

Huntington, S. P. (1996). *The clash of civilizations and the remaking of world order*. Simon and Schuster.

Hurley, P. (1968). The confirmation of continental drift. *Scientific American, 218*, 53–62.

Hussey, E. (1999). Heraclitus. In A. A. Long (Ed.), *The Cambridge companion to early Greek philosophy* (pp. 88–112). Cambridge University Press.

Hynan, R. (2007). Evaluating parapsychological claims. In R. J. Sternberg, H. L. Roediger. III, & D. F. Halpern (Eds.), *Critical thinking in psychology* (pp. 216–231). Cambridge University Press.

Iverson, P., & Jacks, D. J. (2012). A life of its own: The tenuous connection between Thales of Miletus and the study of electrostatic charging. *Journal of Electrostatics, 70*, 309–311.

James, C. (1989, April 28). Stealing Heaven (1988) Review/Film; Doomed Passion of Aberlard and Heloise. *The New York Times*, p. C14.

James, W. (1894). Discussion: The physical basis of emotion. *Psychological Review, 1*, 516–529.

Janis, I. L. (1972). *Victims of groupthink: A psychological study of foreign policy decisions and fiascoes*. Houghton Mifflin.

Jenkins, H. M. (1976). Animal learning and behavior theory. In E. Heard (Ed.), *The first century of experimental psychology* (pp. 177–228). Routledge.

Jennings, H. S. (1906). *The behavior of the lower organisms*. Macmillan.

Jensen, R. (2006). Behaviorism, latent learning, and cognitive maps: Needed revisions in introductory psychology textbooks. *The Behavior Analyst, 29*, 187–209.

Johanson, D. (n.d.). *Origins of modern humans: Multiregional or out of Africa?* http://www.actionbioscience.org/evolution/johanson.html

Johns Hopkins University. (1876). *Gilman's inaugural address. Johns Hopkins University.* https://www.jhu.edu/about/history/gilman-address/

Johns Hopkins University. (n.d.). *Gilman's inaugural address. Johns Hopkins University,* https://www.jhu.edu/about/history/gilman-address/

Johnson, M. R. (2019). Aristotle on kosmos and kosmoi. In P. S. Horky (Ed.), *Cosmos in the ancient world* (pp. 74–108). Cambridge University Press.

Johnson, P. (1976). *A history of Christianity.* Atheneum.

Johnson, P. (1988). *A history of the Jews.* Harper & Row.

Johnson, R. C., McClearn, G., Yuen, S., Nagosha, C. T., Abern, F. M., & Cole, R. E. (1985). Galton's data a century later. *American Psychologist, 40,* 875–892.

Johnson, T. M., Zurlo, G. A., Hickman, A. W., & Crossing, P. F. (2016). Christianity 2017: Five hundred years of Protestant Christianity. *International Bulletin of Mission Research, 41,* 41–52.

Jones, M. C. (1924). A laboratory study of fear: The case of Peter. *Pedagogical Seminary, 31,* 308–315.

Joyce, N., & Faye, C. (2010). Skinner air crib. *Observer, 23,* 26.

Jung, C. G. (1965). *Memories, dreams, reflections* (Rev. ed.) . Vintage Books.

Kacki, S., Velemínský, P., Lynnerup, N., Kaupová, S., Jeanson, A. L., Povýšil, C., Horák, M., Kučera, J., Rasmussen, K. L., Podliska, J., Dragoun, Z., Smolík, J., Vellev, J., & Brůžek, J. (2018). Rich table but short life: Diffuse idiopathic skeletal hyperostosis in Danish astronomer Tycho Brahe (1546–1601) and its possible consequences. *PLoS One, 13,* e0195920.

Kagan, J. (2009). *The three cultures: Natural sciences, social sciences and the humanities in the 21st-century,* Harvard University Press.

Kalachanis, K., Panou, E., Theodossiou, E., Kostikas, I., Manimanis, V. N., & Dimitrijeví, M. S. (2015). The cosmic system of the Pre-Socratic philosopher Anaximenes and stars and their formation. *Bulgarian Astronomical Journal, 23,* 41–44.

Kalat, J. W., & Shiota, M. N. (2012). *Emotion* (2nd ed.). Cengage.

Kandel, E. R. (2009). The biology of memory: A forty-year perspective. *The Journal of Neuroscience, 29,* 12,748–12,756.

Kardas, E. P., & Henley, T. B. (2021, May 26–27). *Dealing with racism and misogyny in psychology's history* [Poster session]. Association for Psychological Science Virtual Convention.

Karin-D'Arcy, M. R. (2005). The modern role of Morgan's canon in comparative psychology. *International Journal of Comparative Psychology, 18,* 179–201.

Kashima, Y. (2014). How can you capture cultural dynamics? *Frontiers in Psychology, 5,* 1–16.

Kasparov, G. (2010). The chess master and the computer. *New York Review of Books, 57,* 16–19.

Kelley, D. R. (1991). *Renaissance humanism.* Twayne -Publishers.

Kemp, S. (1996). *Cognitive psychology in the Middle Ages.* Greenwood Press.

Kennedy, C. H. (2004). Recent innovations in single-case designs. *Journal of Behavioral Education, 13,* 209–211.

Kenny, A. (2010). *Ancient philosophy: A new history of Western philosophy* (Vol. 1). Oxford University Press.

Kenny, A., & Pinborg, J. (1982). Medieval philosophical literature. In N. Kretzmann, A. Kenny & J. Pinborg (Eds.), *The Cambridge history of later medieval philosophy*, (pp. 11–42). Cambridge University Press.

Khalifa, R. (n.d.). *The authorized -English translation of the Quran, Sura - 3.* http://www.submission.org/suras/sura3.htm

Kichigina, G. (2009). *The imperial laboratory: Experimental physiology and clinical medicine in post-Crimean Russia.* Editions Rodopi B. V.

Kihlstrom, J. F. (2019). Lewin, Kurt. In V. Ziegler-Hill & T. K. Shackelford (Eds.), *Encyclopedia of personality and individual differences* (pp. 1–5). Meteor Nature.

Kim, A. (2006). *Wilhelm Maximilian Wundt. Stanford Encyclopedia of Philosophy.* http://plato.stanford.edu/entries/wilhelm-wundt/

Kim, K. H. S., Relkin, N. R., Lee, K. M., & Hirsch, J. (1997). Distinct cortical areas associated with native and second languages. *Nature, 388,* 172–174.

Kimura, D. (1992). Sex differences in the brain. *Scientific American, 267,* 118–125.

Kimura, D. (2004). Human sex differences in cognition, fact, not predicament. *Sexualities, Evolution, & Gender,* 45–53. *6.1*

King, D. B., & Wertheimer, M. (2005). *Max Wertheimer and Gestalt theory.* Transaction Publishers.

Kitcher, P. (2012). The trouble with scientism. *The New Republic, 243,* 20–25.

Knobe, J. (2010). Person as scientist, person as moralist. *Behavioral and Brain Sciences, 33*(4), 315–329. doi:10.1017/S0140525X10000907

Koffka, K. (1922). Perception: An introduction to the *Gestalt-theorie. Psychological Bulletin, 19,* 531–585.

Koffka, K. (1935). *Principles of Gestalt psychology.* Harcourt, Brace & World.

Köhler, C., Hoffmann, K. P., Dehnhardt, G., & Mauck, B. (2005). Mental rotation and rotational invariance in the rhesus monkey. *Brain, Behavior, and Evolution, 66,* 158–166.

Köhler, W. (1925). *Mentality of the apes.* Harcourt, Brace & World.

Konner, M. (2001). Evolution and our environment: Will we adapt? *Western Journal of Medicine, 174,* 360–361.

Konner, M. (2020). Before, after, and alongside the excavation. In T. B. Henley, M. J. Rossano, & E. P. Kardas (Eds.), *Handbook of cognitive archeology: Psychology in Prehistory* (pp. 19–35). Routledge.

Konstan, D. (2009). *Epicurus. Stanford Encyclopedia of Philosophy.* http://plato.stanford.edu/entries/epicurus/

Koontz, N. A., & Gunderman, R. B. (2008). Gestalt theory: Implications for radiology education. *American Journal of Roentgenology, 190,* 1156–1160.

Kramer, P. D. (2006). *Freud: Inventor of the modern mind.* HarperCollins.

Krause, J., Lalueza-Fox, C., Orlando, L., Enard, W., Green, R. E., & Burbano, H. A. (2007). The derived FOXP2 variant of modern humans was shared with Neandertals. *Current Biology, 17,* 1908–1912.

Kraut, R. (1993). Introduction to the study of Plato. In R. Kraut (Ed.), *The Cambridge companion to Plato* (pp. 1–50). Cambridge University Press.

Kraut, R. (2004). *Plato. Stanford Encyclopedia of Philosophy.* http://plato.stanford.edu/entries/plato/

Kreshel, P. J. (1990). Walter Thompson: The legitimation of "science" in advertising. *Journal of Advertising, 19*, 49–59.

Kuhl, P. K. (2000). A new view of language acquisition. *PNAS, 97*, 11850–11857.

Langewiesche, W. (1991). The world in its extreme. *Atlantic Monthly, 268*, 105–129.

Lashley, K. S. (1950). *In search of the engram.* In In Society for Experimental Biology, *Physiological mechanisms in animal behavior. (Society's Symposium IV.)* (pp. 454–482). Academic Press.

Laven, M. (2006). Encountering the Counter-Reformation. *Renaissance Quarterly, 59*, 706–720.

Lawler, A. (2007). Middle Asia takes center stage. *Science, 317*, 586–590.

Lazari-Radek, K., & Singer, P. (2017). *Utilitarianism: A very short introduction.* Oxford University Press.

Lee, M. R., Hayes, T. C., & Thomas, S. A. (2008). Regional variation in the effect of structural factors on homicide in rural areas. *The Social Science Journal, 45*, 76–94.

Lemann, N. (1995, September). The great sorting. *The Atlantic Monthly, 276*, 84–100.

Lennox, J. G. (2006). *Aristotle's biology. Stanford Encyclopedia of Philosophy.* http://plato.stanford.edu/entries/aristotle-biology/

Lesher, J. (2008). *Xenophanes. Stanford Encyclopedia of Philosophy,* http://plato.stanford.edu/entries/xenophanes/

Lewin, K. (1917/2009). The landscape of war. *Art in Translation, 1*, 199–209.

Lewin, K., Lippitt, R., & White, R. K. (1939). Patterns of aggressive behavior in experimentally created "social climates." *The Journal of Social Psychology, S.P.S.S.I Bulletin, 10*, 271–299.

Lewin, M. A. (1998). Kurt Lewin: His psychology and a daughter's recollections. In G. A. Kimble & M. Wertheimer (Eds.), *Portraits of Pioneers in Psychology,* (Vol. 3, pp. 105–118). American Psychological Association.

Lewontin, R. C. (2009). Why -Darwin? *The New York Review of Books, 56*, 19–22.

Ley, R. (1990). *A whisper of espionage.* Avery Publishing Group.

Ley, R. (1997). Köhler and espionage on the island of Tenerife: A rejoinder to Teuber. *American Journal of Psychology, 110*, 277–284.

Li, J. Z., Absher, D. M., Tang, H., Southwick, A. M., Casto, A. M., & Ramachandran, S. (2008). Worldwide human relationships inferred from genome-wide patterns of variation. *Science, 319*, 1100–1104.

Li, X., Harbottle, G., Zhang, J., & Wang, C. (2003). The earliest writing? Sign use in the seventh millennium BC at Jiahu, Henan Province, China. *Antiquity, 77*, 31–44.

Lindberg, D. C. (1992). *The beginnings of Western science.* Chicago University Press.

Linné, C. V. (1707–1778. 1964). Systema naturae. In *Tomus II: Vegetabilia,* (10, 1759 ed.). Stechert-Hafner Service Agency.

Little, S. G., & Akin-Little, A. (2008). Psychology's contributions to classroom management. *Psychology in the Schools, 45*, 227–234.

Livio, M. (2002). *The golden ratio: The story of phi, the world's most astounding number.* Random House.

Lockard, R. B. (1968). The albino rat: A defensible choice or bad habit? *American Psychologist, 23*, 734–742.

Locke, J. (1975/1689). *An essay concerning human understanding*. Clarendon Press.

Loeb, J. (1911). The significance of tropisms for psychology. *Popular Science Monthly, 79*, 105–125.

Loftus, E. (1979). *Eyewitness testimony*. Harvard University Press.

Luchins, A. S. (1942). Mechanization in problem solving: The effect of Einstellung. *Psychological Monographs, 54*, i–95.

Ludwig-Körner, C. (2017). Anna Freud and observation: Memoirs of her colleagues from the Hampstead War Nurseries. *Journal of Infant, Child, and Adolescent Psychotherapy, 16*, 131–137.

Lundin, R. W. (1989). *Alfred Adler's basic concepts and implications*. Accelerated Development.

MacCorquodale, K. (1970). On Chomsky's review of Skinner's *Verbal Behavior*. *Journal of the Experimental Analysis of Behavior, 13*, 83–99.

Mackintosh, N. J. (2003). Pavlov and associationism. *The Spanish Journal of Psychology, 6*, 177–184.

Maggin, D. M., Chafouleas, S. M., Goddard, K. M., & Johnson, A. H. (2011). A systematic evaluation of token economies as a classroom management tool for students with challenging behavior. *Journal of School Psychology, 49*, 529–554. 10.1016/j.jsp.2011.05.001

Malik, A. H., Ziermann, J. M., & Diogo, R. (2017). An untold story in biology: The historical continuity of evolutionary ideas of Muslim scholars from the 8th century to Darwin's time. *Journal of Biological Education, 52*, 3–17.

Mallon, R. (2016). Experimental philosophy. In H. Cappelen, T. Gendler & J. P. Hawthorne (Eds.), *The Oxford handbook of philosophical methodology*, (pp. 411–443). Oxford University Press.

Manicas, P. T. (2002). John Dewey and American psychology. *Journal for the Theory of Social Behaviour, 32*, 267–294.

Marentette, P. (2014). Achieving "good article" status in Wikipedia. *Observer, 25*, 27.

Marshack, A. (1972). *The roots of civilization*. McGraw-Hill.

Martin, T. R. (2000). *Ancient Greece*. Yale University Press.

Martinez, J. A., & Smith, N. D. (2017). Socrates' aversion to being a victim of injustice. *Journal of Ethics, 22*, 59–76.

Martinich, A. P. (1999). *Hobbes: A biography*. Cambridge University Press.

Marx, M. H., & Hillix, W. A. (1963). *Systems and theory in psychology*. McGraw-Hill.

Mattox, M. (2017). *Martin Luther: Student of the creation, Sapienta*. https://henrycenter.tiu.edu/2017/06/martin-luther-student-of-the-creation/

McCabe, I. (2018). *Carl Jung and alcoholics anonymous: The twelve steps as a spiritual journey*, Routledge.

McConnell, D. S., & Fiore, S. M. (2017). A place for James J. Gibson. In B. B. Janz (Ed.), *Place, space, and hermeneutics: Contributions to hermeneutics*, (Vol. 5, pp. 261–273). Springer International Publishing.

McDougall, W. (1912). *Psychology: The study of behaviour*. Williams & Northgate.

McDougall, W. (1926). *An introduction to social psychology* (Rev. ed.) ed.). John W. Luce & Co.

McEvedy, C. (1988). The bubonic plague. *Scientific American, 258*, 118–123.

McInerny, R. M. (1970). *A history of Western philosophy* (Vol. 2). University of Notre Dame Press.

McKirahan, R. D. (1999). Zeno. In A. A. Long (Ed.), *The Cambridge companion to early Greek philosophy* (pp. 134–158). Cambridge University Press.

McKnight, S. A. (1989). *Sacralizing the secular: The Renaissance -origins of modernity.* Louisiana State University Press.

Medawar, J., & Pyke, D. (2001). *Hitler's gift: Scientists who fled Nazi Germany.* Arcade Publishing.

Meijer, P. A. (2017). *A new perspective on Antisthenes.* Amsterdam University Press.

Mellars, P. (2009). Archaeology: Origins of the female image. *Nature, 459,* 176–177. doi:10.1038/459176a

Merton, R. K. (1949). *Social theory and social structure.* Free Press.

Mikalson, J. D. (2004). *Ancient Greek religion.* Wiley-Blackwell.

Miller, G. A. (1956). The magical number 7 plus or minus two: Some limits on the our capacity for processing information. *Psychological Review, 63,* 81–97.

Miller, G. A. (2003). The cognitive revolution: A historical perspective. *TRENDS in Cognitive Sciences, 7,* 141–144.

Milton, K. (2000). Hunter-gatherer diets—a different perspective. *American Journal of Clinical Nutrition, 71,* 665–667.

Mithen, S. (1996). *The prehistory of the mind.* Thames & Hudson.

Mithen, S. (2004). *After the ice: A global human history, 20,000–5,000 BC,* Harvard University Press.

Mjøset, L. (2001). Theories: Conceptions in the social sciences. In N. J. Smelser, P. B. Baltes, (Eds.), *International encyclopedia of the social and behavioral sciences* (pp. 15641–15, 647).

Molnar, M. (2002). John Stuart Mill translated by Sigmund Freud. In G. van de Vijver & F. Geerardyn (Eds.), *The pre-psychoanalytic writings of Sigmund Freud* (pp. 112–123). H. -Karnac Ltd.

Moncrieff, C. K. S. (1933/2018). *Abelard & Heloise.* Mineola.

Moore, A. M. T., Hillman, A. J., & Legge, A. J. (2000). *Village on the Euphrates: From foraging to farming at Abu Hureyra.* Oxford University Press.

Moore, J. (2001). On distinguishing methodological from radical behaviorism. *European Journal of Behavior Analysis, 2,* 221–244.

Moore, J. (2013). Methodological behaviorism from the standpoint of a radical behaviorist. *The Behavior Analyst, 36,* 197–208.

Moore, M. K., Williams, J. L., & McCarley, N. G. (2019). George Berkeley through history: Multimodal perception from the 1700s to present. *North American Journal of Psychology, 21,* 361–372.

Morawski, J. (2020). Psychologist's psychologies of psychologists in a time of crisis. *History of Psychology, 23,* 176–198.

Morgan, C. L. (1894). *Introduction to comparative psychology.* Charles Scribner's Sons.

Morgan, E., Fogel, A., Nair, A., & Patel, A. D. (2019). Statistical learning and gestalt-like principles predict melodic expectations. *Cognition, 189,* 23–34.

Moroz, L. L. (2011). *Aplysia. Current Biology, 21,* R60–R61.

Morris, E. K., Lazo, J. F., & Smith, N. G. (2004). Whether, when, and why Skinner published on biological participation in behavior. *The Behavior Analyst, 27,* 153–169.

Morris, E. K., Smith, N. G., & Lazo, J. F. (2005). Why Morris, Lazo, and Smith (2004) was published in *The Behavior Analyst. The Behavior Analyst, 28,* 169–179.

Morris, I. (2010). Latitudes not attitudes: How geography explains history. *History Today*, *60*, 27–33.

Morris, W. E. (2009). *David Hume. Stanford Encyclopedia of Philosophy*, http://plato.stanford.edu/entries/hume/

Morrow, J. L. (2015). Secularization, objectivity, and Enlightenment scholarship. *Logos*, *18*, 14–32.

Mosak, H. H., & Maniacci, M. (2011). Adlerian psychotherapy. In R. Corsini (Ed.), *Current psychotherapies* (pp. 67–112). Cengage.

Moyer, G. (1982). The Gregorian calendar. *Scientific American*, *246*, 144–153.

Mumford, L. (1956). The natural history of urbanization. In W. L. Thomas (Ed.), *Man's role in changing the face of the Earth* (pp. 382–398). University of Chicago Press.

Nadler, S. M. (2008). *Baruch Spinoza. Stanford Encyclopedia of Philosophy*. http://plato.stanford.edu/entries/spinoza/

Napier, M. R., & Adams, S. H. (2002). Criminal confessions. *FBI Law Enforcement Bulletin*, *71*, 9–15.

Narvaez, D. (2020). In search of baselines: Why psychology needs cognitive archeology. In T. B. Henley, M. J. Rossano, & E. P. Kardas (Eds.), *Handbook of cognitive archeology: Psychology in prehistory* (pp. 104–119). Routledge.

Nathan, P. E. (2000). The Boulder model: A dream deferred—or lost? *American Psychologist*, *55*, 250–252.

National Research Council. (1991). *Performance Assessment for the Workplace: Volume I*. The National Academies Press.

Neisser, U. (1967). *Cognitive psychology*. Appleton-Century-Crofts).

Neisser, U., & Hyman, I. E. (2000). *Memory observed: Remembering in natural contexts* (2nd ed.). Worth Publishers.

Neitz, J., Geist, T., & Jacobs, G. H. (1989). Color vision in the dog. *Visual Neuroscience*, *3*, 119–125.

Nelson, J. M. (2006). Missed opportunities in dialogue between psychology and religion. *Journal of Psychology & Theology*, *34*, 205–216.

Neuringer, A., & Englert, W. (2017). Epicurus and B. F. Skinner: In search of the good life. *Journal of the Experimental Analysis of Behavior*, *107*, 21–33.

Newborn, M. (2003). *Deep Blue: An artificial intelligence milestone*. Springer.

Newell, A., & Simon. (1956). The logic theory machine—A complex information processing system. *IRE Transactions on Information Theory*, *2*, 61–79.

Newell, A., & Simon, H. A. (1972). *Human problem solving*. Prentice-Hall.

New York Times. (1999, January 2). *The Stoics have a stand on everything, even on dinner parties and sex*. New York Times. https://www.nytimes.com/1999/01/02/books/think-tank-the-stoics-have-a-stand-on-everything-even-on-dinner-parties-and-sex.html

Nielsen, M. (2020). The human social mind and the inextricability of science and religion. In T. B. Henley, M. J. Rossano, & E. P. Kardas (Eds.), *Handbook of cognitive archeology: Psychology in prehistory* (pp. 296–310). New York.

Noland, R. W. (1999). *Sigmund Freud revisited*. Twayne Publishers.

Norcross, J. C., & Castle, P. H. (2002). Appreciating the PsyD: The facts. *Eye on Psi Chi*, *7*, 22–26.

Nubiola, J. (2011). The reception of William James in continental Europe. *European Journal of Pragmatism and American Philosophy*, 1–13.

Nuñez, R., Allen, M., Gao, R., Rigoli, C. M., Relaford-Doyle, J., & Semenuks, A. (2019). What happened to cognitive science? *Nature Human Behavior, 3*, 782–791.

O'Meara, D. J. (2016). Gerson. L (Ed.), *Plotinus The Cambridge history of philosophy in late antiquity* (pp. 301–324). Cambridge University Press.

Osborne, T. M. (2014). *Human action in Thomas Aquinas, John Duns Scotus, & William of Ockham.* Catholic University of America.

Ozment, S. (1980). *The age of reform 1250–1550.* Yale University Press.

Pajares, F. (2003). William James: Our father who begat us. In B. J. Zimmerman & D. H. Schunk (Eds.), *Educational psychology: A century of contributions* (pp. 41–64). Lawrence Erlbaum.

Panegyres, K. P., & Panegyres, P. K. (2016). The ancient Greek discovery of the nervous system: Alcmaeon, Praxagoras, and Herophilus. *Journal of Clinical Neuroscience, 29*, 21–24.

Parry, R. (2005). *Empedocles. Stanford Encyclopedia of Philosophy*, http://plato.stanford.edu/entries /empedocles/

Pavlov, I. (1904). *Nobel lecture.* http://nobelprize.org/nobel_prizes/medicine/laureates/1904/ pavlov–lecture.html

Penner, T. (1993). Socrates and the early dialogues. In R. Kraut (Ed.), *The Cambridge companion to Plato* (pp. 121–169). Cambridge University Press.

Petit, J. R., Jouzel, J., Raynaud, D., Barkov, N. I., Barnola, J.-M., & Basile, I. (1999). Climate and atmospheric history of the past 420,000 years from the Vostok ice core, Antarctica. *Nature, 399*, 429–436.

Pettitt, P. (2020). From corpse to to symbol: Proposed cognitive grades over the long-term evolution of hominin mortuary activity. In T. B. Henley, M. J. Rossano & E. P. Kardas (Eds.), *Handbook of cognitive archeology: Psychology in prehistory,* (pp. 512–525). Routledge.

Pfeiffer, J. E. (1982). *The creative explosion.* Harper & Row.

Pfungst, O. (1911). *Clever Hans* (C. L. Rahn, Trans.). Henry Holt and Company.

Pieper, J. (1964). *Scholasticism: Personalities and problems of medieval philosophy.* McGraw-Hill.

Pizlo, Z. (2008). *3D shape: Its unique place in visual perception.* MIT Press.

Plato. (1969). *Plato in Twelve Volumes* (P. Shorey, Trans.). Harvard University Press. Vols. 5–6 (Original work published n.d.)

Pojman, P. (2009). *Ernst Mach. Stanford Encyclopedia of Philosophy*, http://plato.stanford.edu/entries /ernst-mach/

Prochazka, A. (2017). Neurophysiology and neural engineering: A review. *Biology of Neuroengineering Interfaces, 118*, 1292–1309.

Pyle, A. (2003). *Malebranche.* Routledge.

Quinn, S. (2019). *A mind of her own: The life of Karen Horney.* Plunkett Lake Press.

Rachlin, H. (2005). What Müller's law of specific nerve energies says about the mind. *Behavior and Philosophy, 33*, 41–54.

Randall, K., Isaacson, M., & Ciro, C. (2017). Validity and reliability of the Meyers-Briggs Personality Type Indicator: A systematic review and meta-analysis, *Journal of Best Practices in Health Professions Diversity:. Education, Research & Policy, 10*, 1–27.

Reisz, R. D. (2018). Göttingen in Baltimore or the Americanization of the German university? *Journal of Research in Higher Education*, 23–44.

Rescorla, R. A. (1968). Probability of shock in the presence and absence of CS in fear conditioning. *Journal of Comparative and Physiological Psychology, 66,* 1–5.

Reyes, M. G. (2006). The rhetoric in mathematics: Newton, Leibniz, the calculus, and the rhetorical force of the infinitesimal. *Quarterly Journal of Speech, 90,* 159–184.

Richardson, R. D. (2006). *William James,* Houghton Mifflin.

Riesman, D. C. (2006). Al-Farabi and the philosophical curriculum. In P. Adamson & R. C. Taylor (Eds.), *The Cambridge companion to Arabic philosophy* (pp. 52–71). Cambridge University Press.

Roberts, P., & Knobe, J. (2016). Interview on experimental philosophy with Joshua Knobe. *Exchanges: The Warwick Research Journal, 4,* 14–28.

Robichaud, D. J., & -J. (2018). *Plato's persona: Marsilio Ficino, Renaissance humanism, and Platonic traditions.* University of Pennsylvania Press.

Robinson, A. (2017). Scientist, theologian, and heretic. The *Lancet, 390,* 1638–1639.

Robinson, D. N. (1981). *An intellectual history of psychology* (Rev. ed.). Macmillan.

Robinson, D. N. (1982). *Toward a science of human nature.* Columbia University Press.

Robinson, D. N. (2001). Reaction-time experiments in Wundt's Institute and beyond. In R. W. Rieber & D. K. Robinson (Eds.), *Wilhelm Wundt in history: The making of a scientific psychology* (pp. 161–204). Kluwer/Plenum.

Rock, I. (1992). Comment on Asch and Witkin's "Studies in space orientation II." *Journal of Experimental Psychology: General, 121,* 404–406.

Rock, I., & Palmer, S. (1990). The legacy of Gestalt psychology. *Scientific American, 263,* 84–90.

Rodkey, E. N. (2010). Profile of Eleanor Gibson. A. Rutherford (Ed.), *Psychology's Feminist Voices Multimedia Internet Archive.* http://www.feministvoices.com/eleanor-j-gibson/

Roediger, H. L. (2004). What should they be called? *Observer, 17,* 46–48.

Roediger, H. L. (2004, March). What happened to behaviorism? *The APS Observer, 17,* 5, 40–42.

Roediger, H.L., & Yamashiro, J. (2019). History of psychological approaches to studying memory. In R.J. Sternberg & W. Pickren (Eds.), *Handbook of the intellectual history of psychology: How psychological ideas have evolved from past to present* (pp. 165–215). Cambridge University Press.

Rohrer, J. M., Egloff, B., & Schmukle, S. C. (2017). Probing birth-order effects on narrow traits using specification-curve analysis. *Psychological Science, 28,* 1821–1832.

Roitblatt, H. L. (1982). The meaning of representation in animal memory. *The Behavioral and Brain Sciences, 5,* 353–406.

Rolian, C., Lieberman, D. E., Hamill, J., Scott, J. W., & Werbel, W. (2009). Walking, running and the evolution of short toes in humans. *Journal of Experimental Biology, 212,* 713–721.

Rosen, E. (1966). Galileo and Kepler: Their first two contacts. *Isis, 57,* 262–264.

Rosen, F. (2017). Bain, Alexander (1818–1903). In J. E. Crimmins (Ed.), *The Bloomsbury encyclopedia of utilitarianism* (pp. 39–40). Bloomsbury Publishing Plc.

Ross, B. (1991). William James: Spoiled child of American psychology. In G. A. Kimble, M. Wertheimer, & C. L. White (Eds.), *Portraits of pioneers in psychology* (Vol. 1, pp. 13–25). Lawrence Erlbaum.

Rowe, J. H. (1965). The Renaissance foundations of anthropology. *American Anthropologist, 67,* 1–20.

Rudgley, R. (1999). *The lost civilizations of the Stone Age.* Free Press.

Russell, B. (1927). *Philosophy*. Norton.

Russell, B. (1937). *Philosophy of Leibnitz*. George Allen & Unwin Ltd.

Russell, B. (1945). *The history of western philosophy*. Simon and Schuster.

Ryle, G. (1967). John Locke. *Crítica: Revista Hispanoamericana de Filosofía, 1*, 3–19.

Sagan, C. (1977). *The dragons of Eden: Speculations on the evolution of human intelligence*. Random House.

Samelson, F. (1981). Struggle for scientific authority: The reception of Watson's behaviorism, 1913–1920. *Journal of the History of the Behavioral Sciences, 17*, 399–425.

Sansone, D. (2009). *Ancient Greek civilization* (2nd ed.). Wiley-Blackwell.

Sayers, J. (1991). *Mothers of psychoanalysis*. W. W. Norton & Company.

Scarborough, E., & Furumoto, L. (1987). *Untold lives: The first generation of American women psychologists*. Columbia University Press.

Schacter, D. L. (2001). *Forgotten ideas, neglected pioneers: Richard Semon and the story of memory*. Psychology Press.

Schmandt-Besserat, D. (1996). *How writing came about*. University of Texas Press.

Schmid, B. V., Büntgen, U., Easterday, W. R., Ginzler, C., Wallee, L., Bramanti, B., & Stenseth, N. C. (2015). Climate-driven introduction of the Black Death and successive plague reintroductions into Europe. *PNAS, 112*, 3020–3025.

Schmitt-Pantel, P. (1999). Greek meals: A civic ritual. In J. L. Flandrin, M. Montanari, & Sonnenfeld. A (Eds.), *Food: A culinary history from antiquity to the present* (pp. 90–95). Columbia University Press.

Schnädelbach, H. (1984). *Philosophy in Germany, 1831–1933*. Cambridge University Press.

Schorske, C. E. (1980). *Fin-de-siècle Vienna*. Alfred A. Knopf.

Schwartz, S. (2000). A historical loop of one hundred years: Similarities between 19th century and contemporary dream research. *Dreaming, 10*, 55–66.

Schwartz, S. I. (1999). *The French and Indian war 1754–1763: The imperial struggle for North America*. Castle Books.

Scott, E. (2002). The nature of change. *Natural History, 111*, 79.

Seattle Union Record. (1918, April 24). *Protecting the working mothers. Seattle Union Record*. University of Washington. https://depts.washington.edu/labhist/laborpress/Union_Record_1900 –1928.htm

Seay, B., & Gottfried, N. (1978). *The development of behavior*. Houghton Mifflin.

Sedley, D. (1999). Parmenides and Melissus. In A. A. Long (Ed.), *The Cambridge companion to early Greek philosophy* (pp. 113–133). Cambridge University Press.

Sedley, D. (2003). The school, from Zeno to Arius Didymus. In B. Inwood (Ed.), *The Cambridge companion to the Stoics* (pp. 7–32). Cambridge University Press.

Segal, E. M., & Lachman, R. (1972). Complex behavior or higher mental process: Is there a paradigm shift? *American Psychologist, 27*, 46–55.

Sellars, J. (2006). *Stoicism*. University of California Press.

Semaw, S., Renne, P., Harris, J. W. K., Feibel, C. S., Bernor, R. L., & Fesseha, N. (1997). 2.5-million-year-old stone tools from Gona, Ethiopia. *Nature, 385*, 333–336. doi:10.1038/385333a0

Sexton, V. S., & Hogan, J. D. (1992). *International Psychology*. Lincoln University of Nebraska Press.

Seyhan, A. (2009). What is Romanticism, and where did it come from? In N. Saul (Ed.), *The Cambridge Companion to German Romanticism* (pp. 1–20). Cambridge University Press.

Sharps, M. J., & Wertheimer, M. (2000). Gestalt perspective on cognitive science and on experimental psychology. *Review of General Psychology*, *4*, 315–336.

Sharratt, M. (1996). *Galileo: Decisive innovator*. Cambridge University Press.

Shepard, R. N., & Metzler, J. (1971). Mental rotation of three-dimensional objects. *Science*, *171*, 701–703.

Shettleworth, S. J. (2009). The evolution of comparative cognition: Is the snark still a boojum? *Behavioural Processes*, *80*, 210–217.

Silverman, I., Choi, J., & Peters, M. (2007). The hunter-gatherer theory of sex differences in spatial abilities: Data from 40 countries. *Archives of Sexual Behavior*, *36*, 261–268.

Simmons, D. (2016). Imposter syndrome: A reparative history. *Engaging Science, Technology, and Society*, *2*, 106–127.

Simon, H. A., & Newell, A. (1971). Human problem solving: The state of the theory in 1970. *American Psychologist*, *26*, 145–159.

Singer, P. N., van der, Ejik., & P, J (Eds.). (2019). *Galen: Works on human nature*. Cambridge University Press.

Singh, S. (1999). *The code book*. Doubleday.

Skinner, B. F. (1945). Baby in a box; the mechanical baby-tender. *Ladies' Home Journal*, 135–136, 138. *62*, 30–31.

Skinner, B. F. (1948). *Walden two*. Macmillan.

Skinner, B. F. (1953). *Science and human behavior*. Free Press.

Skinner, B. F. (1957). *Verbal behavior*. Appleton-Century-Crofts.

Skinner, B. F. (1970). B. F. Skinner, an autobiography. In P. B. Dews (Ed.), *Festschrift for B. F. Skinner* (pp. 1–21). Appleton-Century-Crofts.

Skinner, B. F. (1971). *Beyond freedom and dignity*. Alfred A. Knopf.

Skinner, B. F. (1981). Selection by -consequences. *Science*, *213*, 501–504.

Skinner, B. F. (1990). Can psychology be a science of mind? *American Psychologist*, *45*, 1206–1210.

Skinner, C. E. (1929). [Review of the book *The battle of behaviorism*]. *Journal of Educational Psychology*, *3*, 253–254.

Smith, D. E., & Karpinski, L. C. (1911). *The Hindu-Arabic numerals*. Ginn and Company.

Smith, R. (1995). Logic. In J. Barnes (Ed.), *The Cambridge companion to Aristotle* (pp. 27–65). Cambridge University Press.

Snodgrass, A. M. (2001). *The dark age of Greece*. Routledge.

Sobel, D. (1999). *Galileo's daughter*. Walker & Company.

Sockol, M. D., Raichlen, D. A., & Pontzer, H. (2007). Chimpanzee locomotor energetics and the origin of human pedalism. *PNAS*, 104, 12265–12269.

Sokal, A. (2010). *Beyond the Hoax: science, philosophy and culture*, Oxford University Press.

Sokal, M. M. (2016). Launching a career in psychology with achievement and arrogance: James McKeen Cattell at the Johns Hopkins University, 1882–1883. *Journal of the History of Behavioral Science, 52*, 5–19.

Sorell, T. (1988). Descartes, Hobbes and the body of natural science. *The Monist, 71*, 515–525.

Spade, P. V. (2006). *William of Ockham. Stanford Encyclopedia of Philosophy*, http://plato.stanford.edu/entries/ockham

Spatz, C., & Kardas, E. P. (2008). *Research methods in psychology: Ideas, techniques, and reports*. McGraw-Hill.

Sperling, G. (1960). The information available in brief visual presentations. *Psychological Monographs, 74*, 1–29.

Staats, A. W. (1991). Unified positivism and unification psychology: Fad or new field? *American Psychologist, 46*, 899–912.

Staes, N., Sherwood, C. C., Wright, K., de Manuel, M., Guevara, E. E., Marques-Bonet, T., Krützen, M., Massiah, M., Hopkins, W. D., Ely, J. J., & Bradley, B. J. (2017). FOXP2 variation in great ape populations offers insight into the evolution of communication skills. *Scientific Reports, 7*, 16866–16876.

Stark, R. (1996). *The rise of Christianity*. Princeton University Press.

Stearns, P. N. (2008). *Why study history?* http://www.historians.org/pubs/free/WhyStudyHistory.htm

Steinman, R. M., Pizlo, Z., & Pizlo, F. J. (2000). Phi is not beta, and why Wertheimer's discovery launched the Gestalt revolution. *Vision Research, 40*, 2257–2264.

Stepnisky, J. (2019). Sociological theory. In J. M. Ryan (Eds.), *Core concepts in sociology* (pp. 295–308). John Wiley & Sons Ltd.

Sternberg, R. J. (2005). Unifying the field of psychology. In R. J. Sternberg (Ed.), *Unity in psychology: Possibility or pipedream?* (pp. 3–14). American Psychological Association.

Sternberg, R. J., & Grigorenko, E. L. (2001). Unified psychology. *American Psychologist, 56*, 1069–1079.

Stevens, S. S. (1961). To honor Fechner and repeal his law. *Science, 133*, 80–86.

Stigler, S. M. (1999). *Statistics on the table*. Harvard University Press.

Strasser, B. J. (2019). *Collecting experiments*. University of Chicago Press.

Strickland, L. (2006). *The shorter Leibniz texts: A collection of new translations*. Continuum.

Strodach, G. K. (1963). *The philosophy of Epicurus*. Northwestern University Press.

Stuart, D. E. (1997). Power and efficiency in eastern Anasazi -architecture: A case of multiple evolutionary trajectories. In B. H. Morrow & V. B (Eds.), *Anasazi architecture*, (pp. 36–52). University of New Mexico Press.

Stuart, D. G., Schaefer, A. T., Jean Massion, B., Graham, A., & Callister, R. J. (2014). Pioneers in CNS inhibition: 1. Ivan. M. Sechenov, the first to clearly demonstrate inhibition arising in the brain. *Brain Research*, 20–48. *1548*

Sullivan, D. (2010). *Hermann Lotze. Stanford Encyclopedia of Philosophy*. http://plato.stanford.edu/entries/hermann-lotze/

Tattersall, I. (1999). *Becoming human: Evolution and human uniqueness*. Houghton Mifflin Harcourt.

Taylor, C. C. W. (1999). The atomists. In A. A. Long (Ed.), *The Cambridge companion to early Greek philosophy* (pp. 181–204). Cambridge University Press.

Teghtsoonian, R. (1971). On the exponents in Stevens' law and the constant in Ekman's law. *Psychological Review, 78*, 71–80.

Teuber, M. L. (1994). The founding of the Primate Station, Tenerife, Canary Islands. *American Journal of Psychology, 107*, 551–581.

Thomas, N. J. T. (2010). *Mental Imagery. Stanford Encyclopedia of Philosophy*. http://plato.stanford.edu/entries/mental-imagery/

Thorndike, E. L. (1898). *Animal intelligence: An experimental study of the associative processes in animals (Psychological Review, Monograph Supplements, No. 8)*.

Thorndike, E. L. (1911). *Animal intelligence*. Macmillan.

Thorndike, E. L., & Woodworth, R. S. (1901). The influence of improvement in one mental function upon the efficiency of other functions (I). *Psychological Review, 8*, 247–261.

Thorndike, R. L. (1991). Edward L. Thorndike: A professional and personal appreciation. In G. A. KimbleM. Wertheimer & C. L. White (Eds.), *Portraits of pioneers in psychology*, (Vol. 1, pp. 139–151). Lawrence Erlbaum.

The Times. (2005, January 22). *Alexander Marshack*. http://www.timesonline.co.uk/tol/comment/obituaries/article504865.ece

Tinker, C. B. Translator (Trans.). (1912). *Beowulf*. Newson & Company.

Tinklepaugh, O. L. (1928). An experimental study of representative factors in monkeys. *Journal of Comparative Psychology, 8*, 197–236.

Titchener, E. B. (1898). The postulates of a structural psychology. *Philosophical Review, 7*, 449–465.

Todes, D. P. (2014). *Ivan Pavlov: A Russian life in science*. Oxford University Press.

Tolman, E. C. (1932). *Purposive behavior in animals and men*. Century.

Tolman, E. C. (1948). Cognitive maps in rats and men. *Psychological Review, 55*, 189–208.

Tolman, E. C., & Honzik, C. H. (1930). Degrees of hunger, reward and non-reward, and maze learning in rats. *University of California Publications in Psychology, 4*, 241–256.

Tolman, E. C., Ritchie, B. F., & Kalish, D. (1946). Studies in spatial learning: I. Orientation and the short-cut. *Journal of Experimental Psychology, 36*, 13–24.

Toomela, A. (2007a). Culture of science: Strange history of the methodological thinking in psychology. *Integrative Psychology & Behavioral Science, 41*, 6–20.

Toomela, A. (2007b). Unifying psychology: Absolutely necessary, not only useful. In A. V. B. Bastos & N. M. D. Rocha (Eds.), *Psicologia: Novas direcoes no dialogo com outros campos de saber* (pp. 449–464). Casa do Psicologico.

Tošković, O. (2018). Preserving the history of science-Journey of old psychological instruments. *Acta Imeko, 7*, 117–120.

Townsend, J. T. (2008). Mathematical psychology: Prospects for the 21st century. *Journal of Mathematical Psychology, 52*, 269–280.

Trinkaus, C. (1979). *The poet as philosopher: Petrarch and the formation of the Renaissance*. Yale University Press.

Truss, L. (2004). *Eats, shoots, & leaves*. Gotham Books.

Tulving, E. (1972). Episodic and semantic memory. In E. Tulving & W. Donaldson (Eds.), *Organization of Memory* (pp. 382–402). Academic Press.

Tulving, E. (1983). *Elements of Episodic Memory*. Oxford University Press.

Tversky, A., & Kahneman, D. (1974). Judgment under uncertainty: Heuristics and biases. *Science*, *185*, 1124–1131.

Twomey, T. (2020). Domestic fire, domestic selves: How keeping fire facilitated the evolution of emotions and emotion regulation. In T. B. Henley, M. J. Rossano, M, & E. P. Kardas. (Eds.), *Handbook of cognitive archeology: Psychology in prehistory* (pp. 415–430). Routledge.

UNFPA. (2008). *State of world population 2007: Unleashing the potential of urban growth*. http://www.unfpa.org/swp/2007/english/introduction.html

US Department of Labor. (n.d.). *O*NET OnLine*. http://online.onetcenter.org/

Usher, P. (2005). Hamlet's love letter and the New Philosophy. *The Oxfordian*, *8*, 93–109.

Valiunas, A. (2011). Psychology's magician. *The New Atlantis*, *31*, 93–121.

van Nispen, H. (2018). A woven web of guesses: Xenophanes of Colophon. *Apeiron*, *51*, 391–403.

Varden, H. (2015). Kant and women. *Pacific Philosophical Quarterly*, *98*, 653–694.

Varden, H. (2017). Kant and women. *Pacific Philosophical Quarterly*, *98*, 653–694.

Varki, A. (2013). Thought experiment: Dating the origin of us. *The Scientist*, *27*, 28–29.

Varki, A., & Gagneux, P. (2016). How different are humans and "great apes"? A matrix of comparative anthropogeny. In M. Tibayrenc & F. J. Ayala (Eds.), *On human nature: evolution, diversity, psychology, ethics, politics and religion*, (pp. 151–160). Elsevier.

Vater, M. G., & Wood, D. W. (2012). The trajectory of German philosophy after Kant, and the "difference" between Fichte and Schelling. In M. G. Vater & W. Wood. D (Eds.), *J. G. Fichte/F.W. Schelling: The philosophical rupture between Fichte and Schelling: Selected texts and correspondence (1800–1802*, (pp. 1–20). State University of New York Press.

Vaughn, S. N. (2017). Anselm of Le Bec and Canterbury: Teacher by word and example, following the footprints of his ancestors. In B. Pohl & Gathagan. L (Eds.), *A companion to the abbey of Le Bec in the central Middle Ages (11th-13th centuries*, (pp. 57–93). Brill.

Verduin, K. (n.d.). *A short history of probability and statistics*. http://www.leidenuniv.nl/fsw/verduin/stathist/stathist.htm

Volmar, A. (2014). In storms of steel. In D. Morat (Ed.), *Sounds of modern history: Auditory cultures in the 19th and 20th century* (pp. 227–255). Berghahn.

von Frisch, K. (1967). *The Dance Language and Orientation of Bees*. Harvard University Press.

Waller, J. (2002). *Einstein's luck*. Oxford University Press.

Wang, H., Feng, J., Bu, Q., Liu, F., Zhang, M., Ren, Y., & Y, Lv. (2018). Breast mass detection in digital mammogram based on gestalt psychology. *Journal of Healthcare Engineering*, 2018, 1–13.

Watson, J. B. (1913). Psychology as the behaviorist views it. *Psychological Review*, *20*, 158–177.

Watson, J. B. (1914). *Behavior: An introduction to comparative psychology*. Henry Holt.

Watson, J. B. (1928). *The psychological care of infant and child*. Norton.

Watson, J. B., & McDougall, W. (1929). *The battle of behaviorism*. Norton.

Watson, J. B., & Rayner, R. (1920). Conditioned emotional reactions. *Journal of Experimental Psychology*, *3*, 1–14.

Watson, P. (2005). *Ideas: A history of thought and invention, from fire to Freud.* HarperCollins.

Weichselbraun, A. (2018). Containment. Directed by Peter Galison and Robb Moss. *Environmental History, 23,* 393–396.

Weier, J. (2002). *Urbanization's aftermath, NASA Earth Observatory.* http://earthobservatory.nasa.gov /Features/Lights3/printall.php

Weiten, W. (2010). *Psychology: Themes and variations* (8th ed.). Wadsworth.

Weller, C. R. (2018). Al-Farabi's world historical travels: From Central Asia and the Middle East, to Europe and Russia, and back again. *Eurasian Journal of Religious Studies, 3,* 30–34.

Wells, B. (2018). Nightmarish romanticism: The Third Reich and the appropriation of romanticism. *Constellations, 9,* 1–10.

Wells, G. L., Memon, A., & Penrod, S. D. (2006). Eyewitness evidence: Improving its probative value. *Psychological Science in the Public Interest, 7,* 45–75.

Wertheimer, M. (1923). Untersuchungen zur lehre von der Gestalt, II. *Psychologische Forschung, 4,* 301–350.

Wertheimer, M. (1945). *Productive thinking.* Harper & Brothers.

Wertheimer, G. (1999). Gestalt theory reconfigured: Max Wertheimer's anticipation of recent developments in visual neuroscience. *Perception, 28,* 5–15.

Whitehead, A. N. (1978). D. R. Griffin & W. Sherburne). D (Eds.), *Process and reality: (Corrected* ed.). Free Press.

Whitehead, A. N., & Russell, B. (1910). *Principia mathematica.* Cambridge University Press.

Wicks, J. (1983). Roman reactions to Luther: The first year (1518). *The Catholic Historical Review, 69,* 521–562.

Wight, R. D. (1993). The Pavlov-Yerkes connection: What was its origin? *Psychological Record, 43,* 351–359.

Wildberg, C. (2019). *Neoplatonism. The Stanford Encyclopedia of Philosophy,* https://plato.stanford. edu/archives/sum2019/entries/neoplatonism/

Wildner, M. (1999). In memory of William of Occam. *The Lancet, 334,* 2172.

Windholz, G. (1989). The discovery of reinforcement, extinction, generalization, and differentiation of conditional reflexes in Pavlov's laboratories. *The Pavlovian Journal of Biological Science, 24,* 35–42.

Winovski, R. (2006). Avicenna and the Avicennian Tradition. In P. Adamson & R. C. Taylor (Eds.), *The Cambridge companion to Arabic philosophy* (pp. 92–136). Cambridge University Press.

Winston, A. S. (1990). Robert Sessions Woodworth and the "Columbia Bible": How the psychological experiment was redefined. *The American Journal of Psychology, 103,* 391–401.

Witkin, H. A., & Asch, S. E. (1948). Studies in space orientation: IV. Further experiments on perception of the upright with displaced visual fields. *Journal of Experimental Psychology, 38,* 762–782.

Wolfe, T. (1998). *A man in full.* Farrar, Straus, and Giroux.

Woodruff, P. (1999). Rhetoric and relativism. In A. A. Long (Ed.), *The Cambridge companion to early Greek philosophy* (pp. 290–310). Cambridge University Press.

Woodward, W. R. (2015). *Hermann Lotze: An intellectual biography.* Cambridge University Press.

Woodward, W. R. (2018). G. T. Fechner (1801–1887) in and for psychology. *Archives of Psychology,* https://archivesofpsychology.org/index.php/aop/article/view/71

Woodworth, R. S. (1921). *Psychology*. Holt.

Woodworth, R. S. (1930). Autobiography of Robert. In S. Woodworth. In C. Murchison (Ed.), *History of psychology in autobiography* (Vol. 2, pp. 359–380). Clark University Press.

Woodworth, R. S., & Schlosberg, H. (1954). *Experimental psychology*. Holt, Rinehart and Winston.

World Hunger Education Service. (2009). *World Hunger Facts*. http://www.worldhunger.org/articles/Learn/world%20hunger%20facts%202002.htm

Wrightsman, B. (1975). Andras Osiander's contribution to the Copernican achievement. In R. S. Westman (Ed.), *The Copernican achievement* (pp. 213–243). University of California Press.

Xie, Y. (2011, May 13). *How do we measure scientific productivity?* https://www.aaas.org/how-do-we-measure-scientific-productivity

Yerkes, R. M., & Morgulis, S. (1909). The method of Pavlov in animal psychology. *Psychological Bulletin, 6*, 257–273.

Young, J. L. (2018). The long history of big data in psychology. *The American Journal of Psychology, 131*, 477–482.

Young-Bruehl, E. (2008). *Anna Freud* (2nd ed.). Yale University Press.

Zaretsky, R., & Scott, J. T. (2009). *The philosophers' quarrel: Rousseau, Hume, and the limits of human understanding*. Yale University Press.

Zhmud, L. (2016). Greek arithmology: Pythagoras or Plato. In A. B. Renger & A. Stavru (Eds.), *Pythagorean knowledge from the ancient to the modern world: Askesis, religion, science* (pp. 311–336). Harrassowitz.

Zhmud, L. (2017). Heraclitus on Pythagoras. In E. Fantino, U. Muss, C. Schubert, & K. Sier (Eds.), *Heraklit im kontext* (pp. 173–187). Walter de Gruyter.

Zhmud, L. (2018). What is Pythagorean in the Pseudo-Pythagorean literature? *Philologus, 163*, 72–94. doi:10.1515/phil-2018-0003

Zimmer, C. (2005). *Smithsonian intimate guide to human origins*. Madison Press Books.

Zimmer, C. (2011). The brain. *Discover*, 22–24.

Zollikofer, C. P. E., León, Ponce de., S, M., Lieberman, D. E., Guy, F., Pilbeam, D., & Likius, A. (2005). Virtual cranial reconstruction of *Sahelanthropus tchadensis*. *Nature, 434*, 755–759. doi:10.1038/nature03397

Zupko, J. (2018). Nothing in nature is naturally a statue: William of Ockham on artifacts. *Metaphysics, 1*, 88–96.

GLOSSARY

Algorithm: An effective procedure that guarantees a result.

Alienation: The feeling of being an outsider or of being isolated even while living inside of society or a social group.

Analysand: In Jungian psychotherapy, the person seeking analysis.

Anima, Animus: In Jungian theory, the archetypes that helped men understand women and women understand men, respectively.

Animism: The belief that physical objects are alive or they contain some type of life force.

Aphasia: Loss of the ability to speak or to comprehend spoken language following a brain injury.

Apperception: Being conscious of one's own perceptions.

Applied behavior analysis: The design, application, and assessment of environmental modifications that lead to improvements in human behavior in the real world using principles derived from Radical Behaviorism.

Archetype: in Jungian theory, one of many inherited mental images or patterns found in the collective unconscious.

Asceticism: the pursuit of a life of self-denial and personal austerity.

Baseline: The environmental situation or context that exists before a treatment or intervention is applied.

Behaviorism: The approach to psychology spearheaded by Watson that sought to eliminate consciousness and introspection and substituted objective methods that focused on animal and human behaviors only.

Causal determinism: The doctrine that all events are caused by other antecedent events.

Collective unconscious: Jung's expansion of the unconscious to include a primordial layer filled with universal "psychic structures" common to all of humanity.

Comparative psychology: The branch of psychology that explores the behavior of all animals (including humans) and attempts to demonstrate phylogenetic linkages of those behaviors between species and assess their adaptive value.

Compensation: In Adlerian theory, when a person makes up for a real or perceived personality deficit by becoming more competent in another way.

Conditioned emotional responses: Terminology first introduced by Watson and Rayner to describe the acquisition of emotional responses in children through classical conditioning.

Continuity: The idea that all living things are related to each other to some degree.

Cosmopolitanism: The view that all peoples in the world belong to a single community.

Creationism: The belief that God created all things in substantially the same form as they presently exist and that they did not evolve from distant ancestors.

Determinism: The belief that all present or future events are the consequence of past events.

Dialectic: The belief that every proposition (the thesis) contains its own negation (the antithesis), and that their resolution produced an advance in knowledge (the synthesis), which in turn becomes a new thesis, causing the process to repeat itself, but at a new level of knowledge.

Dogmatism: Excessively positive belief in the truth of one's convictions.

Doppler Effect: The phenomenon first discovered by Christian Doppler in 1842 where a constant sound emanating from a moving object changed its pitch as it approached or receded from a stationary observer.

Double-aspectism: A solution to the mind–body problem in which the mental and physical parts are considered to be separate representations of the same substance.

Dualism: The philosophical idea that there are two types of phenomena, usually described as mental (mind) or physical (body).

Dynamic psychology: Woodworth's attempt to define psychology as an eclectic discipline of activity and thought that could not be approached by any single methodology.

Ego: In Freudian theory, the part of the personality closest to the outside world yet also able to observe and assess the contents of the conscious and the preconscious.

Eminence: Possessing superior skills, abilities, or status.

Empiricism: The view that holds that all knowledge comes from experience, especially from sensory experience.

Enlightenment: The period spanning the midpoints of the seventeenth and eighteenth centuries characterized by radical changes in thinking about science, politics, and the arts.

Environmentalism: The view that individual differences in behavior are mostly due to experience and other environmental factors.

Exegesis: The critical analysis of texts.

Expectancy: An internal state in which an organism anticipates an event based upon prior learning trials.

Fellowship: A form of payment for students by which part or all of tuition and/or other expenses are paid by the school. In exchange, fellows provide hours of service, usually by teaching or conducting research.

Field theory: The physical theory that describes the movement of objects when influenced by forces such as electricity or magnetism.

Force field: A region surrounding a magnet or electric current influencing other objects or fields without actually coming into physical contact with them.

Free association: A therapeutic technique in which patients are encouraged to speak freely in the presence of their therapist who listens and, later, interprets the content of their utterances.

Functionalism: An early school of thought in American psychology that sought to discover ways to improve the match between organisms, their minds, and their environments.

Gestalt: A unified whole that cannot be predicted from summing its component parts. Gestalts may be perceptual, cognitive, or social.

Grand tour: The traditional finishing point of an English gentleman's education consisting of a lengthy (e.g., several years) guided tour of European cities conducted by a knowledgeable tutor.

Gymnasium: The most academically advanced level of secondary education in Germany, roughly equivalent to the college preparatory track of American high schools.

Hedonism: The pursuit of pleasure and the avoidance of pain.

Heliocentrism: The astronomical model in which the planets revolve around the Sun in elliptical orbits.

Hellenization: The spread of Greek ideas about the structure and origin of the natural world and the search for lawful causation within it.

Hereditarianism: The view that individual differences in behavior are mostly due to innate and inherited factors.

Heuristic: A procedure that may likely yield a solution but not necessarily the best one, a rule of thumb.

History: The study of events, people, and ideas from the recorded past.

Hominin: Member of one of the primate genera in the line of descent to modern humans, or a member of the subfamily: Hominini.

Humanism: The study and application of worldly knowledge for and about secular concerns instead of sacred ones, especially as applied to art and literature. Humanism was inspired by a renewed reverence for classical thinking, especially that of Plato and the Neoplatonists.

Humorism: The belief that health was maintained by a balance of the four humors: blood, black bile, yellow bile, and phlegm.

Hunter-gatherer: A human lifestyle based around males hunting animals and women gathering plant materials. The lifestyle demands constant movement from place to place as local conditions change.

Hypothetico-deductive system: A system using logic derived from a small, restricted set of given truths used to deduce new, derived, and logically consistent statements. After, those deductions are tested experimentally. Statements experimentally confirmed are kept, and the others are discarded.

Id: In Freudian theory, home of the two sources of biological energy. The id manifested the pleasure principle, which was primarily sexual while thanatos represented the aggressive urges inherent in human behavior.

Idealism: The belief that reality lies within an abstract and nonphysical realm accessible only through introspective analysis.

Inferiority complex: In Adlerian psychology, when individuals develop such profound feelings of social inadequacy that they either become extremely discouraged or overcompensate by exhibiting aggressive behavior.

Insight learning: A type of learning in which a solution to a problem appears suddenly, usually after a period of time has passed since the problem was first presented.

Intelligent design: The theory that all living things on earth were created by a designer because no other mechanisms can account for the observed complexity of nature.

Interactionism: The belief that there exists a separation between the physical world and the mental world and that each can mutually affect the other.

Intervening variable: Unobservable variables such as internal states or cognitions assumed to influence behavior.

Intervention: A specific alteration to the baseline condition designed to change the response rate initially observed.

Learning curve: A graphical representation of the progress of learning over time with the dependent variable shown on the *y*-axis and time shown on the *x*-axis.

Mach Bands: The illusion created in a visual stimulus when an abrupt change in color or brightness creates illusory light or dark lines next to each band.

Materialism: The belief that everything in the universe must consist of matter, including minds and mental states.

Mentalism: Explaining behavior by recourse to variables such as cognitions, memories, or motivations.

Methodological behaviorism: The most prevalent form in contemporary psychology, it requires the elucidation of observable stimuli and behaviors along with a commitment to formal theory testing.

Monasticism: The lifestyle of Christian men and women who chose to live in single-gender religious communities and devote their time to work and prayer.

Natural selection: The competitive process by which organisms that are better adapted to survive the environmental conditions around them survive, and thus, reproduce more successfully leaving more offspring, and gradually altering the population characteristics of their own species.

Nature-nurture: The philosophical problem regarding the sources of knowledge.

Neobehaviorism: The modification of Watson's Behaviorism that allowed for the experimental analysis of operationally defined unobservable variables related to cognitive states and emphasized the study of learning along with the use of animal models for human behavior.

Nihilism: The belief that nothing that exists can be known or communicated.

Nominalism: The belief that universals are cognitive categories of mind, not rigid relationships between universals and particular events.

Ockham's razor: The modern interpretation of "entities should not be multiplied unnecessarily" revolves around explanatory simplicity, sometimes called the "Law of Parsimony." In modern science, this means using the minimum amount of explanation necessary. So, if two theories each adequately explain a set of phenomena, modern scientists will accept the simpler theory.

Operationism: The idea that science is best understood as a public, operationally defined enterprise in which phenomena may only be analyzed via methods that yield concrete results.

Papal infallibility: The belief that the Pope, after prayer and meditation, may formally and without question reveal God's intentions to the Church.

Pavlovian conditioning: (also known as Classical conditioning) The pairing in time between a neutral stimulus (e.g., any stimulus in any modality that does NOT naturally cause a consistent physiological response) and a stimulus that DOES cause a consistent physiological response (e.g., food and salivation) so that, over time, the neutral stimulus comes to cause nearly the SAME physiological response.

Persona: In Jungian theory, the public face of the personality that conformed to social mores. The persona developed during childhood and typically disintegrated as people aged.

Phenomenalism: The philosophical system that examines conscious experience itself directly, intentionally, and from one's own point of view.

Phenomenology: The philosophical system that examines conscious experience itself directly, intentionally, and from one's own point of view.

Philology: The study of texts with the goal of determining authorship, priority, authenticity, and relationship to other texts. The term originally meant love of learning. Today the term *linguistics* has largely replaced it.

Positivism: Comte's antimetaphysical and antitheological view that argued that knowledge can only be sought through empirical means verifiable by the senses.

Pragmatism: The approach to philosophy developed by Charles Sanders Peirce, William James, and later, John Dewey that argued that truth is always a practical compromise between empiricism and idealism.

Preestablished harmony: The mind–body solution in which mental events affect other mental events and physical events affect other physical events but each cannot affect the other. God willed the apparent coordination between mind and body at the time of creation.

Prehistory: The period of human existence prior to the existence of recorded information.

Psychophysical parallelism: The mind–body problem solution that allows for two separate systems— one for physical events and the other for mental events—but prohibits them from affecting each other.

Psychophysiology: The scientific study of the relationships between the physiological mechanisms of the body and corresponding cognitive states.

Purposive behaviorism: Tolman's version of neobehaviorism that emphasized goal-directed activity in animals and humans while only relying on objective behavioral data.

Quadrivium: The advanced curriculum of the medieval university consisting of the four courses: arithmetic, music, geometry, and astronomy.

Rationalism: The universe, including physical events, can only be explained through the action of human thought.

Realism: The belief that universals are real entities and possess physical existence.

Relativism: The belief that no universal values exist and that instead values vary by individuals, groups, or historical era.

Schema: A dynamic cognitive unit based on previous knowledge that reconstructs memories and knowledge.

Scholasticism: The dominant mode of thought in Christian Europe during the Middle Ages that attempted to reconcile faith and reason using scripture and recovered Aristotelian sources.

Science: A method of inquiry that combines empirical observations, reliable results, public dissemination, and theory to investigate the universe.

Secularism: The search for explanation within the confines of the world and its reality, combined with a rejection or diminishment of revealed or otherworldly concepts.

Sedentism: A human lifestyle associated with largely remaining in one place or locality with food production based on farming plants and livestock.

Shadow: In Jungian theory, the personality structure that holds one's true motives and desires.

Shaping: The reinforcement of successive approximations of a final, desired response.

Social contract: An agreement between the governed and the government to provide security, welfare, and laws agreeable to both.

Social Darwinism: The misapplication of Darwinian principles of evolution to explain observed differences between societies or human groups, especially to justify the status quo.

Stimulus error: Reporting anything other than a quality of a sensation, image, or affect while introspecting, especially reporting things already known through experience.

Structuralism: An early approach to psychology that used controlled introspective methods to infer the elements of the mind.

Superego: In Freudian theory, the part of the personality that forms from the repression of the Oedipus Complex (the ego-ideal) and socialization (the conscience).

Tachistoscope: A device that can display visual stimuli for extremely brief periods.

Taxonomy: The discovery, naming, and classification of animals, plants, and other living things.

Teleology: Explaining something by appealing to its final use as the reason for its creation.

Theories: The constructions scientists create to explain and organize phenomena as well as to direct their future research.

Threshold or Limen: Herbart's conception of a limit below which an idea will be out of consciousness, and conversely, in consciousness when above it.

Topological psychology: Lewin's approach to psychology that used diagrams to symbolize and explain the relationships of variables such as learning, motivation, and tension on behavior.

Transducer: In physiology, transducers are the specialized organs, such as the eye and ear, that convert physical energy into neural information

Transposition: Learning the relationship between two stimuli and subsequently transferring that learning to other pairs of stimuli.

Trivium: The basic curriculum of the medieval university consisting of the three courses: grammar, logic, and rhetoric.

Vitalism: The doctrine that physical and chemical forces alone are insufficient to explain living things, hence an additional and unknown life force is required.

Voluntarism: The system of psychology developed by Wundt that emphasized the role of unconscious and conscious choice of certain parts of consciousness based upon personal feelings, history, and motivations.

Word association test: An early psychological test first devised by Sir Francis Galton in which participants responded to a long list of words by saying the first word that entered their mind after hearing the test word.

Zeigarnik Effect: The finding that people are much more likely to remember uncompleted tasks than completed tasks.

Zeitgeist: How it feels to live in a particular time or place and to experience its particular culture, morals, and intellectual surroundings.

INDEX